Rising Damp

Dedicated to the memory of
Walter Jackson, 4th Bn, Lincolnshire Regiment
who died at Bayeux, Normandy, 1st July 1944

Rising Damp:
THE COMPLETE SCRIPTS

Eric Chappell

Edited by Richard Webber

GRANADA

First published in Great Britain in 2002

By Granada Media, an imprint of André Deutsch Limited
20 Mortimer Street
London W1T 3JW

In association with Granada Media Group

A catalogue record for this book is available from the British Library.

ISBN 0 233 99944 2

Typeset by
Derek Doyle and Associates, Liverpool
Printed and bound in the UK

10 9 8 7 6 5 4 3 2 1

CONTENTS

INTRODUCTION

BY ERIC CHAPPELL

When I decided to publish the scripts of *Rising Damp* my first thought was, did I have them all? What followed was a desperate search in the loft amongst piles of mildewed papers until I found them. They were dog-eared, held together with rusty staples, covered with nicotine stains (I smoked endless panatellas in those days in my search for inspiration), scratchings out and mysterious arrows pointing this way and that, all reflecting the urgency of the time.

The scripts were written in feverish haste by someone who didn't really know what he was doing, and who was finding things out as he went along. I didn't admit this at the time, even to myself. I took the view that sitcom writers fell into two categories: the quick and the dead, and I didn't intend to be one of the latter!

I was hardly prepared for the hurly-burly of situation comedy, where shows had to be written in a fortnight, rehearsed in a week, recorded in an hour and a half, and put out in twenty-five minutes, and then the process repeated all over again.

A few months before I'd been an auditor with the Electricity Board. Most people thought I was mad when I left to become a playwright, but were too polite to say so. I had taken this decision on the strength of my first play: *The Banana Box* – that was to have an all too brief run in the West End.

The Banana Box was the play that inspired *Rising Damp*, and although there was a great deal wrong with it, I was encouraged by its modest success. It was the first full-length play I'd written and I had always had a special feeling about it. I remember posting it off one sunny Saturday morning and thinking: 'At last I'm a playwright, life will never be the same again.' And it wasn't.

I never felt I had the stamina for situation comedy – I still don't. I intended to write plays in a leisurely way and starve in a garret. Nevertheless, I had submitted, somewhat diffidently, two sitcom pilots to ITV. I then had the horrifying thought that they may be accepted. My agent was wryly amused.

7

He pointed out that I'd be damned lucky to get one pilot accepted, never mind two. In the event they were both accepted and I found myself writing *Rising Damp* and *The Squirrels* in tandem. All this at the kitchen table, constantly harassed by two small children demanding food, whilst their mother was out doing a 'proper' job. A popular song on the radio at the time was 'Bridge Over Troubled Water' – and I took some comfort from this. I revenged myself on the children by giving them a lifelong aversion to beans and mashed potatoes.

Inspiration came slowly under these circumstances. I'd stare at the blank page for hours without thinking of a single sentence. I remember reading once that Michael Frayne stared so hard at his typewriter in search of inspiration that he discovered how the tabulator key worked. I know how he felt.

Some weeks I could think of only one funny line and I'd roll it along like a snowball until it became bigger and bigger, and eventually became a script. The completion of a script always seemed a miracle. I never actually thought I'd finish a series, until one glorious day, I looked at the pile of completed work and thought, 'If I'm not careful I'm going to finish this series.' It was a great moment.

I did, however, have one stroke of luck during all this: Leonard Rossiter. Len had been in *The Banana Box* and loved his character. He was fiercely loyal to the series and although he consumed my words at an alarming rate, he had an armoury of looks, leers, shrugs and incredulous expressions that earned me laughs I never had to write.

Len, and a brilliant cast, guaranteed the success of the series. And it was a success. Six number one spots, beating the mighty *Coronation Street* and I think the first ITV sitcom to win the BAFTA. Our success was assured, as long as I didn't blow up. And when I did throw my pen down in exhausted desperation it was Len who stood by me. He said he wouldn't work with any other writer – and the studio had to wait.

As I look back over the scripts, some of them over twenty-five years old, they appear to have been written by someone else, from another world, which, in a way, I suppose they were. They couldn't have been written now, and certainly not by me. Why are they still being shown? Possibly because we always tried to tell a story, and people never tire of stories.

I have been asked why we only made four series when the show was so hugely popular, the reason is simple. Len and I didn't come from theatrical backgrounds: he worked for years at an insurance company – I worked for years at the electricity board – we'd both had enough of long-running shows. We knew it was time to move on – what we didn't know was that *Rising Damp* would become a little part of TV history.

ERIC CHAPPELL ON THE PERFORMERS

Leonard Rossiter

Len was the driving force behind *Rising Damp*. He was a powerful and very physical actor. I may have written the words but he provided the punctuation. His whole body would form a question mark, the twist of his head was an exclamation, his eyes blazed italics, and the open-mouthed stare was a line of dots going into infinity.

Len also had an astonishing verbal dexterity – this seems to be a Liverpudlian tradition from Tommy Handley through to Ken Dodd – and it allowed him to deliver long speeches with speed and clarity, very important in a situation comedy where time was of the essence.

I never found Len particularly impressed or affected by his sudden fame, which was refreshing. He still enjoyed a pint, still retained that earthy, irreverent sense of humour and he never sought the company of cabinet ministers or appeared on high profile chat shows. He was his own man – take him or leave him. I can still hear him saying, 'It's funny, Eric – let's leave it in.'

Richard Beckinsale

Richard's laid-back manner and his minimalist style of acting, which would have made him a great film actor had he lived, were not only complementary to Len's frenetic performance, they were essential. He was able to absorb all Len's energy and then disperse it with great naturalism. It would have been fatal if they'd both conducted their scenes at the same high pitch. Richard was one of those actors who appeared to be doing very little whilst a good deal was going on under the surface.

Although not the oldest, he was the most experienced sitcom actor of the quartet, having already appeared in *The Lovers* and *Porridge*. This allowed him to be something of a calming influence on the show – a calming

9

influence that was often needed. The role of Alan was not Richard's favourite – he told me once that he was tired of playing innocent young men, especially as he was in his early thirties, married, with children but still playing frustrated virgins. He felt he was ready for more mature roles, and having seen him in these parts I knew he was right. But he was a victim of his youthful looks. I always said, 'Never mind, Richard, enjoy it while you can – there's plenty of time.' Unfortunately there wasn't.

Frances de la Tour

The Banana Box, in which Frances appeared, was my first play and Miss Jones was my first female creation. At that time I wasn't even sure I could write a female character – a fear which haunts most male writers. The character was a little sketchy and there were gaps, but Frances filled these gaps with a wonderful display of gauche innocence, coupled with an underlying sexual repression. When people complimented me on this fully-rounded character I was never sure how much was me and how much was Frances. I do know that the more scenes I wrote between Frances and Len the easier they became and they were always immaculately performed. They may have been politically opposed, they may never have kissed, but together they were magic.

Don Warrington

Don came to the play, and the series, straight from drama school. Imagine how intimidating it must have been to be plunged into the hurly-burly of sitcom with three enormously talented and experienced actors. Confronted with this, Don showed grit and determination, and a great deal of savvy. He didn't try to compete for laughs, he performed with sardonic coolness, sometimes aloof, sometimes with icy reserve, but always regal, when all the time he must have been quaking in his boots.

I always felt Don and I were in the same position – we were both beginners. We had to learn quickly or we were lost.

SERIES ONE

Rising Damp was based on a play I wrote called *The Banana Box*. With the exception of Richard Beckinsale, the actors who brought the show to life on the small screen appeared in the play, so when it came to the television series they knew their characters inside out.

We kicked off with the pilot episode, *The New Tenant*. I had originally titled it *Rooksby*. It was named after the play's central character, and I had intended to use the name not just for the pilot, but the actual series too. But then Len Rossiter gave an interview and described the character as a mean, lascivious landlord. He was quoted in one of the popular papers and a man, who not only shared the same name but was also a landlord, objected strongly. At the eleventh hour, I was forced to change the name. While I opted for *The New Tenant* for the episode, I needed some inspiration for the central character's name, so I trawled the phone book. I wanted something which sounded similiar and Rigsby caught my eye.

Changing the name also impacted the title of the series. For some reason Rigsby didn't sound right, so I put my thinking cap on again. I wanted something that sounded downbeat yet, at the same time, comical. Eventually I arrived at *Rising Damp* and as soon as I mentioned it, everyone leapt at the idea.

One difference between the sitcom and the play was that on the stage Philip was in possession of the flat and Alan was the new arrival, but here I wanted to introduce Philip in a different way to make more of an impact, so I swapped the situations around.

In the early episodes of the first series I was borrowing ideas from the play and fitting them into a framework suitable for television. An example of this in the second episode, *Black Magic*, is where Rigsby talks to Philip about their cultural differences, and enquires about what women are like in his part of the world. In this episode you'll notice plenty of one-liners and isolated comic situations, little moments pieced together, perhaps not telling much of a story; this is because I was still extracting the 'goodies' out of the play and establishing the relationships.

When I first saw Len playing Rigsby, I knew I had a winner. But we faced a scheduling problem because *Rising Damp* was being shown on Friday evenings, not the best time. Those who saw it felt it was great, but an awful lot of people missed it. Consequently, viewing figures grew very slowly and we were desperate for a better slot.

To the horror of the producer, the third script, *A Night Out*, saw Rigsby and his tenants leaving the house for the first time. It was a very claustrophobic show and I wanted to prove that we could take the show outside the house and it would still work. When I submitted the script, everyone was nervous, probably because they felt more secure if events unfolded in familiar settings.

After it had been recorded, Len said, 'Thank god that's over.' I was surprised, because the episode had gone very well and I felt my exercise had been a success, but because everyone had been so alarmed by filming away from the house, I didn't make a habit of it. The only other times we ventured out were for scenes in a pub, during *Pink Carnations* in the fourth series, out onto the roof and in the garage.

I introduced my first extra character, a wrestler called Spooner, in *A Night Out*. He was used as a device to embarrass Rigsby, who'd borrowed his jacket to take Miss Jones to The Grange. But I liked him and he was seen again in *All Our Yesterdays*. Derek Newark was perfect in the role, just the sort of guy I wanted. Sadly, the stories didn't continue to lend themselves to using the character and he was never seen again.

When it came to recording the episode the final scene was cut. The show finished with Rigsby and Alan exiting The Grange, whereas I'd written a scene just outside where they're attempting to put people off entering the restaurant. It might have been cut for time reasons or Ronnie Baxter, the director, thought it a better way to finish, I'm not sure.

A scene in *A Night Out* was written at the last minute. Ronnie Baxter, the director, phoned to say the script was short and another scene was required. I didn't have a clue what to write, but the scene I eventually penned was vitally important because it highlighted the chemistry between Len Rossiter and Frances de la Tour.

To help me come up with an idea for the scene I flipped through magazines and books. I spotted an advert for perfume, so I thought why doesn't Rigsby give Miss Jones perfume as a birthday present. I hurriedly wrote the scene – which also involved Rigsby stepping on Miss Jones's false eyelashes after mistaking them for a spider – but as time was short, I phoned it in. As it was done in haste, I half expected Ronnie to reject the scene, but when I arrived at the studio a couple of days later, Richard Beckinsale came up to me and said, 'We've decided you must phone in all the scenes at the last minute because it's the best one in the episode.' I soon realised you didn't have to write a lot for Len and Frances. They had a natural diffidence, and the gaucheness of Miss Jones and the repressed feelings of Rigsby were pure comedy. Recognising how well they could work together, I went on to write more scenes like that one. But you won't find this scene in the script, it was never written down.

One of the ideas behind the plot for *Charisma* came from real life. When I was a little boy I visited a friend's house and swallowed some tablets, thinking they were sweets. Next morning, I got up and filled the toilet only to find the urine was turquoise – my mother nearly had a fit! It remained vivid throughout the day, and everyone at school was coming to the toilet to watch. The colour gradually faded, thank goodness, but it's a story I had fun with in this episode.

Although the episode contained fresh material, I was still leaning heavily on the play for storylines I could jiggle around to make some sort of story. For example, the 'love wood' scene which caused a big hoot on stage. I had started writing the play in 1969 and when I needed to establish some background for the black character, I read a lot of anthropological titles on Africa. I discovered something about a tribal custom involving the burning of wood to help attract the opposite sex. It was a lovely story, so I made sure I fitted it into the play, and it worked like a dream.

Up to the time when I wrote *All Our Yesterdays* I still wasn't sure I could complete an entire series of scripts. But this became the first episode where I didn't draw on ideas from the play, which gave me the boost of confidence needed to go on and finish the run.

Spooner made his final appearance in this one. Once again he was used as a device. Rigsby was always talking about the war, how heroic he'd been, and Spooner provided a test of courage. The wrestler had a broken leg and was in a very mean, troublesome mood; he was playing his radio at full volume and someone had to tell him – but nobody wanted to. The scenario presented a challenge for Alan and Rigsby. While Alan had never been tested under fire, and Rigsby was the so-called hero, they both failed when it came to telling off Spooner.

I shocked everyone with the penultimate episode, *The Prowler*, by being my own man. I wrote the script, submitted it and everyone liked it. Then I decided I didn't like the way I'd done it, so I rewrote it. I sent it in a week later and Duncan Wood, the executive producer, asked, 'What are you doing? We've accepted that one already.' I can't remember why I rewrote it, and it cost me valuable time, but I knew the revised version was better.

The episode had a well-constructed plot, and a solid story. A pilot programme – involving an American cast – was made for the U.S. market and the script was based on this episode. Sadly, it never worked out and no series was commissioned. The decision didn't surprise me; it was the wrong type of show to be shown over there, partly because the bedsitland I portrayed in *Rising Damp* didn't exist in America, so people couldn't relate to it.

The first series closed with *Stand Up and Be Counted*. Having frequently worried about my ability to write beyond the pilot episode, finishing the series was like reaching a pinnacle. By this time I'd settled into a writing pattern, although my working day was very frenetic. It took about two or three drafts before I was happy with a script, and I always got up at about six each morning to begin work. But I never wrote much in the afternoon, it's never been the most productive part of my day. With my wife working full-time at this point, I also had two children to look after most of the time, so there were a lot of pressures. Looking back, I wonder how I did it. I've now reached the age when I need more peace and quiet to write, as well as pens and paper. But back then I was scratching away on old bits of paper on the kitchen table with the children running around shouting – it felt like I was going mad. I have never considered myself a patient man, so I probably released any anger and frustration by shouting louder than they did!

This final episode contained a political theme and was written at a time of great political dissention. There was industrial unrest all over the place, and television was riddled with it, so it was a good parody to do. If my memory serves me right, a strike was in danger of affecting *Rising Damp*, there was a risk of having the plugs pulled on us, but I started to notice there always seemed to be a lot of loyalty towards the show – even when industrial arguments were rife everyone made sure they completed *Rising Damp*!

We finished the series with Rigsby, Alan and Philip all singing 'The Red Flag'. There was a sense of unity, not just in the storyline but almost as a way of saying: 'We've finished the series, we're celebrating and we're all together.'

Pilot Episode

The New Tenant
by
Eric Chappell

PART ONE

SCENE 1: *Int. vacant room. Afternoon. Rigsby enters. He walks around the room with evident satisfaction. Gives a casual flick with his duster.*
Alan, a long-haired student, enters. His clothes are untidy. He is clutching a shawl around his shoulders.

ALAN: (*anxiously*) I was wondering, Rigsby – have you thought anymore about the room?

RIGSBY: Oh, yes – I've thought about it. (*continues dusting*)

ALAN: (*hopefully*) Only you said you'd consider me.

RIGSBY: Did I?

ALAN: Yes, you did say that.

RIGSBY: (*stares at him*) You couldn't afford a room like this.

ALAN: How much is it?

RIGSBY: Six.

ALAN: You can't charge six for this.

RIGSBY: Why not?

ALAN: It's too small.

RIGSBY: I know it looks small – that's the heavy wallpaper. I should have used paler colours. But you couldn't get a room like this for less than six. Look at it. (*Proudly*) Functional, with just a hint of luxury. It should appeal to the professional class. All I've got to do is put a phone in and—

ALAN: You do that, Rigsby, and it'll look like a telephone box!

RIGSBY: (*frowns*) If you think it's so small why do you want it?

ALAN: Because it's freezing up there – and it's damp.

RIGSBY: I've told you before – it's not damp.

ALAN: I've got rising damp – my furniture's coming to pieces.

RIGSBY: How can you have rising damp in the attic? You're higher than the crows up there. It should be very healthy – like Switzerland.

ALAN: (*groans*) Switzerland! Rigsby, my suits are going green.

RIGSBY: (*studies him*) I don't deny your suits are going green. You've got mould – I can see that. But it's not rising damp.

ALAN: Well, what is it then?

16

RIGSBY: Condensation.

ALAN: Condensation!

RIGSBY: And do you know why? Because you will try to cook a five course meal on one gas ring. I can't see you for steam some nights.

ALAN: That's because it's so cold up there.

RIGSBY: Of course it's cold. I've never said it wasn't. There's nothing between this house and the Urals. You're breathing the same air as the Tartars up there and look how long they live. I should charge you extra.

ALAN: (*desperately*) Rigsby, I can't go on like this. I've forgotten what it's like to wear open-necked shirts. I can't spread my butter. I tear great holes in the bread. How can I study under these conditions? The brain won't work at low temperatures.

RIGSBY: (*winks*) That's not the only thing that won't work – which in your case isn't a bad thing. Besides, when did you last study? The only thing you study is your navel. You even shave lying down. And when did you last go to the college? They must have forgotten what you look like down there.

ALAN: Of course they haven't. I go regularly.

RIGSBY: How can you? Your hair's never dry.

ALAN: I thought so. That's what you've got against me, isn't it? It's because I've got long hair. Well, just you remember, Jesus Christ had long hair.

RIGSBY: (*sharply*) That's enough of that.

ALAN: What?

RIGSBY: Don't go comparing yourself with him. You show a bit of respect.

ALAN: But it's true – he did have long hair.

RIGSBY: He didn't have a hairdryer though, did he? He didn't give himself blow waves.

ALAN: Look, if Jesus Christ came down on earth today he wouldn't get this room.

RIGSBY: Why not?

ALAN: Well, for one thing he couldn't afford it and for another he'd have to have his hair cut.

RIGSBY: Now wait a minute. I've got nothing against long hair – it's what's hiding behind it that worries me.

ALAN: What do you mean?

RIGSBY: This room contains my own personal property – most of this furniture belonged to my father. He died on that settee.

Alan removes his hand rather quickly from the settee.

ALAN: Well, what's that got to do with it, Rigsby?

RIGSBY: It's a question of respecting his memory.

ALAN: I'll respect his memory.

RIGSBY: You don't understand. He was a man of high principles. He was superintendent of the Sunday School. I remember he once got off a bus sooner than sit against a woman with bare arms. That's the sort of man he was.

ALAN: So?

RIGSBY: How's he going to feel when the 1974 Sex Olympics start on that settee?

ALAN: (*protests*) But I'm not like that, Rigsby.

RIGSBY: I know what you students are like – sex mad.

ALAN: Now, listen, have I ever brought a girl back here?

RIGSBY: Not yet. But you're only waiting your chance – just like the rest of them.

ALAN: I couldn't get a woman to come back here – I've tried. They take one look at this place and suddenly remember a previous appointment.

RIGSBY: You needn't blame this place for your lack of success with women, mate. I keep telling you – it's your hair. You want to get it cut. It might improve your chances if you didn't look so much like Rasputin.

ALAN: There you are you see – it is my hair. That's what you've got against me. That's why you won't let me have the room.

RIGSBY: It's got nothing to do with your hair. I fought Adolf Hitler for five years but it wasn't because I disliked his moustache. I think you only grew your hair long so that you could say that was why people disliked you. I think they disliked you before.

ALAN: Is that so?

RIGSBY: Yes.

ALAN: Well, they don't dislike me as much as they dislike you.

RIGSBY: (*belligerantly*) Who dislikes me? I'll punch their heads in.

Ruth Jones knocks timidly on the open door and enters. She is a woman about thirty. Pale. Sensitive. Refined.

RUTH: Hello, Alan. Oh, Mr Rigsby, I wonder if I could have a word?

Rigsby's manner becomes mild.

RIGSBY: (*beams*) Of course, Miss Jones – would you like to come down to my room?

RUTH: (*hastily*) Oh, no – it won't take a moment.

RIGSBY: Certainly. (*To Alan*) Excuse me.

Alan crosses to the door.

ALAN: (*whispers to Ruth*) I'll leave the door open.

Alan exits.

RUTH: I was wondering, Mr Rigsby – I have a student at the college who needs a room – is this one available?

RIGSBY: (*frowns*) A student. I don't know about that.

RUTH: (*appealing*) I wouldn't normally ask but accommodation is such a problem at the college and it is my responsibility—

RIGSBY: Well, I'd like to do you a favour, Miss Jones, but look what happened the last time – we got *him* up there.

RUTH: You mustn't be too hard on Alan. I think he's shy and lonely.

RIGSBY: Yes – so was Crippen. Oh, I'm not blaming you, Miss Jones. He looked quite presentable when he arrived. You didn't know he was going to turn into a flaming werewolf. Do you know he had the nerve to ask for this room? I wasn't having him down here – not next to you – taunting you with his rock music. It wouldn't be fair – not to a woman of your refinement. (*Looks at her hungrily*) There are some men, Miss Jones, who'd try to take advantage of a single woman – living on her own.

RUTH: (*innocently*) Do you think so, Mr Rigsby?

RIGSBY: Look what happened to your custard creams.

RUTH: We don't know that was Alan.

RIGSBY: Of course it was – he's always eating.

RUTH: That's because of his nerves.

RIGSBY: Nerves! Is that what he's been telling you? There's nothing wrong with his nerves – you try getting the rent out of him. You know, Miss Jones – if you don't mind me saying, you waste too much time on these students. You should think of yourself. You need the companionship of someone nearer your own age. A man who's seen something of the world. Who's understanding – with a sense of humour.

RUTH: (*shrugs*) But I just don't meet people like that, Mr Rigsby.

Rigsby winces at this rebuff.

RIGSBY: This student – has he got long hair?

RUTH: Oh, no. In fact it's quite short. I believe he comes from a very good family.

RIGSBY: Good family – then he'd appreciate a room like this.

RUTH: I'm sure he would.

RIGSBY: (*muses*) A good family you say?

RUTH: Yes. Mr Smith's rather aristocratic.

RIGSBY: Smith. Hmm. Aristocratic. Well, we could do with someone like that around here. Someone with standards – someone who'll clean the bath out after him.

RUTH: And he's so conscientious and hard-working – in fact he's a very mature student.

RIGSBY: (*suspiciously*) Is he a friend of yours, Miss Jones?

RUTH: Oh, no. I've only met him briefly but I must say he seems a perfect gentleman.

RIGSBY: Well, it's a long time since we've had one of those – they're a dying breed around here. All we get are Communist infiltrators. All right – send him along.

RUTH: I do appreciate this, Mr Rigsby.

RIGSBY: Anything for you, Miss Jones.

RUTH: (*backing away*) Oh, what about the rent?

RIGSBY: Should we say £4?

RUTH: That seems very reasonable.

RIGSBY: Well, my name's not Rachman, Miss Jones. I don't want to make money out of these poor students. I don't want to be a landlord – I want to be a friend.

RUTH: (*backing away*) Well, that certainly does you credit, Mr Rigsby. I'll send him along.

Ruth exits hurriedly. Rigsby picks up cat and strokes it.

RIGSBY: What about that then, Vienna? I think I did myself a bit of good there.

* * *

SCENE 2: *Int. attic flat. That evening. Alan is sitting at the table. He still has the shawl around his shoulders. He is surrounded by test tubes, microscopes, books, etc. A skeleton is hanging in the corner of the room. Alan is looking intently at a retort. Cut to retort. It contains vegetable soup. Rigsby and cat enter.*

RIGSBY: I want that table.

ALAN: What for?

RIGSBY: It belongs downstairs.

ALAN: But I'm eating off it.

RIGSBY: I warned you I might need it at any time.

ALAN: Can't you wait until I've finished.

RIGSBY: I can't wait for you to stop eating – life's too short. Every time I come in here you're eating – you never stop. Those choppers of yours are the nearest thing to perpetual motion I've ever seen.

ALAN: I have to eat, Rigsby. It's the only way I can keep warm.

RIGSBY: (*watches him. shakes head*) I've never seen anyone clear a plate faster than you – it's as if you're feeding something under the table. Come on – I'm doing you a favour, really. I ought to take your knife and fork as well.

They start to struggle over the table.

ALAN: Be careful! You'll spill it!

RIGSBY: God! What a mess. Just look at it. (*Peers*) You're not cooking those Surprise peas again?

ALAN: They're not Surprise peas.

RIGSBY: It's surprising where I keep finding them. They come drumming down the stairs like grape-shot. It's all right for you, you don't have to clean them up. Now come on I've got to get on.

ALAN: Why are you in such a hurry?

RIGSBY: I've got a gentleman coming this evening.

ALAN: (*incredulous*) A what?

RIGSBY (*angrily*) A gentleman.

ALAN: (*innocently*) What's he coming here for?

RIGSBY: (*jaw snaps*) As a matter of fact he's coming for the room.

ALAN: So that's it.

RIGSBY: Yes, that's it.

ALAN: He won't stay.

RIGSBY: Oh, yes he will – just as long as you keep away from him. You're not getting that room.

ALAN: What do you mean?

RIGSBY: Don't think I don't know why the other one left.

ALAN: He went for a cheaper room.

RIGSBY: No – he didn't. He left because he found a jar marked 'Diptheria Germs' in his bed. So keep away from him. Now let's have this table.

ALAN: What about my friend? He was looking forward to a meal – he hasn't eaten for weeks.

RIGSBY: What? (*Rigsby turns and sees the skeleton for the first time. Starts back*) My God! Where did he come from?

ALAN: (*mischievously*) Don't you recognise him, Rigsby? He had the room before me. He was the one who kept saying it was cold up here. (*Moves skeleton's arm*) Shake hands with Rigsby.

Rigsby draws away.

RIGSBY: You get him out of here.

ALAN: Why?

RIGSBY: Because it's morbid, that's why.

ALAN: I'd have thought you'd have been used to sights like this – after your exploits in the Western Desert.

RIGSBY: Don't worry, I've seen more of those bleached by the desert sun than you've had hot dinners. You should have been there, you wouldn't think it was so funny then.

ALAN: I wasn't even born then.

RIGSBY: What about your father?

ALAN: He was in the RAF.

RIGSBY: Brylcreem boy!

ALAN: He's bald.

RIGSBY: I remember him. Didn't he have dizzy spells when he was here?

ALAN: That was the climb – well, it is high up.

RIGSBY: That's typical – typical of the RAF – none of them could stand heights. You couldn't get half of them up a ladder. How we ever won the war I'll never know. (*Stares at skeleton*) I've seen plenty of these, don't you worry, but I'm not having one in the house. So get him out.

ALAN: But I've got to study anatomy, Rigsby. How can I set bones if I don't know what they look like?

RIGSBY: They'll never let you set bones. Look what happened when you examined Vienna. He only had a slight limp, by the time you'd finished he had a dislocated hip. If they ever make you a doctor I'm going to write to the Medical Council. You'd be more dangerous than the Black Death. You get him out of here.

Rigsby drags the table to the door. Alan follows.

ALAN: At least he's someone to talk to – and he's musical. (*Picks up fork*) Should we give you a tune?

RIGSBY: That's not funny.

Exits with table.

* * *

SCENE 3: *Int. Landing and stairs. Alan follows Rigsby*

ALAN: It won't do you any good.

RIGSBY: What do you mean?

ALAN: With Miss Jones. I know why you're doing it. Dirty old man.

RIGSBY: Why you—! (*Starts back but is handicapped by table*) She's a respectable woman. Nothing could be further from my mind.

ALAN: Oh, then why do you clean her windows three times a week?

RIGSBY: Just thank your stars I'm holding this table. You'd better watch your step. This place is looking up – there may not be room for you – not now I'm getting a better class of tenant.

Philip Smith, a young negro, appears on the landing. He is handsome, cool, self-possessed. Carrying a case.

PHILIP: Excuse me. My name's Smith. Is this my room?

Rigsby stares. Alan starts to smile. Philip looks puzzled.

END OF PART ONE

PART TWO

SCENE 4: *Int. Attic. Late evening.*
Alan is reading. Rigsby enters looking worried.

RIGSBY: Well, that's done it.

ALAN: Done what?

RIGSBY: Did you see him? She said he was aristocratic. Aristocratic! He's probably never had a pair of shoes on until he came here.

ALAN: (*drily*) Don't tell me you're prejudiced, Rigsby. After all, we're all supposed to be brothers.

RIGSBY: He's not my brother – my brother lives in Accrington. Besides, this one's different. (*Lowers voice*) Did you see that mark on his cheek – initiation ceremony.

ALAN: So what? That's no different from the Germans and their duelling scars.

RIGSBY: He didn't get that in Heidelberg. That's a tribal mark – he's straight out of the bush. It's not his fault but what's going to happen when he hears the drums?

ALAN: What drums?

RIGSBY: You wait until the next full moon – we'll all be locking our doors. You wait until we get the washing of spears.

ALAN: Rigsby – you ought to be ashamed of yourself. He's a stranger here. We should be making him feel at home.

RIGSBY: (*looking along the shelves*) Yes, I suppose you're right.

ALAN: What are you lookinig for?

RIGSBY: Where's that jar marked 'Diptheria Germs'?

* * *

SCENE 5: *Int. Philip's room. Later.*
Philip has unpacked. He looks around him with a fastidious air. He is clearly unimpressed. He picks up a book. Starts to read.
Rigsby enters. He sees a spear and shield on the wall. Tests point. Winces.

RIGSBY: I see you've made yourself at home then?

PHILIP: Er … yes.

RIGSBY: What do you think of it?

PHILIP: (*politely*) It seems very nice.

23

RIGSBY: Yes – it seems nice. That's the wallpaper – very good quality – it has to be to hold the bricks together. (*Crosses to the window*) Come here – see how these bricks have come away from the woodwork? You can get your hand in there. Of course, we're very high up here – this house holds back half the town. I'm insured against low flying aircraft.

PHILIP: (*smiles*) And there's nothing between this house and Russia.

RIGSBY: (*frowns*) Who told you that?

PHILIP: Miss Jones did happen to mention—

RIGSBY: (*suspiciously*) How well do you know Miss Jones?

PHILIP: Not very well but she's in Administration—

RIGSBY: I know that. I know all about Miss Jones. She's a friend of mine but I'm not rushing it. (*Sharply*) All right with you?

PHILIP: (*surprised*) Yes.

RIGSBY: As long as we understand each other. Nothing personal but we don't want any misunderstandings. That's what I told young Lenin up there.

PHILIP: Who?

RIGSBY: The one with the long hair. Did you see it? Right down to his shoulders.

PHILIP: Is he at the university?

RIGSBY: Yes.

PHILIP: I don't think I know him.

RIGSBY: No, you wouldn't. (*Evil grin*) He only goes out after dark. Take my tip – keep away from him. He's training to be a doctor – mixes with sick people all the time. I think he's a germ carrier. (*Philip approaches stove*) Watch that gas – it'll take your head off. If it starts hissing like a snake, don't try and light it, send for me. (*Rigsby looks out of the window*) Hello – they're at it again.

PHILIP: Who are?

RIGSBY: Come here. See those curtains twitching? See those shapes moving?

PHILIP: Where?

RIGSBY: The window opposite. See?

PHILIP: Yes, I think—

RIGSBY: The old ladies. If they give you any trouble stick your backside out of the window.

PHILIP: (*stares*) What sort of trouble?

RIGSBY: They make rude signs – put their fingers to their noses. Very funny family. (*Sharply*) Did I mention the rent?

PHILIP: Yes. (*He goes to wallet*)

RIGSBY: I insist on a month in advance.

PHILIP: Miss Jones didn't mention that.

He hesitates but pays Rigsby. Rigsby notices a full wallet. Takes money, a shade disappointed. Picks up cat.

RIGSBY: Come on, Vienna.

PHILIP: Isn't that a strange name for a cat?

RIGSBY: We don't think so.

PHILIP: Why do you call him Vienna?

RIGSBY: Ah, well you take this cat to the door on the coldest night of the year. When you'd have to kick a polar bear out never mind a cat. You show him the door and if he sees a pair of ears out there – it's goodnight, Vienna.

Exit Rigsby.
Philip stares after him with a bemused expression on his face. Returns to his work. There is a knock on the door. He sighs. Alan enters.

ALAN: Hello. Welcome to Bleak House. Mind if I come in for a warm? My name's Alan Moore. I live upstairs. (*Extends hand*).

PHILIP: Philip Smith.

Philip takes Alan's hand rather reluctantly. Then he crosses room and wipes it surreptitiously on a towel.

ALAN: You know – I think this is great.

PHILIP: What is?

ALAN: You coming to live here.

PHILIP: (*suspiciously*) Why?

ALAN: (*uncertainly*) We've never had a—

PHILIP: What?

ALAN: I've never known a ... (*Hesitates*) It'll be an experience.

PHILIP: What sort of experience?

ALAN: I don't know.

PHILIP: Let's get one thing straight – I'm not an experience.

ALAN: No, of course not. (*Pause*) What do you think of Rigsby.

PHILIP: I don't know. Is he mad?

ALAN: Probably. He lives all alone down there – except for his cat. No one's ever been in his room. Some say he was jilted on his wedding day – that he sits down there every night with the remains of the cake. The other story is that he's murdered his wife and that he's got her walled up somewhere – staring at us.

PHILIP: (*wearily*) I was hoping to get some peace and quiet here. I do have a lot of work to do. (*Pointedly*)

ALAN: Yes, of course. Well, I won't disturb you. (*Pats Philip's shoulder. Philip moves away*) Just let me know if you're short of anything. If you want to borrow any cups.

PHILIP: (*hastily*) No – I've got some.

ALAN: Well, goodnight, Philip.

PHILIP: Goodnight. (*Alan exits*).

Philip sighs. Shakes head. Returns to his books. There is a tapping on the wall. Philip groans. Crosses to the wall. Listens. Taps back. He is still listening at the wall when Ruth enters and glides across to him.

RUTH: Philip – at last. (*She kisses him*). I've been so impatient waiting for the others to go. I wanted to give you a proper welcome. Are you all right for butter?

PHILIP: Yes. (*Looks anxiously at the door*) Do you think we should be doing this?

RUTH: Do you realise it's the first time we've been alone since that night.

PHILIP: What night?

RUTH: That night. You haven't forgotten, Philip?

PHILIP: (*uncomfortably*) Oh, that night.

RUTH: Don't you remember? You said my skin was like the skin of fruit. I thought that was lovely – so poetical. (*Pause. Feels cheek*) What fruit did you mean, Philip?

PHILIP: Ruth, I am rather busy at the moment. And we've got to think of appearances.

RUTH: I don't care about appearances – not anymore. Let's be impulsive … drink life to the dregs. (*Stops. Listens*) Was that Rigbsy?

PHILIP: Rigsby?

RUTH: We shall have to be careful. He can be very funny about this sort of thing.

PHILIP: What will he do?

RUTH: He cuts my water off. (*Shrugs*) Not that I care – not any more. (*She puts Philip's hand over hers. Sighs*) Black on white, Philip.

Philip moves away.

What's the matter?

PHILIP: Nothing. I've just remembered how much work I've got to do.

RUTH: Do you ever think about that night? The way we ran hand in hand through the pouring rain. (*Intensely*) Don't you find the rain primitive, Philip?

PHILIP: Very – I wanted to get a taxi.

RUTH: Do you remember what we said to each other?

PHILIP: You said you could get me a flat. I didn't know you were going to be next door. How am I going to get any work done?

RUTH: Work can wait, Philip.

She begins to enfold him. Rigsby enters. They move apart. Rigsby eyes them suspiciously.

Well, if there's nothing else I can get you, Mr Smith. (*She pauses at the door*) Perhaps we can exchange our supplements sometime?

PHILIP: Er … yes.

Ruth exits.

RIGSBY: What was she doing here?

PHILIP: She came to see if there was anything I wanted.

RIGSBY: I see. (*Sharply*) You don't want anything, do you?

PHILIP: No.

RIGSBY: Good. If you want anything, you come to me. Here's your rent book.

Rigsby exits.

* * *

SCENE 6: *Int. landing.*
Rigsby aims an angry kick at the cat who departs screeching.

* * *

SCENE 7: *Int. attic.*
Alan is drying his hair with a hairdryer. Rigsby enters. Looks at him in disgust.

RIGSBY: It gets more like a Ladies' Hairdressers every day. (*Sits down*) Well, he's staying. Just can't get rid of him. The trouble is he can't take a hint. I've tried to be diplomatic. Now I shall have to get nasty.

ALAN: Rigsby – I keep telling you. We've all got to learn to live together—

RIGSBY: How can we? Their ways aren't our ways. They're different.

ALAN: No, they're not. You're prejudiced.

RIGSBY: No, I'm not.

ALAN: You don't even like people with heavy suntans.

RIGSBY: Oh, yes, well, look at the trouble I had with that Indian. All that cooking. And bringing his friends in. He used to arrive here with twenty-four of them in the back of a taxi. But I never complained and what happened? He left owing a month's rent.

ALAN: I bet you squeezed him out.

RIGSBY: No, I didn't. He went on a day trip to Boulogne and they wouldn't let him back in again.

ALAN: Well, that wasn't his fault.

RIGSBY: All I got left with was the *Hindu Guide to Love* and that was in Hindustani. Mind you you should see the pictures – no wonder they all look undernourished.

ALAN: Don't you realise, Rigsby, they come from a civilisation much older than ours. Take Philip down there. He's probably more civilised and cultured than we are.

RIGSBY: Civilised! Cultured! Have you seen the size of that spear?

ALAN: Well, I like him and I happen to believe that black and white should learn to live together. I know he seems distant, but that's because of people like you, Rigsby.

RIGSBY: (*scowls*) I don't know why Miss Jones had to bring him here in the first place.

ALAN: Perhaps she fancies him.

RIGSBY: You watch your tongue. She's not like that. She's a respectable woman. She's saved herself.

ALAN: What for?

RIGSBY: For the right man.

ALAN: (*amused*) Not you, Rigsby.

RIGSBY: Why not?

ALAN: I thought you said she was respectable?

RIGSBY: She is but underneath … You see she's untapped. There's a lot of pent up force there. She's fighting against it but one day she's going to burst like a dam – and I'll be waiting. (*Scowls*) And if anyone tries to come between me and her—

He leaves the threat unfinished. He picks up the jar marked Diptheria Germs from the shelf.

* * *

SCENE 8: *Int. Philip's room.*

Philip enters in dressing gown on return from Bathroom. Stares. Cut to Rigsby who turns around hurriedly.

PHILIP: (suspiciously) Did you want something, Rigsby?

RIGSBY: No, just came to see if you'd settled in, that was all.

PHILIP: Well, if you don't mind—

RIGSBY: You see the previous tenant … he never did settle. He seemed to sense an atmosphere.

PHILIP: (*stares*) What sort of an atmosphere?

RIGSBY: You know. (*Moves closer*) Bad spirits.

PHILIP: What?

RIGSBY: You see – years ago a man died in here – in horrible circumstances. Killed himself while the balance of his mind was disturbed.

PHILIP: I think I know the feeling. I'm only surprised that he found the time.

RIGSBY: (*disappointed*) It doesn't worry you then?

PHILIP: No.

RIGSBY: Well, I thought I'd just mention it – in case you were of a nervous disposition. Look at the cat. See how his hair's standing on end? He can sense it. We wouldn't spend a night in here – not for a fortune.

PHILIP: I'm relieved to hear it – now if you don't mind—

Rigsby crosses to door. Pauses.

RIGSBY: Horrible circumstances.

Rigsby exits.
Philip breaths a sigh of relief. Sees jar marked Diptheria Germs by the bed. He recoils for a moment then drops it in wastepaper basket. There is a knocking on the wall.

PHILIP: Oh, no.

He covers his ears. A moment later Ruth enters.

RUTH: What's the matter, Philip? You look worried.

PHILIP: Worried! This is like being in the middle of a sponsored walk. How can I work? Everyone keeps coming in and out. If it's not you it's Rigsby. Now he's even started germ warfare! How can I work under these conditions?

RUTH: You're working too hard, Philip. You should try to relax. Why don't you come and lie down?

Ruth crosses to the bed. Sits on it. Looks at him flirtatiously.

Should I turn the covers back for you?

She leans back and sexily draws the covers. The skeleton is lying there grinning at her. Ruth jumps up with a loud scream.

RUTH: What's that doing there?

PHILIP: It's not mine.

RUTH: Then why do you sleep with it? Why couldn't you have had a teddy bear or something?

Rigsby bursts in.

RIGSBY: All right – don't worry, Miss Jones, I'm here. Now then Monolulu, what's your little game? My God! You haven't wasted much time. You haven't even had the grace to let the dust settle. Well, you needn't think you're going to get away with it around here. This is a respectable house.

RUTH: Don't be ridiculous, Mr Rigsby. Philip is perfectly respectable. He happens to be the son of a chief.

RIGSBY: What?

RUTH: The son of a chief – a paramount chief.

PHILIP: Oh, my God. (*Turns his back and looks out of the window*).

RIGSBY: Son of a chief. I didn't know that. He never said anything to me.

RUTH: He doesn't want anyone to know.

RIGSBY: Well, if he wants to be bloody secretive.

PHILIP: I'm trying to lead an ordinary life. (*Looks hard at Ruth*) All I want is to be left alone.

RUTH: (*sighs tremulously*) If that's how you feel, Philip.

Ruth exits.
Rigsby looks at Philip with new respect.

RIGSBY: Son of a chief, eh?

PHILIP: It's not important.

RIGSBY: (*sharply*) I know it's not important. You don't have to tell me that. Just your luck, isn't it? I suppose you come from an old family?

PHILIP: Yes.

RIGSBY: Yes. Born to it. Same in the war. My old captain – he came from a good family – not like these tu'penny ha'penny gentlemen you get today. He always carried a stick and smoked a pipe. I never saw him ruffled. When Jerry opened up he'd just lean on his stick and say, 'Where do you think that's coming from, sergeant?' Everyone would leap for cover but not the captain.

PHILIP: What happened to him?

RIGSBY: (*winces*) He got blown up by a shell. (*Pause. Studies Philip*) I suppose being the son of a chief ... you can have your pick?

PHILIP: What?

RIGSBY: (*confidentially*) You know – women.

PHILIP: (*smiles*) Oh, yes.

RIGSBY: I thought so. I've always understood that women out there

are more ... you know. (*Winks*).

PHILIP: (*winks*) Oh, much more.

RIGSBY: Yes. I've heard that. Ours are always getting headaches. Do yours get headaches?

PHILIP: No, I don't think so.

RIGSBY: Miss Jones gets headaches. Terrible headaches. She has to wear blue glasses. She wouldn't be much good to you. You're hard on your women aren't you?

PHILIP: What do you mean?

RIGSBY: You make them walk miles in the hot sun with pots on their heads.

PHILIP: Oh, yes.

RIGSBY: I couldn't see Miss Jones doing that.

PHILIP: Nor could I.

RIGSBY: I've heard that out there – you can have as many wives as you like.

PHILIP: Yes.

RIGSBY: I should have thought one would have been enough—

Philip starts to pack.

RIGSBY: What are you doing?

PHILIP: I'm going. Isn't that what you wanted?

RIGSBY: Oh, I see – the place isn't good enough for you.

PHILIP: What?

RIGSBY: Just because you're the son of a chief, you needn't look down your nose at this place.

PHILIP: (*bewildered*) But—

RIGSBY: This is a fashionable place. We had the manager of the Co-op Drapery here last year and he never complained. We're getting breezes straight off the Urals here—

PHILIP: (*hesitates*) I can't stop here, Rigsby. (*Points at Ruth's wall*) I'll never get any work done.

RIGSBY: Mmm. I suppose not. It's you being the son of a chief. She's the same about the Prince of Wales.

PHILIP: I can assure you there's nothing between us.

RIGSBY: No, of course not – she wouldn't last five minutes in the jungle. She had sunstroke at Bournemouth last year.

PHILIP: Well, if you'd just return my rent.

RIGSBY: (*frowns*) Now there's no need to be hasty. There is another room. A very salubrious spot. Get your things.

* * *

SCENE 9: *Attic landing.*
Alan is climbing stairs from bathroom. He has a couple of curlers in his hair. He sees Rigsby emerge from the flat.

ALAN: (*suspiciously*) What were you doing in there, Rigsby?

RIGSBY: Actually, I was just returning your table.

ALAN: What? Thanks, Rigsby, that's great. (*Pause*) Wait a minute, you're not still trying to squeeze him out, are you?

RIGSBY: No, I'm trying to squeeze him in.

ALAN: Because if you are, I'll report you. I happen to believe that black and white should learn to live together.

RIGSBY: I agree with you—

ALAN: What?

RIGSBY: I've been thinking about what you said. You were right.

ALAN: I'm very glad to hear it.

Alan puts hand on door knob

RIGSBY: You've left your curlers in.

ALAN: What?

RIGSBY: I wouldn't go in there with your curlers in.

Alan stares at him, his suspicions fully aroused. He opens door.

* * *

SCENE 10: *Int. flat.*
Philip is placing his spear on wall over fireplace.

ALAN: Hey! What's going on here. This is my room.

PHILIP: I beg your pardon but this is my room.

They both look at Rigsby who begins to disappear down the stairs.

ALAN: Rigsby! I'm not sharing.

Alan crosses to landing followed by Philip.

* * *

SCENE 11: *Int. stairs.*
Alan and Philip follow Rigsby onto the landing.

ALAN: You can't do this, Rigsby.

RIGSBY: You said black and white

should be able to live together.

ALAN: Not in the same room!

PHILIP: What about my privacy?

ALAN: And mine.

RIGSBY: You'll get used to it. You can be like brothers—

He glances at Alan's hair.

… or sisters—

He passes down the stairs.
Alan and Philip stare at each other in horror.

BOTH: Rigsby!

They pursue Rigsby down the stairs.

THE END.

Series One

EPISODE 1

Black Magic
by
Eric Chappell

PART ONE

SCENE 1: *Top flat. Late evening.*

Alan is standing looking in the mirror. He is wearing a smart, well cut blazer. He studies himself. He begins to try various expressions in the mirror. Haughty, cynical, amused. Rigsby enters silently. Creeps up behind Alan and stares over his shoulder.

Alan gives a start.

ALAN: Rigsby! Do you have to creep up like that?

RIGSBY: (*chuckles*) You never get tired of looking at yourself, do you? You'll wear that mirror out the way you're going on.

ALAN: I was just running a comb through, that's all.

RIGSBY: You were trying to make your eyebrows go up and down again, weren't you?

ALAN: No, I wasn't.

RIGSBY: Yes, you were. You looked as if you were having a fit. You won't get a woman that way.

ALAN: That's what you think. (*Returns to mirror*) As a matter of fact this sort of detached, cynical expression pulls the birds. I get quite a few looks.

RIGSBY: I'm not surprised – they're probably waiting for someone to throw a net over you.

ALAN: There's nothing wrong in having an expressive face, Rigsby. It shows character.

RIGSBY: Cobblers.

ALAN: All right. How do you suggest I express my personality?

RIGSBY: Why don't you go out and get tattooed. That's what we used to do.

ALAN: That's typical. That's your idea of expressing yourself, is it? Go out and get tattooed. Perhaps I'd look better with a dancing girl on my chest?

RIGSBY: (*grins*) It's the only way you're going to get one on there.

ALAN: Not any more (*returns to mirror*) I've decided to change my image.

RIGSBY: Well, I'm all for that. Is the new image going to clean the bath out after him?

ALAN: (*ignores him*) I've neglected myself long enough. You can let yourself go without noticing it. You stop using the after-shave,

34

dispense with the underarm, stop changing your socks and one day you find you're an old man. (*Looks hard at Rigsby*)

RIGSBY: (*frowns*) This new image – it wouldn't have anything to do with our friend, would it. (*He points at spear*)

ALAN: No – why should it?

RIGSBY: Isn't that his jacket you're wearing?

ALAN: I was just trying it on.

Returns jacket to wardrobe.

RIGSBY: (*sharply*) That's not the only thing you're trying on.

ALAN: What do you mean?

RIGSBY: I understand you've been telling Miss Jones that conditions up here are disgusting.

ALAN: (*clears throat*) Well, as a matter of fact, Rigsby, we feel—

RIGSBY: Oh, *we* feel. He's only been here five minutes and it's *we* feel. I knew he'd cause trouble.

ALAN: He's not causing trouble. Philip just feels that we're overcrowded.

RIGSBY: Overcrowded! He's never known luxury like it. He never had a pair of shoes on until he came here.

ALAN: Rigsby – not again.

RIGSBY: He hasn't. They're pinching his feet – you can see.

He has them off as soon as he can. They've got to feel the ground under their toes.

ALAN: Rigsby, those shoes are handmade. He's the son of a chief.

RIGSBY: All right – so he's the son of a chief. All that means is that his mud hut's a bit bigger than all the other mud huts. Well, he needn't think he can come here causing trouble. I only let him stay out of the kindness of my heart.

ALAN: You let him stay because you'd got hold of the rent money.

RIGSBY: He could have had it back.

ALAN: How could he? Most of it's gone over the counter at the Blue Ram. You haven't drawn a sober breath since he arrived.

RIGSBY: Well, I wouldn't get too attached to him if I were you.

ALAN: Who said I was attached to him?

RIGSBY: (*shrewdly*) I notice you haven't gone home this weekend.

ALAN: You know what my parents are like. We'll only spend Saturday night rug-making or insulating the roof. At least Philip's interesting.

RIGSBY: What's interesting about him?

ALAN: He's got ten wives.

RIGSBY: What?

ALAN: That's what I heard at university. Ten wives, Rigsby.

RIGSBY: (*deeply affected*) Bloody hell! (*Pause*) Well, marriage doesn't mean the same to them. They get married each time there's a hurricane. When they think God's angry with them.

ALAN: Still, ten wives.

RIGSBY: Yes, well, that's the sort of thing he's going to miss in the small hours. And what's going to happen then? He'll go on the rampage. No one'll be safe. He's probably already planned his first all-night party.

ALAN: Well, I won't mind – it'll make a change.

RIGSBY: Are you mad? They're not like our parties you know. It won't be a dry sherry and a waltz on the terrace. It could go on to the next bloody rains.

ALAN: Well, we could do with a bit of excitement around here.

RIGSBY: You might get more excitement than you bargained for. You've seen the state of the brickwork. This house holds back half the town – you hold a party up here and you'll all slide out into the middle of the road with the rest of the town on top of you. (*Pause. Looks out of the window. Possibly sees Philip*) No, I'm going to keep a very close eye on him. He's already made himself a nuisance with Miss Jones. Hanging around – flashing his teeth at her.

ALAN: You're not jealous, are you, Rigsby?

RIGSBY: Of course I'm not jealous. (*Reassuring himself*) She wouldn't give him a second look.

ALAN: (*mischievously*) Oh, I don't know. A white woman could have a lot of status out there. We don't know how many bags of salt she might be worth.

RIGSBY: You watch your tongue.

ALAN: I can just see her with a few hoops round her neck, making her way down to the river with a pile of washing.

RIGSBY: I've told you before – she's a shy sensitive woman. She wouldn't get involved with someone like him.

* * *

SCENE 2: *First floor landing.*
Philip is tiptoeing up the stairs. He sees Ruth's door is slightly open. He hesitates then creeps quietly by. A hand reaches out from behind the door seizes the end of his scarf and drags him in.

* * *

SCENE 3: *Int. Ruth's flat.*
Ruth is putting her arms around Philip.

RUTH: What's the matter, Philip?

You promised to come down last night. What happened?

PHILIP: I couldn't. Rigsby was painting your door.

RUTH: I know. That was the fifth coat. I think he suspects. He even paints the door knob.

PHILIP: There you are – we must be careful.

RUTH: Then there's only one answer. I must come to you.

PHILIP: No! I mean, what about Alan?

RUTH: He always goes home on Fridays.

PHILIP: (*backing towards door*) I must go, Ruth.

Philip opens the door. Rigsby almost falls into the room.

* * *

SCENE 4: *Int. first floor landing.*

RIGSBY: Just checking the paintwork, Miss Jones. (*Glares at Philip who is edging by*) I think it needs another coat.

RUTH: But it's had five already, Mr Rigsby.

RIGSBY: I know. (*Shakes head*) It's groaning out for it, Miss Jones.

RUTH: But do you have to do it at midnight?

RIGSBY: It's the best time. No one's

moving about then. (*Another glance at Philip*) At least they shouldn't be.

Philip hurries upstairs. Enters top flat.

* * *

SCENE 5: *Int. top flat.*
Philip enters. Sees Alan has put on dressing gown.

PHILIP: (*surprised*) I thought you went home at the weekend?

ALAN: Not every weekend. You don't mind?

PHILIP: (*relieved*) No – not at all. (*Pause*) Rigsby's going to paint Ruth's door again.

ALAN: Not again!

PHILIP: He says it's groaning for it.

ALAN: It's not the door that's groaning for it. He's getting worse. We may as well be in college. We won't be able to do any entertaining.

PHILIP: Do you mean women?

ALAN: Er … yes, of course.

PHILIP: (*studies him*) You didn't say so. You're not against them are you?

ALAN: (*hastily*) No. (*Sadly*) I'm not against them often enough.

PHILIP: I'm quite active in that respect.

He slips shoes off. Alan watches him.

ALAN: Yes. I thought you would be.

PHILIP: (*sharply*) Why?

ALAN: Pardon?

PHILIP: Why did you think that?

ALAN: Well, I didn't think you'd got my inhibitions.

PHILIP: I've got inhibitions you haven't even heard of.

ALAN: Oh. They say you've got ten wives.

PHILIP: Yes.

ALAN: (*grins*) Ten wives!

Philip stares at him. The smile fades from Alan's face.

ALAN: Don't you find ten rather intimidating?

PHILIP: No. It's like driving in traffic. You only see the one in front.

Alan watches Philip admiringly as he begins to undress.
Becomes curious.

ALAN: Are you circumcised, Philip?

Philip freezes in the act of removing his trousers.

PHILIP: My God!

ALAN: I just wondered. Are you?

PHILIP: (*irritably*) Yes.

ALAN: So am I. Rotten isn't it?

PHILIP: You should have it done when you're thirteen – in the bush – with a blunt knife.

ALAN: Was it painful?

PHILIP: It does make your eyes water a little.

ALAN: I suppose it's the custom.

PHILIP: Yes. They're mad about it in my country. They even do the girls.

ALAN: Crikey! (*Frowns*) How do they do the girls?

PHILIP: I don't know. I don't stare as hard as you do.

ALAN: Sorry.

Philip retreats to living area.

PHILIP: I could do with a little more privacy around here.

ALAN: Don't worry. No one ever comes up here.

Philip attempts to remove his trousers again.
Rigsby makes an abrupt entrance.

RIGSBY: Whoops! Mind your backs.

Philip pulls trousers up in alarm.

PHILIP: Don't you ever knock, Rigsby?

ALAN: It's time we had a key to that door.

RIGSBY: We don't need keys here.

(*Glance at Philip*) At least we didn't. Besides, I've got to have access.

ALAN: We can't even lock the bathroom door – we have to wedge a chair against it.

RIGSBY: I've told you before – if you're in there all you've got to do is keep whistling.

ALAN: We can't whistle all the time.

RIGSBY: What's the matter – frightened someone's going to come in and sink your boats?

PHILIP: We have a right to some privacy.

RIGSBY: Oh, yes, and I suppose you're used to better things?

PHILIP: That wouldn't be difficult.

RIGSBY: (*Frowns, studies Philip*) There's something I don't understand about you, Sunshine. If you're the son of a chief why are you called Smith?

PHILIP: That's not my real name.

ALAN: Of course not, Rigsby.

RIGSBY: Then what's your real name?

PHILIP: I can't tell you that. My real name is known only to the elders. You see, my people believe that if a man has your name he can do you harm. That he can take your name and work evil with it.

RIGSBY: We have people like that in this country – we call them the police.

ALAN: Rigsby – you don't understand. Philip's name's taboo.

RIGSBY: Well, if his name's Taboo, why can't he say so instead of being so secretive about it? I think he's just trying to get away from those ten wives. Ten wives! Have you ever heard anything like it?

PHILIP: Why shouldn't I have ten wives? I'm not poor. I'm not sick.

RIGSBY: Well, I think it's indecent. I'm surprised the missionaries didn't put a stop to it.

PHILIP: (*angrily*) Missionaries. We don't need missionaries.

ALAN: Why not?

PHILIP: Because I happen to be a god – that's why not.

Alan and Rigsby stare at him in surprise.

RIGSBY: You what?

ALAN: He's joking.

PHILIP: You ask my people – they don't think it's a joke.

RIGSBY: I don't know how you've got the nerve to stand there and say it. (*Looks up*) It's a wonder he doesn't strike you dead.

ALAN: (*anxiously*) I suppose it's a primitive belief is it, Philip?

PHILIP: No it isn't. It's simply that

my people believe that I've inherited certain supernatural powers from our ancestors.

RIGSBY: Oh, yes. Well, you're not dealing with ignorant savages now, you know. You're dealing with educated white men. And I can prove you're not a god. Do a miracle.

PHILIP: What?

RIGSBY: Go on – do a miracle. If you've got magic powers what are those dirty pots doing in the sink? I should have thought you could have had those washed and stacked. Come on, Mary Poppins, what are you waiting for?

PHILIP: My powers relate mainly to the forest and the hunting of animals.

RIGSBY: I bet they do. That's very convenient isn't it? Well, I don't think you're a God. What are you going to do about it? Go on – strike me down – give me the evil eye.

Sound of train.
Rigsby starts.

RIGSBY: What was that?

ALAN: (*laughs*) It was only a train passing.

RIGSBY: You see. You can't do anything. Because you're dealing with twentieth-century man, mate, not a relic from the stone age.

PHILIP: All right. I'll work a miracle. (*He takes spear from the wall*)

RIGSBY: (*retreating*) What are you going to do with that?

PHILIP: This spear belonged to my ancestors – it has considerable power.

ALAN: What are you going to do, Philip?

PHILIP: I'm going to make something appear. But you must be very still.

He switches the light out. Gets down on his knees. Brings the spear down three times on the floor.

ALAN: What's supposed to happen?

RIGSBY: Nothing.

PHILIP: Shush!

Silence.

RIGSBY: (*laughs*) You see. Nothing's going to happen. I told you.

Ruth enters the flat in her nightdress. She is slightly breathless and is carrying a bottle of wine. She switches on the light. Sees Alan and Rigsby.

RUTH: Oh. Oh dear. I've come to the wrong room. (*Puts bottle of wine behind her*) I must have been dreaming. I shall really have to stop taking those red tablets. Do excuse me.

Ruth backs out of door.
Close up of Rigsby's anguished face.
Fade out.

END OF PART ONE

PART TWO

SCENE 6: *Int. top flat. Following evening.*

Philip is reading. Alan is watching him over the newspaper. Philip gets up, looks out of window.

PHILIP: I see it's raining again.

ALAN: Yes. (*pause*) Do you like England, Philip?

PHILIP: It's all right.

ALAN: What do you like best?

PHILIP: (*considers*) I think the telephone boxes – they're rather nice.

ALAN: (*disappointed*) Is that all?

PHILIP: I like the swimming pools. I suppose that's because there are no crocodiles.

ALAN: Do you have many crocodiles in your country?

PHILIP: There's more water than land in my country – and more crocodiles than people.

ALAN: Do they attack you?

PHILIP: (*impatiently*) Of course they attack you. What do you think they do? Swim up and give you a big kiss?

ALAN: What do you do?

PHILIP: You wrestle with them.

ALAN: Crickey!

PHILIP: (*frowns*) Can you smell paint?

ALAN: (*sniffs*) Yes – it's coming from the door.

Alan opens the door. Rigsby stands there with a paint brush.

ALAN: Hello, Rigsby. Painting the door?

RIGSBY: Yes – thought I'd give it a quick coat.

He gives a final dab at the door knob. Returns brush to pot. Enters.
Philip returns to reading. Rigsby looks over his shoulder.

RIGSBY: See you're soaking up the white man's knowledge. Oh, they're *always* criticising us, but they know where to come for a decent education – cradle of civilisation this place.

ALAN: What are you taking, Philip?

PHILIP: I'm specialising in Town and Country Planning.

Rigsby howls with laughter. Can hardly stop.

41

RIGSBY: Oh, yes. I've heard there's a real demand for that in the jungle. One thing they're crying out for is a regular dustbin collection.

PHILIP: (*seriously*) Do you know what I plan to do with the jungle, Rigsby? I'm going to tarmac it.

RIGSBY: (*surprised*) The jungle?

PHILIP: (*earnestly*) Well, the worst parts. What do you think?

RIGSBY: (*uncertain. Uneasy glance at Alan*) I suppose it's an idea.

PHILIP: A master stroke. Where there was once only the mosquito there'll be trees growing out of black velvet tarmac.

RIGSBY: Well, yes I suppose—

PHILIP: There'll be decent bus shelters – plenty of white lines. Can you see it, Rigsby?

RIGSBY: Yes.

PHILIP: And flourescent street lighting.

RIGSBY: Yes – why not?

PHILIP: And of course zebra crossings.

Rigsby, who has been carried away by the image, stares at Philip. Alan laughs. Rigsby scowls.

RIGSBY: You know you've got a very peculiar sense of humour. I mean look at last night.

PHILIP: You think that was a joke?

RIGSBY (*derisively*) Magic powers! Oh, your people may believe it. You may believe it but don't expect us to believe it. After all, it wasn't so long ago when you lot were eating each other.

PHILIP: What do you mean not so long ago?

RIGSBY: God! You don't still eat people?

PHILIP: Only people we admire.

RIGSBY: That's a funny reason.

PHILIP: My people believe that if you eat a brave person – particularly his heart – you become brave too. We eat his eyes for a fierce stare – sweetbreads for virility.

RIGSBY: Well, don't look at me – I wouldn't be any good to you. No point in having a dip in my gravy. Honestly – eating people – I think it's disgusting. And don't think I swallowed all that mumbo-jumbo last night. Miss Jones coming up here was a pure coincidence.

ALAN: Is that why you're painting the door, Rigsby?

RIGSBY: You couldn't do anything to me, could you? And do you know why? Because it's all in the mind. Superstition that's all that is.

Exits. Muttering. Loud crash. Alan and Philip open door.
Landing.
Rigsby has tripped over paint tin and fallen down stairs.

Alan and Philip return to room laughing.
Philip slips on jacket.
Alan returns to paper.

ALAN: Going out, Philip?

PHILIP: Yes.

ALAN: (*casually*) I thought I might go out tonight. There's a good film on at the Plaza. They all have their clothes off in the first ten minutes. I don't know if you'd thought of seeing it?

PHILIP: No.

ALAN: Of course we could always go to the flea-pit. They're showing *Zulu* again.

Philip stares at him.

ALAN: No, perhaps not. I don't know if you've got any ideas?

PHILIP: I've got a date.

ALAN: Oh.

PHILIP: If you're on your own—

ALAN: No. I could always go and see one of my birds. It's just that I normally go home at the weekends.

PHILIP: Why don't you take Ruth to the pictures?

ALAN: Ruth? (*Shakes head*) No – I don't think she'd like clothes off in the first ten minutes. Besides, she wouldn't come.

PHILIP: Why don't you ask her? I think she likes you.

ALAN: Do you? She's older than me.

PHILIP: But more experienced.

ALAN: Miss Jones? She's so reserved.

PHILIP: You'd be surprised. We have a flower in my country. It's very remote – very inaccessible. You have to climb the mountain to see it. It only flowers once every ten years. But when it does … (*draws in breath*)

ALAN: As good as that?

PHILIP: All I can say is it's well worth the climb.

Philip exits.
Alan stares after him.

* * *

SCENE 7: *Int. top flat. Later.*
Alan is dressed in Philip's blazer again. He is moving around the flat in a bored manner. Looks in mirror, tries to raise eyebrow. Sighs. Approaches skeleton.

ALAN: Would you care for the next dance? (*Dances with skeleton*) Do you come here often? I can recommend the food. They serve the best smoked salmon in London. Oh, you're still slimming. You should be careful – you can overdo it.

Rigsby enters.

ALAN: Do you like the jacket? Saw

it in the King's Road and simply had to have it.

He twirls around and comes face to face with Rigsby.

RIGSBY: You morbid sod.

ALAN: Rigsby.

RIGSBY: They'll be taking you away if you go on like this. I shall have to write to your parents. It's about time you got back to the rug-making. (*Looks around*) Where's your mate?

ALAN: He's gone out.

RIGSBY: (*grins*) Oh, he's left you on your own, has he? I thought you'd have both been out limbo dancing tonight.

ALAN: As a matter of fact he's got a date.

RIGSBY: He's not bringing her back here. I'm not having Miss Jones tormented by creaking bed-springs. They're the noisiest beds in the house – you can hear them even when the trains are passing.

ALAN: Philip's not like that.

RIGSBY: How do you know what he's like? You think he's marvellous, don't you?

ALAN: No.

RIGSBY: Yes, you do. You should have seen your face last night. You didn't believe all that rubbish did you? All that talk about supernatural powers?

ALAN: Didn't you?

RIGSBY: I wasn't taken in for a minute.

ALAN: He said he'd make something appear.

RIGSBY: Not Miss Jones – that was pure coincidence.

ALAN: Getting Miss Jones up here in her nightie was more than a coincidence – it was a miracle.

RIGSBY: (*shakes head*) I'm surprised at you. You're supposed to be a medical man. You'd believe anything.

ALAN: Speaking as a medical man, I've found that there are a great many things that can't be explained away. We see miracles in the wards everyday. We know so little, Rigsby.

RIGSBY: You're telling me. Look what happened when the man in the basement collapsed. You examined him and pronounced life extinct – three hours later he started snoring.

ALAN: We all make mistakes.

RIGSBY: Well, you're making another one now. Hanging about after him. (*Pause*) Why don't you come down to the Ram? Last half hour? Come on I'll take you – as long as you don't ask for red wine.

ALAN: No. The last time you took me there my eyes wouldn't focus for a week. And you left me in the garden all night.

RIGSBY: I told you before – I forgot where I'd put you.

ALAN: I woke up covered in dew.

RIGSBY: Well, it's no good sitting here. You ought to do something.

ALAN: I'll read a book.

RIGSBY: Suit yourself.

Rigsby exits.
Alan picks up a book. Yawns. Looks around. Notices spear. Becomes thoughtful. He takes spear down. And switches out light. He gets on his knees taps on floor three times. The knocking is returned. Alan looks surprised. Taps back. He is still staring at the floor when Ruth enters. She embraces Alan. Alan kisses her. She recoils. Puts on light.

RUTH: Alan! What do you think you're doing? You've made my ear go funny. Did Philip put you up to this?

ALAN: No.

RUTH: Where is he?

ALAN: He's gone out.

RUTH: He's so inconsiderate some-times. You wouldn't believe we're almost engaged, would you?

ALAN: (*surprised*) No.

RUTH: We're keeping it quiet at the moment. Well, you know what people are like. I don't know what Daddy would think. He wanted to keep Britain white.

ALAN: Haven't you told him?

RUTH: I can't. Poor Daddy's no longer with us.

ALAN: Has he moved?

RUTH No – he died three years ago – on Guy Fawkes' night. He had a heart attack in the street – people kept stepping over him, they thought he was a guy.

ALAN: Oh, I'm sorry.

RUTH: No, please don't worry. I'm sure he'd have seen the funny side of it. He had a marvellous sense of humour. (*Pause*) I must say I'm surprised Philip hasn't said anything to you.

ALAN: So am I.

RUTH: But then you don't really know him. He can say such won-derful things. Wild poetic things. I'll never forget that night. He said I was a pool without water – yet men may drown in me. He said I had the skin of fruit and beautiful milk. That's very basic isn't it.

ALAN: I think the bit about the milk is very basic.

RUTH: I knew you'd understand. You're so sensitive, Alan. (*She puts her hand on his*)

Rigsby enters. He watches them. Silent. Threatening. Ruth sees him. Starts.

RUTH: Well, I must go, Alan. I can't stop chattering here. Goodnight.

(*Edges by Rigsby*) Goodnight, Mr Rigsby.

Ruth exits.
Rigsby watches her go in silence.

RIGSBY: (*coldly*) What was she doing here?

ALAN: (*uneasily*) She brought something up.

RIGSBY: (*prowls around*) Was it the butter?

ALAN: Yes.

RIGSBY: (*fiercely*) Liar! So this is why you didn't want to go home at the weekend.

ALAN: (*backing away*) What do you mean?

RIGSBY: You've been planning this all along. I should have known. You students are all the same. Sex mad.

ALAN: Now wait a minute, Rigsby. How do you know she came up to see me.

RIGSBY: What do you mean?

ALAN: I'm not the only one who lives up here.

RIGSBY: Why, you—! So that's it. It's slander now is it? Do you think Miss Jones would involve herself with someone like that? A woman of her refinement. Have you seen that woman's washing? She still wears harvest festivals – all is safely gathered in, mate. Don't you cast aspersions at her.

ALAN: What are you doing to do, Rigsby?

RIGSBY: I'm going to split you down the middle.

Alan snatches up a bottle.

ALAN: Stand back, Rigsby. You know what's in this bottle? Micro-organisms. Millions of them. Enough to wipe out a whole city. I only have to remove the stopper.

RIGSBY: (*stops*) I don't believe you.

ALAN: Millions of them, Rigsby. And not one of them over-lapping.

RIGSBY: I can't see anything.

ALAN: You won't see anything. But they'll come hopping out after you just the same. I've only got to remove this stopper and within ten minutes you'll be foaming at the mouth – twenty minutes you'll be praying for death.

RIGSBY: Keep that away from me.

Alan reaches the door. Turns.

ALAN: Here, catch.

Alan throws the bottle to Rigsby who drops it. Rigsby sees something on his hands. Whimpers and recoils. Stops. Looks hard. Smells his hand. Licks it.

RIGSBY: Salad cream! I should have known. He couldn't tell the truth if his life depended on it. (*He picks up spear and is about to put it* back). As if Miss Jones would come up here to see him. Wild horses wouldn't—

He looks at spear. Hesitates. Looks around.

RIGSBY: Mumbo-jumbo – that's all it is.

Hesitates. Looks around again. He gets down on his knees. Raises the spear and brings it down three times with great solemnity.
The door opens, Philip stands on the threshold watching. Alan joins Philip and looks over his shoulder. Rigsby is about to raise the spear once more. Hears a chuckle. Turns. Sees them. They burst into laughter.

RIGSBY: Now wait a minute. What are you laughing at? I didn't say I believed it. Wait a minute.

They retreat laughing, followed by Rigsby brandishing the spear.

THE END

Series One

EPISODE 2

A Night Out
by
Eric Chappell

PART ONE

SCENE 1: *Int. top flat. Early evening. Alan and Philip are reading their books. Rigsby enters rather self-consciously. He looks unnaturally smart but dated. He is wearing a suit, white silk scarf and kid gloves. He coughs. They don't look up. He checks his lacquered hair in the mirror. Alan looks up. He sees Rigsby and does a double take.*

ALAN: Good heavens! (*Rigsby scowls*) Look at this, Philip. Who is this well-dressed stranger? Can it be Count Dracula back from the dead? Dropping in for a quick bite?

RIGSBY: Why don't you give it a rest?

ALAN: Why – it's Rigsby. I didn't recognise him, did you?

PHILIP: No. It must be the suit. I've never seen you in a suit before, Rigsby. Has there been a bereavement?

RIGSBY: (*angrily*) Look, I came to see what you thought – if you're going to be funny about it … (*He makes for the door*)

ALAN: (*hastily*) No – come back Rigsby. Let's have a look at you. (*Rigsby stands awkwardly in the middle of the floor. They study him. Alan looks closely at the suit.*) When did you last wear this, Rigsby – V.J. night?

RIGSBY: This is a good suit – real quality. You feel the material (*Alan feels the cloth*) It's thorn-proof.

ALAN: It feels bullet-proof to me.

PHILIP: (*smiles*) Don't listen to him, Rigsby. You look very smart.

RIGSBY: (*pleased*) Well, I knew you know more about clothes than he does. That's why I came up. Go on – tell me what you think. I don't mind.

PHILIP: Well … (*hesitates*) If I may make a criticism – it is a little dull.

RIGSBY: (*sharply*) Dull?

PHILIP: Yes.

RIGSBY: Well, it would be for you, wouldn't it?

PHILIP: What do you mean?

RIGSBY: Not enough bright colours I suppose.

PHILIP: I'm not talking about bright colours. I don't like bright colours.

RIGSBY: What! Give you a bale of coloured cloth and you'd dance till sunset.

PHILIP: As a matter of fact my favourite colour happens to be black, Rigsby.

RIGSBY: You couldn't wear black. You'd disappear.

PHILIP: Rigsby, when I said your suit was dull I wasn't referring to the colour – I meant there's no flair – no style. It's dull.

RIGSBY: Oh, yes. I suppose you'd improve it with a few beads and a shrunken head.

PHILIP: I think one shrunken head is enough, Rigsby.

Philip returns to his book.

RIGSBY: (*disappointed*) I knew I was wasting my time coming up here. What do you two know about fashion anyway?

ALAN: We know enough not to wear white scarves and kid gloves.

RIGSBY: There's nothing wrong with a silk scarf and gloves, mate. I could go anywhere in these. That's more than you could do. I was walking behind you yesterday – it was a bloody disgrace.

ALAN: What do you mean?

RIGSBY: There were blokes outside the Blue Ram making bets on which sex you were. All you needed was a handbag. And those trousers!

ALAN: What's wrong with them?

RIGSBY: They're too tight.

ALAN: No, they're not.

RIGSBY: They're crippling you. You keep wearing those and in two years you'll be singing soprano. (*Pause. Pulls up trousers*) At least there's plenty of room in this suit.

PHILIP: Where did you get it from Rigsby? Off a dead German?

RIGSBY: As a matter of fact I got it from Spooner. He was throwing it out because it wasn't flared enough for him. He's very fussy about his clothes.

ALAN: (*gets close. Sniffs*) Hmm. I can smell his cologne.

RIGSBY: Get off.

ALAN: Are you sure he's a wrestler? He smells more like a male model.

RIGSBY: Don't let him hear you say that. He'll tear your head off. They call him the Animal.

PHILIP: Rigsby, you haven't told us why you're all dressed up.

RIGSBY: What?

PHILIP: What's the special occasion?

RIGSBY: (*contemptuously*) Don't you know? Haven't you any idea?

They look at each other.

PHILIP: No.

RIGSBY: You're a heartless pair, aren't you? Today happens to be Miss Jones's birthday.

ALAN: Are you sure?

RIGSBY: I saw the cards arrive this morning.

PHILIP: (*shocked*) He's right. She mentioned it last week. I've just remembered.

RIGSBY: Well, it's a bit late now. She's had two cards that's all. I bet she's down there sobbing her socks off. Not that you two care. She hasn't even got a cake – just a bit of swiss roll. Well, it's not good enough. A birthday can be a very emotional time for a woman like that – living on her own. She'll be sitting there in her blue glasses looking back over the years – and what's she got to show for them, hey? Two cards and a swiss roll.

ALAN: I wonder how old she is.

RIGSBY: That's none of your business. The point is, what are we going to do about it?

PHILIP: What can we do about it now?

RIGSBY: I've already done something.

ALAN: What?

RIGSBY: (*slightly anxious*) I've booked a table at the Grange.

ALAN: The Grange! You must be joking. They'll never let you in.

RIGSBY: What do you mean?

ALAN: You've already been banned from the British Legion for poking that stripper with a stick of celery. What makes you think you'd be welcome at the Grange?

RIGSBY: Look, I know the manager.

ALAN: Don't tell me. He was in your mob during the war.

RIGSBY: No – he should have been. Actually, he spent most of the war in the false roof – behind the water tank.

PHILIP: Have you asked Ruth if she wants to go?

RIGSBY: Ah, well, that's one of the reasons I came up. I'm not going to ask her – you are.

PHILIP: What?

RIGSBY: You see if I ask her – she might get the wrong idea.

ALAN: (*innocently*) What do you mean – the wrong idea?

RIGSBY: (*uncomfortably*) Well, she might think … She might get the idea. You know – she might. (*Sees them grinning at each other*) Never mind what wrong idea – are you coming?

ALAN: I can't go to the Grange, I haven't got any money.

RIGSBY: You've never got any money. Have you taken a vow of poverty or something?

ALAN: You know I can't manage on my grant.

RIGSBY: Oh God! Not that again. I can feel the tears coming to my eyes. (*Pause*) All right – I'll pay for you.

ALAN: (*impressed*) Thanks, Rigsby.

RIGSBY: I'll add it to the rent.

ALAN: What about you, Philip?

PHILIP: Yes, why not?

RIGSBY: Good. (*Takes Philip's arm*). Now go down there and ask her.

Opens door and pushes Philip out on to landing.

* * *

SCENE 2: *Int. stairs and landing.*
Alan and Rigsby watch Philip go down stairs.

PHILIP: (*pauses*) Suppose she refuses?

RIGSBY: Tell her she's prejudiced.

PHILIP: (*frowns*) What?

RIGSBY: Go on – before she gets her blue glasses on.

Philip reaches the door and knocks on it. The others retreat.

RUTH: (*from behind door*) Who is it?

PHILIP: It's Philip. Can I see you for a moment?

RUTH: (*tremulous*) No.

PHILIP: Come on, Ruth, open the door.

RUTH: You don't want to see me.

PHILIP: I do.

RUTH: No, you don't – go away.

PHILIP: Well, if that's how you feel.

About to go.

RUTH: (*opens door quickly*) Well, if you're going to stand there all night I'll have to let you in.

* * *

SCENE 3: *Int. Ruth's flat.*
Philip enters. Ruth turns away, she is wearing her blue glasses.

RUTH: I suppose you've just remembered it's my birthday.

PHILIP: Many happy returns, Ruth.

RUTH: Oh, be quiet. I feel old.

PHILIP: You're not old.

RUTH: I'm older than you.

PHILIP: (*curiously*) How old are you?

RUTH: (*sharply*) Never mind that. (*She removes her blue glasses, looks in the mirror*) I look old.

PHILIP: Ruth, you're an attractive woman.

RUTH: (*turns profile to him*) You know you don't mean that.

PHILIP: I do. You're very attractive.

RUTH: (*quietly*) Well, I'm not going to argue with you, Philip. (*Pause, smiles*) A man did call after me as I was coming home.

PHILIP: What did he say?

RUTH: He said, 'Hello, Beautiful.'

PHILIP: There you are you see.

RUTH: I think he was drunk.

PHILIP: Why should you think that?

RUTH: Because after he said it he sank down in the middle of the road.

PHILIP: Well, you're still an attractive woman. You are. You don't look a day over thirty.

RUTH: (*angrily*) I'm not a day over thirty. And if I'm so attractive why am I sitting alone on my birthday? I should be exchanging repartee with beautiful friends. I should be surrounded by laughter and clinking glasses. Instead of which I'm deciding whether to try another mud pack or do some steam ironing.

PHILIP: Ruth – you're not alone.

RUTH: I may as well be. No one ever talks to me here. I wish I'd never left the Badminton Club.

PHILIP: But they never talked to you there.

RUTH: At least we shouted the score to each other. And they'd have remembered my birthday.

PHILIP: But I have remembered your birthday.

RUTH: What?

PHILIP: We're going to the Grange.

RUTH: Oh, Philip. Why didn't you tell me before. You shouldn't have let me go on like this. The Grange. There'll be dancing by candle-light. It'll be so romantic – just the two of us.

PHILIP: (*uneasily*) Well, not just the two of us.

* * *

SCENE 4: *Int. Spooner's room. Alan and Rigsby enter cautiously.*

RIGSBY: Er … Mr Spooner. Are you sure he's out?

ALAN: Yes.

RIGSBY: (*shakes head*) I don't know about this. Spooner's funny about his clothes. He knocked a bloke down three flights of stairs once just for wearing his hat.

ALAN: He never gets back before two. You'll have returned it by then. (*Alan opens wardrobe. Takes out tuxedo*) What about that, then, Rigsby?

RIGSBY: I'm not wearing that.

ALAN: Why not?

RIGSBY: I'll look like a fairy.

ALAN: No, you won't.

RIGSBY: Look, I'm going to eat there – not play in the band.

ALAN: This is the sort of thing they wear there. Try it on.

Rigsby puts it on.

ALAN: Well, what do you think?

RIGSBY: Um.

ALAN: Think of it. The candlelight. The orchestra playing in the background. You in a tuxedo. She won't be able to resist you.

RIGSBY: (*hesitates*) I don't know. I look like Gary Glitter.

ALAN: Rigsby – this is the thing to wear. You don't want to look out of place do you?

RIGSBY: Wait a minute. It won't be me who'll look out of place. What about our friend.

ALAN: Why should Philip look out of place?

RIGSBY: Well, it may have escaped your notice but he's a bit on the dark side … They notice things like that at the Grange. You'd better tell him to stick close to me.

ALAN: And who are you going to stick close to, Rigsby?

RIGSBY: Then there's going to be the knives and forks.

ALAN: What about the knives and forks?

RIGSBY: What's he going to make of them? They'll be stretched out there like surgical instruments. I mean it's going to be a bit different from a dip in the tribal stewpot.

ALAN: Rigsby – what do you think he's going to do? Eat with his bare hands?

RIGSBY: We don't know what he's going to do. That's what I'm saying. For all we know his favourite meal's probably a handful of maize and a bit of burnt Christian. We'll have to keep an eye on him. We don't want him dropping any clangers. We don't want him drinking out of the finger bowl.

Alan is reaching into the wardrobe. Takes out a bow tie.

ALAN: What do you think to this?

RIGSBY: Does it light up?

ALAN: Of course, it is a clip on. (*Puts it on*) I'd sooner tie one myself.

RIGSBY: Spooner'll tie one for you if he finds out. He won't like this.

ALAN: Well, are you going to wear it or not?

RIGSBY: I suppose it's not too bad. I've got a feeling tonight's the night. I think she's going to be surprised when she sees me.

END OF PART ONE

PART TWO

SCENE 5: *Ext. The Grange. Evening.*
A taxi draws up outside. Ruth is the
first to emerge. She looks back at the
taxi, obviously displeased. She enters
through the swing doors. Alan
follows. Philip and Rigsby are
paying the driver.

RIGSBY: Trust him to show a clean
pair of heels when it comes to the
fare. (*Rigsby takes Philip's arm*)
Now, listen. Before we go in –
there's no need to be nervous.

PHILIP: (*puzzled*) What?

RIGSBY: Just stick close to me. All
right?

PHILIP: Yes.

RIGSBY: Good. Now watch these
swing doors. You'll find them a bit
different from the old beaded curtains. You'll have to be sharpish or
they'll take your foot off.

Rigsby enters the swing doors the
wrong way. He is involved in a
struggle with a party leaving and is
finally propelled onto the pavement
again.

Bloody peasants. You can tell
they've never been anywhere.

Rigsby enters once more followed by
Philip.

* * *

SCENE 6: *Int. Grange.*
The Grange is in period style.
Panelled. Heraldic devices. Old
torture instruments. Rigsby and
Philip enter.

RIGSBY: (*turns to Philip*) Don't
worry. If anyone says anything to
you – tell them you're with me.

Rigsby advances towards restaurant
where Alan and Ruth are waiting.
The manager appears. He gives
Rigsby an icy stare.

MANAGER: Hey! You.

RIGSBY: Who, me?

MANAGER: Yes, you. Where do
you think you're going?

RIGSBY: I'm going in there.

MANAGER: Oh, no you're not.
Outside.

RIGSBY: What do you mean
outside? I've got a table.

MANAGER: Tables are all taken.

RIGSBY: Now wait a minute—

PHILIP: Hello, Charles. Is there
some difficulty?

56

MANAGER: Hello, Mr Smith. (*Looks from Philip to Rigsby*) Is this gentleman with you? I'm sorry. Would you like your usual table. This way. (*He ushers them through. Confidentially to Philip*) I'm sorry about that, sir. But we can't be too careful these days.

Close up of Rigsby bringing up the rear – fuming.

* * *

SCENE 6a. *Int. restaurant. Late evening.*
Rigsby, Ruth and Philip are sitting at a table. They have finished their meal. Rigsby is drawing on a cigar.

RIGSBY: Have some more wine, Miss Jones.

RUTH: Do you think I should? My face is glowing.

RIGSBY: (*leers*) You look radiant, Miss Jones. (*He pours more wine*)

RUTH: Not too much. I feel quite light-headed. If I have any more I shall do something silly.

RIGSBY: We'd better have another bottle. Hey!

He tries to get attention of waiter. He is ignored. Philip raises a languid hand. The waiter appears as if by magic.

Same again, waiter. (*The waiter sniffs and departs*) You know I've never seen you by candle-light before, Miss Jones. The effect is magical.

RUTH: (*coyly*) Mr Rigsby.

RIGSBY: Yes. A woman like you, you really grace a dinner table. Stimulating the conversation – pushing around the mints. We should do this more often.

RUTH: Yes. It was such a nice idea of yours to come here, Philip. (*Pats Philip's hand*)

PHILIP: (*uncomfortably*) I'm glad you're enjoying it.

Rigsby frowns at Philip. Gestures with his head for him to leave.

RUTH: This place has such an ambience – don't you agree, Mr Rigsby?

RIGSBY: Er … yes.

RUTH: (*solemnly*) Do you know we're sitting in old church pews?

RIGSBY: It feels like it.

RUTH: I mean everything's so Gothic. And those torture instruments on the wall as we came in – they're absolutely genuine.

RIGSBY: (*laughs*) Of course they're genuine. That's in case you can't pay. They don't make you wash the pots anymore – just screw you up in an iron boot.

The music starts.

RUTH: Oh, they're dancing. It's simply ages since I've danced.

RIGSBY: Of course, Miss Jones.

Rigsby stands up and extinguishes his cigar. Ruth meanwhile dances away with Philip. Rigsby scowls.

Bloody cheek. (*Tries to relight cigar. Alan returns to the table*) Where have you been?

ALAN: Don't go to the bogs.

RIGSBY: Why not?

ALAN: There's a man in there brushing you down and asking you if you've had a nice holiday. It costs you 10p to get out.

RIGSBY: You should have shown him your Barclay card.

ALAN: It's the dearest one I've ever had. Mind you, he said I looked well.

RIGSBY: (*eyes him coldly*) Some people would say anything for 10p. What can you expect? You won't get it for a penny here. You're paying for the ambience – whatever that is. It reminds me of a visit to my Aunt Hilda's – a big hello and a small sherry. The only difference is her cobwebs are genuine.

ALAN: Well, at least it makes a change from the Blue Ram. At least they don't spit on your shoes here.

RIGSBY: I wouldn't mind but I'm still hungry.

ALAN: You can't be.

RIGSBY: I could go a bag of chips.

ALAN: (*looks around*) Where are Ruth and Philip?

RIGSBY: Over there – dancing. He's taking a lot on himself. I still want to know why he ordered the meal.

ALAN: Well, you couldn't – it was in French.

RIGSBY: I was managing – until he stuck his oar in.

ALAN: Rigsby – we didn't come here to have plaice and chips four times.

RIGSBY: I don't know why he can't take a hint. I've been giving him the nod all night. How am I going to get her on her own? Look at him? Leaping around flashing his choppers. He'll be arching his back and passing under the table in a minute. I feel sorry for Miss Jones – she can't be enjoying it.

ALAN: She looks as if she's enjoying it.

RIGSBY: No. She's being polite. She'd much prefer a slow waltz. That's where I'm going to score. He couldn't do a slow waltz. His feet are all wrong. If he tried a reverse turn he'd be arse over elbow. You wait until they play a waltz – if this lot can play it without electrocuting them-selves. (*Shouts through cupped hands*) What about a waltz?

People stare. The manager approaches. He gives Rigsby a stony stare.

MANAGER: Is everything to your satisfaction, gentlemen?

ALAN: (*hastily*) Fine – thank you.

RIGSBY: Yes. You've come a long way from that tea urn in the market, Charlie.

MANAGER: I beg your pardon?

RIGSBY: I'll never forget you and your dad. Standing behind that tea urn – with those plates of curly sandwiches.

MANAGER: (*angrily*) There was nothing wrong with those sandwiches.

RIGSBY: Well, I can understand you being loyal to them, Charlie – they were in the family a long time but you couldn't call them fresh, could you?

MANAGER: We never had any complaints.

RIGSBY: Never had any complaints? You couldn't get near the counter for food inspectors. And what about that tea?

MANAGER: What was wrong with the tea?

RIGSBY: It could hardly crawl out of the spout. It was Charlie's job to dash by the urn at high speed with a tea bag.

The manager looks around in embarrassment.

MANAGER: Would you mind keeping your voice down? You're annoying the other guests.

RIGSBY: Don't they know about the stall, Charlie?

MANAGER: And don't call me Charlie. (*Low menacing*) Listen, I know you. You're a troublemaker. Well, I'm going to keep a very close eye on this table and if there's any trouble from either of you – you're out.

The manager stalks away.

RIGSBY: Poor old Charlie – he never did have much sense of humour.

ALAN: We haven't had the bill yet.

RIGSBY: It'll be worth it. Just look at Miss Jones. She's radiant. I should have done this before. It's a new environment. She's looking at me as a man not a landlord for the first time.

ALAN: Are you sure?

RIGSBY: Yes. You just watch for the signs. If she leaves her hand on mine just that shade too long – make yourself scarce.

ALAN: (*starts*) Rigsby! Is that Spooner over there?

RIGSBY: What?

ALAN: It is! He's coming this way.

RIGSBY: God! He'll murder me if he sees me in his jacket. Look the other way.

Rigsby hides behind the menu. Spooner, built like a wrestler, passes the table. Stops.

SPOONER: Hello, Alan.

ALAN: (*covers tie*) Hello, Spooner.

SPOONER: I didn't know you came here.

ALAN: Now and then.

SPOONER: You'd better not let that old skinflint find out – he'll be putting your rent up. (*Rigsby glares behind menu. Spooner turns away then turns back again.*) Wait a minute – that's my tie.

ALAN: What?

SPOONER: You're wearing my tie.

ALAN: I only borrowed it, Spooner.

SPOONER: Nobody borrows my things.

He leans forward and snatches the tie from Alan.

ALAN: Spooner!

SPOONER: And in future – keep out of my room.

Spooner walks away. Rigsby peers out from behind menu. Sees Alan covering his throat.

RIGSBY: What happened?

ALAN: He's taken the tie.

RIGSBY: I thought he'd cut your throat.

ALAN: He may as well have done. They don't let people in here without a tie.

RIGSBY: Well, you're in now.

ALAN: Do you think they'll throw me out?

Looks around nervously.

RIGSBY: For not wearing a tie? No. Probably give you a couple of turns on the rack, that's all. Don't worry. I'll get him. Calling me a skinflint. You wait until he takes a bath – there's going to be a sudden absence of hot water.

The music stops, Philip and Ruth return to the table.

RUTH: Thank you, Philip. I enjoyed that. You're such a natural dancer.

RIGSBY: So that's what it was. Dancing. I thought he was trying to bring rain.

ALAN: Well, I wish I could do it.

RIGSBY: That's not dancing. Letting yourself go like that. It's indecent.

PHILIP: (*mocking*) Well, you know what it's like when we hear da music, Rigsby. Am hopin' to have a go on da bongos later.

RIGSBY: Not if I can help it. What we want now is a bit of Strauss – civilised music. Couples gliding across the floor as one.

The music starts again. Slower this time.

ALAN: Now's your chance, Rigsby.

RIGSBY: All right. Don't rush me. (*Formally*) Miss Jones, would you care for the next waltz?

RUTH: (*rising hesitantly*) Er ... certainly, Mr Rigsby.

They cross onto the floor.

RIGSBY: If it gets a bit tricky, Miss Jones – don't worry, just follow me.

Rigsby guides Miss Jones across the floor with great dignity.

PHILIP: What's he doing?

ALAN: Dancing. That's how they used to do it years ago.

Rigsby spins around with Miss Jones.

PHILIP: Will he be able to stop?

ALAN: I hope so. If he lets go of her now she'll end up in the kitchen.

Cut to Rigsby. He's dancing with a blissful smile on his face. He lets go of Ruth's hand, promenades, twirls around and rejoins her. Other dancers watch in admiration.

ALAN: He's not the same man, is he?

PHILIP: It's incredible.

ALAN: Crikey! There's Spooner.

Spooner is standing on the dance floor with his arms folded. Rigsby breaks away from Ruth spins round and takes an angry Spooner into his arms.

RIGSBY: Spooner!

SPOONER: What are you doing in my tuxedo, Rigsby?

RIGSBY: I'm dancing. What do you think I'm doing? Let go!

SPOONER: You've been in my wardrobe.

RIGSBY: Sling your hook, Spooner. I'm with a lady.

SPOONER: I want my tuxedo.

RIGSBY: I've only borrowed it. I'll have it back by twelve.

SPOONER: Will you? (*He pulls the jacket down over Rigsby's shoulders*) Well, I've got news for you, Cinderella – the ball is over and your coach has turned back into a pumpkin.

RIGSBY: Let go.

An undignified struggle takes place. There is a ripping sound. A sleeve comes away in Spooner's hand. Ruth turns on her heel and returns to the table.

RUTH: I've never been so humiliated in my life. I shall never be able to come here again. Take me home, Philip.

She exits. Philip shrugs at Alan and follows her.
Cut to Spooner who is examining sleeve. He is almost tearful.

SPOONER: Look what you've done. You've ruined it. I don't want it back now. And you won't get any more rent out of me until it's paid for.

He throws the sleeve down and stalks off the floor. Rigsby picks up

the sleeve rather sadly. People look the other way.
He returns to his table.

RIGSBY: Where's Miss Jones?

ALAN: She's gone, Rigsby.

RIGSBY: Was she annoyed?

ALAN: What do you think?

RIGSBY: It's a good thing for Spooner the magistrates won't allow me one more punch. Why did he have to come along? I was near to it there. She was definitely weakening.

The manager approaches them. He is wearing a triumphant, sadistic smile. He circles the table. Alan tries to hide his missing tie. Rigsby tries to put on sleeve.

MANAGER: I understand there's been a disturbance on the dance floor.

RIGSBY: No, I wouldn't call it a disturbance. (*To Alan*) Would you call it a disturbance?

ALAN: Not a disturbance. Just a gentle ripple really.

MANAGER: (*stares at Alan*) Excuse me, sir, but you're not wearing a tie.

ALAN: Er … no … I—

MANAGER: We have a strict rule about gentlemen wearing ties here, sir. It's to keep out the riff-raff (*glance at Rigsby*). I'm afraid I must ask you to leave. And

you'd better take your friend with you.

RIGSBY: Wait a minute – I've got a tie.

MANAGER: Yes. Well, it may have escaped your attention but you only appear to have one sleeve. You're both improperly dressed and I must ask you to settle your bill and leave.

ALAN: Come on, Rigsby.

RIGSBY: Why should we?

MANAGER: Of course if you wish us to use force.

RIGSBY: (*raising voice*) That's right. Throw us out. I should have expected this. This is the way the country treats its heroes. It was different when I was standing between you and Hitler. Where were you in 1940? I'll tell you – in your false roof.

MANAGER: What do you mean? I went in.

RIGSBY: I know what you were in – the 49th Deserters. The red caps were round your house every Monday morning – they spent half the war fighting your mother.

MANAGER: Get out of here at once.

Waiters move forward.

RIGSBY: Be careful. If this shrapnel moves another half inch you'll have a death on your hands. (*They draw back*) Of course I can understand it. You were making a fortune until the GIs found out that half a crown wasn't the same as a penny.

MANAGER: (*almost wringing hands*) Will you please go – quietly.

RIGSBY: Don't worry – I'm going. We don't want to disturb the ambience, do we? (*Moves to go. Pauses at next table*) Watch what you're eating. What do you think he's got the candles for? So that you can't see. You're eating the only four-legged chicken in captivity. Anyone lost a cat lately?

The waiters close in on Alan and Rigsby. They are evicted.

* * *

SCENE 7: *Ext. Grange. Night.*
Rigsby and Alan are precipitated onto the pavement.

RIGSBY: (*darts back up the steps*) Meeow!

ALAN: Come on, Rigsby.

RIGSBY: I've been thrown out of better places than this. It's a dump. (*Shouts*) I'm still hungry!

ALAN: So am I. Do you fancy a bag of chips?

RIGSBY: With plenty of vinegar.

ALAN: And some scollops.

RIGSBY: And some soggy peas. What are we waiting for?

ALAN: Wait a minute.

He crosses to where a party has just arrived.

ALAN: (*businesslike*) Ah. Excuse me, has the stomach pump arrived? Damn. I'll have to ring the hospital again. Four down with food poisoning. No warning, just sudden convulsions at the table. I wouldn't go in there – it's not a pretty sight.

The guests stare at him in horror. Alan rejoins Rigsby.

RIGSBY: Well, I don't suppose it's been too bad. At least we've given Miss Jones a night to remember.

Alan stares at him. They set off down the street.

THE END

Series One

EPISODE 3

Charisma
by
Eric Chappell

PART ONE

SCENE 1: *Int. Ruth's flat. Evening. Ruth is clearing away the tea things. There is a knock and Rigsby peers around the door.*

RIGSBY: I've come to fix your drip, Miss Jones. (*Enters*)

RUTH: Oh, thank you, Mr Rigsby. I don't know what I'd do without you.

RIGSBY: That's all right – that's what I'm here for. Any little thing, Miss Jones. (*Leers, crosses to sink*)

RUTH: (*follows*) I'm afraid I'm not very practical.

RIGSBY: (*tightening tap*) No, well, you're the more artistic type – you like beautiful things (*motions to draining board*). Look at your cups – willow pattern plate. Lovely theme – separates you from the rest, Miss Jones. And your table mats. Scenes from the ballet. How many people around here eat off scenes from the ballet? You're lucky if you get a beer mat. No, you've got that indefinable something called good taste, Miss Jones.

RUTH: Do you think so, Mr Rigsby?

RIGSBY: Oh, yes. You've made a difference to this place. Shades on the bulbs, blue water in the toilet. You've really raised the standard.

RUTH: I hope the others don't think I'm too fussy. I mean, I do want them to accept me.

RIGSBY: They'll accept you all right – that's what worries me. (*Stands back*) There, that's fixed it. Anything else, Miss Jones?

RUTH: Yes. I wonder if you'd have a look at the doorknob?

RIGSBY: Again? I looked at it last week. What's the matter with it now?

RUTH: (*apologetically*) People keep walking off with it.

RIGSBY: Do they? (*Examines knob*) Huh! You can see why – it's been vandalised. What can you expect with that lot upstairs. (*A few turns of screw*) There, that's fixed it.

RUTH: Oh, good. I don't know how to thank you, Mr Rigsby.

RIGSBY: (*slowly*) I was thinking, Miss Jones. Spooner's given me a couple of tickets for the wrestling – for tomorrow night (*diffidently*) I was wondering if you'd like to come?

66

RUTH: (*surprised*) Me, Mr Rigsby? Oh, I don't know … I —

RIGSBY: (*hastily*) They're not too near the front – well, you don't want a fifteen-stone wrestler in your lap, do you?

RUTH: (*quietly*) Does that happen?

RIGSBY: It can do. And Spooner has got this nasty habit of spitting his drinking water over the crowd. All in the heat of battle, of course.

RUTH: (*doubtfully*) Well, it's very nice of you to ask me but—

RIGSBY: You'll enjoy it. It's a grudge fight. Spooner against the Russian. It ended with a broken leg last time.

RUTH: How awful! Mr Spooner or the Russian?

RIGSBY: Neither – I think it was somebody in the third row. You see, the Russian comes on in ballet tights and pelts Spooner with flowers. This infuriates Spooner and he belts the Russian with the stool.

RUTH: Surely the referee wouldn't allow that?

RIGSBY: No, this is before they shake hands. Of course everyone starts booing Spooner while the Russian keeps blowing him kisses.

RUTH: Poor Mr Spooner.

RIGSBY: You don't understand, Miss Jones. They're supposed to boo him. He's the villain.

RUTH: Doesn't he have any supporters?

RIGSBY: Not many – you see they're the ones he spits at. Well, what do you say, Miss Jones? Perhaps we could have a spot of supper afterwards.

RUTH: I'm sorry, Mr Rigsby, but I've just remembered. I'm working late tomorrow night.

RIGSBY: Ah. (*Crushed*)

RUTH: (*anxiously*) I hope you don't mind?

RIGSBY: No. No, of course not. I quite understand, Miss Jones.

RUTH: It was nice of you to ask me. I'm sorry.

RIGSBY: That's all right. It was just a thought. I can always get rid of them. After all it's all fixed, isn't it?

Rigsby exits with an attempt at jauntiness. Ruth stands guiltily by the door. Sighs. Crosses room deep in thought. Pauses. Looks down at doorknob in her hand.

* * *

SCENE 2: *Int. attic flat.*
Alan is looking in the mirror as Philip enters. Alan turns.

ALAN: Well, what do you think?

PHILIP: What about?

ALAN: The earring (*points to his ear*)

PHILIP: Oh yes. (*Examines earring*) It's not very big, is it?

ALAN: It doesn't want to be – catch it in anything it could tear your ear off. (*Anxiously*) Do you like it?

PHILIP: Yes. You look as if you don't give a damn.

ALAN: Well, I don't.

PHILIP: Has Rigsby seen it?

ALAN: No, I've been covering it with my hand. Well, you know what he's like. He thinks a signet ring's flashy. Do you want a coffee? (*Crosses to cooker*)

PHILIP: I need something.

ALAN: What's the matter?

PHILIP: I've just said goodnight to the most beautiful girl I've ever met – there were tears in her eyes.

ALAN: Why, what happened?

PHILIP: Nothing – that's the trouble. I wanted to bring her back here but how could I with Rigsby prowling around?

ALAN: Couldn't you go back to her place?

PHILIP: No, she's in college. It's driving me mad. I've got a big scene going here.

ALAN: Again?

PHILIP: What do you mean – again? This is different. I'd go through fire and flood for this girl.

ALAN: What about the park?

PHILIP: And get covered in moss and dead leaves. Do you want me to ruin my clothes?

ALAN: I thought you'd like the park. Just you and her under the stars.

PHILIP: Would you stop talking as if I was the last of the Mohicans? As far as I'm concerned the park is strictly for the ducks. (*Drinks*) What's the matter with Rigsby anyway?

ALAN: Ruth keeps turning him down. It's made him bitter. He's down there right now asking her to go to the wrestling. (*Shakes head*) She won't go. She's afraid the main bout will be her versus Rigsby.

PHILIP: (*Still concerned with his problem*) I think I'll tell him straight out that I'm bringing a girl back.

ALAN: You do that and you'll find your cases in the hall. Besides, what about Ruth. She'll have the vapours if you bring a girl back here. No, what we should do is try and get Ruth and Rigsby together.

PHILIP: And how do we do that?

ALAN: We've got to give Rigsby some advice.

Philip stares at him and starts to laugh.

PHILIP: What sort of advice could you give him?

ALAN: (*frowns*) How to make it with Ruth.

PHILIP: But you've never made it with anyone.

ALAN: Yes, I have.

PHILIP: Alan, I've never seen you with a girl.

ALAN: Wait a minute. What about that girl who's been following me?

PHILIP: What girl?

ALAN: The one on the racing bike.

PHILIP: You can't count her – she never dismounts.

ALAN: She will – you wait and see. Besides, just because you haven't seen me with a girl that doesn't mean there hasn't been one. As a matter of fact I've just been getting over a very big scene.

PHILIP: Oh, I didn't know.

ALAN: I don't talk about it much but it was pretty steamy while it lasted.

PHILIP: Like that?

ALAN: They say I was the reason she failed her O levels.

PHILIP: You mean she was still at school? And you're going to advise Rigsby?

Sound off. Rigsby approaching coughing.

ALAN: Don't you think he needs it?

Rigsby enters coughing. He gives them a sour look.

ALAN: Want some coffee, Rigsby?

RIGSBY: I need something – my guts are in a turmoil.

ALAN: Do you take anything for it?

RIGSBY: No – deep breathing – that's the only thing that helps. Deep breathing – every morning.

ALAN: You should see a doctor.

RIGSBY: (*shakes head*) No. You start worrying about your health and you're finished. We had a bloke like that downstairs. He thought his shoulder blades were deformed. Kept asking me to look at them. Spent hours trying to see them in the mirror. By the time he was finished they *were* deformed. (*Drinks coffee*) That's better.

PHILIP: (*clears throat*) Rigsby – there's something I wanted to ask you.

RIGSBY: (*lowers cup*) My God! (*Stares at Alan*) What's that?'

ALAN: What?

RIGSBY: On your ear – something's glinting. What is it?

ALAN: It's an earring.

RIGSBY: An earring! Stop the world I want to get off.

ALAN: What's wrong with it?

RIGSBY: What's wrong with it? You

look like the gypsy's warning! You know I'm getting worried about you. You're getting more effeminate every day – it must be all that red wine you're drinking.

ALAN: Everyone's wearing them, Rigsby.

RIGSBY: Then God help England. Let's hope the Russians don't find out. I can just see us all marching into battle in bloody earrings – that'll really send a thrill of fear through the enemy.

ALAN: Philip thinks it's all right.

RIGSBY: Well, he would, wouldn't he. He thinks a bone through the nose is all right.

PHILIP: (*controls himself*) Rigsby, I wanted to ask you—

RIGSBY: Here's some tickets for the wrestling. (*Hurls the tickets down savagely*)

The boys stare at him.

RIGSBY: Ask me what?

PHILIP: Er … it doesn't matter.

ALAN: (*picks up tickets*) Has she turned you down, Rigsby?

RIGSBY: Mind your own business. (*Sighs. Sits down*) I can't understand it. I've tried everything with that woman.

ALAN: (*Puts hand on Rigsby's shoulder*) Do you want some advice, Rigsby?

RIGSBY: From you? Who do you

think you are – bachelor of the month? I don't need your advice.

ALAN: Rigsby, you've got to change your image. You've got to get with it.

RIGSBY: Perhaps I should borrow your earring.

ALAN: You know what I mean.

RIGSBY: I know what you mean. You mean medallions – shirt open to the waist and drinking Campari while some bird in a nightie's helping you off with your boots. Well, life's not like that. (*Bitterly*) Besides she's too busy with good causes to worry about me. (*Glance at Philip*) Too busy worrying about his mates in Africa. The trouble is I'm not a good cause.

PHILIP: Oh, I don't know – what about Help the Aged?

ALAN: (*hastily*) You know what you need, Rigsby? Charisma.

RIGSBY: I'm not spraying myself with that stuff, mate – it dries up all your juices.

ALAN: No. Charisma. It means personal charm – appeal.

RIGSBY: Well, I haven't noticed much charisma around here.

ALAN: Ruth doesn't want to go to the wrestling. You know what she'd like? A quiet evening listening to Perry Como.

RIGSBY: Oh yes.

ALAN: Look, I've got his latest record here. (*Gets record*) Why don't you take it down there? Give it a twirl – get her in a romantic mood and then give her a gentle squeeze.

Rigsby looks down at the record and then back at Alan.

RIGSBY: Perry Como?

ALAN: It never fails.

RIGSBY: (*sighs*) I don't know. The trouble is she's a sensitive woman and my stomach being what it is – it starts to roll whenever I get near her!

ALAN: That's all right. Take a couple of these (*hands Rigsby a small bottle*). They'll settle your stomach and tone you up at the same time.

RIGSBY: (*examines bottle suspiciously*) They haven't got any hormones in them, have they?

ALAN: No.

RIGSBY: Only that bloke down the road – the one who got the cheap turkey at Christmas – that was full of hormones. Three days later his wife had a deeper voice than he'd got.

ALAN: I can assure you they're perfectly harmless, Rigsby.

Rigsby pockets bottle.

ALAN: Don't forget the record.

RIGSBY: I don't suppose it would do any harm.

PHILIP: Wait a moment, Rigsby.

Philip advances and slips a medallion over Rigsby's neck. Rigsby winces but does not object.

RIGSBY: (*anxiously*) Who did you say this was by?

ALAN: Perry Como.

RIGSBY: Perry Como. (*Nods*)

Rigsby exits.

PHILIP: What were those tablets?

ALAN: Mild tranquillisers – perfectly harmless. The big thing is they'll give him confidence – you see he's put Ruth on a pedestal.

PHILIP: As long as they don't put him on a pedestal. How did you get hold of them?

ALAN: They were taken off the market.

PHILIP: I thought you said they were harmless?

ALAN: Well, they do have this side effect.

PHILIP: What sort of side effect?

ALAN: They turn your water green.

Philip stares.

* * *

SCENE 3: *Int. landing.*
Rigsby, his hair slicked is standing outside Ruth's door. Hesitates. Takes out bottle. Swallows several tablets. About to knock. Pauses. Undoes top button of shirt. Knocks. Enters.

* * *

SCENE 4: *Int. Ruth's flat.*
Rigsby enters, gives Ruth an oily grin.

RUTH: (*puzzled*) Yes, Mr Rigsby?

RIGSBY: I thought you'd like to hear this record, Miss Jones. Perry Como.

RUTH: Oh, Perry Como. Yes, I do like him. He does things to me.

RIGSBY: Does he? I'll slip it on.

Rigsby crosses to record player. He blinks and has great difficulty in putting record over the spindle. Stands back.

RIGSBY: Where's the handle?

RUTH: It works by electricity.

RIGSBY: Yes, of course. I've got it. Why don't you sit down, Miss Jones? Just let it flow over you.

Rigsby joins Ruth on the couch. A slurred voice comes from the record player.

RIGSBY: (*smiles*) He's got a lovely voice, Miss Jones.

RUTH: Mr Rigsby, it's on the wrong speed.

RIGSBY: What?

RUTH: I'll do it. (*She rises slowly then abruptly as if pinched*) Mr Rigsby! (*Ruth crosses to the record player looking shocked*) I hope we're not going to go in for that sort of male chauvinism. Whatever you may think, I'm not a sex object – nor do I abandon myself to the strains of Perry Como. I don't know who's given you that impression. (*Worried glance at ceiling*) If someone's shown you those cuff-links bought in a weak moment, I can only— (*turns*) Mr Rigsby!

Cut to Rigsby.
He is asleep, a fixed glassy smile on his face, his jaw set. He slides gently onto carpet.

END OF PART ONE

PART TWO

SCENE 5: *Int. attic flat. Next evening. Alan is pacing anxiously. He gives a start as Philip enters.*

ALAN: Have you seen Rigsby?

PHILIP: Yes.

ALAN: Was he awake?

PHILIP: Yes.

ALAN: (*relieved*) Good.

PHILIP: But he can't feel his teeth.

ALAN: What!

PHILIP: He's been to the doctor's. (*Listens*) I think that's him now.

ALAN: I'd better go.

Alan moves to the door as Rigsby enters.

RIGSBY: Where do you think you're going?

ALAN: What's the matter, Rigsby?

RIGSBY: You ask me that after nearly poisoning me.

ALAN: You're exaggerating.

RIGSBY: I was drugged to the eyeballs. I slept for twenty-four hours. I still can't feel my teeth.

And that's not all – do you know what I found when I went to the bathroom? My water's turned green!

ALAN: (*nervously*) Green?

RIGSBY: Bright green. I've taken those pills to the doctor's. He said they were for women in early pregnancy. Do I look as if I'm in early pregnancy? I'd sue you if you'd got any money. Of course you've finished me with Miss Jones. She thinks I'm stark staring mad – and I don't blame her. Why did I have to listen to you?

ALAN: I was only trying to help.

RIGSBY: You! My God! What do you know about the opposite sex? If a woman so much as looked at you you'd have a nose bleed. The only thing you've ever taken to bed is your Mickey Mouse hot water bottle.

ALAN: As a matter of fact I'm seeing a woman tonight, Rigsby.

RIGSBY: There he goes again. You know, I think you live in a dream world. I don't think these women exist. Sometimes I don't think you exist. Sometimes I think you came out of the bloody wallpaper.

Alan musters his shattered dignity.

ALAN: I am seeing a woman tonight. You believe me don't you, Philip?

Philip looks silently out of the window. Alan looks from one to the other.

ALAN: Well, it's true anyway.

Alan exits to bedroom.

PHILIP: (*almost sympathetic*) There'll be another time, Rigsby.

RIGSBY: I'm not so sure about that. It's all right for you. I mean, it's different in Africa. You're closer to nature. I haven't been close to nature since last Christmas – I wasn't that close then. (*Sighs*) I don't get many chances these days. There was this woman at the pub. They all said don't give her a lift home or she'll interfere with you. She was supposed to interfere with you while you were driving. So I gave her a lift home.

PHILIP: What happened?

RIGSBY: Nothing. She was a washout. All she did was talk about her feet.

Philip smiles. Rigsby regards him thoughtfully.

RIGSBY: What would you do in my position?

PHILIP: What?

RIGSBY: What would they do in your country?

PHILIP: In my country, if a man was in your position he'd get the wood of the love tree and burn it outside the girl's hut. When she smelled the smoke she'd appear at the door. He'd look deep into her eyes and she'd fall in love with him.

RIGSBY: Just like that? (*Hesitates*) Have you got any of this wood?

PHILIP: Why – would you like some?

RIGSBY: I'm not saying I believe it.

PHILIP: Well, I don't have it.

RIGSBY: Look, anything's worth a try. I'm desperate. I'll do you a favour sometime … Philip.

PHILIP: That may be sooner than you think, Rigsby. (*Winks*) I'll get it for you.

Philip enters bedroom as Alan emerges. Alan looks curiously at Rigsby, who hovers uneasily.
Philip returns and hands Rigsby a piece of wood. Rigsby takes it surreptitiously and makes for the door. Stops.

RIGSBY: Hey! This has been planed.

PHILIP: (*shrugs*) Everything's commercial these days, Rigsby.

Satisfied, Rigsby exits.

ALAN: What was that all about?

PHILIP: (*smiles*) I've given Rigsby some love wood. He's going to burn it outside Ruth's hut.

ALAN: Do you think it'll work?

PHILIP: I shouldn't think so – it came off the wardrobe.

Alan stares.

* * *

SCENE 6: *Int. attic flat. Late evening. Alan enters. Switches on the light. He appears breathless. He is followed by a rather defiant girl in jumper and shorts.*

ALAN: Well, this is it, Beryl.

BERYL: (*astonished*) You mean you live up here? Where do you keep your oxygen?

ALAN: You get used to it. Come and sit down.

BERYL: Aren't you forgetting something?

ALAN: (*sighs*) In here?

He crosses to landing and returns with a racing bike which he leans against the wall.

ALAN: You could have left it downstairs – it would have been perfectly safe. We're quite respectable here.

BERYL: (*coldly*) That's not what I heard. (*Circles room. Pauses at skeleton*) Who's your friend?

ALAN: I've told you – I'm a doctor.

BERYL: Who was he – one of your patients?

ALAN: Sit down – let me get you a drink.

Alan takes out several nasty-looking bottles. He blows dust from the soda syphon.

ALAN: What'll you have?

BERYL: No thanks. I can always have a drink from my canisters. (*Suspiciously*) You look very young for a doctor.

ALAN: Yes. Everyone says that. Do you know I've even been taken for a student. You should hear them in the Operating Theatre. 'Good God! You're not going to let that boy cut me open.'

BERYL: Why are you whispering?

ALAN: I'm not whispering. I've got a low voice.

BERYL: Are you frightened of the landlord?

ALAN: Who, Rigsby? No – he knows his place. You have to humour him of course. He's a bit simple – he had a bad war. Burst a paper bag behind Rigsby and he'd be straight over that settee. Would you like a sweet?

He offers Beryl a crumpled bag. She peers in.

BERYL: They don't look like sweets. They look like those things my sister had – they turned her water green.

Alan hastily puts the bag away.

ALAN: What about a cigarette?

Alan takes out two cigarettes, puts them in his mouth and lights them. He hands one to Beryl.

BERYL: I'm not smoking that.

ALAN: Why not?

BERYL: The end's all soggy. Besides, I'm in training.

ALAN: (*desperately*) Should I put on a record? Do you like Perry Como?

BERYL: Yes.

ALAN: (*brightens*) Good.

Alan puts the record on the turntable and joins Beryl on the couch.

ALAN: Just let it flow over you.

BERYL: Flow over me. I can hardly hear it.

ALAN: Well, we don't want to wake everyone up do we?

BERYL: What's that in your ear?

ALAN: An earring. They're very fashionable at the moment.

BERYL: Yes, our coalman's got one. His went septic. (*Sniffs*) Can you smell burning?

ALAN: Look, why don't you relax and just enjoy the music.

Alan puts his arm around her.

BERYL: Hey! What's your game?

ALAN: What?

BERYL: Listen, doctor, when I want you to examine me I'll let you know.

ALAN: I wasn't examining you.

BERYL: Then what were you doing – trying to guess my weight?

ALAN: Hey, why do you ride that bike all the time?

BERYL: Oh, it's my dad. He doesn't like me going with boys, so he follows me. It's the only way I can outdistance him. He says the first boy who touches me – he's going to wring his neck. What was that?

ALAN: What?

BERYL: Well, it sounded like someone coming up the stairs.

ALAN: Quick. Under the bed.

BERYL: Wait a minute.

ALAN: It may be the landlord. He hasn't seen a woman in years – it could upset him.

Alan ushers Beryl into bedroom as Ruth enters.

RUTH: Alan, can you smell burning?

ALAN: No.

RUTH: I've been smelling it all evening. It's very strong on the stairs. Are you sure it's not up here? What about the bedroom?

Ruth moves to bedroom.

ALAN: (*hastily*) I'll check it.

Exits to bedroom.
Ruth moves around the room sniffing.
Stares at bike. Continues sniffing.
Ruth has her back to the door as
Rigsby enters. He is holding a piece of
smoking wood in his hand. Ruth
sniffs, turns and stares at Rigsby.
Rigsby approaches Ruth wafting the
wood around her.

RUTH: What on earth's that?

RIGSBY: (*advancing*) This? It's a piece of wood.

RUTH: I can see that. For heaven's sake stop wafting it around like that – you'll start a fire.

RIGSBY: It'll do that all right.

RUTH: Mr Rigsby, have you been drinking?

RIGSBY: Haven't you noticed anything yet?

RUTH: Yes, the most appalling smell.

RIGSBY: This isn't ordinary wood – this is special. Breathe in deeply – see what happens.

RUTH: Mr Rigsby, I don't know what you've got in mind but I can assure you nothing's going to happen. You've been acting most strangely just lately.

RIGSBY: (*advancing*) Don't fight it, Miss Jones – just let yourself go.

RUTH: Keep away, Rigsby. I'm warning you.

RIGSBY: Don't struggle, Miss Jones. You can't quench this fire.

RUTH: (*halting at table*) We'll see about that.

Ruth picks up soda syphon and
sprays Rigsby. Rigsby stares at her
in blank astonishment. Ruth turns
on her heel and sweeps out. Alan
peers around the door. Enters.

ALAN: What happened?

RIGSBY: Nothing. Nothing happened – as usual. It was a washout – a bloody washout.

ALAN: What was?

RIGSBY: Mind your own business.

Wafts stick pensively in front of him.

ALAN: You can stop wafting it around, Rigsby. It didn't come from Africa. It came off the wardrobe.

RIGSBY: (*roars*) What! I should have known – he's going through this place like a whirling dervish. (*Hurls stick away*) No respect for property at all. Mind you, I wasn't taken in. I just went along with it. He didn't fool me for a minute.

Rigsby slumps in chair. He stares
mournfully at the bike. It slowly reg-
isters.

RIGSBY: What's that doing here? You know I don't allow bikes in the house – get it out of here.

Beryl emerges from the bedroom.

BERYL: You leave that bike alone.

RIGSBY: (*eyes narrow*) So that's it. You've had a woman in. (*Sees bottles*) And drinking!

ALAN: No – she only drinks out of her canisters, Rigsby.

RIGSBY: It's an orgy – the only thing I can't work out is what the bike's for.

ALAN: I assure you it was all perfectly harmless, Rigsby.

RIGSBY: You didn't bring her up here just to ring her bell.

BERYL: I wouldn't let him talk to you like that, doctor.

RIGSBY: Doctor!

BERYL: Even if he is simple.

RIGSBY: What! Do you know who I am?

BERYL: Well, if he's the doctor – I suppose you must be the body-snatcher.

RIGSBY: You get her out of here. Go on – before I kick her spokes in. Bodysnatcher! I'm the landlord. I'm responsible for this place. I'm not having sex on wheels in here.

BERYL: Don't worry, I'm going.

Beryl flounces by Rigsby.

BERYL: And you can keep Golden Ear-rings over there. I knew he couldn't be a doctor – not living in a dump like this.

Exit Beryl.
They stare at each other speechlessly.

RIGSBY: (*short laugh*) Is that what you call charisma?

ALAN: You can't win them all, Rigsby.

RIGSBY: You don't win any of them. (*Amusement fades. He stares at Alan*) What gave her the idea I was simple?

ALAN: What? I don't know, Rigsby.

RIGSBY: Simple am I? Bodysnatcher am I?

Rigsby becomes threatening. He picks up soda syphon.

ALAN: Now wait a minute, Rigsby. Put that down.

Philip enters.

PHILIP: (*cheerfully*) Oh, Rigsby, is it all right if I bring a girl back tonight?

RIGSBY: Oh, it's you, is it? I wondered when you were coming back.

Rigsby advances on them with the syphon. There is a dangerous gleam in his eye. They back away.

PHILIP: Rigsby, what's the matter?

ALAN: Keep calm, Rigsby.

PHILIP: Put that down.

Rigsby attacks them with the soda syphon. The boys defend themselves with the furniture.

THE END

Series One

EPISODE 4

All Our Yesterdays
by
Eric Chappell

PART ONE

SCENE 1: *Int. attic flat. Evening.*
There is the distant sound of a radio.
Alan, who is trying to read, throws
the book to one side as Philip enters
the room from the bedroom.

ALAN: It's no good – I can't con-
centrate. Spooner's got his radio
on again.

PHILIP: I hadn't noticed.

ALAN: You're not trying to read.
Didn't you hear it last night? It
was on for hours.

PHILIP: No, well, I didn't get in until
three and I was so exhausted.

ALAN: (*irritably*) I don't want to
hear about that.

PHILIP: (*smiles*) Well, you know
how it is.

ALAN: No, I don't. I was here on
my own last night. If things go on
like this I'll have to take up raffia.
(*Angrily*) And I didn't sleep a
wink for that radio.

PHILIP: Why don't you tell him
about it?

ALAN: Spooner? I'm not going to
tell him. He's a professional
wrestler – and my body doesn't
bend that easily these days.

PHILIP: I'm sure he'd be reasonable.

ALAN: Well, I'm not. Ever since
he's had his leg in plaster he's
been impossible. He blames the
whole medical profession just
because it itches. I don't think
he'd have been quite so angry if
it had happened in the ring, but
tripping over the cat – that's
what really annoys him.

PHILIP: Yes, he blames Rigsby. He
says that cat's Rigsby's evil spirit.
He's going to wring its neck.

ALAN: He'll do it too. Spooner was
a Red Devil.

PHILIP: Who are they?

ALAN: Airborne.

PHILIP: Oh, the ones who jump by
parachute?

ALAN: I don't think Spooner
bothered with a parachute. He's
as hard as nails. He's the one they
lay across the barbed wire for the
others to run over. He used to
break doors down with his head.
I'm not telling him to turn his
radio down.

* * *

SCENE 2: *Int. stairs and landing.*
Rigsby is walking upstairs. He bends and picks up Vienna.

RIGSBY: Now, Vienna, don't stand about on the stairs. We don't want another accident. (*Evil grin*) Who's a naughty boy?

Ruth emerges from her room.

RUTH: Mr Rigsby, I really must complain about Spooner's radio. It was on all last night.

RIGSBY: I'll tell him about it, Miss Jones. It's his leg you see – he can't scratch it.

RUTH: Well, I don't see how Radio Luxembourg's going to help. I hardly closed my eyes last night.

RIGSBY: I'd never have known that, Miss Jones. You look morning fresh as usual.

RUTH: Well, I don't feel it – I feel shattered.

RIGSBY: I'm not surprised, the stuff you get on the wireless these days. At least we used to have decent programmes. What happened to *In Town Tonight*?

RUTH: I'm sure I don't know, Mr Rigsby. That was before my time.

RIGSBY: Well, what about Uncle Mac then? 'Goodnight children – everywhere.' Still brings a lump to the throat. Not like the flared trouser brigade you get these days. Slopping their tea into the microphone and telling you about their love life.

RUTH: Yes, well, if you could have a word with Spooner.

RIGSBY: No sooner said than done, Miss Jones. And if you find you can't sleep, knock on my door. I don't sleep much – not since Anzio. I'll make a cup of tea – we can talk about the old days.

RUTH: Mr Rigsby – I don't think our old days are quite the same ones. (*Pause, frowns*) In fact I've got very few old days.

Ruth exits.
Rigsby continues up the stairs.

* * *

SCENE 3: *Int. top floor landing.*
There is the sound of music as Rigsby listens outside Spooner's door. He puts the cat down.
RIGSBY: Off you go, Vienna. I don't think Uncle Spooner wants to see you at the moment – in fact he'd have your tripe out.

Rigsby squares his shoulders. Knocks and enters.

* * *

SCENE 4: *Int. Spooner's room*
Spooner is sitting by the radio. He is sipping moodily at a scotch and staring at his foot, which is in plaster and resting on a stool. He turns the radio off.

SPOONER: What do you want?

RIGSBY: (*nervously*) Hello, Spooner. How are you feeling?

SPOONER: (*unsmiling*) I'll give you three guesses, Rigsby.

RIGSBY: Does it hurt?

SPOONER: (*stares*) Of course it hurts. What do you think it's doing? It's throbbing like fury. And all I can do is sit here staring at the goldfish.

RIGSBY: (*peers into bowl*) Hmm, Funny pets, goldfish.

SPOONER: At least they don't trip you up on the bloody stairs, Rigsby.

RIGSBY: Never mind, Spooner. That throbbing's a good sign. It means it's getting better. You'll be back in the ring in no time. (*Pause*) Do you want me to autograph it?

SPOONER: (*surprised*) What?

RIGSBY: Your leg. They do that in the hospital – well, it provides a bit of amusement.

SPOONER: (*sharply*) You touch that leg, Rigsby, and I'll split you down the middle.

RIGSBY: I hope you're not bearing a grievance, Spooner. You can't blame me. And you can't blame Vienna. It's not his fault you didn't see him. I can't put lights on him, can I? And I know he's sorry. He likes you, Spooner – that's why he rubbed against your legs.

SPOONER: (*grimly*) He rubbed against my legs all right.

RIGSBY: I'd have brought him in but I know his fur gets up your nose. But as long as you don't bear him any ill will.

SPOONER: (*low voice*) You know what I'm going to do when I get out of this plaster, Rigsby? I'm going to get hold of that flea-ridden monster and wring it's bloody neck.

RIGSBY: Spooner—

SPOONER: And then you know what I'm going to do? I'm going to beat you to death with the carcase.

Rigsby breaks away and backs to the door.

RIGSBY: I wouldn't touch Vienna if I were you, Spooner. Anything happens to him and what about his little friends? Where will they go? They'll be after you, mate. Thirty thousand of them. You'll hear the sound of marching feet, then, Spooner.

SPOONER: Get out, Rigsby.

Spooner picks up a tumbler to throw. Rigsby darts out. Spooner turns the radio on again.

* * *

SCENE 5: *Int. attic flat.*
Rigsby enters.

ALAN: When are you going to tell Spooner about his radio?

RIGSBY: I've told you – you've got to make allowances – the man's suffering.

ALAN: So are we.

RIGSBY: If you think I'm going to deprive him of his last remaining source of pleasure—

ALAN: You could tell him to turn it down.

RIGSBY: You know your trouble? You can't stop complaining. Nothing suits you. The room doesn't suit you, the furniture doesn't suit you.

ALAN: What furniture?

PHILIP: I think he's talking about that dusty couch and the table with the word Apples coming through.

RIGSBY: (*frowns*) I know you haven't got much furniture – that's deliberate. I could have crowded this room with furniture but you'd have only been tripping over it. I've furnished it in light and space.

PHILIP: Well, I'd prefer an easy chair.

RIGSBY: (*angrily*) What do you expect for the money you pay? G-Plan? I suppose you'd like lights shining through Polystyrene – little coffee tables and velvet drapes.

ALAN: I'd settle for a few cushions.

RIGSBY: (*outraged*) Cushions! You won't be satisfied until this place looks like the inside of a Turkish brothel. If I'd put any more furniture in this room you'd have been overcrowded.

ALAN: Whose fault's that?

RIGSBY: (*slyly*) Of course, I know tensions must arise up here – under the circumstances.

PHILIP: (*suspiciously*) What circumstances?

RIGSBY: Nerves are bound to get taut. Different ethnic groups – alien cultures.

PHILIP: Do you mean because I'm black, Rigsby?

RIGSBY: Did I say that? Did that word pass my lips? Oh, no – we have to be very careful these days. Look what happened to Enid Blyton.

ALAN: What's Enid Blyton got to do with it?

RIGSBY: She got into trouble because Noddy didn't like Gollywog.

PHILIP: Are you talking about me?

RIGSBY: No – I'm talking about Enid Blyton.

ALAN: We're perfectly happy here, Rigsby.

RIGSBY: Good. Because if there's any trouble you'll be the one to go. He's fire-proof. A victimised minority. He's got rights.

ALAN: What about my rights?

RIGSBY: You haven't got any.

ALAN: You never said that when I came with my father. You made us a cup of tea.

RIGSBY: Yes, I remember him. He kept jumping up and down to see if the floorboards creaked – ended up with his foot through the plster. What was he in?

ALAN: What?

RIGSBY: In the war.

ALAN: The Air Force.

RIGSBY: A Brylcream boy!

ALAN: He's bald.

RIGSBY: They were a shower – fought the war in carpet slippers.

ALAN: Well, my father didn't.

RIGSBY: What did he think to the room?

ALAN: (*hesitates*) He thought it was high up.

RIGSBY: (*laughs*) That's typical – typical of the RAF. None of them could stand heights. You couldn't get most of them up a ladder. How we ever won the war I'll never know. We were on parade with them in Manchester – five hundred of them and they never made a sound – do you know what they were wearing? Rubber boots. They were a disgrace – they couldn't march to save their lives. The Women's Land Army marched better than they did – and they were pushing wheelbarrows.

PHILIP: Surely the RAF were meant to fly not march, Rigsby.

RIGSBY: Oh, you're referring to those mysterious objects that stood on the runway – held together with canvas and string. They didn't go near them – they went everywhere by luxury coach.

ALAN: What about the Battle of Britain?

PHILIP: What was that?

RIGSBY: Surely you must have heard about that – even in your remote outpost? They must have beaten that out on the drums – the battle of the great iron birds. The First of the Few.

ALAN: Churchill said, 'Never was so much owed by so many to so few.'

RIGSBY: Oh, yes, and what did we owe your father?

ALAN: What do you mean?

RIGSBY: Where was he when this glorious page of history was being written? He wasn't doing victory rolls over Biggin Hill.

ALAN: He was in the Stores.

RIGSBY: I thought so – never saw an angry man. Well, he's not the type – most of them were public school – born leaders.

ALAN: You mean just because my father doesn't talk with a plum in his mouth?

RIGSBY: No, I mean they were born to it. All that rugby and flicking each other with wet towels.

ALAN: I think they're twits.

RIGSBY: Don't let that foppish manner fool you. Underneath they had nerves of steel – even if they did get into their Spitfires with Teddy bears under their arms. Don't underestimate them – the *Luftwaffe* made that mistake. No, you could always depend on those lads when the pressure was on.

ALAN: Well, how do you know I wouldn't be like that when the pressure was on?

RIGSBY: (*laughs*) You?

ALAN: It wasn't my fault I missed the war. Perhaps I'd have been doing victory rolls over Biggin Hill.

RIGSBY: (*shakes head*) No. You see you're not a man of action.

ALAN: You don't know, Rigsby – perhaps I could have been a war hero.

RIGSBY: It's not likely though is it? (*Craftily*) I mean, you've done nothing but complain about Spooner's radio but you won't tell him about it, will you? You want me to do it.

ALAN: That's not the same thing. He's a professional wrestler.

RIGSBY: He's a professional wrestler with one leg at the moment, and you're still frightened of him.

ALAN: But I can't wrestle – I've never been any good at it.

RIGSBY: Well, you know what they say? If you can't fight, wear a big hat.

ALAN: What does that mean?

RIGSBY: You've got to assert yourself – look him straight in the eye and tell him to turn the bloody thing off.

ALAN: And suppose he won't? Suppose he turns nasty?

RIGSBY: Well, get his crutch off him and kick him in the leg.

PHILIP: And what's going to happen when he gets out of plaster? He's going to remember all these little slights like being kicked in the leg.

RIGSBY: (*shrugs*) Of course, if he's afraid—

ALAN: I'm not afraid.

Alan makes for the door.

PHILIP: Alan, don't be a fool. Spooner's been drinking – it's not just his leg that's plastered.

Alan exits.
Philip and Rigsby stare after him in surprise.

* * *

SCENE 6: *Int. Spooner's room.*
Alan enters bravely.
Spooner looks up and turns off radio.

ALAN: (*nervously*) Hello, Spooner.

SPOONER: (*sourly*) What do you want?

ALAN: Er … how's your leg?

SPOONER: (*mournfully*) I've been looking at it. I think they've turned it the wrong way. I'll be walking like a bloody penguin.

ALAN: No, you'll be all right. They know what they're doing. (*He moves the crutch out of Spooner's reach*) Spooner, can I borrow your transistor?

SPOONER: (*puts hand on radio*) Why?

ALAN: I want to listen to the Proms.

SPOONER: No. It's all I've got left. That and the bloody goldfish.

ALAN: Cheer up. You'll be laughing about this in a few weeks.

SPOONER: (*reaches for bottle*) Do you think so?

ALAN: Let me do that.

Alan reaches to pour Spooner a drink. He treads on the injured foot.

SPOONER: (*groans*) Get away from me, you quack. It had just stopped throbbing. Go on, before I shake your teeth out.

Alan backs towards door.

ALAN: Honestly, Spooner, just look at you. A fifteen-stone wrestler and you're acting like a baby. You know what you are? A fake. I always thought wrestling was fixed.

Spooner tries to reach crutch and falls.
Alan exits hurriedly.

* * *

SCENE 7: *Int. attic flat.*
Alan enters adjusting his tie.

RIGSBY: Well, what happened?

ALAN: You can't hear it can you?

RIGSBY: You mean you told him?

PHILIP: You're very pale.

ALAN: I usually am when I'm angry.

RIGSBY: I don't believe it.

ALAN: Don't be fooled by the foppish manner, Rigsby – underneath there are nerves of steel. I could have been up there – over the Weald of Kent – a couple of 109s before breakfast. I looked him straight in the eye and told him he was a fake.

RIGSBY: You said that? I can't believe it.

Exits shaking his head in disbelief.

PHILIP: Did you really say that?

ALAN: Yes.

PHILIP: I didn't know you had the nerve.

ALAN: (*modestly*) It's only when we're under pressure that we find these things out about ourselves, Philip. What was that?

There is the sound of a crutch and the dragging of a foot approaching the door.

ALAN: My God! It's Spooner he's coming for me.

Alan moves behind Philip. The sound gets nearer.

PHILIP: It's stopped.

ALAN: Don't let him get me, Philip. (*He takes spear down from the wall*). Hold him off with this.

The door opens, Rigsby enters grinning and using sweeping brush as a crutch.

RIGSBY: Hello – Biggles.

END OF PART ONE

PART TWO

SCENE 8: *Int. attic flat. Evening.*

Alan and Philip are trying to read. Rigsby is flicking around with the sweeping brush. He is chuckling to himself. Sound of Spooner's radio. Rigsby chuckles louder.

RIGSBY: Well, you turned out to be a right Naafi candle didn't you?

ALAN: Shut up, Rigsby.

RIGSBY: Mind you, it doesn't surprise me. I saw them go like that in the war – all talk until the first sign of danger and then they fell apart. You'd have been one of the first to crack.

PHILIP: And what about you, Rigsby? Why don't you go and tell Spooner?

RIGSBY: (*blusters*) It's not me who's complaining is it? A bit of music doesn't worry me.

PHILIP: You won't go because Spooner's threatened to wring your neck. I'm surprised that someone who faced the might of the German army should be afraid of Spooner – that's if you did face the might of the German army.

RIGSBY: What are you getting at?

PHILIP: Only that I always thought English heroes were supposed to be modest.

ALAN: That's right. They say men who really saw action never talk about it, Rigsby.

RIGSBY: Well, you know why, don't you? Because nobody listens anymore. (*Busy with brush*) They're not interested – they want to forget. A few poppies on Armistice Day and that's about it. The parades are getting shorter every year. They can't even keep quiet for the two minutes silence. They'd sooner hold a Pop Festival any day. I often wondered what we saved this country for. What's happened to the old traditions? What happened to British grit?

PHILIP: (*drily*) I think you're sweeping most of it under the carpet, Rigsby.

RIGSBY: I was one of the first, mate. I didn't take any notice of old Chamberlain – 'In my hand I have a piece of paper.' We all knew what he could do with that. I was there when they were needing them not feeding them. And I saw action. If you don't believe me – what about this? (*He bares his chest*). What do you think this is?

88

ALAN: (*peers*) It looks like your nipple.

RIGSBY: What? (*Looks down*) Oh, wrong side. (*He opens his shirt wider*) What do you think that is?

ALAN: That's your other nipple.

RIGSBY: That's shrapnel, mate. If that moves another inch I'll be the last casualty of World War II.

Ruth enters. Rigsby hurriedly buttons his shirt.

RIGSBY: Ah, here's someone who'll remember what it was like. You went without during the war didn't you, Miss Jones. There was no orange juice for you was there?

RUTH: (*winces*) I was only a baby, Mr Rigsby.

RIGSBY: But you must remember it. The ration books, the gas masks, Potato Pete and Doctor Carrot and Victory Pie.

RUTH: Well, I was very small.

RIGSBY: Still, you made sacrifices. Not like these two – they don't know what it's like to go without.

ALAN: I wouldn't say that.

RUTH: I hardly remember. I mean, I was still in my pram.

RIGSBY: Ah, but it was the people's war, Miss Jones. Everyone suffered.

RUTH: Well, it was some years before I saw a banana.

RIGSBY: (*triumphantly*) There you are, you see.

RUTH: And mother always insisted we were machine gunned coming from the vicarage. She was pushing me in my pram and this *Messerschmitt* dived very low. She saw the pilot quite clearly – in fact she swore it was someone she'd met in Germany before the war. What she'd said to make him go to those lengths I can't imagine.

RIGSBY: Did you hear that? Miss Jones even defied the Luftwaffe from her pram. That's what life was like in those days. Blood, sweat and tears – and sacrifice. you don't know you've been born.

ALAN: Well, it wasn't my fault I was born too late. I could have made sacrifices.

RIGSBY: You! You go into a tantrum if you have to go without your puffed rice. You couldn't have made sacrifices – you're too soft – your hair's too long, and you eat too many sticky sweets. The trouble is you never did your National Service.

ALAN: So what?

RIGSBY: So what! You could have seen the world. You could have had your own Bren gun carrier at eighteen and a good bunch of mates. And you wouldn't have been frightened of Spooner.

RUTH: Oh, that's what I came up about. We really must do something about Spooner.

RIGSBY: Well, don't ask him – he came back terrified.

PHILIP: I wouldn't say that.

ALAN: He's right, Philip.

RIGSBY: Of course I'm right. You know what he's like. Who has to get the spiders out of the bath for him? I do.

ALAN: It's true. I'm a physical coward. It was the same at home. All the dogs on the road used to bark at me – even ours.

RUTH: There are different kinds of courage, Alan. He wouldn't like to go into a ward full of smallpox.

ALAN: Neither would I.

PHILIP: It was all a long time ago. You don't want to listen to Rigsby's stories – how do we know what really happened?

RIGSBY: Are you calling me a liar?

PHILIP: All I'm saying is that the memory can play tricks, Rigsby.

RIGSBY: We'll see about that. I'll show you whose memory can play tricks. You wait here.

Rigsby exits.

RUTH: (*sighs*) Oh, dear – now we're in for it.

PHILIP: What do you mean?

RUTH: He'll be bringing up his burnished shell cases.

ALAN: And his letter from Monty.

RUTH: He's going to be fighting World War II all over the house again. Kicking the door open and shouting at us in German. Telling us all those bloodthirsty stories.

ALAN: How he attacked that German machine gun nest with an empty beer bottle. He never shuts up about the war.

RUTH: And he always insists on treating me as a contemporary – I can't think why.

Rigsby enters with a small trunk.

RIGSBY: I'll show you a thing or two.

PHILIP: What's that?

RIGSBY: Evidence, mate. (*He opens the lid*) Mementoes of five years of conflict.

RUTH: (*hastily*) Well, I can't stop, Mr Rigsby. I only came up to complain about Spooner. I wish you'd talk to him.

RIGSBY: (*doubtfully*) Yes – I'm working round to it, Miss Jones. Only you know what he's like – he can be a bit hasty.

PHILIP: (*smiles*) Spooner was a Red Devil.

RUTH: But weren't they on our side?

RIGSBY: We were never quite certain.

ALAN: He's an expert in the martial arts – his hands are lethal weapons.

RUTH: Couldn't we talk to him under a white flag?

PHILIP: Do you want me to do it, Rigsby?

RIGSBY: (*hastily*) No. Don't worry, I'll have a word with him. After all, it's my job.

RUTH: I'd be very grateful, Mr Rigsby.

RIGSBY: Would you, Miss Jones? Don't worry I'll see him.

RUTH: Thank you. (*Makes for the door*) Oh, Philip, could you come down for a moment? I want you to help me with the curtains – they're stuck again.

Philip sighs and follows Ruth out. Rigsby stares after them moodily while Alan examines the contents of the trunk.

RIGSBY: She never asks me to help her with the curtains. Why does she have to ask him? Thought she'd have been interested in these. The trouble is, no one's interested anymore. They soon forget. There were no flags out when I came home. No banners across the street saying 'Welcome Home' for me. They hoped I wasn't coming. What did they ever do for the war effort on this road except fill the pig's swill bin? Oh, I know they took the railings down across the road – and put them back up

again when it was all over – kept them in the garage.

ALAN: What's this?

He holds up a dagger.

RIGSBY: That's an SS dagger. Sharp, isn't it? How many throats did that slit on the night of the long knives?

Alan hurriedly returns the dagger. Rigsby grins.

RIGSBY: (*cont'd*) You see you're not used to cold steel – it's all this electric shaving. (*Crosses to door. Listens.*) God! He's started singing now. I suppose I ought to see him. I did promise her.

ALAN: Yes – you could do yourself a bit of good there. She said she'd be very grateful.

RIGSBY: (*brightens*) Yes. (*Hesitates*) Suppose he sets about me?

ALAN: Show him what you're made of, Rigsby.

RIGSBY: I won't have to – it'll be all over the floor.

ALAN: You're not frightened of him are you, Rigsby?

RIGSBY: No.

ALAN: Of course he was a Red Devil.

RIGSBY: So he says. It must have been a long time ago. He gets dizzy stepping off the kerb these days.

ALAN: Then what are you worried about? You want to win her respect don't you?

RIGSBY: Yes.

ALAN: Well, go on then.

Rigsby exits.

* * *

SCENE 9: *Int. landing.*
Rigsby approaches Spooner's door. He is about to knock, then hesitates and stands back.

RIGSBY: (*shrugs*) Who wants respect anyway?

He turns to go back to attic. Alan is standing at the top of the stairs. He is wearing a German helmet and tunic. Rigsby jumps back.

RIGSBY: (*cont'd*) For God's sake! Did you have to do that? That took me right back, that did. You frightened the life out of me.

ALAN: Where did they come from?

RIGSBY: Off a dead German.

Alan quickly removes the helmet. Rigsby sees that he is holding a revolver.

RIGSBY: Where did you get that from?

ALAN: Out of the case.

RIGSBY: I'd almost forgotten that.

That's my old 45 – had that all through the war.

ALAN: Is it loaded?

RIGSBY: Of course it's not loaded. You don't leave guns loaded – don't you know anything?

ALAN: (*points gun at Rigsby*) Reach for the sky, marshal.

Rigsby ducks hastily.

RIGSBY: Don't point it at me.

ALAN: But you said it wasn't loaded.

RIGSBY: It isn't. But you never point a gun at people. That's the first rule.

ALAN: Then how did we win the war?

RIGSBY: (*takes gun*) You've got to treat them with respect. (*Clicks gun*) See that action? That's as smooth as the day it was made.

He pulls the trigger again and there is a loud explosion.
They stare blankly at each other.

ALAN: I thought you said it wasn't loaded?

RIGSBY: I could have sworn I emptied it. I must have left one in.

ALAN: The point is where has it gone?

RIGSBY: (*frowns*) Ah, well, we'll have to follow the line of flight. It shouldn't be difficult.

They move along the landing getting nearer Spooner's door as they talk.

It's probably embedded in the plaster somewhere.

ALAN: (*hisses*) Rigsby. There's a hole in Spooner's door.

RIGSBY: What are you talking about? (*Examines hole*) My God!

ALAN: And there's something else.

RIGSBY: What?

ALAN: He's stopped singing.

RIGSBY: (*mouth drops*) But it couldn't have ... (*Taps on door*) Spooner? (*Stares at Alan. Opens the door slowly*). Spooner?

* * *

SCENE 10. *Int. Spooner's room. Spooner is stretched out in a grotesque shape across the couch. His eyes are closed. Rigsby closes the door hurriedly.*

* * *

SCENE 11: *Int. landing.*

RIGSBY: I've shot him.

ALAN: Are you sure?

RIGSBY: I know a dead man when I see one. What am I going to do? I couldn't face prison. I'm an old man. My heart wouldn't stand it.

ALAN: (*feels own pulse*) You know

I'm surprisingly calm. I thought I'd be more upset.

RIGSBY: You should have been where Spooner was. Poor old Spooner. What are we going to do? I need time to think.

Philip and Ruth enter.

RUTH: (*firmly*) I've made up my mind, Mr Rigsby. I'm not standing for this any longer. I'm going straight in there to tell Spooner to turn that radio down.

RIGSBY: He won't listen to you, Miss Jones.

RUTH: I don't care.

She moves towards door.

RIGSBY: (*desperately*) You can't go in there, Miss Jones.

RUTH: Why on earth not?

ALAN: Rigsby's just shot him.

RUTH: (*shocked*) What! Because he wouldn't turn his radio down? Isn't that rather drastic, Mr Rigsby?

RIGSBY: I didn't mean to do it. It was an accident. I didn't do it on purpose. I couldn't hit a barn door.

ALAN: I thought you said you were trained to kill?

RIGSBY: Whose side are you on?

PHILIP: Hadn't we better take a look at him?

RIGSBY: I can't go in there. I never could stand the sight of blood. You go. Poor old Spooner. He was so alive only a few minutes ago.

Philip, Ruth and Alan enter Spooner's room. Rigsby does a nervous dance up and down the landing. He aims a kick at Vienna, who departs screeching. Ruth puts her head around the door.

RUTH: Mr Rigsby, I think you'd better come in.

RIGSBY: No, I couldn't. Is he … ?

RUTH: Come along.

* * *

SCENE 12: *Int. Spooner's room. Spooner is now laid on the couch. The others are gathered solemnly around him. Rigsby advances humbly towards Spooner. He kneels by him.*

RIGSBY: (*hopefully*) He doesn't look too bad – under the circumstances, does he? Spooner, Spooner, I'm sorry. I didn't mean it. It was an accident. It won't happen again. (*Winces as he bites off the words*) Say something, Spooner. Don't leave me without a word. Spooner, can you ever forgive me!

Spooner opens one eye and stares at Rigsby. He grabs him by the collar.

SPOONER: No, I can't! I've been trying to get to sleep for two days

– and when I finally do, you start whispering in my ear. And shooting bullets through the door.

The others start to laugh. Spooner joins in. Rigsby breaks away furiously.

RIGSBY: Why you! You could have given me a heart attack! I've aged ten years.

SPOONER: I'm sorry, Rigsby. I didn't think I'd ever smile again. This is the best laugh I've had since I tripped over the bloody cat. Don't worry, Rigsby – I forgive you.

RIGSBY: I don't care what you do.

SPOONER: Now where's your sense of humour, Rigsby? Can't you see the funny side of it?

RIGSBY: No, I can't.

PHILIP: I wonder where the bullet went?

ALAN: That's a point.

They look around.

RUTH: Oh. Your poor little goldfish.

She is standing over the fragments of the bowl.

SPOONER: What!

RUTH: I'm afraid they're on the carpet, Mr Spooner.

SPOONER: Well, don't just stand there – get them in water!

Rigsby moves cautiously to the door. Opens it.

RIGSBY: Oh, Spooner – if they don't come round … do you think I could have them for the cat?

SPOONER: (*roars*) Let me get at him.

Spooner struggles to get up and is restrained by the others.

Rigsby exits.

Spooner follows, hopping on one foot and struggling with the others.

THE END

Series One

EPISODE 5

The Prowler
by
Eric Chappell

PART ONE

SCENE 1: *Int. hall. Late evening.*
Rigsby is standing by the open front door. He is peering uneasily into the darkness.

RIGSBY: Come on, Vienna. You don't want to be out in this – it's getting foggy. This is the night the cat men come. You don't want to end up stretched across a tennis racquet, do you? Come on. Where are you? What are you doing? (*Plaintive howl from the cat. Rigsby sighs*) I might have known. You'll get your ears torn off one night – they're like bloody clothes pegs now. (*Second howl*) No wonder you haven't got strength to get out of that chair all day – lucky sod.

Rigsby is about to close the door when he hears a muffled scream. He peers outside. Second scream. He realises it is coming from inside the house.

Miss Jones?

Rigsby dashes upstairs.

* * *

SCENE 2: *Int. first floor landing.*
Rigsby enters as Ruth opens her door. She looks pale and distraught.

RIGSBY: Miss Jones! What's the matter?

RUTH: It was awful. I came in from the bedroom and saw this shadow. I— (*sways*).

RIGSBY: You'd better sit down, Miss Jones. You've gone ashen.

He takes her arm and they enter flat.

* * *

SCENE 3: *Int. Ruth's flat.*
Rigsby helps Ruth to a chair.

RUTH: I feel quite faint.

RIGSBY: Are you all right, Miss Jones? Should I loosen your clothing?

RUTH: (*hastily*) No. No, that won't be necessary.

RIGSBY: Perhaps if you put your head between your knees?

RUTH: I always think that looks so ungainly, Mr Rigsby. Besides, I feel better now.

RIGSBY: What happened?

RUTH: I came in from the bedroom. There was this shadow by the window ... and these horrible staring eyes. That's when I screamed. I covered my face and screamed. When I looked again he was gone.

RIGSBY: (*doubtfully*) Well, he's certainly not here now. (*Looks around*) Are you sure you saw someone, Miss Jones? I mean the firelight can play tricks.

RUTH: Of course I'm sure. I saw these horrible staring eyes.

RIGSBY: Could it have been a reflection?

RUTH: (*Indignantly*) No, certainly not. If you don't believe me, Mr Rigsby—

RIGSBY: Of course I believe you, Miss Jones. (*Looks out of window*) I was just wondering how he got up here – there's no drainpipe—

RUTH: (*wildly*) I don't know how he got up here. Perhaps he used a trampolene. Perhaps he's a nocturnal pole vaulter. All I know is he was in my room.

RIGSBY: (*soothingly*) Now you must try and keep calm, Miss Jones. I know you've had a nasty shock but you must keep calm. The question is, where is he now?

RUTH: Do you think he's out there?

RIGSBY: He could be. Then again, he could be in the house.

RUTH: (*alarmed*) Mr Rigsby! (*Clutches his arm*)

RIGSBY: (*pleased*) I don't think I

should leave your side tonight, Miss Jones.

RUTH: (*nervously*) What do you mean?

RIGSBY: I mean what was he doing in your room?

RUTH: You don't mean—?

RIGSBY: He didn't come up here to leave a box of Milk Tray. You could have been another victim of the permissive society, Miss Jones.

RUTH: Are there really people like that?

RIGSBY: You'd be surprised. There's a lot of it about. (*Looks upwards*) Funny *they* never came when you screamed. I suppose they could be in bed. They are suffering from another energy crisis.

RUTH: You mean they've no heating?

RIGSBY: I mean they've no energy. I think I'd better take a look round. Keep your door locked, Miss Jones.

RUTH: Be careful, Mr Rigsby.

RIGSBY: Don't worry about me, Miss Jones. I'm not easily frightened. And after Anzio every day's a bonus.

Rigsby exits.

* * *

SCENE 4: *Int. landing.*
As the door closes Rigsby's smile fades. He looks around nervously. Hurries upstairs glancing over his shoulder.

* * *

SCENE 5: *Int. attic flat.*
Alan is reading. Rigsby enters.

RIGSBY: I don't know what this place is coming to. Miss Jones has just had an intruder.

ALAN: (*amused*) What?

RIGSBY: She's very upset about it.

ALAN: Why, did he get away?

RIGSBY: It's not funny. If a respectable woman can't get a night's sleep without a sex maniac bursting in. (*Looks around*) Where's your mate?

ALAN: Philip. He's having a bath.

RIGSBY: He's always having a bath.

ALAN: There's nothing wrong with having a bath, Rigsby.

RIGSBY: How would you know? You've been here six months and the name hasn't gone off your soap yet. I think you only keep it in there as a status symbol. (*Pause. Frowns*) I suppose he is having a bath.

ALAN: Of course he's ... Rigsby. You're not suggesting it was Philip? (*Laughs*) She didn't say it was Philip?

RIGSBY: No, it was dark. She couldn't distinguish his features. Well, she wouldn't, would she? As long as he remembered not to smile.

ALAN: Philip's not like that.

RIGSBY: How do we know what he's like?

ALAN: He's no different from me, Rigsby.

RIGSBY: That's no recommendation.

ALAN: Just because he's black. We're all the same underneath – we're all seventy per cent water.

RIGSBY: You speak for yourself.

ALAN: It's true – we're seventy per cent water.

RIGSBY: No – we'd ooze all over the floor.

ALAN: Rigsby—

RIGSBY: They're not the same as us.

ALAN: They are.

RIGSBY: All right. If they're the same as us – why do they always break down on the M1?

ALAN: (*surprised*) Do they?

RIGSBY: Haven't you seen them – staring with childlike bewilderment at their steaming radiators? No, they're not the same as us. And we didn't have any of this trouble before he came.

ALAN: You're being ridiculous.

RIGSBY: (*side glance*) Of course, it needn't have been him down there.

ALAN: Well, I'm glad you admit it.

RIGSBY: It could have been you.

ALAN: What do you mean? I've got examinations. I haven't got time for that sort of thing.

RIGSBY: Oh? (*Snatches book*) What about this? You've only got to turn to the first page with the gravy stains. (*Reads*) 'She felt his hot breath on her neck – they embraced passionately.' (*Reads on*) Blimey!

ALAN: Do you mind? (*Snatches book back*)

RIGSBY: You know it's bad for your eyes, don't you?

ALAN: What?

RIGSBY: (*grins*) The small print.

ALAN: This book has considerable literary merit.

RIGSBY: Considerable literary merit! That's hard porn that is – handed over at midnight in a plain wrapper. No wonder a woman's not safe anymore.

Philip enters with towel. He is dressed in shirt and jeans.

PHILIP: (*glances at them*) What's the matter?

ALAN: Ruth's had an intruder.

PHILIP: (*shocked*) What?

RIGSBY: Yes. She saw this dark— shadowy figure in her room. Now I don't think there's anyway he could have got into her room – except from the stairs. That's why I'm checking up. Now Spooner's wrestling at Wolverhampton so it can't be him – besides, he's frightened of the dark. So that just leaves the people in this room. (*Looks from one to the other*)

PHILIP: Yes. I see what you mean. Where were you when this happened, Rigsby?

RIGSBY: I was trying to get the cat— (*Indignantly*) Wait a minute – I'm asking the questions.

PHILIP: (*disgusted*) My God! What a country.

RIGSBY: Oh, yes. I suppose it doesn't happen in your country?

PHILIP: No – not with the skinning men.

RIGSBY: I didn't think— (*frowns*) Who are the skinning men?

PHILIP: We hand people like that over to the skinning men – and they skin them.

RIGSBY: (*shocked*) You mean alive?

PHILIP: Of course. There wouldn't be much point in it if they weren't alive. It's an art. You're not supposed to break the skin – it's considered unlucky.

RIGSBY: Unlucky! Who for? (*Chuckles*) I bet that cures them. I bet they don't feel like sliding down drainpipes after that. (*Glances at other two*) We ought to have skinning men in this country.

ALAN: Well, don't look at us, Rigsby. We're studying – we haven't time to fool around like that – have we, Philip?

PHILIP: Of course not.

RIGSBY: Oh, well, the one who had the room before you, he was studying. I found him very studious – until he made the hole.

ALAN: What hole?

RIGSBY: The hole in the floor. Miss Jones was getting ready for bed one night – next minute she was covered in plaster. I found him peering through this hole in the floor. I moved him on after that.

ALAN: Why? Wasn't there room for both of you?

PHILIP: Where is this hole?

RIGSBY: Never you mind.

PHILIP: I suppose you've thought that the intruder needn't be one of us. That he could be a burglar.

RIGSBY: What?

PHILIP: He could be after all that money you've got under the floorboards.

RIGSBY: I've told you before, I haven't got any money under the floorboards. I'm a poor man – always have been.

ALAN: Rigsby, you don't think you've fooled anyone with your tattered appearance? Everyone knows about the miser's hoard. It's probably a London mob.

RIGSBY: (*frowns*) Perhaps I'd better have a look round. Be on the safe side.

Exit Rigsby.

* * *

SCENE 6: *Int. landing.*
Rigsby comes downstairs. He peers nervously into the gloom. Moves the sideboard and lifts floorboard to get at his money box.
He hears footsteps.

RIGSBY: Who's that?

A man emerges from gloom. Smartly dressed. A weary cynical manner.

BAKER: (*displays card*) DC Baker, sir. Regional Crime Squad. I hope you don't mind but your front door was open. Not very wise this time of night – especially since we've had reports of a prowler in the vicinity.

RIGSBY: A prowler!

BAKER: You haven't seen him have you, sir?

RIGSBY: No, but Miss Jones has – he was in her room.

BAKER: She actually saw him.

RIGSBY: Well, only his shadow – I

thought it was one of them upstairs.

BAKER: Have you checked to see if there's anything missing?

RIGSBY: I was just going to do that.

BAKER: I would, sir. It's important to know what sort of villain we're looking for.

Rigsby takes out the money. Counts it. Watched in silence by Baker.

RIGSBY: (*weakly*) Just my holiday money.

BAKER: Is it all there, sir?

RIGSBY: Yes. Should I put it back.

BAKER: I don't see why not. It's safer than unit trusts. I wish mine was in there. We'll all need a little hole like that the way things are going.

Rigsby moves back furniture.

Of course he needn't be after money. You said he was in Miss Jones's room?

RIGSBY: Yes.

BAKER: I'd better see her. After that, I'll question the others. For all we know the prowler could be somone living in this house. (*Glance at Rigsby*)

* * *

SCENE 7: *Int. attic flat.*
Philip is putting on his coat.

ALAN: Where are you going?

PHILIP: I think I'll take a look round.

ALAN: Be careful – you're already under suspicion.

PHILIP: But I was having a bath.

ALAN: I told him that, but you know what he's like.

PHILIP: Actually, I thought he suspected you.

ALAN: No, it was you he suspected.

PHILIP: The whole thing's ridiculous.

ALAN: Of course – who wants to see Miss Jones in her harvest festivals?

PHILIP: Yes. (*Pause by door*) Where were you when it happened, Alan?

ALAN: I was up— (*stops*) Now just a minute. I was here the whole time.

Philip smiles. Exits.
Alan picks up book with disgruntled air. Starts to read. Glances at floor. Lifts carpet back with his foot.
Rigsby enters. Alan pushes carpet back.

RIGSBY: Well, that's done it. We've got the police here now.

ALAN: Oh, no – not the police.

RIGSBY: What's the matter? Is your library book overdue? As a matter of fact we could do with some law and order around here. Where's our friend? Has he packed his bags?

ALAN: No.

RIGSBY: He'd better watch out. He's going to see British Justice at work. Painstaking and implacable.

ALAN: The police are only the tools of the Establishment, Rigsby. Dedicated to preserving the Capitalist system.

RIGSBY: Just because they caught you riding without lights. Well, I only hope that's all you've got on your mind. He's asking Miss Jones for a statement right now. You might get your collar felt before the night's out. He'll be coming up to ask you a few questions so you'd better straighten yourself up – and keep your hands out of your pockets.

ALAN: You think he'll believe me if I keep my hands out of my pockets?

RIGSBY: He might.

ALAN: Of course, you're right, Rigsby. I've never thought of it like that before. If only Crippen had straightened himself up and kept his hands out of his pockets he'd have never been arrested. Well, just remember to keep *your* hands out of your pockets.

RIGSBY: (*frowns*) What are you getting at?

ALAN: What about those British Railway towels in the bathroom? And all that stuff you get cheap at the Blue Ram?

RIGSBY: Now wait a minute. Don't you point the finger at me. I'm a respectable citizen. I'm a rate payer. It's people like me who are paying for your education. And what do we get? Beards and bloody beads.

Exit Rigsby.

* * *

SCENE 8: *Int. landing.*
Rigsby comes downstairs. He listens at Ruth's door.
Baker emerges.

BAKER: Ah, Mr Rigsby. I've taken a statement from the lady. Now where are the others?

RIGSBY: Upstairs. (*Leads way*) I wouldn't trust either of them.

BAKER: What do they do, sir?

RIGSBY: As little as possible. They're supposed to be students.

BAKER: Students.

RIGSBY: Yes, I thought that would furrow your brow. Pair of trouble makers. Nothing they'd like better than rolling marbles under police horses.

BAKER: I wonder if I know them?

RIGSBY: I wouldn't be surprised. You must have seen them around. (*Confidentially*) One of them's got long hair and surgical boots. The other one's black – with tribal marks. He could turn nasty if it's a full moon. If he gives you any trouble – kick him in the groin, they're sensitive there.

BAKER: So am I, sir. This way?

* * *

SCENE 9: *Int. attic flat.*

Alan is peeling back the carpet. He finds the hole. Puts his eye to it. Baker enters. Stares at Alan. Walks over and bends down beside him.

BAKER: Looking for something, sir?

Alan looks up in dismay.

END OF PART ONE

PART TWO

SCENE 10: *Int. attic flat.*
Alan and Baker are sitting opposite each other. Baker is consulting his notebook.
Rigsby enters with a mug of tea. Hands it to Baker.

BAKER: Thank you, Mr Rigsby. (*Refers to notebook*) And you were up here when the incident took place, sir?

ALAN: Yes.

BAKER: Is there anyone who can substantiate that?

ALAN: Well, no.

BAKER: And you didn't hear the scream?

ALAN: No.

RIGSBY: I'm not surprised – with all that foliage. He can hardly see – never mind hear. Like a bloody sheep dog.

BAKER: (*frowns*) Please, sir.

ALAN: That's what he's got against me. He doesn't trust me because of my long hair—

RIGSBY: What do you mean? Look, I didn't trust Hitler but it wasn't because of his moustache.

BAKER: If you don't mind, Mr Rigsby, I'm trying to ask a few questions.

RIGSBY: Of course.

Baker stands up. Circles the room. Examines skeleton. Glances at Alan. Opens sexy book. Reads for a moment. Raises eyebrows at Alan.

BAKER: I suppose it's pretty lonely up here, sir?

ALAN: Yes – I mean no, not really.

Baker begins to inspect pin-up calender. Raises eyebrows at Rigsby.

BAKER: Are you sure you're getting enough exercise, sir?

ALAN: Yes. I go out for walks late at night I— (*quickly*) Well, not that late.

BAKER: I understand you're a student?

ALAN: Yes.

BAKER: And what are you studying? (*Turns from calender with a smile*) Not Divinity I hope.

ALAN: I'm studying medicine.

106

BAKER: Ah, very worthwhile. A real vocation.

RIGSBY: He'll never make a doctor. He lays on that bed all day protesting about unemployment. He gets his orders straight from the Kremlin.

ALAN: Rigsby.

RIGSBY: You know what they're going to do when they get in power? They're going to hang me from the nearest lamp-post. He's told me that. And I fought to save democracy. We were going to make a land fit for heroes and what do we get? Streakers!

ALAN: Well, there's nothing shameful in the human body, Rigsby.

RIGSBY: No, but we don't want it in the middle of bloody Woolworth's do we? What's the country coming to? Suppose you were taking your mother out? Her first walk in the spring sunshine. Leaning on her stick – admiring the flowers. And what happens? Some silly sod comes dashing out of the bushes stark naked with flowers in his hair. It would be enough to give her a heart attack.

BAKER: Yes, well, if you don't mind—

RIGSBY: Of course, it's you and me who are paying for it all. We're keeping these students. Supposed to be the cream of the country and what do we get? Football hooligans in sandals.

BAKER: (*coldly*) My son happens to be a student.

RIGSBY: Eh? Ah, well, I'm not saying they're all like that. There are some decent ones – some very nice lads. Have a cigarette.

BAKER: Well, I don't normally but – thank you.

Rigsby lights Baker's cigarette. Baker inhales. Smiles at Alan.

Tell me, have you ever been in trouble with us before?

ALAN: Yes.

BAKER: And why was that?

ALAN: I was summonsed for a faulty rear light.

BAKER: Oh. Well, we don't really call that form, sir.

Baker begins to look round the room.

RIGSBY: What are you doing? Looking for prints? Pieces of fibre? A strand of hair?

BAKER: Actually, I was looking for an ash tray. Perhaps it would be an idea if we went back to Miss Jones's room.

RIGSBY: Ah, returning to the scene of the crime.

BAKER: I thought it might be a bit warmer down there, that's all. And I did want to ask Miss Jones a few more questions. If you could follow me.

Baker exits followed by Alan and Rigsby.

* * *

SCENE 11: *Int. stairs and landing. Rigsby takes Alan's arm.*

RIGSBY: He's playing it cool.

ALAN: What do you mean?

RIGSBY: He knows who it is. Going to confront him with the principal witness. Normal police tactics. Can you feel the net tightening?

ALAN: Rigsby!

* * *

SCENE 12: *Int. Ruth's flat. Ruth is close to Philip. She moves away as the others enter.*

RUTH: Well, have you solved the mystery?

BAKER: Not yet, Miss. (*Glance at Philip*) And who's this gentleman?

RUTH: This is Mr Smith. He's from Africa.

RIGSBY: (*aside*) Well, he didn't think he was from the arctic.

RUTH: (*proudly*) He's the son of a chief.

BAKER: Is that so? I hope you've settled in all right, sir.

PHILIP: Yes, thank you.

BAKER: Not too cold for you?

RIGSBY: (*disgusted*) Aren't you going to ask him any questions?

BAKER: Mr Rigsby, *I'm* conducting this investigation.

RIGSBY: Investigation! It's more like a diplomatic exchange. If this had been his country it would have been straight over to the skinning area – we'd have been down to the bone by now. Ask him where he was when it happened.

PHILIP: I was having a bath.

BAKER: Well, there'll hardly be a witness to that, would there, sir?

PHILIP: No.

They both laugh.

RIGSBY: (*scowls*) We'd have done better with Securicor.

BAKER: Now, Miss Jones, I know you say the intruder was in shadow but is there anything you can remember about him?

RUTH: Only those horrible staring eyes.

BAKER: Oh, yes. Those eyes.

He glances at the three of them. His gaze lingers on Rigsby who glares back indignantly.

You haven't noticed anything suspicious in the last few days – you haven't been followed – no one's made advances?

RUTH: (*regretfully*) No. (*Pause*) There was a man on the train. He had a leather jacket with his name on the back. Steve, I think it was.

BAKER: Yes, Miss?

RUTH: He was singing 'They tried to tell us we're too young'. I could feel his eyes burning into me.

BAKER: What happened?

RUTH: He began experimenting with the light switch so I moved to another compartment. I thought he might be a Hell's Angel.

BAKER: I don't think that's likely – they usually travel by motorbike.

RUTH: I thought he may have had a puncture.

BAKER: Of course, it needn't be an outsider. It could be someone in this room.

Protests.

It's a known fact that we're in greater danger from the people we know. There's many a woman who expected to receive a warm embrace only to feel the slash of cold steel.

Ruth gives a little scream.

RIGSBY: You're a bundle of fun you are.

BAKER: Since nothing's missing – we must look for darker motives.

I wonder if we could try an experiment? Perhaps we could get some idea of the height and shape of the intruder. If you could stand over there, gentlemen. I'm going to put the light out. Miss Jones, if you could touch the person most like the intruder.

RIGSBY: Now we're getting somewhere.

RUTH: Isn't this exciting? Like Paul Temple.

BAKER: Er— yes, miss.

Baker puts out light.

Now off you go. (*Pause*) No, that's me, Miss.

RUTH: Sorry. I'll start again. I should say— this one.

Baker puts on the light. Ruth is holding Rigsby's arm.

RIGSBY: Now wait a minute.

BAKER: Don't worry, sir. We're just trying to build up a picture – nothing personal.

RIGSBY: I should hope not.

BAKER: By the way, where were you when you heard the scream, sir?

RIGSBY: I was getting the— I thought you said there was nothing personal?

PHILIP: Officer, I wonder if this has any significance? I found it outside – below the window.

He hands Baker a rather bedraggled comb.

BAKER: Hmm. A comb … rather dirty … several teeth missing.

RUTH: Just the sort of thing you'd expect.

ALAN: (*examines it*) It's yours, isn't it, Rigsby?

RIGSBY: What? (*Looks at comb*) Yes. (*Uneasily*) It must have dropped out of my pocket when I was cleaning the windows. What are you all staring at?

BAKER: I wonder if you'd excuse us for a few minutes? I would like to ask Mr Rigsby one or two more questions.

RUTH: Yes, of course.

They all exit on to the landing darting uneasy glances back at Rigsby.

BAKER: Sit down, Rigsby.

RIGSBY: Hey, what's happened to the Mister all of a sudden?

BAKER: Now I only want to ask you a few questions. (*He angles table lamp slightly into Rigsby's face*) Nothing personal.

RIGSBY: Not much! You shouldn't be asking me questions – you should be asking them out there. I'm a rate payer. I'm a respectable member of the community. (*Sighs*) You try being a good citizen. You try to help the police and what does it get you?

Trouble. I was coming back from the pub one night and this woman was knocked off her bike by a car. She hadn't got any lights but it wouldn't have made any difference because the driver was pissed. Well, I didn't just walk by, mate, I stopped and helped. I told the driver what I thought of him and went and phoned for an ambulance.

BAKER: You did the right thing.

RIGSBY: While I was in the box the driver got in his car and drove off. I didn't even get his number.

BAKER: I still don't see—

RIGSBY: I haven't finished yet. When I came out of the box, the woman got up, shook herself, jumped on her bike and pedalled off down the road. She went like the wind – no one could have caught her. When the police and the ambulance arrived I was the only one there.

BAKER: What happened?

RIGSBY: I was arrested for being drunk and disorderly.

BAKER: I see. (*Pause*) Do you live here alone?

RIGSBY: Yes.

BAKER: I suppose you're pretty lonely.

RIGSBY: Well, I— (*indignantly*) No, I'm not.

BAKER: Is there a Mrs Rigsby?

RIGSBY: There was. She's gone.

BAKER: Do you mean disappeared?

RIGSBY: No, I mean gone. She left me.

BAKER: I'm sorry.

RIGSBY: I'm not. It was a mistake. Glamour of the uniform. We were married during the war. We were on rations then – I've been on rations ever since.

BAKER: I hope you realise I have to ask these questions.

RIGSBY: Questions! This is the third degree. You've made your mind up haven't you?

BAKER: What?

RIGSBY: When are you going to get it over with? When are you going to slip the bracelets on? When are you going to take me down to the station and knock hell out of me?

BAKER: Mr Rigsby—

RIGSBY: Are you going to hit me where it doesn't show or am I going to have one of those nasty accidents in the cell door?

BAKER: But we don't do things like that.

Baker leans forward to put hand on Rigsby.

RIGSBY: Take your hands off me, you fascist. I fought five years against blokes like you. The only difference is they were covered in swastikas. Five years honourable service for King and country – and you don't even believe what I say.

BAKER: But I do.

RIGSBY: What?

BAKER: I do believe you.

RIGSBY: (*surprised*) Do you?

BAKER: Of course. I consider myself a good judge of character. You don't spend twenty years in the Force without knowing when someone's telling the truth. I go by the face. You're an honest man, Mr Rigsby, I can tell that. (*Gets up. Pats Rigsby on shoulder.*) If everyone was like you we'd be out of business. Well, I'd better start a search of the area.

RIGSBY: You mean you're going?

BAKER: Yes. We're not going to find our man in this house, Mr Rigsby. Don't worry, I'll let myself out.

RIGSBY: I've always said our police are the best in the world.

BAKER: (*smiles*) Thank you, sir. Goodnight.

Exit Baker.
Rigsby sits there staring in front of him, still numb from the compliment. The others return. They stare at him.

ALAN: What happened, Rigsby?

RIGSBY: Do you know what he said to me? He said I was an honest man. He could tell by my face. That's the nicest thing anyone's ever said to me.

ALAN: He can't make many arrests.

RIGSBY: What do you mean? Blokes like him are the backbone of the country.

PHILIP: Yes, well, don't forget he believed us as well, Rigsby.

RIGSBY: Yes. (*Sniffs*) Well, I don't suppose he can be right all the time.

RUTH: Well, I don't think I shall sleep until they catch this man.

RIGSBY: Don't you worry, Miss Jones. If he tries it again he'll have me to reckon with.

RUTH: (*sharply*) What's that?

RIGSBY: (*starts*) What?

RUTH: There's someone on the stairs.

ALAN: It's the prowler!

RUTH: He's coming in.

RIGSBY: Come on – Help me hold the door. Keep back! We've called the police.

VOICE: Don't be silly, sir. We are the police.

The door opens and two uniformed policemen enter.

PC: Sorry to disturb you but we're looking for a man who's been entering houses in this vicinity.

RIGSBY: (*laughs*) Oh, we know all about that, don't we? (*The others join in*)

PC: He's been posing as a police officer. Has anyone seen him?

The smile fades from Rigsby's face. He gives a cry and dashes out to landing to check his money.
The others laugh harder for a moment and then their expressions change to ones of horror. They dash off to check their possessions, watched by surprised policemen.
Cut to Rigsby in despair over the open floorboard.

THE END

Series One

EPISODE 6

Stand Up and Be Counted
by
Eric Chappell

PART ONE

SCENE 1: *Int. landing – afternoon.*
Alan is coming upstairs. He looks nervous and furtive. His top coat is draped over his shoulders in an air of mystery. He enters the attic flat.

* * *

SCENE 1A: *Int. attic flat – afternoon*
Alan enters attic flat.

* * *

SCENE 1B: *Int landing – afternoon.*
Rigsby enters. He is also in top coat and is wearing a blue rosette. He gazes after Alan and follows him. Enters attic flat.

* * *

SCENE 2: *Int. attic flat.*
Alan is peering nervously out of the window. Rigsby creeps up behind him.

ALAN: (*startled*) Oh! It's you.

RIGSBY: What are you looking for?

ALAN: I wish you wouldn't creep up like that, Rigsby.

Rigsby lifts Alan's empty sleeve. Stares at him.

RIGSBY: You been biting your nails again? I don't know why you can't wear that coat properly. You look like the Count of Monte Christo. It's got sleeves in. Why can't you use them?

ALAN: (*removes coat*) The police are after me.

RIGSBY: (*laughs*) Yer what—

ALAN: It's not funny – I hit one of them.

RIGSBY: (*incredulously*) You hit a policeman?

ALAN: I didn't know he was a policeman. Someone had knocked his helmet off – I thought he was a porter.

RIGSBY: And you hit him?

ALAN: We were making a political protest.

RIGSBY: Not again.

ALAN: We tried to enter this meeting of the National Front, and they called the police. I didn't actually hit him, I pushed him in the back. When he turned round he was quite pale. He said,

'What did you do that for?' I don't think he was very strong.

RIGSBY: What did you say?

ALAN: I said, 'I'm sorry, I thought you were someone else.' He said, 'I'll get you for that.' So I came away.

RIGSBY: I don't think Lenin would have left it like that.

ALAN: I was the only one who stood up to the police dog. I wasn't frightened. I patted it and I got a cheer.

RIGSBY: (*suddenly*) Hey, they're here.

ALAN: (*startled*) Oh— (*Checks landing – looks relieved*) Do you think they'll come here?

RIGSBY: They'll try the airports first. You'll be all right. You wouldn't be the first. We had a man downstairs – got into the wardrobe everytime I opened the door. I don't know what he'd done but he spent more time in that wardrobe than out of it.

ALAN: I wouldn't like that much.

RIGSBY: If you're going to be a revolutionary you'll have to get used to wardrobes.

ALAN: No, I don't think I'd make a revolutionary. I keep wanting to go to the lavatory all the time. You can't keep rushing off in the middle of a demonstration.

RIGSBY: I warned you, didn't I? You should never have got involved with them. If you go on like this I'll have to give you notice.

ALAN: Wait a minute, Rigsby. What about free speech?

RIGSBY: That's not the point. You're giving this place a bad name. I've got my position to think of. I'm a member of the Conservative Club – I can't get on the billiard table as it is.

ALAN: You know your trouble, Rigsby? You're a social climber.

RIGSBY: Well, I haven't climbed very far, have I? There's only one bloke down there who speaks to me and he washes the glasses.

ALAN: (*fingers rosette*) Is that why you've been canvassing for them?

RIGSBY: Well, I did a bit this morning. Won them a few votes – I didn't get many arguments.

ALAN: I'm surprised at that.

RIGSBY: (*sly grin*) Well, I had the megaphone. Any trouble and I gave them a thousand decibels straight between the eyes. Left them with their ears ringing. I think I did myself a bit of good there. I'll be playing a thousand and one up with De Vere-Brown before the week's out.

ALAN: That lot will never get in – Conservative twit.

RIGSBY: (*frowns*) Mind you, what the commitee are going to say when they find out I'm sheltering a Marxist—

ALAN: I've told you before, I'm not a Marxist.

RIGSBY: Oh, no? Then who's that on the wall, hey? It's not your granny is it? It's another sworn enemy of Capitalism and shaving. What have you Marxists got against shaving anyway?

ALAN: I'm not a Marxist. (*Importantly*) As a matter of fact I'm a Maoist.

RIGSBY: It must be all the crispy noodles you've been eating. I've noticed your eyes are getting quite horizontal these days. Anyway, how can you be a Maoist in a local council election? As far as I can see it, we've got a straight fight between Conservative and Labour with a modest intervention from the Liberals. Unless they've put someone up from the Lotus House, your vote's going to be wasted.

ALAN: I shall vote Labour of course.

RIGSBY: What do you mean – 'Of Course'? You've never had a pair of overalls on in your life.

ALAN: The students and workers must unite – we've got to link arms against a common enemy.

RIGSBY: You won't get anyone linking arms with you – not in those trousers. (*Laughs*) I can just see you linking arms with a six-foot steel worker. Swapping your cucumber sandwiches for his three-inch jam butties. Offering him a glass of red wine and a whiff of your after-shave. He wouldn't know what to make of you.

Philip enters. He is wearing a red rosette and carrying a revolutionary poster.

RIGSBY: Oh, my God! Not you as well. I thought *he* was a funny looking Maoist, but you're ridiculous.

PHILIP: What do you mean?

RIGSBY: Only that as a Chinaman you leave something to be desired. You see, the Chinese believed that when God made us he put us all in the oven. Apparently he took us out before we were ready – they were done to a turn – and you were burnt to a bloody crisp, mate. So you see, whatever way you look at it, to the Chinaman you're a definite failure.

PHILIP: We're not talking about race, Rigsby – we're talking about a political philosophy.

ALAN: Right!

RIGSBY: Well, you can't vote – you're not eligible.

PHILIP: At least, I can lend my support.

RIGSBY: But why? I mean you're the son of a chief. (*Pause*) I know what it is. You feel guilty.

PHILIP: (*hotly*) No, I don't.

RIGSBY: (*teasingly*) You've been beastly to the servants.

PHILIP: Now look, Rigsby—

RIGSBY: You want to be popular. You want to be carried shoulder-high round the mud huts. Well, you start talking about equality and they're going to start thinking. They're going to notice that your mud hut's a bit bigger than theirs – they'll carry you shoulder high then, mate – right down to the crocodile pool.

PHILIP: I didn't expect you to understand, Rigsby – you're a reactionary.

RIGSBY: No, I'm not.

PHILIP: You want to bring back hanging.

RIGSBY: So what? A lot of people want to bring back hanging.

PHILIP: Not in public, Rigsby.

RIGSBY: You can talk. When you want a change of government you just send for the skinning men.

PHILIP: That's not true. We have democratic elections, Rigsby. (*Sly pause*) It's what happens to the losers.

RIGSBY: What do you mean?

PHILIP: It's not a pretty sight.

RIGSBY: What happens to them then?

PHILIP: Well they take two saplings and tie them together – then they tie a leg to each and cut the rope.

RIGSBY: (*winces*) Urgh! That's one way of losing your deposit.

ALAN: Hey, that's not a bad idea. I saw that in a Tarzan film once. We can do that to the Tories. I can just hear the sound of ripping pin stripes.

RIGSBY: Shut up! I don't know what you've got against the Tory party.

ALAN: What about the three-day week?

RIGSBY: I don't know what you're complaining about – the five-day one never suited you. Besides, it wasn't our fault – you can blame those mates of yours with the little lights on their heads.

ALAN: You can't blame the miners, mate – all they wanted was a living wage.

RIGSBY: You'd believe anything. Don't you know what's behind all those strikes – all this political unrest? Russian gold.

PHILIP: Russian gold?

ALAN: For heaven's sake, Rigsby.

RIGSBY: They've certainly taken you in, haven't they? You've only got to see the Red Army Ensemble dancing around singing Little Brown Jug and you think they're marvellous. Well, I'm not having this house used as a centre for subversion.

ALAN: Subversion!

PHILIP: Rigsby—

RIGSBY: Well, you're not having any more meetings here – and you can stop giving that clenched first salute to the baker. I've got my position to think of. I was hoping to get into the Round Table canoe race this year.

ALAN: Rigsby – all we want is a fairer society. We want things to be shared.

RIGSBY: Is that why you keep squeezing Miss Jones's tooth-paste? (*Shakes head*) I don't know what she thinks to all this.

PHILIP: Ruth agrees with us.

ALAN: Yes.

RIGSBY: What do you mean? Miss Jones is a 'don't know'.

PHILIP: She was a 'don't know' but I had a long session with her the other night. She knows now.

RIGSBY: Oh yeah? (*Frowns*) Well, listen *I* had a long sessions with her and she agreed with every word *I* said.

ALAN: That's because she's frightened you'll cut her water off.

RIGSBY: We'll see about that.

Rigsby exits.

* * *

SCENE 3: *Int. Ruth's room.*
Ruth is studying circulars of the three candidates. She looks worried and is wearing her blue glasses. Rigsby knocks, enters.
Ruth hurriedly shuffles papers away.

RIGSBY: Excuse me, Miss Jones.

RUTH: Yes, Mr Rigsby?

RIGSBY: I've just heard some very disturbing news – in fact I could hardly believe my ears.

RUTH: (*quickly*) It's not true, Mr Rigsby – we're just good friends. I – what?

RIGSBY: (*frowns*) I was talking about the election, Miss Jones.

RUTH: Oh, the election.

RIGSBY: They've had the nerve to suggest that you're going to vote Labour.

RUTH: Yes, I know. Philip can be so persuasive.

RIGSBY: But you can't – not a woman of your background.

RUTH: To tell the truth I just can't make up my mind. I feel so responsible – especially after seeing *Shoulder to Shoulder*. I keep thinking of all those women chaining themselves to railings.

RIGSBY: But I explained it all to you yesterday, Miss Jones.

RUTH: I know.

RIGSBY: I showed you how we were going to balance the payments, encourage investment, eradicate unemployment, and cure inflation. You remember – I did it on the back of that cigarette packet.

RUTH: I know, but you see I keep having doubts.

RIGSBY: I can understand that. But you must remember our world's in danger, Miss Jones.

RUTH: (*stares*) What world is that, Mr Rigsby?

RIGSBY: You know, Miss Jones. The Sunday afternoon game of tennis – the sound of ball against gut – the scattered applause from the deck chairs—

RUTH: I didn't know you played tennis, Mr Rigsby.

RIGSBY: I was never off the courts before my strings went. I still remember those days. The sun slanting through the French windows as we sipped our iced lemonade. That's our world, Miss Jones.

RUTH: Well, I did used to go with the Young Farmers, only Daddy didn't approve. They tended to be a little robust – I think it came from watching the animals.

RIGSBY: Yes. After the poll closes Col. De Vere-Brown and his good lady will probably have a few of us back to the Manor for a celebration drink – served by the butler in the library. Perhaps you'd like to come?

RUTH: (*doubtfully*) I don't know. I'm not sure about Col. De Vere-Brown.

RIGSBY: But what have you got against him, Miss Jones?

Rigsby picks up picture of de Vere-Brown

RUTH: I'm afraid I don't like his eyes.

RIGSBY: You can't vote against him because you don't like his eyes. What's wrong with his eyes?

RUTH: Don't you think they look rather cold?

RIGSBY: (*studies picture*) It's probably the glossy paper.

RUTH: You're sure it's not all those blood sports he follows?

RIGSBY: I don't know anything about that, Miss Jones. I know he watches Leeds United.

RUTH: I've seen pictures of him in *Country Life*. He's usually standing knee-deep in a pile of bloodstained feathers with both barrels smoking.

RIGSBY: Well, he's got to relax sometime.

RUTH: But I thought they were trying to get away from the grouse shooting image?

RIGSBY: Ah, but most of those sort of men go shooting, Miss Jones – it takes their mind off things.

RUTH: I'm sure it does the same for

the grouse but that's no excuse. (*Opens door*) Now if you don't mind, Mr Rigsby.

RIGSBY: (*hastily*) I can promise you, he's not inhuman Miss Jones – he's got two lovely labradors.

RUTH: I'll have to think about it.

RIGSBY: But I was counting on you. I've put you down for a car.

RUTH: (*indignantly*) I don't need a car. I'm not quite decrepit.

RIGSBY: No of course not – I'm sure.

RUTH: I *do* have a pair of legs.

RIGSBY: Yes, of course – very nice legs, if I may say so.

* * *

SCENE 4: *Int. landing.*
Rigsby sees Vienna. Vienna has a sign saying vote Labour on her back. Rigsby picks up Vienna and goes upstairs.

* * *

SCENE 5: *Int attic flat.*
Alan and Philip are working on posters. Rigsby enters.

RIGSBY: How many times have I told you about putting those red ribbons on Vienna? That cat's Conservative – at least he is in the daytime. And I'm not having those posters up at the windows. (*Snatches at a poster*)

The boys start to sing The Red Flag.

RIGSBY: And you can stop that bloody row. I don't know what De Vere-Brown would say if he knew. Shut up!

ALAN: You know your trouble, Rigsby? You're a snob. The way you worship the upper classes.

RIGSBY: At least they know how to behave. At least they're gentlemen.

ALAN: (*derisively*) Gentlemen!

RIGSBY: Of course, you don't know the meaning of the word.

ALAN: And what happens inside those rugby scrums, Rigsby? When they all stand back and there's an ear on the floor.

RIGSBY: That's character-building.

ALAN: You should remember the Depression.

RIGSBY: I don't have to. I get it every time I come up here.

ALAN: And the hunger marches—

RIGSBY: Hunger marches! The only hunger marches you've been on is when you creep down for Miss Jones's custard creams. (*He comes face to face with poster of Labour candidate in characteristic pose on wall. Laughs.*) Oh dear. Oh dear. Just look at him. What a face! Would you buy a second-hand car from this man?

PHILIP: You'd have a job – he sells baby clothes.

RIGSBY: Just look at him.

ALAN: He's a good speaker.

RIGSBY; He's a demagogue.

Jones, the Labour candidate, enters. He is wearing a red rosette. Smoking a cigarette rather affectedly. Dressed as the picture.

RIGSBY; You can see it in his eyes. Ranting and raving – whipping the audience into a frenzy. I don't know what gets into him. It must be all those years amongst the soft toys. Just look at those wild eyes – drunk with power. You couldn't trust a man like that, could you?

He appeals to Jones. Looks back at poster then back to Jones. Confusion.

END OF PART ONE

PART TWO

SCENE 6: *Int. landing.*
Rigsby creeps up on attic door. He is carrying megaphone. Grins evilly. Raises megaphone to his lips. Nothing happens. Finds end stuffed with socks, etc. or something nasty on mouthpiece. Splutters. Bursts into flat angrily.

* * *

SCENE 7: *Int. attic flat.*
Jones and the boys are studying voter lists. Look up as Rigsby enters.

ALAN: Hey, Rigsby -- you've lost the top off your cornet.

RIGSBY: You can't hold political meetings here. This is a private house.

JONES: Mr Rigsby, we may be on opposite sides but there's no reason why we shouldn't be friends. I just popped in to see how the boys were getting on. They've been invaluable. I really think I've got the support of the students this time.

RIGSBY: Why – are you legalising pot?

JONES: Now, Mr Rigsby – they're a fine bunch of chaps. (*Pats boys on the shoulders*) I get on with them very well.

RIGSBY: (*drily*) I'm sure you do.

JONES: You mustn't be too hard on them. I know they can be a little wild but they're only seeking richer experiences – trying to become more complete persons.

RIGSBY: Yes and we know what that means – contraceptives on demand!

JONES: (*coughs*) I must say I'm really very surprised that a man of your intelligence should be voting for De Vere-Brown.

RIGSBY: What do you mean?

JONES: (*picks up Tory poster*) Well, look at him. He's got no chin.

RIGSBY: Don't be so— of course he's got a chin.

JONES: Oh, he's a decent enough chap – quite sound on swine fever and Dutch elm disease, but he's completely lost on the broader national issues.

ALAN/PHILIP: Hear hear!

RIGSBY: We're not interested in the broader national issues – we're

122

more interested in who's been fouling the footpath.

JONES: Well, with those two labradors of his you won't have to look very far.

RIGSBY: At least he'll get rid of those gypo's at the end of the lane.

JONES: I'm sure he will – he's had a lot of experience. His ancestors roasted peasants over open fires. Of course, he's too remote. He's no idea of the sacrifices that have to be made.

RIGSBY: What do you mean? When we had the last crisis there was one light burning in that house. And he shared the bathwater with his wife.

ALAN: Yes, that's about all he would share – and I bet he got in it first. And what did he tell the striker's wives? No sexual relations until they went back to work.

RIGSBY: He never said that. (*Pause*) He said no more hot dinners.

JONES: Well, we all know what he meant by that, don't we?

RIGSBY: Oh yes – and what about you? What about that cottage in Wales and the Filipino house boy.

JONES: What do you mean?

RIGSBY: Well, they're going to be a definite embarrassment when the Russians land – not to mention all those shares in ICI.

JONES: I've no intention of discussing my private affairs with you, Rigsby. That is a cheap Tory jibe. I see what you mean about him. Now I must get down to the committee rooms. Keep up the good work, dear boys.

Jones exits.

RIGSBY: Keep up the good work, dear boys. Oh dear. Oh dear.

Alan and Philip watch him suspiciously.

ALAN: What's so funny, Rigsby?

RIGSBY: Did you see the way he was holding that cigarette? He shouldn't be with you – he should be with the Gay Liberation Front.

ALAN: (*angrily*) That's typical of you, Rigsby.

PHILIP: What are you trying to say?

RIGSBY: He's a middle-class poof anyone can see that.

ALAN: That's right – you can't win a political argument so you resort to that.

RIGSBY: Look – you know as well as I do he's off every weekend to the ballet.

ALAN: A lot of people go to the ballet.

RIGSBY: Yes – but not with a twenty-five-year-old milkman they don't.

PHILIP: That's a cheap smear, Rigsby.

RIGSBY: Well, I can't stand here arguing. I've got to get people out to vote. The party's depending on me – and no more posters up anymore alright?

PHILIP: (*disarmingly*) Of course not, Rigsby. (*Arm on shoulder*) After all, it is your house.

RIGSBY: All right then. As long as you remember that.

Rigsby turns away from Philip. He has a 'Vote Labour' sign on his back. Exits.

* * *

SCENE 8: *Int Ruth's room. Early evening.*
There is a knock on the door. Ruth opens the door. She is confronted by a breezy, open-faced young man. He is wearing an orange rosette.

RUTH: Oh!

PLATT: Excuse me – my name is Platt, I'm your Liberal candidate.

Platt enters.

RUTH: Oh … you're much nicer than the other two.

PLATT: Of course I'm rather new to it.

RUTH: Well, I think you're doing awfully well. Won't you sit down?

PLATT: I see you've been studying form – Can I depend on your vote, er … um?

RUTH: Miss Jones. Of course, I've always been rather liberal – it's my nature. On the other hand I suppose I'm what people would call a political virgin. I just don't seem to be able to take the plunge.

PLATT: Ah, you mean you're a 'don't know'.

RUTH: I wouldn't say that exactly. I just need a little convincing.

PLATT: Well, of course, the personal approach is important. That's why I've been out meeting people, shaking hands. We always say you can't beat skin to skin.

RUTH: (*moves closer*) Oh yes – I do agree about that.

* * *

SCENE 9: *Int. hall.*
Rigsby enters. He puts the mega-phone down rather wearily. Climbs the stairs.

* * *

SCENE 10: *Int. Ruth's room.*
Ruth has Platt trapped on the couch.

RUTH: I do think it's important to get to know your candidate thor-oughly, don't you?

PLATT: (*uneasily*) Er … yes. Would you like a pen?

RUTH: Oh, thank you. Are you married, Mr Platt?

PLATT: No.

RUTH: Isn't that a coincidence? Neither am I. Of course it's early days yet. In a way I suppose we're both 'don't knows' … waiting for the right candidate.

PLATT: Well, I really think I must be going.

RUTH: Oh, no, please stay and have a coffee. You must be quite parched after all that public speaking.

Pats hand. She looks surprised as if she's discovered something exceptional.

RUTH: Oh, what warm hands you've got.

The door opens and Rigsby enters. He sees them holding hands. Scowls suspiciously.

RUTH: Oh, Mr Rigsby – this is Mr Platt, our Liberal candidate.

PLATT: Hello, Mr Rigsby.

Rigsby stares.

RUTH: Er … I was just getting a coffee, Mr Rigsby. Would you like one?

RIGSBY: I could do with something, Miss Jones.

RUTH: I won't be a moment.

Ruth moves into the kitchen area.

Rigsby and Platt sit awkwardly eyeing each other's rosettes.

Platt clears throat nervously.

PLATT: I thought it would be a good thing if I introduced myself.

RIGSBY: I saw you speak at the Corn Exchange.

PLATT: Oh yes. What did you think?

RIGSBY: I was riveted. I couldn't take my eyes off you.

PLATT: Really? That's most encouraging.

RIGSBY: Your flies were undone.

PLATT: Actually, I'm rather a new boy at this. I thought I'd go on a walkabout – meet the people – kiss a few babies.

RIGSBY: You're taking a chance around here – even their mothers daren't do that. You can catch anything from chicken pox to beri-beri.

PLATT: (*earnestly*) But I do think it helps – getting around – shaking flesh.

RIGSBY: (*sharply*) You haven't been doing that here, have you?

PLATT: I beg your pardon?

RIGSBY: Because you're wasting your time. She's spoken for.

PLATT: But I thought she was weakening.

RIGSBY: Did you? I've thought that for a long time – probably another false dawn.

PLATT: Look, Mr Rigsby, I know you've got your beliefs but we do have your interests at heart. (*Pats shoulder*) We intend to do a lot more for the pensioners. Cheaper bus fares – meals on wheels—

RIGSBY: (*indignantly*) I'm not a pensioner.

PLATT: Oh.

RIGSBY: That's 12 months of Labour government. I looked quite young before they got in. And I don't know why they have to keep going on about old age pensioners. What we want is euthanasia.

PLATT: Surely, Mr Rigsby, that's going too far.

RIGSBY; All these bonuses at Christmas. You should have seen them in the Blue Ram. You couldn't get to the bar for pensioners. And they were all on shorts. (*Sharply*) Is that your car out there?

PLATT: Yes.

RIGSBY: You should have left it under the light. They use hub caps for ashtrays around here. They're all communists. They don't believe in private property unless it's their own.

PLATT: Oh. I didn't know. Is that the time? I must get off. I have so much to do.

Platt rises as Ruth enters with coffee.

PLATT: I'm terribly sorry, Miss Jones. I must get down to the committee rooms. You did mean the mini?

RIGSBY: Yes.

PLATT: Oh! it's not mine, it's my mother's. I'm very sorry Miss Jones – perhaps another day.

Platt exits. Ruth stares after him.

RUTH: What a pity – he's such a charming man.

RIGSBY: You can't vote for him, Miss Jones.

RUTH: He had such a lovely handshake.

RIGSBY: Skin to skin they call that.

RUTH: It wasn't just that – he gave me something.

RIGSBY: Oh! what was that?

RUTH: A ball point pen.

RIGSBY: Isn't that contravening the regulations?

RUTH: And he's got a lovely smile.

RIGSBY: You can't vote for a lovely smile. This isn't Miss World. You've got to vote for party and principle. You must have party loyalty.

Alan and Philip enter. They are wearing red rosettes and are carrying placards.

ALAN: Are you coming to vote, Ruth?

RIGSBY: You never give up do you?

PHILIP: Have you decided, Ruth?

RUTH: No, I'm absolutely torn. Everyone's so convincing.

RIGSBY: Well, you can't vote for all of them. It's not the three draws.

PHILIP: But you promised, Ruth.

RIGSBY: You keep out of this. This isn't your country. You can't bribe her with sunshade and a few beads. She's got a mind of her own.

PHILIP: I told you which way to vote.

RIGSBY: Did you hear that, Miss Jones? Where he comes from the woman does as she's told. There's no Women's Lib, out there. You'd have to walk ten paces behind with a pot on your head.

RUTH: (*reproachfully*) Actually, I have got a mind as well as a body, Philip.

PHILIP: Of course, I just thought you were too intelligent to be influenced by Rigsby.

Knock on front door.

RIGSBY: Now that's someone else come to see if we've voted. You'd better make up your mind, Miss Jones.

Rigsby exits.

* * *

SCENE 11: *Ext. front door.*
Rigsby opens the door. A tall distinguished man stands on the threshold. He is accompanied by two labradors.

* * *

SCENE 11A: *Int. hall.*

RIGSBY: Colonel De Vere-Brown. This is an unexpected pleasure – come in.

BROWN: Thank you. (*Enters*) Roper, Bella, Heel. (*Consults list*) I've just called Mr … er—

RIGSBY: Rigsby – don't you remember me?

BROWN: What?

RIGSBY: You must have seen me – standing around the billiard room.

BROWN: What?

RIGSBY: You must have seen me – standing around the billiard room.

BROWN: I don't quite—

RIGSBY: At the club.

BROWN: Yes, I thought your face was familiar.

RIGSBY: You'll know me better once we've met over the green baize.

BROWN: What? Oh. Of course. Glad to see you're one of the faithful, Ragsby.

RIGSBY: Oh yes, Col. De Vere-Brown you can depend on me.

BROWN: Good man. I was just doing the rounds – trying to flush a few more out. Roper! Come here. Oh, sorry about that.

RIGSBY: (*winces*) That's alright. It'll clean up. He's a lovely dog.

BROWN: Yes. Wonderful mouth – have you got your people out yet?

RIGSBY: I've tried, Colonel – but it's been hard work.

BROWN: Yes – but we mustn't give up.

RIGSBY: No – of course not—

BROWN: I've flushed quite a few out down the road.

RIGSBY: Well, you've got the labradors.

BROWN: What?

RIGSBY: Er … How's the shooting gone this year, Colonel?

BROWN: Not too good. The birds all got this dreadful disease – all flapping around on the floor.

RIGSBY: Ah! That would be fowl pest.

BROWN: What?

RIGSBY: Dreadful disease. Of course, I'm something of a shot myself.

BROWN: Oh? I didn't know that.

RIGSBY: Oh yes. Very good eye reflexes. A sudden movement, the whirr of feathers and – one for the pot.

BROWN: Yes. That's very interesting – well – having trouble getting your people out?

RIGSBY: Yes it's an uphill job. They don't appreciate the finer things in life around here – most of them are communists.

BROWN: I'm not surprised, Ragsby – just look at this place – see the damp? You know what this is, don't you? The unacceptable face of capitalism.

RIGSBY: (*astounded*) What?

BROWN: (*confidentially*) How much does he charge for these places?

RIGSBY: What do you mean?

BROWN: What are the rents?

RIGSBY: Well … six.

BROWN: Scandalous! You should take him in front of the rent tribunal.

RIGSBY: Now wait a minute.

BROWN: Don't worry, Ragsby, I understand – frightened of the landlord – nasty piece of work I suppose. Well, we intend to do something about this place when we get in. Probably have it pulled down. Build some flats for single tenants. Stop all this exploitation.

RIGSBY: You can't demolish this – it's my home.

BROWN: Don't worry – you'll be all right, we'll find a place for you.

RIGSBY: How can you? I'm the landlord, you great puddin'!

BROWN: What!

RIGSBY: You're supposed to be on my side – you should protect the landlords.

BROWN: Not your sort of landlord, Ragsby. (*Stares at him*) I remember you now. You're the chap they disqualified from the billiards competition – for wetting the end of your opponent's cue.

RIGSBY: That was a lie.

BROWN: The party can do without people like you, Ragsby.

RIGSBY: Rigsby! And I can do without you – you public school twit. You wouldn't play billiards with me, would you? I wasn't good enough. Well, I don't care. Just because I wasn't born with a silver spoon in my mouth. Well, I don't need you lot. I'm a self-made man. Now get out of here and take those dirty tykes with you.

BROWN: Don't worry, Rigsby. I'm going. Roper. Bella. Heel. And don't bother to come into the billiard room again.

Rigsby picks up megaphone and blows a massive raspberry after him. He moves upstairs.

* * *

SCENE 12: *Int. Ruth's room.*

ALAN/PHILIP: Ruth, you promised.

RIGSBY: (*angrily*) Where are those placards?

PHILIP: Up here – why?

RIGSBY: I'll tell you why – because there's just been a ten per cent swing to the left.

Rigsby reaches for placards.

RUTH: But Mr Rigsby, you said—

RIGSBY: Never mind what I said. I can change my mind can't I? How does that song go?

Rigsby leads them down the stairs singing The Red Flag.

THE END

SERIES TWO

During the first series, the hierarchy at Yorkshire had been clever in not giving me an entire series to write in the first place: the episodes were commissioned piecemeal, so I didn't experience the sort of strain I faced whilst writing the second series. To add to the pressure, I was fearful because time was at a premium. While I was penning *Rising Damp*, I was also busy writing *The Squirrels*, a sitcom for ATV. Being an office-based show, I found the scripts more difficult to write and I consequently spent more time on them. This caused a knock-on effect as far as *Rising Damp* was concerned, and as a result we lost Frances de la Tour before the end of the series. However, before the problems came to a head, I settled down and wrote three scripts.

The series couldn't have got off to a better start. *The Permissive Society* went like a bomb. It contained a lot of sexual jokes and scenes exploring permissiveness, with Rigsby trying to learn from the boys. It was fun to do and, again, dealt with old themes like Rigsby's jealousy of the students' lifestyles – he was adamant they were living the good life and he was missing out, especially as far as women were concerned.

Food Glorious Food was also easy to write. Rigsby has a wager with Philip that he can go without food for 48 hours. I shall never forget Rigsby having to bite into plastic fruit, suffering a hot potato, and his egg smuggling. Another good episode.

So was *A Body Like Mine*, which everybody loved. The episode contains the famous boxing match and a lot of the success was down to Len. I simply described the match, it was Len's inventiveness that brought it to life. His performance was, once again, excellent and I just loved those ridiculous shorts!

I'd now delivered three scripts but only had about ten days to do the next before they moved into production. I didn't think I could finish it in time; the pressure of having to think quickly made my mind go blank and I couldn't come up with any ideas for the storyline. I rang my agent and told him I couldn't continue like this. Luckily, everybody was very understanding and the production schedule was put back. But that's why we lost Frances de la Tour for the last three shows in the series. I'd taken on too much work and

Len gave me a lecture about saying no to people, but when you're new to the profession you hate turning people down because you're frightened you'll never be asked again.

When it came to writing *Moonlight and Roses*, it was clear what the storyline was going to be because I had to cover Frances' departure. Stage commitments meant she was no longer free to finish the series and I had to come up with a good reason for Miss Jones leaving. So I brought in Desmond, with whom Miss Jones falls in love. By the end of the episode she leaves to marry her librarian lover. As far as I knew, Frances wasn't coming back, so I took the opportunity to introduce Brenda (played by Gay Rose) because I needed a female replacement. It wasn't an easy task because I hadn't written many female characters and found them extremely difficult. People say Miss Jones is well drawn but I felt she was very sketchy, simply a caricature, it's just that Frances was so good playing her.

Brenda was very much a caricature, too. She was rough and ready but didn't have much depth. Fortunately, that's not terribly important in sitcom so long as people can relate to the character from the moment they appear. Of course, I was lucky again because Gay played her beautifully.

A Perfect Gentleman was the first episode without Miss Jones. She was missed, but the strength of the other characters carried us through and I didn't have people coming up asking, 'What's happened to Miss Jones?' Everybody liked Ruth, but the other main characters – plus those who appeared briefly (like Seymour) – were equally well liked.

I'd worked before with Henry McGee, who played Seymour, and he was a great encouragement; I think he was one of the first people who spotted that I might have some talent. So when it came to casting this episode, I suggested Henry because I liked him and knew he would do well. In a sense, this episode was almost a perfect show; it was solidly written and recorded beautifully without any real effort. It was probably the easiest episode to write.

Next came *The Last of the Big Spenders*. In this episode I decided it was time for Rigsby to splash out on some furniture to impress Brenda, whom he tried to seduce on his new sofa. But at the same time I thought it would be a good twist if we saw the bailiffs coming to reclaim the goods because Rigsby had bought it all on credit and hadn't kept up the payments.

The series finished with *Things that Go Bump in the Night*. I've always liked spooky comedy since I was a boy, and films of the 1930s and 1940s depended a lot on ghosts. I've always wanted to write something about the supernatural and this was my first attempt. I enjoyed creating the grey lady and the idea of getting them into drag was fun, especially during rehearsals, which were always professionally handled; I've been to read-throughs since where they've been uproarious with everyone laughing at the jokes. It was never like that on *Rising Damp*; there was always a solid professionalism from the *Rising Damp* brigade. I got the feeling they all wanted to win their laughs later; they were simply reading to check it worked structurally.

I was relieved when the second series came to an end as I'd come through a very difficult period. I was also shattered. It was like I'd competed in the Olympics. I was low physically and although I had to get on and write some more episodes for *The Squirrels*, I made sure I left myself plenty of time. But before I could really relax, I had to complete the Christmas Special, *For The Man Who Has Everything*. As it turned out, I ended up with five weeks to complete the script, a real luxury! I took my time over it and enjoyed the process. The episode focused heavily on Rigsby because I got the idea from *Scrooge*. Playing Philip's girlfriend in the episode was Elizabeth Adare, who'd appeared in *The Banana Box*. She did a good job and had a nice impish way about her; I was pleased to use her again because she's a lovely girl.

Series Two

EPISODE 1

The Permissive Society
by
Eric Chappell

PART ONE

SCENE 1: *Int. attic flat. Evening.*
Alan and Philip are getting ready to go out.
Alan is nervous.

ALAN: What time did you tell these girls we'd be there?

PHILIP: About nine.

ALAN: Well, it was nice of you to ask me, Philip. I appreciate it.

PHILIP: That's all right.

ALAN: What's mine like?

PHILIP: She's a very sweet, sensitive girl.

ALAN: (*suspiciously*) You mean she's ugly.

PHILIP: She's not ugly – she's very attractive.

ALAN: (*smiles*) Good. (*Frowns*) Then why am I getting her?

PHILIP: Because she's a friend of this girl I'm seeing. They wanted a foursome. They said if I knew someone reasonably presentable – with a pleasing personality – to bring him along.

ALAN: (*Flattered*) And you thought of me.

PHILIP: No. He couldn't come.

ALAN: Oh. (*Pause*) What about Ruth?

PHILIP: Ruth?

ALAN: Does she know you're seeing this girl?

PHILIP: That doesn't matter anymore. You see I've told her.

ALAN: (*surprised*) About the ten wives?

PHILIP: Yes.

ALAN: How did she take it?

PHILIP: Well, she wasn't very pleased. You know how she hates crowds. (*Worried*) She was quite upset about it.

ALAN: You don't think she'll start reaching for the aspirins?

PHILIP: I hope not. But what else could I do? I had to make a clean break.

ALAN: You did the right thing, Philip. You have to be cruel – it's kinder in the long run. (*Stares into mirror*) Good looks can be a curse sometimes. (*Pause*) Where are we going tonight?

PHILIP: I thought we'd go for a drink and then back to their place. They've got a self-contained flat.

ALAN: A self-contained flat! I'd better put a clean vest on.

PHILIP: (*smiles*) Alan – don't get in a state about it.

Philip exits.

ALAN: I'm not getting in a state about it.

Alan begins to take out various lotions and sprays.
Rigsby enters. He gives the bottles a jaundiced look.

ALAN: Is the water hot, Rigsby?

RIGSBY: What do you want to know for?

ALAN: I'm going to have a bath.

RIGSBY: Wait a minute – I'm not going to have you in there all night preening yourself. Once you get in front of that full-length mirror you lose all track of time.

ALAN: No point in having a good body if you can't appreciate it, Rigsby.

RIGSBY: I wouldn't mind if it stopped there. Last time you were trying to see how high you could get your footmarks up the wall. You left the place swimming in water.

ALAN: (*over toiletry*) I think I'll use my Soap Bunny. (*Picks up soap figure*)

RIGSBY: (*surprised*) Are you sure? You've had him a long time.

ALAN: He's got to get wet sometime – and it is a special occasion. (*Quotes*) 'The masculine, scented soap to brighten up a man's bathtime'.

RIGSBY: You'll need more than masculine, scented soap. I know you. You'll come out that bathroom looking like Veronica Lake.

ALAN: Who's Veronica Lake?

RIGSBY: Don't you know anything? She was a film star – had long flowing hair. You're a lot like her – except she wore less jewellery.

ALAN: Don't you worry about me. Times have changed. You don't have to smell of old socks any more, Rigsby. You just make sure there's plenty of hot water.

RIGSBY: (*stares at bottles*) Are you sure there's going to be room? Just look at this stuff. You know you're damaging the atmosphere with this, don't you? (*Uses spray*) God! What's this? Fly spray?

ALAN: No – that's to keep my hair in place. It's useful if I'm caught in the rain.

RIGSBY: You're never caught in the rain. You won't go out until you've heard the weather forecast. Besides, if you want to keep your hair in place why don't you do what I do? Use soap and water.

ALAN: You know why, Rigsby. Because when you get caught in

the rain you come out in little bubbles. I can't afford that. I've got a date tonight.

RIGSBY: I thought so. I wondered why we were having this sudden interest in personal hygiene. What's she like?

ALAN: I haven't met her yet. Philip's arranged it.

RIGSBY: You mean she hasn't seen you?

ALAN: No.

RIGSBY: She's in for a shock.

ALAN: Now listen, Philip asked me because I happened to be the sophisticated type they were looking for.

RIGSBY: Oh yes, and what are you going to wear – your Donald Duck shirt – or those jeans with 'come and get me' on the crotch?

ALAN: That's a point – what should I wear?

Philip enters.

What do you think I should wear, Philip?

PHILIP: (*sighs*) I don't know. Wear what you like – it doesn't matter.

ALAN: Ah, but I believe in preparation. I want this to be like a well-planned military campaign.

RIGSBY: Why don't you wear your RAF overcoat? (*Sneers*) Well-planned military campaign.

ALAN: You're only jealous, Rigsby. Did I tell you they've got a self-contained flat? I can see it all now. Three vodkas, a few packets of flavoured crisps and Geronimo!

RIGSBY: My God! Just listen to him. He never talked like that before you came. He's changed – even his voice has got deeper.

PHILIP: Well, it's better than being furtive about it, Rigsby.

RIGSBY: No, it isn't. I preferred him when he was being furtive. Do you know he arrived here with an ivory prayer book and a teddy bear? Now look at him. A fully paid-up member of the permissive society.

ALAN: I haven't changed that much, Rigsby.

RIGSBY: Yes, you have. Before *he* came all you knew about women was what you saw in those magazines.

ALAN: No, it wasn't.

RIGSBY: I used to see him in Smith's – pretending he was looking for *Practical Woodworker*. Always turning to the centre pages. He thought all women were like that. It must have come as a big surprise to him when he found they hadn't got staples across their stomachs.

ALAN: There's nothing wrong in admiring the perfection of the female figure.

RIGSBY: That's not perfection –

that's all accomplished by body make-up and Sellotape. That's sex-ploitation.

PHILIP: I couldn't agree more, Rigsby. In my country we find that sort of thing degrading. We don't feel that sex is something to be sniggered at. We don't read those sort of magazines.

RIGSBY: Of course you don't. You don't have time to read about it – you're too busy doing it.

PHILIP: At least they don't have to draw diagrams for us, Rigsby. We don't have to be shown on the blackboard. No one has to tell us where the erogenous zones are.

RIGSBY: The what?

ALAN: The erogenous zones, Rigsby. (*Grins*) He doesn't know what they are.

RIGSBY: Yes, I do. (*Hesitates*) Somewhere near the equator, aren't they?

ALAN: (*laughs*) I knew you didn't know. The erogenous zones are those parts of the body most sensitive to sexual stimuli.

RIGSBY: Ah – *those* erogenous zones.

ALAN: I mean, take the ear for example. That's an erogenous zone. You blow in Miss Jones's ear, Rigsby – you'd be staggered at the results.

RIGSBY: (*angrily*) Now you watch your tongue. I'm not having that sort of talk around here. This is a respectable house.

ALAN: It's nothing to be ashamed of, Rigsby. It's even discussed in schools these days.

RIGSBY: Well, if we'd tried that in my day we'd have received a sharp blow from a heavy ruler, mate.

ALAN: Times have changed, Rigsby. We believe in love without fear.

RIGSBY: Oh yes. I seem to remember the last time you indulged in love without fear – you spent three days hiding under that bed from her father.

ALAN: That was different. He was a reactionary. Always going on about the permissive society. He didn't like me.

RIGSBY: Didn't he? You do surprise me. I wonder what he could have possibly had against you?

ALAN: He said I was damaging his hedge. We used to lean against it.

RIGSBY: I can understand how he felt. He's spent years raising his daughter to perfection – to the flower of womanhood – and what happens? Along comes this long-haired Herbert in surgical boots who starts swinging on his gate – damaging his hedge – and chatting up his daughter.

ALAN: It wasn't just that. He found these letters ... and they were open to ... er ... certain interpretations.

RIGSBY: I bet they were.

ALAN: He said he was going to wring my neck.

PHILIP: He shouldn't have read your letters.

ALAN: That's what I said.

RIGSBY: What do you mean? Of course he should have read them. It's his duty to protect his daughter. She's his responsibility. He's got to shelter that innocent girl from the likes of you. When I was your age that was important – the purity of a woman. It was the finest gift a woman could give to a man on their wedding night. Now he has to make do with a set of cuff-links. (*Pauses by door*) Well, just remember the permissive society stops at that front door – we don't want it in here.

Exit Rigsby.

* * *

SCENE 2: *Int. landing.*
Rigsby pauses by Ruth's door. Listens. Knocks gently. Enters.

* * *

SCENE 3: *Int. Ruth's room.*
Ruth is drying her eyes. Sniffing. Rigsby regards her anxiously.

RIGSBY: Are you all right, Miss Jones?

RUTH: Yes, thank you, Mr Rigsby.

RIGSBY: If you don't mind me saying, Miss Jones – you look a little distraught. Should I make you a cup of tea?

RUTH: Tea! (*Laughs harshly*) Why do we always think that a cup of tea will solve everything? My God! Tea!

RIGSBY: I can see you're a coffee drinker, Miss Jones.

Rigsby starts to prepare coffee whilst Ruth applies handkerchief. Rigsby darts another anxious glance.

RIGSBY: Been watching the television, Miss Jones? Enough to get anybody down. Depression moving in from the North Sea. There's another run on the pound. And Valerie Singleton's shopping basket's gone up again.

RUTH: (*sighs*) I walked by the canal tonight. It looked so inviting.

RIGSBY: (*surprised*) Did it? You do surprise me. I mean, inviting's not the word I'd use to describe that canal – no, the word I'd use is filthy.

RUTH: Just a splash and a short struggle and it would all be over.

RIGSBY: What? (*hastily*) No – you wouldn't get much of a splash out of that canal – it's full of prams. If you wanted to do something like that, it would be quicker to drink it. But you shouldn't be having these morbid thoughts, Miss Jones. I know things look black at the moment—

RUTH: I just can't take any more.

RIGSBY: I understand. Is it the Social Contract, Miss Jones?

RUTH: No, Mr Rigsby. It's something more personal than that.

RIGSBY: Ah. It's a man isn't it? An affair of the heart?

RUTH: I'm afraid so, Mr Rigsby.

RIGSBY: (*gently*) If there's anything I can do, Miss Jones. If you want him filling in.

RUTH: No – that won't be necessary. (*Sighs*) It's the deception I can't stand.

RIGSBY: You're too trusting, Miss Jones.

RUTH: I suppose so. What hurts even more – I've done his washing for three months. He said no one could get his collars as white as I did. Now I suppose he's got someone else.

RIGSBY: Now you don't know that, Miss Jones – he could be using a launderette. You just tell me his name and—

RUTH: No, I can't do that. It'll only lead to unpleasantness. No – I must try and forget him, but it's difficult when you've had your finest feelings trodden on. It's moments like this, Mr Rigsby when I envy the simple amoeba.

RIGSBY: The amoeba, Miss Jones?

RUTH: Yes. You see, when they want to reproduce – they just wander off and split themselves in two. I know it doesn't sound much fun but at least life would be less complicated. Don't you agree, Mr Rigsby?

RIGSBY: I hadn't really thought about it. It'd certainly put the lid on Marjorie Proops.

RUTH: You see this isn't the first time it's happened.

RIGSBY: I didn't know that, Miss Jones.

RUTH: I don't often talk about it. The memory is still quite painful. He was plausible too. So charming and considerate. Until he saw the wedding presents then something seemed to snap. He went, and so did the presents. The last I saw of him he was driving down the road in a hired mini-van with my father clinging from the roof.

RIGSBY: You seem rather unfortunate in your choice of men, Miss Jones.

RUTH: What do I do wrong? Perhaps if I was more … permissive?

RIGSBY: No, Miss Jones. You're an example to us all. Someone to look up to.

RUTH: Thank you, Mr Rigsby. You're a tower of strength.

RIGSBY: (*Trying to blow gently in her ear*) The trouble is, there's no respect anymore. They don't know how to treat a woman of your refinement. I'd consider it a privilege to help you pick up the pieces.

RUTH: You're very kind. Is there a draught in here?

RIGSBY: I hadn't noticed, Miss

Jones. If you'd like me to stay for a while – under the circumstances—

RUTH: No – that won't be necessary. I've taken a sleeping tablet.

RIGSBY: Oh.

RUTH: I'm afraid I shall soon be asleep.

Rigsby sighs and rises.

But it is nice to know that there's someone in the house I can depend on. Someone with standards.

RIGSBY: Of course. There's not many of us left, Miss Jones. Goodnight.

Rigsby exits.

* * *

SCENE 4: *Int. landing.*
Rigsby scowls. Aims kick at the cat. Screech.

* * *

SCENE 5: *Int. attic flat. Late evening. Alan and Philip enter taking off coats. Philip is angry.*

PHILIP: (*stares at Alan*) My God!

ALAN: What's the matter?

PHILIP: You know what's the matter. It was a disaster – and it was your fault.

ALAN: I don't know what you're talking about.

PHILIP: I thought it was going to be three vodkas – a few packets of flavoured crisps and Geronimo.

ALAN: Well, yes – but I hadn't met them then. They were too sophisticated for that.

PHILIP: Is that why you spent all evening telling them how to remove the gall bladder? All those gory details – I began to wonder if I should have worn a white shirt!

ALAN: Well, they seemed interested.

PHILIP: Interested! They were mesmerised. And when we got back to the flat and they said what should we do – and you suggested Scrabble.

ALAN: Well, what about all those four-letter words? That could have led to something.

PHILIP: Well, it didn't tonight. They couldn't wait for us to go and I don't blame them.

ALAN: Perhaps I should have told you, Philip. I don't usually try anything on the first date.

PHILIP: On the first date! You mean you get a second? Well, you won't this time. (*Pause*) You're frightened of women, aren't you?

ALAN: No.

PHILIP: You've never really known a woman, have you? Not intimately.

ALAN: Now wait a minute – why do you think I had to hide under that bed for three days?

PHILIP: Because the family wanted you to get married and you got cold feet.

ALAN: Yes, well, I didn't want to get married. They kept saying, 'Come on in the water's lovely.'

PHILIP: But you were frightened?

ALAN: No. I didn't mind a dip – I just didn't want to swim the Channel.

PHILIP: You haven't had a dip though – have you?

ALAN: (*hesitates*) No.

PHILIP: I thought not. Then why do you tell so many lies?

ALAN: Well, you know what they say about students. I just didn't want to get a bad name – that was all.

PHILIP: It's nothing to be ashamed of.

ALAN: No, I suppose not. Oh, it's all right for you. You've got ten wives – no one can challenge your experience. (*Curiously*) How old were you when you first—?

PHILIP: Oh, it was all part of my initiation. Went with the tribal mark. On my fourteenth birthday.

ALAN: On your fourteenth birthday! (*Shrugs*) All I got was a bike.

PHILIP: Well, don't worry about it. You're going through a phase. You're just a little immature, that's all.

Philip exits.

ALAN: I'm not immature.

He crosses to bed and places his teddy bear inside the sheets.

END OF PART ONE

PART TWO

SCENE 6: *Int. attic flat. Next morning. Alan is alone.*
Rigsby enters. Hovers. He eyes Alan enviously. Finally brings himself to speak.

RIGSBY: Did you have a good time last night?

ALAN: Oh yes – very good – very successful. Remind me to carve another notch on the bedpost, Rigsby.

RIGSBY: (*scowls*) That's just like you, isn't it? Keeping a record. You know what you'd have been in the war, don't you? A sniper. You students – you're all the same – it's disgusting. Where are your standards? How can you be so depraved?

ALAN: It isn't easy, Rigsby. You have to work at it. Last night, for example, it was all a question of technique.

RIGSBY: Technique?

ALAN: Yes. You see you can compare a woman with a finely tuned piano.

RIGSBY: What?

ALAN: You have to approach her like a concert pianist. It's no good just sitting down and playing chopsticks. Look at these long tapering fingers, Rigsby – musician's hands these are.

RIGSBY: My God. You're off again. Don't you ever stop?

ALAN: Well, if you're not interested.

RIGSBY: This girl you met last night – was she like a finely tuned piano?

ALAN: Of course. Mind you – I did experience some resistance.

RIGSBY: You mean you couldn't get the lid up?

ALAN: That's where technique comes in, Rigsby. I remembered to look deep into her eyes – made her feel a woman – the only woman – woman, the eternal mystery. Then I whispered a few French phrases in her ear – that always gets them going.

RIGSBY: Then what happened?

ALAN: Well, at first she was quite cool. But after a while I could see I was having an effect. She began polishing her glasses in an agitated manner. The Scrabble board fell to the floor.

RIGSBY: The Scrabble board?

ALAN: She began to shake like an aspen leaf.

RIGSBY: My God! Then what happened?

ALAN: You can't expect me to tell you any more, Rigsby.

RIGSBY: No – I suppose not.

ALAN: But the old sea began pounding against the rocks, Rigsby. Factory chimneys started falling – there were coloured lights in the background – Tchaikovsky.

RIGSBY: Tchaikovsky. He was there as well was he?

ALAN: You know what I mean, Rigsby.

RIGSBY: Hmm. I wonder if that would work with Miss Jones?

ALAN: Of course it would.

RIGSBY: I don't know. She's a bit depressed at the moment. I don't think she's in the mood for the sea pounding up against the rocks – that sort of thing. You see she's just been let down by this bloke.

ALAN: So what? You could restore her faith in men, Rigsby.

RIGSBY: Yes – there's only one snag. I happen to be married.

ALAN: (*surprised*) You are, Rigsby? I didn't know that.

RIGSBY: It was during the war. I should never have done it. It was a military blunder on the scale of Anzio. The only woman I ever really fancied in those days was Greer Garson. I used to see all her films – her and Walter Pigeon – they don't make films like that anymore. I always meant to marry a woman like that.

ALAN: Was your wife like Greer Garson?

RIGSBY: What? (*Frowns*) No – she was more like Walter Pigeon, actually.

ALAN: Well, I wouldn't worry about being married, Rigsby. Marriage is an outmoded custom. We live in a modern society – it's a question of personal freedom.

RIGSBY: Perhaps you're right. (*Pauses by door*) A few French phrases?

ALAN: That's right, Rigsby.

Rigsby nods and exits.

* * *

SCENE 7: *Int. attic flat. Evening. Philip is getting ready for bed. Alan enters in dressing gown.*

PHILIP: Have you see Ruth?

ALAN: Yes.

PHILIP: How did she seem?

ALAN: Not very happy. She's wearing her blue glasses.

PHILIP: (*worried*) Well, there's nothing I can do about it.

ALAN: No, of course not. You've got to be cruel.

PHILIP: Absolutely. (*Pause. Regards Alan*) You know this could be your big chance, Alan.

ALAN: What? Oh, no. You're not getting me involved.

PHILIP: Alan – Ruth's a wonderful woman.

ALAN: (*surprised*) Is she?

PHILIP: A wonderful woman – and she's lonely.

ALAN: (*Frowns*) If she's so wonderful, why is she lonely?

PHILIP: Because you don't appreciate her.

ALAN: You mean, *you* don't appreciate her.

PHILIP: I'm not good enough for her.

ALAN: You've never said that before.

PHILIP: I think you need each other. This could be your big chance. After all, she's a great believer in charity – always prepared to help a worthy cause – to aid the deprived. And there's no one more deprived than you, Alan.

ALAN: Now wait a minute—

PHILIP: After all, you've got something special, Alan.

ALAN: What's that?

PHILIP: Your innocence.

ALAN: Well, I'll keep it for the moment if you don't mind.

PHILIP: Alan, you can't go on like this – you'll pop your cork. Why don't you go to her?

ALAN: What – like this?

PHILIP: Why not? Think about it. You won't have to tell all those lies anymore. They'll be the truth.

ALAN: Suppose she gets angry.

PHILIP: She won't. After all, it's a compliment.

ALAN: Is it?

PHILIP: You're going there to make a humble offering.

ALAN: Yes, and suppose she tells me what to do with my humble offering?

PHILIP: She won't. But of course if you really are afraid of women—

ALAN: I'm not afraid.

PHILIP: Just a little immature.

ALAN: We'll see about that.

Alan exits.

*   *   *

SCENE 8: *Int. Ruth's room.*
Ruth is asleep in a darkened room. Alan enters. He gropes his way to the bed. He puts his hand forward to touch Ruth. Hesitates. Draws back.

Is about to retreat. Door creaks. Alan looks around fearfully. Steps into wardrobe.
Rigsby enters.

RIGSBY: (*whispers*) Miss Jones. (*Louder*) Miss Jones.

RUTH: (*wakes*) Mr Rigsby. (*Switches on light*) What are you doing here at this time of night?

RIGSBY: I had to see you, Miss Jones.

RUTH: Surely it could have waited until the morning? (*Puts on dressing gown*)

RIGSBY: No – I've waited too long already. Time's running out for me, Miss Jones.

RUTH: I don't think I quite understand, Mr Rigsby.

RIGSBY: This is my September song, Miss Jones.

RUTH: (*stares*) You're not going to sing, Mr Rigsby – not at this time of night?

RIGSBY: Miss Jones – I've been meaning to say this for a long time. You're a very attractive, desirable woman.

RUTH: Mr Rigsby, this isn't the time … (*stops*) Go on.

RIGSBY: Seeing you last night – alone and almost suicidal – it made me realise just what you mean to me.

RUTH: Mr Rigsby—

RIGSBY: Of course I always knew there was someone else but now he's out of the way, it's just you and me. He could never appreciate you, Miss Jones. You're like a finely tuned piano

Suppressed chuckle from wardrobe.

RUTH: I beg your pardon?

RIGSBY: You need a very light touch, Miss Jones. (*Moves closer*)

RUTH: Mr Rigsby – not at this time of night – what would people think?

RIGSBY: (*with effort*) *Honi soit que mal y pense*, Miss Jones.

Chuckle from wardrobe.

What was that? Is there someone in this room, Miss Jones? Someone who shouldn't be here?

RUTH: Yes – you, Mr Rigsby.

RIGSBY: But you must know how I feel. You must have felt my eyes on you. I've always admired you.

RUTH: Mr Rigsby – I don't know what to say.

RIGSBY: (*hoarsely*) *Respondez s'il vous plait.*

RUTH: Mr Rigsby!

Rigsby moves into powerful embrace.

RIGSBY: *Dieu et mon droit!*

Ruth struggles free.

Why should we live alone, Miss

Jones? Say you'll come down to the ground floor.

RUTH: Please, let me get my breath, Mr Rigsby. This is so unexpected. Don't think it's not appreciated. You've paid me the finest compliment a man can pay a woman. To ask her to marry you.

RIGSBY: What?

RUTH: You are asking me to marry you?

RIGSBY: Well, not exactly, Miss Jones.

RUTH: What do you mean – not exactly?

RIGSBY: Well, there is a bit of a drawback where marriage is concerned. You see, unfortunately, I happen to be married already.

RUTH: Mr Rigsby! And I thought you were different. You come up here with your talk of finely tuned pianos and all the time – you ought to be ashamed of yourself – you know I'm at a low ebb.

RIGSBY: But, Miss Jones – marriage is an outmoded custom. This is the permissive society.

RUTH: Not in this room, it isn't.

RIGSBY: You don't understand.

RUTH: Oh, I understand. You thought you could come up here and take advantage of a woman crushed by fate. But I've still got my values, Mr Rigsby.

RIGSBY: I know – that's what attracted me, Miss Jones. I don't meet many women like you.

RUTH: I'm not surprised. You know what you're like, Mr Rigsby? You're like these men who go around shooting pheasants and then complain when they're scarce. Now get out.

Laughter from wardrobe.

RIGSBY: Miss Jones – there's someone in the wardrobe.

RUTH: Oh yes, didn't you know – I keep a man in there. Would you like to see him?

Throws open the wardrobe door.
C/U of Alan.
There is a stunned silence.

* * *

SCENE 9: *Int attic flat. Morning.*
Alan nervously putting on coat.
Rigsby enters.

RIGSBY: (*dangerously*) Where do you think you're going?

ALAN: I'm going out, Rigsby.

RIGSBY: How can you be going out? I mean, the sun's not up. You should be resting in your coffin – you bloody vampire.

ALAN: Now get out of my way, Rigsby. I've got to meet Philip.

RIGSBY: Oh yes, and who are you going to deceive this time with your three vodkas and your flavoured crisps?

ALAN: What are you doing, Rigsby?

RIGSBY: I'm moving the furniture. I want plenty of room.

ALAN: What for?

RIGSBY: To swing you round in.

ALAN: Now wait a minute – about last night.

RIGSBY: What about last night? What can you possibly say?

ALAN: Evil is in the eye of the beholder, Rigsby.

RIGSBY: Not last night it wasn't. I wasn't the one in the wardrobe. Poor Miss Jones didn't know where to put herself. I've always suspected you?

ALAN: What?

RIGSBY: I think it's because of your small forehead. Well, you're not going to trifle with Miss Jones's feelings anymore.

ALAN: I haven't trifled with Miss Jones's feelings.

RIGSBY: Then what were you doing in that wardrobe? You weren't looking for woodworm.

He closes with Alan.

ALAN: (*desperately*) It was just an impulse – nothing happened. I didn't trifle with her. I've never trifled with anyone.

RIGSBY: (*surprised*) What?

ALAN: It's true.

RIGSBY: You mean there's been no sea crashing up against the rocks – no coloured lights?

ALAN: (*sadly*) No – it was just talk.

RIGSBY: But you're a member of the permissive society. You know where the erogenous regions are.

ALAN: I know where the Himalayas are but I've never been there.

RIGSBY: My God! You must have a very vivid imagination.

ALAN: Yes – I have to have. And you've got to exaggerate a bit – it attracts the birds. I'll never be Bachelor of the Month if I tell them the truth.

Cooper enters unnoticed. He is a square, hard-looking man in middle age.

That's why I put it around I like my girls long and leggy – with funny little mouths. I dine them in dimly lit Greek restaurants and then whip them back to my bachelor pad for a few records and a bit of how's your father—

Alan sees Cooper for the first time.

Oh, hello, Mr Cooper.

COOPER: I've been looking for you.

ALAN: (*nervously*) Have you?

COOPER: Yes, in fact we've all been looking for you. You're a very difficult man to find. Sandra's very upset.

ALAN: Is she?

COOPER: She seemed to have got this idea in her head that you two were engaged.

ALAN: Well, we did have a sort of understanding.

COOPER: No, she had the understanding. I want to know what you had.

ALAN: I don't quite understand.

COOPER: Don't you? You come to my house, you eat your way through the deep freeze, you damage my hedge and then you calmly walk off leaving Sandra in tears. I want to know what you're going to do about it.

ALAN: I think there must be some misunderstanding.

COOPER: There's no misunderstanding. I've got a letter here.

ALAN: You shouldn't have read that – it's not addressed to you.

COOPER: (*glances at Rigsby*) It's written in green ink. (*Rigsby raises his eyebrows. Cooper reads*) 'I can't wait to see you, *mon cheri*. Your body is like a highly tuned piano – what music we will make together. (*They both glance at Alan*) Meet me tonight by the hedge. Make sure old misery guts is out of the way. Do not fail me, I am burning with desire. *Au revoir, mon petite*. Etcetera, etcetera. And that's just a sample.

Rigsby starts to laugh.

I suppose you think it's funny. I expected more concern from his father.

RIGSBY: What?

COOPER: I should have known better. You've both got the same depraved expression. I only have to look at you to see where he gets it from.

RIGSBY: Hey! Now wait a minute.

COOPER: It's people like you who are responsible for all this permissiveness. Well, I don't believe in it. I came up here to insist that he went through with the marriage, but after seeing you I've changed my mind. I realise Sandra's had a very narrow escape. Fancy having you for a father-in-law.

RIGSBY: Now just you listen to me. (*Pokes Cooper in the chest*) He's right. You shouldn't have read that letter. You people are all the same. You keep rabbiting on about the permissive society but have you seen it? No, because it's all in the mind. It doesn't exist. I should know, I've looked. So don't keep telling me how things have changed because they haven't. Now just take your nasty little thoughts and get out of here.

Rigsby advances, still poking Cooper in the chest.
Rigsby shouts down the stairs.

Go on – before you get more than you bargained for.

He closes the door.

ALAN: Hey, Rigsby – you didn't half tell him.

RIGSBY: There you are, you see. Just the same during the war. When the chips are down—

ALAN: (*admiringly*) Thanks, Rigsby. Don't know what I would have done without you.

RIGSBY: That's all right, anytime.

Alan looks out of the window.

ALAN: Hey – there he goes.

RIGSBY: With his tail between his legs.

ALAN: He's going to his car.

RIGSBY: Is he getting in?

ALAN: No – there are two other fellows getting out—

Rigsby joins him at the window.

RIGSBY: Big buggers, aren't they?

ALAN: (*alarmed*) Rigsby – they're Sandra's brothers!

BOTH: They're coming up!

RIGSBY: Quick! The key – the key—

They look around for somewhere to hide.

THE END

brute – no one would go near him. Who befriended him? Who put his hand out to that animal?

ALAN: You did, Rigsby. He bit you, didn't he?

RIGSBY: (*frowns*) Yes, well, you don't expect gratitude – you do it because it has to be done.

ALAN: What's Ruth collecting for anyway?

RIGSBY: (*confidentially*) I'm not sure – but I think it's people.

ALAN: (*laughs*) Ah, that explains it.

RIGSBY: What do you mean?

ALAN: Well, you don't like people.

RIGSBY: I've got nothing against people—

ALAN: Oh, you'd give to animals because they're soft and cuddly—

RIGSBY: I give to cancer.

ALAN: Only because you think you might get it.

RIGSBY: No, I don't.

ALAN: What about the time you came up here clutching your throat? Thought you'd got a growth. You were nearly wetting yourself – it was only your adam's apple.

RIGSBY: Look, I've got nothing against people but I'm a poor man. I can only give so much – and she'll expect more for people.

ALAN: You don't give that much, Rigsby. I notice you always cover the money with your fingers when you put it in. You don't let anyone see it.

RIGSBY: Of course I don't. You're not supposed to. That's your bad breeding showing that is. Just because you go around making an exhibition of yourself – covering people with flour, smashing up pianos, seeing how many you can squeeze into a phone box. At least I've got a bit of dignity.

ALAN: Well, you don't look very dignified at the moment – skulking up here.

RIGSBY: I'm not skulking, I'm skint. Look at me. I'm the one she should be collecting for. I've hardly got a button left on this jacket.

ALAN: I wondered what you'd been putting in the tins.

RIGSBY: (*listens*) She's coming up here. I'll just stay out of sight.

Rigsby crouches behind furniture.
Sound of collecting tin.
Ruth enters.

RUTH: Hello, Alan. Have you seen, Mr Rigsby? I saw his feet flying up the stairs. (*Sees Rigsby's feet. Shakes tin.*) Hello, Mr Rigsby.

RIGSBY: (*rises*) Oh, hello, Miss Jones – just checking the woodworm.

RUTH: (*shaking tin*) I thought you might be avoiding me.

RIGSBY: Avoiding you, Miss Jones – the very idea. What's that you've got in your hand, Miss Jones? Is that a collecting tin?

RUTH: Yes, it's for Famine Relief. I thought you might like to help others less fortunate than yourself, Mr Rigsby.

RIGSBY: Of course, Miss Jones. A very worthy cause – allow me to contribute.

Rigsby fishes around in pocket. Makes a great fuss of putting money in, shaking tin vigorously.

RUTH: That's very kind of you, Mr Rigsby.

RIGSBY: It was nothing, Miss Jones.

ALAN: That's what it sounded like.

RIGSBY: (*ignores him*) In the words of the song, Miss Jones, 'If I can help somebody as I pass along, then my living shall not be in vain.'

RUTH: I wish more people felt like that, Mr Rigsby. Let me pin the flag on you. I'm afraid I'm not very good. (*Rigsby backs apprehensively*) I've transfixed several people already. One screamed so loudly I almost dropped the tray. Now keep still. That's the trouble. I've had to practically harpoon some of them. There.

Rigsby winces with pain.

Of course, some don't intend to stop – they just quicken their pace. You certainly see the worst side of human nature selling flags. Do you know, some even pretend they haven't got any money – even when they're carrying three carrier bags from Tesco's.

ALAN: I think that's terrible.

RUTH: (*smiles. Shakes tin*) Alan?

ALAN: Oh yes – of course.

Alan feels awkwardly in his pockets. Turns them out. Crosses. Shakes piggy bank. They watch him in silence.

Do you know – I don't think I've got any change at the moment.

RIGSBY: Surprise. Surprise.

ALAN: I'm sorry, Ruth.

RUTH: That's all right, Alan. I'll see you later. Thank you, Mr Rigsby.

RIGSBY: My pleasure, Miss Jones.

Ruth exits.
Rigsby snatches flag from his chest.

RIGSBY: Another one straight through the skin.

ALAN: It's for a good cause, Rigsby.

RIGSBY: I don't know about that. She's always ready to help our little brown brothers – she never gives a thought to me.

Philip enters unnoticed.

You've got to be black to get any

sympathy around here. I'm the wrong colour.

PHILIP: I've always said so, Rigsby. Do you want to borrow the lamp?

RIGSBY: Oh, it's you. No thanks. After all, there are some slight disadvantages in your pigmentation – like a dimly lit street and a ten-ton lorry. I mean they'd never pick you out on sidelights, would they?

ALAN: Don't take any notice, Philip. He's in a bad mood. He's just given to Famine Relief. He didn't want to – he only did it to impress Miss Jones.

RIGSBY: No, I didn't. I can't help having a warm, impulsive nature. All I'm saying is these people should learn to look after themselves. It's time we laid down the white man's burden.

PHILIP: What do you mean, Rigsby? How can you lay it down? We're the ones who do all the carrying. We're the ones who've been exploited.

RIGSBY: We haven't exploited you. Where would you have been without us?

PHILIP: Rigsby – it was paradise before you came. Unspoilt, unpolluted.

RIGSBY: You can't tell me about those places. I've been there. Oh, they've got a nice climate, clear skies, blue sea. The only trouble is, the beach goes back five hundred miles. Just strips of sand. And did they do anything about it? Did they find the oil? Did they build the railways and dig the canals? No, they just laid out under the palms and read the Kama Sutra.

PHILIP: As a matter of fact, Rigsby, not only did they do the digging but they had to do it on an empty stomach.

RIGSBY: Well, that's their religion, isn't it? They're so fussy. They won't eat the sacred cow, will they? And the other half believe in reincarnation – they won't eat anything in case it's someone they know. That's why they won't do any digging – if they put their spade through a worm they think they've cut Granny in half. You can't be like that about animals.

ALAN: That's good coming from someone who spends a fortune on tinned cat food.

PHILIP: Yes, how can you object to feeding the poor when you spend so much on that fat, greasy thing.

RIGSBY: Hey! Keep your voice down. He understands every word you say. You've hurt his feelings now. Never mind, Vienna – the dark gentleman didn't mean it.

PHILIP: But I did mean it. Just look at him. What use is he?

RIGSBY: What use is he? He's not supposed to be any use – he's a pet.

PHILIP: Would you eat him if you were starving, Rigsby?

RIGSBY: I shall have to cover his ears if you go on like this. Of course I wouldn't eat him. We don't do that sort of thing in this country.

PHILIP: He's your sacred cow, Rigsby. He has the best of everything.

RIGSBY: Of course he does. He has that stuff they show on television. The one the cat picks out – he always goes for that bowl – unerring he is.

ALAN: Well, he gets his tail trodden on if he doesn't.

PHILIP: Don't argue with him, Alan. He's riddled with prejudice. He's never seen drought. He doesn't know what it's like to be hungry.

RIGSBY: What do you mean? When I was in the desert we went without food for three days. But we stood it. We were iron men. We were the only battalion who didn't eat the mascot.

PHILIP: Three days! You couldn't go without food for forty-eight hours, Rigsby.

RIGSBY: Who says so?

PHILIP: Here's five pounds that says you couldn't.

RIGSBY: You're on.

PHILIP: There'll have to be conditions.

RIGSBY: Any conditions you like. It'll be money for jam.

PHILIP: There won't be any jam, Rigsby. And no sweets – not even a glacier mint … I know you've got a sweet tooth.

RIGSBY: You needn't worry.

PHILIP: We'll have to confiscate your food. You won't be able to leave the house.

RIGSBY: That's all right. That money's as good as mine.

PHILIP: Perhaps. It doesn't really matter, Rigsby, because I'm going to enjoy watching you sweat. You're going to know what it's like to go hungry and I shall watch you like a cat watches a mouse. Now I'm going to collect your food. I hope you haven't eaten.

Philip exits laughing.

Rigsby stares after him in silence.

RIGSBY: You know – I think he's got something against me.

* * *

SCENE 2: *Int. Rigsby's flat. Day.*
Alan and Rigsby are sitting opposite each other.

RIGSBY: I don't know what you're sitting there for.

ALAN: I'm supposed to keep an eye on you.

RIGSBY: Well, it's been a waste of time hasn't it? I told you I could do it. All a question of will power. How long is it now?

ALAN: (*checks watch*) Forty-five minutes.

RIGSBY: Is that all? I thought it was longer.

ALAN: Do you think you're going to make it?

RIGSBY: Of course I'm going to make it. You don't understand, do you? You've never learnt self-discipline. You'd never last in an open boat – you'd be drinking the sea water, crying out for your sticky sweets.

ALAN: Well, it's all right for you. I'm still growing.

RIGSBY: Yes – like a big black cloud. What you don't understand is that it's all a question of mind over matter. (*Pause. Sharply.*) Are you eating a sweet?

ALAN: Yes. You don't mind, do you?

RIGSBY: No, it doesn't worry me. (*Pause*) Are they those little chocolates that don't mark your gloves?

ALAN: Yes.

RIGSBY: I thought so. Sort of honey-combed with a soft centre?

ALAN: This one's got a bit of hazelnut.

RIGSBY: Yes, they're the ones. You're better off buying them like that – you're not paying for the box.

ALAN: Yes – you get no end.

RIGSBY: Yes. (*Pause*) I can hear you chewing.

ALAN: Sorry.

RIGSBY: (*gets up*) I don't know why he asked you to keep an eye on me. He's got a very suspicious nature. I'm going to enjoy watching his face when I take the fiver off him. I think I'll get a drink.

ALAN: Now wait a minute, Rigsby.

RIGSBY: We said food – we never said anything about drink. (*Opens cupboard*) Hey! He's taken the milk stout.

Philip enters.

PHILIP: What's the matter, Rigsby?

RIGSBY: You've taken the beer.

PHILIP: Yes. I'm afraid you can only drink water.

RIGSBY: (*appalled*) Water! You never said anything about water.

PHILIP: Rigsby, if you were in a drought you wouldn't even get that.

RIGSBY: But I don't drink water.

PHILIP: I'm afraid you'll have to get used to it.

RIGSBY: Well, it's not the water you see – it's the fluoride.

ALAN: It'll harden your teeth.

RIGSBY: I don't want my teeth hardening. I'm not going to be eating anything, am I? Besides, it's a matter of principle. No one asked me if I wanted fluoride.

ALAN: It won't do you any harm.

RIGSBY: What! You haven't seen the inside of my kettle. I don't want those little bits jumping around in me.

PHILIP: Well, if you want to call it off, Rigsby. If it's too tough for you—

RIGSBY: Too tough! You're talking to an old desert rat, mate. I'll survive. It's just a question of will-power.

PHILIP: Mind over matter.

RIGSBY: That's right.

PHILIP: I quite agree. My great uncle always said that. Of course, he was the witch doctor – but he could go without food.

RIGSBY: There you are you see. (*Pause. Frowns.*) Do you mean altogether?

PHILIP: Oh yes. Never touched a crumb.

RIGSBY: He must have had incredible powers. What was the secret?

PHILIP: He never told us. But he'd just perfected it when he died.

Fade out on Rigsby's face.

END OF PART ONE

PART TWO

SCENE 3: *Int. Rigsby's room. Next morning.*
Rigsby enters from bedroom.
He groans and rubs his stomach.
Cat meows.
Rigsby opens cupboard.

RIGSBY: Looks as if they've taken your food as well. Well, don't look at me. I've got nothing. I've been chewing my pyjama cord all night. You'll have to go out and catch yourself a sparrow – that's if you know how. (*Holds Vienna up to window*) You're supposed to creep up on them and pounce. Pounce! You can't even win a fight with the cushion these days. Just look at you. It must be years since you went in for the kill. You couldn't catch a sparrow – you'd have to speed up to catch a rubber duck.

Alan enters.

ALAN: Talking to yourself, Rigsby?

RIGSBY: No, I wasn't. I was talking to Vienna. I suppose you know you've taken his tins. You'd better start feeding him or he'll have your arm off. See the way his tail's moving from side to side.

ALAN: What about you, Rigsby? How are you feeling?

RIGSBY: I'm all right. Don't worry about me. What time is it?

ALAN: It's almost dinner time.

RIGSBY: (*scowls*) I've noticed something about you. You can never open your mouth without mentioning food.

ALAN: Sorry, Rigsby. (*Studies him*) It's getting to you, isn't it?

RIGSBY: No, it isn't. I don't give way that easily – I've got a bit of backbone, mate.

ALAN: Did you sleep all right?

RIGSBY: Yes. Why not?

ALAN: Weren't you hungry?

RIGSBY: Of course I was hungry but I mastered it. Not that you helped. Taunting me with your cooking smells. (*Sharply*) You've been wafting them down the stairs, haven't you?

ALAN: No, Rigsby.

RIGSBY: I must say I didn't expect that sort of sadism. Frying sausages and bacon. At least you could have shown some respect and had a salad. You've been playing havoc with my taste buds.

ALAN: That's funny, Rigsby.

RIGSBY: What is?

ALAN: We haven't been doing any cooking. You know what's happening? You're beginning to hallucinate.

RIGSBY: No – it's the cat.

ALAN: I mean, you're thinking about food so much, you're beginning to imagine it. I shall probably turn into a boiled ham right in front of your eyes.

RIGSBY: What do you mean, *turn* into a boiled ham?

ALAN: You'd better try and take your mind off it. Why don't you watch television? They'll be doing the Yoga.

RIGSBY: (*brightens*) You mean those birds in the leotards. I don't mind watching that.

Rigsby switches on television. They watch.

RIGSBY: There she is. What's she doing.

ALAN: She's assuming the lotus position.

RIGSBY: Is she? Look at her now. She can't be very comfortable.

ALAN: That's where you're wrong. She's achieved total serenity – she's completely relaxed.

RIGSBY: That's more than I am. Where's her head gone? I should have thought that was physically impossible. (*Sighs*) Oh, no – here comes Charlie Chan. How's that for cruelty? He's left her in a knot while he's talking – a typical Chinese refinement that.

ALAN: You should try it – it would do you good.

RIGSBY: Now we've got the commercials.

Seductive music.

ALAN: Hey, look. They came in search of paradise. Just look at that walk – look at that shape.

RIGSBY: Look at that chocolate. Flaky white coconut in rich syrup. This is agony. Oh, now we've got the Arab scene – shot on the dunes at Skegness. You can tell he's not an Arab – his nose is too straight.

ALAN: He's going to snatch up her handkerchief from his horse. See the way her eyes are burning into him over her veil. Full of Eastern promise. Now she's invited him into the tent to sit with her on the silk cushions.

RIGSBY: She's opening the casket.

They hum jingle.

ALAN: I wonder if he ever gets round to the chocolate?

RIGSBY: What do you mean? It's the best bit. I'm not watching any more of this. It's all bloody food. Try the other side. (*Switches over*) Oh no. It's the Galloping Gourmet! Why doesn't he get back to Australia?

ALAN: He's just finishing. Look, they're going up to taste it.

RIGSBY: Stand by with the stomach pumps. Look at her – rolling her eyes in simulated ecstasy. You can tell it's free. I can't stand anymore. (*Switches off*) You know the trouble these days? Everyone's preoccupied with food. Running around in striped aprons and cooking in wine. What's the country coming to?

ALAN: Well, I'd better be going – it's dinner time.

RIGSBY: (*winces*) What are you having?

ALAN: Nothing much. Just roast beef and Yorkshire pudding. Followed by apple pie, custard and cream.

Rigsby groans. Vienna meows.
Alan exits.
Vienna meows at the door.

RIGSBY: I see. You want to go now, do you? My God! It doesn't take you long to desert a sinking ship. That's all you've ever wanted from me – food. There's never been any love or affection. If you could handle a tin opener I wouldn't see you for smoke.

Ruth enters carrying dish.

RUTH: Hello, Mr Rigsby. I've found I've cooked too much fish.

RIGSBY: (*brightens*) Have you, Miss Jones?

RUTH: I thought Vienna might like it.

RIGSBY: (*disappointed*) I'm sure he would. (*Tries to edge cat away from dish*) It seems a pity though, when you think about it. What those fishermen went through to get that. Mountainous seas – heaving decks – force eight gales – black ice on the rigging – and all for that.

RUTH; But you've always said nothing's too good for him, Mr Rigsby.

RIGSBY: Well, I'm beginning to change my mind – there's a lot of hungry people in the world, Miss Jones.

RUTH: Now you're making me feel awful, Mr Rigsby.

RIGSBY: Well, I shouldn't worry about it. You could hardly send that to Bangladesh.

RUTH: No, but you're right. We all eat too much. People are starving and what are we doing? Spending a fortune on trying to lose weight.

RIGSBY: (*leers*) Well, you've got nothing to worry about there, Miss Jones – if I may say so.

RUTH: Thank you, Mr Rigsby.

RIGSBY: You've got a superb figure.

RUTH: Actually, I sometimes wish I was a little more—

RIGSBY: A little more what, Miss Jones?

RUTH: You know. (*Gestures*) A little more—

RIGSBY: No, that would be fatal, Miss Jones. You've got an hour glass figure.

RUTH: (*surprised*) Do you think so? (*Sighs*) I can't help wishing I held a little more sand.

RIGSBY: Ah, but you've got poise – elegance.

RUTH: Well, I was once asked to do modelling.

RIGSBY: There you are you see – you could have burst on the fashion scene.

RUTH: It was only for gloves, Mr Rigsby.

RIGSBY: That would have just been the beginning. You could have been doing commercials by now. I can see it all. Early morning – birds twittering and you coming out of the wood in your gum boots and your saucy little rain hat. There's a mysterious little smile playing around your lips. Where have you been? Where are you going? What have you been doing? Slowly you take an object from your pocket – deliberately you peel back the wrapping and your white teeth sink into rich flaky chocolate.

RUTH: Er … yes … well, I must be going, Mr Rigsby. I've got to dress the bird table.

Ruth exits.
Rigsby darts for the dish. Drives cat away.
Philip enters.

RIGSBY: Here, pussy, pussy. (*Uneasily*) Miss Jones brought it down.

PHILIP: Well, Rigsby – how are you feeling?

RIGSBY: I'm all right. Don't worry about me.

PHILIP: I wondered if you wanted to call it off.

RIGSBY: Why should I want to call it off?

PHILIP: You don't look very good. Your eyes have gone yellow.

RIGSBY: What! No, they haven't. You're just trying to scare me.

PHILIP: Well, it could be dangerous – a man of your age.

RIGSBY: I'll worry about my age – you just worry about your five quid.

PHILIP: As long as you don't get a vitamin deficiency.

RIGSBY: What do you mean, a vitamin deficiency?

PHILIP: You'll soon know. Your teeth start getting loose – and your hair falls out.

RIGSBY: What? (*Sits down uneasily*) Look – there's nothing wrong with me.

PHILIP: No, of course not. (*Stares*) How long have you had those little white bits in your finger nails?

RIGSBY: Where? I don't know.

PHILIP: That's a bad sign, Rigsby.

RIGSBY: Is it?

PHILIP. Lack of calcium. Your bones are going brittle. Whatever you do, don't stand up in the bath. If you fall we'll never get you together again.

RIGSBY: Now wait a minute.

PHILIP: (*rising*) No, don't get up. You're bound to feel weak. That's the trouble with scurvy.

Philip exits.

RIGSBY: Scurvy! (*Hesitates. Takes comb and crosses to mirror. Combs hair. Examines teeth of comb.*) Oh, my God!

* * *

SCENE 4: *Int. attic flat. Early evening.*
Alan is consuming a plate of meat pie and sausages.
Rigsby enters. Sees food. Groans.

ALAN: Are you all right, Rigsby?

RIGSBY: All right! Do I look all right? I've been without food for thirty-six hours. Look at my nails – see the bits of white in them?

ALAN: I wouldn't worry about that.

RIGSBY: Oh, it's all right for you – they're not your nails.

ALAN: Come on, Rigsby. Where's your Dunkirk spirit? Where's your backbone?

RIGSBY: If I go on like this you won't have to ask – you'll be able to see it. (*Points at skeleton*) He's in better shape than I am. I can count every one of my ribs. And I think I've got rickets.

ALAN: You haven't got rickets.

RIGSBY: That's what you think. I've been looking at my legs in the mirror – if I put any weight on them they start to bend.

ALAN: You know what it is? You're becoming demented – it's lack of food.

RIGSBY: I know it's lack of food.

ALAN: Did you try the Yoga?

RIGSBY: Oh, yes. I assumed the lotus position – it took me half an hour to get out of it.

ALAN: Never mind. I'll get you a nice glass of water.

Alan crosses to get water.
Rigsby takes a sausage from plate and pops it into mouth. It's too hot. Tries to blow on it. Alan returns with water. Rigsby snatches glass drops sausage into it. Throws contents out of window.

RIGSBY: Water! It tastes terrible.

ALAN: Why don't you give up, Rigsby? Have something to eat.

RIGSBY: No – I shall go on to the end now. The die is cast. (*Seriously*) A man of my age – anything can happen. (*Solemnly*) If anything does happen – I don't want you to blame yourself. Don't feel responsible.

ALAN: (*calmly*) No, I won't. (*Carries on eating.*)

RIGSBY: (*Scowls*) I don't want you to interfere. I've got to fight this alone. If the worst happens, (*catch in voice*) if they say to you, 'Why did you let him do it?', you tell them – that's what he wanted.

ALAN: Yes, I'll tell them that.

RIGSBY: (*explodes*) God! Haven't you got any feelings?

ALAN: Well, what do you want me to do?

Rigsby closes door. Lowers voice.

RIGSBY: You know what I want. I want some help. I mean, we're both white Caucasians.

ALAN: You mean?

RIGSBY: If you were to get some food down – say some of that meat pie – I'd show my appreciation.

ALAN: How?

RIGSBY: I'd split the fiver.

ALAN: (*considers*) No – it wouldn't be honest.

RIGSBY: Listen – my teeth are loose – my hair's falling out – my stomach's sending urgent messages to my brain and you've decided to turn honest. You've picked a fine time to turn honest.

ALAN: But Philip's watching you like a hawk.

RIGSBY: I know – that's because he likes to see me suffer. He's never forgiven us for the slave trade. You know what's going to happen if I quit now? It's going to be black supremacy in this place.

ALAN: Well, can't you ask Ruth for something?

RIGSBY: And suppose she mentions it to him? Where would I be then?

ALAN: (*ponders*) She's dressed the bird table.

RIGSBY: I might have expected that from you. I suppose you'd like to see me upside down chewing a bit of bacon rind? (*Pause*) Listen, we don't even have to meet. But if I was to find something outside my door—

ALAN: I'll have to think about it.

RIGSBY: Well don't leave it too long or you'll be finding my bones on the stairs.

Philip enters. Stares suspiciously.

RIGSBY: (*hastily*) Well, thanks very much for the water, it was delicious.

Exit Rigsby.

* * *

SCENE 5: *Int. landing.*
Rigsby stops outside Ruth's door. Inhales deeply. Opens door. Creeps into empty room.

* * *

SCENE 6: *Int. Ruth's room.*

RIGSBY: (*softly*) Miss Jones.

He approaches cooker. Tries to put hand in. It is too hot. Takes egg from box and slips it into top pocket. He sees bowl of fruit.

Vitamin C!

He crosses and takes savage bite at apple. Recoils in horror.
Ruth enters.

RUTH: Ah, I see you're admiring my wax fruit, Mr Rigsby.

RIGSBY: Er … yes – very decorative, Miss Jones.

RUTH: I've just been arranging some flowers in the hall. I hope you don't mind.

RIGSBY: Not at all.

RUTH: Is anything the matter, Mr Rigsby?

RIGSBY: No – I thought I could smell something burning, Miss Jones.

RUTH: I hope not. I don't want to be slicing the gravy again. (*Opens cooker*) No, I think it's all right.

RIGSBY: Don't move, Miss Jones.

RUTH: What?

RIGSBY: You look a picture standing there. Your face flushed from the cooking – that lock of hair on your cheek – the trace of flour on your arms. And smelling of steak and kidney. You're going to make someone a very lucky man.

RUTH: I'm not a very good cook, I'm afraid.

RIGSBY: Oh, I'm sure you'd rise to the occasion. I can see it now. The thoughtless phone call from the office telling you that the boss is coming to dinner. Your wry smile as you pop in a casserole – not forgetting your oxo cube. At seven o'clock there you are in a low cut dress sipping a sherry. You'd certainly give a meal man appeal, Miss Jones.

RUTH: Oh, Mr Rigsby – you're just saying that.

She pushes him playfully on chest. Rigsby winces as egg breaks.

RIGSBY: Excuse me, Miss Jones. I must go now.

Rigsby exits.

* * *

SCENE 7: *Int. Rigsby's room. Evening. Rigsby enters. He is carrying a vase of flowers. He sits down at the table with them. Salts and peppers them. Removes head of flower.*

* * *

SCENE 8: *Int. hall.*
Philip enters from the stairs. He is calling the cat softly. Carrying a

bowl of food he clearly finds unsavoury.

PHILIP: Here, Vienna.

Puts dish outside Rigsby's door. Exits.

* * *

SCENE 9: *Int. Rigsby's room.*
Rigsby throws away flower. Pauses. Listens. Opens the door and takes in the bowl. Sits down with it wearing a triumphant smile. Eats. Considers. Nods.

RIGSBY: Could have given me a bit more crust.

* * *

SCENE 10: *Int. attic flat. Morning.*
Alan and Philip are preparing fried breakfast.

PHILIP: (*looks at watch*) Well, he's done it. I didn't think he would.

ALAN: Neither did I. Did you hear his shout of triumph? He'll be up in a minute. I suppose he deserves some breakfast.

Rigsby bursts in.

RIGSBY: I told you I could do it.

PHILIP: Come in, Rigsby. Have some eggs and bacon.

RIGSBY: Never mind that. What about the money?

PHILIP: Yes, of course. (*Hands over money*) I must say I'm surprised, but you've earned it. I only hope it's taught you something – what it's like to go hungry. Perhaps you'll give more freely in future.

RIGSBY: What do you mean? I'm the soul of generosity. I'm all heart – you ask anyone.

Ruth enters angrily.

RUTH: Mr Rigsby – I've just emptied my collecting tin and found this.

RIGSBY: What's that, Miss Jones?

RUTH: A button, Mr Rigsby. (*Holds it against his jacket*) It appears to have come from your jacket.

RIGSBY: Good heavens, Miss Jones – so it does. Must have got in with my change. Soon put that right.

ALAN: Yes. Do you know what he's been doing, Ruth? Starving for the cause. He's raised five quid. You were going to give it to Oxfam weren't you, Rigsby?

RIGSBY: What?

RUTH: Oh, Mr Rigsby – that's wonderful. (*Takes money*) I could hug you.

RIGSBY: Could you, Miss Jones? (*Makes best of it*) Well, you know me – all heart.

RUTH: I always knew there was something, Mr Rigsby. Under that rough exterior – there's pure gold.

ALAN: Well, come on, let's eat.

PHILIP: You'll join us, won't you, Ruth?

RUTH: Oh yes.

They sit down.

And you went without food, Mr Rigsby?

RIGSBY: For forty-eight hours, Miss Jones.

RUTH: Heavens. You make me feel humble.

RIGSBY: Just a question of will-power. Mind you – I'm looking forward to this.

Raises knife and fork.

RUTH: Yes – you must be.

PHILIP: Oh, by the way, Rigsby – don't forget to bring the dish back.

RIGSBY: (*lowers fork*) What dish?

PHILIP: The one I brought the cat food down in.

ALAN: I hope Vienna enjoyed it.

PHILIP: Yes – he had all the left overs for the week.

ALAN: Yes – all that old bacon rind.

PHILIP: And those sausages we thought were off.

ALAN: And that foul-smelling meat.

PHILIP: He must have an iron con-stitution.

Rigsby turns a sickly green. He stands up.

RUTH: What's the matter, Mr Rigsby? Aren't you hungry?

THE END.

Series Two

EPISODE 3

A Body Like Mine
by
Eric Chappell

PART ONE

SCENE 1: *Int. Ruth's room. Evening. Ruth is doing exercises. Rolling head. Grimacing. Going limp. Studies effect in mirror. Takes up a skipping rope and begins skipping.*

RUTH: Jelly on a plate.
Jelly on a plate.
Wibble wobble, wibble wobble.
Jelly on a plate.

Knock on the door. Ruth puts away the skipping rope as Rigsby enters.

RIGSBY: Ah, Miss Jones, I thought you might be feeling lonely and I wondered if you'd like to come down and watch the television.

RUTH: Well, I don't know, Mr Rigsby. I—

RIGSBY: David Attenborough's on at the moment. I know you've always had a weakness for him, Miss Jones.

RUTH: Oh, yes, I have. It's those lovely dimples of his that do something to me when he smiles.

RIGSBY: Yes. Mind you, his dimples aren't very prominent at the moment – he's standing in a pile of bat droppings.

RUTH: Oh, how awful.

RIGSBY: I don't know how he does it. He's standing in this cave, his eyes are watering, bats swooping all around him – nothing on his head. And he's talking about the joys of nature!

RUTH: Still, I do think he's incredibly brave. There aren't many men who'd go through the jungle with their socks rolled down.

RIGSBY: That's very true, Miss Jones. His legs look surprisingly pale under the circumstances. (*Proudly*) Of course that's the thing about colour television – it opens up new dimensions.

RUTH: I'm sure it does.

RIGSBY: You'll come down then, Miss Jones? I've done some potted meat sandwiches—

RUTH: Well, it's very kind of you, Mr Rigsby, but I must do my exercises.

RIGSBY: Exercises, Miss Jones?

RUTH: Yes, I've decided to improve my figure.

RIGSBY: You don't need to do that. You've got an exquisite figure, Miss Jones.

170

RUTH: Some people wouldn't agree with you, Mr Rigsby.

RIGSBY: Who's been saying otherwise? Just give me the word, Miss Jones – if you want me to sort him out—

RUTH: No, that won't be necessary. But certain things have happened – they've forced me to take a long hard look at myself. I took an inventory of my body, Mr Rigsby – and I was shocked.

RIGSBY: There was nothing missing, was there?

RUTH: My whole body was in a state of muscular tension – that's why I've been getting these recurring headaches.

RIGSBY: But I thought you were taking tablets for that, Miss Jones?

RUTH: That's not the answer, Mr Rigsby – there are dangers. Look what happened last night. I awoke – took a tablet. I thought at the time it seemed rather large. It was only when it became lodged in my throat that I realised I should have dissolved it in water.

RIGSBY: What on earth did you do?

RUTH: I lay there and fizzed for three hours! Still, it gave me time to think. I've been letting myself go, Mr Rigsby. I've been neglecting my body. That's why I thought I'd do a few gentle exercises. Philip suggested some.

RIGSBY: (*grimly*) Did he? Well, I'd be careful if I were you – you could do yourself a serious injury. I must say I don't care for this fetish for physical fitness that's going around here at the moment. You can get carried away with that sort of thing. You don't need to do exercises, Miss Jones. I mean, I don't do exercises and look at me.

RUTH: (*doubtfully*) Yes, well—

RIGSBY: (*stares*) What?

RUTH: If you don't mind me saying so, Mr Rigsby. I think you could do with a little exercise.

RIGSBY: You can't be serious. I'm in superb condition.

RUTH: What about your back?

RIGSBY: (*touchily*) There is nothing wrong with my back.

RUTH: Then why did those two men have to carry you home from the supermarket?

RIGSBY: That was an isolated incident. It could have happened to anyone. I went down a shade too quickly for some dried peas and just locked.

RUTH: You ought to be careful, Mr Rigsby – a man of your age.

RIGSBY: A man of my age! I'm in my prime, Miss Jones.

RUTH: I've heard you on the stairs. The slightest exertion and you're wheezing and coughing.

RIGSBY: We'll see about that. Stand back, Miss Jones.

RUTH: What are you going to do, Mr Rigsby?

RIGSBY: I'm going to show you what clean living and a balanced diet can do. I'm going to raise this chair aloft by one leg.

RUTH: Please be careful.

RIGSBY: Don't worry. I used to do this twenty years ago – and I can still do it today—

Rigsby raises the chair with great effort.

RUTH: (*impressed*) Mr Rigsby!

Rigsby holds the chair for a moment. The chair wobbles. Rigsby collapses in a fit of coughing. Chair falls to the ground.

RIGSBY: (*gasps*) Nothing to it—

* * *

SCENE 2: *Int. attic flat.*
  Alan is lifting weights.
  Philip is reading.
  On the wall is a muscular body with Alan's head superimposed.

ALAN: (*pauses*) Are you sure this is going to work?

PHILIP: Of course it will, but you've got to keep it up.

ALAN: I'm shattered.

PHILIP: You're putting far too much effort into it. Try and relax.

ALAN: How can I relax? I've got veins standing out all over my body.

PHILIP: Remember, there's a giant inside you waiting to get out.

ALAN: Then why doesn't he give me a hand with these weights?

PHILIP: There's a giant inside all of us.

ALAN: I bet mine's got varicose veins. (*He studies the picture*) Do you really think I'll look like that?

PHILIP: You will if you work hard. Haven't you noticed any difference?

ALAN: (*puts weights down and considers*) I think my arms are getting longer. I don't want that. I don't want my hands brushing the ground as I walk along.

Philip studies him.

PHILIP: I think your deltoids are getting larger.

ALAN: Do you? (*Looks in mirror*) I think you're right. That should pull the birds. Wait until I get on the beach this summer. I can see it now – lounging around in my striped shorts – a couple of birds in bikinis rubbing the old Ambre Solaire into me – their screams of delight when they get to my deltoids.

PHILIP: (*smiles*) It means a lot to you, doesn't it?

ALAN: Yes. Well, it's all right for

you, Philip, but I was a delicate child. When you were in the bush having adventures and living off wild berries, I was having vapour rubs. Well, all that's going to change now. Just let Rigsby try pushing me around. He's going to get a surprise – especially if he tries that handshake.

PHILIP: You mean when he tries to crush your fingers?

ALAN: Yes. Why does he do that?

PHILIP: He relates it to his virility. He looks on us as a challenge. That's why he's always trying to prove he's fitter and stronger than we are.

ALAN: He's got a bad back.

PHILIP: I know, but he won't admit it.

ALAN: He has to wear a knee bandage to get up the stairs. He's a physical wreck. I feel sorry for the poor old sod—

Rigsby enters carrying Vienna.

Oh, hello, Rigsby.

Rigsby eyes Alan in his vest.

RIGSBY: My God! It's Strang the Terrible. Don't be alarmed, Vienna. Don't be disturbed by all that rippling muscle. I'm sure the gentleman means us no harm.

Rigsby walks around Alan and shakes his head.

What do you think you're doing?

ALAN: I'm developing my body.

RIGSBY: The only thing you going to develop's a hernia. You're wasting your time, you know – it won't do you any good.

ALAN: Why not?

RIGSBY: Because you won't be able to keep it up, that's why. You're not the type. You get tired brushing your hair. And then what's going to happen. All that muscle's going to turn to fat. You're going to look like something that's been left out of the fridge all night.

ALAN: That's where you're wrong. I'll keep it up, don't you worry. You wait, you'll see a difference. When I disrobe on the beach this summer there's going to be a buzz of excitement. And do you know why?

RIGSBY: You've forgotten your trunks?

ALAN: No. I shall have a perfectly developed body.

RIGSBY: Perfectly developed body! You'll look a freak. (*Points at picture*) You weren't meant to look like that. You were meant to be puny. I don't believe in this preoccupation with the body – it's not natural.

PHILIP: There's nothing wrong with exercise, Rigsby. You should try it sometime.

RIGSBY: Listen, if he wants exercise why doesn't he go and kick a ball around?

ALAN: I don't like football.

RIGSBY: (*aghast*) What! Don't like football? You're talking about a national sport. What's this country coming to? When I was your age I was out every night playing football.

Alan and Philip exchange glances. Philip winks.

PHILIP: Were you good at it, Rigsby?

RIGSBY: Good? I was brilliant. If it hadn't been for the war – who knows? I could have been another Tommy Lawton.

ALAN: Who was Tommy Lawton?

RIGSBY: (*shocked*) Who was Tommy Lawton? Only the finest centre forward who ever breathed – that's all.

ALAN: How can you compare him with players today?

RIGSBY: He'd have made mincemeat out of that lot. Have you see them? Prancing around the field like a bunch of male models, kissing and cuddling. In my day when you scored a goal all you got was a brisk handshake – now you get covered in love bites. We used to tackle hard then – hard but fair. The full backs used to come at you like butcher's dogs. If they caught you right you could end up in the stand.

ALAN: Aye, it was a man's game in those days—

PHILIP: Aye, it were that, lad.

RIGSBY: Are you two trying to be funny?

ALAN: No, I envy you, Rigsby. I wish I was good at sport.

RIGSBY: Ah, but you see I was a natural.

PHILIP: It's a pity we can't put the clock back. See how good you really were – before you began to slow down—

RIGSBY: I haven't slowed down! I'm still a hundred per cent fit. And I don't have to develop my body either. Let's face it, I happen to be very well endowed. Nature has showered her blessings on me. I've never had much money but I've always had my health and strength.

ALAN: What about your bad back?

RIGSBY: I haven't got a bad back. I'm as fit as a fiddle. Why do you think Miss Jones is attracted to me. She's sensed the latent power – the almost feline grace.

ALAN: Feline grace!

PHILIP: He means like Vienna.

RIGSBY: And what's wrong with Vienna?

PHIILIP: Well, look at him, Rigsby. He's not very agile, is he?

RIGSBY: That's what you think. He may not bother much these days but he hasn't lost his reflexes, anymore than I have.

ALAN: (*derisively*) Reflexes!

RIGSBY: I'll prove it to you.

He picks up Vienna.

Now gather round because I'm going to show you something—

They gather around Rigsby.

I'm going to hold this cat four feet from the floor – face upwards. Observe his relaxed manner. Now, if I let him go, what do you think will happen?

ALAN: He'll go through the floorboards.

RIGSBY: Oh no, he won't. He'll land on his feet. And do you know why? Because he's got perfect reflexes. It's a scientific fact. Now watch carefully – it'll all happen very quickly. Right – here we go—

Rigsby releases the cat. Vienna falls with a loud thud followed by a screech and bolts out of the room.

They stare after him in silence.

Rigsby looks puzzled.

That's funny – he usually lands on his feet. He couldn't have been awake.

Ruth enters.

RUTH: I wonder if one of you strong men could get the lid off the pickle jar for me.

ALAN: Of course, Ruth. Allow me.

Alan takes the jar with new-found

confidence. *He struggles with the lid.*

RUTH: Can you manage?

As Alan struggles his confidence turns to panic.

RIGSBY: Your face has gone red.

ALAN: It won't budge.

RIGSBY: Isn't that marvellous? All these weeks of training and he can't get the lid off a pickle jar. Come on, give it to me. It's all a question of pressure—

He takes the jar. He begins to struggle.

ALAN: What's the matter, Rigsby?

RIGSBY: It won't budge. Must be a crossed thread.

PHILIP: May I try?

Philip takes the jar.

RIGSBY: It's no good. You won't move it. We need a vice . .

Philip removes the lid.

PHILIP: There you are, Ruth.

RIGSBY: I must have loosened it.

RUTH: (*admiringly*) I didn't realise you were so strong, Philip. Come downstairs – you can be the first to indulge—

She leads Philip out of the room leaving Rigsby scowling.

END OF PART ONE

PART TWO

SCENE 3: *Int. Rigsby's room.*
Rigsby is waiting impatiently. Alan
enters with weights and equipment.

ALAN: I've got them, Rigsby.

RIGSBY: He didn't see you, did he?

ALAN: No. Does it matter?

RIGSBY: Of course it matters. Right.
I'd better get started.

He tries to pick up weights. Fails. He
tries chest expanders. Fails. Continues
with smaller weights.

ALAN: I'm glad you've decided to
get fit, Rigsby.

RIGSBY: What do you mean? I am
fit. I'm just putting a fine edge to
it, that's all.

ALAN: What made you decide to do
it?

RIGSBY: Why do you think?
Because of him up there. Did you
see that look of superiority when
he got the lid off the pickle jar?
My God, that was a definite
setback for the white races, that
was. And that's not the only
reason. Did you see Miss Jones?
She was impressed. I think he's
getting ideas in that direction.

ALAN: He doesn't need Ruth. He's
got ten wives already.

RIGSBY: Yes but they're black. Miss
Jones is white. She could be
useful to him.

ALAN: What as – a marker?

RIGSBY: She could give him prestige
out there. Help them with their
diplomatic exchanges – show
them how to fold their serviettes.

ALAN: You can't be serious, Rigsby.
It won't happen.

RIGSBY: You're dead right – because
I'm not going to let it. I've told
you before. Anyone who comes
between me and Miss Jones can
expect trouble.

Rigsby starts doing press-ups.

He'd better watch out now I'm
getting myself in shape.

He collapses gasping.
Philip enters.

PHILIP: What are you doing,
Rigsby?

ALAN: He was doing press-ups.

They help Rigsby to his feet.

176

PHILIP: You shouldn't be doing that, Rigsby – not at your age. Think of your heart.

RIGSBY; There's nothing wrong with my heart. (*He breaks free*) What do you want anyway?

PHILIP: I was hoping to watch the cricket. The West Indies are playing.

RIGSBY: I'm not watching the West Indies. It may have escaped your attention but I'm now the proud owner of a colour television. I've got all the colours of the spectrum there. I'm not watching something that looks just the same in black and white.

ALAN: That's not the reason. He just doesn't like to see them win.

RIGSBY: Now wait a minute. I don't mind seeing them win. We still know how to lose in this country. We can still face defeat with a smile.

ALAN: What about when Leeds lost to Bayern Munich? Your smile slipped a bit that day. You threw a bottle at the television.

RIGSBY: That was different. We were robbed – robbed at the last gasp – and after our valiant-hearted lads had run themselves into the ground. You could see it in their faces – they were drained. I hadn't seen expressions like that since Dunkirk. And as for the Germans – you could see all that Teutonic arrogance coming back. When they put that second goal in, I thought they were going to break into the goose step.

PHILIP: All right, Rigsby. If you're so sporting why don't you watch Muhammad Ali?

RIGSBY: I'll tell you why – because he can't box.

PHILIP: Then how did he become world champion?

RIGSBY: He talks them to death. He gets them in a clinch – engages in a bit of witty repartee and while they're trying to think of an answer, he clouts them round the ear. It wouldn't work with me.

Alan and Philip exchange glances.

PHILIP: Don't tell me you were a boxer as well?

RIGSBY: I was brilliant. If it hadn't been for the war. Who knows?

ALAN: (*doubtfully*) You don't look like a boxer.

RIGSBY: Of course I don't. The best ones never do. They're the ones you've got to watch out for. You don't worry about the ones with the broken noses and cauliflower ears. But when you come across someone like me – who still has his good looks – who still retains an almost classic profile – that's when you've got to watch out.

PHILIP: You know, it's amazing – you appear to have been good at everything, Rigsby.

Rigsby rummages in his cupboard.

He produces an old pair of boxing gloves.

RIGSBY: Well, what do you think these are? They're not to stop me biting my nails. These gloves have seen me through many a bout. One punch from these and you'd go down like a roll of lino.

He thrusts them in Philip's face.

PHILIP: Don't do that, Rigsby.

RIGSBY: A few rapier-like lefts – the old one-two – you wouldn't know what hit you.

PHILIP: You don't have to prove anything to me, Rigsby.

RIGSBY: Listen, if we had another pair of gloves I'd prove something.

PHILIP: Well, I can get a pair of gloves.

RIGSBY: All right. You get them. Bring them down tonight. We'll see whether I'm past it.

PHILIP: (*smiles*) All right, Rigsby. I'll see if I can find them.

RIGSBY: You do that.

Philips exits.

That showed him. Did you see how pale he went?

ALAN: No.

RIGSBY: No, well, it's difficult to tell.

ALAN: Are you sure you're doing the right thing?

RIGSBY: Don't worry – he won't lay a glove on me.

He dances around Alan

Look at that footwork. I'll float like a butterfly and sting like a bee.

He taps Alan on head and body. Falls back breathing heavily.

ALAN: You're floating like a bee and stinging like a butterfly at the moment.

RIGSBY: I'm not punching my weight.

ALAN: Suppose he punches his weight?

RIGSBY: He won't hurt me. Do you know why? Because I know how to ride a punch. I'll show you. Here, put these gloves on. (*He thrusts the gloves onto Alan's hands*) Now, go on – hit me.

ALAN: No, I'd rather not, Rigsby.

RIGSBY: Come on – straight on the chin – as hard as you like.

ALAN: I don't want to.

RIGSBY: I know what it is. You can't work up any aggression. I'm too likeable. Well, just try and imagine I'm a thoroughly nasty, objectionable piece of work. I know it's difficult, but do your best.

ALAN: It's not that, Rigsby.

RIGSBY: What is it then?

ALAN: You might hit me back.

RIGSBY: No, I won't. I haven't got any gloves on, have I? Now come on – right on the chin.

ALAN: All right then.

Alan punches Rigsby on the chin. Rigsby spins round and falls on the settee.

ALAN: Rigsby?

Rigsby lies motionless, his eyes shut and his mouth open.

* * *

SCENE 4: *Int. Rigsby's room. Evening. The room has been prepared for the contest. The furniture has been shoved back and a rope strung around the room. Rigsby is shadow boxing nervously. Alan enters.*

RIGSBY: Where is he? Changed his mind, eh? Well, I don't blame him. Let's get the furniture back.

ALAN: No. He's coming. He's just getting ready.

RIGSBY: (*disappointed*) Oh. Still, I suppose he's getting nervous – starting to sweat – showing signs of strain?

ALAN: I don't think so. He says he's looking foward to having the gloves on again.

RIGSBY: Yes, well ... (*stops*) Again! Did you say again? You mean he's done it before?

ALAN: Yes. When he was in Africa he did a lot of boxing. He was champion of his region.

RIGSBY: My God! Why didn't you tell me? I thought he was a novice. Champion of his region. He'll murder me.

ALAN: But you've got the experience, Rigsby.

RIGSBY: Shut up, will you? (*He begins to pace*) Of course he's planned this. He's going to duff me up.

ALAN: You'll be all right, Rigsby. I'm going to be the referee. At the first sign of blood I shall stop the fight.

RIGSBY: Don't give me that. The first sign of blood and you'll faint. (*Pause. Considers*) Still, I suppose you could always disqualify him—

ALAN: What for?

RIGSBY: For a low punch.

ALAN: Suppose he doesn't punch low?

RIGSBY: I could always jump in the air.

ALAN: Look, if you want to call it off – I'll go and talk to him.

RIGSBY: How can I call it off? What will Miss Jones say if she finds out. She might give the white feather.

ALAN: Then what are you going to do?

RIGSBY: I shall have to go and put the frighteners on him.

ALAN: How are you going to do that?

RIGSBY: Well, you know what they say? If you can't fight – wear a big hat—

Rigsby swaggers out.

* * *

SCENE 5: *Int. attic flat.*
Philip is punching a punch bag furiously. Rigsby enters. He watches and winces.

RIGSBY: I see you're getting ready then?

PHILIP: Yes.

RIGSBY: A funny world, isn't it, Phil? Two grown men getting ready to knock seven bells out of each other. And we say we're civilised. (*Side glance*) It's a funny world. (*Pause*) When you think about it.

Philip ignores him and continues punching.

I mean you're black and I'm white. If we can't get on – what chance has the world got. It makes you think, Philip—

PHILIP: Do you want to call it off?

RIGSBY: (*indignantly*) Who said anything about calling it off. I was just thinking aloud, that's all.

PHILIP: I thought you seemed nervous.

RIGSBY: I'm not nervous. There's only one thing that worries me, and that's if I lose my temper. That's why I had to give up boxing. Nearly killed a bloke once. I get this red mist in front of my eyes and there's a singing in my ears. And when it clears – there's someone stretched out on the canvas.

PHILIP: Is it you, Rigsby?

RIGSBY: All right. You've had your chance. Don't say I didn't warn you.

He crosses to the door. Looks back at Philip pounding the punch bag. Winces. Exits.

* * *

SCENE 6: *Int. Ruth's room.*
Ruth is doing her exercises. Rigsby knocks and enters.

RIGSBY: Ah, Miss Jones.

RUTH: Yes, Mr Rigsby?

RIGSBY: There's something you ought to know. I don't know how to tell you this – a woman of your sensitivity and refinement – but there's going to be a fight.

RUTH: A fight?

RIGSBY: Downstairs. Philip and me – we're having the gloves on. It's going to be a fight to the finish. I'm afraid the blood's going to flow. I thought it was only fair to let you know.

RUTH: Thank you, Mr Rigsby. I'll come down. I love a good fight.

RIGSBY: What? No, you don't understand. It's not an ordinary fight – it's over you, Miss Jones.

RUTH: Over me? Oh! How exciting.

RIGSBY: Somebody could get hurt – possibly maimed for life. Now I know you want peace in the world – and that you're against the polaris missile – and in the circumstances, out of consideration for you, I'm prepared to call it off. It'll be a disappointment of course—

RUTH: No – I wouldn't dream of it.

RIGSBY: You wouldn't?

RUTH: It's a wonderful compliment. And just to show you how much I appreciate it, I shall go out this evening with the winner. That's if he can stand. What do you think of that, Mr Rigsby?

RIGSBY: Er, yes, I shall look forward to it, Miss Jones.

Rigsby exits looking queasy.

* * *

SCENE 7: *Int. Rigsby's room.*
Alan and Philip enter. Philip is dressed for the contest.

PHILIP: Where's Rigsby?

ALAN: He's probably in there putting on his knee bandage or hiding his teeth. I'll go and get him.

Alan exits into bedroom.
Ruth enters.

PHILIP: Ruth! What are you doing here?

RUTH: Philip, I didn't know you could be so jealous. Fighting over me.

PHILIP: What! Is that what Rigsby told you?

RUTH: Yes. And I told him I'd go out with the winner. Will the Grange suit you?

PHILIP: (*horrified*) How do you know I'll win?

RUTH: Of course you'll win. All you've got to do is soften him up inside. He won't last. He lives on suet puddings.

PHILIP: I didn't know you knew anything about boxing.

RUTH: Oh yes. I love Henry Cooper. That's what you want to do. Give him Henry's hammer – the old left hook—

Alan and Rigsby enter.
Rigsby is dressed in baggy shorts and singlet. He looks anxious.
Philip shadow boxes briskly.
Alan leads them into the middle of the room.

ALAN: (*with gusto*) Right. I want a clean contest. No holding, no butting – no punching with the inside of the glove – no gouging – biting – or punching on the break—

RIGSBY: My God! You're enjoying this, aren't you?

ALAN: Now, come out fighting.

RIGSBY: You just note where my belt is – anything below that and he's disqualified.

RUTH: (*sweetly*) I'll ring the bell.

Ruth rings the bell.
Rigsby and Philip approach each other cautiously. They do a full circuit. Rigsby contrives to keep Alan between them. He gets in a sneaky punch and then goes into a clinch with Philip, hanging on grimly. Alan separates them and Rigsby throws himself into a clinch with Alan.

ALAN: Hey! That's me!

RIGSBY: Well, get out of the way.

Rigsby rings the bell. Prepares to sit. Alan throws water over him. He splutters. Ruth rings the bell.

RUTH: Now's your chance, Philip. Kill him!

Rigsby stares round at Ruth in shocked surprise.
Philip looks even more apprehensive. A night out with Ruth is clearly weighing on his mind.
Rigsby finds his retreat cut off. He closes his eyes and sticks out a despairing left. Philip runs onto it and

with a great show of histrionics falls to the ground. Rigsby opens his eyes.

RIGSBY: (*amazed*) I've got him! I'm the winner!

He raises his hand in triumph as Ruth sweeps angrily from the room.

* * *

SCENE 8: *Int. attic flat. Later.*
Alan shakes his head at Philip.

ALAN: But why did you have to take a dive?

PHILIP: I've told you – I wasn't going out with Ruth. I'm not starting that again.

ALAN: But Rigsby will never let us forget it. Oh, Lord, here he is now.

Rigsby enters. He is dressed to go out. He grins triumphantly.

RIGSBY: I told you, didn't I? I haven't lost the old magic. I hope I didn't hurt you.

PHILIP: No, you didn't hurt me.

RIGSBY: The trouble is, I don't know my own strength.

ALAN: Rigsby, he took a dive.

RIGSBY: Is that what he told you? He didn't take a dive. He's just a bad loser. I put him down fair and square. He met me in the peak of condition. And Miss Jones and I are off to the Grange. How about that? I feel I could accomplish anything tonight. Nothing's beyond my powers.

He seeks the weights. He picks them up and holds them above his head.

Look at this. I can do it!

ALAN: That's very good, Rigsby.

Rigsby puts the weights down but remains bending.

PHILIP: That's great, Rigsby. You should take it up.

Silence. They stare down at him.

ALAN: Rigsby, what's the matter?

RIGSBY: It's my back – it's locked!

Ruth enters.

RUTH: (*resignedly*) Well, are you ready, Mr Rigsby? Mr Rigsby, what's the matter?

ALAN: He's locked. He can't straighten up.

RIGSBY: It'll pass, Miss Jones. I can still make it.

RUTH: I'm not entering the Grange with you in that condition, Mr Rigsby. It would be like walking in with a chimpanzee. (*Smiles*) I'm afraid it will have to be Philip after all.

PHILIP: What?

RUTH: Come along, Philip. We'll be late—

She takes Philip by the hand. They exit.

RIGSBY: But, Miss Jones—

He tries to hobble after them but fails. Alan takes his hand.

ALAN: (*sympathetically*) I'll take you back to your room, Rigsby. (*He leads Rigsby to the door*). Cheer up. There's always the second prize—

RIGSBY: (*hopefully*) I didn't know there was a second prize. What is it?

ALAN: (*winks*) Two nights out with Miss Jones.

Rigsby tries to get at him. Groans.

THE END.

Series Two

EPISODE 4

Moonlight and Roses
by
Eric Chappell

PART ONE

SCENE 1: *Ext. front door. Moonlight. Ruth and Desmond are standing on the porch. Desmond is smaller than Ruth. Lock of hair over forehead. Poetical manner.*

RUTH: I thought you were going.

DES: How can I go when you look so enchanting?

RUTH: Oh, Desmond.

DES: Oh, Ruth – why do you exert this cruel power?

RUTH: I don't mean to be cruel.

DES: Just one kiss.

RUTH: No, Desmond, not here.

DES: It's this place, isn't it? It's always the same.

RUTH: It's just that I can feel these eyes watching me. (*Starts*) Desmond – you're not leaning against the doorbell?

DES: Just one more kiss.

RUTH: (*struggles*) No.

DES: You know, you're beautiful when you're angry.

RUTH: (*softens*) Desmond.

DES: You get these little lights in your eyes – like stars reflected in limpid green pools.

RUTH: Oh, Desmond – you say the most beautiful things.

DES: You inspire me.

RUTH: My eyes are just like anyone else's really.

DES: Then why do they set my pulses racing?

RUTH: Desmond, please don't.

DES: I can't help. It's this damned moonlight. You're like an ivory statue – cold and unapproachable. The beautiful brow – the proud arch of the neck – the superb ripeness—

RUTH: (*sharply*) Desmond.

* * *

SCENE 2: *Int. attic flat. Evening. Alan is at window. Philip is reading.*

ALAN: (*excitedly*) Just look at them. They can't take their eyes off each other.

Philip joins Alan at the window.

PHILIP: Oh yes. (*Pause*) Ruth looks different somehow.

ALAN: Of course she does. She's a woman in love.

PHILIP: Who is he?

ALAN: His name's Desmond.

PHILIP: (*amused*) Desmond!

ALAN: He works in the library. Hangs about the poetry section. He's got all the chat.

PHILIP: I wondered why she'd stopped coming up.

ALAN: Yes – she's crazy about him.

PHILIP: He doesn't look much.

ALAN: He doesn't have to. He's got the *Oxford Book of English Verse* behind him. He's only got to recite a couple of stanzas and she's away – it's like giving her double vodkas.

PHILIP: How do you know?

ALAN: I've been listening.

PHILIP: Alan – how can you do it?

ALAN: It's easy – I get behind those bushes in the front garden.

PHILIP: No, I mean spying on them like that.

ALAN: I'm not spying. I just happen to have a natural curiosity about my fellow man – no harm in it.

PHILIP: Oh yes – and what about that couple in the park?

ALAN: I wasn't spying on them. I was just tying my shoelace.

PHILIP: At night? Behind a laurel bush?

ALAN: Well, I didn't know they were on the verge, did I? It was a pure coincidence.

PHILIP: Then why did he chase you through the park with a starting handle. And come away from that window. I don't want anything to go wrong. This is the first time I've been able to get on with my work since I came here. (*Pause*) Does Rigsby know about it?

ALAN: I shouldn't think so – he'd be out there with a shotgun.

PHILIP: Poor Desmond – he'll have him for breakfast. I hope he doesn't see them holding hands.

ALAN: Oh, they hold hands all the time. You should see them in restaurants. They have to cut their meat up together.

PHILIP: You don't follow them into restaurants?

ALAN: I'm studying his technique. I wonder if it would work with this girl I know. She might respond to poetry – she hasn't responded to anything else. Hey! Wait a minute – I think they're coming to the boil. I must hear this.

Alan opens window gently. Listens. Rolls eyes.
Philip, intrigued, edges casually to

window, struggling not to lose dignity.

DES: You're such a tantalising creature. Why do you torment me? (*Frowns*) You know what I want, Ruth.

RUTH: Yes, I think so, Desmond.

DES: I want to take you away from here.

RUTH: Oh.

DES: But you don't love me enough.

RUTH: I do.

DES: No, not as much as I love you. Perhaps you don't think I'm being serious?

RUTH: I know you're being serious, Desmond. You're making those finger marks on my arm again.

DES: I can't help it. I'd go to the ends of the earth for you – brave any dangers – endure any hardships.

RUTH: Oh Desmond.

DES: Just one kiss, Ruth. Before my bus comes.

RUTH: Just one then – quickly before someone sees us.

DES: Oh, Ruth.

RUTH: Oh, Desmond.

They embrace.

* * *

SCENE 3: *Int. attic flat.*
Philip is dragging Alan away.

PHILIP: Come away, Alan – we shouldn't be listening to this.

ALAN: (*dramatically*) It's this damned moonlight – it's so cruelly deceptive.

He moves across the room in slow motion ballet of two lovers meeting. Sings.

'Sweeter than springtime are you. Gayer than laughter are you.' You know, it's amazing how potent cheap music can be.

He whirls around the room, hand outstretched, and meets Rigsby at door. Rigsby stares grim-faced.

RIGSBY: My God! What do you think you're doing? You know, if you go on like this you'll get that room of your own all right – the only trouble is it'll be made out of rubber.

Rigsby moves towards window.

PHILIP: (*quickly*) What do you want, Rigsby?

RIGSBY: I was looking for Miss Jones. You haven't seen her have you?

Alan and Philip exchange glances.

ALAN: I think she's gone out.

RIGSBY: Again? That's the third time this week. (*Sighs*) Pity really – it's a lovely evening and I'd put a couple of chairs out on the patio.

ALAN: (*amused*) Patio!

RIGSBY: (*fiercely*) That's what I said.

ALAN: Do you mean the backyard?

RIGSBY: I mean the patio.

ALAN: Rigsby – four fairy lights and a plant-stand don't make a patio.

RIGSBY: Well, I don't say you haven't got to use your imagination. You've got to ignore the tin bath and the mangle.

PHILIP: And the drains.

RIGSBY: There's nothing wrong with those drains. No, it's very nice down there – bathed in moonlight. It's like a fairy grotto.

ALAN: And you were hoping to take her down for a lucky dip, were you?

RIGSBY: You mind your own business.

Rigsby crosses to window.

I wonder where she's got to?

PHILIP: (*hurriedly*) Rigsby.

RIGSBY: What?

PHILIP: Would you like a coffee?

RIGSBY: Thanks. (*Studies Philip*) You know you've changed – you're much more considerate these days.

PHILIP: Thank you, Rigsby.

RIGSBY: Yes, and you're not the only one who's changed. Have you noticed Miss Jones lately?

ALAN: Miss Jones?

RIGSBY: Haven't you noticed a change in her? All that mooning around – sighing and sniffing flowers – that extra dab of scent behind the ears – the mysterious smile of the Mona Lisa.

ALAN: No, Rigsby.

RIGSBY: It's finally happened.

ALAN: What has?

RIGSBY: She's fallen for me. Oh, it was bound to happen eventually – they can't resist this sort of charm for long.

Sips coffee.

ALAN: Are you sure, Rigsby?

RIGSBY: Oh yes. The flower is finally turning its face towards the bee. That's why I wanted to get her out on the patio.

He glances out of the window. He almost chokes on coffee. He is quivering with rage.

Who's that?

ALAN: Where?

RIGSBY: There. That man twining himself around Miss Jones.

PHILIP: Oh, he's just a friend, Rigsby.

RIGSBY: He's being too bloody friendly. I'll murder him.

Rigsby exits, followed by Alan and Philip.

* * *

SCENE 4: *Int. landing.*
Rigsby is struggling to get free of Alan and Philip.

RIGSBY: Let me get at him.

ALAN: You can't go out there, Rigsby.

RIGSBY: You saw what he was doing.

PHILIP: No – it was the shadows moving – just a trick of the light.

RIGSBY: (*hesitates, uncertain*) But I saw him.

ALAN: He's not like that, Rigsby. He works in the library.

RIGSBY: I don't care where he works.

PHILIP: His name's Desmond.

RIGSBY: (*stops*) Desmond! (*Grins from one to the other*) Bloody Desmond.

ALAN: Yes.

They all start to laugh.

RIGSBY: But what does he want with Miss Jones?

ALAN: They have a mutual interest in John Betjeman.

RIGSBY: God! Don't tell me there's another one. She's been leading a double life.

PHILIP: No – they're just friends, that's all.

RIGSBY: And you think it was a trick of the light?

PHILIP: Yes.

ALAN: You've got nothing to worry about there. After all – with a name like Desmond—

RIGSBY: (*grins*) Yes. I ask you – Desmond.

They start to laugh.
Ruth enters.
She is walking slowly. She is sniffing at a flower. Smiling pensively.

RUTH: (*sighs*) Oh, hello. Isn't it a lovely evening. Doesn't it make you feel glad to be alive. On such a night as this—

Smiles. Exits humming quietly to herself. Rigsby stares after her open-mouthed.

RIGSBY: Let me get at him. I'll murder him.

He struggles with Alan and Philip.

* * *

SCENE 5: *Int. attic flat. Evening.*
Alan and Philip are working. Alan looks out of the window.

ALAN: They're still out there.

PHILIP: Well, come away.

ALAN: Hey! He's gone down on one knee.

PHILIP: What?

ALAN: Wait a minute – he's gone down on both knees. He's either dropped something or he's proposing. He *is* proposing.

PHILIP: Are you sure?

ALAN: He's slipping something onto her finger. She's examining it in the light. She can't believe it. She's getting her eyeglass out.

PHILIP: Good old Ruth – she's done it at last.

ALAN: Yes, after all these years. It's like winning a Cup Final medal. Hey – she's coming in.

PHILIP: She can't wait to show us.

ALAN: I can hear her size nines coming up the stairs.

PHILIP: Remember – complete surprise.

Ruth bursts excitedly into the room.

RUTH: You'll never guess what's happened.

ALAN: No – what's happened.

RUTH: Look. (*She holds up hand*)

ALAN: You've painted your nails.

RUTH: Oh, Alan.

ALAN: Wait a minute. What's that on your finger? It's a diamond ring. Philip, she's wearing a diamond ring.

RUTH: We're engaged.

PHILIP: Congratulations, Ruth. I'm delighted. (*He kisses her on cheek*)

RUTH: Thank you, Philip. (*Squeezes hand*) I know what that must have cost you. Never mind, you'll forget me – in time.

ALAN: Yes. We'll miss you, Ruth. I wonder who'll get your room.

RUTH: Don't say anything yet. I don't want Rigsby to know. He'll only cut my water off.

PHILIP: You'll have to tell him sometime.

RUTH: Not yet. I must go.

ALAN: Of course.

They escort her to door humming the bridal march.
Rigsby enters. Smiles, eager to be included.

RIGSBY: What's this? Some sort of celebration?

RUTH: Oh hello, Mr Rigsby. I must go. Desmond's waiting.

Exit Ruth.

RIGSBY: (*scowls*) Did you hear that? Desmond's waiting. She hasn't even got time to talk to me these days. I shall have to do something about that Desmond.

PHILIP: (*anxiously*) What are you going to do, Rigsby?

RIGSBY: I'll think of something. He works in the library, doesn't he? He's used to peace and quiet – I could shatter that for him. I could go and make a rude noise in the reading room – I could bend down the pages of my library book – I could write something nasty in the fly leaf. I could do a lot of things. He won't take much discouraging.

PHILIP: Rigsby – you've already thought of something. What are you going to do?

ALAN: He's going to give him a fat lip.

RIGSBY: No, he's an intelligent man. He'll see reason – I shall just have a quiet word with him, that's all – tell him to stay away from her.

PHILIP: And what if he doesn't?

RIGSBY: Then I'll give him a fat lip.

PHILIP: A fat lip – that's your answer to everything, isn't it?

ALAN: It won't do any good. You'll only drive them into each other's arms.

RIGSBY: Thank you, Marjorie Proops.

PHILIP: But she prefers Desmond.

RIGSBY: No, she only thinks she does. We're destined for each other. I can feel it. What do my stars say?

Alan opens magazne.

ALAN: What are you, Rigsby?

RIGSBY: I'm Libra. Denoted by the sign of the scales. That means I'm well balanced, in harmony with myself, tolerant, with a sense of justice.

PHILIP: What!

ALAN: Are you sure your scales haven't gone wonky, Rigsby.

RIGSBY: What does it say?

ALAN: (*reads*) You will have plenty of opportunity to indulge your love of pleasure this month.

RIGSBY: There you are.

ALAN: You are ready for a new and exciting love affair.

RIGSBY: What did I tell you?

PHILIP: But Ruth's not new.

RIGSBY: She would be to me. What else does it say?

ALAN: You should try out your new glamorous image and give thought to beauty treatment.

RIGSBY: What!

ALAN: You'll find no shortage of men, particularly towards the end of the month.

Rigsby snatches the magazine from Alan.

RIGSBY: This is for women! Still I suppose you've got to reverse it.

PHILIP: I don't suppose you've

The way we were: Eric Chappell at the
time he was writing *Rising Damp*.

Food Glorious Food: Five pounds says that Rigsby can't go without food for 48 hours.

Food Glorious Food: After 36 hours without food, Rigsby can't help comparing himself with Alan's skeleton.

Food Glorious Food: Rigsby is tempted
by Miss Jones's fish.

Food Glorious Food: 'I shall go on to the end now.
The die is cast.'

Food Glorious Food: Never one to go
without if he can possibly help it, Rigsby
resorts to eating ancient sausages.

Rigsby and his beloved Vienna — nothing
was ever too good for him.

If only Ruth felt half as much passion for Rigsby
as she did for Philip when he first arrived.

A Body Like Mine: Egged on
by Philip, Alan searches
for the giant inside.

A Body Like Mine: Rigsby attempts to impress Ruth with a rigorous training programme for his boxing match with Philip.

Romancing the new tenant: Rigsby tries his best with Brenda, the artists's model in *Moonlight and Roses*.

Is anybody there? Philip, Rigsby and Brenda in search
of The Grey Lady in *Things That Go Bump in the Night*.

For the Man Who Has Everything: Rigsby misses his
chance with Gwen the postwoman.

Wrong again! Somehow, Rigsby thinks that Lucy is Philip's Christmas present to him in *For The Man Who Has Everything*.

Setting the scene: Rigsby's little world was brought alive in Colin Pigott's sets.

ever stopped to wonder why she prefers Desmond?

RIGSBY: Well, no.

ALAN: He's got the chat, Rigsby. He can express his feelings. Have you ever taken Ruth out into the moonlight and told her exactly what's in your heart.

RIGSBY: Oh, my God.

ALAN: Well, have you?

RIGSBY: (*uncomfortably*) You mean … you mean the … you mean the three little words.

PHILIP: He can't even say it!

RIGSBY: Well, we don't go in for that sort of talk around here. This is Andy Capp country. All that moonlight and roses – that was all right for Noel Coward but he never went with the women around here … You try creeping up on them in a silk dressing gown and saying 'The moonlight becomes you, darling' and you'd get a belt round the ear.

PHILIP: But you've got to be able to express your feelings, Rigsby.

RIGSBY: (*embarrassed*) Shut up, will you?

ALAN: He's embarrassed.

RIGSBY: No, I'm not.

ALAN: Why don't you say it with flowers, Rigsby?

RIGSBY: What?

ALAN: You've never done that.

Desmond sends her fresh flowers every day.

RIGSBY: I wondered what was wrong with him – it must be green fly.

ALAN: I suppose you think sending flowers is soppy?

RIGSBY: I didn't say that. She knows how I feel. She knows I fancy her.

ALAN: Fancy her! Is this the language of Shakespeare and Byron. Where's your sense of romance, Rigsby?

RIGSBY: Don't talk to me about romance – there's no such thing. It's all a racket. You spend a fortune on flowers and chocolate and where does it get you? You find yourself in an expensive restaurant with a glass full of chopped fruit and eating meat off a flaming sword. The waiters are hovering like vultures and you're wondering what it's all going to cost and if you can beat them to the door. And then what happens? Up come the genuine gypsy violinists – day workers from Fords – and they play your tune – and you hold hands in the candle-light – and they shake their earrings. All very romantic – until you forget to tip them – then you get a violin bow up your nostril.

ALAN: I'm not talking about that, Rigsby. I'm talking about the beauty of the language. Poetry. Do you know any poetry?

RIGSBY: Only 'The Charge of The Light Brigade'.

ALAN: You should learn a bit of poetry. That's the only way you'll compete with Desmond.

RIGSBY: I think I'd sooner give him a fat lip.

PHILIP: (*anxiously*) You can't do that, Rigsby. If I were you, Rigsby, do you know what I'd do?

RIGSBY: What?

PHILIP: I'd take her in my arms – hold her close and tell her that the lights in her eyes are like stars.

RIGSBY: Stars?

PHILIP: Stars reflected in limpid green pools.

ALAN: Philip, he can't say that.

RIGSBY: Why not? That's beautiful. There's only one snag – she never lets me get that close.

PHILIP: Then tell her she's like an ivory statue – cold and unapproachable. Talk about her beautiful brow – the proud arch of her neck – the superb ripeness of her—

RIGSBY: (*swallows*) You're right. She couldn't resist that, could she? Now that's what I call poetry. The superb ripeness … I can't wait … Thanks Philip. You know you have changed. You can be quite likeable sometimes.

Rigsby exits.

ALAN: Why did you tell him that? She'll murder him.

PHILIP: That's better than him murdering Desmond.

Rigsby returns.

RIGSBY: Oh Philip, mind if I have a dash of your aftershave?

* * *

SCENE 6: *Int. Ruth's room. Evening. Ruth has just returned. She is examining ring.*
Rigsby enters. He is holding a bunch of flowers.

RIGSBY: Oh, Miss Jones – I've just brought you a few flowers.

RUTH: Why thank you, Mr Rigsby. Aren't they nice? Very similar to those ones in the park.

RIGSBY: Er, yes.

RUTH: I'll put them in water.

Ruth crosses to vase which contains a superior bouquet from Desmond. Rigsby winces.

Was there anything else, Mr Rigsby?

RIGSBY: My word, Miss Jones.

RUTH: What's the matter, Mr Rigsby.

RIGSBY: Your eyes.

RUTH: What about them?

RIGSBY: Those little lights – like stars reflected in limpid green pools.

RUTH: (*angrily*) I beg your pardon, Mr Rigsby?

RIGSBY: No, don't move away, Miss Jones. You're like an ivory statue – cold and unapproachable.

RUTH: Mr Rigsby!

RIGSBY: The proud arch of the neck – the superb ripeness of—

RUTH: How dare you, Mr Rigsby?

RIGSBY: What?

RUTH: You've been listening. I thought I saw those bushes move. You gooseberry! How could you do it? How can you mock the finest feelings two people could have for each other?

RIGSBY: But Miss Jones – you don't understand.

RUTH: Oh, I understand. I'm engaged and I'm leaving here – as soon as possible. Now get out.

She throws vase. Rigsby ducks and exits hurriedly.

* * *

SCENE 7: *Int. landing.*
Rigsby comes face to face with Alan.

ALAN: What's the matter, Rigsby?

RIGSBY: Nothing's the matter. Why should anything be the matter?

ALAN: I thought I heard shouting.

RIGSBY: No, I didn't hear any shouting.

Ruth's door opens. The flowers fly out and land at Rigsby's feet.

END OF PART ONE.

PART TWO

SCENE 8: *Int. Ruth's room. Day.*
Rigsby enters nervously.

RIGSBY: Miss Jones – I've just come
to say—

He sees the cases standing in the
corner. Sighs. The door opens.
Rigsby ducks nervously as Alan
enters.

ALAN: Ah, Rigsby – about this
room. I thought now that Ruth's
going—

RIGSBY: My God! You can't wait,
can you? Haven't you got any
feelings?

ALAN: Yes, of course, I'm sorry.
(*Pats Rigsby's shoulder*) You've
had a tough break, Rigsby.

RIGSBY: (*touched*) That's all right.

ALAN: No, I should have been
more sensitive. (*Pause*) Now
about this room. You see this girl
I know – she's looking for a
room. She's very respectable –
got an O level in Divinity – wears
skirts down to here – very studious – you wouldn't know she
was here—

RIGSBY: You never stop trying, do
you? You're about as sensitive as
a rubber cosh. Don't you realise

that this room means something
to me. That I might want to sit
alone with my memories – and
think what might have been.

ALAN: (*gently*) Why don't you let
them come, Rigsby?

RIGSBY: Let what come?

ALAN: The tears. You'd feel better.

RIGSBY: There's only one thing
that'll make me feel better and
that's shaking hands with your
windpipe.

ALAN: What have I done?

RIGSBY: You and your stars. 'A new
and exciting love affair' you said.
'Indulge your love of pleasure'
you said. You never said anything about dodging bloody
vases. I was nearly decapitated.

ALAN: It was your idea to look at
the stars, Rigsby. Anyway,
perhaps your destiny lies elsewhere. You shouldn't let this
make you bitter. After all, there
are plenty more pebbles on the
beach.

RIGSBY: (*seizes Alan*) How dare you!
What sort of man do you think I
am? You think I can switch my
feelings off and on like that? You
think because I don't go around

sighing and groaning and carving hearts on trees that I don't feel things.

ALAN: I didn't say that.

RIGSBY: You know your trouble – you don't know the real thing when you see it. You're so bloody shallow. 'Plenty more pebbles on the beach.' You'd have said that to Romeo and Juliet, you would. 'Don't take the poison, Romeo – plenty more pebbles on the beach.'

ALAN: I didn't know you felt so strongly about it, Rigsby.

RIGSBY: Well, I do. And I'll tell you this – she hasn't gone yet – and until she does, I'm not giving up. And if I ever get hold of that Desmond—

Desmond enters.

DES: Oh, hello. I hope I'm not interrupting anything.

RIGSBY: (*silkily*) No, not at all – come on in.

ALAN: About the room, Rigsby—

Rigsby pushes Alan to the door, his eyes still on Desmond.

RIGSBY: I'll think about it – let you know.

Alan exits.

DES: (*nervously*) You must be Mr Rigsby.

RIGSBY: (*friendly*) Yes, that's right.

DES: I … er … came for the cases.

RIGSBY: They're over there.

DES: I hope you don't mind.

RIGSBY: Mind? Why should I mind?

DES: Well, I had the impression – just an impression – that you didn't approve of me.

RIGSBY: I wonder how you got that idea. No – as a matter of fact I'm delighted. We all are. It's nice to know she's finally managed it.

DES: Managed it?

RIGSBY: You know what I mean – that she's finally managed to hook – to get someone at last. We shall all go to the wedding of course.

DES: Oh, that's splendid.

RIGSBY: (*grins*) Well, we won't believe it unless we actually see it.

DES: What?

RIGSBY: Just my little joke. You see this isn't the first time. Miss Jones has had several disappointments. Something always seems to go wrong.

DES: Well, it won't this time, Mr Rigsby.

RIGSBY: Well, it's all in the stars I suppose. What star were you born under?

DES: What? Oh, I'm a Virgo.

RIGSBY: Yes, I thought you might

be. Just your luck I suppose. (*Proudly*) I'm a Libra.

DES: Yes – well, I'd better get the cases.

RIGSBY: Yes – I'm surprised she went for a Virgo. Still, if you don't mind the drinking.

Des puts down cases.

DES: Drinking. What drinking?

RIGSBY: Oh, didn't you know about that?

DES: I haven't noticed her drinking.

RIGSBY: Well, you wouldn't – unless she gets violent.

DES: Does she get violent?

RIGSBY: Very rarely. You've got to watch out for the signs of course. The level starts to drop in the decanter – and it's not evaporation – there's a faint whiff of peppermint on the breath and the clink of her hip flask.

DES: But mother doesn't approve of drinking – we're going there tonight.

RIGSBY: Well, just keep her off the sherry trifle – unless you want her sliding gracefully under the table.

DES: Does she do that?

RIGSBY: No – well only at Christmas.

DES: But why does she drink?

RIGSBY: Ah, it's a sad story. You see she's afraid of men.

DES: I didn't know that.

RIGSBY: Oh yes – happened years ago – when she was younger – she saw something nasty in the woodshed. Now she always carries a knitting needle in her handbag.

DES: Good heavens!

RIGSBY: Not that that'll worry you of course.

DES: Er … no.

RIGSBY: Still, marriage is a bit of a gamble really. A mate of mine married a woman like that – the honeymoon was a disaster.

DES: What happened?

RIGSBY: She jumped off the balcony on their wedding night.

DES: What on earth for? What did he do?

RIGSBY: He didn't do anything. He wasn't even there. He was in the bar having a last drink – he actually saw her pass by the window. She went home with her leg in plaster.

DES: You don't think Miss Jones would do anything like that?

RIGSBY: Of course not. Mind you, it is a bit worrying – you being a librarian – you don't want her coming in the library and pulling all the books off the shelves.

DES: (*stares wildly*) Excuse me.

RIGSBY: Where are you going?

DES: I've just remembered something.

RIGSBY: What about the cases?

DES: I shall have to leave them.

Ruth enters.

RUTH: Desmond – what's the matter?

DES: I'm sorry. I've just found out – the flat's been taken. We'll have to call it off for the time being. Excuse me – I'll have to go – I've left a tap running.

Exit Desmond.

RUTH: Desmond! What's happened? Why is he acting so strangely?

RIGSBY: I've no idea, Miss Jones. He's been acting like that ever since he arrived – a very strange character if you don't mind me saying. I think you've had a very narrow escape there.

RUTH: Desmond.

Ruth exits in pursuit.

RIGSBY: (*shakes head*) True love never runs smooth.

* * *

SCENE 9: *Int. Ruth's room. Evening. Alan enters with a jaunty young woman. Attractive. Faintly tarty.*

ALAN: Well, this is it, Brenda. What do you think?

BRENDA: Yes, it's all right. Are you sure you can get it for me?

ALAN: You leave it to me. I've got a lot of influence around here. The landlord eats out of my hand.

BRENDA: Well, I do appreciate it. After all, I hardly know you.

ALAN: (*closes*) Well, we can soon alter that.

BRENDA: (*moves away*) I hope there's not going to be any of that. I hope you're not getting this room with an ulterior motive.

ALAN: (*closer*) No, of course not. I just thought we could drink our cocoa together – play Scrabble – listen to the Proms.

BRENDA: Don't do that.

ALAN: You know you're beautiful when you're angry – you get these little lights in your eyes.

BRENDA: (*surprised*) What?

ALAN: They're like stars reflected in limpid green pools.

BRENDA: Blimey! Who rattled your cage?

ALAN: What?

BRENDA: Listen. I've been taken in by that kind of talk before. And what happened? He walked out on me.

ALAN: I'm not like that.

BRENDA: Then you'd better stop that sort of talk.

ALAN: What if I don't?

BRENDA: I'll swipe you with my handbag.

ALAN: Oh. Well, I tell you what. You have a look round – get the feel of the room and I'll make you a cup of tea.

Alan exits.
Brenda examines the room.
Rigsby enters silently. He studies her figure with more than passing interest.
Brenda starts.

BRENDA: Oh, hello.

RIGSBY: Hello.

BRENDA: I'm looking at the room.

RIGSBY: So I see.

BRENDA: It's not yours is it?

RIGSBY: No.

BRENDA: Alan says he can get it for me. Apparently the landlord eats out of his hand.

RIGSBY: Oh, does he?

BRENDA: Alan says he's a bit weird but perfectly harmless. Do you know him?

RIGSBY: Oh, yes. You could say we're just like that.

BRENDA: Who're you then?

RIGSBY: I'm the landlord.

BRENDA: Oh dear. I suppose that means I don't get the room.

RIGSBY: I wouldn't say that. I mean, I might be in a position to help you – if it becomes vacant.

BRENDA: I'd be very grateful.

RIGSBY: Would you? I must say you look a very nice sort of person – the sort that would clean their bath out after them. I do like to keep up the standard.

BRENDA: Yes of course. There's only one thing that worries me. Alan upstairs. I don't think he's quite normal.

RIGSBY: No he's not.

BRENDA: He's been saying the most peculiar things.

RIGSBY: Oh yes, he would. I'd keep away from him if I were you. (*Confidentially*) It's not my nature to speak ill of people but he's as foul as a box of frogs.

BRENDA: Is he really?

RIGSBY: Don't worry – you'll be perfectly safe. I'll be here all the time.

BRENDA: Oh good. (*Looks around*) I must say, it's a lovely room.

RIGSBY: Yes – and quite a nice view – now they've painted the gasometer. And down there, of course, is the lawn and patio. You can sunbathe down there – you have to watch out for the red ants but apart from that it can be very pleasant. Yes – get out there in your bikini ... Have you got a bikini?

BRENDA: Well, yes.

RIGSBY: I'm sure you'd look very nice in it.

BRENDA: Oh, Mr Rigsby.

They laugh. Ruth enters.

RUTH: My word – you haven't wasted any time, Mr Rigsby.

RIGSBY: Miss Jones!

RUTH: I've barely packed my cases and you're installing another woman.

RIGSBY: I can explain, Miss Jones.

BRENDA: Perhaps I'd better go.

RUTH: I think you'd better.

Brenda exits.

RIGSBY: I can explain.

RUTH: You don't have to. I was considering staying, but not now.

RIGSBY: I didn't bring her here. She heard about the room – came to enquire. No one can replace you, Miss Jones – you know that. I can see you're upset, Miss Jones. He's let you down, hasn't he?

RUTH: (*sits down*) Yes. I can't find him anywhere.

RIGSBY: I could have told you. These blokes are all the same – all talk. You need someone solid and dependable.

RUTH: I don't know anyone like that.

RIGSBY: He's been leading you on, Miss Jones.

RUTH: I suppose you're right.

RIGSBY: Well, if you need a shoulder to lean on—

RUTH: Thank you, Mr Rigsby.

RIGSBY: I'm not a great one for talk, Miss Jones. There's just three little words I want to say to you.

RUTH: What's that Mr Rigsby?

RIGSBY: (*with effort*) I ... I ... I—

RUTH: Is that it?

Desmond enters.

RUTH: Oh, Desmond.

DES: Oh, Ruth.

RIGSBY: Oh hell!

RUTH: I thought you'd gone for good.

DES: No, I couldn't. I love you. I don't care what the world thinks. I don't care how much you drink. You can drink barrels for all I care.

RUTH: What!

DES: I've been thinking it over. I'll help you. It's a sickness really – nothing to be ashamed of. We'll face the problem together. We'll see the best doctors. You can be helped – I'm sure of it.

Rigsby starts for the door.

RUTH: Desmond, what on earth are you talking about?

DES: Mr Rigsby told me. There's no need to be afraid. You can put away the knitting needle. We'll face things together.

RUTH: Mr Rigsby!

Rigsby turns from door in attitude of surprised innocence.

RIGSBY: Yes, Miss Jones?

* * *

SCENE 10: *Int. attic. Later.*
Alan is alone.
Philip enters.

PHILIP: She's gone then.

ALAN: Yes, the end of an era. He's taken it badly.

PHILIP: (*shrugs*) Who needs women?

ALAN: You do. You've got ten of them. (*Pause*) Have you stopped to think what would happen if all the time we spent chasing birds was devoted to research?

PHILIP: No.

ALAN: We'd have cured the common cold and found a substitute for oil. Instead of which there's old Rigsby eating his heart out.

PHILIP: I've never seen him like this before.

ALAN: It'll take him a long time to get over this—

* * *

SCENE 11: *Int. Ruth's room.*
Rigsby leads Brenda into the room.

RIGSBY: Here we are then.

BRENDA: Well, what is it?

RIGSBY: I just wanted a quiet chat. I like to take a personal interest in all my tenants—

They sit down on the settee.

BRENDA: I suppose you're like a father to them.

RIGSBY: No, not exactly, no, but I like to get to know them.

BRENDA: Well, what do you want to know?

RIGSBY: For example, why did you want to leave your present place?

BRENDA: It's the landlord. He was trying it on.

RIGSBY: Typical. A woman's not safe anymore.

BRENDA: He thinks he can try it on because I'm a model.

RIGSBY: A model. Of course, I should have realised. The poise, the elegance, the daring use of colours. Furs? Paris originals?

BRENDA: I'm not that sort of a model.

RIGSBY: Oh, the commercial. The chocolate one. That desert scene – those two Arabs wrestling in the rays of the dying sun and you on your silk cushions, full of Eastern promise – your eyes glittering.

BRENDA: That's not me. I'm an artist's model. And just because I take my clothes off for a living some men try to take advantage. You should see the photographic club – I can feel their eyes burning into me. Half of them haven't even got film in their cameras.

RIGSBY: How disgraceful. I can see what you mean. I've an artistic bent myself. I can under-stand exactly how you feel. I can admire the perfection of the female form without having to throw a leg over it. It's no more than a good sunset to me. Talking about the artistic trade, I'm quite handy with the camel hairs myself – and you've got this English rose quality. I'd love to get you down on canvas—

* * *

SCENE 12: *Attic flat.*
Ruth enters.

ALAN: Ruth. What are you doing here?

RUTH: I've just come to say goodbye.

They embrace her.

ALAN: Goodbye, Ruth.

PHILIP: Take care, Ruth.

RUTH: I'll miss you two. Bye, Philip. Bye, Alan.

PHILIP: We'll miss you.

ALAN: Have you said goodbye to Rigsby?

RUTH: After what happened?

PHILIP: He's very upset about it.

ALAN: He's down there feeling things very deeply—

RUTH: Is he really upset?

ALAN: Shattered.

PHILIP: Why don't you just say goodbye. I'm sure it will make him feel better.

RUTH: All right. I'll pop in and see him on the way out.

Ruth crosses to the door. Turns.

I sometimes wish I'd never been given this power over men—

* * *

SCENE 13: *Ruth's room.*
Rigsby is sitting very close to Brenda.

RIGSBY: ... I can just picture you knee-deep in ferns, bathed in moonlight, like an ivory statue, cold and unapproachable, the beautiful brow – the proud arch of the neck – the superb ripeness.

And those littls lights in your eyes—

Ruth is standing regarding them from the door.

RUTH: (*mockingly*) … like stars

reflected   in   limpid   green pools—

Rigsby looks up in alarm.
Ruth advances menacingly.

THE END.

Series Two

EPISODE 5

A Perfect Gentleman
by
Eric Chappell

PART ONE

SCENE 1: *Int. Rigsby's room. Evening. Rigsby is cleaning shoes. Alan enters – disgruntled – towel around shoulders. He throws down sponge bag.*

RIGSBY: What's the matter with you?

ALAN: I've got a complaint, Rigsby.

RIGSBY: I'm not surprised – you should eat more fresh vegetables.

ALAN: I'm talking about Seymour. He's monopolising the bathroom again.

RIGSBY: No, he's not.

ALAN: He's been in there for hours.

RIGSBY: Well, you can't expect him to just dash in and out – not Seymour.

ALAN: He's reading the paper. I could hear him turning the pages.

RIGSBY: Ah, he's probably studying the financial section. (*Confidentially*) He's thinking of getting out of gilt edged.

ALAN: I'm glad he's thinking of getting out of something. I wish he'd get out of that bathroom.

RIGSBY? Look, he's not like you, you know. He's got a lot on his mind – as a matter of fact, he's very concerned about his Krugerrands.

ALAN: He's not looking at them in there, is he? I mean, if he wants a medical opinion.

RIGSBY: Don't you know what Krugerrands are?

ALAN: Of course I know what Krugerrands are. I also know he hasn't got any. He has to borrow 10p for the gas.

RIGSBY: (*witheringly*) My God! It hasn't taken long, has it?

ALAN: What do you mean? What hasn't taken long?

RIGSBY: It hasn't taken long for you to show your resentment. Just because he's had a public school education – just because he's a gentleman.

ALAN: (*derisively*) A gentleman.

RIGSBY: Yes. I knew that word would stick in your throat. He's a gentleman – he's got breeding.

ALAN: So has our cocker spaniel, Rigsby, but we don't let him take over the bathroom.

RIGSBY: I might have known – that's a typical working-class reaction.

ALAN: Wait a minute. How do you know I haven't got breeding?

RIGSBY: You! You haven't got breeding.

ALAN: Why not?

RIGSBY: Because you suffer from one grave disadvantage.

ALAN: What's that?

RIGSBY: You're common.

ALAN: I'm not common. In what way am I common?

RIGSBY: You eat with your mouth open.

ALAN: Everybody eats with their mouth open. What do you expect me to do? Stuff it in my ear?

RIGSBY: (*patiently*) No – all I'm saying is that once it's in there that's the last we should see of it. Not with you though – you're like those things on the back of dust carts – your teeth rotate.

ALAN: Well, that's great – that's charming. How long have you been watching me like this?

RIGSBY: Ah, you see, it's these little things that give you away in civilised society. That and covering everything in tomato sauce. I can just imagine the confusion at the high table with you shouting for the sauce bottle and wiping your butter knife on the table cloth.

ALAN: I don't wipe my butter knife on the table cloth!

RIGSBY: Your trouble is you don't know what it's all about. You wouldn't even know which way to pass the port – assuming it ever got by you. Now I've made a point of studying these things.

ALAN: (*sarcastically*) Of course, you've got breeding, haven't you, Rigsby?

RIGSBY: You've noticed, have you? Well, you don't get features like this by accident. This is the result of breeding.

ALAN: Oh, and where does all this breeding come from, Rigsby?

RIGSBY: (*confidentially*) Well, this isn't generally known – so keep it to yourself, but my grandfather was a bastard.

ALAN: You mean he was cruel to you?

RIGSBY: No. I mean he was a real bastard – he was the natural son of (*hestitates*) of someone.

ALAN: Who?

RIGSBY: I can't tell you that – suffice it to say, I'm related to one of the most powerful families in this country.

ALAN: I don't believe it.

RIGSBY: It's true – how else do you think Granddad got the horse and cart? Hush money. I shall never want. I've only got to show myself at the drawbridge –

they'd recognise the family features and I'd be made.

ALAN: I bet you would.

RIGSBY: You're only jealous – just because I've got a dash of nobility in me.

ALAN: How can you tell?

RIGSBY: It's in the blood. I've only got to hear that hunting horn and I feel my ears pricking – my nostrils begin to twitch and I'm away.

ALAN: It sounds as if you've got a dash of foxhound to me.

RIGSBY: You can laugh but I've always known I was different – someone set apart. It's the same when the Royal coach goes by and She sees me – and our eyes meet and she waves just that little bit longer. I know what she's thinking. She's thinking 'He's one of us.'

ALAN: Don't you mean 'one of them'?

RIGSBY: No, I don't. I've always felt at ease with the gentry – they usually take to me. It's the same with Seymour – we took to each other at once. I'm glad he's come here – at least now I can enjoy some civilised conversation.

ALAN: So that's it. You're hoping he's going to get you in the golf club.

RIGSBY: No, I'm not.

Philip enters angrily.

PHILIP: Rigsby – what are you going to do about Seymour? He's in the bathroom again.

RIGSBY: Well, don't be so impatient. Your trouble is you're too hot-blooded – I suppose it comes from being born in the tropics.

PHILIP: I am not hot-blooded, Rigsby.

RIGSBY: Now come on, let's face it – you are inclined to dash for the drums at the slightest provocation. Look what happened yesterday – you flew into a rage just because Seymour borrowed your soap.

PHILIP: Rigsby – he borrows everything. He's a scrounger.

RIGSBY: He's not a scrounger. He came here at short notice. He forgot to pack a few things, that's all.

ALAN: Rigsby won't hear a word against him. He'll do anything for Seymour. He's getting special treatment.

RISGBY: Now wait a minute – no one can accuse me of having favourites. I treat everyone the same.

Seymour enters. He is a distinguished man in late-forties. Under a bland exterior there is a calculating hardness.

SEYMOUR: Ah, there you are. Have you finished the shoes yet? I say, you've got a real shine on those.

He takes the shoes much to Rigsby's embarrassment.

SEYMOUR: It's jolly decent of you.

RIGSBY: That's all right, Seymour.

Rigsby tries to usher him to door. Seymour pauses by Philip and addresses him in something that sounds like Swahili. Exits. Philip stares.

ALAN: Did you see that? He's even cleaning his shoes for him.

RIGSBY: I was just putting a shine on them, that's all.

PHILIP: I wish he'd stop talking to me like that – I can't understand a word he says.

RIGSBY: That's why you resent him, isn't it? Because he was out there. You hold him responsible for our colonial past. Well, he got malaria working for you lot, the least you could do is make him feel at home.

PHILIP: What do you want me to do – take his letters up in a cleft stick?

RIGSBY: There was a time when you'd have been glad of Seymour Bwana. What happened when you wanted the tigers killing – who did you send for then?

PHILIP: We didn't send for anyone. We don't have tigers in Africa.

RIGSBY: (*uncertain*) Yes, well, that's thanks to men like Seymour. He protected you. Seymour Bwana and his stick that spoke thunder – who represented the great white mother across the sea, who stopped you eating each other and shrinking heads, who sorted out your little problems.

PHILIP: My little problem at the moment is how to get back that five pounds I loaned him.

ALAN: I didn't know he'd borrowed money off you. You see, he's a con man.

RIGSBY: No, he's not. I can judge character. He's genuine.

ALAN: Then why is he always short of money?

RIGSBY: That's because of your lot. They've bled him white. Crippled him with death duties. When he came home from Africa he found the estate in ruins. He'd got dry rot in the panelling – moth in the tapestry and the moat had dried up. And where were his faithful retainers? Clocking on at British Leyland. That's why he had to get a job.

ALAN: What job?

RIGSBY: He's a financial consultant.

ALAN: I wouldn't trust him with my finances.

RIGSBY: What finances?

PHILIP: Has he paid the rent yet, Rigsby?

RIGSBY: (*hesitates*) Well, no.

ALAN: I thought not.

PHILIP: (*innocently*) I thought you always asked for it in advance?

RIGSBY: Well, this is different.

ALAN: You won't get it, Rigsby.

RIGSBY: What do you mean? I've only got to ask for it.

ALAN: You ask him. I bet you won't get it. I bet he makes an excuse about mislaying his cheque book.

RIGSBY: That's what you think. I'll show you.

Exit Rigsby.

* * *

SCENE 2: *Int. Seymour's room.*
Seymour is getting ready to go out.
Whistling cheerfully.
Rigsby enters rather uneasily.

RIGSBY: Ah, if you're going out I'll come back later.

SEYMOUR: No, come in, old boy. Always glad to see you. I look forward to our little chats.

RIGSBY: Yes, well, so do I, Seymour, so do I. I don't often have the chance to talk to someone like you. Someone I can respect – who'll pay his rent promptly.

SEYMOUR: That's just the way I feel. As soon as I saw you, Rigsby, I felt this rapport. I thought 'There's a chap I could have a good yarn with', and I was right.

RIGSBY: (*shyly*) Yes, well, I find I can talk to you, Seymour.

SEYMOUR: Can you? That's a damned nice thing to say, Rigsby.

RIGSBY: Well, I don't want you to think I'm just someone who comes up for the *rent*.

SEYMOUR: No, of course not. The fact is you don't seem like an ordinary landlord to me – they're usually money grabbing, mercenary types. You're different – you've got style. I can't explain it – something about you.

RIGSBY: Probably the way I hold my coffee cup – it's things like that that give you away. But for an accident of birth, Seymour, who knows? We could have been chums.

SEYMOUR: Ah, I thought so.

RIGSBY: We could have shared our tuck together – held rags in the dorm. And after that – Oxford. Dreaming spires – punting on the Isis – chatting up the birds from Lady Margaret's and then back to Balliol for crumpets and plover's eggs.

SEYMOUR: But it wasn't to be, Rigsby?

RIGSBY: No – never got through my eleven plus.

SEYMOUR: You know, Rigsby, you'll have to come down and spend the weekend with us sometime.

RIGSBY: (*thrilled*) At the manor? I

should like that, Seymour. You don't think your lady wife would mind?

SEYMOUR: Of course not. We could put you in the Chinese room.

RIGSBY: The Chinese room. You mean in the four poster – carved by Grinling Gibbons? My word, I shall have to get the cord back in my pyjamas now. Wait until I tell the others – they'll be green with envy.

SEYMOUR: I wouldn't say anything to them. I know they resent me.

RIGSBY: I wouldn't say that.

SEYMOUR: Philip's been giving me some very black looks.

RIGSBY: Well, he couldn't give you any others, could he?

SEYMOUR: It hurts, Rigsby. I gave them the best years of my life. Twenty years I spent out there, and do you know what thanks I got? The natives peed in the drinking water. I've never got over it.

RIGSBY: I'm not surprised.

SEYMOUR: And then there's the other one – the one with the long hair – looks like a bloody red to me.

RIGSBY: You've put your finger on it there. He won't be satisfied until we're all swinging from the nearest lamp-post.

SEYMOUR: Yes, that's typical –

their answer to everything – mindless violence. They should be put against a wall and shot. Well, must be off.

RIGSBY: Where is it tonight then?

SEYMOUR: Golf club. Thought I might pick up a few investors. I've some very attractive stocks. (*Pause*) I suppose you've got your little pile safely invested, Rigsby?

RIGSBY: Oh yes.

SEYMOUR: I thought so. ICI? Unilever? Shell?

RIGSBY: No. Premium Bonds, actually.

SEYMOUR: Oh. We shall have to have a talk sometime. Do you play golf?

RIGSBY: Well, no – never got round to it.

SEYMOUR: You'll have to come out with me sometime – you'll soon pick it up.

RIGSBY: Yes, well, I've always had a feeling for the game – did very well on the sea front at Skegness, until I got stuck in one of those little wooden windmills.

SEYMOUR: Yes – splendid. Well, I must fly.

RIGSBY: (*awkwardly*) Oh, Seymour. I don't like to mention this but I was wondering – about the rent.

SEYMOUR: Oh, of course.

RIGSBY: I hope you don't mind.

SEYMOUR: No, completely slipped my mind. You should have mentioned it earlier. Ah, wait a minute – I've left my cheque book at the office. Isn't that silly of me? I'll see you later.

Seymour exits.
Rigsby winces.

* * *

SCENE 3: *Int. attic flat. Later.*
Alan is reading.
Rigsby enters a shade thoughtfully.

ALAN: Well, Rigsby – did you get it?

RIGSBY: No, he hadn't got his cheque book with him.

ALAN: I knew it.

RIGSBY: He left it at the office – nothing unusual in that.

ALAN: Well, it doesn't matter. I wouldn't take a cheque if I were you. You'll probably find it's got certain rubbery qualities.

RIGSBY: Listen, I could have had the money any time – I just didn't want to bother him. He's got a lot on his mind – his west wing's crumbling.

ALAN: He hasn't got a west wing – nor an east wing. He's only got one suit and he lives on fish fingers and peas.

RIGSBY: So you're spying on him now. Your trouble is you don't know a gentleman when you see one.

Philip enters. Searches in his pockets and looks around.

PHILIP: That's funny. I can't find my wallet. I'm sure I had it in this jacket.

ALAN: Are you certain?

PHILIP: Yes. I had it earlier.

They look around.

ALAN: (*stops*) Did you have it when Seymour came in?

PHILIP: Alan, you don't think?

ALAN: He brushed against you – I saw him.

RIGSBY: My God! You don't care do you? That's slander that is.

ALAN: Well, this has never happened before, has it?

PHILIP: Well, that's no reason to jump to conclusions.

RIGSBY: Of course it isn't.

ALAN: You're right – we shouldn't be hasty.

RIGSBY: No.

ALAN: He's a crook.

RIGSBY: There you go again.

PHILIP: You haven't got any proof, Alan.

ALAN: We don't know anything about him though, do we? Only that he hasn't paid his rent. And he's already borrowed money.

RIGSBY: (*reluctantly*) That's true, I suppose – well, there's nothing we can do about it.

ALAN: We could search his room.

PHILIP: We can't do that.

ALAN: He won't know – he's gone out.

PHILIP: Perhaps it would be simpler to call the police.

RIGSBY: (*hastily*) No – we don't want them around here. (*Pause*) I suppose it wouldn't hurt just to take a look. I mean we could be proving his innocence.

ALAN: Come on then.

They exit.

* * *

SCENE 4: *Int. Seymour's room. Alan, Rigsby and Philip enter.*

PHILIP: Are you sure we should be doing this?

RIGSBY: I'll never be able to look him in the face again.

ALAN: Come on – you'll thank me for this. When I've exposed him. He's probably a master criminal.

RIGSBY: Where are we supposed to look?

ALAN: Under the mattress – top of the wardrobe – rip the lining of his jacket.

Philip and Rigsby stand helplessly as Alan searches.

Seymour enters. Watches for a moment.

SEYMOUR: What are you looking for?

ALAN: A wallet. (*Stops. Turns and sees Seymour*) Oh.

RIGSBY: Ah, I don't know how to put this, Seymour but you see this wallet's missing and—

SEYMOUR: And you suspect me?

RIGSBY: No.

ALAN: No – everyone's under suspicion.

SEYMOUR: But most of it falls on me I suppose. (*Protests*) No – I quite understand. I'm a stranger – you don't know anything about me. Perhaps you'd like to search me? (*More protests*) No – I'd feel better if you did. In fact I insist. Please. (*Alan taps his pockets sheepishly*)

ALAN: No – it's not there.

SEYMOUR: Now what about you?

ALAN: Me?

SEYMOUR: You did say everyone was under suspicion.

ALAN: Well, yes.

SEYMOUR: Good. You don't mind
  then?

ALAN: No. (*Grins and shrugs at
  others*)

SEYMOUR: (*searching*) Hello.

What's this? (*He takes wallet from
Alan's pocket*) Is this what you're
looking for?

Alan stares.

END OF PART ONE.

PART TWO

SCENE 5: *Int. Seymour's room. Next day.*
Seymour is shaving cuffs of shirt with razor blade. Hears noises off. Opens door. There is a shout of 'Fore!' followed by a golf ball whizzing past Seymour's head. Rigsby enters carrying golf club.

RIGSBY: Sorry about that, Seymour. I didn't know you were going to open the door.

SEYMOUR: That's all right, old boy. What are you doing?

RIGSBY: Just getting in a bit of practice.

SEYMOUR: Yes – don't think I'm being critical, old man but wouldn't it be easier if you played outside?

RIGSBY: I thought I'd iron out the rough spots first. After all, I don't want to look a fool.

SEYMOUR: Er ... no, of course not.

RIGSBY: (*swings club*) Well, what do you think?

SEYMOUR: Yes. Your backswing's a little short.

RIGSBY: Ah, well, I've got to be careful there, Seymour. I've hit the cat twice. Mind you, I think I'm improving – I can pitch seven out of ten into the downstairs lav from the landing.

SEYMOUR: That's very good.

RIGSBY: Of course, you have to watch out for ricochets.

SEYMOUR: I can see you're going to make a very useful addition to our foursome, Rigsby. I know the mayor's dying to meet you.

RIGSBY: The mayor. You play golf with the mayor? I wonder if he could get my paving slabs done? (*Shakes head*) Well, you've certainly cracked it, Seymour. You've only been here five minutes and you're playing golf with the mayor. I suppose it's the old tie – and the accent and the old tweeds – you've certainly got into an exclusive circle. (*Confidentially*) I suppose they've all bared the left breast?

SEYMOUR: I beg your pardon?

RIGSBY: Rolled up the old trouser leg – exchanged the magic word Boaz.

SEYMOUR: Oh, I see. Well, you can't expect me to discuss that, Rigsby.

215

RIGSBY: No, of course not. (*Hesitates*) It won't be too expensive this golf, will it?

SEYMOUR: Oh, you can afford it, Rigsby.

RIGSBY: Only I haven't got all the rent in yet.

SEYMOUR: Well, if it worries you, Rigsby—

RIGSBY: No, I do appreciate the invitation. Especially after last night. I hope you didn't think I had anything to do with it.

SEYMOUR: That's all right. It was perfectly natural for you to doubt my probity.

RIGSBY: What? No, it wasn't me who had doubts. It was those two going on about you not paying your rent.

SEYMOUR: Oh, the rent. Do you know that slipped my mind again. Here you are, Rigsby. (*He hands money to Rigsby*)

RIGSBY: (*surprised. Delighted*) Thank you, Seymour. I hope you didn't think I was hinting.

He stuffs money into his wallet.

SEYMOUR: No, of course not. (*Glance at wallet*) Do you think you're wise carrying all that money around?

RIGSBY: What do you mean?

SEYMOUR: I was thinking of last night's little incident.

RIGSBY: Ah, well, that was explained – they must have got their jackets mixed up. (*Seymour shakes head*) You're not suggesting?

SEYMOUR: I don't trust him, Rigsby. Something about that young man's features.

RIGSBY: Well, his eyes are a bit close together but you can't mean—

SEYMOUR: (*arm around Rigsby's shoulder*) Well, far be it from me to cast the first stone but I advise you to watch your pockets, Rigsby.

RIGSBY: Well, I'll keep my eye on him of course but—

SEYMOUR: Good man.

Rigsby exits.
Seymour smiles. Takes Rigsby's wallet from his pocket and removes money.

* * *

SCENE 6: *Int. attic flat.*
Philip is alone reading. Rigsby enters looks around.

RIGSBY: Where is he?

PHILIP: Gone to the shop.

RIGSBY: Funny about last night.

PHILIP: What do you mean?

RIGSBY: Funny how that wallet got into his pocket.

PHILIP: I must have got the wrong jacket.

RIGSBY: Funny though.

PHILIP: Are you suggesting that Alan took it?

RIGSBY: Well, we don't know, do we? I don't want to cast the first stone—

PHILIP: But you're going to.

RIGSBY: It does look suspicious.

PHILIP: You mean like the time your brother was caught with that sports jacket?

RIGSBY: (*sharply*) That was a misunderstanding. He only took it out of the shop to see how it looked in the daylight.

PHILIP: They picked him up three streets away.

RIGSBY: Well, the light was better there. Look, I'm not saying he did it on purpose. He could have had a blackout. A mate of mine had one of those – found himself outside Marks and Spencers clutching a black chiffon nightie.

PHILIP: Listen, Rigsby. I share a room with Alan. I've got to know him. I trust him.

RIGSBY: I still think we ought to keep an eye on him.

PHILIP: No we're not, Rigsby. We're going to act as if nothing's happened – we're going to treat him perfectly naturally. After all, he's bound to feel awkward.

RIGSBY: I know that. Give me credit for a bit of sensitivity. I won't say anything – he won't notice any change in my manner.

Alan enters.
They both start guiltily.

PHILIP: Hello, Alan.

RIGSBY: Hello.

ALAN: (*looks from one to the other*) You've been talking about me. (*They protest*) Yes, you have. You think I had that wallet. You don't trust me.

PHILIP: Of course we trust you.

RIGSBY: You know your trouble? You're too sensitive. (*Arm on Alan's shoulder*) Of course we trust you. We've known you long enough to trust you.

ALAN: Do you really, Rigsby?

RIGSBY: I'd trust you with my wallet anytime. Here, take it. (*He feels in his pocket. Can't find the wallet. Panics.*) Wait a minute! It's gone! He's got my wallet. (*Seizes Alan*) He never stops. (*Shakes Alan*) Come on. Give it back.

ALAN: I haven't got it.

PHILIP: Of course he hasn't (*grabs Rigsby's arm*).

RIGSBY: (*stops*) What? No – he couldn't have, could he? (*Doubtfully*) No – I'm sorry – I got carried away. I don't know what came over me. I must have dropped it somewhere.

ALAN: (*angrily*) Oh no – you don't think that really, Rigsby. It's going to be like this from now on, isn't it? I'm always going to be under suspicion.

Alan slams out.

PHILIP: Now you've done it, Rigsby.

RIGSBY: Yes. Mind you, he's right you know – we'll never be certain – not now.

PHILIP: Well, I'm certain – and I'll prove it.

RIGSBY: You'll never prove it – not that he's honest (*pause*) that's if he is honest—

* * *

SCENE 7: *Int. Rigsby's room. Day. Seymour is examining ornament from mantelpiece. About to slip it in pocket as Rigsby enters.*

SEYMOUR: (*smoothly*) Ah, hello, old boy. Nice piece.

RIGSBY: Yes. Crown Derby – been in the family for years.

SEYMOUR: Yes. (*Replaces ornament reluctantly*) By the way, I bought those shares for you. Should be through in a few days.

RIGSBY: Good. Lucky you told me about them, Seymour. I didn't even know there was oil in the Pennines.

SEYMOUR: Shush! We don't want

it to get out – not until we've bought up the issue.

RIGSBY: Of course not – my lips are sealed.

SEYMOUR: Good. (*Looks around*) You know this is a very well appointed room, Rigsby.

RIGSBY: Do you think so?

SEYMOUR: Yes – ideal room for entertaining. You know you ought to do more entertaining – now you're going up in the world. Have a few people back for drinks – ask the mayor.

RIGSBY: The mayor – do you think he'd come?

SEYMOUR: He would if I asked him.

RIGSBY: I wonder if he'd wear his chain?

SEYMOUR: I wouldn't be surprised.

RIGSBY: The mayor – having drinks here. I'd really be in the swim then, Seymour. Accepted at last. I can just see myself swanning down to the golf club in my chunky sweater – with two matching terriers, like little bookends – being greeted on all sides in the changing room. Just wait until I tell those two.

SEYMOUR: I wouldn't do that if I were you, Rigsby. You'll only arouse their envy. It's people like that who've been holding you back all these years.

RIGSBY: You're right as usual, Seymour. They've always resented me taking my proper place in society. They'd spoil everything – probably come down in their string vests. And there's another thing – I still haven't found that wallet. We don't want anything like that to happen – not with the mayor. Suppose he lost his insignia?

SEYMOUR: Well, don't worry, old boy. Just leave everything to me. You're in good hands.

RIGSBY: Thanks, Seymour.

Seymour exits.
Rigsby picks up Vienna.

RIGSBY: Vienna – we've got the mayor coming. So don't do anything in any dark corners.

* * *

SCENE 8: *Int. attic flat. Evening.*
Philip is pretending to read but he is watching Alan who is slamming around in a deep sulk. Alan crosses to door.

PHILIP: Where are you going?

ALAN: I'm going to the bathroom – do you mind? Or do you think I'm going to steal the towels?

PHILIP: Alan – don't be ridiculous.

ALAN: You're watching me, aren't you?

PHILIP: No – well, yes but I'm worried about you—

ALAN: Worried about your wallet you mean.

PHILIP: Look, no one thinks you had that wallet.

ALAN: Don't tell me you haven't had doubts. Well, you'll never know, will you?

PHILIP: Alan.

Alan exits, slamming door.
Philip stares after him for a moment.
Takes a five pound note from wallet.
Exits.

* * *

SCENE 9: *Int. landing.*
Philip enters. Places five pound note on the floor. Withdraws behind door. Rigsby enters. Crosses landing. Sees note and puts his foot smartly over it. He looks around carefully. About to pick it up as Philip enters. Straightens.

PHILIP: Hello, Rigsby. Found your wallet yet?

RIGSBY: No – I've looked everywhere.

PHILIP: What are you waiting here for?

RIGSBY: Oh, just looking around. We'll soon need some decorating – my word yes – just look at that ceiling.

Philip looks up.
Rigsby stoops. Philip sees him.
Rigsby straightens – rubs leg.

PHILIP: What's the matter, Rigsby?

RIGSBY: Just a sudden spasm. Shrapnel must have moved.

PHILIP: I didn't know it was in your leg, Rigsby.

RIGSBY: Travels around – never know where it is these days.

PHILIP: Rigsby – what's that under your foot?

RIGSBY: What? (*picks up wrong foot*) I can't see anything.

PHILIP: The other one, Rigsby.

RIGSBY: Good heavens! A five pound note.

PHILIP: Were you going to keep it?

RIGSBY: No, I wasn't. I shall have to hold it of course – for it to be properly claimed.

PHILIP: That won't be necessary – it's mine.

RIGSBY: Yes – that's very easy to say but how do we know that? No – I shall have to make enquiries. (*Sly grin*) Now of course – if you knew the number.

Philip smiles and quotes the number.

RIGSBY: (*stares*) You're right. My God! You don't take any chances, do you?

PHILIP: Rigsby – I put that note down for Alan to find.

RIGSBY: What did you do that for?

PHILIP: To prove his honesty – to prove I could trust him.

RIGSBY: Oh yes. Well, if you can trust him why did you take the number?

PHILIP: In case someone else picked it up. (*Derisively*) 'Not for me to cast the first stone'. I'm not surprised – you could start an avalanche, Rigsby.

RIGSBY: Now wait a minute – you don't think he'll hand it in, do you? He'll be straight down to the Chinese.

PHILIP: That's what you think. Quick – he's coming.

Philip replaces note. He and Rigsby exit to attic flat.
Seymour enters from his flat. He puts his foot over the note.
Alan enters. He sees Seymour leaning against wall. He stares curiously.

ALAN: Are you all right, Seymour?

SEYMOUR: Just getting my breath, old boy. A touch of the old malaria – teeth will be going like castanets any moment now.

ALAN: Anything I can do?

SEYMOUR: No – I'll be all right in a moment.

ALAN: (*hesitates*) By the way – I'm sorry about the other night – jumping to conclusions like that.

SEYMOUR: Don't worry about it, old boy. All perfectly natural.

ALAN: Now they suspect me.

SEYMOUR: I don't, old boy. I can tell by the face. You're a decent type anyone can see that.

ALAN: Thanks, Seymour. Are you sure you're all right?

SEYMOUR: Just leave me alone for a moment.

Alan exits. Seymour takes note.

* * *

SCENE 10: *Int. attic flat.*
Philip and Rigsby look expectantly as Alan enters.

ALAN: (*cheerfully*) Hello, you two.

PHILIP: You sound more cheerful.

Philip glances outside, confirms money has gone.

ALAN: I feel more cheerful. I've just had a very nice experience out there. I tell you what – let's all go down the Chinese.

PHILIP: (*angrily*) No thanks. I've lost my appetite.

Philip exits.

ALAN: What did I say?

* * *

SCENE 11: *Int. Rigsby's room. Evening.*
A table is spread with food. Rigsby is fussing over table. Seymour enters.

SEYMOUR: They should be here soon. Everything all right?

RIGSBY: Yes. I've got everything here. Sausages on sticks – flavoured crisps – mixed nuts – salmon sandwiches – food for the gods.

SEYMOUR: Splendid. Wait a minute. We've slipped up, Rigsby. No champagne.

RIGSBY: Champagne! You never said anything about champagne.

SEYMOUR: They're bound to expect champagne. It'll be a disaster.

RIGSBY: Will it?

SEYMOUR: They'll laugh at us.

RIGSBY: I've got two crates of stout.

SEYMOUR: That won't do. We'll have to get some. You'd better leave this to me.

RIGSBY: (*relieved*) Oh good.

SEYMOUR: Give me thirty pounds.

RIGSBY: Thirty pounds!

SEYMOUR: Can't do it for less. Of course if you want to call it off.

RIGSBY: Oh, all right then. But I'm getting a bit short. (*He pulls up shirt to reveal money belt*) I keep it in here now. Can't be too careful after all that's happened.

SEYMOUR: I think you're very wise. Here let me help you.

Seymour helps Rigsby to tuck his shirt in.

SEYMOUR: That's it. I'll be back as soon as possible.

RIGSBY: I don't know what I'd do without you.

SEYMOUR: That's all right, old boy.

Exit Seymour.

* * *

SCENE 12: *Int. landing.*
Seymour looks around. Takes money belt from under jacket. Hurries to room.

* * *

SCENE 13: *Int. landing. Later.*
Seymour appears around door. He is carrying suitcase. Looks around cautiously. Philip appears on landing.

PHILIP: Well, if it isn't Seymour Bwana. Is the great white hunter off on yet another safari?

SEYMOUR: What? Oh yes, old boy. Darkest Birmingham – the whiteman's grave.

PHILIP: Well, before you go – what about the five pounds you owe me?

Philip puts arm across the passage.

SEYMOUR: Oh yes, of course. Completely slipped my mind. Here you are. It's a bit crumpled – hope you don't mind.

PHILIP: (*studies note*) What? No, I don't mind at all, Seymour. It's a lovely five pound note. (*He catches Seymour's arm*) You're not going, are you?

* * *

SCENE 14: *Int. Rigsby's room. Later. Rigsby enters from bedroom. Vienna is on the table astride a plate of sandwiches.*

RIGSBY: Get out of it, you flea-bitten monster. Don't you get enough to eat? How can I give these to the mayor now that you've been on them? (*Pause. Examines plate*) Still – he won't know. Must remember to keep off the salmon paste. I wish they'd hurry up. I'm sure those sandwiches are beginning to curl.

Knock on door.

RIGSBY: Ah, there he is.

Rigsby opens door.
Alan and Philip enter smiling.

ALAN: Hello, Rigsby. Having a party?

RIGSBY: No, what makes you think that?

ALAN: All that food – you're not going to eat it all yourself?

RIGSBY: As a matter of fact I'm having a few friends in so buzz off.

PHILIP: What sort of friends?

RIGSBY: Very influential friends. (*Proudly*) I've got the mayor coming.

ALAN: The mayor!

RIGSBY: Yes – and he's dying to meet me. They all are. We're going to have a civilised evening of wit and good conversation – so sling your hook.

PHILIP: I suppose Seymour's invited?

RIGSBY: Of course – the evening wouldn't be complete without Seymour. He's just gone for the champagne.

PHILIP: Yes – well, he won't be coming back, Rigsby.

RIGSBY: What do you mean?

PHILIP: He's gone. Packed his cases and gone.

RIGSBY: I knew it – you've driven him away. You've always resented our friendship. Just when I was trying to better myself. He was worth two of you – he'd got the lot – wit – sophistication—

Alan takes out Rigsby's money belt and begins examining it.
Rigsby gasps and feels his middle.

RIGSBY: Where did you get that from?

PHILIP: Seymour had it. And your wallet. We've got most of the money.

RIGSBY: (*crushed*) Not Seymour. He was always a perfect gentleman.

PHILIP: I'm sorry, Rigsby. But there was no country house – no mayor – no champagne.

RIGSBY: Oh my God! Do you think there's any oil in the Pennines?

PHILIP: What?

RIGSBY: Never mind. It doesn't matter. I shall never trust anyone again.

ALAN: You can trust us, Rigsby. (*Cheerfully*) Should we start on the grub?

RIGSBY: It doesn't worry you, I suppose, that I've been cut to the quick?

ALAN: Of course, but life goes on, Rigsby. Now where should we start?

RIGSBY: (*slyly*) The salmon paste's rather nice.

Alan tucks in.
Rigsby watches him.

RIGSBY: You know there was one thing about old Seymour – at least he didn't eat with his mouth open.

They start to argue.

THE END.

Series Two

EPISODE 6

The Last of the Big Spenders
by
Eric Chappell

PART ONE

SCENE 1: *Int. Rigsby's room. Teatime. Rigsby is examining several new articles of furniture with evident satisfaction. There is a drinks trolley, coffee table, couch, modern floppy chair, etc. He is in a good humour.*

ALAN: Hello, Rigsby.

RIGSBY: (*cheerfully*) What's the matter with you? You look dead miserable. Don't tell me they've cancelled the revolution again.

ALAN: No – I wondered if you could help me, Rigsby?

RIGSBY: What? Of course I can help you – that's what I'm here for. I'm not just a landlord, you know – I'm a counsellor and friend. Now, what's your little problem?

ALAN: (*hesitates*) I don't know how to put this – it's a bit delicate.

RIGSBY: (*suspiciously*) It's not bed wetting, is it?

ALAN: No – it isn't.

RIGSBY: A bit delicate. Ah, I know, you've been having thoughts.

ALAN: (*mystified*) What?

RIGSBY: Don't worry about it. It's all part of growing up. You're going through a difficult time.

The sap's rising – mysterious changes are taking place inside your body – there's a sudden lack of interest in football.

ALAN: I've never been interested in football.

RIGSBY: No – that's true, you haven't, have you. It's always been Karate or Kung Fu or something else from the land of the bandy legs. Still, you have become aware of the opposite sex.

ALAN: Well, yes.

RIGSBY: You've no doubt noticed that they don't throw a cricket ball as well as we do and wondered why, hey?

ALAN: Listen, Rigsby – this has got nothing to do with women – well, not directly.

RIGSBY: Well, what is it? You're not getting that prickly heat again, are you?

ALAN: No! Look, if you're going to be like this—

RIGSBY: All right. Come on. Sit down. (*Sits Alan down*) You can talk to me. That's what I'm here for. Now, what is it?

226

ALAN: I want to borrow some money.

Rigsby's smile fades. His expression hardens.

RIGSBY: What?

ALAN: I want to borrow some money. Should we say £5?

RIGSBY: You can say what you like. I'm not saying anything.

ALAN: You mean you won't help me?

RIGSBY: It's not that. Listen, let me give you some advice. (*Sententiously*) 'Neither a lender nor a borrower be.' If I was to lend you money what would happen? Friendship would fly straight out of the window.

ALAN: What friendship? If you were a friend you'd lend me the money.

RIGSBY: All right – since we're talking about friendship – what about your mate upstairs? Why don't you ask him? I mean he's not exactly short, is he? I'm sure he could run to a few bags of salt or an elephant's tusk.

ALAN: I can't ask Philip. I borrowed from him last week.

RIGSBY: That's your trouble, you see. You're improvident. You're spending too much on bangles and bloody beads.

ALAN: What do you mean? Most of my money goes in that gas meter – just to keep warm. Sometimes I wonder if there's a roof on this house. Haven't you ever thought of central heating, Rigsby?

RIGSBY: Central heating – are you mad? Price of fuel today. Never.

ALAN: No, I suppose you're waiting for solar energy, are you, Rigsby?

RIGSBY: Listen, you be satisfied with that gas fire. Before the North Sea yielded up its riches we had to make do with a pile of nutty slack. And during the war even that was scarce – you had to share a fire with a friend.

ALAN: Did you find one, Rigsby?

RIGSBY: I had plenty of friends – don't you worry.

ALAN: You've never had any friends, Rigsby – and do you know why? Because you're a grotty miser.

RIGSBY: I'm not a miser.

ALAN: Then why do you stick all the bits of old soap into the new soap? Why do you jump up and down on the toothpaste tube?

RIGSBY: Well, that's different. That doesn't mean I'm a miser. I'm just being more careful with the world's resources. You can laugh but it's five minutes to midnight. This is spaceship earth. And you're too wasteful. I could live on the contents of your dustbin.

ALAN: You don't have to do that, Rigsby. Just come up and ask.

RIGSBY: You throw crusts away that thick.

ALAN: Well, I can't eat them if they're stale.

RIGSBY: You could make bread and butter pudding.

ALAN: I don't like bread and butter pudding.

RIGSBY: That's got nothing to do with it. You've been spoiled by the welfare state. You're not prepared to make sacrifices. What have you done to raise the money?

ALAN: (*hesitates*) Well, I've taken all the lemonade bottles back.

RIGSBY: Is that all? Couldn't you get a job?

ALAN: (*shocked*) What?

RIGSBY: My God! You've gone ashen.

ALAN: Look, Rigsby – I'm studying medicine – that is a full time job. I can't help it if I'm a victim of inflation.

RIGSBY: You're a victim of inflation! What about me? I was hoping to retire one day – perhaps to Bournemouth. Get a bit of sun – dip my feet in the gulf stream. But your lot have put paid to that. I shall end up clinging to the radiators in the public library – trotting down to the supermarket with a wheelbarrow full of pound notes.

ALAN: You're not doing so badly, Rigsby – all this new furniture you've been getting.

RIGSBY: That's the reward for thrift, mate – years of bread and butter puddings. I'm entitled to a bit of gracious living. And get out of that chair – you've been in it long enough – you'll dent it.

ALAN: (*rises*) All right. I can see I'm wasting my breath. I should have known you wouldn't break the habits of a lifetime.

RIGSBY: Wait a minute. I'll tell you what – I'm not a hard man. (*Shakes couch*) Did you hear that? There's some money down there – if you can get your hand in – you can have it.

ALAN: (*indignantly*) If you think I'm going to stoop to that—

RIGSBY: Please yourself. (*Sadistically shakes couch again*) Sounds like a couple of 50ps to me.

ALAN: (*listens*) Well – (*hesitates*) I suppose if it's 50p.

Alan slides his hand down the back of the couch. Gets himself into a contorted position.
Brenda enters. She stares at Alan curiously.

BRENDA: What's he doing?

RIGSBY: Nothing. He always sits like that – he finds it more comfortable.

Alan rises, sheepishly rubbing wrist.

ALAN: Hello, Brenda. (*Covers up*) Yes – well, you'll be all right with that, Rigsby. Beautifully sprung. (*Pats couch*) Just let me know if you have any more trouble.

Alan exits awkwardly.

BRENDA: Is this the new furniture?

RIGSBY: (*proudly*) Yes – I wanted you to have a look at it. Well, I know you've got an artistic nature. What do you think? Functional with just a hint of luxury. Skilfully fashioned by the craftsmen of Evesham.

Brenda stares at beanbag-type chair.

BRENDA: What do you do with that?

RIGSBY: You sit in it. It moulds to the contours of your body. In your case it's got a lot of moulding to do.

BRENDA: (*sits*) It must have cost a lot of money.

RIGSBY: Well, that's what money's for. I've always enjoyed the good things in life. I've never been frightened to spend. What do you think of the drinks cabinet? See the wheels? See how it glides. I shall find it very useful when I want to sip a martini in the bath.

BRENDA: (*relaxes*) It's lovely. When you've been standing in front of a paraffin stove all day with nothing on, this is luxury.

RIGSBY: Yes – I suppose it must be. Have a grape.

BRENDA: Thank you.

RIGSBY: Yes – I like to indulge myself. I always think life should have a bit of style, don't you? You can spit the pips in the ashtray. Yes, I must have elegance.

BRENDA: (*looks round*) Oh, is that your cat? Isn't he nice.

RIGSBY: (*surprised*) Is he? I wouldn't pick him up if I were you. He's been scratching all day. I shall have to get after him with the powder. (*Pause*) I'm glad you like the furniture, Brenda. I was wondering if you'd like to come down one evening.

BRENDA: What for?

RIGSBY: Well, we could talk about art. I do a bit you know.

BRENDA: Don't talk to me about art. I stand there for hours stark naked and when they've finished I've got two eyes on the side of my head – a hole through the middle and legs like matchsticks. Do you see me like that?

RIGSBY: No – I don't see you like that. I see you knee-deep in ferns – with perhaps a bit of lace. I should like to do you in oils sometime – well, it would make a change – I'm getting tired of bowls of fruit. Perhaps we could go out for a meal … and discuss it—

BRENDA: Do you mean tonight?

RIGSBY: (*taken aback*) Well, yes.

BRENDA: Thanks – I'd love to. It's

ages since I had a slap-up meal. We could go to a really flash place. We could have Dover sole – and fat juicy steaks – and a real go at the sweet trolley.

RIGSBY: (*nervously*) Er … do you eat much?

BRENDA: Like a horse.

RIGSBY: (*uneasily*) I thought models just had grapefruit and a slice of toast.

BRENDA: Oh, I don't. I eat and eat. Ooh, I'm looking forward to this. I bet you know some nice places.

RIGSBY: Well, yes.

BRENDA: I'll go and see what I've got to wear. Better be my best dress – with a big spender like you. I'm glad you're not mean. I can't stand mean men – you know, the sort that squeeze the toothpaste tube right up and carry their money in a purse. I'll see you later – my mouth's watering already.

Exit Brenda.
Rigsby takes out his purse and looks with horror at the contents.

* * *

SCENE 2: *Int. attic flat.*
Philip is reading.
Alan enters.

ALAN: (*hesitantly*) Er … Philip – you couldn't lend me a fiver until the end of the week?

PHILIP: Not again! (*Sighs*) What's it for this time?

ALAN: I want to take Brenda out.

PHILIP: No – definitely not.

ALAN: Why not?

PHILIP: Listen, Alan. I've told you. She's not your type. Brenda's been around – she likes a good time – you couldn't keep pace with her.

ALAN: I could try.

PHILIP: No, Alan. She wouldn't be good for you. Brenda is for the more experienced man.

ALAN: You know, you can be irritating sometimes. How am I going to get experience if you take this attitude. You keep saying 'Come on in the water's lovely' and just when I'm going to take the plunge you stop me.

PHILIP: Alan – I don't mind you taking the plunge – I just don't think you're ready to swim the Channel. Look, what would happen if you did get off with her? How would you get your work done? You imagine it. You get your books out at night – there's a knock on the door. Brenda's standing there in a negligee. She beckons you seductively … (*pause*)

ALAN: Well, go on.

PHILIP: You see, you're distracted already. You don't want that sort of thing.

ALAN: Don't I?

PHILIP: It would be another night wasted.

ALAN: You speak for yourself.

PHILIP: I was talking about your education.

ALAN: So was I. Look, I know Brenda's been around but she's not after my money.

PHILIP: Good – because she's not getting any.

ALAN: (*angrily*) You know, Philip – where women are concerned, you're a bit of a big head.

PHILIP: (*angrily*) Oh, am I?

ALAN: Yes.

Rigsby enters.

RIGSBY: Hello. What's this? An acrimonious dispute? Is this an example of the white backlash?

ALAN: No, it's not. And you can both keep your money. I wouldn't take it now if you begged me.

RIGSBY: Oh, he's on the scrounge again, is he?

PHILIP: I don't mind lending you the money – but not to spend on Brenda.

RIGSBY: So that's it. I didn't think it was for text books. Well, he's right – you keep away from her – she's too rich for your blood. She's a model. Girl about town.

ALAN: So what?

PHILIP: I've told him – a girl like that could bleed you white.

RIGSBY: (*stares*) Yes, well, you've got a definite advantage there, haven't you?

PHILIP: What do you mean by that?

RIGSBY: I mean, you've got the money – he hasn't. Besides, she's not his type. He could never take her home.

ALAN: Why not?

RIGSBY: Well, for one thing she never does her top button up. You walk in with a girl like that and your father's going to jump straight out of his carpet slippers. And what about your mother? She could hardly introduce her to the knitting circle, could she?

ALAN: I don't see why not.

RIGSBY: Listen, they didn't make these sacrifices for you to throw it all away on a woman like that. This could be the first step on a downward path ending in dissipation and an early death.

ALAN: For heaven's sake, Rigsby!

RIGSBY: Some lonely plot in a deserted churchyard – watered by a mother's tears.

ALAN: Just because she poses in the nude.

RIGSBY: Oh, that doesn't worry you? But suppose you married her? It would worry you then –

all those hot little eyes staring at her over the easels – her most intimate details displayed on ten foot posters – small boys drawing moustaches on her.

ALAN: I'm not listening to any more of this. The only reason you won't lend me money is because you're too mean.

RIGSBY: I am not mean!

ALAN: (*suddenly*) Hey, Rigsby – you've got a money spider on you.

RIGSBY: What? Where? Be careful – don't crush it.

ALAN: See what I mean?

Exit Alan.

RIGSBY: I don't know why he says things like that. I'm not mean.

PHILIP: Neither am I.

RIGSBY: (*sideways glance*) Of course not, Philip – I know that. I know if it had been something worthwhile you wouldn't have hesitated. (*Pause. Second glance*) Did you notice me just now? When I mentioned his mother – how my voice went sort of husky?

PHILIP: (*puzzled*) No.

RIGSBY: Oh, it did – quite a little tremor. You see, it made me think of my mother. Lovely dark hair she used to have – white as snow now. She'll be sitting there – in front of the black lead grate – her

gnarled old hands clasped in her lap. She'll be looking at that text over the mantelpiece – 'A boy's best friend is his mother' – waiting for that knock that never comes. I've always been too busy. I'd forgotten how she scrubbed floors for me and took in washing.

PHILIP: You should go and see her, Rigsby.

RIGSBY: I almost went tonight. I thought it would be nice to surprise her – take a few presents.

PHILIP: Then why don't you?

RIGSBY: Pride, I suppose. No money. And in my letters I've always said how well I've been doing.

Rigsby turns away and blows nose. Philip takes out money, approaches Rigsby.

PHILIP: Look, Rigsby – would this help?

RIGSBY: No – I couldn't.

PHILIP: Go on – you can pay me back.

RIGSBY: Well, if you insist. (*Takes money*)

Brenda enters in best dress.

BRENDA: Ah, there you are. What about this then, Rigsby? Will it do for tonight? (*Twirls around*).

RIGSBY: (*hurriedly*) Yes, that's fine.

BRENDA: Good. See you later.

Exit Brenda.
Philip removes money from Rigsby's hand.

PHILIP: So that's the white-haired old lady, is it? I should have known better. Why did I fall for a story like that?

RIGSBY: Well, I couldn't tell you the real reason, could I? Not after what you said. What am I going to do? She's expecting an expensive evening.

PHILIP: You'll have to do what you normally do. Empty the meters.

RIGSBY: I can't take her out with a hundred weight of silver in my pockets – it plays hell with the linings. Besides, suppose she sits on my knee? I'll cut her to ribbons.

PHILIP: Hard luck, Rigsby.

Philip exits.
Rigsby sighs. Starts to empty meter.

* * *

SCENE 3: *Int. landing.*
Rigsby enters. He slips some more silver into his already overloaded pockets. A man enters in Gas Board uniform. He has a plump sad face and carries a collector's bag.

RIGSBY: What do you want?

COLLECTOR: Er ... I'm from the Gas Board.

RIGSBY: Well, I hope you wiped your feet. Do you want to read the meter?

COLLECTOR: Er ... no. I don't quite know how to put this, but I've come to cut off your supply.

RIGSBY: What!

Collector starts nervously.

COLLECTOR: I've come to disconnect you.

RIGSBY: You can't do that.

COLLECTOR: I've got to.

RIGSBY: Why?

COLLECTOR: You haven't paid your bill for three quarters.

RIGSBY: Well, there's no need to get nasty.

COLLECTOR: I'm not being nasty. I've got a job to do – it's my duty.

RIGSBY: Oh yes – the old excuse – doing your duty. Just like the Gestapo – they were only doing their duty.

COLLECTOR: I'm not like the Gestapo.

RIGSBY: You come here late at night – making threats, in a peaked cap – and say you're not like the Gestapo. (*Peers closely*) You remind me of Himmler.

COLLECTOR: I'm nothing like Himmler. He wore glasses. I don't like doing this.

RIGSBY: Well, don't do it.

COLLECTOR: I've got to.

RIGSBY: It could mean trouble for you. Do you want me to write to my MP?

COLLECTOR: I shouldn't – we cut him off last week.

RIGSBY: Oh. Well, it won't end here. I've got influential friends. I've got an African chief upstairs. He feels the cold something dreadful. You cut his gas off and there could be a diplomatic incident. He'll probably go straight home and turf out the missionaries.

COLLECTOR: Well, I'm sorry.

RIGSBY: You're sorry – what about my tenants? They're getting their suppers. They're going to be sorry when their beans start to coagulate.

COLLECTOR: Perhaps they could have a salad.

RIGSBY: My God! You're hard-hearted. I suppose nothing's going to stop you.

COLLECTOR: I'll take money.

RIGSBY: Look, I haven't got two ha'pennies to rub together. (*Clink of silver*) Well, hardly. I wouldn't mind but I'm never warm these days. What with the shrapnel – and I never had a pension. And it gets so cold at night now.

COLLECTOR: I know, it was bitter last night – there was an inch of frost on the lawn.

RIGSBY: Yes well, where does that leave me? Hey, come here – feel these feet.

Rigsby sits on the stairs and removes shoes.

RIGSBY: Come on – feel them.

Collector feels feet.

COLLECTOR: Oh, they're like little blocks of ice.

RIGSBY: You know what that is, don't you? Trench foot. Anzio – up to my knees in mud for three days.

COLLECTOR: You poor soul. The country's got a lot to answer for.

RIGSBY: I try to make the best of it. At least I've always had my self-respect – until now.

COLLECTOR: I'm sorry. Oh, I do hate this job. I shall be tossing and turning all night.

RIGSBY: What about me? I shall be disgraced.

COLLECTOR: No you won't.

RIGSBY: What?

COLLECTOR: It's no use – I can't do it. There comes a point when a man has to make a choice. I shall go back and hand in my cap.

RIGSBY: Will you? I don't know what to say. I'm sorry I made that remark about the Gestapo.

COLLECTOR: That's all right.

RIGSBY: No, it was hurtful. I shall never forget this.

They shake hands.
Brenda enters from bathroom in curlers and underslip.

BRENDA: Hey, Rigsby – I can't wait for tonight. We'll really have a ball. The best of everything.

She whirls Rigsby round. The money crashes through his pockets. The collector stares. His expression changes. He opens his bag.

COLLECTOR: My word. It looks as if we've hit the jackpot.

END OF PART ONE.

PART TWO

SCENE 4: *Int. Rigsby's room. Later. Rigsby scowls at Vienna.*

RIGSBY: It's all right for you. If you want a night out, all you've got to do is go up on the tiles. You don't need money – not with me around. The money I've spent on cat food over the years – it's enough to make you believe in vivisection. (*Sighs*) I wish I had it now. I don't know what I'm going to do.

Brenda enters.

BRENDA: Well, I'm ready.

RIGSBY: Oh yes, very nice too. But I'm afraid we can't go.

BRENDA: Why not?

RIGSBY: Er ... the cat's not well.

BRENDA: He looks all right to me.

RIGSBY: Ah, I know he looks all right, but he's not. It's all that scratching. I think he's lacerated himself. No, I'm as disappointed as you are but I'm afraid it's out of the question.

BRENDA: (*disappointed*) Oh dear. I suppose it's back to the baked beans.

RIGSBY: Not necessarily. I mean, we could dine here. You wouldn't get more luxurious surroundings than these. I could send out for something – we could have drinks from the trolley, (*spins trolley around*) munch a few grapes.

BRENDA: (*doubtfully*) Yes. Well, all right. But I think I'll go and change.

RIGSBY: Yes, slip into something comfortable. I'll get into my smoking jacket.

Brenda exits.

RIGSBY: (*chuckles*) Well, Vienna, I think I handled that pretty well. And just remember – you're not very well so don't drop any dead mice in her lap.

He slips on smoking jacket.
Alan enters.

ALAN: I just saw Brenda come out of here again. What are you up to, Rigsby?

RIGSBY: As a matter of fact Brenda and I are going to spend the evening together. We're going to have music – a little wine – good food. You wouldn't like to go out

236

and get us some cod and chips, would you?

ALAN: No, I wouldn't. I know what you're planning, Rigsby. My God, you've even got grapes. Well, she's not like that, Rigsby. All right, she may know all the answers, but underneath there's something fine and decent.

RIGSBY: I hope not – that's going to be a big disappointment.

ALAN: That's why you've got all this new furniture, isn't it? You're trying to impress her.

RIGSBY: I've got news for you – I have impressed her. Afterwards we shall have a few drinks off the trolley, then settle down on the settee – fashioned by the craftsmen of Evesham – and who knows?

ALAN: (*bitterly*) I hope it collapses.

RIGSBY: Go on – eat your heart out.

Rigsby bustles Alan out of the room. He switches off main light. Puts on music. Sprays perfume in the air. There is a gentle tap on the door. Rigsby selects a single stemmed rose.

RIGSBY: Come, my love.

He opens door. He presents flower to a cynical looking man in a bowler hat.

RIGSBY: (*stares*) Who are you?

FLINT: My name's Flint, Mr Rigsby.

He slides by Rigsby followed by broad man in blue serge.

FLINT: This is Charlie.

Flint looks around, taking in subdued lighting, smoking jacket etc. Glances at Charlie.

FLINT: My word.

RIGSBY: What do you want? What are you doing here?

FLINT: I must say – you certainly live in style, Mr Rigsby. Soft lights – sweet music.

CHARLIE: Hey – he's even got grapes.

FLINT: (*crosses*) So he has. Just like the last days of ancient Rome, Charlie. (*Takes grape*)

RIGSBY: Hey! You leave those alone.

CHARLIE: (*sniffs*) What's the smell?

FLINT: Perfume, Charlie. (*They look at Rigsby*) I think we're in the presence of a trendsetter. That's the thing about this job – we do meet such interesting people.

RIGSBY: Well, don't think I'm being curious but what is your job? You can tell me and then get out. I haven't time to stand talking to you; I've got company.

FLINT: Should we tell him, Charlie? I hope you've got a sense of humour, Mr Rigsby, because there's a certain delicious irony in this. (*Hands Rigsby document*) We've come to take the furniture back.

RIGSBY: Wait a minute – you can't do that.

FLINT: Oh, yes we can. You see, you've not paid your instalments and we've got an order to repossess.

RIGSBY: Oh, I see. Look, there's no need to be hasty – have another grape. I'm sure we can sort this out. Just an oversight on my part. Let me see what I've got. (*He empties purse and pockets. Hands money to Flint*)

FLINT: (*unimpressed*) Thank you, Mr Rigsby. (*Pockets money*) I'll tell you what – we'll let you keep the promotional ashtray.

RIGSBY: What!

FLINT: This isn't enough, Mr Rigsby – it barely covers my time – it certainly won't pay off the craftsmen of Evesham.

RIGSBY: But you can't do this to me.

FLINT: There's nothing you can do about it, Mr Rigsby – you haven't got a leg to stand on – which is unfortunate since we're taking the chairs.

RIGSBY: You don't understand – tonight's special. (*Confidentially*) Look, I can see you're men of the world. Well, I happen to be ... er ... entertaining a young lady down here.

Flint and Charlie exchange glances.

FLINT: Did you hear that, Charlie? Hence the subdued lighting and the seductive music. You naughty boy. (*Much elbowing and laughter*) How the other half live,

Charlie. And you were hoping to ... hey?

RIGSBY: (*sheepishly*) Yes, that's right.

FLINT: Well, you're not doing it on our springs.

RIGSBY: You rotten lot. You're sadists that's what you are.

FLINT: If you don't mind, Mr Rigsby. Charlie doesn't like that sort of talk. After all, we're only doing our job. I can't afford a drinks cabinet. I have to move the settee – get down on my hands and knees and fish around in the sideboard.

RIGSBY: But what am I going to say to her? She'll be down in a minute. She's expecting a night of unbridled luxury, not a roll on the lino.

FLINT: I do sympathise but we'll be as discreet as possible. She won't even know we're here.

RIGSBY: She'll have a bloody good idea when the furniture starts disappearing. Look, what have I done wrong? I only wanted to live now and pay later. My God! They were smarmy enough in the showroom. They said I was reflating the economy – getting the wheels of industry turning again. Well, look where it's got me. She'll never talk to me again. I'll be an object of contempt.

FLINT: Yes, you will. It doesn't bear thinking about.

RIGSBY: What if I can get the money? I do have friends here.

FLINT: Well, that's different. I mean, we're not vindictive men. I'll tell you what we'll do. We'll go outside for a smoke – give you five minutes – then if there's nothing doing, we'll start.

RIGSBY: Thanks – I appreciate that.

FLINT: That's all right. We always operate with tact and diplomacy. (*Pause*) Oh, and don't try locking the door or we'll kick the panels in. (*Stops at door*) Oh, and if the worst comes to the worst, don't worry – you'll hardly notice us. We removed a table last week – they didn't even know we'd been – and they were eating off it.

They exit followed by Rigsby.

* * *

SCENE 5: *Int. attic flat.*
Philip alone reading.
Rigsby enters breathlessly.

PHILIP: I thought you were going out, Rigsby. Your white-haired old mother will be waiting – she'll be ringing those gnarled old hands – waiting for that knock that never comes.

RIGSBY: Listen, I want some money quickly.

PHILIP: Oh, yes. What is it this time? Let me guess. I know, she needs an operation. There's only one surgeon who can perform it and he lives in Switzerland.

RIGSBY: Shut up, will you? I'm serious.

PHILIP: All right. Come on. What is it this time?

RIGSBY: They're taking my furniture away.

Philip laughs.

PHILIP: Rigsby, you can do better than that.

RIGSBY: It's true. They'll be standing it on the pavement any minute now. You know I've always had a good name around here. Do you want to see me humiliated?

PHILIP: Listen, Rigsby, I know why you want that money. You're taking Brenda out.

RIGSBY: (*starts*) Brenda! Oh my God!

Rigsby exits hurriedly.

* * *

SCENE 6: *Int. Rigsby's room.*
Brenda is sitting on the couch.
Rigsby bursts in.

RIGSBY: (*halts*) Ah, there you are.

BRENDA: (*puzzled*) Yes.

RIGSBY: Yes. You know, I've been thinking – perhaps we should go out after all.

BRENDA: What about the cat?

RIGSBY: Oh, he's made a wonderful recovery. (*Flicks cat with his foot*) Look how lively he's getting.

BRENDA: Well, I wish you'd make up your mind. First we're going out and then we're not – now we're going out again. You don't mind if I get my breath, do you?

RIGSBY: Of course. Let me get you a drink. I've got a very nice sherry. (*Pours drink*) This'll really assault your taste buds.

Brenda takes drink, looks round.

BRENDA: Where's the coffee table?

RIGSBY: What? (*Looks around in horror*) Oh, I must have put it down somewhere. Don't worry. Drink up. Then we can go out – perhaps have a walk by the canal.

BRENDA: Canal!

RIGSBY: Well, if you don't want to do that we could go have a look at that hole in the High Street – that's if they haven't filled it in.

Flint enters with great stealth, unseen by Brenda. He holds a tactful finger to his lips. Removes table lamp. Exits.

BRENDA: (*frowns*) Is it getting dark in here?

RIGSBY: Or we could go up to the by-pass – there's usually an accident this time of night. And I love a good walk don't you?

BRENDA: Is that your idea of a night out?

RIGSBY: Well, there's always plenty to see.

BRENDA: You mean it's cheap.

RIGSBY: No, I didn't mean that. But after all, the best things in life are free.

BRENDA: That's what you think.

Flint enters unseen. Silently removes drinks trolley.

RIGSBY: I hope you don't think I'm mean. But I thought you'd enjoy a walk and it is a lovely evening.

BRENDA: Yes. What do you want to do? See the Midland Bank by moonlight?

RIGSBY: What? No. Come on – have another drink.

BRENDA: The cocktail cabinet's gone!

RIGSBY: Has it? Goodness, so it has. I knew I shouldn't have oiled those wheels. (*Nervous laugh*) Probably half-way down the road by now. Should we go?

BRENDA: Do you mind if I finish my drink?

Flint and Charlie enter. Start to remove chair. Brenda sees them.

BRENDA: (*whispers*) Mr Rigsby, there are two men taking your chair away.

RIGSBY: So there are.

FLINT: Oh, excuse me, Miss. (*He removes cushion from behind Brenda*)

Brenda leaps to her feet.

BRENDA: I've had enough of this. First you want to go out – then you want to stop in – then you want to look at a hole in the road. Now they're taking your furniture away. The last of the big spenders! I'll be lucky to get a bag of crisps.

RIGSBY: No, wait.

Brenda sweeps out.

FLINT: I hope it was nothing we said, Mr Rigsby.

* * *

SCENE 7: *Int. attic flat.*
Philip reading.
Alan enters.

ALAN: (*restlessly*) I wonder what he's doing down there.

PHILIP: Alan, for heaven's sake, stop worrying.

ALAN: You haven't been down there. He's got seductive music – subdued lighting – it's like a spider's web. Poor Brenda – if only there was some way I could protect her.

PHILIP: I think Brenda can look after herself.

ALAN: There you go again.

PHILP: Well, you don't think he's having his evil way with her?

ALAN: Why not? It's the only way he knows. And Brenda doesn't realise.

PHILIP: Why don't you face facts? She realises. She knows what it's all about. Rigsby's been up here twice to borrow money. She's a gold digger.

ALAN: No, she's not.

PHILIP: Alan, be guided by me. You know I have this radar where women are concerned.

Brenda enters.

ALAN: (*surprised*) Hello, Brenda. What's the matter.

BRENDA: I'm fed up. Are you two coming across the road for a drink?

Alan glances at Philip.

ALAN: Well, I'd love to, Brenda, but I haven't got any money.

BRENDA: That's all right. I'll treat you. After all, it's only money.

ALAN: (*triumphantly*) Well, what do you think of that, Philip?

PHILIP: No definitely not. (*Smiles*) I'm going to buy you a drink, Brenda – it's the least I can do.

ALAN: What about Rigsby?

BRENDA: I don't think he'll be coming – they're taking his furniture away.

PHILIP: What!

They burst into laughter.

PHILIP: And I didn't believe him.

BRENDA: I wouldn't have minded if he hadn't tried to be so flash. I can't stand that. I'll get my coat. I could just sink a pint.

Exit Brenda.

ALAN: Did you hear that? She could sink a pint.

PHILIP: What a girl.

ALAN: What are we waiting for? (*They cross to door*) I'll go first. After all, you're radar's not so good.

They exit.

* * *

SCENE 8: *Int. Rigsby's room.*
Rigsby is sitting dolefully on couch – the only item of new furniture remaining. Alan enters in top coat. Looks around incredulously.

ALAN: Blimey! They haven't left much, have they?

RIGSBY: No – and they haven't finished yet. Where are you going?

ALAN: We're going across to the pub for a drink – with Brenda. Hey – she drinks pints.

RIGSBY: I wish I'd known. I could just go a pint. (*Eyes Alan*) But of course, I'm broke.

ALAN: (*innocently*) Are you, Rigsby?

RIGSBY: Haven't got two ha'pennies to rub together.

ALAN: That's rotten – I know how it feels.

RIGSBY: I don't suppose you could lend me 50p, Alan? All I need's a latchlifter.

ALAN: Well, I would, Rigsby, but you know how it is – if I was to lend you money friendship's going to fly straight out of the window.

RIGSBY: Why you little rotter.

ALAN: Let me give you some advice, Rigsby. 'Neither a lender nor a borrower be.'

RIGSBY: That's great, isn't it. And I'm on my beam ends – flat broke.

ALAN: Well, not flat broke, Rigsby. (*Alan rocks couch gently with his hand – chinking sound*) You know that does sound like 50p to me.

RIGSBY: If you think I'm going to grovel down there for it … I've got my pride you know. (*Alan rocks couch again*) It does sound like 50p.

Rigsby gets down on his knees. Plunges his hand deep into the cushions.

RIGSBY: Wait a minute. I've got it. It is 50p. Ouch! I've got my hand stuck – it's like a vice. Hey! Give us a pull.

ALAN: Sorry, Rigsby. I can't hang about here.

Flint and Charlie enter.

FLINT: Hello – what's this, Mr Rigsby? Now this isn't very sporting, is it? I thought you were going to take it like a man. After all, possessions aren't everything. Now come on – let go.

RIGSBY: I'm trying to. I can't let go, you puddin'.

FLINT: Can't bear to part, Charlie. Please, Rigsby – this job's dif-

ficult enough. I can't bear to see grown men cry. Let go.

RIGSBY: I can't. Help!

FLINT: Nothing for it, Charlie. He'll have to come with us.

They start to struggle over couch. Brenda and Philip enter.

PHILIP: Is he coming?

ALAN: (*grins*) No – he's giving them a hand.

They exit, leaving Rigsby struggling with Flint and Charlie.

THE END.

Series Two

EPISODE 7

Things that Go Bump in the Night

by

Eric Chappell

PART ONE

SCENE 1: *Ext. Porch. Night.*
Alan and Brenda enter. Alan is nervous whilst Brenda looks faintly bored.

BRENDA: Aren't we going in? It's cold out here.

ALAN: We'll have to watch out for Rigsby – he doesn't like it when we're late in.

BRENDA: It's only half-past ten.

ALAN: Is that the time? My word, it's just flown by, hasn't it? What a night, hey, Brenda?

BRENDA: (*without enthusiasm*) Yes.

ALAN: I thought you'd like *Dr Zhivago*. I've seen it three times. (*Pause. Clears throat*) I hope you didn't mind the kiss.

BRENDA: (*stares*) What kiss?

ALAN: (*surprised*) I kissed you on the cheek. You know – when the Cossacks were cutting up the peasants.

BRENDA: Oh, I'm sorry, Alan. I thought you'd caught me with your ice lolly.

ALAN: No – that was me.

BRENDA: Well, I was a little dis-

tracted at the time. Omar Sharif's eyes had just started to fill with tears. He was lovely.

ALAN: Yes but he was up there, Brenda. Celluloid. I was next to you.

BRENDA: (*without enthusiasm*) Yes.

ALAN: I couldn't take my eyes off you. I'll tell you this – if those streetlights hadn't been on when we came home – anything could have happened.

BRENDA: We could have cut through the churchyard.

ALAN: Ah, well, I didn't like to – not with all the deceased lying around.

BRENDA: I don't think they'd have disturbed us. Were you scared?

ALAN: No.

BRENDA: You're scared of Rigsby.

ALAN: No, I'm not.

RIGSBY: (*off*) Who's that out there?

ALAN: (*opening door*) Quick – up the stairs.

Brenda exits.

* * *

SCENE 2: *Int. Rigsby's room.*
Rigsby is peering out of door.

RIGSBY: Oh, it's you. Another five minutes and I'd have locked that door. (*Returns*) Mind the milk bottles. (*Crash*) Clumsy twit.

Alan enters indignantly with remains of empty milk bottle.

ALAN: You left them there deliberately. I'm surprised you don't have barbed wire and searchlights. It's like being in Stalag Luft 7, this is.

RIGSBY: I like to know who's prowling about.

ALAN: Well, I wish you'd stop waiting for me to come home, Rigsby. You're getting just like my mother.

RIGSBY: You should be glad I take an interest in you. (*Frowns*) You haven't been drinking, have you?

ALAN: No, I haven't. And if I had – it's got nothing to do with you. If you don't mind I would like to lead my own life.

RIGSBY: I just don't want you getting into bad company, that's all. I owe it to your parents. You've already knocked off Holy Communion and the Scouts. Where's it going to end?

ALAN: I just don't want you spying on me all the time – do you mind?

RIGSBY: (*angrily*) Who's spying? I'm not spying. If you want to be bloody secretive.

ALAN: I'm not secretive.

RIGSBY: Where have you been then?

ALAN: As a matter of fact I've been to see *Dr Zhivago*.

RIGSBY: Oh. (*Pause*) Well, what did he say?

ALAN: What?

RIGSBY: (*shakes head*) And you say you're not secretive. I didn't know there was anything wrong with you. Is it the prickly heat again?

ALAN: Rigsby – *Dr Zhivago* is a film. It's about a man's disillusionment with the Russian revolution.

RIGSBY: You didn't have to go out to see that. I've been disillusioned with it for years.

ALAN: You should have seen it, Rigsby. It was a good film. You ought to get out more.

RIGSBY: I can see all the films I want to see on the television.

ALAN: What sort of films can you see on there?

RIGSBY: Good films.

ALAN: Such as? What good films have you seen lately?

RIGSBY: Well ... recently I've seen ... *Dracula* ... *Brides of Dracula* ... *Frankenstein and the Monster—*

ALAN: (*aghast*) Is that all you've watched?

RIGSBY: No. (*Pause*) I've seen *The Mummy's Hand* as well.

ALAN: Good Heavens! Doesn't that tell you anything about yourself, Rigsby?

RIGSBY: What do you mean?

ALAN: They're all horror films.

RIGSBY: I like horror films.

ALAN: But what does it indicate? I mean, what's the state of your mind?

RIGSBY: There's nothing wrong with my mind.

ALAN: Well, you wouldn't catch me watching that sort of rubbish.

RIGSBY: Yes – and we all know why. You watch anything like that and we'd have to leave the lights on all night. You get frightened watching *Scooby Doo*.

ALAN: It doesn't frighten me, Rigsby. I just happen to find it all rather childish.

RIGSBY: Oh, yes. Well, look what happened when we watched *Psycho* – you went to the lavatory fourteen times. You hardly saw any of it.

ALAN: I saw most of it.

RIGSBY: You didn't see the murders though, did you?

ALAN: Yes, I did. I saw them through a crack in the door.

RIGSBY: I shall never forget you that night. You went to bed shaking like a leaf and clutching your panda. Mind you, one good thing – it's stopped you hanging about the bathroom.

ALAN: Well, that film ought to be a lesson to you – the murderer had a split mind – probably got it from watching too many horror films.

RIGSBY: What do you mean? Those films are very interesting – very educational.

ALAN: Oh, yes, if you want to know how to kill a vampire, or hold a black mass, or invoke the devil.

RIGSBY: As a matter of fact these films are a manifestation of the eternal struggle between good and evil – revealing the darker side of human nature.

ALAN: (*incredulously*) Where did you get that from, Rigsby?

RIGSBY: I heard it on *Film Night*.

ALAN: But, Rigsby, it's all superstition – these things just don't exist.

RIGSBY: I wouldn't be so sure.

ALAN: Have you ever met a vampire?

RIGSBY: You go down to the tax office.

ALAN: I'm being serious.

RIGSBY: Listen – anyone could be a vampire. Except for having two rather prominent choppers and sleeping in a coffin, there's nothing to distinguish him from anyone else. Of course, if you do have any suspicions, try garlic – he won't come near you.

ALAN: Neither will anyone else.

RIGSBY: And watch your jugular vein. Oh, and carry a sharp wooden stake – but not in your trouser pocket.

ALAN: All right – you can joke, but I think you half believe it, Rigsby.

RIGSBY: Why not? You take the werewolf. By day a humble bank clerk. But at night he turns rather hairy – removes his white collar and cuff-links and dashes onto the Common – you'd probably take him for an Alsatian.

ALAN: I wouldn't take him for anything. I'm a man of science. You can't expect me to believe in the supernatural.

RIGSBY: You won't cut through the churchyard though – not at night. Not with all those bodies about.

ALAN: They don't worry me. I'm a medical man – when they're dead they're dead.

RIGSBY: They are when you've finished with them. Oh, it's all right talking like this with the lights on. But when you're on the stairs – under the forty watts – it'll be different. This is an old house. Strange things can happen. There's been a lot of unhappiness here.

ALAN: I've got news for you, Rigsby – there still is.

Alan exits.

* * *

SCENE 3: *Int. landing.*
Alan enters. Pauses by Brenda's door. Looks around nervously and scuttles upstairs.

* * *

SCENE 4: *Int. attic flat.*
Philip is reading. Puts down book as Alan enters.

PHILIP: (*eagerly*) Well? How did you get on?

ALAN: All right.

PHILIP: Where did you go?

ALAN: I took her to see *Dr Zhivago*. I thought it would get her in a nice romantic mood.

PHILIP: That was good thinking. Did it work?

ALAN: Oh yes. She fell in love with Omar Sharif.

PHILIP: (*disappointed*) You mean you blew it.

ALAN: I didn't blow it. This isn't a loose ball in the penalty box, Philip. This is a woman – mysterious and complex. And I was competing with Omar Sharif. Did you know he could make tears come to his eyes just like that?

PHILIP: I think I know the feeling.

ALAN: I wouldn't have minded but it was me who was buying the chocolate and ice-cream.

PHILIP: Did you kiss her?

ALAN: Yes.

PHILIP: Where?

ALAN: In the balcony.

PHILIP: I mean, whereabouts?

ALAN: On the cheek.

PHILIP: On the cheek!

ALAN: She was eating a lolly – I wasn't keen on the flavour. Look, it wasn't easy, I had to snatch a moment after she'd finished with the ice lolly and she was struggling with the cellophane on the milk tray.

PHILIP: Well, what happened?

ALAN: There was this big sigh.

PHILIP: That could have been a sign of encouragement.

ALAN: It wasn't Brenda. It was this bloke sitting behind. He couldn't see the film. He prodded me in the shoulder blades with his pipe. Spent the rest of the night spitting bits of tobacco in my neck.

PHILIP: You blew it. After all the trouble I went to.

ALAN: I didn't. The cinema's not the right place. And where else can we go? I haven't got a car – and that's a disadvantage. I'm

the first pedestrian she's ever been with. I could see her eyebrows go up when we caught the bus. Oh, let's face it, Philip – I'm not even sure she likes me.

PHILIP: Of course she likes you. Why do you think she went out with you?

ALAN: Probably did it for a bet.

PHILIP: You've got to get more confidence, Alan. After all, she prefers you to Rigsby.

ALAN: That's not saying much. She'd prefer King Kong to Rigsby. I think he's half the trouble.

PHILIP: What do you mean?

ALAN: He keeps watching me all the time. He won't let me get near her. He's like a Red Coat at Butlins. Now he's trying to tell me the place is haunted.

PHILIP: That's just to make sure you stay in your room.

ALAN: Yes – and he keeps lecturing me on morals.

PHILIP: He's playing on your guilt complex.

ALAN: I've got nothing to be guilty about yet.

PHILIP: That's what he wants. He's playing on your psychological fears.

ALAN: Is that why he's always on about my prickly heat?

PHILIP: Precisely. He wants you to

associate prickly heat with Brenda. Well, he's not getting away with it. I'll see her again – put a good word in for you.

ALAN: What will you say?

PHILIP: I'll tell her that underneath you're a very interesting and exciting person.

ALAN: Thanks. (*Frowns*) Underneath what?

PHILIP: Your shyness. I'll tell her it's your natural modesty.

ALAN: You're right. Too much modesty – that's my trouble. Hey – and don't forget to mention my exceptional good looks.

PHILIP: I won't.

Philip exits.
Alan crosses to the mirror. Checks his appearance. There is a hollow groan from direction of stairs. Alan moves away from door. There is a second groan. Alan seizes Panda. The door opens slowly. Rigsby staggers into room. He has one hand behind his back.

ALAN: It's you, Rigsby. What's the matter?

RIGSBY: I don't know. I had this nasty turn coming up the stairs.

ALAN: You'd better sit down. I'll get you a drink.

RIGSBY: It must have been that conversation we had. They don't like it when you're frivolous about them.

ALAN: Who don't?

RIGSBY: Them. I had this strange sensation – as if I was being taken over – transformed. I still feel quite strange.

ALAN: Drink this.

Alan hands Rigsby cup. Rigsby takes hand from behind his back. He has a monster hand. Alan screeches and drops cup.

ALAN: Rigsby! Your hand.

RIGSBY: Oh, my God! I knew it. I'm being taken over.

He groans and reels out of the door. Appears a moment later wearing a hideous mask.
Alan recoils in horror.

RIGSBY: (*laughs*) You should just see yourself. (*Removes mask*) A medical man! Physician heal thyself.

ALAN: You've got a distorted sense of humour, Rigsby.

RIGSBY: It was just a little experiment. You see, when your eyes tell you one thing and your brain tells you another – you always end up believing your eyes.

ALAN: Look, I know your game, Rigsby. You're just trying to frighten me. Philip was right.

RIGSBY: I wouldn't take any notice of him. He'd have been worse than you.

ALAN: No, he wouldn't.

RIGSBY: He's riddled with super-stition. You know what happened when they first had petrol stations out there? They spent three years worshipping the pumps. He'd have gone down on his knees if he'd seen me like this.

ALAN: No, he wouldn't.

RIGSBY: He would. His hands would have started flapping – his eyes would roll – 'Oh Lordy, Lordy', he'd have gone. Hey! He's coming – you see.

Rigsby puts on hand and mask and hides behind the door.
Philip enters.
Rigsby puts monster hand on his shoulder.
Philip turns.

PHILIP: Hello, Rigsby.

Rigsby makes threatening noises.
Philip peers closer.

PHILIP: Rigsby, I'd change that soap if I were you.

Rigsby removes mask. Philip recoils in mock horror.

RIGSBY: Ah, well, of course you knew it was me, didn't you? But if I'd been some ghastly apparition – that would have been different.

ALAN: What do you mean, dif-ferent?

RIGSBY: If I'd been some dreadful mutation – some alien being.

PHILIP: You watch too many horror films, Rigsby.

ALAN: It's infantile rubbish.

RIGSBY: Hm. Of course, you've never met the Grey Lady, have you?

ALAN: (*uneasily*) What do you mean? The Grey Lady?

RIGSBY: She's supposed to haunt this place.

PHILIP: Have you seen her, Rigsby?

RIGSBY: No, I'm glad to say. Because if you do they say your days are numbered. But some-times I have noticed a sudden coldness in the room and heard the swish of her dress. I think she's supposed to be walled up somewhere.

Looks around.

ALAN: Well, it doesn't worry me.

RIGSBY: It doesn't worry me – except when I'm stripping the wallpaper.

ALAN: I don't believe you, Rigsby.

RIGSBY: All right. But I wouldn't go roaming about – not late at night. You never know. (*Turns*) Goodnight.

Reveals vampire teeth. Alan starts. Rigsby exits laughing.

PHILIP: He never stops, does he?

ALAN: Just trying to frighten us.

PHILIP: I've seen Brenda. She says why don't you go down. She's made some coffee.

ALAN: Oh, I don't know – it's getting late.

PHILIP: He has frightened you.

ALAN: It isn't that. He's watching me all the time. I'll never get to the door.

PHILIP: You know – he's very keen on ghosts. I think we ought to give him one.

ALAN: What do you mean?

Philip crosses to wardrobe and takes out long dress and bonnet.

ALAN: (*laughs*) Philip, I never knew! When do you wear these? When you're smoking your pipe?

PHILIP: (*Frowns*) It's for the Rag parade.

ALAN: I can't wait to see you in it. Why don't you slip it on?

PHILIP: No. (*Holds it up against Alan*) I was thinking of the Grey Lady.

* * *

SCENE 5: *Int. Brenda's room.*
Brenda is making coffee.
Rigsby knocks and enters.

RIGSBY: My word, Brenda – that smells good. And two cups, hey?

BRENDA: (*coldly*) Yes.

RIGSBY: Hmm. Been out this evening, Brenda?

BRENDA: Yes. Been to see *Dr Zhivago*.

RIGSBY: (*frowns*) Oh. (*Recovers*) Yes, that film's always been a favourite of mine – particularly the way it deals with a man's disillusionment with the Russian revolution.

BRENDA: So that's what it was about. I thought Omar Sharif was good.

RIGSBY: Oh, yes. She's lovely – always liked her. Brenda – I was wondering if you'd like to come down for a bite to eat? I could send out for something—

BRENDA: What – meals on wheels?

RIGSBY: (*weak laugh*) I'm glad you've got a sense of humour, Brenda. I like that. (*Glance at cups*) Alan won't be coming. He gets a little jittery this time of night. You must have noticed. He thinks the place is haunted. Keeps talking about the Grey Lady.

BRENDA: I don't like the sound of that. (*Shudders*) Ghosts.

RIGSBY: Nothing to worry about. As long as you're not on your own.

BRENDA: What was that? I thought I heard a sort of moan.

RIGSBY: (*Grins*) Have no fear – Rigsby's here.

Sound of moaning off.

BRENDA: There it goes again.

RIGSBY: (*nervously*) Yes. (*Licks lips*) Probably the cat. Touch of hard pad.

BRENDA: Hadn't you better go and see?

RIGSBY: Yes. I'll investigate. You just wait here. (*Rigsby hesitates then exits boldly*)

* * *

SCENE 6: *Int. landing.*

RIGSBY: Is that you, Vienna?

A grey figure with bonnet appears on the staiars.

RIGSBY: Oh, my God!

Rigsby dashes downstairs.

* * *

SCENE 7: *Int. Brenda's room.*
Brenda is standing petrified staring at door. Grey Lady appears. Brenda screams.

ALAN: It's all right, Brenda. It's only me.

BRENDA: Alan! What are you dressed like that for?

ALAN: I did it to frighten Rigsby.

BRENDA: (*smiles*) Well, you certainly succeeded.

ALAN: You're not angry?

BRENDA: No. (*Closes door. Puts arms around Alan. Draws back slightly at bonnet. Gently*) Well, now you're here – why don't you take your frock off?

END OF PART ONE.

PART TWO

SCENE 8: *Int. landing. Hour later.*
Rigsby enters nervously. His head moving in ninety-degree turns. He approaches Brenda's door. Hears low female laughter. Uncertain, he turns on his heel and darts upstairs.

* * *

SCENE 9: *Int. attic flat.*
Philip is reading.
Alan's bed appears to be occupied. Mound of blankets.
Rigsby enters abruptly.

PHILIP: Shush. Alan's asleep.

RIGSBY: He's lucky. I wish I was.

PHILIP: What's the matter, Rigsby? You look as if you've seen a ghost.

RIGSBY: What! Yes. (*Forced laugh*) Er … you haven't had a woman up here, have you?

PHILIP: No, Rigsby – I thought that was against the rules.

RIGSBY: It is. But I wouldn't mind this once – not if you were to tell me the truth. Biggish girl – rather old-fashioned – wearing a bonnet? Sort of distressed – moaning and ringing her hands.

PHILIP: (*shakes head*) Doesn't sound like my type, Rigsby.

RIGSBY: No, I must have been mistaken. Probably the Double Gloucester. I knew I shouldn't have had it – not this time of night.

PHILIP: If you saw a woman, Rigsby – there's bound to be some logical explanation.

RIGSBY: That's what I thought. She had this bonnet on. I suppose it could have been the Salvation Army – mind you, there was no sign of a tambourine. And there was this wailing noise.

PHILIP: It doesn't sound like the Salvation Army.

RIGSBY: I don't know – you should hear them on Sundays.

PHILIP: It was probably the wind in the chimney.

RIGSBY: Yes.

PHILIP: Where did you see her?

RIGSBY: Now wait a minute – I only thought I saw her. She was going towards Brenda's room.

PHILIP: That's it.

255

RIGSBY: (*starts*) What!

PHILIP: It was probably Brenda.

RIGSBY: It couldn't have been – I'd only just left her. I suppose we ought to go down and see if she's all right.

PHILIP: Oh, I wouldn't disturb her now. It's late.

RIGSBY: (*grins*) Scared, hey? I might have known. The old voodoo's rearing its ugly head – thought I could see the whites of your eyes. You can't eradicate a thousand years of superstition over-night. Well, I'm not afraid – you'd better leave this to me.

* * *

SCENE 10: *Int. Brenda's room.*
Alan and Brenda are embracing by the door. They separate. Alan looks dazed and disheveled.

BRENDA: (*smiles*) Don't you think you'd better go now?

ALAN: (*blinks*) What? Yes, I suppose so. Brenda, you know we ought to do this more often. It's been terrific.

BRENDA: Yes. What's showing next week?

ALAN: What?

BRENDA: At the pictures?

ALAN: The pictures? Oh yes. (*Frowns*) What did we see tonight?

BRENDA: *Dr Zhivago.*

ALAN: Yes, of course. You know I think I've gone off the pictures. (*Solemnly*) Brenda – you're terrific. (*Loosens tie*)

BRENDA: Do you feel all right?

ALAN: Yes.

BRENDA: Has your prickly heat gone now?

ALAN: Yes. I don't think I'll ever have it again. It's meeting you. You've made me feel … feel—

BRENDA: Terrific?

ALAN: Yes. You see, I've never had much confidence. When I get alone with a girl I always think she's going to do something terrible – you know, like fall asleep. You've made me feel different. You treat me like a man. Those two don't think I'm a man.

BRENDA: Don't be silly, Alan, of course you're a man. Now don't forget to put your dress on before you go.

Brenda starts to help him into dress.

* * *

SCENE 11: *Int. stairs and landing.*
Rigsby is coming down stairs slowly. Alan is coming up in dress and bonnet. They see each other and both turn on their heels.
Rigsby gives a hoarse cry.

* * *

SCENE 12: *Int. attic flat.*
Rigsby bursts in.

PHILIP: What's the matter now, Rigsby?

RIGSBY: I've seen it again!

PHILIP: Well, keep your voice down. Alan's trying to sleep.

RIGSBY: God! She's a size. She's got wild hair and feet like barges. No wonder they walled her up.

PHILIP: Come on, Rigsby. I can see we won't get any peace until we've solved this.

RIGSBY: After you.

Philip exits followed by Rigsby.

* * *

SCENE 13: *Int. Brenda's room.*
Alan enters breathlessly.

BRENDA: What's the matter?

ALAN: Rigsby's coming.

BRENDA: What are we going to do?

ALAN: I'll have to hide.

BRENDA: I thought you weren't afraid of him.

ALAN: I can't fight him in a dress, Brenda. I'd never live it down.

BRENDA: You'd better hide in the back.

Brenda hides Alan behind kitchen curtain. There is a knock on door. Brenda opens the door stifling exaggerated yawn.
Philip and Rigsby enter.
Rigsby looks around nervously.

BRENDA: What's the matter?

PHILIP: Rigsby thinks he's seen a ghost.

RIGSBY: What do you mean 'thinks'? I saw it all right. It was a woman with great big feet. You're sure she didn't come in here?

BRENDA: I haven't seen a woman in here.

RIGSBY: Well, I saw it.

BRENDA: Perhaps you're psychic.

PHILIP: (*sharply*) That's it!

RIGSBY: (*starts*) What! (*Sighs*) I wish you'd stop doing that.

PHILIP: It's the Grey Lady. She's trying to get in touch with you.

RIGSBY: Well, I wish she'd give me a ring instead of jumping out and frightening me to death.

PHILIP: You know what we ought to do? Hold a seance.

RIGSBY: (*hesitates*) I don't know. How do we do that?

PHILIP: We put the lights out and hold hands.

RIGSBY: You must be joking.

BRENDA: Well, I'm game.

RIGSBY: Well, I don't suppose it's a bad idea under the circumstances. What do we do?

PHILIP: Put the lights down. (*Switches off main light*) Now we get around the table and join hands.

They gather around the table in gloom.

BRENDA: Ooh!

RIGSBY: Oh, was that you, Brenda? Sorry.

PHILIP: Are you ready?

RIGSBY: What do we do now?

PHILIP: We'll try and get in touch with her.

BRENDA: She might manifest herself.

RIGSBY: She won't be the only one.

PHILIP: Are you there, Lady in Grey? Do you wish to speak to us? Knock once for no and twice for yes.

Two knocks.

RIGSBY: (*starts*) Which one of you did that?

PHILIP: How could we? We're holding hands. Who is it you wish to speak to?

RIGSBY: Oh God! Not me.

PHILIP: Is it Rigsby?

Two knocks.

RIGSBY: Tell her I'm out.

PHILIP: What is it you wish to say to Rigsby?

Faint crooning.

RIGSBY: What's she saying?

ALAN: (*behind curtain in sing-song*)
Roses are red
Violets are blue
Sugar is sweet
What happened to you?

RIGSBY: What's she getting at?

ALAN: I'm alone and unhappy.

RIGSBY: I'm not surprised with feet like that.

ALAN: You make me unhappy, Rigsby. You are cruel. Be kind to them.

RIGSBY: Who does she mean?

ALAN: Those dear young people. I've seen their misery. Be kind to them before it's too late, Rigsby. Give them warmth – give them affection. Money isn't everything. Don't be an old skinflint.

RIGSBY: Now wait a minute.

ALAN: I shan't rest until you do. A man was cruel to me once.

RIGSBY: You should have done something with your hair.

ALAN: Repent, Rigsby – or I shall return.

Voice fades.

RIGSBY: Oh yes. You two think you've been very clever, don't you?

BRENDA: What do you mean?

RIGSBY: Don't think I don't know what's behind that curtain. You've set this up. It's a tape recorder.

Rigsby pulls curtain aside. He sees Alan silhouetted in the gloom. He gives loud cry and dashes from the room.

* * *

SCENE 14: *Int. Rigsby's room. Next evening.*
Rigsby is alone. He is reading book of ghost stories. He hears a noise – turns head very slowly. Comes face to face with cat.

RIGSBY: God! I wish you'd stop doing that. And stop staring over my shoulder. I know you're trying to frighten me – you're just like the others. (*Pause*) Still, I think I'll leave Edgar Allan Poe for tonight. With a name like that no wonder he had the horrors. (*Puts book down*) What was that? (*Listens*) Someone outside the door – trying it on again. Well, I'll show them. (*Opens door violently*) You can cut that bloody game out! Oh. Hello, Vicar.

A middle-aged, pleasant man in clerical clothes enters the room.

VICAR: Ah, Mr Rigsby. You left a message at the Vicarage – they said it was a matter of some urgency.

RIGSBY: Yes, that's right, Vicar. I'm in need of your services.

VICAR: (*beams*) My word, Mr Rigsby, this is good news. (*Laughs*) I didn't expect to see you until the last rites. I'm delighted. Does this mean you're going to join our little congregation?

RIGSBY: Ah, well, I've never been a big church-goer.

VICAR: Yes, I had noticed, Mr Rigsby.

RIGSBY: Well, it's the old leg wound. I can't get in the pews. I'd be forced to stand during prayers.

VICAR: We wouldn't mind, Mr Rigsby.

RIGSBY: Yes, well, it's not just that. I had a nasty experience in your church. Not your fault. Vicar before you. He was a decrepit old … he was rather frail. Dropped me in the font during the christening. Never been back since – except for Remembrance Sunday. I do most of my praying walking about – have to with the leg. Still, you can be a good Christian without going to church – look at the curate.

VICAR: Er … yes. Well, what exactly did you want to see me about, Mr Rigsby?

RIGSBY: (*closes door*) I want you to do a bit of exorcising.

VICAR: I beg your pardon?

RIGSBY: You see this place is haunted.

VICAR: (*starts*) Haunted! (*Nervously*) Oh dear – I don't like the sound of that.

RIGSBY: Well, I must say – your reaction's a shade disappointing, Vicar. This could be a big opportunity for you. There'd be a lot of publicity in it. National Press. Pictures. Vicar flays evil spirit. I mean, I could have gone to the Catholics – they'd have been here like a shot.

VICAR: It's just that I'm a little nervous of that sort of thing.

RIGSBY: If you're nervous how do you think I feel? You've got no right to be nervous. If I send for an electrician I don't expect him to tell me he's terrified of electricity.

VICAR: Tell me – has anyone seen this … er … manifestation?

RIGSBY: Only me. In the room above. It's a woman in a grey dress with wild hair and large feet. I don't know why she chose me. I suppose I'm sensitive to spirits.

VICAR: (*side glance*) Yes, I had heard.

RIGSBY: (*sharply*) You don't believe me, do you?

VICAR: I didn't say that, Mr Rigsby. It's just that there must be some natural explanation.

RIGSBY: I see. Well, I hope you're not going to take this attitude on the Day of Judgement, Vicar. You'll certainly be found wanting. I know where you'll be at the last trump – under the bloody bed.

VICAR: Now there's no need to get angry, Mr Rigsby – it's just that I like to avoid too much spiritual excitement – bad for the digestion. Why don't you see the curate? He's more experienced with unquiet spirits – runs the whist drives.

RIGSBY: Him? You mean the one who's always playing cricket?

VICAR: Well, the season is over, Mr Rigsby.

RIGSBY: Yes, I suppose he'll have his pads off by now. Well, as long as he doesn't come here talking like Peter West. Hitting the devil for six and playing a straight bat.

VICAR: I'm sure he won't.

RIGSBY: I was hoping for a professional job. Perhaps even the Bishop. Looks as if all I'm getting's a vicar's runner. Well, I want the full service – place sprinkled with holy water – the lot.

VICAR: (*stiffly*) Well, we'll have to see – we aren't the National Health, Mr Rigsby. I can't make any promises.

RIGSBY: You've certainly changed your attitude. You were all smiles when you came about the organ fund.

VICAR: Well, does this apparition say anything?

RIGSBY: Yes. (*Hesitates*) She told me to be kinder to people.

VICAR: Oh. She sounds rather nice.

RIGSBY: She's not. If she's so nice why hasn't He let her in? She's not nice – she's horrible. Besides, no one could be kinder than me. I'm a fool to myself – you ask anyone.

VICAR: I simply thought it may be the voice of your conscience, Mr Rigsby.

RIGSBY: My conscience is clear, don't you worry. The point is what are you going to do about it?

VICAR: (*rises*) I'll see my curate – see what we can do. But in the meantime, remember what I said. Search your conscience, Mr Rigsby. Have we left undone things which we ought to have done?

RIGSBY: Yes. Yes. (*Bustles vicar out. Locks door*) I thought we'd get the commercial.

Rigsby crosses. Sees reflection in mirror. Starts violently.

RIGSBY: No doubt about it. I shall have to take myself in hand.

Door rattles.

RIGSBY: Who's that?

PHILIP: Philip.

Rigsby lets Philip into room.

PHILIP: Why did you lock the door?

RIGSBY: Well, you never know who's about these days.

PHILIP: Do you mean the Grey Lady?

RIGSBY: No – I don't mean the Grey Lady. She doesn't worry me. (*Anxiously*) Are you going out?

PHILIP: Yes, I'm going to post a letter. Have you got any change?

Rigsby fumbles for change.

RIGSBY: Do you have to go? I mean it's late. They'll be switching the street lights off soon. Those lorry drivers'll never see you. We don't want you to get knocked down. You should wear something light at night, Philip.

PHILIP: I'll be all right, Rigsby.

He turns to leave.

RIGSBY: Oh, Philip. In the past ... er. I may have seemed hard on you – almost cruel sometimes. But that's just my way. I'm just a rough old soldier. Underneath I'm a very affectionate person. I've always been very fond of you. (*Squeezes arm*) I want you to remember that.

PHILIP: (*stares*) I'll try to, Rigsby.

RIGSBY: Same with Alan. We've had our differences, but deep down there's a bond. Where is he by the way?

PHILIP: He's … er … asleep.

RIGSBY: He would be the lazy s— Well, of course he needs the rest. He works too hard – I've often told him.

PHILIP: Well, I'd better go.

RIGSBY: Hurry back.

Philip stares. Exits.
Rigsby hears door close. Shivers.

* * *

SCENE 15: *Int. attic flat.*
Rigsby enters quietly.
Crosses to mound of bedclothes on Alan's bed.

RIGSBY: (*gently*) Alan, old chap. Are you asleep? I just wanted to say … well … I may have said some unkind things to you in the past. Well, if I have – I'm sorry. I think you've got a lovely head of hair. And you can use that hairdryer as long as you like. Forget the electricity. I just want you to be happy here. Alan? Alan?

Rigsby pulls blanket and comes face to face with panda. He stares. Scowls thoughtfully around the room. Opens wardrobe. Discovers dress and bonnet. Evil smile crosses his face.

* * *

SCENE 16: *Int. Brenda's room. Dark. Alan and Brenda are cuddling on settee.*

BRENDA: What was that?

ALAN: What?

BRENDA: I heard a noise on the stairs.

ALAN: (*grins*) Perhaps it's the Grey Lady.

BRENDA: Alan – the door!

Brenda switches on standard lamp as door opens.
The vicar appears around the door followed by eager young curate with camera.

VICAR: Ah. Do excuse me. We're looking for Mr Rigsby.

BRENDA: (*pulls down jumper*) Well, he's not here.

CURATE: Ah. (*To Alan*) Is this the room where she reveals herself?

BRENDA: (*alarmed*) What?

CURATE: The Grey Lady?

ALAN: (*straightens tie*) Oh. Yes.

CURATE: I thought so. (*To vicar*) Can't you sense the air of excitement?

VICAR: Steady, Gordon. Don't let's get carried away.

CURATE: I suppose you two were sitting here in the dark waiting to see what would develop?

Alan and Brenda look at each other.
Vicar winces.

ALAN: Yes – that's right.

CURATE: Splendid. Well, I'd like to take a few pictures. I've got my flash. You don't mind?

BRENDA: No.

CURATE: Good. We're hoping to get something really interesting for the parish magazine. Make a change from the over-sixties.

BRENDA: I'm sure it would.

VICAR: Now, Gordon – just don't get over-excited.

CURATE: Should we put the lights off again? Then we can all get stuck in.

VICAR: Gordon.

Curate switches off light.

CURATE: I'm sure we're going to get a manifestation.

VICAR: You're just building yourself up to another big disap-pointment.

ALAN: I think he's right, Gordon.

CURATE: I can hear something. Listen. She's coming.

Sound of moaning. Rigsby enters room in dress and bonnet.
Flash of camera. Screams.

RIGSBY: What the hell!

Vicar switches the light on.

VICAR: Mr Rigsby! It's you!

CURATE: Oh gosh! We're on a sticky wicket.

RIGSBY: Now wait a minute, Vicar. I can explain.

VICAR: Please don't bother.

CURATE: The things people do to draw attention to themselves.

RIGSBY: I said I can explain.

CURATE: Don't bother, Mr Rigsby – you've been clean bowled.

Vicar and curate exit.
Rigsby follows.

* * *

SCENE 17: *Int. landing.*

RIGSBY: Listen, they'll tell you.

Turns back. Alan closes the door. He shouts down the stairs.

RIGSBY: That's right. Cast the first stone. Typical Church of England. Well, I don't like your sermons. They're rubbish!

Philip enters from stairs. He looks hard at Rigsby.
Rigsby, forgetting he's in drag, fishes for cigarette still grumbling.

RIGSBY: I wouldn't mind but they

only work one day a week. Got a light?

Philip lights Rigsby's cigarette.

PHILIP: You know something, Rigsby?

RIGSBY: What?

PHILIP: We just can't go on meeting like this.

Rigsby realises how he looks.

RIGSBY: Hey! Now watch it.

Follows Philip upstairs protesting.

THE END.

Series Two

CHRISTMAS SPECIAL

For the Man Who Has Everything
by
Eric Chappell

PART ONE

SCENE 1: *Int. Rigsby's room Boxing Day. Afternoon.*

Rigsby is alone except for Vienna. He is sitting drinking, with his feet on the table. There are the remains of a meal. He sighs and looks around at the forlorn decorations. Listens.

RIGSBY: Have you noticed something Vienna? Not a sound – we're all alone. (*Sighs*) No doubt about it – there's been a certain decline in my popularity this year. Boxing Day and not one invitation to share the flowing bowl – not one request for my company around the piano. (*Picks up cracker*) I can't even find anyone to pull my cracker. (*Prods cat with cracker*) You're not bothered, are you? No Christmas spirit that's your trouble. It's just another day as far as you're concerned. Another day, another meal, another hole in the flower bed. (*Sound of bottles*) I suppose I could ask the milkman. (*Hesitates*) No – perhaps not. There is that thorny question of his Christmas box. (*Crouches by window*) Better pretend I'm not in.

The door opens. Fred the milkman enters. About thirty, good-looking, rakish, hat at jaunty angle. He sees Rigsby crouching by window. He approaches from behind and rattles bottles.

FRED: Merry Christmas, Mr Rigsby.

RIGSBY: (*starts*) What!

FRED: I just popped in to wish you the compliments of the season.

RIGSBY: Oh yes.

FRED: I thought you might have missed me this week.

RIGSBY: That would have been difficult – the way you've been rattling those milk bottles.

FRED: Oh, I hope I didn't disturb you. (*Puts milk down*) Well, here we are.

RIGSBY: Hey! Wait a minute. Where's my double cream?

FRED: We've run out. There's been a big demand this Christmas.

RIGSBY: Well, what am I supposed to do? What am I going to have on my pineapple chunks?

FRED: Ah, I'm sorry about that.

RIGSBY: You're not sorry, It's because you haven't had the Christmas box, isn't it? (*Holds up bottles*) I suppose this is what they call the milkman's revenge – two bottles of dirty water.

FRED: I said I'm sorry.

RIGSBY: My God! I don't ask much from life but I thought I could depend on my double cream.

FRED: Well, it's the first time. I've never let you down before.

RIGSBY: What do you mean? We've never had the right milk since you came back from the Costa Brava. Flashing your suntan and singing *Viva España* at six in the morning. I nearly complained to the dairy.

FRED: Oh, I see. I suppose you think milkmen shouldn't go to the Costa Brava?

RIGSBY: No, they shouldn't. It gives them ideas. They get an attack of the *mañanas* and start forgetting the double cream. You know what you've become, don't you? A lotus eater.

FRED: I've never touched the stuff.

RIGSBY: I'm not talking about food, mate. I mean you've become what they call a pleasure seeker. That's why your van's been standing outside Mrs Bailey's all morning.

FRED: What are you getting at?

RIGSBY: It's always there. The council have been waiting three months to sweep that gutter.

FRED: I haven't had any complaints.

RIGSBY: I'm sure you haven't – not from Mrs Bailey. I notice she's been getting her curlers out very early these mornings.

FRED: Look, I don't know what you're suggesting

RIGSBY: I'm suggesting that a suntan isn't the only thing you picked up in Spain. You've acquired some very nasty Latin habits, in fact you've become the fastest milkman this side of Madrid.

FRED: (*shakes head*) I should have known better. I shouldn't have come in. I knew I'd get insulted. No wonder you're spending Christmas on your own, Rigsby. No wonder there aren't any Christmas cards.

RIGSBY: You mind your own business. As a matter of fact I prefer spending Christmas alone. I've already spurned a number of invitations. I happen to believe this is a religious festival. I prefer to spend it in quiet contemplation – not guzzling myself stupid.

FRED: Don't give me that. You're on your own because they won't let you in the British Legion – not after poking that stripper with a stick of celery.

RIGSBY: Listen, I don't want to go to the British Legion. I'm quite happy here – away from all the greed and hypocrisy. Christmas is too commercial these days.

FRED: Not around here it's not.

RIGSBY: All right. I suppose I'd better give you something – you'll only say I'm mean.

Hands Fred a coin.

FRED: Thanks. (*Stares at coin*) Are you sure you can afford it?

RIGSBY: Well, if you feel insulted you can give it back.

FRED: Oh no. I'm keeping this. I'll put it on my watch chain.

RIGSBY; Good idea – perhaps it'll help you to remember the double cream.

FRED: Merry Christmas ... Scrooge.

Fred exits.

RIGSBY: (*shouts*) Same to you, Speedy Gonzales. (*Shakes head*) I don't know what they're coming to these days. No double cream, Vienna. (*Meow*) No use working your claws now – you should have pounced on him. Still, at least he was company. I'm beginning to jump at the sound of my own voice. And that mistletoe was a waste of money. I can't see Sophia Loren popping in for a hot mince pie and a sherry at this late stage. I think I'll put my feet up.

Gwen, postwoman, attractive and pleasant, around forty, puts her head around the door. Enters.

GWEN: Mr Rigsby?

RIGSBY: Yes – that's right.

GWEN: I simply had to pop in with this. (*Excitedly*) I think it's a Christmas card.

RIGSBY: (*stares*) What's so unusual about that? After all, it is Christmas.

GWEN: Yes but—

RIGSBY: I'll just put it with all the others that have deluged upon me this festive season.

They both look around, there are no cards to be seen.

GWEN: (*Gently*) There aren't any cards, are there? You see I pass this house everyday. I couldn't help noticing. I've seen your face pressed against the window and I've longed to bring you a card. I was so delighted when this one turned up.

RIGSBY: (*coldly*) Have you been drinking?

GWEN: No – certainly not.

RIGSBY: Only it is unusual to get a delivery by hand these days. I thought perhaps you couldn't find the letter box.

GWEN: I don't drink, Mr Rigsby – not when I'm riding my bicycle.

RIGSBY: Well, it is Boxing Day – I thought you might have taken the odd stirrup cup – and your manner is a little strange.

GWEN: (*stiffly*) I'm sorry – I didn't mean to intrude.

RIGSBY: As a matter of fact, there's a perfectly logical explanation why I haven't had any Christmas cards. I told everyone I was spending Christmas with my brother – they've probably sent the cards there.

GWEN: But why did you tell them that?

RIGSBY: Because I didn't want anyone coming here. I hate Christmas. (*Hastily removes cracker*) I prefer to spend it on my own.

GWEN: (*doubtfully*) Well, I'm surprised your brother didn't send the cards on.

RIGSBY: You don't know my brother. He's probably working on them with an ink rubber right now. He'll use them next year. It was the same when he was at home. He'd have the silver paper off your tangerines before you could say knife.

GWEN: And so you're all alone. What about your tenants?

RIGSBY: They're all away for Christmas – and good riddance. I don't want them here – steaming the place out with their Christmas puddings. Besides, they're not bothered about me – they haven't given me a second thought.

GWEN: I think that's very sad.

RIGSBY: Do you? (*Gazes from Gwen to the mistletoe*) Perhaps you're right. I hadn't thought about it like that. You know, I can see you've got a very sweet nature. What's your name?

GWEN: Gwen.

RIGSBY: That's a nice name. Why don't you have a drink, Gwen?

GWEN: Well, I shouldn't really. I am on duty.

RIGSBY: Come on – the Postmaster General won't mind. (*Pours drink*)

GWEN: Thank you.

RIGSBY: (*idly*) Are you married, Gwen?

GWEN: (*surprised*) No.

RIGSBY: No – I suppose you've never found the time. Out in all weathers fighting your way through snow drifts. Mind you, it's done wonders for your complexion – certainly brought the roses to your cheeks.

GWEN: Why, thank you, Mr Rigsby.

RIGSBY: (*looks up*) Goodness me!

GWEN: What?

RIGSBY: We're under the mistletoe.

GWEN: (*nervously*) Are we?

RIGSBY: Isn't that a coincidence? Well, we can't waste an opportunity like this, can we? It wouldn't be right. You can't quarrel with fate—

GWEN: But Mr Rigsby – I'm in uniform.

RIGSBY: I don't mind. It's not as if you're a policewoman. I wouldn't fancy that – their feet are too big anyway. No – it only serves to make you more provocative, Gwen.

GWEN: (*firmly*) No, Mr Rigsby, please. You're tampering with the Royal Mail – that's a criminal offence.

RIGSBY: (*draws back*) I see, it's like that, is it?

GWEN: (*apologetically*) I am on duty.

RIGSBY: Of course. Well, if you don't mind I'd like to open my correspondence.

GWEN: Yes. (*Pause*) I'm sorry.

RIGSBY: No skin off my nose. Could have been your lucky day, that's all.

GWEN: (*hesitates by door*) Merry Christmas, Mr Rigsby.

Rigsby gives her a sour look.
Gwen exits.
Rigsby opens card.

RIGSBY: One miserable, solitary card. (*Reads*) 'All the best, Rigsby. Happy Christmas and a … (*peers*) and a prosperous New Year.' (*Shakes head*) No doubt about it – my writing's getting worse!

* * *

SCENE 2: *Int. Brenda's room.*
Alan and Brenda enter with suit-cases.

ALAN: (*forced cheerfulness*) Well here we are, Brenda. Alone at last.

BRENDA: What about Rigsby?

ALAN: He's spending Christmas at his brother's. (*Laughs*) Can you imagine those two together? Heating up pennies for the carol singers, setting the dogs on the Salvation Army, helping some poor needy traveller to a bunch of fives. What a Christmas!

BRENDA: Well, what about our Christmas? That wasn't so hot.

ALAN: What do you mean, Brenda?

BRENDA: I spent most of it rolling balls of wool. Your mother doesn't like me, does she?

ALAN: Of course she does. She's just got to get used to you that's all.

BRENDA: Get used to me! You make me sound like greasy food.

ALAN: I didn't mean it like that. I mean she's a bit old fashioned. She's not used to see-through blouses and eye shadow.

BRENDA: So that's it. I'm not good enough. I wondered why she sat me behind that pillar at the carol service. She's ashamed of me.

ALAN: No, she's not.

BRENDA: I'm just as good as she is – even if I don't bottle my own fruit.

ALAN: Of course you are. But you know what mothers are like.

BRENDA: I know what your mother's like. She spoils you.

ALAN: I wouldn't say that, Brenda.

BRENDA: Then why does she blow on your potatoes?

ALAN: She doesn't – well, only when they're hot.

BRENDA: You're going to get a shock when you get married.

ALAN: That's different. I wouldn't expect you to blow on my potatoes, Brenda. The trouble is she's a little bit jealous.

BRENDA: Yes – I suppose that's why she looped all that wool around my hands – in case I made a lightning attack on you.

ALAN: Well, there's no one to disturb us now, Brenda. We're on our own. Why don't you slip into something comfortable?

BRENDA: You must be joking. It's freezing in here. I think I'll go and have a bath and get warm.

ALAN: That's a good idea. Do you want me to bring my loofah?

BRENDA: No thanks.

ALAN: All right, I'll tell you what. You have a bath – I'll go and borrow Rigsby's electric fire – warm the room up a bit.

BRENDA: Will it be all right?

ALAN: Of course, I've told you –

he's at his brother's. I wouldn't have brought you back if he'd been here. He puts up this mistletoe at Christmas and sits around it like a praying mantis. No one's safe.

BRENDA: Well, I'll get my bath.

Brenda exits.

ALAN: (*picks up bath salts etc, sniffs*) Devon violets. I'll bring your bath salts in a minute. I can see we're all set for an undisturbed night of bliss.

Alan exits.

* * *

SCENE 3: *Int. Rigsby's room.*
Alan enters whistling cheerfully.
He crosses. Notices remnants of meal. Stops. Rigsby enters from bedroom.

ALAN: Rigsby!

RIGSBY: Who did you expect – the ghost of Christmas past?

ALAN: I thought you were at your brother's?

RIGSBY: Well, I'm not.

ALAN: You mean you're all on your own?

RIGSBY: That's right.

ALAN: At Christmas?

RIGSBY: What's that got to do with it? It's the same as any other time – except everyone's on the scrounge. I've just had the milkman – then it'll be the newspaper boy. Mind you, he's in for a shock. Do you know what he's written on that front gate? 'Martin Borman lives here.' He won't get anything from me.

Alan glances anxiously upwards.

ALAN: Well, if you go on like this, Rigsby, they will think Martin Borman lives here. You're becoming a recluse. Why don't you go out and get some fresh air? Go and watch United. I hear they're playing four-two-four this afternoon.

RIGSBY: Four-two-four! You must be joking. This is Boxing Day. They've probably been supping since dinner time. They won't be playing four-two-four – there'll be ten of them running around under a cloud of brandy fumes. The only one in position'll be the goalie and he'll be clinging to the upright.

ALAN: Well, you ought to be doing something.

RIGSBY: Just because it's Christmas. I keep telling you, it's one big fiddle. I don't believe in it.

ALAN: Well, if you don't believe in it why have you got the mistletoe?

RIGSBY: Well, it's tradition, isn't it? Old habits die hard.

ALAN: You're telling me. (*Discovers*

cracker) You've even got a cracker.

RIGSBY: Yes, well, I happened to find it lying around, that's all.

ALAN: Hey, should we pull it, Rigsby?

RIGSBY: (*shrugs*) If you want to – I don't mind.

Alan and Rigsby pull at the cracker. They both turn heads away apprehensively.

ALAN: I hate it when they go bang.

RIGSBY: Beginning to tense up, hey? I can see you've never been under fire. (*Loud crack. Rigsby staggers back*) Oh my God!

ALAN: What about you then, Rigsby?

RIGSBY: That's different – that was battle fatigue. (*Enviously*) I see you've got the big end then?

ALAN: Yes.

RIGSBY: What have you got – the usual Hong Kong rubbish?

ALAN: It's a compass.

RIGSBY: Well, you won't need that. You know your way around here. (*Pockets compass*)

ALAN: (*protests*) Hey!

RIGSBY: Well, it's my cracker. You can have the paper hat.

ALAN: I don't want the paper hat.

RIGSBY: Oh dear – what's the matter?

ALAN: Nothing.

RIGSBY: Nothing! Your lower lip's dropping. All right – you can have the plastic ink blot and this – you have to get these little balls into these holes.

ALAN: No – it doesn't matter.

RIGSBY: My God! Christmas and he's got the sulks!

ALAN: No, I haven't. I might have known, Rigsby. You don't change – even at Christmas.

RIGSBY: Then why did you come down? (*Frowns*) That's a point – why did you come down? You thought I was away.

ALAN: Well, I just came in to—

RIGSBY: To what?

ALAN: To leave you your present.

RIGSBY: Present. (*Stares*) You've bought me a present?

ALAN: Yes.

RIGSBY: Well, where is it?

Alan feels in his pockets.

ALAN: Here it is, Rigsby.

RIGSBY: (*stares*) Bath salts?

ALAN: Yes.

RIGSBY: Talcum powder?

ALAN: Devon violets.

RIGSBY: (*threateningly*) Are you trying to be funny?

ALAN: No. I know it's not much but it's the thought that counts.

RIGSBY: It's the thought that worries me. Are you suggesting that I'm lacking in personal freshness?

ALAN: Certainly not. You have a bath every Friday night – I know that.

RIGSBY: Yes, every Friday night – whether I want one or not.

ALAN: Well, I didn't know you were going to take that attitude – I can see I shouldn't have bothered.

RIGSBY: (*hesitates*) No, I'm sorry, it's me. It's been a long time since anybody … took me by surprise, that's all. Have a mince pie.

ALAN: Thanks.

RIGSBY: Have a drink. You know, you're right – it's no fun spending Christmas on your own. I realised that yesterday when I finished my dinner. (*Picks up wishbone*) There was no one to pull the wishbone with. I had to pull it by myself.

ALAN: Well, at least you got the wish, Rigsby.

RIGSBY: But it didn't come true though, did it. Unless you've seen a nubile young woman in a flimsy negligee floating around. Hey?

Rigsby laughs.
Brenda enters in negligee.

BRENDA: How long are you – Oh – Sorry!

Brenda dashes out.
Rigsby stares from her to the wishbone.

END OF PART ONE.

PART TWO

SCENE 4: *Int. Rigsby's room.*
A few minutes later. Alan is fin-
ishing his drink. Rigsby is brushing
his hair. He winks at Alan.

ALAN: What are you looking so
pleased about, Rigsby?

RIGSBY: (*grins*) Nothing – it's just
that I'm getting the Christmas
spirit, that's all.

ALAN: Now wait a minute – you're
not going up there?

RIGSBY: Why not? It's what I wished
for, isn't it? (*Examines wishbone*)
You know, it's never worked
before – must be all those hormones they've been feeding them
on.

ALAN: It was just a coincidence,
Rigsby. You don't think Father
Christmas sent her, do you?

RIGSBY: Well, I did want something
warm for the winter and it certainly beats string-backed gloves
or a chunky sweater—

ALAN: Listen, Rigsby, Brenda
simply decided to come back
early – she hasn't stepped off the
train from Toy Town.

RIGSBY: Yes but why did she come

back early? Because she's been
missing me.

ALAN: Missing you!

RIGSBY: There's something you
don't know. I asked her to spend
Christmas with me.

ALAN: What!

RIGSBY: Well, I could see she was
attracted to the idea but she
couldn't manage it – had to
spend Christmas with these
dreary people in the country.
Well, you can see what's happened. She's missed the
excitement. I have this effect on
women – it's the old animal mag-
netism.

ALAN: Well, the old animal mag-
netism hasn't done you much
good up to now, Rigsby.

RIGSBY: Ah, but this is different.
You see Christmas is a time when
a woman needs a man. It's a very
emotional occasion – they give
you cigarette lighters with your
initials on and sit staring into the
fire and breathing heavy. It's a
time when they lower their
defences. Just like VJ night.

ALAN: Was it like that on VJ night,
Rigsby?

275

RIGSBY: Oh yes. It wasn't only Japan who surrendered that night. There was dancing in the streets. Fireworks erupting against the night sky. The Free World was celebrating the Victory for Democracy.

ALAN: Hey – how did you get on, Rigsby?

RIGSBY: (*frowns*) Not too good. I stood too close to the fireworks – got a rocket up my battle dress. Spent most of the night being treated for first-degree burns.

ALAN: You're not very lucky where women are concerned, are you, Rigsby?

RIGSBY: Oh, I don't know. She did come down in a negligee – and it wasn't to borrow a loaf of bread. She expected to find me alone, mate. (*Pause*) Besides, she promised me a kiss at Christmas.

ALAN: When was that?

RIGSBY: When I unblocked her drains.

ALAN: That was in July!

RIGSBY: What's that got to do with it? A promise is a promise. And she hasn't forgotten, I can tell. I think I'll invite her down for a few drinks – promote the festive spirit – then get her under the mistletoe.

ALAN: What about me?

RIGSBY: You can blow up a few balloons.

Exit Rigsby.

* * *

SCENE 5: *Int. Brenda's room.*
Brenda is finishing dressing. Rigsby enters. Coughs discreetly.

RIGSBY: Did you want to see me, Brenda?

BRENDA: Oh yes. I just looked in to see what sort of a Christmas you'd had, Rigsby.

RIGSBY: (*sighs*) Don't talk to me about Christmas, Brenda. I was all on my own – except for the cat – and I think he's got the mange.

BRENDA: I thought you were staying at your brother's?

RIGSBY: No. That's what I told everyone but it was just pride really. He didn't want me. We had a row over a drumstick last year.

BRENDA: Over a drumstick – wasn't that a bit trivial?

RIGSBY: He didn't think so – I hit him with it. So you see nobody wanted me this year. Peace on earth goodwill towards men – well, there's been very little goodwill towards me I can tell you.

Brenda puts a friendly arm on his shoulder.

BRENDA: I'm sorry, Rigsby.

RIGSBY: That's all right, Brenda. I suppose what I really missed was the warmth of female companionship. That came to me on Christmas Day. I was sitting there all alone and I realised there was no one to crack my nuts for. No joy in getting one out whole if there's no female palm to drop it in, Brenda.

BRENDA: No, I suppose not.

RIGSBY: Not that anyone cares.

BRENDA: I care, Rigsby.

RIGSBY: Do you, Brenda? You would – you're a nice girl. I was wondering if you'd like to come down for a drink?

BRENDA: I'd love to, Rigsby.

RIGSBY: Good. You know, I've always tried to be more than just a landlord to you.

BRENDA: Yes, I know. I haven't forgotten the way you unblocked my drains.

RIGSBY: Ah, I wondered if you'd remember that. I know you were very grateful at the time.

BRENDA: Yes, and just to show you how grateful I am – I've got something for you.

RIGSBY: Oh yes – will I like it?

BRENDA: I hope so.

RIGSBY: I think I know what it is. I knew you hadn't forgotten.

BRENDA: Shut your eyes.

RIGSBY: If you insist. (*Shuts eyes*) I didn't know you were shy.

Brenda holds a packet under his nose. Rigsby sniffs. Opens his eyes.

RIGSBY: Bath salts!

BRENDA: Yes – I didn't know what to get – then I thought of bath salts.

RIGSBY: Did you?

BRENDA: Devon Violets.

RIGSBY: Not you as well.

BRENDA: Don't you like them?

RIGSBY: Oh, yes – very nice. Well, I'll see you later. Brenda.

Rigsby exits crushed.

* * *

SCENE 6: *Int. stairs.*
Rigsby sits down on stairs with a sigh. Examines bath salts. Looks around cautiously and sniffs inside cardigan.

* * *

SCENE 7: *Int. Rigsby's room.*
Alan is trying to blow up balloons. Philip enters cautiously. Looks around.

ALAN: (*surprised*) Hello, Philip.

PHILIP: Is he back?

ALAN: He never went away.

PHILIP: Oh no.

ALAN: I thought you were staying with friends?

PHILIP: I thought he was staying with friends. That's why I came back early. I've arranged to meet this girl here.

ALAN: (*grins*) Hey – you mean you were planning a dirty weekend?

PHILIP: I wish you wouldn't use that phrase, Alan.

ALAN: Sorry, I just assumed—

PHILIP: Well, don't. I have a great regard for this girl. Lucy and I are very fond of each other. I respect her. (*Pause*) Mind you, if our feelings do prove too strong for us—

ALAN: Then you'll have a dirty weekend.

PHILIP: Yes.

ALAN: You're lucky. Brenda and I've been home for Christmas. (*Shakes head*) My parents. Their idea of a dirty weekend is cleaning out the coal bunker.

PHILIP: (*worried*) The trouble is she hasn't booked in anywhere and I promised her that vacant room.

ALAN: Rigsby won't like that.

PHILIP: I don't know – perhaps if I asked him. After all, it is Christmas.

ALAN: What's that got to do with it?

PHILIP: Look, two thousand years ago Jesus was born in a stable because there was no room at the inn. Surely he'll think about that.

ALAN: She's not having a baby is she?

PHILIP: No!

ALAN: Philip, if Rigsby had been the landlord then they wouldn't have even got the stable. You know what it says on that front gate? 'Martin Borman lives here.' And I'm beginning to believe it.

PHILIP: We'll see. Where is he now?

ALAN: He's gone to see Brenda. He wants to get her under the mistletoe.

PHILIP: Do you think he'll succeed?

ALAN: No – he's not very lucky with women. If Rigsby played Blind Man's Buff in a harem he'd get the eunuch. He'll be even more miserable when he gets back.

PHILIP: Never mind – this should mellow him.

Philip produces bottle.

ALAN: What's that?

PHILIP: A present for Rigsby. The wine of my country.

ALAN: You mean the old jungle juice?

PHILIP: Yes. My father sent me six bottles.

ALAN: Is it very strong?

PHILIP: Of course it's strong. They drink this before they undergo the most painful body decorations.

ALAN: I see, it paralyses the nerves.

PHILIP: No, it burns the throat so much they can't cry out – but you feel great afterwards. (Puts bottle down. Looks at watch) Is that the time. She'll be here soon – I'd better go and meet her.

Exit Philip.

* * *

SCENE 8: *Int. hall and stairs.*
Philip is about to put on coat. He hears sound from stairs. Crosses. Finds Rigsby on stairs nursing Vienna.

RIGSBY: I don't know – what a Christmas.

PHILIP: Hello, Rigsby.

RIGSBY: Oh, you're back, are you?

Philip sits down beside him.

PHILIP: What's the matter, Rigsby? You look fed up.

RIGSBY: You'd look fed up if you'd spent Christmas on your own. (*Strokes cat*) He's all I've got now – and he doesn't like me.

PHILIP: Of course he likes you.

RIGSBY: He doesn't. I can feel his claws through my flannels right now. Just because I didn't get the double cream. (*Stares moodily at cat*) If I was six inches high do you know what he'd do? He'd eat me. Mind you, that would suit you a lot, wouldn't it? No one cares about me.

PHILIP: Yes we do, Rigsby – we're very fond of you.

RIGSBY: No you're not.

PHILIP: I've brought you a present.

RIGSBY: I don't care … Have you?

PHILIP: Yes.

RIGSBY: (*frowns*) It's not bath salts, is it?

PHILIP: No.

RIGSBY: Good. Only some people have been dropping broad hints about my personal freshness around here.

PHILIP: (*sniffs*) You've got nothing to worry about there, Rigsby. You have the faintest aroma of Devon Violets.

RIGSBY: Have I? How strange.

* * *

SCENE 9: *Int. Rigsby's room.*
Alan is blowing up balloons. Knock on the door. Lucy, an attractive black girl, enters wearing striking African robes. Alan lets go of balloon in surprise and it whistles away.

LUCY: Hello – I was looking for Philip.

ALAN: Oh no!

LUCY: I beg your pardon?

ALAN: You must be Lucy.

LUCY: Yes.

ALAN: I didn't know you were – I didn't know you were … coming so early. I'm Alan.

LUCY: I thought so. Philip often talks about you.

ALAN: (*pleased*) Does he? What does he say?

LUCY: He says you wear curlers in bed.

ALAN: Oh.

LUCY: What are you doing?

ALAN: Blowing up balloons. I don't think I've got the puff really – I keep getting a lung full of carbon dioxide.

LUCY: Then why do you do it?

ALAN: I don't know – it's an old English custom. I don't suppose you get this sort of thing in Africa.

LUCY: I wouldn't know – I come from Northampton.

ALAN: Oh, I didn't know.

LUCY: Has Philip managed to get the room?

ALAN: Ah – not yet. He's got to see Rigsby.

LUCY: He said it would be all right.

ALAN: Did he? Well, Rigsby can be a bit odd. I wouldn't raise your hopes.

LUCY: Why not?

ALAN: Well, Rigsby doesn't like – he's not very keen on—

LUCY: On what?

ALAN: On people from Northampton. Excuse me – I'd better find Philip.

Alan exits hurriedly.

* * *

SCENE 10: *Int. hall.*
Alan exits through front door. Rigsby and Philip enter from stairs.

RIGSBY: Well, where is it?

PHILIP: What?

RIGSBY: My present.

PHILIP: Oh, I left it in your room, Rigsby.

RIGSBY: I'd better get in there before he gets his hands on it.

Rigsby enters his room.

* * *

SCENE 11: *Int. Rigsby's room.*
Rigsby enters. He sees Lucy. Gapes. Exits hurriedly.

* * *

SCENE 12: *Int. hall.*
Rigsby enters. Abruptly closes his door. He blows out his cheeks. Philip pauses in act of putting on coat. Stares curiously.

PHILIP: What's the matter, Rigsby?

RIGSBY: I don't know what to say. I'm overwhelmed.

PHILIP: It's nothing, Rigsby.

RIGSBY: It may be nothing to you, but it means a lot to me.

PHILIP: Well, they say it's the thought that counts.

RIGSBY: Well, it's a beautiful thought, that is. (*Hesitates*) Are you sure you won't regret it?

PHILIP: Oh no – my father sent me half a dozen.

RIGSBY: (*shocked*) You haven't got them here, have you?

PHILIP: No, I shared them with my friends over Christmas. I found they helped to get the party going.

RIGSBY: I'm not surprised.

PHILIP: Oh yes, and a word of warning. They must be kept at room temperature – they go off in the cold.

RIGSBY: I can understand that – coming from the tropics.

PHILIP: You'll probably find it a bit fiery to start with but you'll soon get used to it. And you'll feel great afterwards.

RIGSBY: I think I'd better get back.

Rigsby exits to his room.

* * *

SCENE 13: *Int. Rigsby's room.*
Rigsby enters. He gives Lucy a faintly simpering smile.

RIGSBY: Hello.

LUCY: Hello.

RIGSBY: Is it warm enough for you? I can't put another bar on—

LUCY: No – that's perfectly all right. Er ... have you seen Philip?

RIGSBY: Yes. He's put me in the picture. Would you like a drink?

LUCY: No, thank you.

RIGSBY: Ah, against your religion.

LUCY: What?

RIGSBY: I must say you speak very good English.

LUCY: Why shouldn't I?

RIGSBY: That's true. After all, the English language is our legacy to the world. You speak it like a native – well, when I say native I don't mean ... You'll have to excuse me – only your ideas of hospitality are a bit different to ours. (*Confidentially*) You'll find things pretty easy around here.

LUCY: Will I?

RIGSBY: Oh yes. You won't have to walk miles with a pot on your head. Water straight out of a tap – see?

LUCY: (*sarcastically*) Isn't that wonderful?

RIGSBY: Just another example of the whiteman's ingenuity. Same with washing – you won't have to heave it down to the river – we've got a launderette just around the corner.

LUCY: You mean I won't have to pound away on those smooth stones anymore.

RIGSBY: No – besides, my drip dries wouldn't stand it.

LUCY: Your drip dries?

RIGSBY: I think you'll like it here. You'll have a room of your own. And of course I shall treat you as an equal.

LUCY: I appreciate that.

RIGSBY: No need to call me Bwana.

LUCY: What!

RIGSBY: We can be quite informal.

LUCY: How informal?

RIGSBY: Well, you won't have to walk ten paces behind me when we go down to Tescos. That's like your market place – rich in colour and echoing with the sound of many tongues.

LUCY: Mr Rigsby, I have no intention of going down to Tescos with you. I intend to lead my own life.

RIGSBY: (*sighs*) Just my luck … Six of them and I get the shop steward. Look, you won't be a beast of burden. I'll carry the baskets. We've got a different attitude. I shan't lie around decorating my body while you do all the work. It's not in my nature. And my needs are very simple.

LUCY: I'm sure they are. (*She moves to a safe distance*)

RIGSBY: (*sighs*) I don't know – I always thought you were supposed to be submissive – averting your gaze and peering shyly around the palms.

LUCY: You'll find there's nothing submissive about me, Mr Rigsby.

RIGSBY: Ah, I know what it is – you're homesick. That's understandable. But you'll soon settle in. You see, we're not so different. Oh, we may appear sophisticated but underneath we have the same strange beliefs and customs. Take that mistletoe – the sacred bough. Know what that is? That's our fertility symbol.

LUCY: Oh yes.

RIGSBY: Yes. That's been placed there by the Arch Druid. Now the custom is that the maidens of the village gather under it and are kissed by the Elder.

LUCY: Who's the Elder?

RIGSBY: I am.

LUCY: I thought you might be. And then what happens?

RIGSBY: We get a good harvest next year.

Rigsby moves closer.
Brenda enters.

BRENDA: Hello, Rigsby. (*Sees Lucy*) Oh, sorry.

RIGSBY: What do you want?

BRENDA: You asked me down for a drink.

RIGSBY: Oh yes. Well, I'm busy at the moment. Could you come back? I might be able to squeeze you in later.

BRENDA: Aren't you going to introduce us, Rigsby.

LUCY: I'm Lucy – I'm a friend of Philip's.

BRENDA: I'm Brenda – I live upstairs.

LUCY: Hello.

RIGSBY: Well, now you've got that over—

Philip and Alan enter.

PHILIP: There you are, Lucy. I've been looking for you. I didn't know you were here – and under the mistletoe!

Philip embraces her.

RIGSBY: Hey! Wait a minute. What do you think you're doing?

PHILIP: It is the custom, Rigsby.

RIGSBY: It's not your custom. Get off!

PHILIP: Why don't you open your present, Rigsby?

RIGSBY: I was trying to do that when you came in.

PHILIP: Allow me.

Philip takes bottle opens it and pours Rigsby a drink.

RIGSBY: (*stares*) Oh. You mean that's my present?

PHILIP: Yes. Is something the matter, Rigsby?

RIGSBY: No – of course not. Very nice. Cheers.

PHILIP: Not too quickly.

RIGSBY: My God! He's trying to poison me.

BRENDA: Pat his back.

They all gather around patting his back.

RIGSBY: That's enough. I should have known. That's bloody jungle juice – it's not meant for the sophisticated Western palate – it's for heathens.

ALAN: How do you feel now?

RIGSBY: Oh fine – except the lining of my throat's gone.

ALAN: That's done it. You won't get the room now.

LUCY: But Mr Rigsby's already offered me the room.

ALAN: I don't believe it.

LUCY: We were just discussing it, weren't we, Mr Rigsby.

RIGSBY: Er … yes. I suppose we were.

LUCY: He has some strange ideas about girls from Northampton – but I think I've put him right.

PHILIP: That's great, Rigsby.

BRENDA: The real Christmas spirit.

RIGSBY: Well, you know me – all heart.

BRENDA: Come on, Lucy. I'll show you the room. And I've got some curtains I can let you have. I'm glad there's going to be another girl – you feel safer.

LUCY: I know what you mean.

They both glance at the men, who look uncomfortable. They exit.

PHILIP: You know, perhaps I've misjudged you, Rigsby. You're not so bad. I always thought you didn't like us.

RIGSBY: I wonder what gave you that idea.

PHILIP: Merry Christmas.

Exit Philip.

ALAN: (*hesitates*) Well, it proves one thing, Rigsby. You can't possibly be Martin Borman.

Rigsby makes threatening gesture.
Alan exits.
Rigsby stares up at mistletoe.

RIGSBY: I think I'll take that down and burn it.

He reaches for stool.
Gwen enters. She is out of uniform.

GWEN: Oh, Mr Rigsby.

RIGSBY: What do you want?

GWEN: (*nervously*) It's about this afternoon. I realised I may have seemed – I don't know – prudish. Lacking in the Christmas spirit. That I may have hurt your feelings.

RIGSBY: You didn't hurt my feelings don't you worry.

GWEN: Well, I'm out of uniform now, Mr Rigsby.

RIGSBY: Good for you.

GWEN: Mr Rigsby – I'm standing under the mistletoe.

RIGSBY: What! Wait a minute. Where's my Devon Violets?

Gwen stands there with her eyes closed. The door opens and Fred enters.

FRED: Hello, what's this? Under the mistletoe. Give us a kiss.

Fred embraces Gwen.

GWEN: Ooh, Fred Baxter. You devil. That's the third time this week but I do like it.

FRED: *Gracias, señorita.*

RIGSBY: Hey! Have you forgotten me?

FRED: No, Rigsby – here's your double cream.

Fred hands Rigsby cream and returns to embrace.

THE END

SERIES THREE

When I turned my attention to the third series of *Rising Damp* I felt much more experienced as a result of the difficulties encountered last time. By now I'd written about twenty-eight shows, including *The Squirrels*, so I knew I could write more. It was still taking me about three weeks to complete an episode, though: the first week was taken up compiling rough notes – but they were often such a mess I struggled to read them myself – then there would be two more drafts, each time becoming clearer. Anyone could write the dialogue, it's the structure that takes the time; most comedy writers can find the lines but can't always find the plot.

Usually the third series of any show goes well because it's established itself with viewers. I found it easier to think up plots for these episodes, and I was probably reaching my peak in terms of generating ideas. The third series also marked Miss Jones's return. I had to find a way of bringing her back, so I made out that her engagement to Desmond, the librarian, hadn't worked out. The opening episode, *That's My Boy*, also involved a baby and there was a big debate regarding whether we should use a real child or not; although you see shots of a child's face, we opted for a dolly for the actual recording. It was fairly lifelike but most people probably noticed it wasn't real. There was a lovely misunderstanding over the baby, which helped ease Miss Jones back into the show. Misunderstandings and false assumptions can lead to pure farce and I used the device throughout the four series.

Next was *Stage Struck*, another solid show. Many people regard it as their favourite, and one or two notable writers have even told me how much they enjoyed it, which pleased me. The question concerning Hilary's sexuality was something we discussed with Peter Bowles, who played the character. We had to decide how camp the character should be. I felt he had to be a bit ambivalent because I wanted people to wonder if he was simply making Rigsby look a fool. All the gay talk was fairly bold at the time, yet it was funny and acceptable; no one took umbrage and the episode went well.

Peter played the character perfectly. Like Leonard, he has a strong personality and from day one I could see them weighing each other up. But it was clear from the start that there was going to be a partnership, with Peter openly expressing his views with Len. I enjoyed working with Peter again in *Only When I Laugh*.

Clunk Click is another classic, and the inspiration for this one came from a conversation with a friend. She knew someone who'd returned from an exciting night out, parked the car, then next morning saw fur under the wheel and thought he'd run over the cat. I liked the story and decided to use it in the episode.

The series had begun with three strong shows and I had people leaning out of car windows, shouting, 'Better than ever!' There was even one chap who told me the show was going to become a classic, which amused me at the time, but he was right.

One of the joys of writing about a guesthouse is that you can introduce new lodgers. As interesting as the main characters were, we'd explored them pretty well by the time I wrote *The Good Samaritans*, and I knew it was the right moment to exploit the setting. We were always in need of something Rigsby and the others could react to and my big advantage was that I could simply open the door and bring in someone new.

To deal with a potential suicide isn't easy. The trouble with delicate subjects is that it's not funny for everybody, but that doesn't mean you shouldn't write about them. In this episode, David Swift played an extremely depressed Mr Gray, and the episode contained some good jokes. One of the scenes involves Mr Gray climbing out onto the roof of the house, which was recorded in the studio, of course. It's all right for me because I simply write the scenes, it's down to the poor designer to build all the sets, but I always had faith in the show's designer, Colin Pigott, and he produced another great set for the rooftop scene.

Fawcett's Python was the next to be transmitted. This episode had a nice African background, allowing Philip the chance to react to the snake and invent a load of tales about the python – it was a lot of fun. I got the idea for this one from an old *Punch* cartoon, which showed a bloke clipping his hedge and accidentally cutting off a snake's head as it popped up through the hedge.

One of the main tasks here was to get a convincing snake, but I think it's pretty obvious it's made of rubber! The episode closed with a great scene: Rigsby, thinking he's been bitten on the behind, pleads with the others to suck the poison out of the wound, but no one volunteers. It's an old joke that goes back hundreds of years, but it worked well.

The penultimate episode, *The Cocktail Hour*, contained a scene where Rigsby shows Alan how a gentleman would enter a room. At the recording, Len gave a brilliant performance but it wasn't as good as when he did it during the dress rehearsal. I said to him, 'That was brilliant!' He turned to me, replying, 'I've been a long time learning the job.' I didn't often praise Len because he didn't want it, but this was one occasion when he glowed because I'd told him how I felt.

The episode finished differently from the original script, but it was well received. As soon as I started playing around with Rigsby's social ambitions, like wanting to be accepted by the town's more affluent members, I couldn't fail. Most towns have a pecking order and many people thought the episode was based on Grantham, near to where I live, but it wasn't.

I brought the series to a close with *Suddenly at Home*, another episode which included a guest appearance, with Roger Brierley playing a hypochondriac. Roger was recommended, I think, by Len and, although Osborne was a straightforward part, he played the character well. By the time I wrote this episode, I was already thinking ahead; I knew *Rising Damp* wouldn't go beyond four series, so I tried out a few medical jokes in the script, which were later encompassed in my next sitcom, *Only When I Laugh*.

Series Three

EPISODE 1

That's My Boy
by
Eric Chappell

PART ONE

SCENE 1: *Int. Rigsby's room. Day.*
*Rigsby enters. He is carrying a
suitcase and wearing a sombrero. He
sighs wearily. He sits down and tips
the hat over his eyes. Alan enters. He
seems a little disturbed to see Rigsby.*

ALAN: You're back then, Rigsby.

RIGSBY: Of course I'm back. Who
did you think it was – the Lone
Ranger?

ALAN: No but I wasn't expecting
you until next week.

RIGSBY: Oh, yes. I thought I could
smell cannabis. (*Suspiciously*)
Everything's all right? Nothing's
happened while I've been away.

ALAN: Well, the surveyor's been
down and put a few more crosses
on the house.

RIGSBY: What!

ALAN: (*grins*) Stop worrying,
Rigsby. Everything's fine. Well,
how does it feel to be back from
the joys of the Costa Brava?
Restored to vim and vigour by
the blue waters of the
Mediterranean?

RIGSBY: Bloody awful. I think I'm
suffering from jet lag.

ALAN: But it must have done you
good, Rigsby. Travel broadens
the mind. Visiting strange lands –
meeting strange people – eating
strange foods—

RIGSBY: Coming out in strange
boils. And what makes you think
I have to travel to meet strange
people? (*sharply*) Did you feed
the cat while I was away?

ALAN: (*guiltily*) Yes. Why?

RIGSBY: Nothing – only I've just
seen him coming out of the
dustbin.

ALAN: (*hastily*) Er … what was the
food like, Rigsby?

RIGSBY: Greasy.

ALAN: Oh. What about the people?

RIGSBY: About the same.

ALAN: You don't sound very
excited.

RIGSBY: I'm not. Well, frontiers
don't mean much to you – not
when you've driven through
them in a Churchill tank with
guns blazing.

ALAN: (*studies case*) You've got a lot
of labels.

RIGSBY: (*proudly*) Yes, I think they'll raise a few eyebrows then I take the washing down to the laundrette.

ALAN: Rigsby – this one says Dubrovnik.

RIGSBY: That's right.

ALAN: But that's in Yugoslavia.

RIGSBY: Is it? I wouldn't know. I got them off a case at London Airport.

ALAN: What did you do that for?'

RIGSBY: Well, you know what they're like around here. Travel snobs. You've got to cross the Sahara on a camel before they take any notice.

ALAN: But, Rigsby, what's the point in putting labels on the case if you haven't been there? You don't change – it was the same last year – you put G.B. plates on to go to the Isle of Man.

RIGSBY: Well, they all do it. What about the milkman? Told me he was taking the night flight to Benidorm – saw him the next day creosoting his mother's fence.

ALAN: (*doubtfully*) I suppose you did go to Spain?

RIGSBY: What do you mean? Of course I went to Spain.

ALAN: You're not very brown.

RIGSBY: No, well, you wouldn't be very brown if you'd spent the last three days in a police station shouting for the British Consul.

ALAN: (*laughs*) You mean you ended up in the cells?

RIGSBY: You can laugh. You wouldn't have lasted five minutes out there. It's not a democracy, you know. You try speaking your mind and you get a well-polished jackboot in the ribs.

ALAN: Why did they arrest you?

RIGSBY: Said I was a troublemaker. Just because I pushed this German in the swimming pool.

ALAN: What did you do that for?

RIGSBY: He was ex-Luftwaffe. All I did was ask him if he knew who'd bombed our Granny's house. He turned into a real little Erich von Stroheim.

ALAN: Rigsby – when are you going to learn that the war's over? The idea of travel is to meet people from others parts – understand their habits and customs.

RIGSBY: Well, I did. I met some very nice lads from Oldham. Mind you, they were turned out in the end – some trouble over a missing bidet. That sort of hotel – everything came away in your hands.

Rigsby starts opening suitcase.

ALAN: Did you bring anything back?

RIGSBY: I didn't forget you if that's what you mean.

ALAN: No, I didn't mean—

RIGSBY: Well, I appreciated you

looking after the place. So I got you some brandy and cigars.

ALAN: You shouldn't have, Rigsby.

RIGSBY: No, you deserve it.

ALAN: I didn't want anything.

RIGSBY: Well, that's fortunate because they took them off me going through customs. I wouldn't have minded but they completely ignored the bloke in front and he had twenty Swiss watches strapped to his arm. I could hear him ticking over the engines. And the lads from Oldham brought the bidet back. Just your luck I suppose.

ALAN: That's all right, Rigsby.

RIGSBY: You had no problems then?

ALAN: No. (*Hesitates*) I let the two empty rooms.

RIGSBY: Wait a minute. I let the rooms around here. What are they like?

ALAN: Two women.

RIGSBY: I thought they would be.

ALAN: (*smiles*) Don't worry – they're quite respectable.

RIGSBY: How would you know? Remember the last woman you let a room to? She turned out to be an erotic dancer.

ALAN: I didn't know she was an erotic dancer.

RIGSBY: You should have had a damned good idea when you

saw the python. (*Shudders*) I'll never forget that python – it kept dropping on me from the lampshade. Then it slithered next door and had three of their garden gnomes. It was nothing but trouble. They haven't got any pets, have they?

ALAN: (*uneasily*) No, I told them we didn't have any pets around here.

RIGSBY: No one's got any pets around here – not after the python. (*Stares*) You're hiding something. I can always tell – it's those shifty eyes.

ALAN: No, I'm not. As a matter of fact you're going to have a nice surprise.

RIGSBY: We'll see about that when I've finished unpacking. Where are you going?

ALAN: I'll just go and warn – tell them you're back.

Alan exits hurriedly.

* * *

SCENE 2: *Int. landing.*
Alan taps gently on a door. Faint baby cry. Alan winces.

ALAN: (*whispers*) Mrs Brent.

A woman about thirty holding a baby opens the door.

MRS BRENT: Yes, Alan?

ALAN: I thought I'd better let you know – he's back.

MRS BRENT: But you said he wouldn't be back until next week.

ALAN: He shouldn't have been. I think he was deported. I did warn you that it could only be for a few days.

MRS BRENT: Doesn't he like children?

ALAN: No. It's nothing personal. He doesn't like grown-ups either.

MRS BRENT: But couldn't we appeal to his better nature.

ALAN: We could but I don't think he's got one. So if you could pack your bags, Mrs Brent—

MRS BRENT: But we've got nowhere to go. You can't do it to us. Just look at his little face.

ALAN: Yes. He's got a lovely little face. He's got lovely little arms and lovely little legs, but he can't stop here.

MRS BRENT: But look at him. He's so happy. He's always smiling – he never stops.

ALAN: He will when he sees Rigsby. He'll probably bite straight through his teething ring. Couldn't you try the Social Security?

MRS BRENT: Well, as a matter of fact, I am going to look at another room today but it's across the town and I can't really manage the baby. (*Pause*) I can see he likes you.

ALAN: (*flattered*) Does he?

MRS BRENT: Oh yes – you can always tell. That's why he's blowing those bubbles.

ALAN: Well, I do have this way with children.

MRS BRENT: Good. Then I can leave him with you. (*Hands Alan baby in carrycot*) Don't forget his bottle. I won't be long.

Mrs Brent exits downstairs.
Alan is left holding the baby. He gives the baby an encouraging smile. The baby cries. Alan panics and dashes upstairs.

* * *

SCENE 3: *Int. Ruth's room.*
Rigsby enters. He gapes when he sees Ruth.

RIGSBY: Miss Jones

RUTH: Mr Rigsby.

They are uncertain whether to embrace, kiss or shake hands. They get in a tangle and settle for a hand-shake.

RIGSBY: You've come back then, Miss Jones?

RUTH: Yes, Mr Rigsby. I hope you don't mind. Only Alan said—

RIGSBY: Mind! Of course I don't mind. It'll be just like the old days. (*Pause*) No wedding bells for you then, Miss Jones?

RUTH: No, Mr Rigsby. I'm afraid it didn't work out. I realised I'd made a mistake. There was someone I was trying to forget but I couldn't.

RIGSBY: (*smirks*) I understand, Miss Jones. I would have written but I don't think letters can really say it. Same during the war. I wrote to this girl all through the desert and Italy – through the heat and the flies and the din of battle. Never missed.

RUTH: How romantic, Mr Rigsby.

RIGSBY: Yes, I must have written her hundreds of letters.

RUTH: But it didn't work out?

RIGSBY: Not really – she married the postman.

RUTH: (*sighs*) We've both had our disappointments, Mr Rigsby.

RIGSBY: Yes. I tried to forget mine. I went to Spain.

RUTH: Yes. Alan told me. You're not very brown.

RIGSBY: (*winces*) No. I tried to lose myself in an excess of gaiety and olive oil but all I got were boils – and then I thought of you, Miss Jones.

RUTH: Surely not, Mr Rigsby. Not surrounded by all those flashing-eyed señoritas.

RIGSBY: They couldn't hold a candle to you, Miss Jones.

RUTH: I've never been to Spain. I understand it's very romantic. And that those Spaniards can be very … hot-blooded.

RIGSBY: That's very true.

RUTH: Yes … I understand they won't take no for an answer.

RIGSBY: I saw it at first hand. No woman's safe out there.

RUTH: Really? Where was this, Mr Rigsby?

RIGSBY: I'll show you. I'll bring up my holiday snaps.

RUTH: Yes. I'd love to see them.

RIGSBY: It'll be just like the old days.

Philip, carrying a suitcase, looks around the door.

PHILIP: Hello, Ruth – so you've come back.

RUTH: Philip! It's lovely to see you.

She throws her arms around Philip. Rigsby glares. Ruth recovers herself.

RUTH: Mr Rigsby's just come back from Spain, Philip.

PHILIP: Oh … You're not very brown, Rigsby.

Rigsby scowls and exits.

* * *

SCENE 4: *Int. attic flat.*
Alan is making soothing noises over carrycot. Rigsby enters. He stares at Alan in astonishment.

RIGSBY: Are you feeling all right?

Alan starts. Screens baby from Rigsby.

ALAN: Rigsby! Do you have to do that?

RIGSBY: Don't get touchy. I've come to thank you. I know we've had our differences in the past and I did have my doubts about leaving you in charge, but I'm very pleased with the way you've looked after Miss Jones. (*Stops*) What's this?

ALAN: What?

RIGSBY: It looks like a baby's bottle.

ALAN: It's a test tube.

RIGSBY: It's got milk in it.

ALAN: I've run out of cups.

RIGSBY: What's that smell?

ALAN: What smell?

RIGSBY: Like new bread. (*Prowls*) And what's this? A rusk. What do you want with a rusk?

ALAN: I like rusks.

RIGSBY: I know you've never grown up but this is ridiculous. Let me give you some advice. If you feel a sudden desire to roll on your back and suck your big toe – resist it.

Rigsby turns to go. There is a gentle burp. Rigsby turns back in astonishment.

ALAN: Pardon.

RIGSBY: Was that you? My God! It must be the rusks – they're affecting you. The sooner you get back on the cannabis the better.

ALAN: (*angrily*) I'm not on cannabis.

The baby starts to cry. Rigsby pushes by Alan.

RIGSBY: It's a baby. What's it doing here? You know the rules.

ALAN: I'm looking after it for someone.

RIGSBY: You? Who in their right mind would trust you with a baby?

ALAN: As a matter of fact he likes me.

RIGSBY: You know why? With all that hair he probably thinks you're his mother. Who is the mother anyway?

ALAN: Just a friend.

RIGSBY: Oh yes. (*Looks at the baby then at Alan and back again*)

ALAN: What are you staring at?

RIGSBY: It's the nose – that's what gives it away.

ALAN: Now wait a minute—

RIGSBY: The likeness is uncanny. No, you don't have to explain – I suppose you just threw caution to the winds.

ALAN: (*hotly*) I didn't throw caution to the winds.

RIGSBY: Why didn't you come to me?

ALAN: Why should I have come to you?

RIGSBY: I could have helped you. I've seen you standing in the chemists – tongue-tied and stammering. You waited half-an-hour for the man to serve you – then you came out with a bottle of Lucozade.

ALAN: Rigsby, he's not mine. His mother's a respectable woman. Her husband's in the Merchant Navy.

RIGSBY: Well, I wouldn't be around when he gets back. (*Pauses at the door. Grimly*) And if that baby's here when I come up again – you're out.

Exit Rigsby.
Alan groans. He picks up baby and strides up and down with it.
Philip enters.

PHILIP: What have you got there?

ALAN: It's a baby.

PHILIP: Well, I didn't think it was your Mickey Mouse hot water bottle. What are you doing with it?

ALAN: I'm looking after it.

PHILIP: Well, it can't stop here. I've got work to do.

ALAN: Don't you start. It won't be for long. (*Indulgently*) Look at his little face.

PHILIP: (*irritably*) I don't want to look at his little face.

ALAN: Go on – look.

Philip looks at baby then at Alan then back again.

PHILIP: Oh. So that's it.

ALAN: (*indignantly*) No – it's not it.

PHILIP: It's the nose.

ALAN: It's not the nose! Look, Rigsby already thinks it's mine. You've got to help me.

PHILIP: How? He's not going to think it's mine. Do you realise this is the first time I won't get the blame around here.

ALAN: Listen, Philip – it belongs to the woman downstairs. If Rigsby finds out I've let the room to them he'll murder me. He mustn't find this baby here when he gets back.

PHILIP: What do you suggest we do – sit on it?

ALAN: We've got to do something.

Baby cries. Philip frowns.

PHILIP: (*brightens*) What about Ruth?

ALAN: Do you think she would?

PHILIP: She's a woman, isn't she?

ALAN: (*doubtfully*) I suppose so.

PHILIP: Come on then.

They exit with baby.

* * *

SCENE 5: *Int. Ruth's room.*
  Philip enters first.

PHILIP: Ruth, I wonder if you could help us?

RUTH: Of course, Philip.

PHILIP: We've got this little problem.

RUTH: And you need a woman's touch. You boys – I don't know how you ever managed without me. Well, what is it?

Alan enters with baby.

RUTH: (*horrified*) Goodness! It's a baby.

ALAN: We wondered if you could look after it for us?

RUTH: No – I don't know anything about babies.

PHILIP: You don't have to. Just follow your instincts.

RUTH: (*backing away*) I am doing.

ALAN: Just hold it, Ruth.

RUTH: No, I'll drop it.

PHILIP: No, you won't.

RUTH: I will. I dropped one at a christening once. It plummeted into the font and saturated the vicar.

ALAN: Come on, Ruth. You must know something about babies.

RUTH: The only experience I've had is with Tiny Tears and that was a long time ago.

Alan manages to place the baby in Ruth's arms.

ALAN: Look at that, Philip. Isn't that incredible?

PHILIP: Yes – the natural way he clings to her.

RUTH: You see – even he thinks I'm going to drop him. (*Panics*) He's gone pink. He wasn't that colour when he came in. He's stopped breathing.

ALAN: He's just holding his breath.

RUTH: He's not the only one. He belongs to the woman across the landing, doesn't he? Well, I've told her, Mr Rigsby won't allow babies.

ALAN: It won't be for long.

PHILIP: (*backing to door*) You know you're a wonderful sight, Ruth.

RUTH: What?

PHILIP: The quiet dignity – the gentle strength. You can see he feels secure.

RUTH: (*Flattered*) Do you think so?

ALAN: Yes. There's a Madonna-like quality about her, Philip. (*They reach the door*) Don't forget to change him

They exit hurriedly.
Ruth holds the baby with pride. Looks in mirror. Gradually her expression changes. She looks at her hand.

* * *

SCENE 6: *Int. Ruth's room.*
Rigsby enters wearing sombrero.
Ruth draws curtain hastily and faces
Rigsby.

RIGSBY: *Buenos noches*, Miss Jones.

RUTH: Er … *Buenos noches*, Mr Rigsby.

RIGSBY: I've brought the snaps.

He hands over the snaps. Ruth tries
to thumb through them quickly but
Rigsby won't let her.

RIGSBY: That's an interesting one – that's the night club – it was attached to the hotel. At least it was when I left.

RUTH: It looks very elegant.

RIGSBY: Yes. Of course that was before the trouble started.

RUTH: What trouble?

RIGSBY: Well, I was indulging in an old Spanish custom – drinking from a goat skin – you're supposed to direct a jet of wine straight into your mouth.

RUTH: I understand that's very difficult.

RIGSBY: It was. Mine went in this woman's ear'ole.

RUTH: Who are these two men in uniform walking towards the camera?

RIGSBY: Ah, they're the police.

RUTH: They seem to be scowling.

RIGSBY: Yes – they never did laugh a lot.

RUTH: And what's this gaunt, ugly building with a cross against one window.

RIGSBY: That was the local police station.

RUTH: Yes. Well, if you don't mind, Mr Rigsby I'll look at them later. I must get ready for work.

Ruth tries to usher Rigsby to the
door. The baby cries.
Rigsby stares at Ruth. Draws
curtain and discovers baby.

RIGSBY: What's he doing here?

RUTH: Er … I'm looking after it for someone, Mr Rigsby.

RIGSBY: (*doubtfully*) I see – looking after it for someone.

RUTH: Yes – so if you'll excuse me—

Rigsby exits in a daze.

* * *

SCENE 7: *Int. landing.*
Rigsby is standing on the landing
looking puzzled.
Alan comes downstairs.

RIGSBY: About that baby—

ALAN: (*cheerfully*) That's all right, Rigsby. It's back with its mother now.

Rigsby stares.

END OF PART ONE

PART TWO

SCENE 8: *Int. attic flat.*
Minutes later. Alan and Philip are reading.
Rigsby enters. He has a faintly menacing air.

ALAN: Not you again, Rigsby.

RIGSBY: (*grim smile*) I hope I'm not disturbing you.

ALAN: Well, we are studying.

RIGSBY: Going all right, is it?

ALAN: Not too bad.

RIGSBY: Good. (*Pause*) What are you like on fractures?

ALAN: What do you mean?

RIGSBY: I mean, could you set a broken arm for example?

ALAN: Certainly.

RIGSBY: And what about lacerations? What are you like on lacerations?

ALAN: I can cope with them.

RIGSBY: And abrasions and heavy bruising?

ALAN: Yes. What do you want to know for?

RIGSBY: (*explodes*) Because you're going to find it very useful when I've done with you. Pick your window.

Alan retreats behind Philip.

PHILIP: (*sighs*) What's the matter, Rigsby?

ALAN: Yes. What's the matter?

RIGSBY: You know what's the matter. And I thought that python was slimy. I should have kept him and got rid of you.

ALAN: But what have I done?

RIGSBY: I've just seen Miss Jones and the baby.

ALAN: I can explain that.

RIGSBY: It's too late.

ALAN: Rigsby, for the last time it isn't my baby.

PHILIP: Besides, violence doesn't solve anything, Rigsby.

RIGSBY: I see, and what would they do in your country then?

ALAN: Tell him, Philip.

PHILIP: Oh, we'd stake him out on an anthill and cover his private parts with honey.

ALAN: Philip!

RIGSBY: Let me get at him.

PHILIP: Rigsby. Look at him. Do you really think it could be Alan?

RIGSBY: (*hesitates*) Well, I know it's hard to believe.

PHILIP: What about the librarian?

RIGSBY: She said it didn't work out.

ALAN: Well, he's not going to buy a book when he can borrow one, is he?

RIGSBY: (*frowns*) You're right. What am I going to do? He's not getting away with it.

ALAN: You could go down and eat celery under his Silence notice.

RIGSBY: It's not funny.

PHILIP: All you can think about is revenge, Rigsby. You could try a little understanding. What about Ruth?

ALAN: Yes and what about the baby?

RIGSBY: I don't like babies.

ALAN: You know, there's something wrong with a man who doesn't like children.

Rigsby looks subdued.

RIGSBY: (*gruffly*) Well, I'll go and see how she is.

Exit Rigsby.

* * *

SCENE 9: *Int. Ruth's room.*
Ruth is bending over crying baby.
Rigsby enters.

RUTH: Oh, I hope he's not making too much noise, Mr Rigsby.

RIGSBY: No, that's all right, Miss Jones. He's only exercising his little lungs. What are you doing?

RUTH: I'm changing him.

RIGSBY: (*looks into cot*) Oh. My word. He's certainly a boy, Miss Jones.

RUTH: (*coyly*) Oh, Mr Rigsby.

RIGSBY: Nothing to worry about there.

RUTH: He's certainly beautifully made.

RIGSBY: Yes – all fully equipped.

RUTH: (*giggles*) Mr Rigsby. (*Pause*) Now for the nappy. Oh. (*Glance at Rigsby*) I think under the circumstances we ought to offer a few words of admiration.

RIGSBY: Admiration?

RUTH: Yes. (*Lowers voice*) It encourages them. Keeps them regular.

RIGSBY: We always had syrup of figs.

RUTH: I think it's best. Who's a clever boy then?

Rigsby joins in words of admiration but looks rather green.

RIGSBY: (*moving away*) You've certainly got a beautiful baby there, Miss Jones. Obviously takes after his mother.

RUTH: Oh, then you know his mother?

RIGSBY: (*knowingly*) I think so, Miss Jones.

RUTH: So our little secret's out?

RIGSBY: Yes.

RUTH: And you don't mind?

RIGSBY: Well, I did at first – I don't deny that. But I'm not going to sit in judgement. It's tough bringing a child up on your own.

RUTH: I think that's very sweet of you, Mr Rigsby.

RIGSBY: Mind you, I would like to know something about the father.

RUTH: He's in the Merchant Navy.

RIGSBY: Is that all you can tell me?

RUTH: Well, I've only seen him once – and then only by the light of his cigarette. He seemed quite nice.

RIGSBY: Quite nice! Is that all you can say, Miss Jones?

RUTH: What's the matter, Mr Rigsby?

RIGSBY: Nothing. After all, these things happen. And I must say I can see you're a born mother. In fact watching you brings a lump to my throat. You see, this may surprise you but I wasn't wanted.

RUTH: I didn't know that, Mr Rigsby.

RIGSBY: Yes, my parents never had any time for me. Times were hard – another mouth to feed. Besides, they always preferred my brother.

RUTH: I'm sure that's not true.

RIGSBY: Oh yes. Whenever we had a bath together I always had the end with the taps. You notice things like that. And my father never showed me the same affection. He kept taking me out in the pram and leaving me.

RUTH: Poor Mr Rigsby. Now for the safety pin. You don't think he's cowering?

RIGSBY: No, he trusts you, Miss Jones. Who's a bonny boy then?

RUTH: I always thought you didn't like children, Mr Rigsby.

RIGSBY: I don't know what gave you that idea, Miss Jones. I was Father Christmas every year at the British Legion – until they set fire to my beard. I love the little … I'm very good with children.

RUTH: I'm so glad. Perhaps you can look after him for a while?

RIGSBY: What?

RUTH: I must pop down to the office. I shan't be long. You'll be all right, Mr Rigsby. (*Hands baby to Rigsby*) Just keep him the right way up.

RIGSBY: But, Miss Jones—

RUTH: I won't be long.

Exit Ruth.
Baby starts to cry. Rigsby panics.

* * *

SCENE 10: *Int. attic flat.*
Alan and Philip are reading.
Rigsby enters with baby in carrycot.

PHILIP: Oh, no. (*Throws down book*)

RIGSBY: He won't stop crying.

ALAN: That's perfectly normal, Rigsby.

RIGSBY: I'm not so sure. (*To Philip*) What do you think?

PHILIP: I don't know. He's a funny colour.

RIGSBY: He's not the only one. The point is what are we going to do?

PHILIP: You mean what are *you* going to do? We're trying to work.

RIGSBY: You can't take that attitude. Just look at his little face. Who's a pretty boy?

PHILIP: He looks rather plain to me.

RIGSBY: Well, he would, wouldn't he. I mean your ideas of physical beauty are different from ours. I suppose if he'd half a dozen rings round his neck and a bit of warpaint you'd think he was marvellous.

ALAN: No, but you can't call him handsome.

RIGSBY: No, well, his veins are standing out at the moment.

ALAN: He looks like a little old man.

RIGSBY: Do you mind? He'll hear you. Anyway, he'll grow out of it. You can't tell at that age. I wasn't very good-looking as a baby. In fact you could say I was an ugly duckling. (*To baby*) Until one day the ugly duckling grew up and what do you think he'd turned into?

PHILIP: An ugly duck.

RIGSBY: (angrily) Are you trying to upset him? Look, I think we'd better sing to him.

ALAN: Why should we sing to him?

PHILIP: Yes, why should we?

RIGSBY: Because if you don't, I'll put your rent up. Let's try 'My curly headed baby' (*starts. To Philip*) Come on. What's the matter? My God! We wouldn't have had this trouble with Paul Robeson.

They sing a refrain. The baby stops crying.

RIGSBY: It's worked. He's stopped.

PHILIP: (*peers into cot*) I'm not surprised.

Baby starts to cry.

RIGSBY: It's you. You're frightening him.

PHILIP: (*indignantly*) No, I'm not.

RIGSBY: Never mind. The dark gentleman means you no harm. He's that colour because he comes from where the sun's very hot – so he has to be heat-resistant – like those non-stick pans. Don't worry – he won't eat you – his father might have done but he won't.

PHILIP: Do you mind, Rigsby.

ALAN: This isn't *Listen with Mother*, Rigsby.

RIGSBY: That's an idea. If we hurry we'll just catch it.

Exit Rigsby.

ALAN: (*worried*) You don't think he's getting carried away do you?

* * *

SCENE 11: *Int. Rigsby's room. Rigsby is entertaining the baby. The radio is on. The programme is something like* Listen with Mother.

VO: Now, children, should we pretend that we're the wind? Let's blow as hard as we can. Come on, puff out your cheeks.

Rigsby glances around to ensure he's alone and then puffs out his cheeks.

VO: Now we'll rush around the field like the wind. Come on – flap your arms.

Rigsby obliges.

VO: And now what's this coming along? A big round ball bouncing in the wind. Should we be a big, round ball, children. (*Rigsby winces*) We're round and we bounce.

Rigsby bounces. Baby cries.

VO: And who's this chasing the ball? It's Rover the dog.

RIGSBY: It would be.

VO: Watch him leap and bark. Should we leap and bark?

Rigsby begins to leap and bark. Alan enters. Rigsby straightens up hurriedly and switches off radio.

ALAN: I wondered if this would help? (*he produces glove puppet*) It's Big Bunny. (*Thrusts it into cot*) Hello, little chap. My word, who's a pretty boy? Here's Big Bunny come to see you.

The baby gurgles with delight.

RIGSBY: (*jealously*) I'll have that if you don't mind.

ALAN: Why?

RIGSBY: Because I said so.

ALAN: You're not his father.

RIGSBY: No, but you'll only confuse

him. Besides, I can see your lips moving.

Rigsby takes over the glove puppet.

ALAN: You know you're getting very possessive, Rigsby.

RIGSBY: I happen to be responsible for him. Anyway, you'd be a bad influence. One day you'd have too much LSD and try walking through a wall with him.

ALAN: Oh, and I suppose you'd be a good influence? What about that night before you went away – you came home drunk.

RIGSBY: What makes you think I was drunk?

ALAN: You had a traffic cone on your head.

RIGSBY: Never mind that. I could do a lot for him.

ALAN: Such as?

RIGSBY: I could give him the things I never had. A good education – I never stood a chance. I was sent to school with a bit of bread and dripping and a stubby pencil. All the other kids had fountain pens in their top pockets but not me.

ALAN: You mean you never even had a fountain pen?

RIGSBY: I never even had a top pocket. That's why I never got invited to parties. That and the gumboots. I used to watch them though. The girls in their silver shoes – the boys in their party slippers – giving each other belters at postman's knock. But not me – I was just a face at the window. It would be different for him. He'd have the best. Perhaps a scholarship – Winchester – Baliol – a seat in the Cabinet.

ALAN: Don't you think you're getting carried away, Rigsby?

RIGSBY: What do you mean?

ALAN: He's got a father. He doesn't need you.

RIGSBY: We'll see about that.

Rigsby starts to entertain the baby with Big Bunny. Alan exits. Brent appears around the door. He is dressed in Merchant Navy uniform. He stares at Rigsby.

BRENT: Hello, there. I wondered where the little shaver had got to.

RIGSBY: (*coldly*) You've come back then?

BRENT: Yes. Who are you?

RIGSBY: I'm the landlord.

BRENT: I thought you were a bit old for a babysitter.

He extends hand. Finds himself shaking hands with glove puppet.

BRENT: How's he been keeping then?

Brent picks up baby.

RIGSBY: Do you mind putting that

baby down? That's not the way to handle him. He's not a duffle bag.

BRENT: I always hold him this way.

RIGSBY: Well, don't blame me if he grows up with his head on one side.

Brent puts baby down.

BRENT: I am his father.

RIGSBY: I know. I'm just surprised you showed up, that's all.

BRENT: What do you mean?

RIGSBY: Do you think it's going to do any good – opening old wounds like this?

BRENT: What?

RIGSBY: Do you mind if I give you some advice, shipmate? Don't tie yourself down. You're not a family man.

BRENT: I'm not?

RIGSBY: No. And do you know why? Because you're wedded to the sea. You're not going to be there when he needs you.

BRENT: I could come ashore.

RIGSBY: What good will that do? The sea's in your blood. Once the wind starts to blow through the shrouds – once you can smell the salt breeze coming off the marshes, you'll be away – to those far away places with the strange sounding names.

BRENT: I don't know about that. I'm only on the cross Channel ferry.

RIGSBY: Well, it's the same thing. (*Sharply*) Don't lean over the cot – you'll frighten him.

BRENT: No, I won't – he knows me.

RIGSBY: Of course he doesn't know you. You're never here. As far as he's concerned you're just a sailor with a big hooter. My God! I'll never know what she saw in you – a woman of her refinement. I know, it was dark.

BRENT: Wait a minute – what's she been saying?

RIGSBY: Not much. To tell the truth I think she's trying to forget it. As far as she's concerned you're just ships that passed in the night. You just moored alongside for a few hours and then went out with the tide.

BRENT: Did she tell you that?

RIGSBY: Well, she was bound to confide in me. I knew her before you came along. We had an understanding.

BRENT: (*angrily*) Oh, did you?

RIGSBY: What are you doing?

BRENT: I'm taking my jacket off.

RIGSBY: (*moving away*) Yes – it is hot in here. My word – what a nice set of tattoos. What's that? A snake twined round an anchor – very tasteful. You haven't got the death of Nelson anywhere, have you?

BRENT: Come here, you.

RIGSBY: Now, no violence – not in front of the child.

There is a scuffle.
Ruth enters.

RUTH: Good heavens! What are you doing? Stop it – you'll upset the baby.

BRENT: I'm sorry, Miss Jones. But it's this geezer—

RIGSBY: It's not me, Miss Jones. It's jolly Jack Tar over there – he's trying to make a clove hitch out of me.

RUTH: Well, stop it, both of you. You'll disturb – oh, what is his name?

BRENT: David.

RUTH: You'll disturb David.

RIGSBY: (*stares*) Surely you can remember his name, Miss Jones? We can all be absent-minded but you are his mother.

RUTH: What are you talking about? I'm not his mother.

RIGSBY: But I thought—

BRENT: (*laughs*) So that's it. You thought David was hers!

RUTH: Really, Mr Rigsby.

RIGSBY: There must have been some misunderstanding.

RUTH: There certainly was.

BRENT: Well, that's a relief – he had me worried for a minute.

Mrs Brent enters.

MRS BRENT: Jim. What are you doing here?

BRENT: It's all right. Mr Rigsby's been looking after David.

MRS BRENT: But I thought Mr Rigsby didn't like babies.

RUTH: Don't worry, Mrs Brent. Mr Rigsby adores babies – don't you, Mr Rigsby?

RIGSBY: (*weakly*) That's right, Miss Jones.

RUTH: He says he can stay as long as he likes. Isn't that kind of Mr Rigsby?

RIGSBY: You know me – all heart, Miss Jones.

MRS BRENT: Well, this is a surprise. Alan said you were such a misery – I mean—

RIGSBY: (*glances up*) Did he really?

Puts on glove puppet.

RUTH: Where are you going, Mr Rigsby?

RIGSBY: (*picks up hammer*) I'm just going to give Big Bunny a bit of exercise.

Rigsby exits up stairs.

THE END.

Series Three

EPISODE 2

Stage Struck

by

Eric Chappell

PART ONE

SCENE 1: *Int. attic flat. Evening.*
Alan is drying his hair at the mirror.
Rigsby enters angrily.

RIGSBY: If he says one word to me –
one more word – I shall have
him.

ALAN: Who's that, Rigsby?

RIGSBY: Hilary – who do you
think?

ALAN: I don't know what you've
got against Hilary. I find him
very stimulating.

RIGSBY: You would. You've liked
him ever since he admired your
earrings.

ALAN: It's not that – we've got a lot
in common.

RIGSBY: Yes, you both share the
same crippling fear of manual
labour. When's he going to get a
job?

ALAN: He's resting.

RIGSBY: I can see that – I'm not
blind. What I want to know is
why he can't wait until nightfall
like the rest of us. Why does he
have to lounge around the house
all day?

ALAN: Rigsby, resting is a show
business term for being out of
work.

RIGSBY: (*scornfully*) Show business.
You don't believe all that
rubbish, do you? He's not in
show business. What's he ever
done? You tell me that.

ALAN: (*defensively*) He's done a lot
of things.

RIGSBY: Such as?

ALAN: You'd be surprised, Rigsby.

RIGSBY: Well, go on – surprise me.

ALAN: He was very nearly in *Oh
Calcutta!*

RIGSBY: Oh, yes. What happened?
Didn't he measure up?

ALAN: He sprained his ankle.

RIGSBY: From what I've heard he's
lucky that's all he sprained.
Anyway, all I know is I've never
seen him in anything.

ALAN: You're not likely to. You
only watch *Crossroads*.

RIGSBY: No, I don't. Besides, I
wouldn't expect to see him in
Crossroads. You have to be good
to get in that.

ALAN: (*amused*) What's so special about *Crossroads*?

RIGSBY: (*shocked*) What's so special? It only happens to be Her Majesty's favourite programme. Everything stops at the palace for *Crossroads*. Just let the corgis start playing up when that's on – they'd soon get a royal toe in the ribs. They say she's riveted to the set. Of course you can understand it – they've got the cream of the acting profession in that – they'd never have Hilary.

ALAN: He was in *I, Claudius*.

RIGSBY: Wait a minute – I watched that – I never saw him.

ALAN: It was only a small part.

RIGSBY: It must have been.

ALAN: He was in the orgy scene. He ran around squeezing his grapes over everyone.

RIGSBY: My God! Is that all he's done – squeezed a few grapes? No wonder he's resting – I suppose the effort was too much for him. (*Frowns*) And I still don't remember seeing him.

ALAN: No, you wouldn't. He was wearing a stag's head.

RIGSBY: How very convenient. You know you'd believe anything. He's completely dazzled you, hasn't he? A bit of show-biz glitter – a bit of tinsel and you're away. I bet he's never been on television.

ALAN: He has. I've seen him in a commercial.

RIGSBY: Which one?

ALAN: You know, the one where these big tough blokes barge into the bar and order their favourite beer.

RIGSBY: (*laughs*) You're not telling me Hilary's one of them?

ALAN: No, he's the one they shove out of the way when they come through the door. Mind you, you only get a glimpse of his back.

RIGSBY: You see – you're so gullible. Well, I've met them before – they're all talk. We had a bloke here once – he said he was in show business. You'd have thought he was Laurence Olivier the way he went on. Turned out to be a human cannon ball. I wouldn't have minded but he was rubbish. The night I saw him they didn't use enough gunpowder – there was a loud bang – a puff of smoke and he fell out the end of the barrel. A real damp squib he was.

ALAN: Well, Hilary's not a damp squib. He read some poetry to us last night. It was great. We all sat around on the floor spellbound. Best night I've had for a long time – finished up with a moussaka.

RIGSBY: A what?

ALAN: A moussaka. Hilary does a terrific moussaka. (*Grins*) You don't know what it is, do you?

RIGSBY: Yes, course I know what it is.

ALAN: It's Greek.

RIGSBY: I know it's Greek. You all join hands and dance in a circle, don't you?

ALAN: No – it's a Greek dish, Rigsby.

RIGSBY: Oh. I should have known. He's got some very fancy ways if you ask me. He's too fond of that striped apron for my liking. He should be out looking for work.

ALAN: Well, he's not been wasting his time. As a matter of fact he's written a play.

RIGSBY: A play! He couldn't write a play – it's all he can do to leave a note for the milkman.

ALAN: Well, he's written one – and it's very good.

RIGSBY: What's it about?

ALAN: It's a psychological drama – full of symbolism and imagery – played out against the backcloth of a dingy boarding house and dealing with contemporary themes.

RIGSBY: My God – it sounds like another *Play for Today*.

ALAN: It's very good. It deals with exploitation – the declining quality of life – the underlying violence in modern society.

RIGSBY: (*snorts*) What does he know about violence? He's only got to break a nail and he's in bed for the rest of the day.

ALAN: It's no good talking to you – you just don't like him. I don't know why.

RIGSBY: Well, for one thing he calls me 'ducky'. If he calls me ducky once more I shall have him.

Hilary enters. He is a man in his late-twenties. He is theatrical – slightly camp but with an underlying toughness which makes him an ambiguous figure.

HILARY: Oh, hello, ducky. Am I interrupting?

RIGSBY: (*frowns*) Yes, you are.

Hilary leans forward and feels Rigsby's cardigan mischievously.

HILARY: Like your cardy – very you, Rigsby. Sort of 'hungry thirties'. I wish you'd let me have the name of your tailor.

RIGSBY: (*pulls away*) Do you mind? We happen to be having a private conversation.

HILARY: I won't keep you. A word in your shell-like, Alan. Could we make it later tonight? Only the evening's been a complete disaster – my soufflé's collapsed. It's just lying there, staring up at me like the creature from the Black Lagoon—

RIGSBY: It's your own fault – that cooker was never designed for soufflés. You should stick to fish fingers like the rest of us.

HILARY: No, it was my agent's fault – kept me on the phone for hours – some tatty review. Want me to take my clothes off again – full frontals – the lot.

RIGSBY: I think it's disgraceful – you wouldn't get me taking my clothes off.

HILARY: You wait until you're asked, cheeky.

ALAN: I think he's got a nerve asking you to do that, Hilary – with all your talent.

HILARY: Well, of course, I refused. I told him 'Over my dead body'. I'm not going through that again. I remember the catcalls from the last time. 'Where were you when they were handed out?' they kept shouting. Couldn't hear a word I was saying. And of course it leaves a scar.

RIGSBY: You mean you got a splinter up your rear end.

HILARY: I mean a mental scar. I've kept the bathroom door locked ever since.

ALAN: Well, you don't need to worry, Hilary. I've just read the play – terrific.

Hilary puts an earnest hand on Alan's arm.

HILARY: Do you really mean that, Alan?

ALAN: Of course I mean it. I particularly like the muscular way you explored the contemporary themes – the underlying passions – the depravity of urban life.

RIGSBY: Hardly goes with his rosebud wallpaper and the chintz curtains, though, does it?

HILARY: I'm so pleased, Alan. You don't mind coming down later?

ALAN: No, suits me. I've just washed my hair – can't do a thing with it.

RIGSBY: (drily) Can't do a lot with the sink either.

Hilary studies Alan's hair.

HILARY: Well, I think it improves it. Gives it more body. I like the way it cascades. Don't you like the way it cascades, Rigsby?

RIGSBY: No, I don't. It gets more like a ladies' hairdressers in here everyday.

ALAN: Don't take any notice of Rigsby. He was the first man to discover short back and sides.

RIGSBY: What's wrong with short back and sides?

HILARY: Nothing, Rigsby. It's just that the 'I-was-a-prisoner-on-Devil's-Island' look doesn't suit everyone. See you later, Alan.

RIGSBY: What's it going to be tonight? Verse reading or home perms?

HILARY: Neither – we're going to read my play. Alan's graciously agreed to play the lead.

RIGSBY: (*astounded*) What!

ALAN: (*hurriedly*) See you later, Hilary.

Hilary exits.
Rigsby stares in astonishment at Alan.
Alan looks uncomfortable.

RIGSBY: You're not serious.

ALAN: (*defiantly*) Yes.

RIGSBY: I never thought it would come to this – acting.

ALAN: What's wrong with it?

RIGSBY: What's wrong with it? Well, I mean, you can't sink much lower than that – acting. A lad of your age should be out kicking a ball about – not poncing around on a stage. I don't know what your mother and father'll say. You've got your future to think about.

ALAN: I am thinking about my future – this could be my big chance.

RIGSBY: You can't act – you can't even speak properly – you can't even sound your aitches.

ALAN: That doesn't matter. Hilary says I've got this basic virility.

RIGSBY: Virility! You've got about as much virility as a wooden rocking horse.

ALAN: I knew you'd put the dampeners on it, Rigsby. Well, I'm still going to do it. I could be another Malcolm McDowell or David Essex.

RIGSBY: Yes, and where are they now?

ALAN: What?

RIGSBY: Forgotten men. I bet they both wish they'd got themselves a trade.

ALAN: Rigsby, there're both big stars.

RIGSBY: Well, I've never heard of them. Take my advice – keep away from Hilary. Don't be taken in by all that show-biz glitter with your name up in lights. You live in a world of make-believe as it is.

ALAN: No, I don't.

RIGSBY: Yes you do. Look what happened when you went out to see that kung fu film – you came home, tried to karate chop the bannisters and nearly took your hand off.

ALAN: I'm not listening to you, Rigsby. This is my big chance and I'm going to take it. And no one's going to stop me.

Alan barges out angrily.
He nearly knocks Philip over as he enters.

PHILIP: What's the matter with Alan?

RIGSBY: Oh, it's the usual – it happens every so often. He gets this yearning for culture. He burns all his pin-ups and starts listening to classical music. It won't last long. He'll soon be down knocking on my door to watch *Tom and Jerry*.

PHILIP: The trouble with you is, Rigsby, as soon as you hear the word 'culture' you reach for your revolver. What's wrong with a cultural evening once in a while?

RIGSBY: Listen who's talking. Before you came here your idea of a cultural evening was running round with someone's head on a pole.

PHILIP: And what's your idea of a cultural evening? Throwing beer cans at the cat?

RIGSBY: Did you know he's going to act in Hilary's play?

PHILIP: Why not? It'll be good for him.

RIGSBY: No, it won't. I've seen these modern plays – they're depressing. They spend all night drinking meths and jumping on the baby.

PHILIP: It's not quite like that – it's more of a love story.

RIGSBY: What? (*pauses by door*) You mean there's a woman in it?

PHILIP: Yes.

RIGSBY: I didn't know that. (*Returns*) Is there any—?

PHILIP: Oh, yes.

RIGSBY: And does he actually get to—?

PHILIP: He never stops. It's a stormy love affair played out in a garret. With lots of searing kisses.

RIGSBY: (*grins*) The crafty little devil. And I was worried about him. I should have known. Lots of searing kisses, hey?

PHILIP: Searing kisses all through the text.

RIGSBY: That's one way of getting to grips with the part. Mind you, I don't think I'd fancy it – not if they do it in the church hall. Not with all those crackling sweet papers. The only time I've ever given a public performance was when someone switched his headlights on in the Odeon car park. Still, they say that actors don't feel anything – it's just a job of work.

PHILIP: You don't believe that, do you, Rigsby? All those torrid love scenes – doing them over and over again.

RIGSBY: Yes, I've seen the beads of sweat standing out on their foreheads. Can't all be simulated. They probably have men in asbestos suits waiting to pull them apart.

PHILIP: And then there are always a few private rehearsals—

RIGSBY: (*leers*) Yes, you certainly wouldn't mind taking your work home with you. (*Pause*) Is she nice?

PHILIP: Who?

RIGSBY: The woman.

PHILIP: Oh, yes.

RIGSBY: Trust him. I bet he picked her out. Who is it?

PHILIP: Didn't they tell you? It's Miss Jones.

RIGSBY: What!

Rigsby's expression changes to one of horror.

* * *

SCENE 2: *Int. Ruth's room.*
Ruth is trying to read a manuscript. She looks bored. Sighs. Puts it down and picks up romantic novel. She hears a fly buzzing. She rolls up manuscript and attacks it furiously. She kills the fly but does considerable damage to the manuscript.
Knock on the door.

HILARY: (*OOV*) Are you there, Ruth?

RUTH: Er … yes, Hilary.

HILARY: (*OOV*) Well? Have you read it?

Ruth straightens the tattered script in alarm.

RUTH: Almost.

Hilary enters.

HILARY: (*eagerly*) What did you think of it? I want you to be brutally honest. A writer must be prepared to accept criticism.

RUTH: Well, it's … er … very interesting.

HILARY: (*sharply*) You don't like it.

RUTH: I do like it. I thought it was

marvellous – but there were one or two things.

HILARY: Let me see – perhaps I can explain. (*Stops. Stares at manuscript*) It's all crumpled.

RUTH: Yes, well, I just couldn't put it down, Hilary.

HILARY: What's this? It looks like a dead fly. Someone's been swotting flies with it.

RUTH: No, it's probably a currant. I couldn't put it down – even at meal times.

HILARY: Do you really mean that?

RUTH: Of course I mean it, silly.

HILARY: Then you'll do it?

RUTH: (*doubtfully*) Well, I don't know. I'm not an actress, Hilary.

HILARY: Nonsense. You'd make a marvellous Maggie.

RUTH: But she keeps attacking people with a bread knife.

HILARY: Well, haven't you ever felt like attacking someone with a break knife?

RUTH: Yes, but I've always fought the impulse, Hilary.

HILARY: Ah, well, don't forget she's been driven mad by drink and she's consumed by this jealous passion for Slim. You could do it, Ruth. I've been watching you.

RUTH: Have you, Hilary?

HILARY: Yes. On the surface cool and aloof, but underneath a seething cauldron of emotion – capable of great passion.

RUTH: (*moves closer*) You're not the first person to have noticed that, Hilary. Of course you're quite right. I once loosened Sandra Plunkett's girth strap because I was jealous of her and the riding instructor.

HILARY: There you are you see. And you're an instinctive actress. That walk, for example – how did you learn to walk like that?

RUTH: (*puzzled*) I don't know – I just sort of put one foot in front of the other.

HILARY: But you must have had some acting experience.

RUTH: Well, I was in an Agatha Christie once.

HILARY: I knew it.

RUTH: It was quite a challenge really. I was strangled in the first scene. I had to lie there for hours with people stepping over me. I wouldn't have minded, but a small boy in the audience kept poking me with a stick to see if I was alive.

HILARY: It must have required a great deal of control.

RUTH: Oh, it did. I received considerable praise. The local paper said 'We have to go a long way to find anyone deader than Miss Jones.'

HILARY: There you are. I know you could do it.

RUTH: Well, since you have such faith in me, Hilary, how can I refuse.

HILARY: Splendid. You'll never guess who's going to play opposite you.

RUTH: (*moves closer*) Oh, I think I can. Someone dynamic and exciting?

HILARY: How did you guess?

RUTH: Just call it female intuition.

HILARY: He's going to make a name for himself one day.

RUTH: He certainly has done with me.

HILARY: He has this virile quality.

RUTH: (*breathlessly*) I know. When do we start?

HILARY: As soon as he comes down.

RUTH: Pardon?

HILARY: He's just washed his hair.

RUTH: Who has?

HILARY: Why Alan of course.

RUTH: Alan!

Ruth's expression changes to one of horror.

END OF PART ONE

PART TWO

SCENE 3: *Int. Hilary's room.*
Two nights later. Hilary is rehearsing Alan and Ruth in their parts.

HILARY: Now, Alan, you must do it with more feeling. And, Ruth – remember when you attack him with the bread knife – look as if you mean it.

RUTH: Yes. Sorry, Hilary.

HILARY: Now, from the top.

RUTH: Oh, my God! I can't go on. Life's a hollow sham – a lousy, hollow sham.

ALAN: No, it's not, Maggie. It's a lousy cage – we're prisoners in a lousy cage – this room's a lousy cage – this house is a lousy cage – life's a lousy cage.

RUTH: It's not a lousy cage, Slim – it's a hollow sham – a lousy hollow sham.

ALAN: It's no good – I must have a fix. Where did you put my syringe?

RUTH: Don't get mad, Slim – I put it down the loo.

ALAN: Why, you no good tramp! I thought so – you've been at the gin again.

RUTH: Take your hands off me you big ape, or I'll carve you up like sliced bread. (*Pause*) Hilary, are you sure this is going to develop into a tender love story?

HILARY: Of course – this is the big scene – let it develop.

RUTH: Take your hands off me you big ape, or I'll carve you up like sliced bread.

ALAN: We'll see about that.

They struggle.

ALAN: Hey! It's sharp.

HILARY: Keep it up – you're doing splendidly. Now kiss her.

Alan forces Ruth to drop the knife and pulls her roughly into an embrace.
Rigsby bursts in. He seizes Alan by the scruff of the neck and pulls him away.

RIGSBY: All right, Miss Jones – I've got him.

HILARY: Do you mind, Rigsby? We happen to be rehearsing.

RIGSBY: Oh, sorry, Hilary. It was Miss Jones – she was so convincing.

316

RUTH: Thank you, Mr Rigsby.

HILARY: Can we get on?

RIGSBY: Of course – don't let me interrupt. (*He sits down and takes out a packet of crisps*)

HILARY: Now, what's the next line?

ALAN: I'm not doing it in front of him.

HILARY: Alan – you must get used to an audience – we had to stop for the window cleaner yesterday.

ALAN: He'll laugh.

RIGSBY: No, I won't.

HILARY: Could we get on? Ruth, you are suddenly aware of this burning desire you feel for Alan.

RIGSBY: Is it a comedy?

HILARY: No.

RIGSBY: Oh.

RUTH: Oh, Slim.

RIGSBY: (*laughs*) Slim!

ALAN: There you are – I told you.

RIGSBY: You can't call him Slim – unless he's going to do it in whalebones. If you don't want any unlooked for laughs you'd better call him something else.

HILARY: Oh, what do you suggest?

RIGSBY: What about Podge?

HILARY: (*angrily*) His name's Slim – now please stop interrupting.

RIGSBY: Sorry, Hilary.

HILARY: Ruth.

RUTH: Oh, Slim, that kiss has opened the floodgates. My whole being's yearning for you.

ALAN: You little fool – I love you madly – passionately – devotedly—

RUTH: Oh, Slim, quench this fire that's burning within me.

Rigsby crunches his crisps.

ALAN: I'm going to take you away from all this – away from this miserable hovel. We'll start a new life. (*Crunch*)

RUTH: Yes, we'll get that white-walled cottage with roses twining round the door. (*Crunch*)

ALAN: Maggie, (*crunch*) is he going to eat those crisps all night?

HILARY: Rigsby!

RIGSBY: Sorry, Hilary.

ALAN: Maggie, I'm going to kiss you as you've never been kissed before.

RIGSBY: This should be interesting.

They kiss. Rigsby reacts jealously.

Call that a kiss?

ALAN: What was wrong with it?

RIGSBY: You're supposed to be kissing her, not licking an envelope.

ALAN: That does it. I'm not rehearsing while he's here.

Alan exits.

RUTH: Now, you've upset him. I'm sure he'll get it right with practice. Alan—

Ruth exits.

HILARY: Rigsby – you've reduced this rehearsal to a shambles.

RIGSBY: Sorry, Hilary. But if you don't mind me saying, you're backing a loser there. Wrong temperament. You need someone with a bit of poise – some experience. And of course the classic profile.

HILARY: Who do you suggest, Rigsby?

RIGSBY: You're looking at him.

HILARY: You, Rigsby?

RIGSBY: I've always had this strange power over an audience. When I was at school they always picked me for the nativity play – every year without fail.

HILARY: Oh, what part did you play?

RIGSBY: Well, Herod, actually. But I've done quite a bit since. It's in my blood – the smell of the greasepaint – the roar of the crowd. During the war I used to do the Hunchback of Notre Dame – without makeup – just a cushion up my shirt – frightened the lads half to death.

HILARY: Yes, I can imagine.

RIGSBY: I used to do this eye-gouging scene with a couple of black grapes – they sent a shiver through the hut I can tell you.

HILARY: Yes, well, I'll let you know, ducky.

RIGSBY: I also do a very good Long John Silver. 'Avast there, Jim'.

HILARY: Quite. Now if you don't mind, Rigsby.

He guides Rigsby to the door.

RIGSBY: (*declaiming*) 'There's a one-eyed, yellow idol to the north of Kathmandu. There's a little marble cross below the town. And a broken-hearted woman tends the grave of Mad Carew. While the yellow god forever gazes down.'

HILARY: Very good, Rigsby. But not quite what I'm looking for.

Hilary opens door.

RIGSBY: (*doggedly*) 'He was known as Mad Carew to the subs at Kathmandu. He was hotter than they felt inclined to tell. But for all his foolish pranks he was worshipped in the ranks. And the colonel's daughter smiled on him as well.'

HILARY: Don't ring us, ducky – we'll ring you.

Closes door on Rigsby.

* * *

SCENE 4: *Int. attic flat.*
Next evening. Alan is learning his part.
Rigsby enters.

RIGSBY: You're going through with it, then?

ALAN: Of course.

RIGSBY: Well, I wouldn't if I were you. I can see the way things are going.

ALAN: Oh, yes. (*Pause. Frowns*) What do you mean – the way things are going?

RIGSBY: I mean Hilary. (*Pause*) Noticed anything odd about him?

ALAN: No.

RIGSBY: Nothing strange in his manner?

ALAN: Well, he's a bit theatrical.

RIGSBY: You could put it that way. Of course they're all the same – putting make-up on every night and wearing wigs. Bound to send them funny.

ALAN: What do you mean, funny?

Rigsby looks around cautiously.

RIGSBY: (*mouths words silently*) He's one of them.

ALAN: What?

RIGSBY: He's one of them.

ALAN: One of them what?

RIGSBY: My God! You're so naïve.

Didn't your parents ever warn you about taking sweets from strangers?

ALAN: They didn't have to – I never got offered any.

RIGSBY: Never?

ALAN: No.

RIGSBY: Surely you've been approached by some kindly gentleman – offering to show you his Hornby train set.

ALAN: No.

RIGSBY: Well, I don't know how to break this to you but Hilary's not as other men.

ALAN: (*grins*) Oh, you mean he's queer.

RIGSBY: Keep your voice down! Yes, that's what I mean. I suppose it never occurred to you.

ALAN: Not really but then again I don't think it's important.

RIGSBY: Of course it's important. In my day it meant prison.

ALAN: Well, we live in more enlightened times, Rigsby. Parliament's made it legal now.

RIGSBY: I'm not surprised with that lot. We're lucky they didn't make it compulsory.

ALAN: You know, I feel sorry for you, Rigsby. You're so reactionary. I'm glad I'm not like that.

RIGSBY: So am I. You know who he's after, don't you?

ALAN: Who?

RIGSBY: You.

ALAN: What!

RIGSBY: I told you to get your hair cut.

ALAN: I don't believe it. How do you know?

RIGSBY: I know the signs. I saw them go that way in the desert – nothing but sand and flies and never the sight of a woman. You had to be very careful who you shared a foxhole with in those days. You had to watch them – especially the one who said, 'Isn't it cold – let's all huddle together!' It wasn't only the Africa Korps you had to fight off in those days. Mind you, you never went to sleep at your post.

ALAN: But what am I going to do, Rigsby?

RIGSBY: There's only one thing you can do. Keep you door locked.

Exit Rigsby.
Alan stares after him appalled.
Philip enters. Stares.

PHILIP: What's the matter, Alan? You look stunned.

ALAN: Rigsby's just told me something terrible.

PHILIP: What's that?

ALAN: (*hesitates*) I can't bring myself to say it.

PHILIP: I think you'd better – you look as if you're going to burst.

ALAN: (*lowers voice*) He says Hilary's that way.

PHILIP: Well, so what?

ALAN: About me.

PHILIP: (*laughs*) Is that all?

ALAN: Is that all! How do you think I feel?

PHILIP: I thought you were broad-minded?

ALAN: I'm not that broad-minded. I don't know what to do about it. (*Pause*) Has this ever happened to you, Philip?

PHILIP: Oh yes. All the time.

ALAN: It's never happened to me.

PHILIP: No, well, you've got to be good-looking.

ALAN: Well, when I say never – not for a long time – not since the choir. What do you do about it?

PHILIP: Just don't encourage him. You haven't been encouraging him, have you?

ALAN: (*indignantly*) No, certainly not. I suppose you think we're decadent.

PHILIP: (*enjoying himself*) Oh, no – we have them out in Africa as well – you can usually tell them – always a bit heavy with the warpaint.

ALAN: Well, what am I going to do? You've got to help me.

PHILIP: Well, I'd get rid of the April

violets for a start. And remember, whatever you do – don't flutter your eyelashes.

Hilary enters.

HILARY: Oh, hope I'm not interrupting. I just wanted a word with Alan.

PHILIP: That's all right – I was just going.

ALAN: Philip.

PHILIP: No, if you two want to be alone.

Philip exits grinning.

HILARY: I hope you don't mind, Alan but I thought we ought to have an extra rehearsal tonight.

ALAN: (*deepens voice*) I don't know about that, Hilary. You see I've got a game of squash with some chaps from the college.

HILARY: I didn't know you played squash.

ALAN: Oh yes. Like to keep fit. A run before breakfast – a cold shower and a rub-down with surgical spirit – keeps you in trim. That reminds me – I've got to get my hair cut.

HILARY: Oh no! Not your hair. That's your crowning glory, Alan.

ALAN: No, I'm afraid it's short back and sides from now on. There's been a lot of banter in the locker room – they've been

flicking me with wet towels again. Besides, it's a bit of a nuisance in the scrum.

HILARY: Don't tell me you play rugger as well?

ALAN: Oh yes. Nothing like punting the leather around on a winter's afternoon. It makes a man of you.

HILARY: But what about rehearsals?

ALAN: (*backing to door*) I've been thinking about that, Hilary. I wonder if it's really my cup of tea. If the rugger team finds out my life wouldn't be worth living – they'd probably scrum down and use me for the ball. (*Opens door*) Besides, to tell the truth I don't reckon all this acting business – I'd sooner see a good stripper anyday.

Alan exits
Hilary is left looking bewildered.

* * *

SCENE 5: *Int. Ruth's room. Later. Rigsby enters.*

RIGSBY: Well, Alan's dropped out then.

RUTH: Yes. (*Cheerfully*) Never mind, Mr Rigsby – the show must go on.

RIGSBY: Yes, fortunately we've got someone who can step into the breach at a moment's notice.

RUTH: That's true.

RIGSBY: (*archly*) Someone with classical good looks – virility – and a great deal of personal charm.

RUTH: I do agree.

RIGSBY: (*smiles*) I thought you'd get my drift, Miss Jones – the part could have been written for him.

RUTH: Oh, yes. Where is he?

RIGSBY: Who?

RUTH: Hilary.

RIGSBY: Hilary! He couldn't play the part. Where's his virility? Where's his inner violence? He nearly ruptured himself putting up his chintz curtains.

RUTH: But he's an actor – surely he can play any part.

RIGSBY: He's an actor with a problem, Miss Jones.

RUTH: What do you mean, Mr Rigsby?

RIGSBY: Nature's played a cruel joke on that man.

RUTH: (*eyes widening*) You don't mean?

RIGSBY: I'm afraid so. Not his fault – an imbalance of chromosomes – he's not as other men.

RUTH: Are you sure, Mr Rigsby?

RIGSBY: You'd be wasting your time there, Miss Jones. Like an empty slot machine – you put your money in but nothing comes out – not even if you kick it.

RUTH: I'd never have guessed.

RIGSBY: I know the signs. The slack wrist – the foppish manner. (*Rigsby starts to camp about the room*) 'Oh, ducky' – the evening's been a complete disaster – my soufflé's collapsed – it's just lying there staring up at me like the creature from the Black Lagoon.'

Hilary enters. Stands behind Rigsby and eyes him coldly.
Rigsby follows Ruth's horrified gaze.

RIGSBY: Oh, hello, Hilary. Well, can't stop here all day chatting, must get on.

Rigsby beats a hasty retreat.

HILARY: Oh, Ruth – about the rehearsals—

RUTH: Er … not just now, Hilary. I'm late for badminton.

Ruth dashes out.
Hilary stares after them. Bewilderment tinged with suspicion.

* * *

SCENE 6: *Int. Hilary's room, later.*
Hilary is reading the play.
Rigsby enters. He has a bright scarf tied around his neck and sandals.

RIGSBY: Hello, ducky – a word in your shell-like.

HILARY: Certainly. You seem to be the only person who's speaking to me these days, Rigsby. What do you want?

RIGSBY: I've just popped in to tell you your problems are over. I'm prepared to play the part of Slim.

HILARY: Not again, Rigsby.

RIGSBY: But nature's designed me for that part, Hilary. The good looks, the physical strength, the silver tongue. I wouldn't be surprised if you hadn't subconsciously based it on me.

HILARY: I'd never thought of it like that. (*Slyly*) Of course, you're a little older but it might just work. Why don't you come and sit down – let me hear you read.

RIGSBY: (*eagerly*) Should I fetch Miss Jones?

HILARY: No, that won't be necessary. I can read her part.

RIGSBY: Oh. All right.

Rigsby sits down by Hilary. Hilary hands him the script.

HILARY: Hmm. What strong, sensitive hands. You may be just the man I'm looking for.

Rigsby looks nervous. Edges away.

RIGSBY: What do you want me to read?

HILARY: Page 90 – from the top.

Rigsby stares in horror at the text.

RIGSBY: (*clears throat*) Oh, Maggie.

HILARY: Oh, Slim, that kiss has opened the floodgates. My whole being's yearning for you.

He puts a hand on Rigsby's thigh.

RIGSBY: (*stares at hand*) You little fool I love you madly – passionately – devotedly.

HILARY: Oh, Slim, quench this fire that's burning within me.

RIGSBY: (*edging away*) I'm going to take you away from this miserable hovel – we'll start a new life.

HILARY: Yes. (*Rests head on Rigsby's shoulder*) We'll get that white-walled cotttage with—

Rigsby almost falls off settee.

HILARY: Go on, Rigsby.

RIGSBY: (*hesitates*) Maggie, I'm going to kiss you as you've never been kissed before – (*Rigsby jumps up in panic*) No – I just haven't got it, have I?

HILARY: Oh, I thought you were rather good.

RIGSBY: No – there's no need to be kind, Hilary. The old magic's gone. It's too late. I couldn't play a romantic lead – not with my feet. Trench foot. I'm a physical wreck really. You can't play an intimate romantic scene – not with foot odour likely to break out at any time. And of course I've never looked after my teeth – you need a full set of choppers for this, Hilary.

Dodge around furniture.

Age is against me. You'll have to find someone else.

Rigsby exits in confusion.
Hilary collapses into laughter.

* * *

SCENE 7: *Int. landing.*
Next night. Rigsby is listening at
Hilary's door.
Alan and Philip enter from street.
Alan is wearing a cap

ALAN: What's going on?

RIGSBY: (*chuckles*)   Hilary's
rehearsing Miss Jones in a love
scene. This should be worth
watching. Come on.

They knock and enter.

* * *

SCENE 8: *Int. Hilary's room.*
Hilary and Ruth are sitting on settee.

HILARY: Rigsby, we're rehearsing.

RIGSBY: That's all right. Don't let us
disturb you. We just want to
watch a professional at work.

Nudges Alan. Takes out crisps.

HILARY: All right. Ruth, we'll try it
just once more.

RUTH: I'm sure I'll get it right this
time, Hilary.

HILARY: Maggie, I'm going to kiss
you as you've never been kissed
before.

They kiss with great passion.
Rigsby's mouth drops open.

PHILIP: Are you sure you're right
about him, Rigsby?

ALAN: Hey! I think she's kissing
with her mouth open.

PHILIP: Rigsby, I can see steam.

Hilary straightens up.

HILARY: Now, Ruth, I'll cross to the
window. Ruth, are you all right?

Ruth is still lying there. A bemused
expression on her face.

RUTH: Yes. Do you mind if we do it
again, Hilary? I don't think I got it
quite right.

RIGSBY: You can't keep doing that,
Miss Jones. You won't have any
lips left!

RUTH: Oh, since Mr Rigsby objects,
perhaps we'd better do it in my
room. Come, Hilary.

They exit.

RIGSBY: Did you see that?

PHILIP: Never mind, Rigsby. He's
only acting.

RIGSBY: He's not acting. He's not one
of them – he's one of us – the dirty
devil. What am I going to do?

ALAN: (*angrily*) Never mind about
you. What am I going to do – I
had my hair cut.

Alan removes cap to show short hair.
He begins hitting Rigsby with cap.

THE END.

Series Three

EPISODE 3

Clunk Click
by
Eric Chappell

PART ONE

SCENE 1: *Int. garage. Day.*
Roar of engine. Screeching brakes.
Cut to Rigsby getting out of white
sports car with canvas hood. He is
wearing a flat cap and string-backed
gloves. He flicks imaginary speck of
dust from bonnet. Alan enters.

RIGSBY: Well?

ALAN: Blimey! It's Dick Dastardly.

RIGSBY: (*scowls*) That's right – be
funny. I wanted to know what
you thought of the car.

ALAN: It's very nice, Rigsby. I've
always wanted a car like this. I
bet it can go.

RIGSBY: Go? I should say it can go.
I was just a blur coming down
the motorway. I was passing
everything – and I'd left the
handbrake on.

ALAN: I thought you were going to
get a Mini?

RIGSBY: No, I decided against it. Too
small. You can lose them in a pile
of dead leaves. No, this is the car
for me – it reflects my personality.
Take your grubby fingers off the
paintwork I've just polished it.

ALAN: How can it reflect your personality? It's a young man's car.

RIGSBY: No, it isn't. You need experience to drive a car like this –
and I was driving before the war.
You could motor then – plenty of
open road. I used to shift in those
days – you could take risks.

ALAN: You don't mean you
overtook the man with the red
flag?

RIGSBY: I mean I had wrists like
steel and instant reactions. The
salesman could see that. He said
he'd been waiting for someone
like me.

ALAN: I bet he had. Where did you
get it from?

RIGSBY: The Car Sales down the
road.

ALAN: I knew someone who got a
car from there. He started hosing
it down and the door fell off.

RIGSBY: Well, there's nothing
wrong with this car. It's only had
one owner – a shy, retiring bank
clerk who collects stamps. He
only used it to take his mother to
church.

ALAN: You don't want to believe
that – they'll say anything to sell
a car.

RIGSBY: Not this one – it's full of

power. You could go fifty miles for a bag of chips in this car and they'd still be warm when you got home.

ALAN: Well, don't get carried away, Rigsby. You weren't that safe in the Anglia.

RIGSBY: What do you mean? Of course I was safe.

ALAN: What about the disqualification?

RIGSBY: Just because I happen to have been victimised by the police. They've always had it in for the motorist around here. That's what I told the constable – I said he should have been out fighting crime not standing in the middle of the road holding up traffic. That's why he did me.

ALAN: No, it wasn't – it was because you ran over his foot.

RIGSBY: I couldn't help it if he'd got big feet. That's the trouble with the police – they're ponderous. They have to have big feet to stop them falling over – he'd got feet like snowshoes. I was victimised. And I won't forget that magistrate – looking down his nose at me – trying to make out I was a bad driver. I've never had an accident in my life.

ALAN: You've hit the gatepost three times.

RIGSBY: I don't count gateposts.

ALAN: Only because they can't jump out of the way.

RIGSBY: I don't know what you're suggesting but I can honestly say that my driving has never given anyone a moment's anxiety—

A small, peppery man enters the garage. He looks at Rigsby indignantly.

MAN: Ah, there you are.

RIGSBY: What do you want?

MAN: You're the man who cut in front of me on the High Street.

RIGSBY: So what?

MAN: I've followed you all the way from the clock tower.

RIGSBY: Why – didn't you know the way?

MAN: I just wanted to tell you that I considered it to be a blatant example of dangerous driving.

RIGSBY: Haven't you been overtaken before?

MAN: Not when the lights are on red.

RIGSBY: They weren't on red – they'd changed. Not that you'd know – you were filling your pipe. I hadn't got time to sit behind you all day. I thought you were training for a funeral.

MAN: How dare you? I knew there'd be trouble as soon as I saw you in the mirror. You sports car drivers.

RIGSBY: How could you see me? You had the dog in the back

window. And the stickers – 'I'm a bloody donor' and 'Come to Jesus'. You must go out expecting an accident.

MAN: With people like you around that's not surprising. I was forced to brake savagely. It may interest you to know the dog's had a fit.

RIGSBY: I'm not surprised. You know what you ought to do? You ought to get in the back window and let him drive.

MAN: I should have expected that attitude from someone who drives a flashy sports car.

RIGSBY: Did you say flashy?

MAN: That's right – flashy. It's ridiculous – a man of your age. I suppose it's a phallic symbol.

RIGSBY: (*puzzled*) A what?

ALAN: A phallic symbol, Rigsby.

RIGSBY: Oh, yes, well, that just shows how much you know about cars. They stopped making them years ago. Now if you don't mind, you're trespassing on private property.

MAN: (*retreats*) I'm going to report you.

RIGSBY: You're wasting your time. You know what you want to do with that car? Take the wheels off and keep chickens in it.

MAN: You'll hear abut this.

Man exits.

RIGSBY: (*through cupped hands*) Sunday drivers! (*Frowns*) What did he mean – phallic symbol?

ALAN: He meant it was a symbol of virility – to attract the opposite sex.

RIGSBY: (*grins*) Yes, well, I'm not saying it won't prove useful where Miss Jones is concerned.

ALAN: So that's the reason. Well, it won't make any difference, Rigsby. Ruth isn't going to be impressed just because you've got a sports car.

Ruth enters.

RUTH: Oh, Mr Rigsby – what a lovely car. I saw it from the window.

RIGSBY: (*glance at Alan*) Do you like it, Miss Jones?

RUTH: I adore it.

She leans on Rigsby's shoulder to look inside.

ALAN: (*snorts*) Women!

Exits.

RUTH: What's the matter with Alan?

RIGSBY: Just jealousy, Miss Jones. After all, he's only got a Raleigh three speed.

RUTH: You've certainly got a lovely shine, Mr Rigsby.

RIGSBY: Yes, I've been waxing her

body. I wondered if you'd like to come for a spin sometime?

RUTH: Oh yes, it's years since I've been in a sports car.

RIGSBY: Perhaps you'd like to take the wheel, Miss Jones?

RUTH: I'd love to, Mr Rigsby – unhappily I've never learned to drive.

RIGSBY: Oh, I didn't know you were a pedestrian, Miss Jones.

RUTH: Yes, I've been a pedestrian ever since they took me out of the pram. And it can be very galling carrying your shopping bags in the pouring rain whilst lady motorists ride by with cigarettes drooping from their lower lips.

RIGSBY: Haven't you ever tried it, Miss Jones?

RUTH: I did once – when I was a young girl. It wasn't very successful I'm afraid. I ran over two cats, a hedgehog and Daddy's leg. It made me realise that the car can be a lethal instrument, Mr Rigsby.

RIGSBY: Not in the proper hands, Miss Jones. Would you like me to teach you?

RUTH: Oh, I don't know, Mr Rigsby. Driving seems to bring the worst out of people. I don't know if I could stand all the bad temper and the swearing.

RIGSBY: You could always try counting up to ten, Miss Jones.

RUTH: (*stares*) I didn't mean me, Mr Rigsby. I was referring to the other motorists.

RIGSBY: Oh. Well, we're not all like that, Miss Jones. I always say if you lose control of yourself – how can you control the car?

RUTH: That's very true, Mr Rigsby.

RIGSBY: I was wondering, Miss Jones, if you'd like to drive out to the country club tomorrow night – they're holding a dance.

RUTH: (*impressed*) The Country Club!

RIGSBY: Yes. There'll be lanterns strung across the terrace – light-hearted banter by the swimming pool – the crunch of tyres on the gravel and the sleek purring of expensive motors.

RUTH: Have you been before, Mr Rigsby?

RIGSBY: No, it never seemed to go with the Anglia somehow.

RUTH: It would mean a long dress. Perhaps I could borrow Aunt Aida's fox fur. It would be so exciting.

RIGSBY: Yes, they usually go on until dawn.

RUTH: Oh, I can just see it. Two people in evening dress, in the early morning – a balloon trailing behind them—

RIGSBY: Yes, the birds singing and dawn breaking over the slag heaps—

RUTH: He hums a tune of the night before and she dances a few steps, her long dress twirling over the dewy grass. It sounds so romantic, Mr Rigsby. I'll go and ring Aunt Aida – ask her to get the fox out of mothballs.

Exit Ruth.
Rigsby smiles and picks up Vienna.

RIGSBY: Well, Vienna, I think we've cracked it at last. (*Feigned surprise*) 'My word, Miss Jones – I had no idea the petrol gauge was so low. I'm afraid we're here for the night.' Ho. Ho.

Rigsby exits chuckling.

* * *

SCENE 2: *Attic flat*
Philip is reading. Alan enters looking dejected.

ALAN: Seen Rigsby's new car?

PHILIP: No but I heard the screech of tyres. Has he killed anyone yet?

ALAN: No.

PHILIP: He will.

ALAN: Aren't you going to look at it?

PHILIP: No. I'm not interested. I consider the motor car to be a threat to the environment.

ALAN: It might be a threat to the environment but it certainly pulls the birds. You should have seen the effect it had on Ruth – she was almost purring. That car's wasted on Rigsby – now if I had it—

PHILIP: But I thought you'd got a girl?

ALAN: You mean Caroline? Yes but how long am I going to keep her? I mean she's got class. You don't catch her sticking chewing gum on the back of the cinema seat. She comes from a good family.

PHILIP: Is that why she's got that funny voice?

ALAN: She hasn't got a funny voice.

PHILIP: She sounds like a cat sliding down a blackboard.

ALAN: They all talk like that. It comes from shouting at the servants. The question is how long is she going to put up with someone who travels by Yorkshire Traction?

PHILIP: I don't see what you're worried about. It obviously doesn't matter to her whether you've got a car or not.

ALAN: That's not strictly true – you see, she thinks I've got a car.

PHILIP: What gave her that idea?

ALAN: Well, I've only met her at the coffee bar. I put my bike round the back and go in throwing these car keys in the air. Now she thinks I've got a car.

PHILIP: I'm not surprised.

ALAN: Now she wants me to take her home for the weekend.

PHILIP: What are you going to do?

ALAN: I don't know. I don't think she's going to fancy fifty miles on my cross-bar.

* * *

SCENE 3: *Int. Rigsby's room. Next Evening*
Sound of engine. Screeching brakes. A moment later Rigsby enters. He is wearing an evening suit. He starts transferring cigarettes to case.
Philip enters angrily.

PHILIP: Rigsby – you could have killed me.

RIGSBY: What are you talking about?

PHILIP: You nearly ran me down out there. You missed me by inches.

RIGSBY: Close as that was it? Well, it was nothing personal – I was swerving to avoid the cat.

PHILIP: The cat! What about me? That's typical of you, Rigsby. You'd swerve to avoid a cat and run down a dozen pedestrians.

RIGSBY: It wasn't like that at all. It's just that I can see him better. His eyes reflect the light – human eyes don't – fact of nature. I can prove it – you go out there and crouch down and I'll put the headlights on you.

PHILIP: That's not the point – you should be more careful.

RIGSBY: Look, I can't help it if you're barely discernible. I've told you before you should wear something light at night – either that or flash your teeth.

PHILIP: That wouldn't make any difference, Rigsby, because I don't think you can control that car.

RIGSBY: How would you know? Let's face it – the internal combustion engine's always been a mystery to your lot. That's why you always break down on the M1.

PHILIP: I'm not interested in cars, Rigsby. As far as I'm concerned they cause pollution – use up the world's limited resources – and in the wrong hands are as lethal as a loaded revolver.

RIGSBY: You don't understand, do you? A car's essential in this country – you can't travel by jungle creeper around here, you know.

PHILIP: You could use a bicycle.

RIGSBY: A bicycle! I'm taking Miss Jones to the Country Club. You're not suggesting we go by tandem? I can just see myself handing my bicycle clips over to the commissionaire. Of course, that's what's annoying you, isn't it? It's because Miss Jones and I are going out. Well, don't worry, as soon as I've filled my cigarette case I'm away – and I won't be home until the morning.

Ruth enters. She is wearing a fox fur complete with head. This head appears to worry her.

RUTH: Do I look all right, Mr Rigsby.

RIGSBY: All right? You look ravishing Miss Jones.

RUTH: I was wondering about this. (*Waggles head of fox*) You don't think it looks ... odd?

RIGSBY: Why should it look odd?

RUTH: It's Aunt Aida's. I suppose it's rather old-fashioned now. I think it's the head. (*Waggles head again*) I keep thinking something's leaped on me from behind.

RIGSBY: I wouldn't give it a moment's thought, Miss Jones. It suits you.

RUTH: Aunt Aida wears it an awful lot. In fact they even look alike. I think it's the teeth. What do you think, Philip?

PHILIP: (*angrily*) What do I think of it? I think it's just another example of the way so-called civilised countries are decimating the animal kingdom. And just to satisfy the whims of fashion – to grace the idle, pampered shoulders of Western women.

RUTH: (*pause*) You don't like it.

PHILIP: I think it's disgusting.

RUTH: Well, I didn't kill it – and I'm sure Aunt Aida didn't.

PHILIP: You can't transfer your guilt as easily as that, Ruth. You're wearing it.

RIGSBY: Wait a minute – how do you know it didn't die of old age? He looks contented enough to me. Aren't you? (*Waggles head*) 'Course I am.'

PHILIP: Well, I think it's obscene, Rigsby. At least we only kill for food and warmth – not for the Country Club.

Exit Philip.

RUTH: Oh, dear – now I've upset him. Perhaps I ought not to wear it.

RIGSBY: No, you'll be all right, Miss Jones – as long as Peter Scott's not there.

RUTH: And you really think it suits me?

RIGSBY: Miss Jones, you look stunning. When we walk through those doors all heads will turn. You know what they'll think? Beauty and the beast.

RUTH: Oh, I don't know – you look very nice too, Mr Rigsby.

RIGSBY: (*winces*) I was referring to the fox, Miss Jones.

RUTH: Oh, of course. Sorry, Mr Rigsby.

RIGSBY: Yes, well, should we go down to the car? The seat belts are a bit tricky and I want to get you strapped down – I mean in.

RUTH: Oh yes. Clunk click every trip, Mr Rigsby.

RIGSBY: (*leers*) I hope so, Miss Jones.

Exit.

* * *

SCENE 4: *Int. garage. Early morning. Sound of car reversing into garage. Cut to sports car. Rigsby is getting out of the car a shade unsteadily. Ruth has her head stuck through the canvas hood and appears to be in a state of shock.*

RIGSBY: (*apprehensively*) How do you feel now, Miss Jones? I know it must have been a nasty shock. Let's see if I can prise you loose. My word, you have got a tight grip on these supports. Let me see if I can loosen your fingers one by one.

He slowly extricates Miss Jones. She struggles clear of the car.

Are you feeling any better?

RUTH: (*hysterically*) Feeling better! I thought my last moment had come.

RIGSBY: Yes, well, I know it said humpbacked bridge – I just didn't think it would be quite so steep.

RUTH: Mr Rigsby – if my foot hadn't caught in the door handle I'd have ended up in the canal.

RIGSBY: Yes, you're probably right, Miss Jones.

RUTH: That was extremely reckless driving, Mr Rigsby.

RIGSBY: Ah, couldn't we look upon it as a minor blemish on what was otherwise a perfect evening?

RUTH: (*hollow laugh*) Perfect evening! The times my past life flashed before me – it was terrifying. Do you always drive like that?

RIGSBY: Oh, it wasn't that bad, Miss Jones.

RUTH: Mr Rigsby – you may think that chasing rabbits down a country lane is the perfect way to round off an evening but I don't.

RIGSBY: Still, the Country Club was very nice, Miss Jones.

RUTH: Oh, yes – the Country Club. You know how sensitive I was about Aunt Aida's fur and what did you say when I handed it in? 'Put a bowl of water down for him – we'll be back later'!

RIGSBY: Just my little joke—

RUTH: I didn't know where to put myself. And later, when you fought over the balloons.

RIGSBY: Well, the red one was mine, Miss Jones.

RUTH: That was no reason to burst everyone else's. My impression was that you'd had too much to drink.

RIGSBY: No, not when I'm driving. Well, I may have had a little over the limit. But actually I usually drive better.

RUTH: Oh, and what about the collision at the crossroads?

RIGSBY: Well, it was only a scratch.

RUTH: A scratch! We dragged his front bumper for three miles. And you didn't stop.

RIGSBY: It was our right of way, Miss Jones. And no one was hurt. It's what we motorists call knock for knock.

RUTH: Well, the way he was chasing us I think he wanted to get his knock in there and then. What happens to you when you get behind a wheel, Mr Rigsby? You were like a man possessed. It was like Death Race 2000. I don't care if I never see that car again. You should be banned.

RIGSBY: Yes. (*Hopefully*) Well, apart from that did you enjoy the evening, Miss Jones.

Ruth gives a gasp of outrage and hurls the fox fur at him. Exits.

RIGSBY: (*sighs*) Apparently not.

END OF PART ONE

PART TWO

SCENE 5: *Int. garage. Morning.*
Rigsby enters. He is clearly suffering from a hangover.

RIGSBY: (*calls*) Vienna. (*Winces. Holds head*) Where are you? You should have been back by now.

Philip enters.

PHILIP: Rigsby – a man called earlier when you were in bed. Said he wanted to see you.

RIGSBY: (*nervously*) A man? What did he want?

PHILIP: He didn't say. He was just looking for someone who owned a white sports car. I told him you were sleeping it off.

RIGSBY: (*alarmed*) What did you have to say that for? What did he look like?

PHILIP: Oh, medium height – well-spoken – expensive clothes – and his front bumper was missing.

Rigsby closes garage door.

RIGSBY: (*covers*) Hmm. Probably wants me to join the Rotary. I know they've been after me for sometime. (*Starts*) Who's that?

Alan enters. He is carrying a battered bicycle.

ALAN: (*indigantly*) Look at this, Rigsby.

RIGSBY: What about it?

ALAN: You've run over it.

RIGSBY: Don't be ridiculous. I'd have known if I'd run over it.

ALAN: You must have run over it last night when you had a skinful.

RIGSBY: I didn't have a skinful!

ALAN: Well, what am I going to do now? The least you can do is let me borrow the car.

RIGSBY: Oh, so that's your game – well, it won't work. You're not getting up to any hanky panky in that car.

ALAN: You couldn't get up to any hanky panky in that car – you'd rupture yourself.

RIGSBY: That's because it's a sports car – not a virgin's hearse. Now, where is that cat? Vienna.

Rigsby catches sigh of the fox fur under the wheel. Turns away abruptly. Gulps.

Vienna! Oh, no!

335

PHILIP: What's the matter, Rigsby?

RIGSBY: (*slowly*) Just look at him, over there. Is … he … dead?

Philip and Alan exchange glances. Philip picks up fur.

PHILIP: Oh yes. I should say he's been dead for sometime—

ALAN: Yes. Do you want to look at him, Rigsby?

RIGSBY: (*hastily*) No. I don't want to see it. Just pick him up and put him in that sack – you'll find one over there.

PHILIP: Certainly, Rigsby.

Philip puts the fox fur into sack.

RIGSBY: Poor Vienna. I told him not to sleep on the garage floor – now it's too late.

ALAN: What are you going to do with him?

RIGSBY: I don't know. He wasn't just a pet you know. He was a companion and friend. I shall probably find some sunny spot – some nook – some dappled bank – where he can sheath his claws for ever. (*Blows nose*)

ALAN: Why don't you put him in the vegetable patch?

RIGSBY: (*frowns*) Why should I put him there?

ALAN: You'll get some big cabbages next year.

RIGSBY: (*angrily*) You know, you can be tasteless sometimes. Besides, I don't want to be digging him up every spring.

PHILIP: Yes, Rigsby's right, Alan. Imagine how he must be feeling.

RIGSBY: Yes, it was all my fault. I'll never drink and drive again. Poor Vienna. It's strange to think he'll never creep up on my lap and sink his claws into my thigh anymore.

PHILIP: Well, perhaps he hasn't died in vain, Rigsby. Perhaps he's a warning. A sacrifice so that others might live.

RIGSBY: You may be right. What kills me is I've just bought twenty tins of cat food.

PHILIP: Alan – I think we should leave Rigsby alone with his thoughts for a few minutes.

ALAN: Yes, of course. (*Hand on Rigsby's shoulder*) Sorry, Rigsby. (*Pause*) I don't suppose you'll feel like driving the car anymore—

RIGSBY: Get out!

Alan and Philip Exit.
Rigsby picks up the sack with a heavy heart. Reaches for a spade. He opens the garage door. Closes it hurriedly. He throws a tarpaulin over the car. French – prosperous, well-groomed, severe expression – enters the garage.

FRENCH: Good morning. My name's French. I'm looking for the owner of a white sports car. I understand he lives here.

RIGSBY: White sports car? No – not around here. Who told you that?

FRENCH: One of the tenants.

RIGSBY: Oh. Was he of a dark complexion? One you'd associate with warmer climes?

FRENCH: Er … yes.

RIGSBY: I wouldn't take any notice of him. He's only been here five minutes. Probably didn't know what you were talking about.

FRENCH: But he spoke perfect English.

RIGSBY: Yes, but he'd say anything to be agreeable. I think he's an illegal immigrant.

FRENCH: Oh. So you haven't seen a white sports car?

RIGSBY: No.

FRENCH: Excuse me for asking but have we met somewhere before?

RIGSBY: I don't think so.

FRENCH: Only I'm a magistrate and I do meet so many people—

RIGSBY: Do you really? That must be very interesting.

FRENCH: And your face is so familiar.

RIGSBY: (*changes expression*) Must be the squint – everyone notices it.

FRENCH: No, I don't think so.

RIGSBY: (*hollow laugh*) Well, as long as it wasn't in court.

FRENCH: My dear sir, I wasn't suggesting—

RIGSBY: No, of course not.

The cover slides from the car, unnoticed by Rigsby.

Well, if I do hear about a white sports car I'll let you know. But it's not the sort of thing you get around here. Now if you'll excuse me – only we've just had a death in the family.

FRENCH: (*points*) That's it!

RIGSBY: (*turns*) Good heavens! A white sports car. How did that get there?

FRENCH: And see these scratches? (*Regards Rigsby curiously*) I have reason to believe that I was in collision with this car late last night. Unfortunately, the driver didn't stop.

RIGSBY: Didn't stop? The swine. What's the world coming to?

FRENCH: I don't suppose you know who owns the car?

RIGSBY: I'll make enquiries. I'll leave no stone unturned.

FRENCH: Yes, well, I would like to meet him. I'll come back this evening. As you can imagine, we have quite a few things to settle.

RIGSBY: Yes, of course.

FRENCH: I'll see you this evening then.

French exits.

RIGSBY: That's what you think.

Rigsby jumps into car. He turns ignition. But the car fails to start. Rigsby's smile fades.

* * *

SCENE 6: *Int. garage. Evening. Alan and Caroline enter. Caroline is breezy – fresh-faced – a little jolly hockey stick.*

CAROLINE: (*admiringly*) What a super little car.

ALAN: Not bad is it? (*Flicks imaginary speck of dust*).

CAROLINE: You've certainly kept this a big secret. To tell the truth – I'd begun to wonder if you'd got one.

ALAN: (*amused*) Had you really? No – just out of commission I'm afraid.

CAROLINE: Couldn't you fix it? After all, you are an advanced motorist.

ALAN: No, I've tried. I think it's the transmission – can't get a peep out of her. It must have been that rally I was on the other night – very hairy. Fog and ice all the way. I aquaplaned three times. Fortunately all that practice on the skid patch paid off. Then my fan belt went – replaced it with my braces and finished third.

CAROLINE: Super. (*Studies car*) Hilary's got one like this. Souped up of course.

ALAN: Hilary?

CAROLINE: You know Hilary.

ALAN: Oh, you mean the one with the GB plates, Sea Link stickers and the BEA shoulder bag?

CAROLINE: Yes. He's driven all over Europe.

ALAN: Super. Mind you, we were going last year. Three of us bought this old van – souped up of course.

CAROLINE: Of course.

ALAN: We were going across Europe – through Turkey – over the mountains into Pakistan – down through India and then shipping to Australia—

CAROLINE: What happened?

ALAN: We got to the end of the road and the wheel came off.

CAROLINE: Oh, hard cheese. Mind if I look inside?

ALAN: No – go ahead.

Caroline gets in driving seat.

CAROLINE: You've left the keys in.

ALAN: What?

Caroline turns the key. The engine starts with a roar.

CAROLINE: It's going! Super. We'll be able to go after all. I'll just go and ring Mummy.

Exit Caroline.

Alan switches off engine.
Rigsby emerges from underneath car. His face is blackened with exhaust fumes. He stares stonily at Alan.

ALAN: (*nervously*) Oh, hello, Rigsby. Sorry about that. (*Dabs at Rigsby's face with a cloth*) I suppose you heard?

RIGSBY: Yes.

ALAN: I wasn't going to take it – just trying to make an impression.

RIGSBY: That's all right. I understand.

ALAN: (*surprised*) You do?

RIGSBY: Yes. I was young once you know. I could lay it on a bit myself. I used to tell them I rode at Brooklyns. Look, I don't want to cramp your style – you can borrow the car – if anyone asks, it's yours.

ALAN: Do you really mean that, Rigsby?

RIGSBY: Yes. Well, after cleaning up Vienna – I don't really feel like driving anymore. As far as the world's concerned, that car's yours. I never owned it. It can be our little secret.

ALAN: That's really nice of you, Rigsby.

RIGSBY: Well, you know me – all heart.

Caroline returns and throws case into car.

Rigsby stands back smiling engagingly.

CAROLINE: Come on, Alan. Get your clog down.

ALAN: I'm coming.

Alan is about to get into the car when French enters.

FRENCH: Excuse me – is this your car?

ALAN: Yes, that's right.

Rigsby turns away, hardly daring to look.

FRENCH: You were in collision with me last night.

ALAN: Was I?

FRENCH: And you didn't stop. You drove on as if nothing had happened.

Alan, with Caroline looking on, realises he's trapped. Looks at Rigsby. Rigsby feigns interest in spanners.

ALAN: Er ... I'm sorry ... I didn't realise—

FRENCH: No, please don't apologise – it wasn't your fault. You had right of way. I was rather careless – I just wanted to clear the matter up.

ALAN: What?

FRENCH: I'm relieved to see there's hardly any damage but you must allow me to make some restitution – if only for your narrow escape. Will ten pounds cover it?

ALAN: Thanks very much.

FRENCH: That's all right. I'm glad you took it so well. Some people would have reported me. And as a magistrate I can't afford a breath of scandal. Good night.

Exit French.
Alan puts the money into his pocket and gets into the car.

ALAN: See you Rigsby.

Alan drives off with a roar.
Rigsby fumes. He looks around for something to kick. He kicks oil drum. Hurts foot.

RIGSBY: I knew I'd miss that cat.

* * *

SCENE 7: *Int. garage. Later.*
Rigsby is standing by open boiler.
He is poking the fire moodily.
Ruth enters.

RUTH: (*coldly*) Oh, Mr Rigsby, have you seen my fur stole? I seem to have mislaid it.

RIGSBY: Ah, it was on the back seat of the car, Miss Jones.

RUTH: Well, I must have it. Aunt Aida's rung up about it.

RIGSBY: The trouble is, Alan's borrowed it.

RUTH: What on earth for? He'll look ridiculous in it.

RIGSBY: No, I mean the car, Miss Jones. I'll let you have it as soon as he gets back.

RUTH: (*coldly*) Thank you, Mr Rigsby.

Ruth turns to leave.

RIGSBY: Oh, Miss Jones, I must apologise for my conduct the other night.

RUTH: (*toss of head*) That's all right, Mr Rigsby – I've stopped shaking now. And I've managed a few hours sleep – with the aid of my red tablets.

RIGSBY: I realise I was reckless but I've learned my lesson, Miss Jones.

RUTH: I should hope so.

RIGSBY: You see, when I returned last night I unwittingly struck down an old friend and companion.

RUTH: Not Mr Baxter from the British Legion?

RIGSBY: No – Vienna, Miss Jones.

RUTH: Vienna! Oh, Mr Rigsby, what can I say? I know how fond you were of each other.

RIGSBY: There is nothing to say, Miss Jones. It was my fault.

RUTH: (*gently*) What have you done with him, Mr Rigsby?

RIGSBY: Well, I was going to bury him in the garden but I just couldn't bring myself to do it.

RUTH: Ah, I understand. Had you thought of having him stuffed?

RIGSBY: I don't think he'd have been very keen on that, Miss Jones. Besides, his coat was never in very good condition.

RUTH: A friend of mine had hers done and put on the mantelpiece. They made a very good job of it. In fact, he looked better dead than he did alive.

RIGSBY: No, I don't think I could have stood him watching me with those sad reproachful eyes. So I decided on cremation.

RUTH: Cremation! You mean he's in there?

RIGSBY: I'm afraid so, Miss Jones. I've got a very nice biscuit tin I can keep him in. It's got the Taj Mahal on the front – and it's air tight. I used to keep the mince pies in it.

RUTH: Poor Vienna.

RIGSBY: (*sighs*) Yes. Do you think cats go to heaven, Miss Jones?

RUTH: I'm sure they do, Mr Rigsby. Who knows, perhaps St Francis will be putting a saucer of milk down for him right now.

RIGSBY: Yes, well, I hope he remembers to put him out every night or there'll be trouble.

RUTH: Do you think we ought to say something, Mr Rigsby?

RIGSBY: Well, I'm not very good with words, Miss Jones.

RUTH: What about a hymn?

RIGSBY: That's a good idea.

Philip enters. Looks at their solemn faces.

PHILIP: What's the matter?

RUTH: We're cremating Vienna.

PHILIP: Why – what's he done? (*Realisation*) Oh no! Rigsby, you haven't!

RIGSBY: Would you be quiet and show some respect.

RUTH: We're trying to think of something to sing.

PHILIP: What about 'Up, up and away'?

RIGSBY: Do you mind? This is a solemn occasion.

RUTH: What about 'Rock of Ages'?

RIGSBY: Very appropriate, Miss Jones.

They begin to sing 'Rock of Ages'.
Philip is forced to join in.
Sound of car.

Alan enters carrying Vienna.

ALAN: Look what I've found.

They ignore him. They continue singing.
Alan joins in. First Ruth and then Rigsby become aware of the cat. The singing dies away.

RUTH: Mr Rigsby! It's Vienna.

RIGSBY: It can't be.

ALAN: It is – I found him in the boot.

RUTH: Mr Rigsby – if that's Vienna – what have you put in the boiler?

RIGSBY: But I saw him – he was under the wheel – his fur all crushed and matted.

Alan and Philip edge to the door.

RUTH: Aunt Aida's fur stole!

Rigsby tries to open boiler. Burns fingers.
Alan and Philip exit.

RUTH: Mr Rigsby, what am I going to do?

RIGSBY: Would you like to borrow the biscuit tin, Miss Jones?

Ruth moves threateningly towards him.

THE END

Series Three

EPISODE 4

The Good Samaritans

by

Eric Chappell

PART ONE

SCENE 1: *Int. Gray's room. Evening. Rigsby enters followed by Gray. Gray is a sad, lacklustre man about forty. He is carrying a small case. He puts it down and looks slowly round the room.*

MR GRAY: (*softly*) Good Lord!

RIGSBY: Yes, well, I know it's not exactly five star, Mr Gray, but it is short notice. I don't normally let rooms at this time of night.

MR GRAY: But there's water running down the walls.

RIGSBY: What did you expect – champagne? I'm not saying you won't find the odd rivulet – it's due to mild condensation. Just don't lean against the wallpaper, that's all – not unless you want covering in regency stripes.

MR GRAY: (*sad smile*) Oh, I'm not complaining, Mr Rigsby, but I have been used to better things.

RIGSBY: Oh, have you? I hope I'm not going to regret this. (*Sharply*) You're not thinking of putting your shoes out, are you?

MR GRAY: Why, no—

RIGSBY: Good. Only the last one who tried that found them replaced by a pair of well-worn tennis shoes. This isn't the Ritz you know.

MR GRAY: (*sighs*) You don't have to tell me that, Rigsby – I've been there. In fact, you may find this hard to believe but you're looking at a man who has reached the heights in his time. I've drunk champagne at Claridges – eaten oysters at the Savoy. I've mixed with the fashionable and the famous – and now I'm reduced to this. I think I've finally touched bottom, Rigsby.

RIGSBY: (*drily*) You haven't seen the basement. Now he's got something to complain about – loose-fitting windows. Every autumn he wakes up covered in dead leaves.

MR GRAY: Well, don't worry, Rigsby. I won't be any trouble. I've long since become immune to my surroundings. I only want the room for tonight and then (*pregnant pause*) I'll be on my way. Now if you'll excuse me – only I must write a few letters before I go.

RIGSBY: Hmm. (*Pause*) Taking a trip?

MR GRAY: Er ... yes. I'm getting out once and for all, Rigsby.

344

RIGSBY: Ah, emigrating. I don't blame you. Where are you going?

MR GRAY: I'm not quite sure – not yet.

RIGSBY: You're leaving it a bit late, aren't you? Somewhere warm I suppose?

MR GRAY: Well, I hope it won't be too warm. Goodnight, Rigsby.

Rigsby exits slightly puzzled.

* * *

SCENE 2: *Int. attic flat.*
Alan is reading.
Rigsby enters. He looks thoughtful.

ALAN: What's the matter, Rigsby? You look worried.

RIGSBY: Just been talking to the new bloke. He's emigrating – at least I think he's emigrating.

ALAN: Not another one. I don't know why everyone wants to emigrate. I wouldn't go.

RIGSBY: They wouldn't have you.

ALAN: Of course they'd have me. With my special skills—

RIGSBY: Special skills! Since when has the ability to lie on your back and blow smoke rings been a special skill?

ALAN: When I'm qualified, Rigsby, I could emigrate anywhere in the world.

RIGSBY: Don't bother – when you start cutting people open we'll all be emigrating.

ALAN: Well, I won't. I feel that in a time of crisis I should put my talents at the disposal of the nation. I shall stay.

RIGSBY: Oh, no – we've got enough Bolsheviks in the Health Service as it is. It's the private patients I feel sorry for. They're already getting cold rice pudding and having to wait for their bottles.

ALAN: No, they're not, Rigsby. They get the same treatment as anyone else.

RIGSBY: Oh, yes? Then why do you let their dahlias wither? They don't even get their flowers put in water these days. And what happens if they complain? They find you're holding a union meeting over their appendix. No, I don't blame him for going. I only wish I was younger.

ALAN: Where's he going?

RIGSBY: (*frowns*) He didn't say. He didn't seem to have much idea – he seemed depressed – it was strange really.

ALAN: That's not strange. They all get depressed when they see that room.

RIGSBY: No, he was depressed before. And he said he wasn't bothered about his surroundings. And there was something else – he didn't have any luggage. You'd have thought if he was emigrating he'd have had some luggage.

ALAN: Well, I agree that's strange. What did he say?

RIGSBY: He said he was getting out once and for all. Then he said he was going to write a few farewell notes … (*Stops. Looks worried*).

ALAN: (*mischievously*) Rigsby, you don't think he's going to do something desperate?

RIGSBY: What do you mean?

ALAN: You know. (*He draws a finger across his throat*).

RIGSBY: (*shudders*) Of course he's not. Why do you always look on the grisly side? You know I've just shampooed that carpet.

ALAN: Don't worry, Rigsby. He wouldn't go to those extremes – not in this day and age.

RIGSBY: I should think not.

ALAN: He'll probably plug himself into the light socket.

RIGSBY: There you go again. You're morbid you are. Just think about me for a change – this is my house – it could play havoc with the wiring.

ALAN: Don't get into a state, Rigsby. He's not going to do anything like that. He's probably got his luggage stored somewhere. And why shouldn't he write a few notes? It's perfectly normal.

RIGSBY: (*reassured*) Of course it is.

You're quite right. I don't know what's getting into me these days. (*Laughs*) Fancy me thinking that.

Philip enters. He is returning from bathroom, a towel slung over his shoulders.

PHILIP: Who's the new man across the passage?

RIGSBY: His name's Gray. He's just arrived. Why?

PHILIP: He's just borrowed my razor.

RIGSBY: What? (*Starts for the door. Stops*) No, I can't. I don't know what I'm going to find.

PHILIP: What's the matter, Rigsby?

ALAN: He thinks Gray's going to hand in his rent book.

He makes throat-slitting motion again.

RIGSBY: Will you stop doing that!

PHILIP: I shouldn't worry, Rigsby. He didn't look the type.

RIGSBY: They never do. The last one didn't look the type. Very quiet he was. Until he went up on the roof in his underpants. He sat up there all afternoon blaming the Labour Government. We had to send for the vicar. He talked to him for three hours through a megaphone. Saved his life.

ALAN: You mean he managed to talk him down?

RIGSBY: Oh no – he still jumped.

PHILIP: Then how did he save his life?

RIGSBY: He landed on the vicar. Mind you, he had a grievance. He was self-employed. I think it was the VAT that did him – that and the National Insurance. If things go on like this we'll all be at it. You'll have a job to find a ledge.

ALAN: Things aren't as bad as that, Rigsby.

RIGSBY: Of course they are. You won't be able to walk down the street without the self-employed dropping on you.

PHILIP: Well, what are you going to do about it, Rigsby?

RIGSBY: Me? (*Cautiously*) I'm not doing anything. After all, it's all supposition. We don't know he's going to do anything. I mean, he could just be sprucing himself up. And why should he do that if he's going to kill himself?

ALAN: Perhaps he wants a good-looking corpse?

RIGSBY: (*winces*) Will you shut up?

PHILIP: But you can't completely ignore the situation.

ALAN: No man is an island, Rigsby.

RIGSBY: I wish you were – somewhere in the North Sea.

PHILIP: Alan's right. Ask not for whom the bell tolls, Rigsby – it tolls for thee.

RIGSBY: (*thoughtfully*) I suppose you're right. If he does do something like that I'll never—

ALAN: You'll never forgive yourself.

RIGSBY: I'll never let that room.

PHILIP: That's all that worries you, isn't it, Rigsby? The bad publicity. You're not really concerned about him.

ALAN: He could be lying there with his throat slit from ear to ear.

RIGSBY: (*groans*) Don't start that again. It's not my fault. I didn't lend him the razor.

PHILIP: He won't use that, Rigsby.

RIGSBY: How do you know?

PHILIP: It's electric.

RIGSBY: (*angrily*) What! Why didn't you tell me before? I'd better have a word with him.

Exit Rigsby.

* * *

SCENE 3: *Int. Gray's room.*
Gray has just finished shaving.
Rigsby enters cautiously.

RIGSBY: Ah, hello, Mr Gray. Had a nice shave?

MR GRAY: Yes. No point in letting myself go – just because the whole world's against me.

RIGSBY: No – that's the spirit, Mr Gray. Would you like some of my aftershave?

MR GRAY: Er … no thank you.

RIGSBY: (*confidentially*) It's that stuff that's supposed to drive the women wild.

MR GRAY: No, I don't think so—

RIGSBY: It's not effeminate. Quite safe in the changing room – boxers use it. It's masculine with just a hint of sensuality. (*Lowers voice*) Now you slap some of that on and go down to a certain little night spot I know. (*Chuckles*) They'll be round you like flies round a jam jar.

Gray suddenly seizes Rigsby by the collar.

MR GRAY: Don't talk about women to me, Rigsby. It was a woman who brought me to this. Before I met her I had a successful business and a contented marriage. She took me for every penny. (*Shakes Rigsby*) I should have seen through her but I was a fool, Rigsby. Now I'm broke and my wife's left me. What have you got to say to that? (*Releases him*).

RIGSBY: (*feels throat*) Well, I can see that 1977 hasn't been your year. But look on the bright side – it can only get better. And now you're smartening yourself up – I always say things can't be too bad while you've still got a pride in your appearance.

MR GRAY: Yes, well, I must prepare for my journey.

RIGSBY: I see. (*Anxiously*) You don't think there'll be time in the morning?

MR GRAY: I think that'll be most unlikely, Rigsby.

RIGSBY: Er … excuse me. I'll be back in a minute.

Rigsby exits hurriedly.

* * *

SCENE 3A: *Int. Ruth's room.*
Ruth is trying nervously to light inside of gas cooker. Loud explosion. Ruth leaps back.
Rigsby enters.

RUTH: Mr Rigsby, I wish you'd get someone to see to this cooker.

RIGSBY: I have rung them, Miss Jones.

RUTH: It keeps exploding.

RIGSBY: They did say they'd send someone round.

RUTH: Well, I hope I can survive until he gets here. My pastry doesn't rise anymore, it disintegrates. I was covered in cake mix yesterday.

RIGSBY: Yes, well, I'm afraid I've got more to worry about than domestic trivia, Miss Jones.

RUTH: Why? What's the matter, Mr Rigsby? You look quite pale.

RIGSBY: It's Mr Gray – the new tenant. He doesn't seem to be quite himself – whatever that is. I wondered if you'd have a word with him? I thought perhaps the soothing balm of a woman's voice?

RUTH: Certainly, Mr Rigsby. What seems to be the trouble?

RIGSBY: Well, not to put too fine a point on it – I think he's contemplating suicide.

Ruth gives a little scream.

RUTH: Suicide! But Mr Rigsby, shouldn't we send for someone?

RIGSBY: Who do you suggest, Miss Jones?

RUTH: What about the vicar?

RIGSBY: He wasn't very successful last time.

RUTH: At least he broke his fall, Mr Rigsby. I thought that was a very Christian thing to do.

RIGSBY: I don't think he meant to, Miss Jones. We had some very unchristian language afterwards. Now if you could have a word with him. It needs the feminine touch. His wife's left him. He's all bitter and disillusioned.

RUTH: Poor man. He must feel terrible. But what can I say? How did you feel when your wife left you, Mr Rigsby?'

RIGSBY: Elated.

RUTH: Still, we must show him that there are people who care. We must persuade him that life can still be wonderful – it isn't all gloom and despondency.

RIGSBY: That's right, Miss Jones. (*Hurries her to door*) Don't forget to mention North Sea oil.

Exit Ruth and Rigsby.

* * *

SCENE 4: *Int. Gray's room.*
Gray has just suspended a noose from a hook in the ceiling.
Ruth enters.

Hello, Mr Gray? I'm Miss Jones. I live downstairs. I wondered how you were settling in.

MR GRAY: That's very kind of you, Miss Jones. Would you like a cup of tea?

RUTH: Why, thank you.

Gray puts out cups.

MR GRAY: Actually, there's not much point in my settling in. I won't be here for long.

RUTH: (*brightly*) Oh, it's not so bad, Mr Gray. You should see it in the daytime. This room gets quite a lot of sun. You'll notice the extra charge for it in the rent book. And the air up here is very fresh and invigorating.

MR GRAY: Yes. We do seem very high up.

RUTH: Yes, there's nothing between us and the Urals.

MR GRAY: Quite a nasty drop from that window.

RUTH: I should say so. We're directly above the compost heap. (*Hollow laugh*) I suppose that's what they call a sticky end. (*Drops catch on window*) But don't let's dwell on such grisly things. Life can be such an adventure don't you agree? It's the simple things – the fragrance of the garden after a summer shower – raindrops dripping like diamonds from the leaves – the birds frolicking in the fresh-smelling earth. Do you know, I have a friendly robin who comes to my window every morning to greet me.

MR GRAY: (*dolefully*) I had a friendly robin once – it used to sit on my spade in the garden and chatter. All day long – chatter, chatter, chatter.

RUTH: How lovely. Didn't that make you feel happier?

MR GRAY: Not really. The cat got it.

RUTH: Never mind. Don't dwell on it, Mr Gray. There's too much gloom and despondency around. Remember it's always darkest before — (*Catches sight of noose*) What's that?

MR GRAY: I was just going to hang out my drip dry. (*Extends rope*).

RUTH: Oh, of course. Mr Gray, I hope you don't think I'm intruding but Mr Rigsby has told me about your misfortune – and if there's anything I can do.

MR GRAY: (*dramatically*) What can anyone do? My wife's left me. My business is in ruins. Debts everywhere.

RUTH: Yes, I know it seems a bad start to the year – but every cloud has a silver lining.

MR GRAY: Not this one.

RUTH: (*gently*) I understand there was another woman?

MR GRAY: Yes, I was a fool.

Ruth observes him drop a tablet into the tea. She stops him as he's about to raise cup to his lips.

RUTH: Tell me about it.

MR GRAY: All she was after was my money. She was attractive and I was flattered. My wife warned me but I wouldn't listen.

Raises cup again. Ruth stops him.

RUTH: Go on.

MR GRAY: I spent money as if there was no tomorrow. I must have been insane. When the money was gone so was she – and so was my wife. I'd lost everything. What made me do it? Just look at this picture.

Gray crosses to get photograph from jacket. Ruth switches cups. Gray returns with picture.

MR GRAY: Look at her, Miss Jones. Tell me, what made me do it?

Ruth examines picture.

RUTH: Oh yes. I can see it all. See the hardness around the mouth? And those cruel little lines near the eyes. A real gold digger. You're better off without her, Mr Gray.

MR GRAY: (*coldly*) That's my wife, Miss Jones.

RUTH: What? Oh, it's the light. I can see it now – you've creased it – she looks very nice.

MR GRAY: I won't hear a word against her.

RUTH: No, of course not.

Gray drinks tea. Stops. Stares at cup and then Miss Jones.

MR GRAY: Miss Jones – have you been sent here to watch me?

RUTH: Watch you? I don't know what you mean, Mr Gray.

MR GRAY: Do you think I might do something desperate?

RUTH: Mr Gray – what on earth gave you that idea? Nothing could be further from my mind.

MR GRAY: Then why don't you drink your tea? It's getting cold.

RUTH: The tea. (*Get up*) Well, do you know – I'm not the least bit thirsty at the moment.

Rigsby bustles in.

RIGSBY: Hello. Tea up. Just what I needed. I'm parched.

Rigsby takes a large gulp. Groans.

RUTH: (*screams*) Mr Rigsby! Is it cyanide?

RIGSBY: No – saccharin.

Ruth darts from room with hysterical laugh.

END OF PART ONE.

PART TWO

SCENE 5: *Int. attic flat.*
Alan and Philip are reading.
Rigsby enters mopping his brow.

ALAN: Well? Has he done it yet?

RIGSBY: I wish you'd take this seriously. He's working himself up to it – I know he is. He's had a shave and put on his drip dry. He's finished his letters – probably one for the coroner. He's poised, I can see it. Miss Jones is fixing him some supper, but I think he'll be gone before her pastry rises.

PHILIP: Why don't you ring the police?

RIGSBY: How can I? I've got no proof. Besides, I've rung the Samaritans.

PHILIP: Who are they?

ALAN: The Samaritans. Of course, we should have thought of them before. They're very good – always standing by – available day and night for souls in distress. What did they say?

RIGSBY: Nothing – they were out. Apparently they've found a wooden leg by the suspension bridge.

ALAN: A wooden leg?

RIGSBY: Yes, they found a note with it saying 'Farewell, cruel world'. Now they're out looking for its owner. They said they'd send someone round as soon as he was available.

PHILIP: There certainly seems to be a sudden rash of suicides at the moment.

RIGSBY: I'm not surprised the way things are going.

ALAN: You'll be next, Rigsby. They'll find your clothes in a neat pile on some deserted beach – a dignified little note written on the back of a final demand. Another victim of the recession.

RIGSBY: (*scowls*) I wish you'd shut up. You're a ghoul, you are. You'd better not talk like that when he comes in.

ALAN: You mean he's coming here?

RIGSBY: Yes, I've asked him along to meet you. I know it's a desperate measure but we've got to keep him occupied and I'm running out of conversation.

ALAN: Well, I don't know what all the fuss is about. He's only trying to draw attention to himself.

That's My Boy: in spite of himself, Rigsby
becomes very fond of the baby.

'There's a Madonna-like quality about her.'
Philip, Alan and Rigsby admire Ruth's
maternal instincts in *That's My Boy*.

'Oh. My word. He's certainly a boy.'

'Not your hair, Alan, that's your crowning glory.'
Alan gets nervous of Hilary's attentions in *Stage Struck*.

'Oh Slim, quench this fire that's burning within me.'
Hilary has some fun with Rigsby in *Stage Struck*.

Clunk Click was Leonard Rossiter's favourite episode.

Rigsby gets bitten by a Fawcett Python.

Ruth is spellbound by Gwyn's welsh eloquence.

Above and Below: Pure farce in *Pink Carnations* as Rigsby and Ruth attempt to spice up their love lives.

The unsuspecting groom is caught in Ruth's
clutches in *Pink Carnations*.

Life in the attic room for students Alan
and Philip was far from salubrious.

Ambrose offers to remove Rigsby's inhibitions
in *Under the Influence*.

Rigsby's long-lost brother Ron turns up and ruins
the wedding day in *Come On In, the Water's Lovely*.

Eric went on to write *Only When I Laugh*, *Home to Roost* and many other award winning comedy series.

RIGSBY: Look, if all he wanted to do was draw attention to himself he could've got a tie that lights up. He doesn't have to go to these lengths.

ALAN: How do we know he's just not trying to get preferential treatment?

RIGSBY: The only preferential treatment he'll get is a free ride in the ambulance.

PHILIP: Rigsby's right, Alan. This could be a cry for help. We ought to make him welcome. Give him a drink.

RIGSBY: Yes, well, not too much of the jungle juice – we don't want to push him over the edge. What we've got to do is cheer him up. You'd better leave that to me.

ALAN: (*amused*) You, Rigsby!

RIGSBY: Yes. I've always been able to look on the bright side. We've had hard times before, you know. I was at my best during the Depression.

PHILIP: I'm not surprised – you've always depressed me.

RIGSBY: Listen, do you know what they used to call me when I was a lad? A little ray of sunshine. Always whistling and singing, I was. And there wasn't much to be cheerful about in those days. My mother had to feed us on a pittance but she managed.

ALAN: Was she a good cook?

RIGSBY: No – bloody terrible but we always managed to look on the bright side.

PHILIP: When have you ever looked on the bright side, Rigsby? You've been predicting the return of the Ice Age for the last two years. You said the Thames would freeze up and there'd be polar bears at the bottom of the garden.

RIGSBY: It'll come, don't you worry – that's if the radiation doesn't get us first.

ALAN: What radiation?

RIGSBY: Radiation brought about by too much ultra-violet – caused by you pushing holes in the atmosphere with your under arm spray.

ALAN: At least I don't smell of old socks, Rigsby—

They are about to argue when they see Gray standing diffidently in the doorway. Rigsby's manner changes.

RIGSBY: Ah, Mr Gray, do come in. I'd like you to meet my boys.

Alan and Philip looked surprised. Introductions.

MR GRAY: I hope I'm not intruding.

RIGSBY: Of course not. We always like to welcome our newcomers. Philip, old chap, pour Mr Gray a drink. Philip has this agreeable little wine from home. Yes – we're one big happy family here. (*Pats Alan on the shoulder*) Isn't that right, Alan?

ALAN: What? Oh, yes.

RIGSBY: Yes. I'm like a father to these two – they could be my own. (*Glance at Philip*) Well, almost.

MR GRAY: Well, I do appreciate this. I must confess I'm at a low ebb at the moment.

RIGSBY: You're bound to be. First night in a strange place. That's why we're extending the warm hand of friendship. Alan, why don't you give Mr Gray one of your nice biscuits?

ALAN: Er … yes – of course.

RIGSBY: (*whispers*) He likes you. He doesn't give his custard creams to anyone.

MR GRAY: I must say it's nice to be in such a warm friendly atmosphere. To see people from such different backgrounds getting on so well.

RIGSBY: All a question of give and take, Mr Gray.

MR GRAY: I suppose so. To tell the truth, my private life has been such a disaster recently I'd almost given up hope.

RIGSBY: Don't do that, Mr Gray. After all, they won't be in for ever.

MR GRAY: I beg your pardon?

RIGSBY: The Labour Government.

ALAN: (*dangerously*) What's wrong with the Labour Government?

RIGSBY: They're a bunch of reds – that's what's wrong.

ALAN: No, they're not. Besides, what have you got against the communists?

PHILIP: He's never forgiven them for winning all the medals in the Olympics.

RIGSBY: Of course they won all the medals, and do you know why? Because they were full of steroids – that's what they give to livestock. They shouldn't have given them medals – they should have had blue rosettes over their ears.

PHILIP: Trust you to come out with that old excuse, Rigsby.

ALAN: They won because they trained harder and had better coaching.

RIGSBY: They don't need coaching. All you've got to do is whisper the magic word Siberia in their ears and they're off like the wind.

ALAN: Well, they've still got a better political system than we've got.

RIGSBY: Did you hear that, Mr Gray. No wonder you want to emigrate. No wonder we're a sinking ship.

ALAN: It's talk like that that's ruining this country. We're not a sinking ship.

RIGSBY: Of course we are. It gets more like the boiler room of the *Titanic* everyday. Confused orders from the bridge – water swirling around your ankles. The only difference is, they had a band.

ALAN: Well if you're so fed up why don't *you* emigrate?

RIGSBY: Don't think I haven't thought about it. I was very nearly part of the brain drain ... I went down to Australia House.

ALAN: Yes and they wouldn't have you. They weren't looking for people like you, Rigsby. You only wanted to go to get out of paying the gas bill.

RIGSBY: No, I didn't. I changed my mind.

ALAN: You didn't change your mind. They threw you out. They wouldn't have had you, Rigsby, when they were taking them with chains round their legs.

RIGSBY: Why, you—

They scuffle. Sound of door closing. They stop.

PHILIP: He's gone.

RIGSBY: Now you've done it. Why can't you have a political discussion without losing your temper?

Exit Rigsby.

* * *

SCENE 6: *Int. Ruth's room.*
Ruth is struggling with the oven. The Samaritan enters. A tall, clean-cut, pipe-smoking man. He sees Ruth crouched over the oven.

SAM: Now that's not the way, old girl.

He pulls Ruth bodily away and dumps her in a chair.

RUTH: I beg your pardon?

SAM: Have you stopped to think what you're doing? What a waste of life it could be?

RUTH: But that's what I've been saying all along. And you've certainly taken your time. I could have killed myself waiting for you.

SAM: Unfortunately I've only just received the message.

RUTH: Isn't that typical? I wouldn't mind, but it's not the first time.

SAM: Ah, you mean this has happened before?

RUTH: It's always happening – always at meal times and usually when I've got visitors. I end up with my head in the gas oven while they eat cold rice pudding.

SAM: Good heavens! I had no idea. I can see this is a serious case. I want you to tell me all about it. I'm prepared to talk all night if necessary. (*Pulls up chair*).

RUTH: (*stares*) Do you do this with everyone?

SAM: Oh, yes.

RUTH: No wonder you're a long time getting around.

SAM: Before I can help you I must get to know all about you.

RUTH: (*surprise. Bewilderment. Coy smile*) Cheeky.

SAM: That's better. You smiled. You have a beautiful smile. You should do it more often. Life's not so bad now, is it?

RUTH: Well, it's certainly looking up at the moment.

SAM: Do you mind if I smoke?

RUTH: No, I love a pipe. You know, you remind me of the man who converted me.

SAM: Ah, was it a crisis of faith?

RUTH: No – North Sea gas. (*Dreamily*) He had this iron-grey curl – it sort of dangled just over his forehead. He came to change my elements – stayed all day – smoked twenty cigarettes and taught me how to play nine card brag.

SAM: I see. Tell me, do you think you're on your own too much?

RUTH: Well, now you mention it, I'm not doing a great deal at the moment.

SAM: I think you should get out more.

RUTH: What about next Tuesday?

SAM: (*coughs*) Now about your little trouble. Perhaps you could give me the symptoms.

RUTH: (*darkly*) Well, I think I've got a leak.

SAM: What!

RUTH: I experience a drop in pressure and then everything goes soggy.

SAM: Have you seen a doctor?

RUTH: No, but I don't think he knows anything about gas cookers.

SAM: Gas cookers! I've not come about the gas cooker.

RUTH: No, I didn't think you had – you monkey.

SAM: I'm a Samaritan.

RUTH: Well, you're certainly doing me a good turn.

SAM: I was summoned here on a matter of life or death.

RUTH: Oh, that must have been Mr Rigsby. I shouldn't bother. I think he's exaggerating the whole thing – there's no hurry.

SAM: (*retreating*) Still, I think I'd better check. Excuse me.

(*Samaritan flees*).

* * *

SCENE 7: *Int. landing.*
Rigsby is standing outside Gray's door.

RIGSBY: Mr Gray? Are you there.

He tries door. Finds it locked.
He takes out key and opens door.

* * *

SCENE 8: *Int. Gray's room.*
Rigsby enters. He discovers room is empty.

RIGSBY: Oh, my God! Mr Gray?

He looks nervously round the room. Samaritan enters.

SAM: Mr Rigsby?

RIGSBY: Yes. Who are you?

SAM: I'm from the Samaritans.

RIGSBY: Well, you've certainly taken your time.

SAM: Well, we have been rather busy. A man's just thrown himself into the canal. Fortunately there was only two feet of water but he cut his leg on a pram.

RIGSBY: Well, now you're here – what are you going to do?

SAM: First of all I want you to relax completely. I'd like to see you lose that wild look around the eyes. It won't solve anything, Mr Rigsby.

RIGSBY: It's not me, you great pudding. I was ringing on behalf of someone else.

Samaritan clearly doesn't believe him.

SAM: Yes, of course. We often get that. Someone ringing up on behalf of a friend. Where is this friend, Mr Rigsby?

RIGSBY: I don't know. I hardly dare look in the wardrobe.

SAM: (*smiles*) Would you like me to look? (*Opens door*) Oh!

RIGSBY: (*alarmed*) What?

SAM: I do like that jacket.

RIGSBY: Did you have to do that? I thought he was hanging up with the suits. I don't know where he could have got to.

SAM: Tell me, Mr Rigsby, what seems to be worrying your friend?

RIGSBY: He's lost all his money and his wife's left him.

SAM: That's very sad.

RIGSBY: Yes, it's no fun being broke.

SAM: I was thinking about his wife. (*Pause*) Where's your wife, Mr Rigsby?

RIGSBY: She's left me – now wait a minute—

SAM: And doesn't that sadden you, Mr Rigsby? Aren't there times when you think about her and feel depressed?

RIGSBY: Why? You don't think she might come back, do you? Now come on, are we going to look for him or not? He must be some-where.

Rigsby opens windows and looks out.

The Samaritan grabs him round the waist.

SAM: Don't do it, Rigsby.

RIGSBY: Let go. I keep telling you – it's not me.

They struggle to the ground. Alan and Philip enter.

ALAN: What's all the din about?

SAM: Keep him away from the window. I'll get assistance.

Exit Samaritan.

ALAN: What's the matter with him?

RIGSBY: Don't take any notice. He's raving mad. No wonder the suicide rate's up.

Ruth enters breathlessly.

RUTH: Oh, Mr Rigsby. I thought I ought to tell you – I've just seen Mr Gray.

RIGSBY: Thank heavens for that. Where is he, Miss Jones?

RUTH: Up on the roof.

RIGSBY: What!

ALAN: What's he doing up there?

RIGSBY: Well, he's not waiting for the last bus.

RUTH: What should we do?

PHILIP: There's only one thing we can do. We'll have to go out there and get him.

RUTH: Oh, Philip – how heroic. Do be careful.

RIGSBY: (*stops Philip*) Wait a minute. Do you mind? This is going to be a bit more difficult than shinning up a coconut tree, you know. You'd better let me lead. Get that rope.

RUTH: Mr Rigsby, are you sure you'll be all right?

RIGSBY: Oh yes. I've done this before, Miss Jones – and under fire.

RUTH: But, Mr Rigsby—

RIGSBY: (*spits on hands*) Don't worry Miss Jones. I'll be up there like a rat up a drain pipe.

ALAN: What should I do with the rope?

RIGSBY: Tie it round your waist.

ALAN: Suppose you slip?

RIGSBY: That's the point. If I slip you'll be at the other end.

ALAN: No, I won't. I'm not ending up in the cucumber frame.

RIGSBY: Come on and stop arguing. Now you follow me, Philip. And don't panic – I'll be with you. And what ever you do – don't look down.

PHILIP: God – it's Tenzing and Hillary all over again.

Rigsby climbs through the window followed by the boys.

* * *

SCENE 9: *Ext. sloping roof/gabled window.*
Gray is sitting on the ridge.
Rigsby and boys make their way up the sloping roof.

RIGSBY: Now then, Mr Gray – what are you doing up here?

MR GRAY: Go away, Rigsby. Leave me alone.

RIGSBY: Why can't we talk this over?

MR GRAY: I don't want to talk it over.

RIGSBY: Don't look down, Mr Gray. It's a long drop – you wouldn't stop rolling until you got to the Town Hall. (*Looks down*) Oh Lord!

MR GRAY: What's the matter, Rigsby?

RIGSBY: Nothing. Philip – don't move.

PHILIP: I'm not moving.

RIGSBY: Where are you? I can't see you. Don't close your eyes for God's sake. Ah, now I've got a foothold.

PHILIP: Rigsby, that's my head.

RIGSBY: Stop complaining. Mr Gray – why are you doing this?

MR GRAY: Go away, Rigsby. You don't care – no one cares.

RIGSBY: Of course we care. Look, there's old Philip and Alan – dif-ferent ethnic groups but roped together – risking life and limb for a complete stranger.

MR GRAY: My wife doesn't care. She'll be sorry when she hears.

RIGSBY: Well, that's not going to do you much good, is it? Oh, she'll probably give you a lovely funeral but don't forget, you won't be going back for the ham tea. Now come on down.

MR GRAY: No, my mind's made up – there's no going back.

RIGSBY: (*shrugs*) All right. I can't stop you. You'd better get on with it.

MR GRAY: What?

RIGSBY: Just do one thing for me.

MR GRAY: What's that?

RIGSBY: While you're up here – straighten that aerial.

MR GRAY: (*blustering*) I'm going, Rigsby.

RIGSBY: Yes, well, try and miss the cucumber frame.

MR GRAY: Aren't you going to try and stop me?

RIGSBY: No, I can see your mind's made up. Before you go – you haven't got any unexpired season tickets? No – well, off you go. I mean, there's a good crowd down there – it'd be a pity to disappoint them. It's not everyone who'd turn out in this sort of weather – they must be perished.

You wouldn't like to hang on until the hot dogs come?

MR GRAY: What are they shouting? Is it 'Go back'?

RIGSBY: Not that lot. I think it's more likely to be 'Jump'. Just look at them. (*Stares downwards*) Oh, my God!

MR GRAY: What's the matter, Rigsby?

RIGSBY: Everything's going round and round.

MR GRAY: He's going to fall. What are we going to do?

ALAN: Should we cut the rope?

PHILIP: No – grab him.

They seize the fainting Rigsby and drag him in.

* * *

SCENE 10: *Int. Gray's room.*
The room is full of people. Press,

ambulance, police.
There is an outburst of applause and cheers.
Cameras flash.

RUTH: Mr Rigsby, are you all right?

RIGSBY: (*shakily*) Of course, Miss Jones. I see you didn't recognise my little stratagem. Just a simple ruse to get him down. Are the press here? (*Beaming smile for cameras*) Try and get my best side. Anyone got a comb? Would they like me to say a few words?

Samaritan moves forward with white-coated attendants.

SAM: Not just at the moment, old chap. He'll be all right once we get him under sedation.

Rigsby is led away struggling.
Everyone begins to laugh, including Gray.

THE END

Series Three

EPISODE 5

Fawcett's Python

by

Eric Chappell

PART ONE

SCENE 1: *Int. Rigsby's room. Morning.*
Rigsby is reading the paper.
Ruth enters looking indignant.

RUTH: Could I have a word, Mr Rigsby?

RIGSBY: Certainly, Miss Jones – what is it?

RUTH: (*closing door*) It's about the new girl.

RIGSBY: Oh, you mean Marilyn?

RUTH: Yes. (*Sharply*) I see it hasn't taken you long to get on first name terms, Mr Rigsby.

RIGSBY: Er … well, you know me, Miss Jones. I always take a keen interest in my tenants.

RUTH: So I've noticed. Is that why you've cleaned her windows three times this week?

RIGSBY: Ah, well, they were rather grimy.

RUTH: You mean you couldn't see through them properly?

RIGSBY: Yes – I mean no—

RUTH: Don't protest, Mr Rigsby. I saw you when you were pruning the apple tree – leering in at her.

RIGSBY: I wasn't leering in, Miss Jones.

RUTH: Of course you were – you fell out of the tree twice.

RIGSBY: I was only giving her a friendly wave, Miss Jones.

RUTH: Yes. You've certainly gone out of your way to be friendly – is that why you've been cleaning her windows on the inside as well? Surely that's not normal practice?

RIGSBY: Well, she had just moved in, Miss Jones, and you know what that room was like. She was in a state.

RUTH: She was also in a negligee, Mr Rigsby.

RIGSBY: So that's what it was! I thought it had a lot of lace. My trouble is I've no idea of fashion, Miss Jones.

RUTH: I'm not surprised you're confused – she certainly wears it a great deal. She came downstairs in it just now – in the middle of the morning. I thought there'd been a fire. I was shocked, Mr Rigsby. And I don't think it's quite the thing – not with young and impressionable minds in the

362

house – they could easily be led astray by a woman like that.

RIGSBY: Oh, I don't think so, Miss Jones – not those two. You haven't seen their calendar – it's disgraceful. They don't go in for views of the Cotswolds or the blacksmith working at his forge – it's all intimate studies of the female form with them. I thought the summer months were bad enough but September's coming in with jack boots and a whip.

RUTH: (*tartly*) How do you know, Mr Rigsby? We haven't reached September yet.

RIGSBY: Ah, well, I was just thumbing through, Miss Jones – I was appalled. No, if you're looking for young and impressionable minds you'd better try the YMCA – there's nothing to worry about round here.

RUTH: But I do worry. We don't know where it's going to end. She went topless in the garden last Sunday – there was a crowd of small boys staring at her through the fence. That sort of thing gives the house a bad name.

RIGSBY: Topless! I didn't know that, Miss Jones.

RUTH: That's surprising – considering how close you were getting to her with the lawnmower. I don't think you're taking the situation at all seriously, Mr Rigsby. The moral climate of this house has definitely taken a turn for the worst. And I've got the curate

coming round this evening – we're rehearsing for the concert. He'll begin to wonder if I'm a fit person to ascend the stage of the church hall. (*Darkly*) After all, birds of a feather, Mr Rigsby.

RIGSBY: (*puzzled*) Birds of a feather? I don't quite understand.

RUTH: Don't you, Mr Rigsby? Have you been able to discover what she does for a living yet?

RIGSBY: (*uneasily*) Er … no, she's still a little reticent on that point.

RUTH: I see. And why do you think she's being so secretive about her work? Unless it's something that she's ashamed of – something that sets her apart from decent respectable people?

RIGSBY: You don't think she's from the tax office, Miss Jones?

RUTH: No, I don't. They don't wear negligees and paint their toenails to administer Schedule D, Mr Rigsby. And why does she sleep most of the day and stay out most of the night?

RIGSBY: (*stares*) Miss Jones – you're not suggesting that she's a loose woman?

RUTH: (*snorts*) Loose! If she got any looser she'd fall apart.

RIGSBY: Aren't you jumping to conclusions, Miss Jones?

RUTH: The facts speak for themselves.

RIGSBY: The facts aren't always

what they appear. There was a woman here once – had a succession of men to her door. Everyone complained, so I called on her posing as a customer. She turned out to be a lady chiropodist. Before I could make an excuse and leave she'd taken a knife to my ingrowing toenail. I've never known agony like it.

RUTH: I still think something ought to be done.

RIGSBY: Well, leave it to me, Miss Jones. I'll have a word with her.

RUTH: Very well, only the last time you had a word with her you were in there for three hours – then you had to go back for your jacket.

Exit Ruth.
Rigsby begins brushing his hair.

* * *

SCENE 2: *Int. attic flat. A few minutes later.*
Alan is brushing his hair and singing. He straightens his tie – picks up newspaper and is about to leave when Rigsby enters.

RIGSBY: Where are you going?

ALAN: I was just taking the paper down to Marilyn. (*Rigsby pushes him back*).

RIGSBY: No, you're not. I want you to keep away.

ALAN: Why?

RIGSBY: Because I said so.

ALAN: That's not a reason. You're always the same, Rigsby. As soon as we get an attractive woman in the house you start going round like the head eunuch.

RIGSBY: Listen, it's for your own good. You'd be out of your depth with a woman like that. You don't want to start the nose-bleeds again, do you?

ALAN: I can look after myself.

RIGSBY: You don't understand. I've had complaints. Miss Jones thinks she's a fallen woman.

ALAN: (*amused*) A fallen woman! And what were you doing in her room last night – trying to pick her up? You know, you're so narrow-minded, Rigsby. A woman's only got to be a bit heavy on the eyeshadow and you think she's a fallen woman.

RIGSBY: (*uncomfortably*) Well, it's not just me. I've got to be careful. Miss Jones has got the curate coming round again tonight. What's he going to say?

ALAN: I thought he was supposed to save fallen women?

RIGSBY: Well, he is—

ALAN: Well, get him to save one for you – this one's mine. You're only jealous because she fancies me.

RIGSBY: No, I'm not. You know your trouble – you think life's like the *Oxford Book of English*

Verse – well, it's not. It has its seamy side.

ALAN: I don't care. I like Marilyn and she likes me. We enjoy each other's company. (*Mockingly*) Fallen woman! We don't use phrases like that anymore. We've thrown off all those old prejudices, Rigsby. We believe in free love.

RIGSBY: Well, I wouldn't go down there then.

ALAN: What do you mean?

RIGSBY: I mean you'd better check the contents of your piggy bank first.

ALAN: What are you talking about, Rigsby?

RIGSBY: Look, I don't want to hurt your feelings. I'm sure she likes you but as far as she's concerned it would just be a commercial transaction.

ALAN: (*shocked*) Rigsby! You don't mean?

RIGSBY: I'm afraid so.

ALAN: (*sits down*) I had no idea. I've never done anything like that, Rigsby. Never.

RIGSBY: I know that. (*Pats shoulder*) They're lucky if they get a packet of cheese and onion crisps out of you. No, it was just one of those unfortunate misunderstanding.

ALAN: I think that sort of thing's degrading. I don't blame the woman, but a man who stoops to that—

RIGSBY: Lowest of the low.

ALAN: Contemptible.

RIGSBY: Yes.

Alan stares at Rigsby.

RIGSBY: What are you staring at?

ALAN: Have you ever … er—?

RIGSBY: (*explodes*) Certainly not. A man in my position – a respected pillar of the community.

ALAN: Sorry, Rigsby.

RIGSBY: I should think so. No, I can put my hand on my heart and say I've never been tempted in that direction. (*Pause*) Not for years.

ALAN: (*grins*) What about the war?

RIGSBY: That was different. That was in France. It was the first time I'd been under fire and I was a virgin soldier – due to the fact that Dolly Myers hadn't come up to scratch on my embarcation leave.

ALAN: What happened?

RIGSBY: We were falling back towards Dunkirk – the Germans had been trying to shoot me full of holes for days. I thought I'd better do something about it while I still had the correct number of apertures. It was strange really – a young man – no more than a boy really – far from home. Outside, the tramp of marching feet and the sound of gun fire and me, poised on the threshold of a new experience.

ALAN: What was it like?

RIGSBY: (*bitterly*) I'll tell you what it was like. The Germans scored a direct hit on the bedroom. The lights went out – the roof fell in and I thought if this is sex they can keep it. I never stopped running till I got to Dunkirk.

ALAN: What are you going to do about Marilyn.

RIGSBY: What can I do. She'll have to go. I can't afford a breath of scandal – not with the curate coming.

ALAN: Do you have to, Rigsby?

RIGSBY: Don't take it to heart – try and forget it – get something to occupy your mind – take up the brass rubbing again.

Exit Rigsby.
Alan snatches off his tie.
Philip enters.
Alan starts to read his paper furiously.

PHILIP: I thought you were going down to see Marilyn?

ALAN: I've changed my mind.

PHILIP: Why?

ALAN: (*shakes paper*) I'm reading the paper.

PHILIP: Anything interesting?

ALAN: Another woman lost her head in the supermarket.

PHILIP: What a country – they'd lift anything.

Alan doesn't smile. Turns pages noisily.

PHILIP: What's the matter? Why aren't you going down?

ALAN: (*throws down paper*) Because I've got principles. I'm not going to pay for the pleasure of her company.

PHILIP: What! Who said she was like that?

ALAN: I wasn't born yesterday, Philip. It's obvious. Painted toenails – black negligee – the way she's chasing me.

PHILIP: Well, she's not going to make a fortune out of you – not with what you've got in the piggy bank.

ALAN: She certainly isn't.

PHILIP: Your trouble is you're too suspicious. You always think women are after your money.

ALAN: No, I don't.

PHILIP: Yes, you do. Look how you were with those girls we met the other night – just because they had arrows on their stockings.

ALAN: That's one of the signs – arrows on their stockings – it's like split skirts and plastic macs.

PHILIP: Is that why you transferred your money to your sock?

ALAN: I was just being careful. There could have been a gang outside. We could have been mugged. I wasn't going to end up in an alley clad only in my Y-fronts.

PHILIP: (*shakes head*) I'll never forget that night. It was the first time I'd seen you spend a pound note. It was as if you were saying goodbye to a dear friend. You spent half the evening trying to peel it in two. Your trouble is you're mean.

ALAN: No, I'm not.

PHILIP: Yes, you are. When we took them to the pictures you insisted on sitting on the front row because you said your eyesight was bad.

ALAN: I'm not mean. It's just that I want a woman to like me for myself – not for my money.

PHILIP: Well, I can understand that but we have a saying in my country; 'He who seeks the bird of paradise must put down a little seed.'

* * *

SCENE 3: *Int. Marilyn's Room*
Marilyn – about thirty – shapely and attractive – a little brassy – is sitting at dressing table.
Rigsby enters. He looks serious.

RIGSBY: Marilyn, could I have a word?

MARILYN: Certainly, big boy – what is it?

RIGSBY: Well, it's a bit delicate.

MARILYN: It usually is.

RIGSBY: No, I've had complaints.

MARILYN: (*eyes narrow*) Complaints? What sort of complaints?

RIGSBY: Well … er … regarding your occupation.

MARILYN: I see – you've found out then?

RIGSBY: Just let's say the pieces have fallen into place, Marilyn.

MARILYN: And you want me to go?

RIGSBY: Well, I am the landlord. I'm responsible for the moral climate around here.

MARILYN: Then why don't you go?

RIGSBY: I'm not blaming you, Marilyn. You're a nice girl, I can see that. But we have got rules.

MARILYN: And you object to my dancing?

RIGSBY: Well, yes. (*Stress*) Dancing? Are you a dancer?

MARILYN: I don't suppose you consider it dancing but I do. It's very artistic. I suppose if I was in the Royal Ballet that would be all right but just because I work the clubs.

RIGSBY: The clubs!

MARILYN: I could have been classical. I had the talent – I just grew too much.

RIGSBY: Yes, I can see that. Of course, they're all skinny birds in the ballet. They have to be. It's the only way they can lift them above their heads without their tights splitting. A well made girl like you would soon make their knees buckle. I shouldn't worry about it – it's their loss.

MARILYN: Then what have you got against me? It's not as if I'm a stripper – more an erotic dancer.

RIGSBY: Erotic dancer. You know, perhaps I've been a bit hasty.

MARILYN: You mean I can stay?

RIGSBY: Let's give it a try.

MARILYN: You're more understanding than my last landlord. He turned me out. Of course, he objected to my partner.

RIGSBY: Partner?

Marilyn produces wicker basket.

MARILYN: Want to see him?

She opens basket. Rigsby peers in. There is a loud hiss. Rigsby freezes.

RIGSBY: (*chokes*) It's a snake!

Marilyn takes Rigsby's hand and pushes it in basket.

MARILYN: You can touch him. He won't hurt you, he's been fed.

RIGSBY: He's got hold of me.

MARILYN: No, he's just extracting warmth from your body.

RIGSBY: I think he's wasting his time.

MARILYN: That's why he's sluggish – too cold for him really – you have to poke him.

RIGSBY: No – don't bother. It seems a pity to disturb him. He looks so peaceful.

MARILYN: He's beautifully marked, isn't he?

RIGSBY: Yes. (*Swallowing*) I particularly like the zig-zags.

MARILYN: Do you really like him?

RIGSBY: Oh, yes – very much.

MARILYN: I think he can sense it. The other landlord didn't like him – that's why he kept dropping on him from the lampshade. He was always in trouble. He crept next door and swallowed two of their garden gnomes – it's amazing what they can cram in. We had to leave after that.

RIGSBY: Yes, well, I must go. Do you think Charlie will mind?

MARILYN: No, he's taken to you.

RIGSBY: By then, Bye, Charlie.

Rigsby exits.

* * *

SCENE 4: *Int. landing.*
Rigsby leans on wall for support.
Alan enters.

RIGSBY: Where are you going?

ALAN: I've made up my mind. I'm going to see Marilyn. I don't care what you say. I'm not going to take a moral attitude – life's too short.

RIGSBY: I think you're right. Go ahead.

ALAN: You don't mind?

RIGSBY: No. I think you'll find it a very stimulating experience.

Alan enters.
Rigsby gives a crooked smile. Lights a cigarette. Counts silently.
There is a piercing shout from inside the room. Alan bursts out the door and dashes up the stairs.

END OF PART ONE.

PART TWO

SCENE 6: *Int. attic flat. Afternoon.*
Alan is reading.
Rigsby enters silently – grinning.
He creeps up behind Alan and hisses.
Alan leaps out of his chair.

ALAN: Rigsby! Don't do that.

RIGSBY: You haven't recovered yet then?

ALAN: No, I haven't.

RIGSBY: You should have seen your face. Talk about blind terror. I haven't seen panic like that since twelve of us tried to get into the same life jacket at Dunkirk.

ALAN: Well, it was horrible – it was coiled ready to spring.

RIGSBY: It was probably more frightened of you than you were of it.

ALAN: I don't think so, Rigsby – it didn't have to spend two hours in the bathroom.

RIGSBY: Of course they can tell when you're frightened of them – they can smell fear. You should have stood your ground – looked it straight in the eye.

ALAN: No, that's what they want you to do. They hypnotise their prey and then swallow it.

RIGSBY: Well, he couldn't have swallowed you – not with those feet. It's really got you going, hasn't it? You're really terrified.

ALAN: No, I'm not.

RIGSBY: Yes, you are. You think it's lurking everywhere. You even ran away from the garden hose this afternoon.

ALAN: Well, I saw it wriggling out of the corner of my eye. I thought it was Charlie. They can move very silently you know. You wait, Rigsby – you'll pick up that hosepipe one day and it'll turn round and stare at you.

RIGSBY: Well, at least I won't panic. And do you know why? Because animals respect me. I've always had this effect – it's a sort of calming influence. Remember that time I had to put those drops in Vienna's ears? I didn't get a scratch.

ALAN: You were wearing gauntlets.

RIGSBY: And what about the time that Alsatian got hold of Miss Jones's joint? Who approached him – spoke a few soothing words and took it from him?

ALAN: You did, Rigsby.

RIGSBY: There you are then. I've always had this way with animals.

ALAN: He bit you, Rigsby.

RIGSBY: I know, but I calmed him in the end.

ALAN: Only after you'd hit him over the head with a broom handle.

Philip enters.

PHILIP: I've just seen the snake. I'd keep away from him if I were you.

RIGSBY: What do you mean?

PHILIP: Well, if I'm not mistaken it's Fawcett's python.

ALAN: Well, I wish he'd take it back.

RIGSBY: No, he means Fawcett was the first to find it.

PHILIP: Well, not exactly, Rigsby. Actually, it found Fawcett. Fawcett was never seen again – except for his boots. Of course, they grow much larger than that – that's a young one.

ALAN: (*panics*) I told you, Rigsby.

RIGSBY: You mean they're dangerous.

PHILIP: Oh yes. When fully grown

they have been known to leap out of the bush and attack a horse and cart.

ALAN: Oh, no!

RIGSBY: Are you sure it's Fawcett's python?

PHILIP: As sure as I can be. Of course, there's only one way to identify the Fawcett python.

RIGSBY: How's that?

PHILIP: From a distance. It was coiled around next door's rabbit hutch – staring in at them. You see it prefers its food fresh.

ALAN: (*gulps*) How fresh?

PHILIP: Moving around if possible. I remember in the old days we presented one to the District Commissioner. He was delighted with it – until it ate the spaniel.

RIGSBY: My God! I'll have to keep an eye on Vienna. He could end up as a bulge in his stomach.

ALAN: He'll have to go, Rigsby.

RIGSBY: You're right. We can't have him wandering loose around here. There's Miss Jones to consider.

ALAN: You don't think he'd eat Miss Jones, do you?

PHILIP: They'd eat anything.

RIGSBY: What do you mean? Miss Jones would prove a very tasty morsel. Besides, she hates creepy-crawlies. She has hysterics if she finds a spider in the bath. Mind you, I wouldn't mind if he had a go at the curate – he's been coming round far too much just lately.

PHILIP: Yes, well we found them very useful for getting rid of the missionaries. Never had much trouble if you kept a Fawcett python handy.

ALAN: Didn't you like the missionaries?

PHILIP: (*smiles*) On the contrary, we found them delicious.

RIGSBY: Well, there's only one thing to do. Someone's got to go down there and tell Marilyn to get rid of it.

Pause.

PHILIP: But who?

ALAN: Well, it's a lucky thing Rigsby's so good with animals.

RIGSBY: What?

ALAN: He has this calming influence.

RIGSBY: Well, yes but—

PHILIP: I think he's afraid.

RIGSBY: No, I'm not.

ALAN: You'd better tie some string round your ankles, Rigsby – you don't want it shooting up your trouser leg.

RIGSBY: You know, I feel sorry for you two. Look at you – you're

shaking in your boots. Well, I'm not. I don't know the meaning of fear I could have been one of the great white hunters.

ALAN: Just like Fawcett.

RIGSBY: Just like Fawcett. (*Stops. Scowls*)

Rigsby exits.

ALAN: Are you really sure it's Fawcett's python.

PHILIP: Oh yes – I can prove it.

Philip opens trunk. Produces stuffed snake.
Alan recoils.

ALAN: Where did you get that from?

PHILIP: It's the Fawcett python. I brought it from Africa. They presented it to me before I left.

ALAN: What did they do that for?

PHILIP: It's supposed to be lucky.

ALAN: What's lucky about it?

PHILIP: It's dead. Beautifully marked, isn't it? You don't see them very often. They're very difficult to stuff.

ALAN: Yes, I can imagine.

Alan takes snake.

PHILIP: What are you going to do with it?

ALAN: (*grins*) I thought of putting

it down the great white hunter's trousers.

* * *

SCENE 7: *Int. Marilyn's room.*
Marilyn is looking through drawers.
Rigsby enters uneasily.

RIGSBY: Ah, Marilyn. Now I hope Charlie's not going to take this personally but I'm afraid he'll have to go. It's not me – it's the tenants – they don't fancy Charlie knotting himself round their windpipes, even with the friendliest intentions.

MARILYN: I knew it. You're all against him. I don't know why. He's just a big soft thing really.

RIGSBY: I know he's a big soft thing – the trouble is he's going to get bigger. If he keeps growing we won't be able to climb the stairs without a machete. You'll have to face facts, Marilyn – he'd be happier in a zoo—

MARILYN: But what about the act?

RIGSBY: Well, couldn't you get something else? Like a couple of ostrich feathers or a few fan-tailed doves? I understand they can be very effective.

MARILYN: It wouldn't be the same.

RIGSBY: I know, but you said yourself, he feels the cold. And the winters here can be cruel – he's not going to let anyone near those radiators. No, I'm afraid he'll have to go.

Marilyn bursts into tears.

RIGSBY: Now, come on, Marilyn. It's not as bad as that. Don't upset Charlie.

MARILYN: It's too late – he's gone.

RIGSBY: What!

MARILYN: I was playing with him in the garden and he just slithered off.

RIGSBY: Oh, my God! Why did you have to take him in the garden? It isn't as if you can throw sticks for him.

MARILYN: (*sniffs*) I thought he'd like the exercise.

RIGSBY: Well, he's certainly getting that. Hadn't you better look for him?

MARILYN: I have done. He's probably miles away by now.

RIGSBY: (*relieved*) Do you think so? Well, you'd better make sure. I don't want to worry you but he's been clipping the hedge next door – one hasty snip and Charlie could be out there looking for his tail.

MARILYN: (*agitated*) Oh, no!

She exits hurriedly.
Rigsby departs whistling.

* * *

SCENE 8: *Int. Rigsby's room. Early evening.*
Rigsby getting tea.
Ruth enters.

RUTH: (*impatiently*) Well, Mr Rigsby, have you seen her?

RIGSBY: Yes, Miss Jones and there's nothing to worry about – she's ... er ... a dancer.

RUTH: Oh. What sort of a dancer?

RIGSBY: Well, not so much classical – more what you'd call modern, interpretive dancing – a sort of glorification of the physical.

RUTH: You mean she takes her clothes off?

RIGSBY: Yes.

RUTH: Well, I hope you spoke to her severely. Remember I've got the curate coming this evening.

RIGSBY: (*sighs*) How can I forget.

RUTH: (*frowns*) What do you mean, Mr Rigsby?

RIGSBY: Er ... will he be singing again tonight, Miss Jones?

RUTH: Yes. I'll be accompanying him in his rendition of 'The Indian Love Lyrics'.

RIGSBY: I must remember to put the cat out.

RUTH: Are you suggesting that the curate's singing disturbs Vienna?

RIGSBY: Well, he does become a little ruffled, Miss Jones. He tries to get behind the cooker.

RUTH: But the curate has a beautiful voice.

RIGSBY: It's only the high notes,

Miss Jones – you know, when he sounds afflicted with a strangulated hernia.

RUTH: I'm afraid there's something of the philistine about you, Mr Rigsby. Well, don't you worry about the curate – you just worry about Marilyn. I don't want anything to disturb his composure. The curate's led a sheltered life. How do you think he's going to react to a woman in a negligee?

RIGSBY: Oh, I shouldn't worry, Miss Jones. He's been trained to resist temptation – a bit of scourging and a couple of hours in a hair shirt and he'll be as right as rain.

RUTH: I'm glad you find this amusing, Mr Rigsby, because I don't.

RIGSBY: I don't think the curate would approve of this attitude, Miss Jones. I think he'd deliver one of his blistering sermons on casting the first stone. After all, he has been subject to malicious gossip himself.

RUTH: What on earth do you mean?

RIGSBY: I was thinking of the time he was seen at *The Last Tango in Paris* without his dog collar – accompanied by an unknown lady.

RUTH: Never mind about that, Mr Rigsby – just remember what I said.

Ruth exits flustered.

Rigsby sighs.

RIGSBY: I don't know, Vienna – who'd be landlord? (*Stares*) What have you got there?

Rigsby feels under curtain. Pulls out snake. Drops it and jumps on the table.

RIGSBY: Oh, my God! It's Charlie. Oh, Lord, look down on your humble servant, Rigsby – and don't let him get me.

Alan enters.

ALAN: What's the matter, Rigsby?

RIGSBY: (*quavering*) Don't take another step. It's on the floor.

ALAN: What is?

RIGSBY: (*points*) That is.

ALAN: Oh, it's the snake.

RIGSBY: Of course it's the snake. What did you think it was – a draught excluder? Now I want you to be a brave lad. Walk slowly out of the room backwards and fetch Marilyn.

ALAN: It's all right, Rigsby.

Picks up snake.

RIGSBY: Be careful! He'll have your arm.

ALAN: No, it's only a stuffed one. Crikey! Talk about the great white hunter – they don't come any whiter than you, Rigsby.

RIGSBY: You mean it's a dummy? What's it doing here?

ALAN: It's Philip's. I thought you'd be interested so I left it down here. Vienna must have got hold of it. I didn't know you were going to panic.

RIGSBY: Panic. Who said I was panicking? I was up here changing the light bulb. (*He examines the snake*) It's very life-like.

ALAN: Yes.

RIGSBY: (*muses*) You know the curate's coming tonight?

ALAN: He's not singing again?

RIGSBY: Yes. Now if this was to get into the room – it might prove very beneficial.

ALAN: (*grins*) Yes – might help him to reach the high notes.

RIGSBY: That's what I thought.

ALAN: (*takes snake*) I'll see what I can do.

RIGSBY: Good lad.

Exit Alan

* * *

SCENE 9: *Int. Ruth's room. Later. Ruth is sitting holding her recorder. Curate is standing in a dignified posture by settee.*

RUTH: Should we run through it once more, Douglas?

DOUGLAS: Very well, Ruth. But please remember it's not a race to see who finishes first – we should try and breast the tape together.

RUTH: (*earnestly*) Yes, of course, Douglas. I think you're singing beautifully.

DOUGLAS: Yes, I do seem in good voice.

RUTH: I'm sure you'll be devastating on the night.

DOUGLAS: Yes. Remember last year? We had a profound effect on the old age pensioners. I swear there were tears in their eyes, Ruth.

RUTH: They were obviously music lovers, Douglas. Some were so overcome with emotion they had to go outside.

DOUGLAS: It was very rewarding.

RUTH: I think it's the best thing in your repertoire, Douglas.

DOUGLAS: Thank you, Ruth. Should we continue?

After a couple of false starts Douglas begins to sing in a strangled tenor voice, accompanied by Ruth on her recorder.

DOUGLAS: 'Pale hands I love beside the Shalimah – where are you now who lies beneath your spell,' etc.

There is a pause, followed by a loud hiss. They glance uncomfortably at each other. They continue. The hiss grows louder. They stop.

DOUGLAS: (*frowns*) Is that you, Ruth?

RUTH: Certainly not.

DOUGLAS: I thought it might be cracked.

RUTH: No. (*Coldly*) I thought it was your breathing.

DOUGLAS: (*stiffly*) There's nothing wrong with my breath control I can assure you.

They begin again, Hissing starts again. Ruth catches sight of snake appearing above back of settee. She freezes. Notes die away.

DOUGLAS: What's the matter, Ruth?

RUTH: (*screams*) It's a snake!

DOUGLAS: What!

They scramble backwards and climb up on the chairs.

RUTH: Where's it gone?

DOUGLAS: I don't know – I think it must be creeping up on us.

Ruth screams again.
Rigsby enters with a smile of triumph on his face.

RIGSBY: Is something the matter, Miss Jones – or do you normally rehearse like this?

RUTH: Certainly not, Mr Rigsby.

RIGSBY: I thought it might be the curate's way of reaching the high notes.

DOUGLAS: There's a snake, Mr Rigsby.

RIGSBY: A snake? Well, don't be alarmed. I'm sure it won't attack a man of the cloth. Now where is it?

RUTH: Do be careful, Mr Rigsby.

DOUGLAS: I think it's coming for us.

RIGSBY: Obviously a music lover. Now where is it? Ah, here it is. I've got him. Lively little chap.

Rigsby makes great play of securing snake. Shakes it a great deal.

RUTH: Oh, Mr Rigsby – take care.

RIGSBY: Don't worry – I had a lot of experience with these out East.

Alan enters. Followed by Philip

RIGSBY: (*Rigsby winks*) You're too late. I've got it. Actually, it put up quite a struggle.

RUTH: How brave of you, Mr Rigsby.

RIGSBY: It was nothing, Miss Jones.

ALAN: Rigsby!

RIGSBY: What?

Alan produces dummy snake out of pocket. Rigsby stares at him for an incredulous moment.

RIGSBY: Oh, my God. It's alive. It's alive.

He runs around the room trying to hand it to everyone. Finally drops it into the laundry basket, closing lid.

RUTH: What's the matter, Mr Rigsby?

RIGSBY: It's bitten me.

ALAN: Are you sure?

RIGSBY: Of course I'm sure.

RUTH: Oh, Mr Rigsby. How do you feel?

RIGSBY: I'm going numb – my eyes— Everything's going glazed.

RUTH: What should we do?

DOUGLAS: Perhaps a prayer?

RIGSBY: Do you mind?

PHILIP: What we've got to do is get a knife – cut open the wound and then suck out the poison. Where is it, Rigsby?

Rigsby undoes shirt.
They stand back in silence.

ALAN: Well, perhaps we ought to ring the doctor.

RIGSBY: Well, don't just stand there. My God! You certainly find out who your friends are at times like this. I'm fading fast. I'm going the same way as poor old Fawcett.

RUTH: I'll get the doctor – mind you, he does hate being called out at this time of night.

RIGSBY: Thanks very much.

Marilyn enters with basket.

MARILYN: Have you found him?

ALAN: He's in with the laundry.

MARILYN: Poor thing. Have they been frightening you, Charlie? (*Recovers snake*).

RIGSBY: What do you mean? He's just bitten me.

MARILYN: Oh, I shouldn't worry about that. He's not venomous – probably just a friendly nip.

RIGSBY: What are you talking about? There's nothing friendly about the Fawcett python.

MARILYN: He's not a Fawcett python.

RIGSBY: How do you know?

MARILYN: Because there's no such thing. Someone's been having you on. No, to tell the truth if he's bitten you I'm more worried for the snake. Poor old Charlie.

Marilyn exits.
Rigsby stares at Alan and Philip.
They edge to the door.

PHILIP: Well, must be off, Rigsby.

ALAN: Yes, see you, Rigsby.

RIGSBY: I'll murder them!

Alan and Philip exit.
Curate and Ruth struggle to restrain Rigsby.

THE END

Series Three

EPISODE 6

The Cocktail Hour

by

Eric Chappell

PART ONE

SCENE 1: *Int. Rigsby's room. Day.*
Rigsby is standing in front of a
cabinet cleaning a paint brush.
Alan enters. He regards Rigsby
uncertainly.

ALAN: (*pleasantly*) Hello, Rigsby.

Rigsby barely grunts.

ALAN: How are you feeling today?

RIGSBY: (*surprised*) What?

ALAN: How are the twinges?

RIGSBY: Not so bad.

ALAN: I'd watch those twinges if I
were you. It could be a strain –
you should take it easy.

RIGSBY: (*gruffly*) I'm all right.

ALAN: (*warmly*) Good. I'm glad to
hear it. (*Pause*) And how's Vienna?
Got over the hard pad yet? You
know, he's quite an attractive cat –
if you ignore the bald patches.
Who's a pretty pussy?

Rigsby stares at the cat and then
back at Alan.

RIGSBY: (*suspiciously*) Did you want
something?

ALAN: (*hastily*) No. (*Pause*) Hey!

You've made a good job of that
cabinet.

RIGSBY: Do you think so?

ALAN: (*admiringly*) Great. Really
professional. First-class job. You
can't see a brushmark.

RIGSBY: I haven't started yet.

ALAN: Oh.

RIGSBY: Now what do you want?

ALAN: What makes you think I
want anything?

RIGSBY: The last time you asked
about my twinges you tried to
borrow five pounds. So what is
it?

ALAN: You'll say no.

RIGSBY: (*disarmingly*) You don't
know that until you ask.

ALAN: You'll refuse – I know you
will.

RIGSBY: I might surprise you – after
all, I'm not inhuman.

ALAN: Can I bring a girl back here
tonight?

RIGSBY: No.

ALAN: I knew it. You're always the

same – this is worse than living at the YMCA—

RIGSBY: I can't help that – this is a respectable house.

ALAN: Well, what's wrong with bringing a girl back?

RIGSBY: The last time you brought a girl back here, I found her sitting on the bed.

ALAN: It wasn't that bad, Rigsby – she had one foot on the floor.

RIGSBY: One foot on the floor doesn't make any difference – that only applies if you're playing billiards.

ALAN: We were only talking.

RIGSBY: All I could hear was heavy breathing.

ALAN: (*accusingly*) Is that why you forced your way into the room?

RIGSBY: I didn't have any choice, did I? You'd wedged a chair against the door.

ALAN: You expected the worst, didn't you, Rigsby? It must have been a big disappointment to find we were only talking.

RIGSBY: You were talking all right – right into her ear 'ole.

ALAN: Well, she was a little deaf.

RIGSBY: Yes, deaf to your proposals. I know you students. A little bit of chit chat and then it's off for the weekend without the benefit of clergy.

ALAN: Well, you were young once, Rigsby.

RIGSBY: I wasn't like you. When I was your age my idea of a dirty weekend was cleaning out the coal-shed. Well, she's not coming back here and that's final.

ALAN: But we've got nowhere to go.

RIGSBY: What's wrong with the Bricklayer's Arms?

ALAN: That's not my idea of a sophisticated evening, Rigsby. They've only got one table and that's under the dartboard. Besides, we want to be alone.

RIGSBY: I bet you do.

ALAN: You don't understand. I've changed. I'm more mature. That's why I want to be alone with her. I want a deeper, fuller relationship.

RIGSBY: Yes, you want to get the other foot off the floor.

ALAN: No, I don't. I simply want a more civilised evening. I respect Angela. She's different from other girls I've met. She's opened my eyes to the good things of life.

RIGSBY: You mean she's on the pill.

ALAN: No, I don't.

RIGSBY: When I was your age they didn't have the pill. All they ever took was a glass of cold water.

ALAN: (*puzzled*) What – before or after?

RIGSBY: No – instead of.

ALAN: Well, Angela's not like that. She's intelligent – well-bred. She has an extensive knowledge of food – wine and music.

RIGSBY: If she goes up there with you she'll need more than that – she'll need an extensive knowledge of karate. Besides, what have you got to offer someone like that? A packet of cheese and onion crisps and a bottle of Cyprus sherry.

ALAN: Well, it's a beginning. What do you say, Rigsby? Angela comes from a very good family. Her parents are very influential—

RIGSBY: I don't care what they are.

ALAN: But what am I going to say to her?

RIGSBY: Tell her it's the butler's night off. Tell her we've run out of gin and tonic. Tell her we're having a sunken bath fitted. I don't care what you say, but she's not coming here.

ALAN: All right, Rigsby, but you'll regret this. I'm moving into influential circles. I'm on my way up.

RIGSBY: Good. Before you go – pass me that paintbrush.

Alan dips the brush savagely into the paint and hands it to Rigsby bristles first. Rigsby takes it without looking and receives the sticky end. Alan exits.

* * *

SCENE 2: *Int. attic flat. Evening. Alan stands back from the mirror. Philip watches him faintly amused.*

PHILIP: You're going ahead with it then?

ALAN: Yes. I should be all right. Rigsby's going to bingo.

PHILIP: I wouldn't be too sure – not with all these preparations. You can smell your aftershave down in the street. It's bound to make him suspicious.

ALAN: You don't think I ought to have another shave?

PHILIP: Alan, you've had two already. I don't think your bristles will show again tonight – they're probably cowering in fear.

ALAN: I don't know. Angela can't stand bristles, she's got very sensitive skin.

PHILIP: Why do you keep walking around like that? Why don't you sit down?

ALAN: No – I've put a jam butty down somewhere – I'd better not take any chances.

Philip rises hurriedly.

PHILIP: Perhaps we'd better cover you with polythene until she comes. I only hope she's going to be worth it.

ALAN: (*studies Philip*) You don't like Angela, do you?

PHILIP: I never said that.

ALAN: You don't have to.

PHILIP: (*protests*) I don't even know her. I've only seen her once. She was with you in the Chinese. I only saw her from a distance. I can't form an opinion from that.

ALAN: But you don't like her.

PHILIP: No. I'm sorry.

ALAN: (*tolerantly*) That's all right. I don't mind. We can't explain these strange prejudices, Philip. (*Sharply*) Why don't you like her? You only saw her face from a distance. You can't form an opinion from that.

PHILIP: Well, she had this expression.

ALAN: What sort of expression?

PHILIP: Miserable.

ALAN: Well, I'm not surprised. She'd just complained to the manager. The rice was burnt – the coffee was cold and when the waiter was clearing the table he shoved a chopstick up her nose.

Alan begins to move lights.

PHILIP: What are you doing now?

ALAN: I'm trying to angle the lights. I want to hide the damp patches.

PHILIP: (*smiles*) I didn't know you had any damp patches.

ALAN: I'm talking about the wall-paper. Angela's very sensitive. She can't stand anything ugly.

PHILIP: (*stares*) Perhaps you'd better switch them off altogether.

ALAN: You could be right. Angela can be very fastidious. (*Frowns*) The trouble is, you can hear the toilet flushing from here. I hope it won't put her off.

PHILIP: I suppose she's used to better things.

ALAN: Oh, yes. You should see their place. Cattle grid – gravel drive – six stone labrador. It's gracious living after this place. There's freshly cut flowers in the hall – the smell of pine – beds made every day – luxury.

Philip prepares to leave.

PHILIP: And what do they think of you?

ALAN: I think they've accepted me. The labrador's stopped pulling me to the ground – and her father let me rake the gravel yesterday. The trouble is, her mother never leaves us alone. Angela's their only daughter and they're frightened of fortune hunters. You can understand it. It would be a tragedy if she fell into unscrupulous hands.

PHILIP: Of course. The money doesn't interest you.

ALAN: Never given it a thought.

ALAN: Is she worth much?

ALAN: Fifty thousand in shares and gilt edged.

Philip smiles and exits.

* * *

SCENE 3: *Int. Ruth's room.*
Rigsby enters silently and mysteriously. He raises a finger to his lips.

RUTH: (*surprised*) Mr Rigsby! I thought you went out on Friday night?

RIGSBY: Not tonight, Miss Jones. You don't mind if I leave the door slightly open? Only I want to listen.

RUTH: What for, Mr Rigsby?

RIGSBY: Anything suspicious. The sounds of a stiletto heel on the stairs – a muffled greeting – the creak of a bedspring. So if I could use your room for a few seconds.

RUTH: You mean this is a stake-out, Mr Rigsby?

RIGSBY: You could put it like that. I'm expecting a woman to come up those stairs at any moment.

RUTH: (*smiles*) Oh, you don't mean the one who's coming to see Alan?

RIGSBY: You know about it, Miss Jones?

RUTH: Well, there were certain tell-tale signs in the bathroom. I noticed he'd discarded his socks – and he'd been in the water so long his soap had turned to a jelly.

RIGSBY: And that's not all. He's put his ivory prayer book away and turned his mother's picture to the wall. That's always a bad sign.

RUTH: Oh, I'm sure there's nothing to worry about, Mr Rigsby. I've always found Alan extremely well-behaved.

RIGSBY: He's a Jekyll-and-Hyde, Miss Jones. He may seem well-behaved in the daytime but as soon as the sun sets over the gasometer he's away. If Hyde's taken over tonight I wouldn't give much for her chances.

RUTH: But surely there's no harm in a visit from a young lady? Anyone would think you were a misogynist, Mr Rigsby.

RIGSBY: I beg your pardon?

RUTH: A misogynist.

RIGSBY: This has got nothing to do with religion, Miss Jones. I've got my reputation to think of.

RUTH: But I'm sure Alan's intentions are honourable.

RIGSBY: If his intentions are honourable why does he always wedge a chair against the door?

RUTH: (*sighs*) I suppose things have changed since my day. Then it was a few stolen kisses behind the tennis club – the tremulous first embrace – the maidenly blush.

RIGSBY: You don't get many maidenly blushes these days, Miss Jones – most of them are on the pill – and they're not taking them for headaches.

RUTH: Just because they're taking the pill, Mr Rigsby, it doesn't mean they're doing anything wrong. It's a precaution – after all, you pay fire insurance but you don't expect the house to burn down.

RIGSBY: Yes, but you are supposed to try and extinguish the blaze, Miss Jones – not lie back and enjoy it.

RUTH: Well, I wouldn't interfere, Mr Rigsby. Young love is a very tender plant – so easily crushed. Daddy always interfered. When I went to the cinema with a young man, he'd flash messages on the screen or hunt us with a posse of usherettes. Don't do it, Mr Rigsby.

RIGSBY: (*starts*) What was that? I heard a foot on the stair.

Sound of steps. They peer round the door. Ruth pulls Rigsby back. Closes door.

RIGSBY: What's the matter, Miss Jones?

RUTH: That's Angela Armitage.

RIGSBY: You know her?

RUTH: I know her mother. She's president of the Women's Guild. Very influential.

RIGSBY: Wait a minute. Her father's not the one who owns half the property around here?

RUTH: Yes.

RIGSBY: And she's come here? My God! We're on the map at last. This could be the turning point. I think I'd better dash around with the air freshener – the wind's off the abattoir again.

RUTH: But I thought you objected to her visit, Mr Rigsby?

RIGSBY: Ah, that was before I saw her. Lovely girl. She's got the clean lines of a young thoroughbred. Breeding, Miss Jones.

RUTH: That's surprising. Her grandfather was a rag-and-bone man.

RIGSBY: Still, I wish I'd known she was coming – I'd have bought that fluffy cover for the toilet seat. I don't suppose you could suggest any last-minute refinements, Miss Jones?

RUTH: Well, you could take the fly papers down, Mr Rigsby. And possibly some fresh towels for the bathroom.

RIGSBY: Good idea. I'll put the blue ones out – they've still got a bit of tread on them.

RUTH: I wonder if they'd like a cup of tea?

RIGSBY: I'm sure they would, Miss Jones.

RUTH: I don't want to make a fuss

– just because it's Angela Armitage.

RIGSBY: No, of course not.

RUTH: I'll just be casual. (*Frowns*) I wonder where I put the Wedgewood?

RIGSBY: That's the spirit. And if I might suggest – perhaps the Earl Gray with a slice of lemon.

RUTH: Yes, and some of my buttered scones.

RIGSBY: Ah. (*Hesitates*) Do you think that's a good idea, Miss Jones?

RUTH: What do you mean, Mr Rigsby?

RIGSBY: (*jocularly*) Well, we won't get through much small talk if we're chewing those scones, Miss Jones. If you remember, last time they played havoc with the curate's dentures.

RUTH: Perhaps you're right. I think I'll stick to the digestives. And whatever you do – don't let me put the milk in first. We must make the right impression.

RIGSBY: (*worried*) I only hope he's making the right impression. I hope he realises he's mixing with the gentry – any hanky panky and Daddy will be round with a riding crop. He could end up looking into the wrong end of a twelve-bore.

* * *

SCENE 4: *Int. attic flat.*
Alan and Angela are sitting on the settee. Angela is a rather snooty young lady who is constantly gazing around the room in disapproval.

ALAN: Are you comfortable, darling?

ANGELA: No, I'm sitting on a spring.

ALAN: Why don't you move closer?

ANGELA: Do we have to stay here? This place is getting on my nerves.

ALAN: I thought we could have a quiet evening – just the two of us.

Sound of toilet flushing. Alan winces.

ANGELA: But it's an awful room. I don't know how you can live here.

ALAN: It's only temporary – until I find something better.

ANGELA: Well, that shouldn't be difficult.

ALAN: We could sit on the bed.

ANGELA: No, Mummy wouldn't like it.

ALAN: (*beams*) I wasn't thinking of asking Mummy, darling. There's only room for two of us.

ANGELA: I wish you wouldn't talk about Mummy like that.

ALAN: Well, she doesn't approve of me, does she, dearest?

ANGELA: What makes you say that?

ALAN: I think it's the way she keeps setting the dog on me.

ANGELA: No, she doesn't. The dog just doesn't like you.

ALAN: But why doesn't he like me?

ANGELA: Because you keep shutting his head in the door.

ALAN: Only because I want to be alone with you, my sweet. And if your mother isn't there she leaves the dog to watch us. I can't understand what she's got against me.

ANGELA: What do you expect – after you made those rings on the coffee table? Poor Mummy was up half the night with the teak oil.

ALAN: Well, it's not the end of the world, Angela. I'm not the first guest to have made rings on her coffee table. I bet other people have done it.

ANGELA: Not with their heels. And then you had the back off the television. You made us miss *The Horse of the Year Show*.

ALAN: I was only trying to adjust the contrast.

ANGELA: Daddy says he's beginning to wonder if it's his house or yours.

ALAN: I don't see how you can say that – they won't let me in the lounge anymore.

ANGELA: Drawing room, dear – lounges are in hotels.

ALAN: I see – I suppose they think I'm a peasant. Was it something I did at dinner? Did I eat the wrong end of the asparagus?

ANGELA: No, you ate all of it. You spent the whole meal lecturing us on the starving millions and how we should be ashamed of having so much when others had so little. Then you asked for a second helping!

ALAN: Well, I'm a growing lad, Angela. And I still don't understand why your mother doesn't like us to be on our own.

ANGELA: Well, she doesn't think it's healthy. She things we ought to be with people.

ALAN: We tried that, Angela – we nearly got turned out the cinema. (*Pause*) Have you thought anymore about … you know?

ANGELA: (*uneasily*) I have thought about it. I think we ought to wait.

ALAN: We can't wait for ever, my sweet. I've not been well. The doctor says it's pent-up emotion – too much frustration. If I was to go suddenly—

ANGELA: Oh!

ALAN: Does that mean yes?

ANGELA: No – I'm on that spring again.

ALAN: Why don't you come and sit on the bed?

ANGELA: (*weakening*) Do you think it'll be all right?

ALAN: Of course.

ANGELA: Then why are you wedging the chair against the door? I thought you said that awful man was out?

ALAN: He is but he can hear the twang of a bedspring from the bus stop.

ANGELA: That's another reason I don't like coming here – Rigsby. He's so common. I saw him the other night. I'm sure he'd had too much to drink.

ALAN: Well, he does get a bit merry but he always knows what he's doing.

ANGELA: He was walking in the middle of the road.

ALAN: Well, there you are. He's no fool. He does that to stop falling into people's gardens. Now stop worrying, Angela. Sit down and relax.

They sit on bed. Alan embraces her.
They sink back on bed.

ANGELA: Alan! I'm lying on some-thing sticky.

ALAN: What!

Angela jumps up. She produces jam butty.

ANGELA: What is it?

ALAN: It looks suspiciously like a jam butty.

ANGELA: Honestly! How could you? Just look at it. My skirt's ruined.

Angela struggles out of her skirt.

ALAN: Let me sponge it down.

Alan takes skirt.
The door opens and Rigsby and Ruth enter breezily with the tea.

RIGSBY: Hello, we've got a surprise for you—

His voice dies away. Ruth and Rigsby stare at scene.

END OF PART ONE

PART TWO

SCENE 5: *Int. attic flat. Minutes later. Alan is standing nervously at the door.*
Rigsby enters. He eyes Alan angrily.

ALAN: Is she all right?

RIGSBY: Miss Jones is sponging her down in the bathroom. I don't know what gets into you. Why did you have to leave it for her to sit on? You know what black-currant's like.

ALAN: I'd forgotten where I'd put it.

RIGSBY: You've got no sense of responsibility. I bet you're the sort who drops his chewing gum on the dancefloor. One minute some poor devil's gliding through the foxtrot, the next he comes to a slithering halt and goes head first through the drum. Well, you've got to mend your ways. Do you know who she is?

ALAN: Of course I know who she is.

RIGSBY: (*busy with air freshener*) Her father's a big man around here. Property developer. Well, he doesn't so much develop it as knock it down. He's cleared more land for car parks than the might of the German Luftwaffe. They

spent two years trying to hit the town hall – he got it down in a week with six Irishmen.

ALAN: Well, that's nothing to be proud of. And what about that ski-slope he built? That was a waste of tax-payers' money.

RIGSBY: Listen, if we win a gold medal in the winter Olympics it'll be due to his foresight.

ALAN: He didn't have that much foresight – it's facing the wrong way. Most of the skiers end up on the M62.

RIGSBY: I hope you don't talk to him like that. We don't want a steel ball coming through the brickwork. I don't fancy my personal assets disappearing down the road in front of a bulldozer. No, you've got to think of the future. You play your cards right and we could all benefit.

ALAN: What do you mean, 'we'?

RIGSBY: Well, you're not telling me that as soon as fortune smiles on you you're going to forget your old friends?

ALAN: Yes.

RIGSBY: Listen, you need me. Without my help you won't get

389

anywhere. You need advice on the social graces.

ALAN: What do you know about the social graces?

RIGSBY: More than you. Just look at those trousers. Do you have to have 'Come and get me' on the crotch? Stand up – let's have a look at you.

Alan stands up.

RIGSBY: Oh dear, oh dear.

Rigsby sprays Alan with air freshener.

RIGSBY: You don't stand a chance in those trousers.

ALAN: They look all right to me.

RIGSBY: You can't see them from behind. They're got more creases than an elephant's backside. (*Frowns*) What's her mother said to you?

ALAN: Well, she doesn't say a lot.

RIGSBY: (*nods*) Speechless. Still, I'm surprised she hasn't asked you a few penetrating questions – like why you always wear the same shirt.

ALAN: I don't!

RIGSBY: Listen – you've got to make the most of this opportunity. It only needs a well-spoken young sprig to come along in a hacking jacket and a pair of cavalry twills and you'll be on your way out.

ALAN: Well, you know I can't afford those sort of clothes – not on my grant.

RIGSBY: Well, perhaps we could arrange a small loan to tide you over – after all, you should be coming into quite a bit – if you ever get her to the altar. In the meantime you've got to look the part. When you enter society you've got to move with a certain elegance. Watch me – I was a past master at it.

Rigsby demonstrates.

When you enter a room – wait for the conversation to die down – then shoot your cuffs, adjusting them so as to leave the diamond cuff-links just visible. When you're bidden to sit down – fingers on the trousers – so. And then to avoid any stiffness throw one leg over the other with non-chalant ease. Right.

Sounds off.

Sounds as if Miss Jones is coming up to pour the tea. Remember, whatever you do, don't slurp it.

ALAN: (*indignantly*) I don't slurp it.

RIGSBY: You do. You sound like a buffalo at a water hole.

Ruth and Angela enter.
Angela still looks aggrieved.
Ruth and Rigsby feign cheerfulness.

RIGSBY: Ah, here we are – the cup that cheers, Angela.

Angela sniffs gloomily.

RIGSBY: Yes. And have you two ladies got to know each other?

RUTH: Oh yes. We had a jolly time – sponging Angela down.

ANGELA: I don't know what Mummy'll say.

RIGSBY: Quite. And how is Mummy these days?

ANGELA: (*coldly*) Do you know her?

RIGSBY: Well, I have brushed against her in Tescos once or twice. Didn't we lock trolleys in front of the frozen food counter?

ANGELA: I've no idea.

RUTH: I know your Mummy quite well. We're both in the Women's Guild. Perhaps she's mentioned me?

ANGELA: No.

ALAN: Hey! Digestive biscuits.

He takes a handful of biscuits. Rigsby winces.

RIGSBY: Wonderfully healthy appetite. (*Lowers voice*) We're all very fond of him. He's got this sort of natural charm. They make a lovely couple, don't they, Miss Jones?

RUTH: Oh yes. And it's so nice to see two young people setting out together down life's highway.

RIGSBY: (*confidentially*) Actually, you've dropped in lucky there, Angela. He's very popular with the opposite sex – it's a wonder he hasn't been snapped up years ago.

Alan starts to dip his biscuits into the tea. Rigsby tries to draw Angela's attention.

RIGSBY: Yes, I'm sure your parents must be very taken with him. What a pity they couldn't have come. We'd have been delighted to see them. Wouldn't we, Miss Jones?

RUTH: Oh, yes.

Alan loses half his biscuit in the tea. Starts fishing for it with a teaspoon.

ANGELA: They're going to Glyndebourne.

RUTH: Ah, Glyndebourne.

RIGSBY: Ah, Glyndebourne. The three-day event no doubt.

ANGELA: I beg your pardon?

RUTH: (*hastily*) Your tea, Mr Rigsby.

RIGSBY: What beautiful cups, Miss Jones.

RUTH: (*modestly*) Oh, just the old Wedgewood.

RIGSBY: Very elegant.

RUTH: They've been in the family for years. In fact they've survived two world wars.

RIGSBY: Did you hear that, Angela? That's quite a thought – that these delicate pieces have survived the might of the German war machine. A thing of beauty is a joy for ever. Don't you agree?

Rigsby frowns at Alan. Alan looks up. Shoots his cuffs. Throws one leg nonchalantly over the other and kicks the tea tray over Angela. Consternation.

* * *

SCENE 6: *Int. attic flat. Two weeks later. Evening.*
Alan is putting finishing touches to drinks table. His appearance has altered in the last two weeks. He is wearing a checked sports jacket and cavalry twill trousers. He is mixing a drink with demonic fervour. Philip eyes him critically.

ALAN: Now taste that.

PHILIP: (*suspiciously*) What is it?

ALAN: It's my cocktail – a little concoction of my own.

PHILIP: (*sniffs it*) I don't think I'll bother.

ALAN: It's good stuff – works wonders with the opposite sex – guaranteed to loosen the strongest elastic. Don't leave the spoon in too long it attacks the metal.

PHILIP: What did you put in it?

ALAN: Everything. It's a real head-shrinker.

PHILIP: Then you'd better drink it.

ALAN: 'Round the teeth – round the gums – Watch out stomach – here it comes.' (*Drinks. Chokes*) I thought so – too much orange juice.

PHILIP: I think I'll stick to wine.

ALAN: You're in luck. I've got a very nice red.

Philip is about to pour a glass.

ALAN: Not yet, Philip. I mean it's barely at room temperature. (*Sniffs bottle*) We'd better let it breathe a while. It's an unassuming little wine but I think we should treat it with respect. We don't want to trample on its feelings.

PHILIP: You're really into this gracious living, aren't you?

ALAN: One has standards, Philip.

Philip surveys table.

PHILIP: I see you've only got five wine glasses.

ALAN: That's right. Angela, Angela's mother, Ruth, you and me.

PHILIP: What about Rigsby?

ALAN: I can't invite Rigsby. This is the cocktail hour – not a get-together over a crate of brown ale.

PHILIP: You mean he's not good enough?

ALAN: Look, I've got Angela's mother coming. I don't want Rigsby slapping her on the back and rattling her gold fillings.

PHILIP: You're ashamed of him, aren't you?

ALAN: No, it's just that I'm moving in different circles these days.

PHILIP: Yes, and who's paying for it?

ALAN: It's only a loan. Look, Angela's mother's coming here to see how I live. I can't take any chances. I'm her prospective son-in-law. Oh, and by the way – the name's Guy.

PHILIP: (*astonished*) Guy?

ALAN: They prefer to call me by my middle name.

Ruth enters carrying tray of pastries.

RUTH: There, that's the last of the vol-au-vents.

ALAN: Well, I must say they look very appetising, Ruth.

RUTH: Would you like to try one?

ALAN: (*hastily*) Er … no thanks. I think I'll wait for the others to come.

RUTH: Philip?

PHILIP: Ah, no – not at the moment – I've just eaten.

RUTH: (*desperately*) Well, someone's got to try them. I put one down

for Vienna but he just sat there and scratched himself.

ALAN: I shouldn't worry, Ruth – you're a very good cook.

RUTH: (*coldly*) Am I? Then why do I keep finding half-eaten pastries in my flower pots? You don't realise – Mrs Armitage is an expert – she cooks in wine not lumpy gravy.

PHILIP: Why don't you ask Rigsby?

RUTH: I can't – he's not invited.

PHILIP: I don't see why he shouldn't come.

RUTH: You don't know what he's like. I remember the last time I had people in for drinks. He completely monopolised the evening. He made us play this dreadful game which involved passing a key on a string through everyone's underwear. I wouldn't have minded but he only came up to complain about the noise.

ALAN: See what I mean, Philip?

PHILIP: (*guiltily*) And after all, it is his night out.

ALAN: (*lowers voice*) We've just got to make sure he doesn't find out.

Rigsby enters silently during this conversation. They turn guiltily and stand in front of the table.

RIGSBY: Hello, what's this then?

ALAN: What's what?

RIGSBY: Having a party?

ALAN: Er … no. I've got Angela and her mother coming for drinks.

RIGSBY: You should have told me. I'd have brought my wine glasses up with the gold rings. (*Surveys table*) Wait a minute. You've only got five of everything.

ALAN: (*deep breath*) That's right.

RIGSBY: Five. (*Looks around. Counts silently*).

ALAN: I can explain.

RIGSBY: No, I understand.

ALAN: You do?

RIGSBY: Yes. (*Nods over Alan's shoulder at Philip. Whispers.*) Left him out, 'ey? I don't blame you. Better to be on the safe side. He'd take a lot of explaining, especially if he starts talking about cannibalism during the pâté – we don't want him recalling the time they ate the missionary, do we?

ALAN: He was only joking.

RIGSBY: Mrs Armitage won't know that. And what about his ten wives? Suppose he starts off about them? She'll certainly clutch at her pearls when she hears that. Hardly the company for a prospective bridegroom. No, you're doing the right thing. Have you told him or do you want me to do it?

ALAN: Rigsby.

RIGSBY: What?

ALAN: Nothing. Ruth, can I borrow a couple of chairs?

RUTH: Yes, of course.

Alan and Ruth exit hurriedly.
Rigsby and Philip stare at each other.

RIGSBY: Look, sorry about the five glasses. I just want you to know it's nothing personal. Don't take it to heart. I'll save you a bit of seed cake.

PHILIP: There's no need, Rigsby. I've been invited.

RIGSBY: (*frowns. Counts again*) Then who's been left out?

PHILIP: You have.

RIGSBY: What! Well, he must have forgotten. It's an oversight. He thought I was going to bingo. Once he knows I'm available it'll be different. I mean the party wouldn't be complete without me.

Alan returns with chairs.

RIGSBY: No, I shan't be going out tonight. I'll be staying in. I'll be down there – tucking into the fish fingers – only Vienna for company. Probably have an early night.

ALAN: We'll try not to disturb you, Rigsby.

RIGSBY: Oh, don't bother about me. You enjoy yourself. (*Sighs*) Don't worry – I'll probably curl up with a bottle of stout – watch the television.

Pauses by the door.

RIGSBY: Did you say something?

ALAN: No.

RIGSBY: Right. I'll get off then.

Rigsby exits. Door closes. Surprised howl from Vienna.

* * *

SCENE 7: *Int. attic flat. Later.*
Mrs Armitage – older version of Angela – is gazing disapprovingly round the room. She puts sherry glass down – sniffs as if there's a bad smell under her nose.
Angela watched her respectfully.
Ruth and Alan flutter around anxiously.
Philip is amused.

RUTH: Could I press you to a vol-au-vent, Mrs Armitage?

MRS A: Why thank you, Miss Jones. I'm glad to see you're sticking at it. I'm sure it'll all come together – eventually.

RUTH: I keep trying, Mrs Armitage.

MRS A: I'm sure these will be splendid.

Mrs Armitage takes a bite. Smile fades, becomes thoughtful.

MRS A: What an interesting room.

Mrs Armitage drops remains of vol-au-vent into plant pot. Ruth observes this and looks crestfallen.

MRS A: I had no idea these buildings were still standing. It's such a long time since I've been in this area. But I thought I should call. Now that these two are thinking of becoming engaged. You see Angela's very precious to us.

ANGELA: Oh, Mummy, honestly.

MRS A: Up until now she's only been interested in slapping a saddle on Muffin and mucking out the stable. (*Perplexed stare at Alan*) Men have never interested her. So you can see my concern. I thought it important to meet Guy's friends. I had no idea he was sharing this room with … er—

ALAN: Philip.

MRS A: Yes. I had no idea you were from the dark continent, Philip.

PHILIP: (*smiles*) You mean he never mentioned it?

MRS A: I don't remember it cropping up.

ANGELA: Philip's the son of a chief.

MRS A: Fascinating.

ALAN: I want him to be best man.

MRS A: (*stares*) Yes. (*Pause*) Well, we were hoping for a white wedding. It would be the social event of the year. That's why I wanted to meet his companions. I think it's such a good guide – don't you?

ALAN: Yes, well, we're up here most nights, Mrs Armitage – talking philosophy – art – literature over steaming hot cups of cocoa.

MRS A: Well, that does seem reasonably civilised. I must confess I always thought this neighbourhood was rather noisy.

ALAN: I wonder what gave you that idea.

Noises off. Sounds of Rigsby singing.

MRS A: What was that?

ALAN: Nothing. Should we put a record on.

Rigsby enters. He has reverted to his former squalor. Old cardigan and baggy trousers.

ALAN: (*loftily*) Did you want something Rigsby?

RIGSBY: Yes – you've left a ring round the bath again.

ALAN: Not now, Rigsby. Can't you see I've got guests?

RIGSBY: Well, I'm not cleaning it off. If you will lie there playing with your rubber duck all afternoon. And stop wafting that serviette about. You don't impress me. You've never used one before.

ALAN: Of course I have.

RIGSBY: No you haven't. Since when have you worried about a few stains? You've always put your faith in biological washing powders.

MRS A: Guy, who is this person?

RIGSBY: (*amused*) Guy! Who's she calling Guy?

ALAN: My middle name, Rigsby. I suppose you always wondered what the G stood for?

RIGSBY: No. It stands for George.

ALAN: (*amused bluster*) Who told you that?

RIGSBY: You did.

MRS A: Guy, has this person been invited?

MRS A: No.

MRS A: Then ask him to leave.

ANGELA: Good for you, Mummy.

RIGSBY: Wait a minute, this is my house. I'll say who's leaving and it might just be you. You look like a troublemaker to me.

MRS A: How dare you?

RIGSBY: (*stares*) Hang on. Don't I know you?

MRS A: I should hardly think so.

RIGSBY: Yes, I do. Mabel Bagworthy that was. You used to live near the skin yard. I remember you riding on your Dad's rag-and-bone cart. Always had a runny nose.

Ruth laughs immoderately.
Mrs Armitage frowns uncomfortably.

MRS A: I think you must be mistaken.

RIGSBY: No – we went to the same school. You were always showing us your knickers behind the caretaker's hut. I couldn't forget you, Mabel. The smell of candyfloss mingling with the faint aroma of dead rabbit.

MRS A: Really. I must protest.

ANGELA: Guy, are you going to let Mummy stand there and be insulted?

ALAN: Certainly not. I'll take you home, Mrs Armitage.

MRS A: Angela, get my coat. I've had quite enough of this dreadful place. If you'll take my advice, Guy – you'll find alternative accommodation at once.

ANGELA: Guy.

ALAN: Coming, Angela.

Alan follows them rather abjectly.

RIGSBY: I hope I didn't spoil their evening.

RUTH: You didn't spoil mine, Mr Rigsby – I was proud of you.

PHILIP: Yes, have a drink, Rigsby.

RIGSBY: Thanks. Looks as if he's gone then.

RUTH: Yes, I'm afraid Alan's changed.

PHILIP: I never thought he'd turn into a snob.

RIGSBY: It didn't surprise me. I've seen it all before – the lust of wealth and power. Thank God I was born humble.

Alan re-enters silently.

RUTH: Alan! Why have you come back.

ALAN: I couldn't abandon my friends. I told Angela, if I'd bought her a ring I'd have been forced to ask for it back.

PHILIP: We've done you an injustice, Alan.

RUTH: Yes, we thought – I don't know how to put it.

RIGSBY: We thought you'd become a social climber.

ALAN: A social climber! No, I haven't changed, Rigsby. Besides, I couldn't have that woman for a mother-in-law.

RIGSBY: That's true.

ALAN: (*winks*) Not someone who rode on a rag-and-bone cart.

Adjusts cuffs foppishly.
They pounce on him.

THE END

Series Three

EPISODE 7

Suddenly at Home
by
Eric Chappell

PART ONE

SCENE 1: *Int. attic flat. Day.*
Alan is reading. Rigsby enters looking disgusted. He peers back around the door.

RIGSBY: Watch yourself – he's coming up.

ALAN: Who is?

RIGSBY: Osborne. I've just dodged him on the stairs. Whatever you do, don't ask him how he is. He's got a list of symptoms as long as your arm.

ALAN: You could show a bit of sympathy, Rigsby – he's not been well.

RIGSBY: (*scornfully*) Not been well! You don't believe all that, do you? He's as fit as you are.

ALAN: I'm not fit.

RIGSBY: Don't you start.

ALAN: I keep having these giddy spells.

RIGSBY: Only when I mention the rent. You want to watch it. You'll be going the same way as Osborne. He's always at the doctor's. He's spent so much time in that surgery they've even consulted him on the new colour scheme.

ALAN: You're exaggerating, Rigsby.

RIGSBY: No, I'm not. He's got his own chair down there. He's only missed once since he's been here – and that was when he was ill.

ALAN: I suppose you think he's a hypochondriac?

RIGSBY: Of course he is. Anyone can see that he's faking.

ALAN: Well, it may interest you to know, Rigsby, that hypochondria is an illness.

RIGSBY: (*triumphantly*) See what I mean? He's even faking hypochondria. It's the doctor I feel sorry for – he's on the verge of a nervous breakdown.

ALAN: That's because he can't keep pace with Osborne's symptoms. You see Osborne needs reassurance – he sits in that surgery listening to everyone's ailments until he thinks he's got the lot. Last night, by the time he got in to see the doctor, he thought he'd got a double rupture – liver failure – a duodenal ulcer.

RIGSBY: I know – and he only went in to get his passport signed. No wonder the National Health is grinding to a halt. It would be different if he had to pay for it.

ALAN: He's entitled to treatment, Rigsby – he's paid in.

RIGSBY: What he's paid in wouldn't cover the X-rays. He must have had every part of his anatomy X-rayed by now. They cover a whole wall down at the hospital – it's like a full-scale map of the underground. And what have they ever found? One collar stud and the top off his pen. It was different in my day. You couldn't afford to be ill. If they didn't see the colour of your money you got the order of the blunt needle.

ALAN: They couldn't make you pay for medical treatment – not even in those days.

RIGSBY: Oh yes, they could. If you didn't pay your bills you came out of that hospital on a set of stumps.

ALAN: But that's the whole point of the NHS. Rigsby. No one should have to pay – there shouldn't be a premium on health – it's your right.

RIGSBY: Well, you wouldn't catch me hanging around the surgery. You start worrying about your health and you're finished.

ALAN: You mean you're afraid of what they might uncover.

RIGSBY: (*uncomfortably*) No, I'm not. There's nothing to uncover.

ALAN: What about your dirty vest? You'd make a terrible patient, Rigsby. You're so afraid. If they wanted to treat you they'd have to bring you down with a drugged dart – like they do in the safari parks.

RIGSBY: Listen, I'm not afraid. What about when I had the abscess on my tooth? The dentist said he'd never seen such spirit.

ALAN: Was that when you bit through his thumb?

RIGSBY: It was a very painful operation. He had his knee in my chest for an hour. And he cracked my jaw bone – I heard it go. Not that he cared.

ALAN: What did he say?

RIGSBY: He said it was a car back-firing. It's a good thing I'm able to endure pain.

ALAN: What! You can't stand pain. You were on your knees most of the time begging for gas. And you can't stand illness. That's why you don't like Osborne – sick people make you nervous.

RIGSBY: No, they don't.

Osborne enters. He is pale, lank and doleful.

OSBORNE: Hello, Rigsby.

Rigsby grunts and moves to the other side of the room.

ALAN: Hello, Ossie. How are you feeling?

Rigsby sighs and looks heavenwards.

OSBORNE: (*gravely*) Not too good, Alan. I've just heard. I've got to go in. They say it's for a minor operation but I think they want to have a good look at me.

RIGSBY: I should have thought they'd have seen enough by now.

ALAN: I shouldn't worry – you'll be in good hands, Ossie.

OSBORNE: Yes, that's what I keep telling myself.

RIGSBY: (*darkly*) Sooner you than me.

OSBORNE: (*nervously*) What do you mean?

RIGSBY: Very bad record that hospital. They don't walk out of there very often – too many rusty scalpels lying around. You haven't booked your holidays, have you?

ALAN: Shut up, Rigsby. It's a very good hospital.

RIGSBY: It used to be – it's never been the same since they lost the key to the poison cupboard.

OSBORNE: Oh dear – I can feel my chest pains coming on.

ALAN: Now don't worry, Ossie. You'll enjoy it – you'll get the best of attention.

OSBORNE: (*hopefully*) Yes. I understand nothing's too much trouble for them.

RIGSBY: It isn't – if you speak Hindustani.

OSBORNE: I don't speak Hindustani. (*Alarmed*)

RIGSBY: Well, you only need a smattering – just to be able to say things like, 'Nurse, I've just drunk from the specimen bottle', or 'Excuse me, gentlemen but you're sawing through the wrong leg'.

OSBORNE: It's not my leg.

RIGSBY: What is it then?

Osborne hesitates. They look at him curiously.

OSBORNE: Well, it's a bit delicate, really.

RIGSBY: (*grins*) Oh, yes? Well, come on, don't be shy – you can tell us.

OSBORNE: Well, it's a sort of ... gentlemen's operation.

ALAN: (*grins*) He's having a vasectomy.

RIGSBY: You watch your language. (*Frowns*) Look, I don't want to be indelicate, Osborne, but you're a single man. You're going to meet a young lady one day – settle down – start a family – you can't do that if you've had your firing pin removed.

ALAN: That's no problem, Rigsby. You can always preserve your seed – keep it in the freezer.

RIGSBY: Oh, yes – and what happens? Someone's only got to

leave the fridge door open and you lose your son and heir along with the kippers.

OSBORNE: It's not a vasectomy.

RIGSBY: What is it then?

Osborne hesitates and then whispers in their ears. Long Pause. Rigsby stares at him.

RIGSBY: You've left that a bit late, haven't you? (*Pause*) Are you thinking of changing your religion?

OSBORNE: No. (*Worried*) I think that's just an excuse to get me in – I think there's more to it than that.

RIGSBY: You think that's just the tip?

OSBORNE: Yes.

RIGSBY: You could be right.

ALAN: I keep telling you – there's nothing to worry about. Operations are perfectly safe these days.

RIGSBY: Not that one – that's the unkindest cut of all. Who's doing it? Singet Khan or Mr Abdullah?

OSBORNE: No, Mr MacAllister.

RIGSBY: Oh, Mac the Knife. Well, you'd better be careful. You know what Scotsmen are like – they like their pound of flesh.

OSBORNE: (*sits down*) Do you mind if I have a glass of water?

ALAN: Certainly. Don't take any notice of Rigsby. MacAllister is a very good man.

RIGSBY: Yes and very genial. You must have seen him around the wards. He's the one who walks through with blood on his boots.

OSBORNE: (*winces*) I think I'd better have one of my tablets.

ALAN: Now you've got to keep calm. The odds are a million to one.

OSBORNE: Against what?

ALAN: Er … against anything happening.

OSBORNE: (*alarmed*) You think something's going to happen.

ALAN: No.

OSBORNE: I have to be careful. I've got this rare blood group – I have to wear this chain around my neck.

RIGSBY: What does it say? 'Do not drain?'

Alan frowns at Rigsby.

ALAN: Now you must keep calm, Ossie.

OSBORNE: (*worried*) They say I have to sign this document.

ALAN: That's only to give the surgeon permission to operate – nothing to worry about.

RIGSBY: Yes – just make sure you

read the small print. You could find you've left your body to medical science.

OSBORNE: They wouldn't do that, would they?

RIGSBY: Oh, yes. You don't know where you are with the medical profession these days. You've heard of spare part surgery, haven't you? Anything goes wrong, it's like a car breaking down on the hard shoulder of the M1. First the battery – then the pump – then the dynamo – that could be you. They've probably already got someone down for your kidneys – and your liver – heart – the lot. You could end up being more active dead than you were alive.

OSBORNE: They couldn't do that, could they, Alan?

ALAN: Of course they couldn't. Not without your permission – or that of your next of kin— (*Checks himself*)

OSBORNE: Next of kin! You do think something's going to happen. You don't think I'll be coming out. I'd better have another tablet. (*Pause. Sadly*) I haven't got any next of kin.

RIGSBY: Well, look on the bright side – at least you won't be missed. And there won't be any awkward questions – like what's happened to your liver.

ALAN: Rigsby! Can't you see you're upsetting Ossie? They can't take any part of you and

put it in someone else. It's out of the question.

RIGSBY: (*soothingly*) Of course. I was only joking. You wouldn't get a respectable surgeon doing a thing like that. Anything left over – he takes home for his dog.

OSBORNE: (*gulps*) Excuse me. I don't feel very well.

Osborne exits hurriedly.

ALAN: Now you've done it. Rigsby. Ossie!

Alan follows in pursuit. Philip enters staring after them.

PHILIP: What's the matter with those two?

RIGSBY: Young Dr Kildare's made another wrong diagnosis. He thinks Osborne's sick.

PHILIP: And you don't think so?

RIGSBY: No – there's nothing wrong with him. He's just malingering.

PHILIP: I don't know – I don't like his colour.

RIGSBY: Well, he probably doesn't like yours but I don't see what that's got to do with it. No, it's all psychological. He talks himself into it – it's all in the mind.

PHILIP: How can you be sure?

RIGSBY: Look, let me explain. It's like when the witch-doctor points the old leopard claw at you. What do you do? Hand in your maize bowl – wrap yourself in a blanket – and off to the happy hunting grounds.

PHILIP: Not anymore, Rigsby. We've come a long way since then. These days we usually ask for a second opinion. And at least we don't suffer from all those ailments that affect Western Society.

RIGSBY: Of course you don't. And do you know why? Because you're closer to nature. Half the trouble in this country is caused by tight underpants. And of course you eat the right food – no fatty substances – no sweets. I've never seen any of your lot with a bad set of teeth – filed to a point sometimes – but never a filling in sight. And they've never seen a nylon toothbrush. You see, you lead a natural existence.

PHILIP: Of course we do, Rigsby. When there's sickness in my village we know exactly what to do.

RIGSBY: Of course you do.

PHILIP: We sacrifice a chicken.

RIGSBY: What! Does it do any good?

PHILIP: Well, not for the chicken but it does wonders for the patient.

RIGSBY: And is that all you do?

PHILIP: Oh no. Then we crush the leaves from the jum-jum tree – mix it with the bile from the horned toad and add the venom

of the cobra. And administer it three times a day.

RIGSBY: Does it work?

PHILIP: They're up and about in no time.

RIGSBY: I'm not surprised. And it really cures them?

PHILIP: Oh, yes. (*Thoughtfully*) Well, it's either that or the penicillin.

RIGSBY: Very funny. Well, Osborne doesn't fool me. He's only doing all this to get out of the basement.

PHILIP: Are you sure, Rigsby? He could have a different motive. He's getting a great deal of attention from Miss Jones.

RIGSBY: What?

PHILIP: Well, you know how she likes to administer succour. How she takes in puppies and birds with broken wings. Well, it's the same with Osborne. She's been making soup for him every day.

RIGSBY: She's been doing what? We'll see about that.

Rigsby exits angrily.

* * *

SCENE 2: *Int. Ruth's room.*
Ruth is making soup.
Rigsby sniffs suspiciously.

RIGSBY: My word, Miss Jones – that smells good.

RUTH: Yes, Mr Rigsby. I'm making it for Mr Osborne – it's been doing wonders for his tubes. I don't feel he's getting enough of the right food. He looks so pale.

RIGSBY: Don't be taken in by that pallid complexion, Miss Jones. There's nothing wrong with him.

RUTH: I'm sure he's anaemic, Mr Rigsby.

RIGSBY: No, he's got as much blood as we have, Miss Jones – it's just that his skin's thicker – it doesn't show through, that's all.

RUTH: I don't see how he can be well, not living in that basement. Not after the wet winter we've had. It's so damp and dark down there – even the mushrooms don't look very good this year.

RIGSBY: Well, I don't see what he's complaining about – he's got a cosy little spot down there – very nice view of the road.

RUTH: Mr Rigsby. He's on a level with the pavement – he can only see people's legs. And when he opens the window he's covered in dead leaves and toffee papers. How can he be comfortable? He's not a mole. And it's so damp.

RIGSBY: I wouldn't say it was damp.

RUTH: Not damp! The last heavy rains we had, his bed started to float. And what about when the coalman mistook it for the cellar? He was engulfed in a ton of nutty slack.

RIGSBY: Well, I'm not saying it doesn't have its drawbacks. But you see, he won't make the best of things. I've met his type before. He enjoys being ill. I mean, we all have aches and pains but we don't go around trying to arouse sympathy.

RUTH: Well, I think it's our duty to help others, Mr Rigsby. We all need a cool hand on our fevered brow sometimes. That's why I'm studying First Aid – so that I'm ready for any emergency.

RIGSBY: And it's a very worthy ambition, Miss Jones, but are you the type? You have to have this ruthless streak for nursing and you're so tender-hearted. Look what happened when we ran over that rabbit – you didn't know what to do.

RUTH: Well, you can't give the kiss of life to a rabbit, Mr Rigsby.

RIGSBY: All right. What about when the window cleaner fell off his ladder? You fainted three times. He had to get off the stretcher to make room for you.

RUTH: I know, but I'm getting better. I'm not so squeamish as I used to be. I'm learning to stand the sight of blood.

RIGSBY: You can't stand the sight of blood, Miss Jones – you're not that good with tomato sauce.

RUTH: You can scoff, but one day all this training will be worthwhile, Mr Rigsby. And I do admire the medical profession – they're so selfless.

RIGSBY: You try getting them out at night. You can never get our doctor – not when he's playing bridge. You have to shout your symptoms down the phone. There was this urgent case the other night – a choking fit. He was on a grand slam – refused to go. And that was his mother. Mind you, you can't blame them – not with people like Osborne ringing up day and night complaining about pains in his chest. He called them out the other night – no consideration.

RUTH: He thought he was dying.

RIGSBY: No, he didn't. As soon as he heard it was the lady doctor he got up and changed into his silk pyjamas.

RUTH: Well, I know Mr Osborne gets into a state but that doesn't mean he's not genuine. Just think how awful you'd feel if he was really ill.

RIGSBY: You don't understand, Miss Jones. I was in the army. I know an old soldier when I see one. We had one in our company – reckoned he had bad eyesight and flat feet. Well, the Army were very considerate about his eyesight – they put him in a forward trench. He saw the Germans before any of us. And his flat feet didn't stop him breaking the United Services' record for the mile.

RUTH: Well, I'd never forgive myself if I turned my back on someone in need.

RIGSBY: (*pause*) Well, actually, I do have this pain in my back, Miss Jones. What I need is a bit of manipulation.

RUTH: Ah, I can help you there, Mr Rigsby.

RIGSBY: (*brightens*) Can you, Miss Jones?

RUTH: Yes, I know a very good osteopath.

RIGSBY: (*frowns*) Thank you very much, Miss Jones – I'll think about it.

Rigsby exits.

* * *

SCENE 3: *Int. basement. Later.*
Osborne is sitting bolt upright at the table staring frontwards.
Rigsby enters scowling. He closes door.

RIGSBY: Now listen, Osborne – while they're out I want a word with you. I'm not having you going to Miss Jones with all your imaginary ailments. I know what your game is – you're trying to take advantage of her good nature. You won't be satisfied until she's doing all your cooking and cleaning. Well, I'm on to you, Osborne. You take pills to make you sleep – pills to wake you up. You've got high blood pressure – low blood pressure. The only things you haven't had are anthrax and Dutch elm disease. (*Pause*) Not talking, hey, Osborne?

You don't like the truth, do you? You're as fit as I am. What do you say to that? Osborne? Look at me when I'm talking to you. (*Stares*) Osborne – Osborne?

Rigsby touches Osborne. Osborne slumps forward onto the table. Rigsby panics.

END OF PART ONE

PART TWO

SCENE 4: *Int. basement flat. Later.*
Rigsby is tidying the room.
Alan and Philip enter in their top-
coats. Rigsby looks at them uneasily.

ALAN: Hello, Rigsby. Where's Osborne?

PHILIP: We wondered if he was feeling better.

RIGSBY: (*emotionally*) I don't know how to say this. Osborne ... Osborne has left us.

PHILIP: What do you mean?

RIGSBY: I mean ... he's gone to a better place.

ALAN: Has he got a council flat?

RIGSBY: (*irritable*) No, he hasn't. He's departed ... we won't see him anymore.

ALAN: I thought you insisted on a fortnight's notice.

RIGSBY: I could hardly do that – not in this case. You see – he's passed over.

Philip and Alan stare at each other.

PHILIP: You mean he's dead?

RIGSBY: If you want to put it crudely – yes.

ALAN: Poor old Osborne. Are you sure, Rigsby? I mean, you always said he was faking.

RIGSBY: Not this time. He was almost rigid. Good thing it didn't happen up there – we'd never have got him down the stairs. I found him – my hands are still shaking. He's dead all right – you can't go through a world war without knowing a stiff – a corpse – when you see one.

PHILIP: Poor Osborne. Does Miss Jones know?

RIGSBY: No. I don't know how to tell her – not after all that's happened. I— (*Stops*)

Ruth enters.

RUTH: Has anyone seen Mr Osborne?

They stare at her in silence.

RUTH: I wondered if he enjoyed the soup. (*Stops*) What's the matter? What are you staring at?

RIGSBY: I'm afraid I have some bad news, Miss Jones.

RUTH: I didn't leave the salt out again?

RIGSBY: No. I'm afraid he's dead, Miss Jones.

RUTH: Oh, my God! (*Stops*) Had he eaten it?

RIGSBY: No, it was untouched. I found him staring at it – the spoon still in his hand – not moving a muscle.

RUTH: (*tearfully*) Poor Mr Osborne.

RIGSBY: I know how you feel, Miss Jones.

ALAN: Let the tears come, Ruth.

PHILIP: It's a terrible shock.

RIGSBY: Yes, we were all very fond of him.

RUTH: (*snaps*) You weren't. Save your crocodile tears, Mr Rigsby. You hounded that poor man – you never showed any sympathy. Keeping him in this miserable hovel. Well, he's gone to a better landlord now. He won't cut his water off and disconnect the gas. (*Tears*) Poor, dear Mr Osborne. You never believed him did you? And now it's too late.

Ruth turns to leave.
Rigsby catches her arm.

RIGSBY: But, Miss Jones—

RUTH: Take your hands off me. Murderer!

Ruth exits.

* * *

SCENE 5: *Int. attic flat. That evening. Alan and Philip are at tea.*
Rigsby enters. He is wearing a black suit and tie. He waits solemnly for comment. They stare at him.

ALAN: Crikey! It's the man in black.

PHILIP: What are you dressed like that for, Rigsby?

RIGSBY: You wouldn't understand. It happens to be a mark of respect—

ALAN: You look like the chief mourner.

RIGSBY: Well, I am in a way. You see, he had no family. No one to mourn his passing. It'll be up to us to give him a good send off.

PHILIP: Shouldn't we ring the hospital first?

RIGSBY: No point. Life was extinct. I know all about the wonders of medical science, but they couldn't do anything for Osborne. No – there's only one thing that'll improve him now and that's embalming fluid.

ALAN: Well, there's no need to be so callous.

RIGSBY: Callous! You sit there stuffing yourself and call me callous. I haven't touched a crumb since I found him. And after what Miss Jones said, how do you think I feel? Who knows? If it hadn't have been for me he might still be alive.

PHILIP: (*kindly*) You can't blame yourself, Rigsby. It could have happened any time.

RIGSBY: Well, I'm going to make it up to him. He's going to have the best funeral this town's ever seen.

ALAN: What's the point, Rigsby? He's not going to be in a position to enjoy it. I happen to believe that when you're dead you're dead.

RIGSBY: Well, that's where you're wrong – you're not dead – only sleeping.

ALAN: (*amused*) Only sleeping! Well, there's going to be some complaints down at the crematorium.

RIGSBY: You can jeer. I'm glad I'm not like you two – at least I believe in something.

PHILIP: I believe in something, Rigsby. I believe that we are part of a cycle. We live – we die – we enrich the soil – crops grow and feed the next generation.

RIGSBY: (*stares*) My God! Is that your idea of a life after death – coming back as a bowl of cornflakes? There's more to it than that.

ALAN: What about reincarnation?

RIGSBY: You don't believe all that rubbish, do you?

PHILIP: Why not? Look on the bright side, Rigsby. Next time you might come back as a human being.

Philip exits.

RIGSBY: I wish you two would show more respect.

ALAN: Why? I think all this weeping and wailing at funerals is morbid.

RIGSBY: You would. That's the trouble with people today – they don't enjoy a good funeral. Death's something we shouldn't talk about. It was different in my day. I'll never forget my father's funeral. The scenes in that churchyard – vivid – etched in the memory. I remember these women weeping – throwing themselves on the coffin – really let themselves go.

ALAN: They must have been very fond of him.

RIGSBY: Didn't even know him – they'd come for a christening. People were like that in those days – you showed your grief. None of those funeral parlours. You had them laid out in the front room – everyone came to have a look. When we had Dad there, it was just like Lenin's tomb. He looked marvellous. Mind you, he'd been at Skegness the week before – came back with a lovely tan.

ALAN: (*takes sandwich from his mouth*) Do you mind, Rigsby? I'm eating.

RIGSBY: Never mind that, I've got something to show you.

ALAN: I haven't finished my tea.

RIGSBY: Come on – it won't take a second.

Alan sighs and follows Rigsby.

* * *

SCENE 6: *Int. basement flat.*
A coffin is standing in the corner of the room.
Alan enters. He turns round and looks at Rigsby.

ALAN: Well, what is it?

RIGSBY: (*proudly*) It's behind you.

ALAN: What? (*He turns and starts back from coffin*) It's a coffin!

RIGSBY: Of course it's a coffin. What did you think it was – a cocktail cabinet?

ALAN: Where did you get it from?

RIGSBY: It's mine. I got it at a closing down sale. Nice, isn't it? Lovely finish. They don't make them like this anymore. I thought it would do for me. I've been keeping it in the garage.

ALAN: (*shudders*) You're macabre, Rigsby.

RIGSBY: No, I'm not. Look at it. Solid oak – see the veneer? Brass handles, and feel this lining – pure velvet. You know, it's almost worth going just to have a ride in one of these. I thought I'd let Osborne have it – it's the least I can do.

ALAN: How do you know he'd like

it? I mean he might have preferred cremation.

RIGSBY: (*shakes head*) No, you don't know where you are with cremations. I've seen them. When it's a nice day I take a few sandwiches up the cemetery. It's peaceful up there. I was sitting in the garden of remembrance one day and this woman came in to spread her husband's ashes. The wind got up and blew them all over the place. I'll tell you this, it was all I could do to finish my sandwiches.

ALAN: (*winces*) Shut up, Rigsby. There's something wrong with you. Anyone who goes up the cemetery for a day out—

RIGSBY: (*amused*) Just look at you – you're twitching all over. You know what's the matter? You're afraid of the trappings of death. I don't know why – we all have to die sometime. ·

ALAN: I don't know about that, Rigsby. Medical science is improving all the time. I may have my body frozen.

RIGSBY: What!

ALAN: They can do that – freeze your body and keep it in cold storage and await the advance of medical knowledge.

RIGSBY: My God! The things they're going to find in your deep freeze. Who's going to be in charge of the funeral arrangements? Birds Eye? And what about the Day of Judgement?

When we're all supposed to stand up and be counted? You'll look ridiculous standing between a leg of ham and a packet of fish fingers.

ALAN: Never mind – I'd sooner do that than end up in one of those.

RIGSBY: (*grins*) Hey, listen.

He makes the coffin lid creak. Alan exits hurriedly.
Rigsby laughs. Starts to polish the coffin.

RIGSBY: I don't know what he's afraid of. When you've got to go – you've got to go.

There is a scratching sound. Rigsby stops abruptly. Listens at lid. Further scratching.

RIGSBY: Oh, no!

He slowly opens the lid. Vienna jumps out and scuttles away.

RIGSBY: That damned cat. You had a narrow escape there – you could have ended up like a crusader's dog. I must watch myself – I felt quite shaky for a moment.

He continues polishing.
Ruth enters silently. She puts a hand on Rigsby's shoulder. He almost jumps out of his skin.

RUTH: What on earth's the matter, Mr Rigsby?

RIGSBY: Miss Jones – you gave me quite a start.

RUTH: I'm sorry, Mr Rigsby. I just came to apologise for my little outburst. I shouldn't have said that.

RIGSBY: (*a little sulkily*) Don't give it a thought, Miss Jones. No doubt a lot of people would agree with you.

Continues polishing.

RUTH: No, Mr Rigsby, I shouldn't have said it.

Ruth takes up a cloth and joins Rigsby in polishing.

RUTH: There, we're getting a lovely shine. What's it for?

RIGSBY: Osborne.

RUTH: (*stares, recoils*) It's a coffin! He's not in there, is he?

RIGSBY: No but I thought I'd get the preparations in hand. No good leaving it until the last moment.

Ruth recovers.

RUTH: You're quite right, Mr Rigsby. It's so important these things go off smoothly. I remember when Uncle Felix was buried at sea – just off Brighton. That was badly planned.

RIGSBY: What happened, Miss Jones?

RUTH: Well, it was a very tasteful service and we came away more than satisfied – unfortunately the next day he popped up at

Worthing. He kept coming in and out with the tide.

RIGSBY: That must have been very distressing, Miss Jones.

RUTH: Yes, it was – he couldn't stand Worthing.

RIGSBY: Well, I've planned a modest little ceremony – up at the cemetary. I've got a reserved plot I can let him have. Nice spot – well back – you don't get many dogs up there.

RUTH: Do we know his religion?

RIGSBY: I don't think he had one. We should be all right – as long as he wasn't Hindu. Don't fancy pushing a flaming pyre up the Humber. And I thought a simple inscription. 'Oh for the touch of a vanished hand and the sound of a voice which is still.'

RUTH: Yes. Or 'A rose has grown over the garden wall and blossoms on the other side.'

RIGSBY: 'My days are gone like a shadow.'

RUTH: 'Boast not thyself of tomorrow for thou knowest not what the day may bring forth.'

RIGSBY: Wonderful sentiments, Miss Jones. I wondered if you'd agree to be principal mourner. I know it would mean a lot to Osborne.

RUTH: (*uncertainly*) Well, I don't know, Mr Rigsby.

RIGSBY: I can see you – all in black

– looking pale and transluscent – dropping a single red rose on the coffin. You'd be very decorative, Miss Jones.

RUTH: Well, I do have this black velvet simply dying to be worn. And that sweet little hat with the veil. I wonder if I've got gloves and handbag to match. I'll go and see.

Ruth exits excitedly.
Rigsby returns to coffin.
Alan and Philip enter.

RIGSBY: What do you want?

ALAN: I wanted Philip to see the coffin. See what I mean, Philip?

PHILIP: Oh yes. Of course. It's a pity. It's such a lovely piece of wood.

RIGSBY: (*anxiously*) What does he mean? What's wrong with it?

PHILIP: It's not big enough.

RIGSBY: Of course it's big enough.

ALAN: Not with all the velvet padding.

RIGSBY: You leave that alone.

PHILIP: Perhaps if we were to double him up a bit?

RIGSBY: No one's going to be doubled up. I tell you it's big enough. There's only one size.

ALAN: Ah, but this is a woman's.

RIGSBY: What! (*stares*) A woman's?

ALAN: See all that fancy work? It's a woman's.

RIGSBY: Well, I'll take a chance if you don't mind.

ALAN: It's not the first time this sort of thing's happened. What about the man who had his own sarcophagus built?

RIGSBY: A what?

ALAN: A sarcophagus. It's a tomb. Beautifully carved in stone with cherubins and seraphins. But he had this feeling it wasn't big enough. They kept saying 'don't worry' until the day he died.

RIGSBY: Well, what happened? Did they get him in?

ALAN: Oh, yes – they got him in all right but they had to cut his feet off.

RIGSBY: (*hesitates*) There's only one thing for it – someone will have to try it.

They look at each other.

PHILIP: Well, you're about his size, Rigsby.

RIGSBY: All right. Give me a hand.

They help Rigsby into the coffin.

RIGSBY: There you are. See what I mean? Plenty of room.

ALAN: You'll never get the lid down.

RIGSBY: Of course you'll get it down.

ALAN: No, it'll squash your nose.

RIGSBY: No, it won't.

PHILIP: Unless we turn his head sideways.

RIGSBY: It's all right. Put the lid down – I'll show you.

They close the lid.

PHILIP: What's it like, Rigsby?

RIGSBY: Very comfortable. Now let me out.

They try to lift the lid. They find it is jammed.

ALAN: It's stuck!

They struggle with the lid.

RIGSBY: Get me out!

PHILIP: Keep calm, Rigsby.

ALAN: We'll get something to force it. Don't go away.

Alan and Philip dash out.

* * *

SCENE 7: *Int. hall.*
Alan and Philip search the hall cupboard.

ALAN: What are we going to do?

PHILIP: We need a heavy screwdriver.

ALAN: He can't stand confined spaces – not after that night in the cells. (*Pause*) You don't think Osborne'll mind, do you? He never liked Rigsby using his things.

PHILIP: I don't think Osborne's worrying about anything at the moment.

ALAN: No. Poor old Osborne – funny to think we'll never hear his voice again.

Osborne enters.

OSBORNE: Hello, Alan, Philip.

ALAN/PHILIP: Hello, Ossie.

Osborne passes them. He almost reaches his door before they realise.

ALAN/PHILIP: Osborne!

They seize him.

ALAN: Are you all right?

OSBORNE: Yes. Mind you, I had a nasty turn. I think I took too many of those tablets. I woke up in the hospital with screens around me. I'll never go there again. I discharged myself. They were all set for open heart surgery – until I started snoring I could have ended up on a slab. Some people can't wait to get rid of you.

He makes for basement.

ALAN: (*hastily*) You can't go in there.

OSBORNE: Why not?

PHILIP: Er ... you can't go in there without seeing Miss Jones. She's been worried about you.

OSBORNE: You're quite right, Philip. That was thoughtless of me.

Osborne exits upstairs.

ALAN: We've got to get rid of that coffin. If Ossie sees it in his condition—

PHILIP: Yes, he could end up in it after all.

Alan and Philip hurry back into basement.

* * *

SCENE 8: *Int. Ruth's room.*
Ruth is in black. She is putting finishing touches to veil.
Osborne enters.

OSBORNE: Hello, Miss Jones.

Ruth slowly raises veil and stares at Osborne.

RUTH: Mr Osborne!

OSBORNE: I thought I'd let you know I've come back.

RUTH: Er ... yes. (*Moistens lips*) Come back from where, Mr Osborne?

OSBORNE: You might well ask. From the edge of the grave, Miss Jones.

RUTH: (*little scream*) Oh, my god!

OSBORNE: I knew you'd be worrying about me – so you're the first person I thought I'd call on.

RUTH: (*backing away*) You needn't have bothered, Mr Osborne.

OSBORNE: I also wondered if there was any soup left.

RUTH: You came back for that?

OSBORNE: And I wondered if you'd ironed those shirts.

RUTH: What! (*Extends trembling hand and touches Osborne. She gives a tremulous sigh of relief*) You're warm. Thank heavens.

OSBORNE: (*puzzled*) What's the matter, Miss Jones? You're distraught. And why are you dressed like that? My dear lady, you're in mourning. How could I have been so insensitive? Who is it?

RUTH: Oh, just a friend.

OSBORNE: Ah, well, I won't disturb you in your hour of grief – I'll leave you.

Osborne exits.

RUTH: Mr Osborne!

Ruth follows.

* * *

SCENE 9: *Int. basement flat.*
Alan and Philip are struggling to raise coffin lid.

RIGSBY: (*muffled*) Get me out of here.

ALAN: Stop shouting – you're using up oxygen. What a design – you could suffocate in one of these.

PHILIP: Well, normally it doesn't matter. It won't budge.

ALAN: We'll have to take it outside – smash it with the sledgehammer.

Muffled protests from Rigsby. They carry coffin to the door. They hear Osborne coming.

PHILIP: Osborne!

They put the coffin down and stand in front of it. Osborne enters followed by Ruth.

OSBORNE: What are you doing here?

ALAN: Er … just moving some furniture for Rigsby.

OSBORNE: But it's a coffin. Has someone died?

RUTH: Er … we thought he had – it appears we made a mistake.

Banging from coffin.

OSBORNE: You certainly have. He's alive and kicking.

Lid flies open and Rigsby appears.

OSBORNE: Rigsby!

RIGSBY: Come on, get me out of here.

RUTH: Are you all right, Mr Rigsby?

RIGSBY: It was a nasty moment, Miss Jones but I kept my head. I learnt that in the war. After all, what's so frightening about a coffin? Look at their faces – white as sheets. Terrified of the grim reaper … (*He*

sees Osborne) Hi, Ossie.

Does a double take. Turns. Spins. Collapses in a dead faint.

THE END

SERIES FOUR

The fourth series saw two big changes: no Richard Beckinsale in the cast and a change of producer. Everybody thinks Richard wasn't in the show because he'd died, but that's not true, he was in a long-running West End show and couldn't be released. It was very late in the day when I heard about it; I'd just started writing the scripts when I received a phone call to say we'd lost Richard. It was a big blow. I'd already had to cope with losing Frances once and thought 'Here we go again.'

One of the important areas I exploited throughout the previous three series were the scenes involving banter between Alan and Philip. We lost all of that with Richard's departure, so it was a relief knowing we were recording the last six shows, although it would have been seven if the bosses at Yorkshire had got their way. They asked if I'd write another one because they'd slipped up and issued a contract for six, but I politely refused – although nowadays I wished I'd accepted because of the repeat fees! Nevertheless, I just had to get through six programmes. I took a lot of time over this series and, even though I say it myself, I think the writing was up to standard, if not better.

Although it was transmitted second in the series, *Fire and Brimstone* was the first script I wrote, so I took the opportunity to explain the absence of Alan. Although he wasn't mentioned by name, Rigsby explained he'd qualified as a doctor. He went on to express his surprise because he wouldn't trust him with a wall chart. Sadly, these lines were cut before the recording.

I brought in a new character, Gwyn Williams, a Welsh theology student, and was going to make him a running character, but even as I wrote the script I knew it wouldn't work, there was no way he could relate to Philip like Alan had. He was also too extreme and it wouldn't have paid off, so I made him into another visiting character. That's taking nothing away from John Clive, he did a good job, but coming into *Rising Damp* at this late stage was like being a substitute in a football match played at a very high speed – you've got to pick up the pace quickly or else you'll be passed by everyone! It's hard on people coming into a show. You're on your own because the rest of the cast know and understand each other, while you're lost for a time until you get used to the atmosphere and proceedings.

I was able to inject a few religious jokes into the script and it was a relief that the episode went well, because with Richard missing I was feeling around for plot ideas in order to fill the vacuum he'd left behind – it wasn't easy. Something always had to be happening so that people didn't stop to think 'Where's Richard?' Fortunately, in *Hello Young Lovers* no one really noticed because they were too busy wondering what the two kids were doing in the house. This episode, which was transmitted first although I'd planned it as second in the run, was easy to write: respectability and marriage are themes that lend themselves to comedy, and opting to focus on two people living together under Rigsby's roof, bearing in mind his starchy ways, was fun.

In *Great Expectations* we saw Rigsby's wife for the first time. It was nice to bring her in and show her to be the dragon he always said she was. We also hear that Rigsby's Christian name is Rupert: I didn't hold back his name deliberately, I just never thought of him as having one. But I realised it was probably an issue I would have to deal with sooner or later.

With Richard's absence, Don and Frances became even more important to the scripts as they were allocated more lines. Miss Jones, in particular, became a much bigger character in this series, as shown in *Pink Carnations*. This episode took a bit of writing because I had to work out how all the misunderstandings between the people wearing flowers could realistically take place. Although I say it myself, it's quite a neat construction and everything worked. It's perfectly logical how the confusion happened: Miss Jones and Rigsby have pink carnations because they're going to meet, everyone else is wearing them because they're part of a wedding party.

We left the house again in this episode but as we were getting near the end of the series, I wasn't going to worry about it. Luckily, everyone else felt the same way and was happy to go along with my plans.

Some of the dialogue in *Under the Influence* is the best I wrote. Sometimes the better dialogue doesn't come off on the screen as well as you think it might, but when I read the script again recently, I realised how good it is. There were some excellent scenes between the late Peter Jeffrey, who played Ambrose, and Rigsby, especially when he's hypnotised.

I closed the door on Rigsby's little world with *Come On In, the Water's Lovely*. I experienced mixed emotions when it came to writing the last episode: there was certainly a sense of relief that we'd maintained a high quality throughout, but what worried Len more than anything, and perhaps made him a little tense towards the end, was that we couldn't let the standard drop. I wanted to keep my writing up to a certain level, he wanted to keep his acting up to that pitch, neither of us could afford to make a bad show. However, the more good shows you get under your belt the more nervous you become about the next. So there was a sense of relief that we got through unscathed. Looking back over all the shows, you can spot a frustrated theatre writer at work, because they could all have been performed on stage, and *Come On In* is no exception.

I never felt Rigsby and Miss Jones would become a couple, probably because I didn't believe she'd capitulate. Anyway, I didn't want to marry them off – it didn't seem logical. I knew something would go wrong and, anyway, it's not funny if they marry. It's funnier that Rigsby went to the wrong church. Fortunately for me, I was never asked to marry them off. In all the years I wrote the show, I didn't get any interference from management. I simply sent the scripts in and they were accepted.

This episode contains, in my view, the best scene between Rigsby and Miss Jones; it's where Rigsby proposes. He puts the ring on the plate only to see it get covered up before it's thrown into the fireplace – pure slapstick. That we had the best scene in the last show proves there was still plenty of life left in the sitcom.

When we finished the show we all knew it was a job well done; it was now time to move on, and within weeks I was writing *Only When I Laugh*. *Rising Damp* finished because Len and I had both had enough of long-running shows; we were ready to do something different. I didn't start writing full-time until I was in my late thirties. I wasn't going to spend all my life writing *Rising Damp*. There were many more things I wanted to do. There wasn't any sadness when I typed the final word. In this business you never look back, you just carry on with the next job. There's time in your dotage to be sentimental. The decision to stop after twenty-eight shows was the right one because today, over twenty years later, it remains unspoilt.

Series Four

EPISODE 1

Hello Young Lovers
by
Eric Chappell

PART ONE

SCENE 1: *Int. Ruth's room. Early evening.*
Ruth is preparing a tea tray and singing 'Younger than Springtime'. Rigsby enters curiously.

RIGSBY: You sound happy, Miss Jones.

RUTH: I am happy. The grass is greener – the flowers are brighter – there's a scent of blossom – and do you know why, Mr Rigsby?

RIGSBY: Horse manure, Miss Jones.

RUTH: I beg your pardon?

RIGSBY: It's that load of horse manure we had last year.

RUTH: It has nothing to do with horse manure, Mr Rigsby. It's love.

RIGSBY: (*stunned*) Love, Miss Jones?

RUTH: Yes, Mr Rigsby. Love – two hearts beating as one – two souls entwined. Love has come to this grim place – lighting up its dark corners – breaking its brooding silence with happy laughter. Love.

She recommences singing and places a rose on the tray.

RIGSBY: (*jealously*) So that's it. Who is it this time, Miss Jones?

RUTH: (*startled*) What do you mean, Mr Rigsby?

RIGSBY: I wondered why you were getting out the Rich Tea. Who is it? Who's being led on by your cold beauty until he thinks happiness is within his grasp – only to find himself discarded like an old sock.

RUTH: An old sock? I don't—

RIGSBY: Until all that's left for him is a quiet moment alone with a safety razor.

RUTH: But, Mr Rigsby – there's no need for all this—

RIGSBY: No need? No need! How many hearts are you going to break, Miss Jones?

RUTH: I haven't broken any hearts, Mr Rigsby.

RIGSBY: Oh yes you have. You break hearts like this. (*He snatches a biscuit and breaks it in half*) And this. And this. (*He breaks several biscuits whilst Ruth watches in horror*) Have you any idea what you leave behind, Miss Jones?

RUTH: It looks like half a pound of broken biscuits.

424

RIGSBY: You leave a man's finest feelings crushed and mangled – like this.

RUTH: Not the flower!

Rigsby seizes the flower and crushes it in his hand.

RIGSBY: But, Mr Rigsby, I wasn't referring to myself. I'm not in love. I was taking this tray to the young couple who've moved in across the landing.

Rigsby stares at her foolishly.

RIGSBY: Oh. (*Releases the flower*) I'm sorry, Miss Jones. I completely misunderstood – got carried away. The young couple – I didn't realise. You'll have to excuse my outburst.

He tries to restore the flower and the broken biscuits.

RIGSBY: Er … what makes you think they're in love, Miss Jones?

RUTH: You've only got to see the way they look at each other – they can't bear to be apart for a moment. She wept when he went to fetch a newspaper. I think they're newly-weds. I saw him carry her over the threshold. Wasn't that romantic?

RIGSBY: (*cynically*) Yes, well, it is early days, Miss Jones – and I can already see a cloud on the horizon. If she weeps when he goes to fetch a paper, what's she going to do when he wants a game of darts? She'll probably have hysterics.

RUTH: (*coldly*) I should have known you'd take that attitude, Mr Rigsby. You've always been cynical about marriage – just because you had a bad experience.

RIGSBY: (*sharply*) What do you mean, 'a bad experience', Miss Jones?

RUTH: (*hesitates*) I mean when your wife left you.

RIGSBY: That wasn't the bad experience – that was the good bit.

RUTH: But there must have been good times – when you first married. Didn't you carry her over the threshold?

RIGSBY: Well, I tried to – unfortunately I banged her head on the door post. You see, she was a big woman.

RUTH: A big woman! Is that all you can say about her? On her wedding day? She must have been beautiful – all brides are beautiful.

RIGSBY: Well, I must admit she was a fine sight – dressed all in white silk – her veil trailing behind – all wispy and gossamer. She seemed to float on air – until I tried to get my arms round her – it was like trying to get hold of a detached barrage balloon.

RUTH: The way you talk about her I'm surprised you ever got married. (*Curiously*) Why did you get married, Mr Rigsby?

RIGSBY: It was a mistake, Miss Jones. I did it for the wrong reason. I got married for security.

RUTH: You mean her father had money?

RIGSBY: No – he had a shotgun. He said I'd been tampering with his daughter. Tampering with her! She was heavier – taller and had a longer reach. I'd have sooner tampered with a rugby league forward.

RUTH: Well, I haven't become quite as cynical as you, Mr Rigsby. I still believe in true love. A young couple setting out on the path of matrimony – so young and vulnerable – it brings a lump to my throat.

RIGSBY: Perhaps you're right, Miss Jones. Just because I had an unhappy experience I shouldn't let it make me feel bitter. Perhaps if I'd met the right woman – someone with charm and breeding – someone not a million miles away—

RUTH: (tosses head) Oh, Mr Rigsby.

RIGSBY: (sighs) Perhaps things might have been different.

RUTH: I'm sorry, Mr Rigsby – I shouldn't have brought it all back. I suppose the wounds never heal properly.

RIGSBY: Well, mine did – I had stitches. I'll tell you what – forget about the tea – let's give them a real welcome. Get out the cut glass, I know where I can lay my hands on a bottle of bubbly.

RUTH: Oh, that would be lovely, Mr Rigsby. (Coyly) After all, they're probably feeling nervous.

RIGSBY: Of course. The strain of the wedding ceremony – the crude jokes at the reception.

RUTH: The aching desire to be alone together.

RIGSBY: And then – the anti-climax.

RUTH: Do you think there'll be an anti-climax?

RIGSBY: Bound to be. (Confidentially) There's always a few shocks on the wedding night. I'm not talking abut the sudden removal of a cork leg or the unexpected sight of false teeth in a glass by the bed. No, it's the realisation that they're going to spend the next fifty years with a total stranger – who gargles. That's why a few romantic touches will make all the difference. Cut some more flowers, Miss Jones – I'll get the champagne.

Exit Rigsby.

* * *

SCENE 2: *Int. attic flat.*
Philip is preparing the tea.
Rigsby enters.

RIGSBY: (ingratiatingly) Ah, Philip, I didn't want to disturb you but I wondered if you could slip me that bottle of champagne?

PHILIP: No, Rigsby.

RIGSBY: Why not? You've had it long enough – it's only gathering dust up here.

PHILIP: I'm saving it for a special occasion.

RIGSBY: What special occasion? What's it for? The first black couple to win *Come Dancing*?

PHILIP: That's my business.

RIGSBY: Look, Philip – Phil. This is a special occasion – there's something to celebrate.

PHILIP: Don't tell me they're restored the death penalty?

RIGSBY: No, it's the young couple downstairs – just got married. Miss Jones and I would like to give them a night to remember.

PHILIP: I should have thought they'd have had a night to remember without you and Miss Jones. What are you going to do – conjuring tricks?

RIGSBY: There's no need to be like that – we're only trying to be friendly.

PHILIP: Look, Rigsby – if it's their wedding night they want to be alone – they don't want you bursting in with champagne.

RIGSBY: Don't you believe it. They'll probably be glad of the company. It's their first night – bound to be tension.

PHILIP: How do you know it's their first night?

RIGSBY: Well, I— (*Shocked*) What do you mean? Are you suggesting—? Wash your mouth out with soap. You've only got to look at them – a couple of innocents. In fact, if there's an opportunity I might take him on one side – give him a little advice.

PHILIP: (*laughs*) You, Rigsby?

RIGSBY: Yes. Why not? It's a serious occasion – he'll need advice. We're not like your lot – we're not polygamous – he didn't get her with a bag of salt. No, you only have one chance in our society – it's like the *Golden Shot*.

PHILIP: And you're going to advise him?

RIGSBY: Yes.

PHILIP: Then here's the champagne, Rigsby. I'm not going to miss this. You giving advice. It'll be like a frog giving singing lessons.

Rigsby scowls. Takes champagne. They exit together.

* * *

SCENE 3: *Int. young couple's room. Robin and Lorna are deep in a passionate embrace.*

LORNA: Oh, Robin – alone at last.

ROBIN: Yes, I never thought I'd ever get you to myself.

LORNA: Yes, there were always people. You don't know how I longed for this moment.

ROBIN: You don't regret it, Lorna?

LORNA: No. To think we've got the whole night before us.

ROBIN: Just you and me and no one to disturb us.

Rigsby enters silently followed by Ruth and Philip. They are clutching champagne glasses and flowers and grinning amiably.

LORNA: And does Squirrel Nutkin still love his Mrs Tiggywinkle?

ROBIN: (*warmly*) Yes, Squirrel Nutkin loves his little Tiggywinkle and he wants to take her to his nice warm nest and keep her there all winter.

He glances over Lorna's shoulder and sees he has an audience.

ROBIN: Er ... Lorna.

LORNA: Yes, Robin? (*Turns*) Oh!

RUTH: Surprise, surprise!

ROBIN: What do you want?

RIGSBY: We thought you might be feeling a bit lonely so we thought we'd join you.

RUTH: We wanted to give you a proper welcome.

PHILIP: I'll open the champagne.

Philip opens the champagne.

RIGSBY: (*admiringly*) Just look at him. You wouldn't think that a few years ago he was pounding coconuts with a sharp stone.

PHILIP: Stand by with the glasses.

LORNA: Do you do this with everyone?

RUTH: No, but this is a special occasion. Don't worry, we won't keep you up – oh! (*Confused*) I didn't mean – I mean you'll probably want to get to bed – after your journey. You must be tired – probably sleep like logs – well, not logs exactly – oh dear. (*More confusion*) I'm doing it again.

RIGSBY: You'll have to excuse Miss Jones – she's a little over-excited. It's the scent of orange blossom.

LORNA: Thank you. This is very sweet of you, Miss Jones.

RUTH: And if there's anything you need. (*She catches sight of Lorna's simple pyjamas on the bed*) My dear. (*Takes Lorna to one side*) You're not going to wear those?

LORNA: What?

RUTH: Those striped things.

LORNA: Well, yes.

RUTH: You can't wear those – not tonight. Come with me – I'll see what I can find.

LORNA: But, Miss Jones—

RUTH: I insist. You can't wear those – they're so old fashioned – he'll think he's in bed with his grand-father. Will you men excuse us for a moment?

Ruth leads Lorna out of the room.

Rigsby and Philip regard Robin with interest.
Robin looks uncomfortable.

PHILIP: (*mischievously*) Nervous?

ROBIN: No.

PHILIP: Never mind – you're in luck. Rigsby's going to give you some advice.

ROBIN: What?

RIGSBY: (*frowns*) All right. All right.

He pours Robin another drink.

RIGSBY: Now, Robin – you don't mind if I call you Robin – unless you'd prefer Squirrel Nutkin?

ROBIN: (*hastily*) No – Robin will be fine.

RIGSBY: Right, Robin. (*Takes him to one side, with Philip desperately trying to hear*) A word of advice. You know about the facts of life I suppose?

ROBIN: Well, yes.

RIGSBY: I thought so. Well, just remember that's not everything – be gentle with her.

Philip nearly convulses.

ROBIN: I beg your pardon?

RIGSBY: You've got to treat her like a bit of Dresden – something precious – above price.

PHILIP: She'll feel like an antique.

RIGSBY: (*scowls*) You keep out of this. What I mean is – take your time. You may be tempted to go completely mad, but don't. Remember you've got your whole life before you. It's like Christmas – you can't wait to get through all your fruit and nuts and then afterwards you wish you'd saved something for Boxing Day. Get my meaning Robin?

ROBIN: I think so – but if you don't mind—

RIGSBY: And try and smarten yourself up a bit.

ROBIN: What?

RIGSBY: After all – first impressions are very important. Now take Philip – he's lethal with the opposite sex but you wouldn't catch him in this position without a silk dressing gown and a dab of aftershave. Am I right, Philip?

PHILIP: (*suppressed laughter*) That's right, Rigsby.

RIGSBY: You got a dressing gown?

ROBIN: Er … no.

RIGSBY: You can borrow mine. Now there's not much privacy around here so when she's changing – look out of the window – sip your champagne and admire the outline of the abattoir against the night sky. What you want is a bit of poise – sophistication. (*Demonstrates*) And when you turn – try and look dazzled.

ROBIN: Dazzled?

RIGSBY: As if you're seeing her for the first time. Then say something complimentary – it's very important at this stage.

PHILIP: (*gleefully*) What do you think he should say, Rigsby?

RIGSBY: Well, something like, 'My dear, you look beautiful – like an ivory statue – your skin is like porcelain – your smile as mysterious as the Venus de Milo—'

PHILIP: I see we're back with the antiques again.

RIGSBY: Do you mind? I'm telling him. Have another drink, Robin.

ROBIN: (*faintly*) Thank you, I think I need one.

* * *

SCENE 4: *Int. Ruth's room.*
Ruth and Laura are looking through the nightdresses.

RUTH: I'm sure this one'll suit you.

LORNA: Are you sure?

RUTH: Oh yes. I … er … bought it for a similar occasion.

LORNA: But it's never been out of the polythene.

RUTH: (*sighs*) Yes – I know the feeling. It wasn't to be, I'm afraid.

LORNA: But then I can't, Miss Jones.

RUTH: Of course you can. It's about time it saw some action. (*Confused*) Oh dear, I've done it again. I don't know what's come over me tonight.

LORNA: Well, if you really don't mind.

She takes the nightdress.

RUTH: Not at all. Oh, and Lorna – if you feel you need any help or advice – don't forget my room's just opposite.

LORNA: (*smiles*) Oh, I'm sure I'll be all right, Miss Jones.

RUTH: Good girl. (*Hesitates*) I don't know how to put this, but you may find things just a little disappointing. If you do – don't worry about it. Remember – a brave smile and keep your dignity – not too much of course – after all, you're not taking tea with the vicar.

LORNA: I'll remember that, Miss Jones, but there's no need to worry.

RUTH: But you're bound to be nervous. It is your wedding night.

LORNA: But it isn't – not really.

RUTH: (astonished) What?

LORNA: We're not married. Daddy doesn't want me to get married – not until I get my degree. He thinks I'm too young. I thought I'd better respect his wishes.

RUTH: But does he know about Robin?

LORNA: Oh no – I wouldn't dare introduce him to Daddy.

Lorna exits.

RUTH: (*shocked*) Good Lord! And she's got my nightie.

Ruth follows hurriedly.

* * *

SCENE 5: *Int. young couple's room. Lorna enters followed by a shocked-looking Ruth.*

LORNA: Look what Miss Jones has loaned me – isn't it beautiful?

RIGSBY: (*admiringly*) In perfect taste, Miss Jones. Just what one would expect from a woman of refinement and breeding – provocative but at the same time, perfectly acceptable in the event of a fire.

RUTH: (*awkwardly*) Er … Mr Rigsby.

RIGSBY: Still, we mustn't keep you two lovebirds any longer. I know what weddings can be like.

Ruth groans.

RIGSBY: I know I was very tired after mine. Well, I did have this nasty fall at the altar rails. The vicar thought I'd had too much to drink but I told him it was my new shoes. Besides, you couldn't get the drink – not during the war. Did you have a nice spread?

Lorna and Robin exchange uneasy glances.

RIGSBY: Of course there were a lot of shortages when we got married but we did our best. The wedding cake had four tiers – mind you, three of them were cardboard. Everything was second-hand – even the confetti had heel marks. You know, that's a funny thing – I didn't notice any confetti. Did you have confetti?

ROBIN: Er … no.

RIGSBY: It wasn't Registry Office, was it?

LORNA: No.

RIGSBY: Don't blame you. Nothing like a church wedding. The pink-faced choirboys – the hushed congregation – the wedding march and the bride – a radiant vision, all in white. Did you wear white?

Lorna sobs and turns away.

RUTH: (*hisses*) Mr Rigsby, they're not married.

RIGSBY: What?

RUTH: They're not married.

PHILIP: (*hastily*) Well, that doesn't matter – I mean, if they love each other—

RIGSBY: (*louder*) What!

PHILIP: (*anxiously*) After all, Rigsby's a man of the world. He knows these things happen—

RIGSBY: (*very loudly*) What!

PHILIP: It doesn't make any difference, does it, Rigsby?

Rigsby takes the glass from Robin and pours it back into the bottle. He replaces the cork with a flourish. Exits.

END OF PART ONE

PART TWO

SCENE 6: *Int. Philip's room. Hour later.*
Philip is reading.
Rigsby enters.

RIGSBY: Who'd have believed it? I never thought it would happen here – the brazen impudence of it – under this roof. My father wouldn't have allowed it – they'd have been out on the pavement bag and baggage. In his day you were lucky if you caught sight of a woman's ankle before you got married – you didn't see that much afterwards.

PHILIP: Oh, come on, Rigsby. It couldn't have been like that – the human race would have died out.

RIGSBY: I'm not saying it didn't take place, but only under cover of darkness. The human body was never displayed in those days. That's why they had bathing machines. They were very fussy. They even covered the legs of the piano stools.

PHILIP: What for?

RIGSBY: Because the sight of a leg could give a sensitive woman a sudden attack of the vapours. The upper classes even had separate changing rooms – like visiting football teams. There was none of this casual attitude to sex. Doctors had to deliver babies with bags over their heads.

PHILIP: Well, times have changed, Rigsby.

RIGSBY: They certainly have.

PHILIP: And it wasn't like that in your day. Don't tell me you didn't know what it was all about.

RIGSBY: (*hesitates*) Well, I had a general idea – I did hear talk in the choir. But we believed in keeping ourselves pure and unsullied for the right woman.

PHILIP: You mean you were pure and unsullied?

RIGSBY: Well, I would have been, if it hadn't been for that night in Paris. But that was the war. No, we always kept ourselves respectable. We didn't leap on the first woman to come along. We believed in long engagements. We had to save up for the black horsehair sofa – the coal scuttle and the aspidistra.

PHILIP: Look, Rigsby, I don't know why you're making such a fuss. I suppose if they'd gone to a registry office and signed a piece of paper everything would have been all right.

433

RIGSBY: Of course, it would. It would have been legal—

PHILIP: Rigsby, they haven't made that illegal – not yet.

RIGSBY: I mean she'd have had security.

PHILIP: Perhaps she doesn't want security.

RIGSBY: Of course she does. How can she relax doing her wifely chores if she knows that the next time she sends him out for a sliced loaf he might not come back?

PHILIP: But that could happen even if you're married.

RIGSBY: And what about her father? He doesn't even know. The first he'll hear about it is when he gets invited to the christening. Of course I should have known they weren't married.

PHILIP: Why?

RIGSBY: They were too happy.

PHILIP: Don't tell me that's illegal as well? Don't tell me we're going to get storm troopers kicking the door in and arresting us for being too happy?

RIGSBY: You don't understand, do you? I've got a responsibility. I'm the landlord.

PHILIP: Well, they're above the age of consent – there's nothing you can do.

RIGSBY: Oh, yes there is – and I've done it. I got her address off the suitcase. Miss Jones is ringing her father right now.

PHILIP: What!

RIGSBY: So if you hear raised voices and the sound of a shotgun being cocked – keep your door shut.

Exit Rigsby.

* * *

SCENE 7: *Int. landing.*
Ruth is waiting for Rigsby at the bottom of the stairs.
Rigsby enters.

RIGSBY: Did you get through, Miss Jones?

RUTH: Yes, he said he'd be here in a couple of hours. He sounded angry. I do hope we've done the right thing.

RIGSBY: I'm sure we have. As long as he doesn't let him have both barrels – we don't want to spend half the night picking pellets out the furniture.

RUTH: Both barrels! Mr Rigsby, you don't think there's any possibility of violence?

RIGSBY: It could happen, Miss Jones.

RUTH: No, I'm sure everything will be all right. They're such a lovely couple. Once he sees them together.

RIGSBY: Well, that rather depends on where he sees them, if you get my meaning. We've got to play for time – before they er ... before they ... er—

RUTH: Before they what, Mr Rigsby?

RIGSBY: Before they celebrate their nuptials, Miss Jones.

RUTH: But what can we do?

RIGSBY: We've got to divert them in some way.

RUTH: Should we ask them over for a game of scrabble?

RIGSBY: (*doubtfully*) No, I don't think they'll be tempted by the intellectual pleasures of scrabble – at least not tonight. No, it'll have to be something more drastic – like setting fire to the bed.

Rigsby has the gleam of an idea.

* * *

SCENE 8: *Int. young couple's room.*

LORNA: It seems very quiet. I think they've gone.

ROBIN: Yes, alone at last.

LORNA: I wish they hadn't gone on about marriage.

ROBIN: Is Mrs Tiggywinkle unhappy?

LORNA: Just a little, Nutkin.

ROBIN: We did agree.

LORNA: I know, but sometimes I think it would have been nice.

ROBIN: You know your father wouldn't have agreed. Come here.

They sit on the bed.

ROBIN: Come to Squirrel's little home in the trees – where it's all cosy and snug.

Rigsby enters with a bag of tools. Gives them a friendly smile. Robin sees him.

ROBIN: Oh, no. What do you want now?

RIGSBY: Just a little job I forgot to do. It won't take long – it just needs fixing.

ROBIN: Well, if it won't take long you'd better get on with it.

RIGSBY: Yes, well, if you'd just excuse me – it's the bed.

LORNA: The bed!

RIGSBY: I've had complaints. It's the springs.

ROBIN: But we don't mind.

RIGSBY: No, I'm sure you don't. But it's the others. The springs squeak – keeps them awake all night. You can hear them even when the trains are passing. Well, you don't want a restless night, do you? Now where's my spanner?

Rigsby begins to bang away at the bed.

LORNA: (*hysterically*) Oh, no! I can't stand anymore.

She exits.
Rigsby gazes after her.

RIGSBY: (*confidentially*) I hope you don't mind me saying but I think she's a little upset.

ROBIN: Yes, just a little.

RIGSBY: I thought so. I suppose it's the disappointment.

ROBIN: (*frowns*) What disappointment?

RIGSBY: Missing the wedding – all the ceremonial – it's a big day in a girl's life. (*Sighs*) You know, she'd look lovely in white.

ROBIN: (*grimly*) Would she?

RIGSBY: And you wouldn't look so bad in pinstripes and a topper. You'd set them off. You've got the figure for it.

ROBIN: That sort of thing doesn't interest me.

RIGSBY: Well, think of the wedding presents – you'd never want for toasters.

ROBIN: I'm not interested in toasters either.

RIGSBY: Well, think about her then. You don't think she wants this? Going like a lamb to the slaughter.

ROBIN: What?

RIGSBY: No wedding march for her – no walk down the aisle on a proud father's arm. The sharp intake of breath from the congregation as she raises her veil – those few simple words – and then the rosy-faced choristers remove their chewing gum and burst into song – you turn and kiss that pink trusting, upturned face and the best man has to separate you for the photographs. That's what you're missing – and all for what? One night of pleasure.

ROBIN: (*weakly*) Rigsby, if you keep going on like this – I'm not going to get one night of pleasure. Have you finished?

RIGSBY: I think so.

Robin sits wearily on the bed. It collapses under him.

RIGSBY: Ah. I think there must be something loose somewhere. Give us a hand with the frame, will you?

* * *

SCENE 9: *Int. Ruth's room.*

LORNA: (*pacing*) How much longer is he going to be?

RUTH: Oh, I shouldn't worry. Have another cup of cocoa – it'll help you sleep. (*Confused*) Well, not sleep exactly – but it does relax the muscles. Oh dear, I'm doing it again.

LORNA: You don't approve of this, do you, Miss Jones?

RUTH: Well, since you mention it – don't you think it would be better if you waited? Think of it – standing there in church next to the man you love – all dressed in white—

LORNA: I couldn't wear white – it would be hypocritical.

RUTH: Oh. Well, if you're not a … I don't think they insist on it … I mean, who in these days? Perhaps you could wear pink?

LORNA: You don't believe in sex before marriage, do you, Miss Jones?

RUTH: My, we are getting down to the nitty-gritty. I don't want you to think I'm a prude. My mother didn't believe in it before marriage – but then she wasn't terribly keen after. Speaking personally, I don't mind before or after – as long as it's not instead of. And think about your poor father, think how disappointed he's going to be.

LORNA: You don't know him. He'd never agree – he'd just get furious.

RUTH: (*nervously*) Oh. Would you say he was a violent man?

LORNA: Oh yes. He's got a filthy temper. And he never listens to me. He's only interested in his collection.

RUTH: What does he collect?

LORNA: Firearms.

RUTH: Oh dear.

LORNA: Is something the matter, Miss Jones? You've gone quite pale.

RUTH: I thought I heard a foot on the stair.

Ruth gives a start as Robin enters.

LORNA: Has he finished?

ROBIN: Oh yes. He's put it together. Only now it slopes and you roll to the bottom of the bed.

RUTH: (*anxiously*) Would you two stay here for a moment? I must see Mr Rigsby.

Ruth exits.

* * *

SCENE 10: *Int. landing.*
Ruth enters closing the door behind her. She comes face to face with Lorna's father. He is carrying a stick.

FATHER: Excuse me, I'm looking for a young couple – moved in tonight. Have you any idea which room?

RUTH: Room? (*Starts*) Is that a gun?

FATHER: What? No, it's a walking stick.

RUTH: Oh. What were you saying?

FATHER: I was asking which room—

RUTH: It's not a sword stick, is it?

FATHER: Certainly not. Now, do you mind? I've had a long journey – I'm in a filthy temper – and I want to see my daughter.

RUTH: Your daughter …? (*Stares at stick*) It's not weighted at one end …?

FATHER: No, it's not weighted at one end. It's a simple, ordinary walking stick. Now which room is it?

RUTH: That one.

She points across the landing and retires quickly.

Father enters.

* * *

SCENE 11: *Int. young couple's bedroom.*
Rigsby is standing surveying the collapsed bed.
Father enters. He grasps the stick firmly in his hand.

FATHER: (*angrily*) So there you are.

Rigsby turns. Father takes in his seedy, unkempt appearance and his eyes widen in disbelief.

FATHER: Oh, no!

RIGSBY: Ah. Are you her father?

FATHER: (*weakly*) Yes.

RIGSBY: We've been expecting you.

FATHER: Have you? I must say you're pretty cool about it.

RIGSBY: Well, nothing shocks me these days. You know what young girls are like. It's not the first time, I can tell you.

FATHER: (*surprised*) You mean it's happened before? I can't believe it.

RIGSBY: Oh, yes. I have to be very careful. No, she's not the first girl to lose her head over a good-looking fellow.

FATHER: (*stares*) You're older than I expected.

RIGSBY: (*puzzled*) What? (*Smiles*) Oh, has she been talking about me on the phone? I'm not surprised. That woman adores me. Well, you can understand it – the two of us being in such close proximity.

FATHER: Do you mind if I sit down? This has been something of a shock.

RIGSBY: Not the bed!

Father observes the bed for the first time.

FATHER: My God! What's happened to the bed?

RIGSBY: It's collapsed. Won't take the strain these days. I've been trying to fix it. You wouldn't like to give me a hand?

FATHER: No, certainly not. (*Brokenly*) It seems I've arrived too late.

RIGSBY: I wouldn't say that. You give up too easy that's your trouble. What you've got to realise is she's headstrong.

FATHER: I knew she was headstrong – I didn't know she was short-sighted.

RIGSBY: You're right – she can't see there's no future in it. That's why you've got to put up a fight. Is that your stick? Very heavy – you could do a lot of damage with this.

FATHER: (*sighs*) I can see the threat of violence doesn't worry you.

RIGSBY: Not a bit.

FATHER: (*pause*) I was wondering – would you take money?

RIGSBY: Who, me? (*modestly*) No, I didn't do this for money. I only did what any man would have done in my place.

FATHER: (*swallows anger*) I don't mean as a reward. I mean would you take money to forget all about it?

RIGSBY: I've forgotten it already. Mind you, if you want to show your appreciation – you can buy me a pint.

FATHER: (*angrily rising*) What! (*Stops*) No, I must think of her. She's not ... She's not—?

RIGSBY: Not what?

FATHER: You know—

RIGSBY: Ah, you mean that delicate question no father likes to ask – is she in the club? I wouldn't know – not my concern really.

FATHER: Good Heavens! How can you be so heartless? (*Hesitates*) What do you feel about marriage?

RIGSBY: Marriage? I don't know – it never worked out for me.

FATHER: You mean you're married.

RIGSBY: Of course I'm married. Do you want to see the scars?

FATHER: You callous, unmitigated swine. Take that!

He attacks Rigsby. They fall struggling.

RIGSBY: Hey! Get off. Get him off me.

Philip bursts in and pulls them apart.

PHILIP: What's happening?

RIGSBY: Keep him away from me – he's unhinged.

FATHER: He's ruined my daughter.

RIGSBY: What? I'm not the man. Tell him, Philip.

PHILIP: He's not the one. He's the landlord. I told you to mind your own business, Rigsby.

FATHER: I think I'm going mad. Where's my daughter?

PHILIP: Probably hiding from you. Can't we sit down and talk this over quietly?

Father stares at Philip.

FATHER: Yes, I'm sorry. Philip, isn't it? Well, I must say I didn't expect ... but then again – if it's what she wants – and we're all the same underneath. Mind you, it'll take a bit of explaining at the Golf Club.

PHILIP: What's he talking about?

RIGSBY: He's going bananas again – watch his stick.

FATHER: It's not important, Philip. It's my daughter's happiness that matters. And Spencer Tracey was ready to accept Sidney Poitier … I'm not against mixed marriages.

RIGSBY: He's doing it again. What are you talking about? He can't marry her he's got ten wives already.

FATHER: Ten wives! I'll kill him.

The struggle begins again.
Ruth, Lorna and Robin enter.

LORNA: Daddy! What are you doing?

FATHER: You can't marry him – he's got ten wives already.

LORNA: Why should I marry Philip? He's not the one.

FATHER: It's not him is it? (*He points at Rigsby*).

RUTH: No. Good Heavens! Not Mr Rigsby – the very idea.

Laughs tactlessly.
Rigsby frowns.

RUTH: No, this is Robin.

Father turns to see Robin, who stands ready to retreat.

FATHER: (*beams*) My dear boy – I'm delighted to meet you.

ROBIN: But Lorna said you'd be angry.

FATHER: After what I've been through? You've made an old man very happy. You must come home – we'll discuss the wedding.

ROBIN: The wedding?

LORNA: (*anxiously*) Robin?

ROBIN: (*smiles*) Why not? We'll never want for toasters.

RUTH: Isn't that wonderful? Isn't that romantic? Let's go to my room – we can celebrate with flat champagne.

ROBIN: (*to father*) But I thought you wouldn't approve of me?

RIGSBY: (*quickly*) Ah well, you can thank me for that. I talked him round. Yes, I convinced him that what we needed was a reconciliation.

RUTH: (*doubtfully*) Mr Rigsby.

FATHER: No, Rigsby's right.

RIGSBY: (*grins triumphantly*) There you are.

FATHER: After seeing him – I'd have approved of Jack the Ripper.

They all exit laughing.
The smile fades from Rigsby's face.

RIGSBY: (*indignantly*) Hey, now wait a minute—

He follows angrily.

THE END

Series Four

EPISODE 2

Fire and Brimstone
by
Eric Chappell

PART ONE

SCENE 1: *Int. attic room. Late afternoon.*
Rigsby enters followed by a man carrying a suitcase. He has an enthusiastic, somewhat excitable manner and speaks with a marked Welsh accent.

RIGSBY: (*defiantly*) Well, this is it.

GWYN: (*approvingly*) Good. This is just what I want.

RIGSBY: (*looks around in surprise*) Is it?

GWYN: Well, I don't want luxury, Mr Rigsby – I just want to live simply.

RIGSBY: (*relieved*) You're right. You can't study surrounded by luxury – it weakens you. You don't want a carpet with a thick pile – you'll tire yourself out crossing the room. Same with the bed. (*Bangs unyielding mattress*) You don't want a spring interior – bad for the posture. Did you say you were studying Theology?

GWYN: That's right, I—

RIGSBY: Well, there you are. None of the saints had spring interiors – they'd never have got out of their pits in the morning. No, if you want simplicity you've come to the right place. (*Helpfully*) How simple do you want it? I could remove a couple of chairs.

GWYN: No, this is just fine.

RIGSBY: Good. It's two pounds – four weeks' rent in advance—

GWYN: Can I see the college from here?

RIGSBY: (*smiles*) Come here. (*He takes Gwyn to the window*) You see that dignified grey building with the arched windows and the sun glinting on the coloured glass – giving off a sort of myriad of light?

GWYN: Yes. Is that the college?

RIGSBY: No, that's the abattoir. But behind it you've got the college – only a stone's throw. Oh, and if you hear the occasional bang, don't worry – it's the humane killer.

GWYN: What!

RIGSBY: (*amused*) It's all right – it's at the abattoir, not the college. Mind you, some people think it should be the other way round. (*Confidentially*) That's where the revolution's going to start.

GWYN: (*puzzled*) At the abattoir?

442

RIGSBY: No, at the college. They've got plans for world revolution down there. They were going to have it last weekend only they found it clashed with Kenny Ball's Jazzmen.

GWYN: (*enthusiastically*) Well, I suppose they're bound to be more politically aware. I can't wait to cross swords in argument. Enjoy the cut and thrust of debate – exchange new and exciting conceptions late into the night. It'll be an enriching experience.

RIGSBY: Yes, well, just make sure you get there before they start on the cannabis.

GWYN: Cannabis?

RIGSBY: They're always at it down there – it's the only thing that keeps them calm. Take my advice and don't accept any hand-rolled cigarettes – you may have an enriching experience you didn't bargain for – like trying to ride your bike through a solid brick wall.

GWYN: Don't worry – I don't smoke. I don't believe we should corrode the senses that God gave us with artificial stimulants. What we need today is a fresh moral attitude.

RIGSBY: My very words. I was only saying that the other day in the bookies – what we need today is a fresh moral attitude. I did say four weeks in advance?

Gwyn has begun to unpack. He takes

a large bible from the case. Rigsby is impressed.

RIGSBY: Ah. The good book. You can't go wrong with that as a friend and counsellor. All the answers are in here. My constant companion during the war – that and a deck of cards.

GWYN: I can see I've come to the right house. Some people would deride me for carrying this, Mr Rigsby.

RIGSBY: You're right. And do you know why? No brotherly love – no humility. That's what we could do with around here. More brotherly love and humility. So if you get any derision you tell me and I'll fill them in.

GWYN: No, that won't be necessary. I look upon it as a challenge. A chance to work with young minds – to grow with them – to find the path of truth together.

Rigsby gives Gwyn a long discerning look.

RIGSBY: You're Welsh, aren't you?

GWYN: Yes. Does it show?

RIGSBY: Just a touch. I don't suppose many people would have noticed, but I was in the Forces – you get an ear for dialects. Soon as you walked in I said to myself, 'He's Welsh', but I thought, 'I'll take a chance.' You can't all be Aneurin Bevans, can you? I suppose you're going to miss it all – hey, Taffy? The welcome in the hillside the male voice choir – the slagheaps—

GWYN: My name's Gwyn – Gwyn Williams.

RIGSBY: Right, Glyn.

GWYN: No – Gwyn.

RIGSBY: (*coldly*) That's what I said.

GWYN: Yes, I suppose I shall miss it. I hadn't thought about it before.

RIGSBY: Never mind, if you get homesick they've got a Welsh collie down the road – perhaps they'll let you take it for walks. Now about the rent—

GWYN: Don't worry, I know I'm going to be happy here. The house seems so full of character. I could sense the atmosphere as soon as I came in.

RIGSBY: Could you? Probably the wind off the abattoir. I'd better close the window – it can turn a delicate stomach.

GWYN: I've never lived away from home before – everything's going to be new and exciting. Are there any rules, Mr Rigsby?

RIGSBY: (*brightens*) Only one. I always insist on four weeks' rent in—

GWYN: Not that rules worry me. I belong to the Primitive Church of the First Day Witness. We're very strict. We don't tolerate drinking, swearing, gambling, bawdiness or fornication.

RIGSBY: (*impressed*) Are there many of you?

GWYN: No, we're dwindling.

RIGSBY: I'm not surprised. Doesn't it get a bit dull – or do they allow Maypole dancing?

GWYN: Oh, I don't want you to think it's all gloom, Mr Rigsby. We know how to enjoy ourselves. There's the harvest supper and the sheepdog trials every August.

RIGSBY: Well, I can see you take your religion very seriously. Of course, that's typically Welsh – all or nothing. You've only got to see them after a rugby ball. Get in their way and they'll bite your legs off. (*Regards him*) Aren't you a bit old for university?

GWYN: Ah, well, you see, we're a small congregation and it's taken a long time to collect the money – and even now they're disappointed – they wanted to send me further. Some wanted to send me abroad – they said distance was no object. They think travel will broaden my mind – bring me up-to-date with modern theology. I suppose we seem pretty old-fashioned to you.

RIGSBY: I don't think you're old-fashioned. I admire anyone who can resist the temptations of the flesh. I did, you know, during the war. Three years – all through the desert – never worried me. Mind you – they used to put this stuff in your tea. No, I think we'll get on very well together. You'll be different from the last one we had up here.

GWYN: Oh, what happened to him?

RIGSBY: They made him a doctor. I still can't believe it. To think they're going to allow him to examine the female form in all its mystery. I wouldn't trust him with a wall chart.

GWYN: Perhaps he'll change. After all, medicine's a sacred calling – it's like the church. There's a sense of vocation.

RIGSBY: You never saw his shifty little eyes. I wouldn't let him examine a woman – not even if she held the stethoscope. He'll go berserk – it'll be a race who has their clothes off first. I never trusted him. And there was Miss Jones to consider.

GWYN: Miss Jones?

RIGSBY: She's got the room below. A woman of refinement – a very close personal friend of mine. But I'm not rushing it. (*Sharply*) All right with you?

GWYN: Of course. I can put my hand on my heart, Mr Rigsby, and say I've always had the greatest respect for womanhood.

RIGSBY: Right, now once we've settled the rent—

Gwyn starts to feel for his wallet. His eyes alight on the second bed. Stares.

GWYN: What's the other bed for?

RIGSBY: Ah. I'm glad you asked about that. That's your – that's the bed for … your room mate.

GWYN: (*astonished*) But I didn't know I'd have to share. To tell the truth I thought the room was expensive enough, but for half a room it's extortionate.

RIGSBY: (*angrily*) Extortionate! You watch your language. You should be thankful I'm squeezing you in.

GWYN: But I haven't enough money as it is.

RIGSBY: Well, that's nothing to be ashamed of – not for a man of the cloth. What do you want – a balance at the Building Society?

GWYN: No, of course not—

RIGSBY: You know, you're a disappointment. You're supposed to embrace poverty – not run a mile. You're not supposed to amass riches on this earth – it's your job to be poor. I'm doing you a favour taking the money.

GWYN: I'm sorry. Mr Rigsby. I'll have to look somewhere else.

Gwyn makes for the door. Rigsby detains him.

RIGSBY: Now wait a minute. Don't let's be hasty. I've got a particular reason for wanting you to stay. (*Confidentially*) I'm worried about him. I think he's on the slide – has been for some time.

GWYN: You mean he's lost faith?

RIGSBY: I don't think he ever had it. Not his fault. He's never had your advantages. He needs the example of someone like you. Someone with principles – it could be the making of him.

GWYN: I suppose it would be a challenge. Is he really in need of saving?

RIGSBY: Degenerate – sunk to the depths – a real little Dorian Gray.

GWYN: Well, I shouldn't turn my back on someone who needs help.

RIGSBY: I wouldn't turn your back on him at all.

GWYN: What?

RIGSBY: I think it's because he's lonely – on his own all the time. I've been worried about him. I pray for him every night but I don't think I'm getting through.

GWYN: I didn't know you were a religious man, Mr Rigsby.

RIGSBY: Well, I try. I don't go to church – it's the leg – an old war wound. I can't get in the pews. But I always listen to *Thought for the Day*.

GWYN: I think I'll stay.

RIGSBY: Good. That'll be four weeks' rent in advance.

Gwyn starts to pay Rigsby the money. Philip enters. He looks at the scene in horror.

PHILIP: Oh no, Rigsby!

RIGSBY: Now let me explain.

PHILIP: You said that when Alan left I could have the room to myself.

RIGSBY: I know, but you'll like him. This is Gwen – make sure you get it right. He's funny about his name.

GWYN: The name's Gwyn.

RIGSBY: See what I mean? Come on – shake hands, Philip.

PHILIP: (*sulkily*) I'm not shaking hands.

RIGSBY: Come on, Phil – shake hands.

Tugs at Philip's sleeve.

PHILIP: No, you've tried this once too often, Rigsby. The room's too small. I was just getting used to a proper supply of oxygen. Now he's going to come along and use up all the air.

RIGSBY: No, he's not a heavy breather. You can tell – just look at him.

PHILIP: He looks like a heavy breather to me. He looks as if he snores.

RIGSBY: You don't snore, do you?

GWYN: No.

RIGSBY: There you are, you see – he doesn't snore.

Philip discovers the bible.

PHILIP: What's this? A bible! That's the last straw.

RIGSBY: Don't talk like that – he won't like it.

PHILIP: *He* won't like it? What about me? I won't stand for it. I'm going to complain. I'll go to the town hall. You won't get away with this, Rigsby.

Philip crashes out. There is the sound of door slamming and Philip's echoing threats and then silence.
They stare at each other for a moment.

GWYN: Do you think I should leave?

RIGSBY: No. I think he likes you.

GWYN: (*surprised*) What makes you think that?

RIGSBY: It was a little thing that gave him away – he didn't try and throttle you – that's a good sign. I think you established a meaningful dialogue.

GWYN: He didn't give me a chance to say a word.

RIGSBY: Well, he'll get used to you. You mustn't get discouraged. I mean if the missionaries had taken your attitude they'd have still been worshipping little yellow idols.

GWYN: But I didn't know he was—

RIGSBY: What?

GWYN: Black.

RIGSBY: Black? Black! Of course he's black. He comes from Africa – what colour did you expect him to be – sky blue?

GWYN: But it alters things.

RIGSBY: You don't think the missionaries took that view, do you? They didn't say, 'Blimey, they're black, let's get the next boat home.' No, they stayed – even when they were in danger of having their heads stuck on a pole.

GWYN: No, you don't understand. I wouldn't like him to feel I'm being patronising. Perhaps he doesn't want to be saved.

RIGSBY: Of course he wants to be saved. It'll be a good experience for you.

GWYN: Perhaps you're right. After all, I mustn't be faint-hearted. I'll stay.

RIGSBY: That's better. You've got that gleam back in your eye.

GWYN: Have I?

RIGSBY: Yes. You look just like Billy Graham. (*Rigsby snatches the money from his hand and makes for the door. Pauses*) Oh, by the way, (*mischievously*) if he starts playing the drums – watch out.

Exit Rigsby.

* * *

SCENE 2: *Int. Ruth's room. Later.*
Ruth is looking despairingly at two
frozen fish fingers she has dropped
woodenly into the pan. She follows
them with a congealed lump of
frozen peas.
Rigsby enters.

RIGSBY: Ah, Miss Jones. I wonder if
you'd like to come down this
evening? I know it's Wednesday
and you're usually a bit brassic –
so I thought I'd send out for
some cod and a bag of chips.
What do you say? Perhaps
washed down with a glass of
chilled white wine?

RUTH: (*impressed*) On a Wednesday,
Mr Rigsby? This is luxury.

RIGSBY: Well, I've had a little
windfall and I feel like casting
my bread upon the waters.

RUTH: (*twinkling*) Don't you mean
cod, Mr Rigsby?

RIGSBY: Ah, very good, Miss Jones.
I can see you're in sparkling form
this evening – the ideal dinner
companion.

RUTH: Well, I must confess the cupboard is rather bare. I was
thinking of applying a blow lamp
to these fish fingers but in view
of your kind offer—

RIGSBY: (*grandly*) Return them to
the pack, Miss Jones. Come and
enjoy the real thing. It's a privilege. If I can help someone as I
pass along this vale of tears then
my living has not been in vain.

RUTH: Should we ask Philip?

RIGSBY: (*frowns*) No, I don't think
he's a fish eater, Miss Jones. He
certainly wouldn't like cod –
perhaps the odd piranha. He's
used to fish with two sets of teeth
– he'd find cod a bit boring.

RUTH: Well, what about the new
tenant? Although he does seem a
little strange. I heard him singing
hymns in the bathroom.

RIGSBY: You can't blame him for
that, Miss Jones – there's no bolt
on the door. You'll like him. A
clean-living man. Studying theology – need I say more?

RUTH: (*doubtfully*) You don't think
he'll be too—?

RIGSBY: Too what?

RUTH: Too religious?

RIGSBY: Is that possible, Miss
Jones?

RUTH: I was thinking of the last
theological student who came
here – the one who went about
with open-toed sandals and a
staff.

RIGSBY: Well, there was no harm in
that.

RUTH: Perhaps not, but I did think
it looked a little out of place in
the Bricklayers' Arms.

RIGSBY: Ah but he had a reason for
being there – he was trying to
reform the barmaid.

RUTH: Yes, but did he have to go
home with her?

RIGSBY: I think he got carried away. He was very dedicated – determined to save her. They say he'd have succeeded if her husband hadn't come home unexpectedly. Still, this one's different. You'll like him.

RUTH: Then should we ask him to join us?

RIGSBY: No, I think he'd prefer to spend his first evening in quiet meditation. They like to live simply – they don't go in for fish suppers. He's not like young Dr Kildare.

RUTH: Do you mean Alan?

RIGSBY: Yes. You only had to unscrew the top off the vinegar bottle and he was down like a shot.

RUTH: Yes. Dear Alan – to think he's practising medicine.

RIGSBY: Yes, it's hard to believe. I'll never know how he got through with those fingernails – he must have worn gloves at the interview.

RUTH: But don't you miss him, Mr Rigsby?

RIGSBY: (*feelingly*) I certainly do. Things are going to be much quieter from now on. I think this one's going to have a calming influence.

Philip bursts in angrily.

PHILIP: Rigsby, have you done anything about that mad Welshman yet?

RIGSBY: Now don't start that again.

RUTH: What on earth's the matter, Philip?

PHILIP: He's put this religious fanatic in my room.

RIGSBY: Just because he's brought a bible with him – it doesn't mean he's a religious fanatic.

PHILIP: He's been singing hymns.

RIGSBY: It'll do you good. He's going to be an example to us all. He doesn't drink – smoke – swear or indulge in carnal practices. I like him.

PHILIP: I don't know why. You've got nothing in common.

RUTH: They do say opposites attract.

RIGSBY: (*indignantly*) What do you mean? I was an altar boy. One day I was snuffing out candles, the next day I was trying to snuff out Hitler. Things could have been different. I could have been like him. He reminds me of what I was like as a young man.

PHILIP: Then why don't you share with him?

RIGSBY: (*quickly*) Ah, well, if you'll excuse me – Miss Jones and I are partaking of a fish supper. I think I'd better get the wine in the fridge.

PHILIP: But what about me, Rigsby?

There is the loud sound of singing

overhead. They stare upwards. The words 'What a friend I have in Jesus' come floating down.

RIGSBY: I think you'd better get up there.

PHILIP: Why?

RIGSBY: It's time for Evensong.

Exits

END OF PART ONE

PART TWO

SCENE 3: *Int. attic room. Late evening.*
The room is in shadows – illuminated by the bedside lamp.
Philip enters. Hesitates.

PHILIP: What are you doing?

GWYN: Nothing.

PHILIP: Have you dropped something.

GWYN: No.

Philip switches on the light.

PHILIP: Oh no! You're not going to do that every night, are you?

GWYN: Surely you don't mind me praying?

PHILIP: Can't you do it in bed?

GWYN: It's not the same in bed.

PHILIP: Of course it is. What's wrong with doing it in bed? It's not like eating biscuits. He won't mind.

GWYN: No, I prefer to do it like this.

PHILIP: (*embarrassed glance at door*) But someone's going to see you.

GWYN: But I want them to see me.

There's no point in bearing witness if no one notices.

PHILIP: (*alarmed*) Well, I hope you're not doing it for me. And you can keep away with that bible. You're not doing any missionary work around here.

GWYN: Oh, I see. (*Smiles*) Didn't you like the missionaries?

PHILIP: (*coldly*) On the contrary I always found them delicious. You see, you're wasting your time with me. I'm a terrible sinner. I'm at it all day long. I get up early in the morning so I can pull in a few before breakfast.

GWYN: Yes, I know.

PHILIP: What?

GWYN: Rigsby told me. He's very worried about you, Philip. He said you'd fallen by the wayside. Never mind, brother – there is more joy in heaven for the sinner who repenteth—

PHILIP: (*outraged*) He said that! I'm going to sue. I'll have him for defamation of character.

GWYN: No, he wants to help you. That's why he persuaded me to stay.

451

PHILIP: You don't think it was the rent?

GWYN: No, he's a good man, Philip. He wants to help you. He thinks I'll be company for you. Should I make some cocoa?

PHILIP: No! So that's what he's been saying. (*Pause*) Look, you've got it wrong. He didn't want you to stay because of me. He's the one who needs help, only he's too proud to ask. You see it's brother Rigsby who's fallen by the wayside.

GWYN: Do you think so?

PHILIP: What you've been listening to is a cry for help. You see, he's transgressed.

GWYN: Ah. (*Uncertainly*) I must say he did have rather a wild look.

PHILIP: A soul in torment – racked by conscience.

GWYN: Are you sure?

PHILIP: Do you know what he's doing at this moment?

GWYN: No.

PHILIP: He's trying to seduce Miss Jones over a fish supper. He's plying her with cheap wine and when she's under the influence—

GWYN: You mean she's in moral danger?

PHILIP: With any luck – yes. Even now it may be too late.

GWYN: But what are we going to do?

PHILIP: I can't do anything. He won't listen to me. But you – he might listen to you.

GWYN: Are you sure?

PHILIP: Perhaps you've been sent here. Perhaps you're the one to save him from himself. Do you hear the call, brother.

GWYN: (*excitedly*) Yes, I think I do. (*Picks up bible*) Hallelujah! Brother.

PHILIP: Hallelujah!

* * *

SCENE 4: *Int. Rigsby's room.*
Rigsby and Ruth are sitting over the remains of a fish supper.

RIGSBY: Have another glass of wine, Miss Jones.

RUTH: Do you think I should?

RIGSBY: Yes, it'll remove the flavour of the salt and vinegar.

RUTH: I must say that was really delicious, Mr Rigsby.

RIGSBY: Well, you have to know where to go for a nice piece of cod, Miss Jones. They don't have any of your frozen fillets – straight from the quayside – still kicking their tails when they arrive.

RUTH: Yes. I thought it must be a high-class establishment when I saw they were wrapped in the *Sunday Times*.

RIGSBY: That's what I like about them – you always get a good read with their stuff – and you get those little wooden forks. They're very hygenic. Look what happened when they found that glass eye in the batter.

RUTH: (*appalled*) A glass eye?

RIGSBY: Yes. They didn't try and blur the issue by saying it belonged to a killer whale, did they. No, they drained the vats and returned everyone's money.

RUTH: (*blanches*) Oh.

RIGSBY: Are you all right, Miss Jones? You've gone quite pale.

RUTH: Perhaps I shouldn't have any more wine – I've had rather a lot.

RIGSBY: Nonsense. There's plenty more where that came from—

RUTH: Should we wash up?

RIGSBY: No, we'll stack them. (*He takes Ruth's hands*) I'm not having those beautiful hands plunged into detergent – it would be a crime, Miss Jones.

RUTH: (*coyly*) My, Mr Rigsby – we have got a silver tongue this evening.

RIGSBY: You inspire me, Miss Jones. Come and sit down here. Bring your glass.

They cross to settee.

RIGSBY: Vienna'll take the rough off

the plates. He's a little marvel for getting the tomato sauce out of the cracks. Sit down by me. (*They sit*) Do you mind if I smoke a cigar? I always think it sets a seal on a meal.

RUTH: Oh, please do, I love a cigar.

RIGSBY: (*worried*) I'm afraid I've only got one, Miss Jones.

RUTH: No, I mean I like the fragrance.

RIGSBY: Good.

He proudly produces a cigar.

RUTH: My word, that's a big one.

RIGSBY: Best quality – hand-rolled. (*Closer*) And you really enjoyed the meal, Miss Jones?

RUTH: Oh yes. I don't think you could have got better fish anywhere.

RIGSBY: (*closer still*) I know where you can get better fish than that.

RUTH: Oh, where?

RIGSBY: (*slight pause*) Yarmouth.

RUTH: (*surprised*) Yarmouth? Isn't that rather a long way to go?

RIGSBY: Not for the weekend.

RUTH: Mr Rigsby, you're not suggesting—

RIGSBY: (*deep gaze*) Get my drift, Miss Jones?

RUTH: But it's out of season.

RIGSBY: Well, there are advantages – at least we'll be able to get a deckchair. What do you say, Miss Jones – just you and me and the seagulls? All expenses paid.

RUTH: (*slowly*) Do you mean a double room, Mr Rigsby.

RIGSBY: Well, it would simplify the booking arrangements.

RUTH: But you're a married man, Mr Rigsby.

RIGSBY: In name only, Miss Jones.

RUTH: But in the eyes of the church—

RIGSBY: (*desperately*) Forget the church, Miss Jones.

RUTH: (*shocked*) Mr Rigsby. How can you say that? Didn't the vicar ask you to love, honour and cherish?

RIGSBY: It was all right for him – he didn't have to live with her. Let's face it, Miss Jones – neither of us is getting any younger – we've got to gather rosebuds while we may—

RUTH: Rosebuds? I don't think it's rosebuds you've got in mind, Mr Rigsby.

RIGSBY: Miss Jones – what if we did go to Yarmouth? Who's it going to hurt? We're not going to be struck by lightning by someone up there – if there is someone up there.

RUTH: Mr Rigsby, you're talking wildly. And stop looking at me like that.

RIGSBY: Like what, Miss Jones?

RUTH: So— so— passionately.

RIGSBY: That's how I feel.

RUTH: Well, you shouldn't. (*Softens*) I must say you can be very plausible sometimes, Mr Rigsby – very persuasive. I don't know if it's the light but you look strangely fascinating this evening.

RIGSBY: Then what do you say, Miss Jones?

RUTH: (*hesitates*) I'll think about it, Mr Rigsby. But don't look like that.

RIGSBY: Have some more wine, Miss Jones.

He continues to stare deep into her eyes.

RUTH: No.

Ruth covers the wine glass with her hand.

RIGSBY: Just a drop.

He continues to stare deep into her eyes and pours the wine. It cascades over the back of Ruth's hand. She stares at him reproachfully.

RUTH: Mr Rigsby – I'm getting wet.

Rigsby leaps to his feet.

RIGSBY: I'm sorry, Miss Jones. How clumsy of me.

RUTH: No, it was my fault. I'll mop it up.

RIGSBY: I'll get another bottle. I've got one in the cellar. I'll be back in a flash. (*Anxiously*) Don't go away.

Rigsby exits.
Ruth mops up the wine.
Gwyn's head appears around the door.

GWYN: Hello.

RUTH: Hello.

GWYN: My name's Gwyn. Gwyn Williams. I've just arrived – I thought I'd introduce myself—

RUTH: Yes, I've heard about you. Do come in. I'm Ruth Jones. Won't you sit down.

GWYN: Thank you. I hope I'm not intruding.

RUTH: Not at all.

Gwyn sits. Finds the settee damp. Frowns. Sniffs. Stares accusingly.

GWYN: Is there a strong smell of drink?

RUTH: Yes, I'm afraid I spilt some.

GWYN: (*accusingly*) The bottle's empty.

RUTH: Don't worry, we've got another bottle. Should I get you a glass?

GWYN: (*shocked*) Not for me, Miss Jones. 'Look not upon the wine when it is red for it biteth like a serpent and stingeth like an adder.'

RUTH: Oh. It's white actually.

GWYN: (*sternly*) The colour is irrelevant – I believe it to be the devil's brew.

RUTH: Do you? Mr Rigsby gets it from the supermarket. I'm sure it's all right in moderation.

GWYN: Is it, Miss Jones? I always think of those words I heard as a child:

'I stand outside the tavern door.
Dad's in there upon the floor.
Life would be grand, life would be sweet,
If he was here upon his feet.'

RUTH: (*smiles politely*) It's catchy, isn't it?

GWYN: That's the effect of strong drink. It makes us forget our responsibilities to ourselves and to others. It turns decent people into monsters – the clear eye becomes bloodshot, a harsh note creeps into the laughter, the brain cells diminish and the liver—

RUTH: (*anxiously*) The liver?

GWYN: Like the sole of an old boot, Miss Jones. I have seen livers that look as if they've been beaten to death with a stick.

RUTH: (*clutches throat*) Good heavens! But we were only having a fish supper.

GWYN: Only a fish supper? (*He surveys the bottles*) A fish supper now but where's it going to lead?

RUTH: Yarmouth.

GWYN: Pardon?

RUTH: He asked me to go to Yarmouth with him.

GWYN: But you refused?

RUTH: Well, not in as many words.

GWYN: Miss Jones, you can't go to Yarmouth.

RUTH: No.

GWYN: It's not worth it, Miss Jones. You won't even get a suntan this time of the year. And the pier will be closed. It'll mean the bingo hall and the slot machines – it's a downhill path, Miss Jones.

RUTH: You're right. Tell me, does that lock of hair always fall forward when you're being eloquent?

GWYN: Miss Jones—

RUTH: Please, call me Ruth.

GWYN: Ruth – that's a beautiful name – a biblical name. A handmaiden of the Lord who gathered in the gleanings of the field.

RUTH: Oh, that's beautiful. You Welsh, you have such a way with words. Of course, my name's Jones – I often wonder if I have

Welsh connections— Look you now—

Rigsby bursts in carrying the bottle of wine.

RIGSBY: I've found it, Miss Jones. (*Stops when he sees Gwyn*) What are you doing here? This is a private party.

RUTH: (*coldly*) I'm afraid the party's over, Mr Rigsby.

RIGSBY: But I've got the wine.

RUTH: You can forget the wine – I don't want a liver like an old boot.

RIGSBY: But, Miss Jones. (*He attempts to recapture the mood by looking deep into her eyes*)

RUTH: (*to Gwyn*) I see what you mean about the eyes becoming bloodshot. Good night. (*Pauses at the door*) Oh, and you can forget about Yarmouth too.

Exit Ruth.

RIGSBY: (*suspiciously*) What have you been saying to her? She was all right when I left. You've had a go at her, haven't you?

GWYN: I persuaded her to see the light.

RIGSBY: (*threateningly*) You'll be seeing lights when I've done with you.

GWYN: I was only trying to save you from a lifetime of regret – from that place of unceasing torment.

RIGSBY: What do you mean? I bet you've never been to Yarmouth.

GWYN: I'm not talking about Yarmouth. I'm talking about the bottomless pit – where the worm dieth not and the fire is not quenched – where there is a wailing and a gnashing of teeth in a lake of fire and brimstone.

RIGSBY: (*uneasily*) Look, I don't believe in all that rubbish. There's no such place. I don't believe there's anyone up there either. So you can't frighten me. You can pack your bags and be out by the morning.

GWYN: I'll pray for you.

RIGSBY: Don't pray for me – you're wasting your time. (*He pushes Gwyn out. Rigsby glances up at the ceiling. Once. Twice*) Well, of course, I didn't really mean that.

* * *

SCENE 5: *Int. attic room. Morning. Gwyn is packing his case. Rigsby enters. He watches Gwyn uneasily, hands in pockets.*

RIGSBY: What's this then?

GWYN: I'm leaving, Rigsby. Isn't that what you wanted?

RIGSBY: Ah, well, there's no need to be hasty, Glen.

GWYN: Gwyn.

RIGSBY: That's right. I mean, we all lose our tempers now and again, don't we?

GWYN: (*surprised*) You mean I can stay?

RIGSBY: Of course you can. (*Pause*) You didn't mean all that about, you know (*Lowers voice*) H-E-L-L? You were having a bit of a joke, weren't you? You don't believe in all that roasting and so on?

GWYN: Yes.

RIGSBY: (*winces*) But you don't believe in all those little demons with forks and the smell of burning flesh?

GWYN: Oh yes. Any idea what that would be like, Rigsby?

RIGSBY: Sounds like a Round Table barbecue – the only difference you get a free ride on the spit.

GWYN: Yes, and the devil wears a chef's hat, Rigsby.

RIGSBY: (*swallows*) Still, I've got nothing to worry about – I've led a good life – well, pretty good – sort of average. It's not been that bad.

GWYN: You're not a religious man, are you, Rigsby?

RIGSBY: (*sighs*) No.

GWYN: (*smiles*) Well, I've got good news for you, brother. There's still time.

RIGSBY: Do you think so?

GWYN: Should we ask Him?

RIGSBY: What now?

GWYN: Yes.

RIGSBY: You mean – pray?

GWYN: Yes.

RIGSBY: Here?

GWYN: Of course.

RIGSBY: Well, it's the leg, you see—

GWYN: Forget the leg. Open up your heart, brother.

RIGSBY: Let's hope it doesn't disturb the shrapnel. (*He struggles down to his knees*)

GWYN: Hallelujah.

RIGSBY: Yes.

GWYN: Lord—

RIGSBY: Are we starting?

GWYN: Yes.

RIGSBY: Should I close my eyes?

GWYN: If it helps. Lord, this is Rigsby. I know he's not much to look at and he's been a miserable sinner.

Rigsby opens his eyes indignantly.

GWYN: He's gambled – used strong language – drunk to excess and lusted after the pleasures of the flesh. (*Pause*) Is there anything else, Rigsby?

RIGSBY: I think that's enough to be going on with. We can leave the half-inching in Woolworth's until later.

GWYN: He asks forgiveness. Now he'd like to make a fresh start and

with your help begin again. Amen.

RIGSBY: Is that it?

GWYN: Yes. How do you feel, Rigsby?

RIGSBY: Yes, do you know – I feel much better. I feel a new man.

Philip enters. He stares curiously at Rigsby crouched on the floor. Rigsby spots him. Hastily.

RIGSBY: Yes. (*Bangs on the floor*) I think that'll be all right. Just a loose floorboard. (*Stamps his foot*) Probably all that dry weather. Shouldn't give you any more trouble. I think that's fixed it. (*Makes for door*) Just a bit of play.

GWYN: Rigsby. (*Rigsby pauses*) Hallelujah.

RIGSBY: (*sheepishly*) Hallelujah.

He exits followed by Philip's surprised stare.

* * *

SCENE 6: *Int. attic flat. Morning. Philip is listening to the radio. He is smoking a cigarette and glancing at the Sunday paper. There is a glass of beer at his elbow. Rigsby enters. He looks at Philip reproachfully. Wafts smoke away. Tut-tuts. Sniffs beer. Tut-tuts. Looks over Philip's shoulder. Tut-tuts.*

PHILIP: Will you stop clucking like an old hen, Rigsby?

RIGSBY: What? Do you mind if I turn the radio down? Only it is the Lord's Day and I don't think he wants serenading with jungle rhythms. Should I get you the Morning Service?

PHILIP: No, I'm reading.

RIGSBY: You know you shouldn't be reading that stuff – not on Sunday. You should be reading about religious matters.

PHILIP: I am doing. 'Vicar and Choirmistress found in Skegness'.

RIGSBY: (*snatches paper*) That's enough. I'm cancelling that paper. You'll have to make do with *The War Cry*.

PHILIP: Rigsby – just because you've got religion it doesn't mean I've got to live like a monk. I'm not supposed to smoke – or drink – or read the Sunday papers. You've started bolting the door at ten-thirty. And when I was saying goodnight to that girl you leaned out of the window and shouted 'Repent ye, the time is at hand.' It's all his fault – it's time he went. He's a fanatic.

RIGSBY: No, he's not. He's an example to us all. He's against all temptations of the flesh.

PHILIP: He likes to get against it rather a lot if you ask me. What about all that time he spends with Miss Jones?

RIGSBY: They're bible-reading – there's nothing wrong with that.

PHILIP: What about all that begatting?

RIGSBY: What?

PHILIP: There's a lot of begatting in the bible, Rigsby.

RIGSBY: Why you – I ought to—No, I shall have to turn the other cheek. I forgive you for those words, brother. Now come with me – and you'll hear the word.

* * *

SCENE 7: *Int. Ruth's room.*
Gwyn and Ruth are sitting on the settee.

GWYN: Now, Ruth, what can I help you with today.

RUTH: (*coyly*) Well, there is one passage I'd like to read to you.

GWYN: Certainly, Ruth.

RUTH: (*clears throat*) 'As the apple tree is among the trees of the wood – so is my beloved among the sons. I sat down under his shadow with great delight and his fruits were sweet to my taste.'

Gwyn's smile fades.

GWYN: Ah, I can explain.

RUTH: I haven't finished. (*Closer*) 'He brought me to the banqueting hall – and his banner over me was love. Stay me with flagons – comfort me with apples, for I am sick of love.'

GWYN: Ruth I— (*He tries to rise but Ruth stays him*)

RUTH: 'His left hand is under my head and his right hand doth embrace me.'

GWYN: Ah, that's the use of an image. What they're doing is comparing er ... physical love with er ... spiritual love. We mustn't take it too literally. I mean, he replies by saying, 'Thy lips are like a thread of scarlet – thy speech is comely – they temples are like pomegranate.'

* * *

SCENE 8: *Int. landing.*
Rigsby and Philip are listening by the door. Rigsby looks horrified.

* * *

SCENE 9: *Int. Ruth's room.*

RUTH: Do go on.

GWYN: (*falters*) 'Thy neck is like the tower of David ... and thy ... thy—'

RUTH: Yes?

GWYN: 'Thy breasts are like two young does that are twins and feed upon the rushes—'

RUTH: Oh, Gwyn.

Ruth throws her arms about him. Gwyn struggles.

GWYN: Ruth, please, control yourself.

He struggles free.

* * *

SCENE 10: *Int. landing.*
Gwyn bursts out of the room.

GWYN: Ah, Rigsby. I'm sorry but I'm afraid I shall have to leave. I feel confined. No room for my books. Sorry. (*Dashes upstairs*)

RIGSBY: (*shocked*) Did you hear what he was saying to her? Is that in the bible?

PHILIP: Yes. Song of Solomon.

RIGSBY: We haven't changed much have we?

PHILIP: What are you going to do, Rigsby?

RIGSBY: (*winks*) I think it's back to the cod supper. Oh, Miss Jones. (*To Philip*) What was he saying? 'Thy lips are like a thread of scarlet – thy speech is comely—' Not bad. Oh, Miss Jones—

Rigsby exits into Ruth's room.

THE END

Series Four

EPISODE 3

Great Expectations
by
Eric Chappell

PART ONE

SCENE 1: *Int. attic flat. Morning.*
Philip is reading.
Rigsby enters the room backwards, casting nervous glances around the door.

PHILIP: (*mystified*) What's the matter, Rigsby?'

RIGSBY: Shush!

PHILIP: Rigsby, I'm busy. I don't want you coming up here. And it's no use walking in backwards – I know you're not just leaving.

RIGSBY: Shush! I'm not visiting – I'm avoiding someone. I think he's from the Council – there's something sinister about him.

PHILIP: What makes you think that?

RIGSBY: I know the type. He's got those hunched shoulders from crouching over figures all day – and those long bony fingers you get from squeezing blood out of a stone.

PHILIP: Well, why should that worry you, Rigsby? Unless you're hiding something.

RIGSBY: Listen, I've got nothing to hide. My conscience is clear, don't you worry. (*Picks up leather*) If he asks for me – I'm the window cleaner.

PHILIP: I thought you'd got nothing to hide?

RIGSBY: I haven't. But that doesn't stop them persecuting you. Once they know you've put a bit of money away for your old age they can't wait to get their thieving hands on it. Coming around here with their rate demands. You've only got to look at his face to see he's absolutely ruthless. The last time I saw someone like him he was handing a branding iron to Vincent Price.

PHILIP: (*smiles*) Haven't you paid your rates, Rigsby?

RIGSBY: (*fiercely*) Who said I hadn't paid my rates? Who told you that? You watch your tongue. I'm in dispute. I'm over-assessed. I'm a poor man. (*Door opens*) I'm the window cleaner.

Rigby starts cleaning the window.
Snell enters. He is wearing a dark jacket and pinstripe trousers and is carrying a briefcase.

SNELL: Excuse me, my name's Snell.

RIGSBY: (*shrugs*) We've all got problems.

PHILIP: Can I help you?

SNELL: I'm looking for Mr Rigsby.

RIGSBY: You've just missed him. Leave your card and we'll tell him you called.

SNELL: Oh, I don't think I have a card.

RIGSBY: No card? You could be anyone. (*To Philip*) Keep your eye on the silver. (*He returns to cleaning the window*)

PHILIP: What do you want Mr Rigsby for?

SNELL: It's a personal matter.

PHILIP: You can tell us – we're his friends.

SNELL: (*hesitates*) Oh, I can't really tell his friends – you see it's strictly confidential – it must be kept within a very small circle.

PHILIP: His friends are a very small circle.

Rigsby scowls.

SNELL: I'm sorry but it's of a financial nature—

RIGSBY: I thought so. And you've just dropped in for a little chat. What have you got in the bag – your thumbscrews?

SNELL: I beg your pardon?

RIGSBY: I don't know why you can't leave him alone. Persecuting an old soldier like this. A man who left his health and strength on the beach at Dunkirk.

SNELL: I really don't think there's any need for all this—

RIGSBY: And what are you doing about the rats – you tell me that?

SNELL: (*nervously*) Rats?

RIGSBY: They're getting bolder everyday. You ask him across the road with the wooden leg. Sitting there reading his Sunday paper – heard this gnawing sound – stood up and collapsed in a pile of sawdust. And what are the Council doing? Nothing.

Rigsby returns to window cleaning.

SNELL: I think there's some misunderstanding. I'm not from the Council – I'm from Hargreaves the Solicitors. And since you insist on knowing, I've come to see Mr Rigsby regarding the estate of his late uncle – George Rigsby.

PHILIP: You mean he's been left something?

Rigsby stops cleaning.

SNELL: Yes, he gets the residue of the estate.

Rigsby's mouth drops open.

PHILIP: Is it much?

SNELL: A considerable sum.

PHILIP: What would you call a considerable sum?

Rigsby strains to hear.

SNELL: A figure not unadjacent to £50,000.

PHILIP: That's a considerable sum.

SNELL: Yes, I hope it won't be too much of a shock for Mr Rigsby.

Rigsby lets out a triumphant roar and capers around the room.

RIGSBY: Rigsby's in the money. He's got the residue. Did you hear that? He's got the residue, as the parrot said when he sat on the vicar's shoulder. (*He opens the door and shouts down the stairs*) Did you hear that? Rigsby's got the residue.

Snell stares at Philip.

SNELL: My goodness – if it has this effect on the window cleaner what's it going to do to Mr Rigsby?

Rigsby returns. He drags Snell to his feet and waltzes him around the room.

RIGSBY: I was wrong about you. You've got a very nice face. I never knew the old devil had any money. Hadn't heard of him in years.

SNELL: (*angrily*) Stop!

Rigsby stops dancing. Snell disengages himself.

RIGSBY: What's the matter – don't you like the waltz?

SNELL: (*coldly*) Mr Rigsby – I presume?

RIGSBY: Yes – how did you guess?

SNELL: I think it was your very natural display of grief on hearing of your uncle's death.

RIGSBY: Oh. Well, of course, I'm very sorry. Mind you, I hadn't seen him in years. (*Sadly*) Poor old Uncle George – I hope it was a peaceful end. To think he thought of me at the last when I'd almost forgotten him. Life can be cruel. Do you know what I'm going to do? I'm going to throw myself on that man's grave and beg his forgiveness.

SNELL: I wouldn't advise that, Mr Rigsby – we've just scattered his ashes on the Mersey. I'll leave you with the necessary papers. Perhaps when you've recovered from your grief, you'll call at the office and advise us on how we should deal with the money.

RIGSBY: You just bundle it into fivers – I'll do the rest. And since you brought the good news—

SNELL: Yes?

RIGSBY: Here's something for your bus fare.

SNELL: (*angrily*) Thank you. Your generosity overwhelms me, Mr Rigsby. Good day.

Exit Snell.

PHILIP: Congratulations, Rigsby. This calls for a celebration. Sit down – have a drink.

RIGSBY: Oh, yes? It's starting already, is it?

PHILIP: What do you mean?

RIGSBY: 'Sit down – have a drink'. You've certainly changed your attitude. It wouldn't have anything to do with the money?

PHILIP: (*angrily*) Certainly not. Rigsby, if you think I'm after your money—

RIGSBY: No, I'm sorry – I shouldn't have said that. I suppose it's suddenly being rich. Do you realise? I'm rich. Rich, rich, rich. But I've got to be careful. Once they get to know they'll all be round.

PHILIP: Who will?

RIGSBY: The fortune hunters – the fast women – the double glazing people. They'll all be after my money. But they won't get it – not a penny. I've waited too long for this.

PHILIP: You'd better watch it, Rigsby – if the money's going to make you miserable—

RIGSBY: You don't understand – it's no fun being rich – it can bring a lot of worry. I mean, what am I going to do about the begging letters?

PHILIP: Oh, I shouldn't worry, Rigsby, I'd keep writing them.

RIGSBY: Yes, that's what I— (*Stops.*

Scowls) Right, that's one less for the champagne reception.

Exit Rigsby.

* * *

SCENE 2: *Int. Rigsby's room. Two days later.*
Rigsby is wearing his best suit and smoking a cigar. He's humming cheerfully as he brushes himself down in the mirror.

RIGSBY: That cat's hairs get everywhere. (*To cat*) If you don't stop moulting I'll give you a coat of varnish. And don't look like that – no one's indispensable. You could find yourself replaced by a Blue Persian – something more in keeping with my status.

Ruth enters carrying Home and Garden *magazine.*

RUTH: Good morning, Mr Rigsby. My word, we do look smart this morning – so distinguished.

Rigsby hides a knowing smile.

RIGSBY: Do you think so, Miss Jones? I take it you've heard about my good fortune?

RUTH: Oh yes. And I must say it couldn't have happened to a nicer person.

RIGSBY: I quite agree. Now, if you'll excuse me – I haven't much time for chit-chat this morning – I have an appointment with my tailor.

RUTH: Oh, I thought you always went to that man on the market – the one by the hotdog stall?

RIGSBY: (*indignantly*) Miss Jones, I'm having a bespoke hacking jacket and cavalry twills – a yellow waistcoat and a tie with fox's heads on it. If you think I'm going to get them from some herbert who stands by the hotdog stall you're mistaken. Besides, everything smells of onions.

RUTH: Well, I must say it's very exciting – seeing you rise in the world like this.

RIGSBY: (*patiently*) I'm not rising in the world, Miss Jones – I've already risen. It's just that now I can enjoy the little luxuries in keeping with my status. Well, time presses and I've also got to see my accountant at eleven for a chat about Capital Gains.

RUTH: I can see you're a very busy man, Mr Rigsby. I don't suppose you have any time for me now.

RIGSBY: Nonsense, Miss Jones. I've always got time for you. (*Glance at watch*) I can give you five minutes.

RUTH: (*hesitantly*) I was wondering, since you've had this windfall – if I could have a new carpet for my room.

RIGSBY: (*frowns*) A new carpet, Miss Jones? What's wrong with the coconut matting?

RUTH: Nothing – it's very nice but it does make these red rings on my knees. I thought if I had something like this. (*Shows him picture in magazine*) Tufty pile – wall-to-wall—

Rigsby studies the picture coldly.

RIGSBY: You mean this one – with the young couple lying across it in their underwear?

RUTH: Er … yes.

RIGSBY: Well, you certainly couldn't do that on coconut matting. You'd get red rings everywhere. Are you planning to do this sort of thing, Miss Jones?

RUTH: Certainly not – I'd just like a little more comfort.

RIGSBY: You don't want a thick carpet, Miss Jones. They're full of static electricity. Very dangerous. Why do you think they're sprawled out like that? Probably been electrocuted.

RUTH: But, Mr Rigsby—

RIGSBY: Besides, if I let you have a fitted carpet they'd all want one.

RUTH: But, Mr Rigsby. (*Fondles his tie*) I always thought I was just a little bit special.

RIGSBY: Don't wheedle, Miss Jones. I know I've paid you some attention in the past but that was when I had more time. (*Sighs*) Women just won't leave me alone these days.

RUTH: (*coldly*) Really?

RIGSBY: That woman who owns the wet fish stand's been making eyes at me again. I think she fancies me.

RUTH: Perhaps she's looking for stock?

RIGSBY: (*indignantly*) What do you mean? She's after me. She took so long counting out the change yesterday the coins smelt of haddock.

RUTH: She's probably heard about the money.

RIGSBY: Well, I don't deny that money plus good looks can be a pretty explosive combination. But I think her feelings are genuine. (*Smirks*) She said she thought I was cracking.

RUTH: Oh really, where?

Ruth crosses angrily to the door.

RIGSBY: What's the matter, Miss Jones?

RUTH: I'm going. I don't want you to think I'm after your money, Mr Rigsby.

Exit Ruth.

RIGSBY: Just as I thought, Vienna. Envy. She's being eaten away by it.

Philip enters with brochure.

PHILIP: What's the matter with Ruth?

RIGSBY: A woman scorned, I'm afraid. Well, you know how it is. I'm moving in different circles these days. I'm already down for the Golf Club. I'll be playing with all those divorcees in ankle socks, twin sets and matching pearls. I'll be mingling with the camel-haired coat brigade – they'll probably invite me over for a rubber of bridge and then I'll be away. You can get a lot of footsy in under those bridge tables.

PHILIP: Er ... Rigsby.

RIGSBY: Well, what is it?

PHILIP: I was thinking. Now you've got some money. What about a heated towel rail for the bathroom?

RIGSBY: (*coldly*) A what?

PHILIP: A heated towel rail.

RIGSBY: You're not getting a heated towel rail. You spend long enough in that bathroom as it is. You won't be satisfied until it's like equatorial Africa in there.

PHILIP: But you can afford it.

RIGSBY: Yes, but where's it going to end? Let me see. (*Studies brochure*) Just look at this. 'Matching suite in Aztec gold – hand-painted mosaic tiles – seascape carpet in aquamarine – sepia-tinted mirror.' (*Stops stares*) Sepia-tinted mirror? What do you want with a sepia-tinted mirror? You'd never see yourself. You know your trouble, you're getting soft. There was a time when you'd have bathed in a jungle stream and wrestled the crocodiles for the soap.

PHILIP: You're just too mean to spend money, Rigsby. All I wanted was a towel rail.

RIGSBY: What's the matter? Have you burned your bum on the paraffin stove again?

Snell enters.

RIGSBY: (*brightens*) Ah, Mr Snell. Has the money come through yet?

SNELL: (*suppressing smile*) No, Mr Rigsby – I'm afraid there's been a complication.

RIGSBY: Don't tell me it was all a mistake – I couldn't bear it.

SNELL: No, there was simply a condition I should have mentioned – a formality – the fine print. (*Bites knuckle*)

RIGSBY: Ah, the fine print – as long as it's nothing serious.

SNELL: (*still concealing mirth*) As you know, George Rigsby was a happily married man.

RIGSBY: I know – his wife had been dead for years.

SNELL: Still, he had fond memories – and he'd lived to see the marriages of his close relatives founder on the roots of acrimony and discord.

RIGSBY: Yes, most distressing.

SNELL: And that's the condition.

That you should be happily married.

RIGSBY: What!

SNELL: Your Aunt Maud, one of the executors is coming tomorrow to ensure that this condition is fulfilled – then we can release the money.

RIGSBY: Aunt Maud! That old bat. But she hates me.

SNELL: (*beams*) Does she really? Still, I'm sure you'll have no difficulty in satisfying her. (*Titters*) You're clearly a man of great personal charm. And you are married?

RIGSBY: Oh yes.

SNELL: She must consider herself the most fortunate of women. Good day, Mr Rigsby.

Exit Snell.
Sound of laughter off.

RIGSBY: Did you hear that? I was right about him. He's sadistic.

Philip screws the brochure into a ball.

RIGSBY: What are you doing?

PHILIP: Well, we can forget the money now.

RIGSBY: That's what you think. I'm not losing that money – not now. I've waited too long. It's all right for Uncle George – he only saw her at the wedding. She was all sweetness and light then – except when she belted me once for standing on her train. He never saw her again – none of them did. (*Stops*) That's it. Aunt Maud won't remember her. All I've got to do is get someone to take her place.

Looks thoughtfully at the ceiling.

PHILIP: You don't mean—? She wouldn't do it.

RIGSBY: (*smiles*) Everyone's got their price.

Exit Rigsby.

* * *

SCENE 3: *Int. Ruth's room. Later. Ruth and Rigsby are talking.*

RUTH: (*horrified*) You mean you want me to impersonate your wife, Mr Rigsby?

RIGSBY: Only for a few hours, Miss Jones.

RUTH: I couldn't – it would be wrong – it would be illegal. You're supposed to be happily married.

RIGSBY: I am happily married – it's just that she lives in Cleethorpes and I live here.

RUTH: (*firmly*) No, I'm sorry. I couldn't do it – and it's no use trying to persuade me.

RIGSBY: (*smiles. Opens magazine. Reads*) 'Sink your feet into the velvet luxury of our deep pile –

enjoy the sensual pleasure of our delicate fibres – choose from our rich autumnal shades.'

RUTH: What do I have to do?

RIGSBY: Just play the affectionate spouse, Miss Jones. I've got some of her old clothes down there.

RUTH: You can't keep calling me Miss Jones. What was her name?

RIGSBY: Veronica.

RUTH: Veronica. (*Grimaces*) I knew there'd be sacrifices. What was she like, Mr Rigsby?

RIGSBY: What was she like? Well, actually she's very difficult to describe. The word evades me at the moment.

RUTH: You must remember what she was like, Mr Rigsby. Don't be horrible.

RIGSBY: That's the word.

RUTH: Did she have any traits they may remember?

RIGSBY: Well, she had this very individual way with a cigarette – she kept it in her mouth while she talked. I don't know if they'll remember that – she did take it out during the service. And then of course there was the bronchial cough – she was always on high tar, you see.

RUTH: I don't know if I could manage that, Mr Rigsby.

RIGSBY: And then there was the distinctive laugh.

RUTH: What was it like?

RIGSBY: Well, it was a sort of cross between a pneumatic drill and someone shooting crows.

RUTH: I certainly couldn't do that.

RIGSBY: I didn't say it would be easy, Miss Jones – not for a woman of your refinement. You see she did have this robust cockney sense of humour – always ready for a quick knees-up. And she did have this habit of slapping you on the back to emphasise a point – she almost put the vicar through the vestry wall. Of course, that was when she was in a good mood – if she was piqued she'd hit you with her handbag.

RUTH: (*horrified*) No, I can't possibly do it. My whole nature would rebel.

RIGSBY: (*hands her cigarette*) Just give it a whirl, Miss Jones.

RUTH: Very well. (*Lights cigarette*) Are you ready? Cor! Luv a duck! (*Inhales greedily and collapses in a fit of coughing. Rigsby pats her back.*)

RIGSBY: You've got the cough, Miss Jones.

＊ ＊ ＊

SCENE 4: *Int. Rigsby's room. Later.*

Rigsby is alone.

Philip enters.

PHILIP: Well, what did she say?

RIGSBY: She's not very happy about it.

PHILIP: (*triumphantly*) I told you. 'Everyone's got their price.' Well, not Ruth. I know her. She's got integrity. She's too decent – too honest—

Ruth enters from the bedroom. She is dressed in suit circa 1946. With shoulder bag. She has a cigarette in her mouth.

PHILIP: (*shocked*) Ruth! How could you?

RUTH: What do you mean, cock? I'd do anything to sink my plates into a soft, velvet pile. Stone the crows – I've gorn out. Give me a light, my old china.

END OF PART ONE

PART TWO

SCENE 5: *Int. Rigsby's rooms. Next afternoon.*
Ruth is setting the table.
Rigsby is preparing to go out.

RIGSBY: How do I look, Miss Jones?

RUTH: Don't you mean Veronica?

RIGSBY: Yes, of course – how do I look, Veronica?

RUTH: Very nice, Mr Rigsby. (*Frowns*) I can't call you that. What is your first name?

RIGSBY: (*awkwardly*) Well, I don't think we need go to those lengths, I—

RUTH: Mr Rigsby, we are supposed to be married. What did she call you?

RIGSBY: Almost everything.

RUTH: I mean at the beginning – when she was being affectionate.

RIGSBY: Well, we didn't go in for endearments – not even in the early days. She'd just smile gently, put her hand on mine and say, 'Now then, ratbag'.

RUTH: I can't call you that. What is your name?

RIGSBY: Rupert.

RUTH: What?

RIGSBY: Rupert.

RUTH: Rupert! (*Stifles laughter*) I'm sorry, Mr Rigsby – only you don't look like a Rupert.

RIGSBY: (*indignantly*) Of course, I don't look like a Rupert. He's a little woolly bear with check trousers and a scarf. I stopped using it. They always used to say 'Oh yes and where's Bill Badger?'

RUTH: Well, I shan't; I think it's a nice name. Now what should I get Aunt Maud for tea? What about some hot buttered scones?

RIGSBY: I don't think so, Miss Jones. I think you'd be courting disaster with her teeth. Besides, she's a martyr to wind and we don't want any social embarrassment. It'd better be something she can dip. Well, I'd better get off – the train should be in by now – unless she's arrived by broom. (*Crosses to the door. Hesitates*) I was thinking. Perhaps we ought to slip into the part now. What about a kiss before I go?

RUTH: I beg your pardon?

RIGSBY: A kiss. After all, you've got to start acting like a wife.

471

RUTH: I don't think there's any need for that sort of thing.

RIGSBY: That's very good, Miss Jones. Only I was thinking of something a little more affectionate. I am going out in the busy traffic. I could have an accident. I could be stretched out in the gutter motionless. What would be your first reaction?

RUTH: Are you wearing clean underwear?

RIGSBY: That's not very affectionate. We're supposed to be a loving couple.

RUTH: (*sighs*) Very well, Mr Rigsby – I mean, Rupert.

They kiss clumsily but tenderly then look embarrassed for a moment.

RIGSBY: (*sighs*) I can't help thinking of what might have been – if fate had been kinder. If our paths had crossed earlier. Where were you, Miss Jones, when I was young and free?

RUTH: In my pram I should think.

RIGSBY: It wasn't to be, was it? And now it's too late.

RUTH: (*quietly*) Is it? They say it's never too late – isn't that what they say?

RIGSBY: Yes, well, what I say— (*Stops*) What? (*Suspiciously*) You've never said that before, Miss Jones. A new warmth seems to have entered our relationship all of a sudden.

RUTH: (*coldly*) Don't look so worried, Mr Rigsby – I'm not after your money.

RIGSBY: Miss Jones—

RUTH: Please, Veronica. Cripes! Look at the gin and lime – you'd better get into the old jam jar and whistle down to the station – can't keep the old bat waiting – she'll have the abb-dabs.

Pushes Rigsby out.

* * *

SCENE 6: *Int. hall. Later.*
Philip enters the hall at the same time as Veronica Rigsby. She is a well-made woman but not as gigantic or grotesque as Rigsby has described.

VERONICA: Hello, sunshine. Is he in?

PHILIP: Who?

VERONICA: Captain Bligh. The old skinflint – or perhaps I shouldn't say that now he's come into money.

PHILIP: Oh, you mean Rigsby. That's his room – there.

VERONICA: Ta. Are you staying here?

PHILIP: Yes.

VERONICA: Well, watch him. Don't take any glass beads. (*Gives celebrated laugh and slaps Philip on the shoulder*)

PHILIP: You must be Aunt Maud. (*Rubs shoulder*).

VERONICA: Stone me! Do I look that old? That comes from being married to him. I was a beautiful girl before he got 'old of me. Of course it was years ago now but I still wake up screaming … (*Laughs*)

PHILIP: I don't understand … who are you?

VERONICA: I'm Mrs Rigsby. Come back to rattle my chains.

Exits laughing.
Philip's amazement breaks into a slow smile.

* * *

SCENE 7: *Int. Rigsby's room.*
Veronica enters.
Ruth gives her a welcoming smile.

RUTH: Hello, dearie. Just in time for a cup of char – or would you prefer a drop of mother's ruin? (*Laughs*)

VERONICA: (*stares*) I'm looking for Mr Rigsby.

RUTH: You must have just missed him. Never mind, all girls together. Park your bum in that chair and get stuck in. And don't worry about the wind – I suffer from it something chronic – just loosen your stays, gel and have a good nosh. We'll all be old one day.

VERONICA: I'm not hungry.

RUTH: Oh. Would you like a fag? (*Veronica takes a cigarette*) That's right. The doctor says they'll be the blooming death of me. But I don't care. You only live once, ain't that right Maud?

VERONICA: (*Coldly*) Who are you? I don't think I've had the pleasure.

RUTH: Haven't you? Must be your age. (*Laughs*) Don't you know me? Veronica.

VERONICA: You've changed.

RUTH: Were you at the wedding?

VERONICA: I thought I was – now I'm beginning to wonder.

RUTH: I'm not surprised. What a day. And when old Rupert fell down in the aisle – laugh – I nearly bust me girdle.

VERONICA: And you're still together. I never thought it would last.

RUTH: You mean because I hit him with me bouquet? Well, he trod on me blooming train, didn't he? Clumsy burke. Still, he's not been too bad, Maud – mustn't grumble.

VERONICA: Yes, now, where did you go for your honeymoon?

RUTH: Where did we go for our honeymoon? You might well ask. (*Laughs*) Where did we go for our honeymoon?

VERONICA: Well, where was it?

RUTH: It was Southend, wasn't it?

VERONICA: I thought it was Blackpool.

RUTH: Southend the first week – Blackpool the second. But to tell the truth by the second week I was past caring. (*Laughs*) Know what I mean, Maud?

VERONICA: I can't get over how young you look.

RUTH: Love of a good man, Maud.

VERONICA: Have you got a photograph of the wedding.

RUTH: No. It was a slosh-up, Maud. All those groups – all that posing – standing there in the bleeding rain – no film in the camera.

VERONICA: That's funny. I've got one.

RUTH: What?

Veronica produces picture.

RUTH: My Gawd! Don't I look a fright. And look at Rupert. Who's holding him up? Glassy eyed and legless. He looks like the condemned man. My, we've certainly changed.

VERONICA: (*bleakly*) You certainly have – you're six inches taller.

RUTH: No, that's the low archway – banged my bonce on it, didn't I?

VERONICA: And you've been together all these years. That's surprising considering he never had a proper job.

VERONICA: Well, he had this back trouble, didn't he? Couldn't get it off the flaming bed. (*Laughs. Slaps Veronica on the shoulder*) But he's a different man these days. He's not the person you once knew.

VERONICA: He's not the only one.

RUTH: What?

VERONICA: You're not Veronica.

RUTH: (*crestfallen. Drops pretence*) How did you know? It was the picture I suppose. I don't know why I agreed to do it. She sounds a terrible woman.

VERONICA: Oh? What's he been saying?

RUTH: (*confidentially*) You don't know the half, Maud. Led him a dog's life.

VERONICA: (*grimly*) She did, did she?

RUTH: Oh yus – I mean yes. Always drawing on a cigarette – he couldn't see her for smoke some nights. And then there was the laugh.

VERONICA: What sort of laugh?

RUTH: (*giggles*) Mr Rigsby said it was a cross between a pneumatic drill and someone shooting crows. I think she must have been a bit common. I only did it so that Mr Rigsby would get the money. He had to prove he was happily married. Happily married! To that woman. Well, I'm glad you found out – I'm glad the pretence is over.

VERONICA: Oh, I knew you couldn't be his wife.

RUTH: Why?

VERONICA: Because I am.

RUTH: (*stares*) What! Oh! (*Rises*) Stone the crows!

Ruth exits hurriedly. Followed by Veronica's celebrated laugh.

* * *

SCENE 8: *Int. hall.*
Rigsby is closing the front door behind a grim-faced Aunt Maud.

RIGSBY: (*approvingly*) Did you hear that? Veronica sounds in sparkling mood.

They enter Rigsby's room.

* * *

SCENE 9: *Int. Rigsby's room.*
The room is empty. Aunt Maud looks around suspiciously.

MAUD: She's not here.

RIGSBY: She'll be through in a minute. Why don't you sit down – dip your bread in something. No need to get suspicious.

MAUD: Of course I'm suspicious. You're hiding something – I can always tell. Always were a shifty little devil. I couldn't abide you, then again, neither could your mother.

RIGSBY: What do you mean? I was a lovely little chap. They used to call me Sunshine.

MAUD: That's not what I called you.

RIGSBY: I was always singing and laughing. Happy as the day was long. Uncle George must have remembered. I hadn't been near him for years but he left me all his money.

MAUD: Yes, it must have been gratitude.

RIGSBY: (*mutters*) You're only jealous, you old bat.

MAUD: (*sharply*) What was that?

RIGSBY: If I don't get the money I suppose it goes to you?

MAUD: No, it goes to the dogs' home.

RIGSBY: The dogs' home! All that money going on nourishing marrow bone jelly! What a waste. If I had that money I could travel the world – enrich my life – see strange and exotic places. (*Temptingly*) And you could share in all that, Aunt Maud.

MAUD: How?

RIGSBY: I could send you postcards.

MAUD: Postcards!

RIGSBY: And I could get your teeth fixed. You could have gold ones. You'd twinkle every time you smiled.

MAUD: Are you trying to bribe a poor old age pensioner?

RIGSBY: No, I've got too much respect for you – you old trout. Besides, I've got nothing to hide.

MAUD: Then where is she? (*Slyly*) I
heard she left you.

RIGSBY: Malicious gossip, Aunt
Maud. Wagging tongues – jealous
of that tender shoot called happiness. Are you there, my love?

VERONICA: (*off*) I'm coming,
dearest, just freshening up.

RIGSBY: She's just freshening up. I
don't know if you'll recognise
her. Marvellous what you can do
with blue eye shadow. Then of
course there was the cosmetic
surgery. And she's lost weight –
which has the strange effect of
making her appear taller – sort of
optical illusion. How is your eyesight these days?

MAUD: There's nothing wrong
with my eyesight.

RIGSBY: (*nervously*) Are you
coming, dearest?

VERONICA: (*off*) Coming, my love.

RIGSBY: So affectionate.

*Veronica enters. Rigsby plants a kiss
on her cheek.*

RIGSBY: Hello, my dear. You
remember Aunt Maud?

*Rigsby halts. Looks again. Freezes in
horror.*

MAUD: It *is* Veronica.

VERONICA: Of course it's Veronica.
How are you, Aunt Maud?

MAUD: I think I'm going to have
one of my turns.

RIGSBY: Well, leave room for me.

MAUD: I thought you'd left him?

VERONICA: No, we're as happy as
two turtle doves. Ain't that right,
Rupert?

RIGSBY: What? Yes, it's been bliss.

MAUD: Well, I don't know how
you've stuck it all these years.
None of us thought it would last.
We all thought it was a bad omen
when the wedding cake collapsed.

VERONICA: Ah. (*Fondly*) You don't
know him. I know he doesn't
look much, but underneath
there's a heart of gold.

MAUD: Well, all I can say is you
deserve some reward, Veronica,
putting up with him all these
years.

VERONICA: You mean we get the
money?

MAUD: Yes, if I had my way you'd
get the George Medal for gal-
lantry as well. (*Rises*)

VERONICA: You're not going?

RIGSBY: (*nervously*) Stay and have a
sandwich.

MAUD: No, I've seen all I want to. I
never could abide him – makes
my flesh creep.

*Maud exits grumbling.
Rigsby eyes Veronica apprehensively.*

VERONICA: (*coldly*) Who was that
woman?

RIGSBY: Aunt Maud.

VERONICA: I mean the woman who was pretending to be me.

RIGSBY: Miss Jones. She lives upstairs.

VERONICA: She'll have to go. There's going to be none of that.

RIGSBY: None of what?

VERONICA: No hugging and squeezing and kissing and cuddling – not while I'm around.

RIGSBY: There never was. I know why you've come back. You've heard about the money. You've come back to pick me clean. All the way from Cleethorpes. You could give flying lessons to vultures.

VERONICA: (*sweetly*) Now, Rupert – that's no way for a happily married man to talk. Remember the good times.

RIGSBY: What good times? I spent most of it dodging saucepans. My ribs have only just healed. After you left I spent three years under an orthopaedic surgeon.

VERONICA: Well, I bet he had more fun than I did. (*Sadly*) Didn't you miss me at all? I missed you.

RIGSBY: Why? You could have always bought a punchbag.

VERONICA: Didn't you miss anything about me? (*Menacingly*) What about my silvery laugh?

RIGSBY: (*nervously*) What?

VERONICA: Or perhaps you don't like my laugh?

RIGSBY: No, I've always found it very melodious.

VERONICA: You don't think it sounds like a cross between a pneumatic drill and someone shooting crows?

RIGSBY: No, the very idea! Who said that?

VERONICA: She did. I suppose she's refined. I suppose her laughter's like tinkling cymbals. (*Picks up handbag*) But then she's not common, is she?

RIGSBY: (*backing away*) No, Veronica – not the handbag.

VERONICA: Not refined, eh? I'll show you bleeding refinement.

RIGSBY: Not the handbag.

Veronica doubles Rigsby up with a blow from her handbag and then knocks him to the ground.

* * *

SCENE 10: *Int. attic room. A few hours later.*
Ruth is sticking a plaster on Rigsby's forehead. Philip is holding the First Aid box.

RUTH: How do you feel now, Mr Rigsby?

RIGSBY: A little dizzy, Miss Jones. God, that handbag gets heavier. I think she must have a brick in it.

RUTH: What are you going to do?

PHILIP: You need police protection.

RIGSBY: I don't need the police. I need the Argyle and Sutherland Highlanders – and I'm not sure they'd stand firm. No, there's nothing I can do. I'm one of that neglected band of battered husbands. They don't ask questions about us in parliament. No one cares.

RUTH: We do, Mr Rigsby. There must be something. Have you tried Marriage Guidance?

RIGSBY: Yes, we tried that. We had this very nice chap – she liked him – until she found he was divorced – then she hit him with a paperweight.

PHILIP: Why don't you try writing to the Problem Page? They might be able to help.

RIGSBY: I did that as well but I had to be careful. I was Nervous of Leeds, Persecuted of Barnsley, and Terrified of Accrington. But they never replied. It was only later I found she was Disillusioned of Doncaster. No, all you can do is turn to your friends at times like this.

RUTH: Oh, I'm sorry, Mr Rigsby – I can't stay, not after what's happened. I don't want to be Mutilated of Cheltenham.

PHILIP: And I can't. It's that laugh – it makes my pen jump across the page.

RIGSBY: That's right, desert a sinking ship. I wish I'd never heard about that money.

Snell enters.

SNELL: Ah, Mr Rigsby. I've been looking for you everywhere. I'm afraid I have some bad news. I want you to take a firm grip of yourself, old chap. Stand by with the brandy.

RUTH: What's happened?

SNELL: I'm afraid there's no money. Apparently George Rigsby never paid any income tax. It all goes to the Inland Revenue.

RIGSBY: You mean I don't get anything?

SNELL: I'm afraid not. Are you all right?

Rigsby begins to laugh.

RIGSBY: That's terrible news. Absolutely terrible. I don't know how I'm going to break it to my wife. (*More laughter*) That poor woman. Stand by with the brandy. It's a shocking disappointment, isn't it?

VERONICA: (*off*) Rupert!

RIGSBY: (*titters*) Coming, dear. It's tragic, really. Oh, Miss Jones – find the time of the next train to Cleethorpes.

Exit Rigsby.

THE END

Series Four

EPISODE 4

Pink Carnations
by
Eric Chappell

PART ONE

SCENE 1: *Int. attic flat. Evening.*
Philip is alone.
Rigsby enters clutching a news-
paper. He hands it to Philip.

RIGSBY: See this?

PHILIP: What?

RIGSBY: In the personal column. Down here – between the surgical appliances and vasectomy without fuss. Look. 'Company director, early forties, cultured, sophisticated, lover of the arts, good food and travel, seeks female of similar background. Object, matrimony. Reply Box 696.' Says it all, doesn't it?

PHILIP: It certainly does. You know, I feel sorry for people like that.

RIGSBY: What do you mean? A company director, cultured, sophisticated and in the prime of his life? He's got the lot, mate. They'll all be reaching for the scented notepaper when they read this. Women find that sort of man irresistable.

PHILIP: Then why does he have to advertise?

RIGSBY: Because they don't know about him, do they? He's probably shy and retiring.

PHILIP: He doesn't sound shy and retiring. He says he's cultured and sophisticated. He seems to have a high opinion of himself.

RIGSBY: Well, there's no point in being too modest. Listen, if you were selling pork pies you wouldn't hide them in the back of the shop, would you? You'd put them on display. All he's doing is putting his pork pies in the window.

PHILIP: We're not talking about pork pies, Rigsby – we're talking about women. And if he's so cultured and sophisticated why can't he get one in the normal way?

RIGSBY: Normal way! You don't know anything about the normal way – not where you come from. When you want a woman all you have to do is dash out and have a quick burst on the drums.

PHILIP: No, we don't. Give us credit for a little finesse, Rigsby.

RIGSBY: Well, what do you do?

PHILIP: Well, we paint ourselves all over in white stripes then hide in the bushes making little whooping noises, and when they come down to fill their water jars, we leap out on them.

RIGSBY: Well, that certainly cuts out the need for a long engagement.

PHILIP: It works, Rigsby.

RIGSBY: Yes, but you can't expect him to cover himself all over in white stripes – he's supposed to be a company director. He'd certainly lose the confidence of the board if he tried that. 'Excuse the white stripes, gentlemen, but I'm off down the laundrette to leap on a few women.' He'd get arrested.

RIGSBY: At least it would be more direct. He'll never get the right woman this way.

RIGSBY: Of course he will. Haven't you ever heard of mail-order brides? In the days of the Empire they did it all the time. All those planters stuck out in remote outposts – the young men in the full vigour of manhood and never the sight of a white woman. Just sitting there night after night listening to the same cracked record of 'Tea for Two', wondering whether to go native or dance with the houseboy. They had to do something or they'd have snapped. So they wrote back home for a woman, giving their full requirements, and she'd come up river with the grand piano and a roll of lino. And they'd be perfectly happy.

PHILIP: How do you know that?

RIGSBY: Because they both know what they're getting. Same with this advert – it gives a clear picture – all there in black and white.

PHILIP: How do you know it's a clear picture? How do we know he's not some poor wretch living out a miserable existence in a back room?

RIGSBY: Of course he's not.

PHILIP: How do you know?

RIGSBY: I know he's not.

PHILIP: You can't be sure.

RIGSBY: I can – I put it in.

PHILIP: You, Rigsby! (*Snatches the paper back*) You're not a company director – you're not early forties – you're not cultured and you're not sophisticated.

RIGSBY: (*pause*) Well, nobody's perfect.

PHILIP: There's not a word of truth in it.

RIGSBY: I supposed I did exaggerate a bit. I was trying to give the right image. Perhaps I should have put 'Company director, cultured, sophisticated, with a slight tendency to exaggeration'.

PHILIP: Yes, and there's something else you've forgotten to mention, Rigsby.

RIGSBY: What's that?

PHILIP: You say here, 'Object matrimony'. You're married.

RIGSBY: Ah, well, you may have put your finger on the one small snag there. I am married but not for long. I filed my petition this morning. I should have done it years ago. In a few months I'll be a free man.

PHILIP: But what about Miss Jones?

RIGSBY: What about Miss Jones?

PHILIP: I always thought that when you got your freedom you two would get together.

RIGSBY: (*sighs*) No, I've got to face facts – for some strange unaccountable reason I don't turn her on. I mentioned I was getting a divorce and hoping to settle down. I couldn't have made it plainer. I said I was looking for the older, more mature woman.

PHILIP: What did she say?

RIGSBY: She offered to put me in touch with the over-sixties. No, the time has come to look elsewhere. That's why I put the advert in. I mean, there's no point in hanging about – I'm not getting any younger.

PHILIP: You are according to this. You're about fifteen years younger.

RIGSBY: Well, I don't want them to think I'm decrepit. When I get the right reply I'll meet her somewhere romantic – some olde worlde pub – a fire blazing in the hearth – the walls covered in horse brasses and warming pans. Our eyes meet across a crowded room—

PHILIP: She makes a dash for the door.

RIGSBY: What do you mean?

PHILIP: You've got to face it, Rigsby. She'll be expecting a much younger man.

RIGSBY: Ah, but I've always carried my age well. You see, I've got what they call an interesting face – it's got character. You must have noticed. (*Pause. Philip remains silent*) All right, you're looking at someone who's known suffering – someone who's been beaten on the cruel anvil of life and worn by experience – but you must admit – that face has been lived in.

PHILIP: It looks as if it's been slept in. I don't know why you've got this thing about your age. Why can't you tell the truth?

RIGSBY: (*angrily*) I haven't got a thing about my age! I may not be as young as I was, but there's more to love than just the physical side. There's such a thing as spiritual attraction. That was my trouble in the old days. I was always influenced by a pretty face and a well-turned ankle. I never looked for what was underneath. We never discussed art, music, literature – the good things of life. If I'd found someone like that things might have been different.

PHILIP: (*Impressed*) I didn't know you felt like that, Rigsby. I'm sorry. I didn't know you were looking for that sort of affinity in a woman.

RIGSBY: Yes – well, that and a decent pair of knockers.

PHILIP: A decent pair of knockers! I should have known. You don't change, Rigsby.

RIGSBY: Listen, culture's all right but you can't talk about Etruscan vases all night. (*Grins*) I like them well-stacked. (*He sways seductively around the room*) I like them to have a bit of this – and a bit of that – and a bit of the other.

Ruth enters during this performance and stares at him coldly.

RUTH: Oh, I'm sorry, Philip. I thought you were alone. I'll come back later.

RIGSBY: (*embarrassed*) That's all right, Miss Jones. I was just leaving.

He snatches up the paper and exits. Ruth ensures that the door is firmly closed.

PHILIP: What's the matter, Ruth?

RUTH: Have you seen this?

She takes a crumpled newspaper from under her coat.

PHILIP: (*studies it*) 'Company director, late forties.' (*Smiles*) Yes, I've just been reading it as a matter of fact.

RUTH: I wonder what sort of person he is? (*Dreamily*) I see him bronzed by travel – steel-grey hair – well manicured hands – sensitive face. Expensive clothes worn with a casual air. Probably sitting alone in an elegant hotel suite listening to Beethoven.

PHILIP: I wouldn't get carried away, Ruth. He could be quite ordinary.

RUTH: What do you mean – ordinary?

PHILIP: Broken fingernails – old cardigan – sitting in a back room, listening to *The Archers*.

RUTH: Don't be ridiculous, Philip. I mean, does he sound like that sort of person? No, he's probably spent his whole life making money and now he's asking himself the question, 'What's it all for?' I think he's lonely. I think he needs someone.

PHILIP: I think you're right. But who's going to reply to something like this? You'd have to be desperate.

RUTH: I suppose you're right. (*Pause*) You haven't got a first-class stamp, have you, Philip?

PHILIP: (*surprised*) Ruth, you're not going to reply to it?

RUTH: Why shouldn't I?

PHILIP: Aren't you taking a chance?

RUTH: I feel like taking a chance. I'm tired of waiting for life to knock on my door, Philip. I've got to get out there and pitch.

PHILIP: But he could be anyone. Suppose you don't like him?

RUTH: I've thought about that. I didn't give my name and address. I just suggested that we should meet somewhere.

PHILIP: Didn't you give him any personal details?

RUTH: Only a brief description – so that he'd recognise me. 'Tall, attractive, late twenties. Cool, self-possessed – with a sort of roguish smile.' Do you think that's enough?

PHILIP: (*drily*) I should think it's more than enough.

RUTH: Well, you're expected to exaggerate a little. I should know – I've been through all this before. I went to a matrimonial agency once. They put me in touch with a fun-loving extrovert with an urge to travel. He sounded fine until I found out he was doing five years in Parkhurst. The next one was better – in fact he was quite nice – what there was of him. The trouble was he only came up to my shoulder. I didn't realise it at first. The first time I saw him he was sitting on a bar stool. How he got up there I'll never know. We had several martinis and we talked – it was so romantic. Until it was time to go and I had to hold the stool while he got down.

PHILIP: It must have been a big disappointment.

RUTH: It was, but even then I thought there was a chance for us. I really tried. I tried so hard I developed a stoop. You see, he was so sensitive about the fact that I was taller. He wouldn't dance with me because we kept walking into the tables and he was too proud to look under my arm. I tried to reassure him. I kept telling him that small was beautiful.

PHILIP: Did he believe you?

RUTH: Yes. He stopped thinking he was beneath me – well, of course he was beneath me – a long way beneath me – but I didn't mind. Then one night I forgot and made this disparaging remark about Napoleon. He got very angry, jumped off his cushions and left. I never saw him again. But this time I think it's going to be different.

PHILIP: I'm sure it will be. All I'm saying is don't raise your hopes too high. Be prepared for a slight disappointment. Remember beauty is in the eye of the beholder.

RUTH: Oh, I do agree – and I can't wait to behold him. I'm sure we're going to like each other. Don't laugh, Philip but I feel I know him already.

PHILIP: Who's laughing?

* * *

SCENE 2: *Int. Rigsby's room. Morning two days later.*
Rigsby is sitting by the phone. He sniffs dreamily at the letter he's holding. Philip enters.

PHILIP: Well, how many replies did you get, Rigsby?

RIGSBY: You'd be surprised.

PHILIP: How many?

RIGSBY: (*scowls*) One.

PHILIP: I thought you were expecting a sackful?

RIGSBY: Yes, well, I told them not to put it down with the surgical appliances. You don't look for a future husband in with the body belts, trusses and hair transplants. They're looking for a replacement not spare parts. Still, I've got one reply – and what a reply. Smell that expensive perfume. Makes your shirt roll right up your back, doesn't it? And look at the stylish hand. She didn't leave school at fourteen – i before the e everytime – and she's writing without lines. You can tell she's got breeding.

PHILIP: I see it isn't signed.

RIGSBY: Of course it isn't signed. You can't expect a woman of quality to identify herself to a box number. For all she knows I could be the phantom flasher. No, she'll want to observe me first before she reveals herself. Once she sees I've got all the social graces – that I can move in any strata of society – I'll be away.

PHILIP: You don't think she'll be disappointed?

RIGSBY: Why should she be disappointed?

PHILIP: Well, for one thing you're supposed to be a lover of the arts.

RIGSBY: That's right.

PHILIP: But you hate modern art – you hate ballet and you hate opera.

RIGSBY: Well, I didn't say I loved them all, did I? Besides, you know what I've got against them – they're not real. Nothing like life at all. How many women do you see with both eyes on the same side and a hole through the middle. It's the same with opera – they stand there beating their chests and ranting away in Italian and all they're saying is 'Pass the spaghetti.'

PHILIP: Rigsby – art interprets life – it's not suppose to be life.

RIGSBY: You're telling me. And what about ballet? You don't dance around a woman in a pair of tights to get to know her, do you? You'd frighten the life out of her. Leaping around thrashing your legs together and trying to get her up on your shoulder. It's ridiculous.

PHILIP: Then what are you going to talk about when you meet?

RIGSBY: Don't worry, I'll find plenty to say. I've been watching Melvyn Bragg. You can always get away with the old chat. You don't have to know what you're talking about – as long as you don't split any infinitives. You won't find me at a loss for words. I can charm the birds off the trees when I want to. You stand by – you won't recognise me. (*Picks up the phone*) She's given me a number to ring – probably her mews flat. (*He dials. Speaks in a low very affected voice*). Hello – What a delightful voice – only you could have written that charming letter – which I've read and re-read and keep close to my heart. Now tell me, where can we meet? (*Stops*) What? You want the Gas Board? (*To Philip*) Must be the maid. Look, forget the Gas Board – just fetch your mistress to the phone, would you? What? You're in a call box. Well, is there a lady outside? Tall, attractive, late twenties, probably wearing a sheepskin coat and a tweed skirt. What? There's a skinny bird in a plastic mac with a shopping bag? Well, would you put her on please? (*To Philip*) She's using a phone box. Probably ex-directory – doesn't want anyone coming round and whipping the old masters. (*Lowers voice*) Hello. We meet at last. This is 696. I was wondering when we could rendezvous? What about lunchtime? The lounge bar at the George? Super. Yes, I'm often there. I'm usually in the corner – with the estate agents. You can usually pick us out – we've all got leather patches. We're always taking the coach horn down and blowing it. (*Rigsby twirls the flex and contorts his body as he talks, adding to his affected manner*) Of course, I do have my more serious side. I love music – poetry – sometimes I just

sit there immersed in a slim volume, lost to the world. Do I know John Betjeman? Does he get in there? Oh, that John Betjeman. Yes, I can see we're going to have a lot to talk about. What do I look like? A sort of well-preserved forty – well, the Mediterranean cruises do me a lot of good. Tall? Yes, well, sort of rangy. Yes, that's a point – how will we know each other. Carry a copy of the *Daily Telegraph*? You couldn't make it the *Daily Mirror*? Only they ran out this morning. I know, what about if we both wore a pink carnation? Yes, it would be awfully romantic. Should we say about one? Perhaps we could have a bite to eat – they have some nice pickled gherkins at the bar. Super. Bye—

Rigsby replaces the phone. Philip stares at him is absolute amazement.

PHILIP: Are you going to talk like that all the time, Rigsby?

RIGSBY: Yes, why not?

PHILIP: You'll give yourself a hernia.

RIGSBY: Don't you worry about me. You just nip out and get a pink carnation. I have to prepare myself. I think this calls for total immersion. I shall have a long soak with my bath crystals. She may sound very refined but underneath I bet she's a raver. Definitely a touch of the Lady Chatterleys there.

PHILIP: Well, don't expect too

much. You haven't seen what she's like.

RIGSBY: Don't worry, I shan't wear my carnation until I've seen what she's like. Not that I'm worried –

not with a voice like that. (*Pauses at the door*) You'll see – all of you. Miss Jones is going to get quite a shock.

END OF PART ONE

PART TWO

SCENE 3: *Int. Old Coaching Inn. Lunchtime.*

Low beams. Brasses. Open fireplace. Coach horns on the wall.

Ruth is sitting tucked away in a corner. She is fidgeting with her carnation and sipping a drink.

Rigsby enters. He is dressed in keeping with his idea of smartness and good taste. He is wearing a flat cap and has top coat draped over his shoulders. He is carrying leather gloves which he slaps against his open hand, his leg and finally the bar. The barman gives him a hostile glance.

BARMAN: Yes?

RIGSBY: A large gin and tonic.

Barman serves the drink sullenly. Rigsby eyes him narrowly.

RIGSBY: With ice.

Barman adds ice.

RIGSBY: And a slice of lemon.

Barman adds lemon. Pauses.

BARMAN: You wouldn't like a cherry in it, would you?

RIGSBY: Yes, please, and pass the crisps down – I'm famished.

Barman slams the bowl down in front of him.

BARMAN: Anything else ... *sir*?

RIGSBY: (*frowns*) Yes, where's the little plastic sword?

BARMAN: (*irritably*) We haven't got any little plastic swords.

RIGSBY: No plastic sword? I always have a plastic sword. No doubt about it, this place is certainly going to the dogs.

BARMAN: Is that it then?

RIGSBY: No, it's not it. (*Pauses. Glances around. Leans forward confidentially*) I'm looking for a young lady.

BARMAN: Aren't we all?

RIGSBY: (*scowls*) Do you mind if we have a little more civility and service around here? It's a good thing you weren't here in the old coaching days – you'd have got a gentleman's glove in your mush.

BARMAN: Is that when you used to come in, sir?

RIGSBY: I've arranged to meet a young lady here. Attractive – late twenties – sort of roguish smile.

488

Probably wearing suede coat – twin set and pearls. Very refined.

BARMAN: Ah. Are you the chauffeur?

RIGSBY: (*indignantly*) No, I'm not the chauffeur. And I haven't got time to bandy words with the likes of you. I'll look for her myself. Riff-raff.

Rigsby strolls across the room. Ruth sees him. She hastily removes her carnation and hides behind her paper. As Rigsby passes, the paper turns in his direction. Rigsby stares. He retraces his footsteps. The paper follows him again. He peers over the paper.

RIGSBY: Miss Jones!

RUTH: Mr Rigsby.

RIGSBY: I didn't know you frequented this place.

RUTH: Oh, I don't – I'm just waiting for a friend.

RIGSBY: So am I.

RUTH: I don't normally drink at lunchtime.

RIGSBY: Ah, well, I won't press you to another – not if you're not used to it – it might upset your metabolism.

RUTH: Do you come here often?

RIGSBY: You could say this is one of my haunts. They all know me here.

The barman removes glasses from the table, scowls at Rigsby.

RIGSBY: Don't take any notice of him. He's one of those lovable eccentrics. People come for miles to be insulted by him. Heart of gold really. Excuse me, Miss Jones – I think that's the Borough Surveyor over there.

Rigsby drifts away. Ruth replaces the carnation.
Cut to bar.
A newly married couple have entered. They are both wearing pink carnations. They are chattering excitedly.

GROOM: Well, how does it feel to be Mrs Smedley?

BRIDE: Oh, absolutely wonderful, darling. I'm so happy. Have we got time for a drink?

GROOM: I think so. They won't be here yet. You look after the drinks – I'll see if the room's ready for the reception. (*Pause*) Darling.

BRIDE: Darling.

They kiss. Groom exits.
Bride pays for the drinks. She turns and is confronted by Rigsby, now wearing his carnation.
Bride stares.

BRIDE: My word, you're early.

RIGSBY: I couldn't wait.

He takes one of the glasses and sips it.

RIGSBY: How did you guess? My favourite aperitif. A dry martini – shaken but not stirred.

BRIDE: (*doubtfully*) Actually – it's a vodka and lemon.

RIGSBY: Is it? Must be the crisps – they play havoc with your taste buds. Should we sit at the bar? Only I'm afraid I have a female admirer over there – I don't want to torture her too much.

BRIDE: You certainly didn't waste any time getting here.

RIGSBY: Well, I didn't see any point in hanging about. I'm a man of quick decisions – impulsive – ready to hazard everything on the throw of a dice. What about a toast?

BRIDE: A toast?

RIGSBY: To love – to love at first sight.

BRIDE: How nice. To love. (*Looks around*) You must be the first.

RIGSBY: (*horrified*) You mean there's going to be others?

BRIDE: Oh yes, there'll be quite a crowd.

RIGSBY: I don't like the sound of that.

BRIDE: Well, you know how it is – once you start asking people— (*Smiles*) Don't worry, there'll be enough to go round.

RIGSBY: (*studies her*) Yes, I'm sure you're right. But I thought we'd just have a quiet chat. Not that I'm frightened of competition but just remember – I was here first. (*Stands back, slaps his thigh with his glove*) Well, what do you think?

BRIDE: I beg your pardon?

RIGSBY: Don't be taken in by this air of cynicism and the world-weary manner. All right, I know I'm a little worn at the edges – it's not been an easy life. But I'm still capable of making a young woman happy. Am I what you expected?

BRIDE: I don't know – who are you?

RIGSBY: (*sighs*) Who do you think I am? Look at me. 'Cultured – sophisticated – company director.' (*Lowers voice*) In surgical appliances.

BRIDE: Oh. That must be very interesting.

RIGSBY: I won't say it's not been an interesting life. But I've never had much time for the opposite sex. I've lived in a man's world.

BRIDE: Yes, I can imagine.

RIGSBY: Of course, I knew you straight away. 'Tall, attractive, roguish smile—'

BRIDE: (*flattered*) Why, thank you.

Groom returns. Stands menacingly behind Rigsby.

RIGSBY: (*lowers voice*) What are you doing tonight?

Bride almost spills her drink.

BRIDE: What?

RIGSBY: What are you doing tonight?

BRIDE: Are you serious?

RIGSBY: Of course I'm serious. What ever it is – put it off. Come back to my place. We could listen to the *Third Programme* – there's an interesting talk on Bronze-age relics. What do you say?

BRIDE: It's out of the question.

RIGSBY: No, it isn't. When life gives you a chance like this you should snatch at it with both hands. (*He puts his hand on hers*)

GROOM: (*outraged*) What do you think you're doing?

RIGSBY: (*half turns*) Do you mind? I was here first.

GROOM: Is he being a nuisance?

RIGSBY: Listen, mush, I'm not being a nuisance, you are. And I'd throw that carnation away if I were you. She obviously prefers an older man.

BARMAN: I've been watching him – he's been at her all the time.

RIGSBY: You get back to polishing your glasses and stop listening to your betters. The lady and I are having a private conversation.

GROOM: How would you like a punch on the nose?

BRIDE: There's no need for that. (*To Rigsby*) Will you please go away and stop annoying me.

RIGSBY: (*astounded*) What! You can't prefer him to me. He's just a callow youth. And look at those shifty eyes. You'd be making a mistake there.

BRIDE: He's my husband.

RIGSBY: (*astonished*) Well, I think you might have told me. Why didn't you mention it in your letter?

GROOM: What letter?

RIGSBY: The letter she sent me.

BRIDE: I didn't send any letter.

Groom grabs Rigsby by the lapels.

GROOM: What's this about a letter?

RIGSBY: 'Hey! Don't stretch the cloth. It's not paid for yet.

BRIDE: Surely you don't believe him?

GROOM: All I know is we've only been married an hour and I find you in intimate conversation with a man who says you've written him a letter.

BRIDE: And you believe him. So this is what married life's going to be like – jealousy and suspicion.

She turns on her heel and exits.

GROOM: I didn't say I believed him, darling. Darling—

Groom exits in pursuit.
Rigsby becomes aware of the hostile face of the barman.

RIGSBY: A case of mistaken identity.

BARMAN: Oh, yes?

RIGSBY: One of those little ironies of fate.

BARMAN: (*menacingly*) We don't like that sort of thing in here. (*Removes crisp bowl*) When you said you were looking for a young lady – I didn't realise you meant any young lady.

RIGSBY: (*backs away*) Er ... excuse me – I've just remembered I'm parked on a double yellow line.

Exits hurriedly.
Cut to Ruth.
Ruth is rising with an air of disappointment. Suddenly she is confronted by the groom looking anxiously for his bride.

GROOM: You haven't seen a young lady wearing a pink carnation, have you?

RUTH: Oh. You've come at last.

GROOM: What?

Ruth draws him to her side.

RUTH: I'd almost given you up.

Groom sees Ruth's carnation.

GROOM: Oh, I'm sorry. You shouldn't be in here. We've got a private room.

RUTH: A private room. (*Coyly*) Wasn't that rather impetuous?

GROOM: Oh, I don't know. You don't get a wife everyday, do you?

RUTH: That's very true.

GROOM: They've done piles of sandwiches. I don't know if we'll be able to eat them all.

RUTH: I don't think I could eat a thing. I'm far too excited. I must say you certainly know how to do things in style. And you look much younger than I expected.

GROOM: (*flattered*) Oh, do you think so?

RUTH: Yes, I suppose it's all those Mediterranean cruises.

GROOM: What?

RUTH: Good heavens! You could be my age.

GROOM: (*doubtfully*) Er – yes.

RUTH: I know what you're thinking. You're thinking she looks older than I expected.

GROOM: (*politely*) No – really.

RUTH: I've always looked older than my years. It's this worried frown. I've had it since I was three. We had a very insecure pushchair – the wheel kept coming off and throwing me into the road. How tall are you?

Bride appears in background.

GROOM: Oh, about six foot.

RUTH: I thought so. And so broad and manly.

GROOM: (*smiles*) Can I get you a drink?

RUTH: Not at the moment. I don't want to dull my senses with drink. I want to savour this moment to the full. Our first meeting.

Ruth takes hold of his hand.
Bride steps forward indignantly.

BRIDE: What are you doing here?

GROOM: I was looking for you.

BRIDE: You weren't. You'd forgotten all about me. You were holding her hand.

RUTH: Why shouldn't he hold my hand? (*Sees bride's carnation*) Oh no! He wasn't meeting you as well? (*Looks around. Sees more women with carnations*) Good heavens! How many are there? No wonder you're providing sandwiches. It's worse than Miss World. He'll be announcing the winners in reverse order. (*To bride*) I'd keep away from him if I were you – the man's an absolute philanderer.

BRIDE: He's my husband.

RUTH: What? He certainly didn't mention that when he rang up.

BRIDE: Have you been ringing this woman up?

GROOM: Certainly not.

RUTH: You fibber. It's obvious he's been deceiving us both.

BRIDE: I should have known. Mother was right about you.

GROOM: Oh, and what's the old battle-axe been saying?

BRIDE: Don't you call my mother a battle-axe. She certainly saw through you. She said you were obsessed with it.

GROOM: With what?

BRIDE: I saw the way you were kissing the bridesmaids. You completely crushed their taffeta.

GROOM: No, I didn't.

BRIDE: Don't ever speak to me again.

Bride turns on her heel once more. Followed by the groom. Mother enters the room. She is a large woman dressed in best finery and sporting a pink carnation.
She smiles fondly at her daughter.

MOTHER: Well, darling – happy is the bride. How does it feel to be married?

The bride bursts into tears and dashes from the room.
Mother turns on groom.

MOTHER: You monster.

GROOM: What have I done?

MOTHER: I don't know, but that girl went out this morning without a care in the world – now look at her. Why couldn't you have waited until you got to Majorca? Things always look better when the sun's shining. Good heavens! We haven't even cut the cake yet. I warned her what it would be like but I'd no idea it would start when you got in the taxi. My poor lamb. What have you done to her?

GROOM: It wasn't me – it was that man.

MOTHER: What man?

GROOM: A sort of slimy, lecherous individual. Pretended to be one of our party. He accosted her.

MOTHER: (*booms*) Accosted her. On her wedding day? Is no one safe anymore? We'll see about this.

Mother strides away.
Cut to Rigsby.
He has returned to the bar for another drink.
Mother approaches him with a grim expression. She taps him on the shoulder. He turns.

MOTHER: I've been looking for you.

RIGSBY: (*turns*) Ah, there you are. And about time— (*stares*) Blimey! Excuse me if I don't get up – my legs have gone weak. You're not what I expected at all. When you said 'late twenties' I didn't know you meant the nineteen-twenties.

MOTHER: I beg your pardon?

RIGSBY: Well, this puts a very different complexion on things. Now I know why you're late – I'm surprised you didn't wait for nightfall.

MOTHER: What!

RIGSBY: Never mind – I understand. It's difficult to be honest about your age. And I did exaggerate myself. Actually, you look quite nice. I like the rinse. And although your figure's a bit ample for my tastes – at least there's plenty to get hold of.

MOTHER: Really!

RIGSBY: Should we go back to my place? I'll draw the curtains and we could listen to Mantovani. (*He leans forward and gives her a gentle squeeze*) After all, they say the best wine comes out of old bottles.

MOTHER: Why, you vulgar little man! How dare you! Do you do this to every woman you meet? You've already accosted my daughter.

RIGSBY: Well, what are you complaining about? You should have got here earlier – twenty years earlier. Late twenties – you wouldn't pass for late twenties in a dark room with a bag over your head.

MOTHER: I've never been so insulted in my life.

RIGSBY: You should get out more.

MOTHER: You're drunk. I shall report you to the manager.

Mother sweeps out of the room.

BARMAN: Another case of mistaken identity?

RIGSBY: (*sighs. Looks round the room. He sees numerous women wearing pink carnations*) My God! It's like looking for a needle in a haystack.

He crosses the room to where Miss Jones is sitting dabbing her eyes. He sits down wearily.

RIGSBY: Mind if I join you, Miss Jones?

RUTH: Not at all, Mr Rigsby.

RIGSBY: Didn't your friend turn up then?

RUTH: No, did yours?

RIGSBY: No. (*sighs*) I think life's passing me by, Miss Jones?

RUTH: That's how I feel.

RIGSBY: In the words of the song 'We're sitting in the station but the train's done gone.'

RUTH: Quite.

RIGSBY: Can I get you a drink, Miss Jones?

RUTH: Thank you, Mr Rigsby – just a small port and lemon.

Rigsby picks up glasses and their eyes alight on each other's carnations.

RIGSBY: Miss Jones!

RUTH: Mr Rigsby!

RIGSBY: You're not 'late twenties, tall, attractive, roguish smile?'

RUTH: Yes. You're not 'company director, early forties, cultured, sophisticated, lover of the arts'?

RIGSBY: Yes.

They stare at each other for a moment and burst into laughter.

RIGSBY: Roguish smile! You've been reading *Woman's Own* again, Miss Jones.

RUTH: Sophisticated! If you're sophisticated what's the pickle jar doing in the bathroom?

More laughter.

RIGSBY: This ought to teach us a lesson. We should be more honest, Miss Jones. Early forties – I'm over fifty.

RUTH: And I shan't see thirty again. I'm plain, ordinary and on the shelf.

RIGSBY: I can't agree, Miss Jones. You're a very attractive woman. There's no one here to touch you. You're the sort who stands out in a crowd.

RUTH: (*sadly*) The last time I stood out in a crowd was when my elastic went at the badminton club.

RIGSBY: Well, I find you attractive, Miss Jones.

RUTH: Thank you. (*Shyly*) I find you attractive too, Mr Rigsby.

RIGSBY: (*hopefully*) Do you, Miss Jones?

RUTH: I wouldn't worry about your age. Some people have got it and some people haven't. And you've got it, Mr Rigsby.

RIGSBY: The trouble is I don't get much chance to use it.

RUTH: I can't believe that, Mr Rigsby. I find you a very stimulating companion.

RIGSBY: (*hoarsely*) Miss Jones.

RUTH: Call me Ruth.

RIGSBY: Ruth, may I kiss you?

RUTH: Yes, Rupert.

Ruth closes her eyes.
Rigsby leans forward. He feels a hand on his shoulder. He find himself surrounded by a hostile crowd. Led by mother, barman, groom, etc.

MOTHER: We're just in time. He's about to strike again – the beast.

RUTH: What on earth's the matter?

MOTHER: Don't worry – you're quite safe, my dear.

BARMAN: You're the third woman he's molested in an hour.

RUTH: (*shocked*) Mr Rigsby!

RIGSBY: (*struggling*) Miss Jones – I can explain.

GROOM: Get him out of here before he tries it again.

RIGSBY: Get off or I'll sue the brewery.

Rigsby breaks free. Snatches coach horn from wall and bends it over barman's head. They both snatch up swords and shields. Rigsby exits across camera, fencing.

RIGSBY: I'll be back, Miss Jones.

Confusion.

THE END

Series Four

EPISODE 5

Under the Influence
by
Eric Chappell

PART ONE

SCENE 1: *Ambrose's room. Teatime. Ambrose is toasting a crumpet. He is a short, swarthy man who looks rather like a gypsy. He has a faintly crafty air about him. When he hears Rigsby on the stairs he puts down the toasting fork and closes his eyes. Rigsby enters in angry mood.*

RIGSBY: Right, Ambrose – my patience is exhausted – where's the rent?

AMBROSE: Rigsby – you shouldn't burst in like that – you could have done untold damage. My mind was in complete repose.

RIGSBY: You're lucky – I wish mine was. Now where's my rent?

AMBROSE: I was about to enter Nirvana – the state of serenity and self-denial.

RIGSBY: Oh yes? (*Picks up toasting fork*) I bet you're the first bloke to arrive toasting a crumpet.

AMBROSE: For a moment I'd forsaken the world of the flesh – pass me the butter, Rigsby.

RIGSBY: You can save all that rubbish for your customers – not that you get many customers these days. I passed your stall on Saturday – it was deserted.

AMBROSE: My gifts aren't for the marketplace, Rigsby. I'm not interested in money. I'm a mystic.

RIGSBY: (*snorts*) A mystic!

AMBROSE: Yes, like the holy men of India. Sitting all day in their simple loin cloths, pushing rusty nails through their hooters. They don't do it for money.

RIGSBY: What are you talking about? Of course they do it for money. You don't push a rusty nail through your hooter just to see it come out the other end. It's a job just like any other. You know what your holy man does after a day's work? He goes home – has a shower – takes one of his hundred suits from the wardrobe and drives round Calcutta in a pink Rolls-Royce. I wouldn't have any trouble getting the rent out of them.

AMBROSE: Well, you'll get your money, Rigsby – as soon as business picks up.

RIGSBY: And when's that? You know why there's no one round your stall – it was the tonic you sold that woman – the one that was supposed to cure her lethargy. It cured her lethargy all right – all her hair fell out.

AMBROSE: Well, that wasn't my fault. She was supposed to swallow it – not rub it in her bonce.

Rigsby takes a bottle from sample case.

RIGSBY: You couldn't swallow this stuff – it'd take the stripes off a zebra. She sat all night with her head in a bucket.

AMBROSE: If she'd followed the instructions everything would have been all right. That's a sovereign remedy. It cures rashes, pimples, flatulence, piles, blushing, stammering, shyness and foot odour. (*Pause*) It's not bad at getting grease marks out of suede either.

RIGSBY: Well, what's in it – apart from liquid dynamite?

AMBROSE: I can't tell you that, Rigsby, it's a Romany secret.

RIGSBY: Romany! You're not Romany. The only time you've been in a caravan was when you had that week at Cleethorpes, then you came back on the Thursday. You don't even look like a gypsy.

AMBROSE: Just because I don't wear a spotted handkerchief and earrings it doesn't mean I'm not a gypsy. I've got Romany blood, Rigsby.

RIGSBY: Then why don't you get out and sell a few clothes pegs instead of sitting around here all day?

AMBROSE: I could tell your fortune.

RIGSBY: You can't tell fortunes.

AMBROSE: I can. I'm the seventh son of a seventh son. We have the gift. We can draw aside the misty veil of time and see the future, Rigsby.

RIGSBY: You can't see the future. Look what happened when that woman lost her hair and her husband came round. We all knew what he was going to do with that starting handle but you just stood there. I mean, he was bound to be distressed, wasn't he? He'd gone to bed with a flaming red head and woken up next to a billiard ball. If you'd been able to read the future you'd have shinned down the drainpipe.

AMBROSE: I don't use these gifts for myself. They're in trust for my fellow man. Go on – let me tell your fortune – would you like the cards or the tea leaves?

RIGSBY: You don't think I believe in that rubbish, do you? You know, I'm always surprised at the gullibility of the British public. If they're not having their palms read – it's their bumps – or their handwriting – even their doodles. There's even a man in Brighton reading women's breast prints. He had a very nice pair through the post the other day – predicted a glowing future – said she was deeply sincere with a sense of humour. She had a sense of humour all right – she'd made them with a pair of oranges. Turned out he's advised a couple of jaffas to invest their money in America.

AMBROSE: Your trouble is you're a sceptic, Rigsby.

RIGSBY: No, I'm not. I can read your future. I'll draw aside the misty veil of time for you. (*Parts the mists and peers into the future*) I can see someone coming through the fog. A short, swarthy man with black hair. He's carrying a suitcase. I see him climbing some steps. He's entering a building. There's an inscription over the door.

AMBROSE: What does it say?

RIGSBY: Salvation Army Hostel.

AMBROSE: Now don't be hasty, Rigsby. I've got something better than money. (*He takes ring from suitcase*) You can have this ring. See the way the colour changes? It changes colour with your mood, Rigsby.

RIGSBY: I don't need a ring to show when I'm in a mood. I'm the one who changes colour.

AMBROSE: (*hopefully*) I can get you something for that – does wonders for the blood pressure.

RIGSBY: No, thanks. (*Peers into case*) Just look at all this rubbish. (*Curiously*) What's this? (*Takes out gadget with a dial*)

AMBROSE: (*wicked grin*) Oh that. That's a sexometer.

RIGSBY: A what?

AMBROSE: It measures your sexual drive. You just hold it in your hand and the arrow moves. See? 'Cold – warm – sexy – very sexy – passionate'.

RIGSBY: (*grins*) And the needle moves along?

AMBROSE: That's right.

Rigsby gives a low confident laugh echoed by Ambrose.

RIGSBY: Just hold it in your hand?

AMBROSE: Yes.

Rigsby takes the sexometer and gives it a confident squeeze. Hands it back.

RIGSBY: What does it say?

Ambrose looks at the dial and back at Rigsby. Frowns.

AMBROSE: You haven't had your hands in cold water, have you?

RIGSBY: No.

AMBROSE: I can't understand it – you're not wearing gloves.

RIGSBY: Well, what does it say?

AMBROSE: It's not very high, Rigsby.

RIGSBY: Well, it must be pointing at something.

AMBROSE: It is— 'Made in Hong Kong'.

RIGSBY: (*angrily*) Just as I thought – more rubbish.

AMBROSE: Don't take it to heart, Rigsby.

RIGSBY: I'm not taking it to heart. If that gadget had been accurate I'd have probably shattered the glass. You know what you are? You're a charlatan. You've never cured anyone in your life.

AMBROSE: Yes, I have – I've cured lots of people.

RIGSBY: How? Not with this. (*Holds up bottle*)

RIGSBY: No. Mainly by manipulation and hypnotism.

RIGSBY: (*derisively*) Hypnotism! You couldn't hypnotise our cat.

AMBROSE: You may not believe in my powers but a lot of people do. I've just completed a very successful case. Professional man – undertaker – kept dressing up in his wife's clothes. Never knew when he was going to roll up at the funeral in a wide-brimmed hat and high heels. It was worrying him to death.

RIGSBY: Yes, it must have been a grave disadvantage. And I suppose you stopped him doing it.

AMBROSE: No – but it doesn't worry him any more. He's even joined the WI. All I did was remove his inhibitions. I could do that for you, Rigsby.

RIGSBY: I haven't got any inhibitions. Besides, you couldn't hypnotise me – you'd be wasting your time. I've got an iron will. No, if you want to prove your powers – you'll have to find someone more susceptible.

Philip enters – also in angry mood.

PHILIP: Where's my money, Ambrose?

RIGSBY: (*amused*) You haven't been lending him money?

PHILIP: You said you'd pay it back today.

RIGSBY: You'd believe anything.

AMBROSE: Ah, well, I've had a bad week, Philip. I shall have to ask for a little more time. Not that I want you to go empty-handed. (*Generously*) You can have one of these.

PHILIP: What is it?

AMBROSE: It's a sexometer. See? 'Cold – warm – sexy – very sexy – passionate.' Amuse your friends – impress the girls.

PHILIP: (*grins*) All I do is hold it?

RIGSBY: You can hold it as long as you like – they don't work – load of junk. (*Takes sexometer from Philip*) See what I mean? 'Passionate'! (*Stares in astonishment*)

PHILIP: (*delighted*) Heh! What about that then, Rigsby? I'm passionate. I'll take it.

RIGSBY: (*jealously*) Just look at him. He's forgotten all about the money now. There's one born every minute. (*Breaks off. Stares thoughtfully at Philip*)

PHILIP: What are you staring at, Rigsby?

RIGSBY: He's just the man we need. Totally unsophisticated – innocent – credulous – subject to primeval forces.

PHILIP: What's he talking about?

RIGSBY: How would you like to assist in a simple experiment?

PHILIP: What sort of experiment?

RIGSBY: He's going to hypnotise you.

PHILIP: Oh no he's not.

AMBROSE: It's perfectly safe.

RIGSBY: Of course it is. We won't make you look silly – this is a serious quest for knowledge.

PHILIP: Then let him hypnotise you.

RIGSBY: No, I'm not the type – too sophisticated. I've seen it all. Of course, if you're afraid.

PHILIP: Why should I be afraid?

RIGSBY: Frightened that he may unleash primitive forces – that we'll strip away that veneer of civilisation and you'll end up dancing starkers under a full moon.

AMBROSE: All you've got to do is relax, Philip. Let your mind go a complete blank.

RIGSBY: There you are – you've got an advantage to start with.

PHILIP: (*considers*) All right, Ambrose, go ahead. See if you can hypnotise me.

AMBROSE: Now, Philip – I want you to relax – close your eyes. I don't want you to resist me. I'm your friend. I'm just going to talk to you. My voice is deep – droning – like the murmur of a summer's day when you were a child. You're very tired. Your arms and legs are like lead – you can't move them. But you don't want to move them – you're just happy to sit in the warm sun. Smile if you're happy, Philip.

Philip smiles.

AMBROSE: Good. You're feeling kind and generous. You don't want that money back from old Ambrose. After all, we're friends, and what's money between friends? What do you say, Philip?

PHILIP: (*opens eyes*) I'll give you until Saturday.

AMBROSE: (*angrily*) You're not cooperating. I knew I was experiencing resistance. (*Turns*) He's not cooperating Rigsby. (*Stops. Rigsby is stretched out in a chair, head on one side, fast asleep*) My God! I've hypnotised him.

PHILIP: He's faking.

AMBROSE: He's not. Rigsby, stand up. (*Rigsby rises*) Rigsby, it's a lovely summer's day. You're a child again. You're running barefoot through an open field. Mummy is picking flowers in a big floppy hat and you're romping in your sailor suit.

Rigsby adopts the attitude of a child. A shifty, calculating child. His voice remains Rigsby. He begins to skip about the room. Stops.

What's the matter, Rigsby?

RIGSBY: I've put my foot in something.

AMBROSE: Never mind. Look over there – some boys are splashing in the river. Why don't you go and play with them?

RIGSBY: (*slyly*) No, I'm going to finish my sweets first. I'm not giving them any. They don't like me. they call me Rotten Rigsby. They give me the Chinese burn. They shut my head in the desk.

AMBROSE: No, they like you – they want you to play with them. And it's a hot day – why don't you take your clothes off and jump in?

RIGSBY: All right – I will.

He removes his shirt and trousers to reveal a startling pair of red combinations. Rather baggy. Philip stares at him in horror.

PHILIP: You're not going to let him take his clothes off?

AMBROSE: It's the only way he'll believe me.

PHILIP: It's going to be a horrible sight.

AMBROSE: I suppose you're right. Wait a minute, Rigsby, there are some girls coming.

Rigsby crouches covering himself.

AMBROSE: It's all right – they're friends of yours.

RIGSBY: No, they're not. A boy's best friend is his mother.

AMBROSE: They're waving to you.

RIGSBY: (*slow smirk*) Is it Molly Baggot? I've got to keep away from her. Mother says if I go with her I won't grow tall and straight. What are they doing?

AMBROSE: They're changing behind the bushes.

RIGSBY: I bet they're playing doctors and nurses again. They only let me play once – then I had to sit outside in the ambulance. They all go behind Molly Baggot's shed. I've seen them. I creep up and blow raspberries. They don't like me.

AMBROSE: Of course they do. Why don't you go and play with them.

RIGSBY: No, I think I'll catch a butterfly and pull its wings off.

PHILIP: He hasn't changed much, has he?

AMBROSE: Look, Rigsby – they're all splashing in the river – boys and girls together. Go and join them.

RIGSBY: No, they'll throw stones at me.

AMBROSE: No, they won't. They like you.

RIGSBY: Right – I will. (*Smiles*) Hello, everyone. (*Smile fades*) They're throwing stones at me! Yeah, and I hate you too. I've seen you, Molly Baggott. Who's got holes in her drawers?

AMBROSE: (*soothingly*) All right, Rigsby. Now sit down. Just relax. When I click my fingers you'll wake up and remember nothing.

Ambrose clicks his fingers. Rigsby opens his eyes.

RIGSBY: Well, come on – get on with it. I can't wait here all night.

AMBROSE: (*smiles*) I'm afraid he's not a very good subject.

RIGSBY: I knew it! You couldn't hypnotise anyone – it's a load of rubbish—

Ruth enters.

RUTH: Excuse me – could someone cross my palm with silver? The gas is running out again.

RIGSBY: Certainly, Miss Jones.

Rigsby feels for his pocket and finds it missing.
Ruth sees him for the first time and takes in the red combinations.

RUTH: Mr Rigsby! Has it come to this?

She averts her face. Rigsby looks down at his combinations.

RIGSBY: Oh, my God!

He snatches up his clothes and dashes from the room.

* * *

SCENE 2: *Int. Ambrose's room. Later. Ambrose and Philip are going through contents of case. Philip trying on rings, etc. Rigsby enters. Ambrose looks at him apprehensively.*

AMBROSE: I'm sorry, Rigsby – I didn't know she was going to come in.

RIGSBY: (*bitterly*) You realise you've ruined my life, don't you? I've always treated that woman with the greatest respect. I've never given her the slightest cause for concern. I hoped that one day she'd come to appreciate the delicacy of my feelings. And what happens? She comes in and finds me dancing around in red combinations.

PHILIP: Well, that's not his fault. I don't know why you wear them, Rigsby.

RIGSBY: Why, what's wrong with them?

AMBROSE: Well, they do look a bit droopy, Rigsby.

RIGSBY: They might look a bit droopy but at least they're warm.

PHILIP: You should get up to date, Rigsby.

RIGSBY: (*confidentially*) Well, I have got this other pair – very brief. They're sort of white with a bull's head on the front.

PHILIP: Pity you weren't wearing those.

RIGSBY: Well, I didn't know I was going to be unveiled, did I? Besides, things were bad enough without her seeing a bull's head staring at her. What would she have said?

AMBROSE: At least she wouldn't call you droopy drawers.

PHILIP: Why did you buy them if you weren't going to wear them?

RIGSBY: Well, I didn't know they were so tight. If I wear them for any length of time I find my voice gets a bit shrill. Actually I was saving them – they were going to be part of my going away outfit. (*Sighs*) Not that I'll need them now.

AMBROSE: I didn't know you felt like that about Miss Jones. I can help you there—

RIGSBY: No, thanks – you've helped me enough. I've lost her respect.

AMBROSE: Your trouble is you treat her with too much respect.

PHILIP: That's right – women like you to be masterful.

RIGSBY: How can I be masterful? I get tongue-tied every time I get near her.

AMBROSE: That's where hypnosis can help you. It'll give you new confidence – a new identity.

RIGSBY: Not if it means taking my clothes off. Besides, it wouldn't work twice – I'd be ready for you.

AMBROSE: Now, just close your eyes – relax – you're feeling tired – very tired – you're very sleepy.

RIGSBY: You're wasting your time – I'm not sleepy, I'm not the—

He drops off abruptly in mid-conversation.

PHILIP: What are you going to do with him this time?

AMBROSE: I'm going to let him live his dreams. Rigsby, listen to me. You're very handsome. Women find you irresistible. You're the great lover – exciting – romantic.

Rigsby gives a confident, sardonic smile.

AMBROSE: You have the continental charm of Charles Boyer. Women fight for your favours. Miss Jones is waiting for you right now – drunk with passion. Go to her, Rigsby.

Rigsby gets to his feet. His manner is assured, confident. He speaks with a French accent – more Clousseau than Boyer.

RIGSBY: If you'll excuse me, gentlemen I 'ave to meet a lady.

PHILIP: Who is it, Rigsby?

RIGSBY: Ah, I cannot say – an affair of the 'eart you understand. All I can tell you is that there is a moon – and a beautiful woman – need I say more? *Au revoir.*

Exit Rigsby.

PHILIP: You don't think you've overdone it?

* * *

SCENE 3: *Int. Ruth's room.*
Ruth is putting finishing touches to a cream gateau.
Rigsby enters. Coat draped over his shoulder in continental style. One eyebrow raised sardonically.

RUTH: (*surprised*) Mr Rigsby!

RIGSBY: 'Ello, my little one. I 'ave come.

RUTH: If you're going to apologise—

RIGSBY: Apologise! (*Laugh*) I never apologise. Life is too short, my pretty. What is past is past – the future is yet to come – all we 'ave is the present.

RUTH: Have you been drinking, Mr Rigsby?

RIGSBY: If I drink it is to forget you. But it is impossible – you 'aunt my dreams.

Lights two cigarettes.

RIGSBY: 'Ave a Gaulois.

RUTH: I don't smoke, Mr Rigsby.

RIGSBY: Don't be afraid of a new experience, *mon petite*. We should pursue new feelings – new sensations. The silky texture of a woman's skin – the fragrance of 'er 'air – the softness of 'er lips.

RUTH: Mr Rigsby! Please. Why are you acting so strangely – are you ill?

RIGSBY: Yes. I 'ave a sickness only you can cure.

RUTH: (*backs away*) Stay away from me.

RIGSBY: Don't fight it, you little fool. This thing is bigger than both of us. You know you are crazy about me. Take my 'and and I'll lead you to the gates of ecstasy.

Ruth raises gateau threateningly.

RUTH: Stay away.

RIGSBY: (*smiles*) What are you going to do with that gateau? You're going to push it in my face? Go ahead. See? I'm defenceless. You cannot do it, because you love me. (*Laughs*) Go on – push it in my face.

Ruth pushes the cake firmly in Rigsby's face. Rigsby stands numbed for a moment. Half gestures as if to speak. Considers. Turns, walks out. Half somnolent, half puzzled.

END OF PART ONE

PART TWO

SCENE 4: *Int. Ambrose's room. Later. Ambrose is packing his bags hurriedly.*
Rigsby enters.

AMBROSE: All, right, Rigsby – don't get mad – I'm going.

RIGSBY: (*disarmingly*) I'm not mad. What makes you think I'm mad?

AMBROSE: Well, for one thing there was that cake in the mush.

RIGSBY: Well, that wasn't your fault, besides I'm quite partial to a bit of cream cake. No, you did your best but you made one simple mistake – you hypnotised the wrong person.,

AMBROSE: What do you mean?

RIGSBY: I'm not the one who needs hypnotising – it's Miss Jones. I don't know why I didn't think of it before. All we've got to do is get her under the influence and I'll be away.

AMBROSE: (*doubtfully*) Wait a minute – I don't know if I could do that, Rigsby.

RIGSBY: Of course you could – ever heard of Svengali? He fancied this bird with the funny name. What was it? Man's hat. Topper.

No – not Topper, Trilby. But Trilby was more interested in these students – until old Svengali offered to cure her headaches. Put her in a trance. Before she knew where she was, she was singing opera in Milan, dripping with jewels, and she thought the sun shone out of old Svengali's eyeballs.

AMBROSE: I don't know if that's ethical.

RIGSBY: It's a bit late for you to start worrying about ethics. Turning that woman's head into a billiard ball wasn't ethical, was it? Neither was stripping me down to my harvest festivals.

AMBROSE: I'll have to think about it.

RIGSBY: There's nothing to think about. My intentions are honourable – almost. My divorce will be through in a few weeks. If you do your job properly she could be the next Mrs Rigsby.

AMBROSE: I can't keep her hypnotised that long! The vicar's going to think it's a bit strange when the three of us go up to take the vows. And what about the honeymoon? I can just see us signing into the hotel. Mr and Mrs Rigsby and hypnotist.

RIGSBY: Look, all I want you to do is lower her resistance – I'll do the rest. Just tell her she's a beautiful woman – that she's been repressing a loving and passionate nature all these years. And if you've got any time left over – put in a good word for me. Mention a few of my good points.

AMBROSE: Well, I suppose I could. (*Pause. Frowns*) What good points?

RIGSBY: (*impatiently*) You know. Good-looking – witty – intelligent. She's probably noticed them already but it won't hurt to remind her. And make her a little bit jealous – after all, I could have my pick.

AMBROSE: All right, Rigsby. I'll do my best. I can't promise anything.

RIGSBY: You get down there while I'm in the mood. I can feel the sap rising. (*Picks up sexometer*) What does it say?

AMBROSE: (*studies it*) I'd loosen your laces if I were you – according to this it's stuck in your boots.

RIGSBY: Don't you worry about me – I think I'll put the silk shirt on and my best braces – the once with the anchors on them – that should prove an irresistible combination.

Exit Rigsby.

* * *

SCENE 5: *Int. Ruth's room.*
Ruth is reading.
Ambrose enters.

AMBROSE: (*beaming*) Hello, pretty lady.

RUTH: Don't you 'pretty lady' me. If Rigsby's sent you to apologise—

AMBROSE: Yes, that's right – he's sent me to apologise – he says his feeling just got the better of him. By the way – his compliments – he says the cream cake was delicious.

RUTH: I don't know what came over him.

AMBROSE: Don't be too hard on him, beautiful lady. (*Poetically*) Blame the willow for leaning towards the pool – blame the bee for robbing the flower of its nectar, but don't blame Rigsby for the way he feels about you … Besides, it was my fault – I hypnotised him.

RUTH: Oh really – you can't expect me to believe that.

AMBROSE: It's true, dear lady – he was deep in a hypnotic trance – all I did was to release his inhibitions.

He places the sexometer slyly before her.

RUTH: I can't understand it – I did nothing to encourage him.

AMBROSE: I gathered that when he came back covered in double cream. That was a dangerous thing to do, Miss Jones. When you're in a deep trance a cream cake between the eyes could prove fatal.

RUTH: I don't believe he was in a trance. (*Sees sexometer*) What's this?

AMBROSE: (*craftily*) Oh, just a trivial toy – purely for amusement. It's supposed to measure a woman's sensuality. You wouldn't be interested.

RUTH: Of course not – the very idea – sensuality. (*They both laugh. Pause*) What do you do with it?

AMBROSE: You simply hold it.

RUTH: How silly. (*Pause*) You mean like this?

AMBROSE: Yes. Not that a woman of your intelligence would take it seriously.

RUTH: No, the very idea. (*Looks at dial. Excitedly*) Good heavens! I'm passionate. Look, I'm passionate – really passionate.

Recovers. Looks embarrassed.

AMBROSE: That doesn't surprise me – when I look into your eyes I can see it all. It's all there, Miss Jones.

RUTH: Is it?

AMBROSE: (*staring hard*) It's the gypsy in you, Miss Jones. Do you feel like running barefoot through the grass – letting your hair fall over your shoulders? Do you want to dance to the sound of a tambourine – to love passionately?

RUTH: Certainly not. And don't look at me like that. You won't hypnotise me. I know Mr Rigsby's put you up to it—

AMBROSE: Look deep into my eyes, Miss Jones. You're feeling very sleepy – you are going into a deep sleep – it's a pleasant sleep.

Ruth reluctantly closes her eyes.

AMBROSE: When you wake we'll meet the real you. Now open your eyes, Miss Jones, and listen to me. You are a beautiful woman – wild – sensual – passionate.

Ruth's face assumes the various emotions in turn.

AMBROSE: You like to feel the earth beneath your feet – the rain upon your face – you are a child of nature – but you are proud – untamed.

Ruth looks proud, untamed.

AMBROSE: You spurn men who would lay jewels at your feet, but when you give, you give freely. When you love – you love fiercely like a tigress. (*Ruth looks like a tigress*) You love Rigsby with the fierce, all-consuming passion of a forest fire. (*Ruth looks troubled*) Rigsby is handsome in his elegant braces and his silk shirt. Women pursue him but he's fickle and you're jealous. Even at this moment he's preparing for an assignation. This may be your last chance. Go to him. Remember – you are wild – fierce – passionate.

Ambrose slips quietly around the door.

* * *

SCENE 6: *Int. Rigsby's room.*
Rigsby is studying himself in the mirror. He is clad in a silk shirt, brightly patterned braces and arm bands.

RIGSBY: What about this then, Vienna? Very sharp. There's a few thousand silk worms given their all for that shirt. And what about the braces? (*Stretches them*) No doubt about it – braces are going to make a comeback—

He catches sight of Ruth in the mirror. She is dressed romany style. Earrings and bracelets jangling. She leans smoulderingly against the door.

RIGSBY: Ah, there you are, Miss Jones. Come in. (*Stares*) Is something the matter? If you don't mind me saying, your breathing seems quite shallow.

RUTH: You know what's the matter, Rigsby. I love you madly – wildly – passionately.

RIGSBY: (*beams*) Right – I'll just close the door—

He attempts to walk by her. Ruth seizes him by the braces, pulls him

round then releases the braces with a mighty twang.
Rigsby gives a cry of pain.

RIGSBY: Be careful, Miss Jones – it's new elastic and that was right on my war wound. Just relax.

RUTH: (*fiercely*) How can I relax – you're driving me insane.

RIGSBY: (*nervously*) Yes, but the door, Miss Jones – the other tenants—

RUTH: I don't care about the other tenants, not with you standing there in your silk shirt and those beautiful braces. I want to shout our love from the roof tops. I want to cover you in burning kisses.

RIGSBY: (*soothingly*) Yes, well, let's get the cat out first – this sort of thing disturbs him – we don't want his fur falling out again.

RUTH: Don't toy with me, Rigsby. I know about the other women. Who are you going to taunt tonight with your bewitching braces and your jaunty arm-bands? Come to me you tantalising, good-looking devil.

Grabs him.

RIGSBY: (*thoroughly alarmed*) Mind the shirt, Miss Jones – think of all those poor silk worms.

RUTH: Why are you so cold – so aloof? Let your braces dangle, Rigsby. Let me run barefoot through your hair. Let me catch one more tantalising glimpse of those red combinations.

RIGSBY: (*desperately*) Miss Jones, I've just remember – I've got a prior appointment—

Ruth pulls him back with his braces once more.

RUTH: I knew it! You're stealing out to meet another woman. God, you're heartless. It's all a game to you, isn't it?

RIGSBY: The shirt, Miss Jones – watch the shirt!

There is a ripping sound and the shirt comes apart.

RIGSBY: Now look what you've done.

RUTH: I don't care. When I love, I love fiercely – wildly – passionately. I'll never let you go. You'll never break another woman's heart. If I can't have you – no one will.

She picks up the carving knife.

RIGSBY: What are you going to do with the knife, Miss Jones?

RUTH: I'm going to cut them off.

RIGSBY: What!

Miss Jones cuts through his braces.

RIGSBY: (*backing away*) Miss Jones, it's all been a terrible mistake – I didn't want it like this. I wanted a sweet, tender woman – not Old Mother Riley. (*He reaches the door*) Help! Someone come quick. Miss Jones has gone berserk!

Exits.

* * *

SCENE 7: *Int. hall.*
Philip and Ambrose arrive at the door together. Rigsby emerges breathless.

PHILIP: What's happened? What's the matter?

RIGSBY: Matter? She's gone mad that's what's the matter. She's got the kitchen knife. Keep her away from me.

He dashes upstairs holding his trousers.
Ambrose and Philip stare at the door. Ruth emerges.

PHILIP: What are you going to do?

AMBROSE: I'll have to bring her round – she's in a deep trance.

Ruth gives them a broad wink.

RUTH: Who's in a trance? I haven't had so much fun in years.

Ruth exits.

* * *

SCENE 8: *Int. Rigsby's room. Next evening.*
Rigsby is swinging a medallion to and fro in front of Vienna.

RIGSBY: You are going to sleep – you're very tired – your eyelids are heavy – your paws are like lead.

Philip enters.

PHILIP: What are you doing, Rigsby?

RIGSBY: I'm practising. I can see it's not good depending on Ambrose. I wanted love and affection – not rent-a-storm. No, if I want her hypnotised I'll have to do it myself.

Philip stares at the cat.

PHILIP: Do you think it's working?

RIGSBY: (*frowns*) It's difficult to say – he's a bit dozy at the best of times. I wish I knew how Ambrose does it – he certainly transformed Miss Jones.

PHILIP: Rigsby, he didn't hypnotise her.

RIGSBY: What?

PHILIP: She was faking. She did it to teach you a lesson.

RIGSBY: What! And I was making allowances for her. I even let her ruin my braces.

PHILIP: But doesn't that give you an idea, Rigsby? There's no need for anyone to be hypnotised. All you've got to do is pretend. She won't be able to blame you – she'll think it's your subconscious.

RIGSBY: I know, but it won't be my subconscious that gets the pie in the face.

PHILIP: Well you'll just have to come on stronger – play it tough.

RIGSBY: I see what you mean. A sort of tough guy – like Alan Ladd. (*Shakes head*) No, he never said

much – even when they trapped his fingers in the door – his eyes used to widen a bit that was all. I don't think I'd get very far with that. There's James Cagney. I could always do James Cagney. But women never liked him very much – he was always pushing their heads in the grapefuit. I know I could be a sort of Edward G. Robinson. (*impersonates*) No one ever crossed him. He'd send the boys round with the violin cases – and they'd play a little tune – a symphony in lead.

PHILIP: That's very good, Rigsby.

RIGSBY: Button your lip, I haven't finished. No floozy's going to mess me around, see. (*Sticks cigarette in his mouth*) When I see something I want – I take it. Light me. (*Philip lights his cigarette*) You can be quicker than that. Now mind the store, Mohammed – I'm going to pay a call on a certain party. And I'll be packing lead.

Exit Rigsby.

* * *

SCENE 9: *Int. Ruth's room.*
Ruth is making cocoa.
The door swings open revealing Rigsby – nonchalant. Hat on back of head chewing gum.

RUTH: (*despairingly*) Oh no – not again!

RIGSBY: Hi, Jonesy. Do you come out or do I come in?

RUTH: I think you'd better come in.

RIGSBY: Yeah, it's time we had a talk, Jonesy. I'm tired of being messed around – I'm not that sort of a guy, see?

RUTH: (*patiently*) Yes, Mr Rigsby.

RIGSBY: Hey! What's all this formality? Call me Rupe.

RUTH: (*hides smile*) Very well, Rupe. Would you like a cup of cocoa?

RIGSBY: Are you kidding? I've brought some hooch. (*Takes out flask*) Wanna shot?

RUTH: I think I'll stick to cocoa.

RIGSBY: Cocoa! You know your trouble, Jonesy? You've been hanging around with too many jerks – too many egg-heads – bleeding hearts – fruit cakes and stuffed shifts. Well, I don't like it, see? I don't like the way they look down their noses at me as if there's a bad smell. They're nothing, see? I take what I want and I want what you've got. So stop thinking with your hips, sister – this is your chance to join the big time.

RUTH: Oh dear, I think you're under the influence again, Mr Rigsby.

RIGSBY: I'll dress you in diamonds and sable. You won't want for nothing. You'll be able to walk up to those society dames and spit straight in their eye. I've been watching you. You've got class. I like the way you chassé around – the way you move like a Swiss clock. So what do you say – how about you and me getting together?

RUTH: I think I'd better fetch Ambrose.

She moves to the door. Rigsby catches her arm.

RIGSBY: Stop playing hard to get. No one takes a powder on Rigsby. You get fresh with me and I'll bust you in the kisser.

RUTH: Don't be ridiculous.

RIGSBY: Right, you asked for it, you dumb broad.

RUTH: What are you going to do?

RIGSBY: Pucker up, sister. I'm going to set fire to your lips.

Rigsby bends her backwards and kisses her hard on the mouth.
Ruth gives a loud scream.
Rigsby is surprised and drops her with a loud bump on the carpet.
Ambrose bursts in.

AMBROSE: What's the matter, Miss Jones?

Ruth picks herself up.

RUTH: It's all my fault. Why did you have to hypnotise him again?

AMBROSE: I didn't hypnotise him.

RUTH: You mean, he's pretending?

They both stare at Rigsby, who stands woodenly before them.

AMBROSE: No, it must be a post-hypnotic trance. Come here, Rigsby.

Rigsby crosses to him.
Ambrose passes a hand in front of his eyes.

AMBROSE: He's hypnotised all right. See that glazed expression?

RUTH: That doesn't mean he's hypnotised. He always looks like that.

AMBROSE: (*sighs*) I see you still doubt my powers. I can assure you he can see nothing – feel nothing – do nothing until I tell him.

RUTH: (*suspicously*) I still think he's pretending.

AMBROSE: Rigsby, lend me a tenner.

Rigsby winces. Takes out wallet and hands Ambrose a ten pound note.

RUTH: Well, I must say I've never seen him take his wallet out before. But how do I know you're not in it together.

AMBROSE: I'll show you. He feels nothing. (*He kicks Rigsby on the ankle. Turns to Ruth*) See what I mean?

Rigsby's face forms into a silent scream.

RUTH: I thought I saw him wince.

AMBROSE: No, you're mistaken.

Ambrose kicks Rigsby even harder.

AMBROSE: You see, he can't feel a thing.

RUTH: He did wince – I saw him.

AMBROSE: You won't be convinced, will you? You want proof? I'll give you proof. Have you got a large hat pin?

Sweat breaks out on Rigsby's brow.

RUTH: (*produces pin*) What are you going to do with it?

AMBROSE: I'm not going to do anything – you are. Just stick it in him.

RUTH: I couldn't.

AMBROSE: Go on – he won't feel it.

Ruth approaches Rigsby.

RUTH: He's sweating.

AMBROSE: That's perfectly normal. Go on – give him a good jab.

RUTH: It seems barbaric.

AMBROSE: He won't feel it – not in his state – we could saw his leg off.

RUTH: Oh, all right.

Jabs pin into Rigsby's bottom.
Silence.

RUTH: Well, I must say, I never would have believed it. How do you do it?

AMBROSE: It's just a gift, dear lady.

Rigsby gives out a tremendous bellow. He bursts by them clutching his rear and dashes out of the room.

THE END

Series Four

EPISODE 6

Come On In, the Water's Lovely
by
Eric Chappell

PART ONE

SCENE 1: *Int. attic flat. Morning. Philip is working. Rigsby enters clutching paper triumphantly.*

RIGSBY: Well, it's arrived.

PHILIP: What has?

RIGSBY: My decree absolute.

PHILIP: Congratulations, Rigsby. What does it feel like?

RIGSBY: What does it feel like? Just look at me. Can't you see a difference? I'm walking erect for the first time in years – it's just like when I had my plaster off at the hospital.

PHILIP: Rigsby – you can't compare your wife to a plaster cast!

RIGSBY: Why not? She was always a dead weight and she certainly stopped me enjoying myself.

PHILIP: But there must have been good times. You must have some happy memories.

RIGSBY: Yes, I suppose so. I mean, we always celebrated our anniversary. Once a year we'd forget our differences and go out to dinner – no expense spared – champagne – the lot.

PHILIP: Well, that was something I suppose.

RIGSBY: Yes. Mind you, we always went to separate hotels. Still, that's all behind me now. Do you realise? I'm a free man. After all these years – I'm free.

PHILIP: Well, what are you going to do with your freedom, Rigsby?

RIGSBY: Get married.

PHILIP: But you've only just got divorced!

RIGSBY: Ah, but it's going to be different this time. I'm going to ask Miss Jones.

PHILIP: How do you know she'll have you? She's never shown much interest before.

RIGSBY: Well, I wasn't free then. That was her objection. She didn't want to share me. Women are funny like that. Besides, I've never actually proposed before. That's the finest compliment a man can pay a woman, a proposal of marriage. It's not like in your country, you know. We don't give them a light tap on the head with a war club and drag them in the bushes. No, it's a candlelit supper, soft lights, sweet music and then, at the right moment, you get down on your knees and plight your troth.

PHILIP: Sounds very romantic. Where are you going to do it – at the transport café?

RIGSBY: No, I'm not. As a matter of fact she's invited me up for a meal tonight. That's when I'm going to seize my opportunity. I'll ask her to make me the happiest of men. She'll give me a maidenly blush – dying to accept but frightened to appear too eager. Then I'll produce something that'll turn the scales.

PHILIP: What's that?

RIGSBY: This. (*Takes out diamond ring*) You'd better shield your eyes. Look at that diamond. Big as a bird's egg. Look at the facets. She won't be able to resist it.

PHILIP: Where did you get it from?

RIGSBY: My brother got it for me years ago. I've been keeping it for just such an occasion.

PHILIP: (*doubtfully*) Your brother? You mean the one who's always finding things?

RIGSBY: (*frowns*) Do you mind? I don't like the tone of that remark. He's not always finding things.

PHILIP: Well, where did he get it from?

RIGSBY: He found it.

PHILIP: He found a diamond engagement ring?

RIGSBY: There's nothing surprising about that, engaged couples are always throwing them at each other. It's a very frustrating time.

He'll make an improper suggestion and she'll threaten to break it off. She'll say she never wants to see him again and throw the ring at him. The next minute they're diving for it in the canal.

PHILIP: Is that where he found it?

RIGSBY: (*impatiently*) I don't know where he found it. All I'm saying is that some are bound to go astray and this is one of them. What are you trying to do – undermine my confidence?

PHILIP: I'm sorry, Rigsby. I just don't want to see you get hurt, that's all. She could still say no.

RIGSBY: (*sadly*) I know. You're right of course. Why should she bother with me – a woman of her refinement.

PHILIP: Rigsby, I didn't mean that.

RIGSBY: Well, never mind – if the worst happens – I've still got my old service revolver and one round of ammunition.

PHILIP: Rigsby.

RIGSBY: Just do me one favour – if things do go wrong – don't forget to feed the cat.

Exit Rigsby.

* * *

SCENE 2: *Int. Ruth's room. Evening. Ruth and Rigsby are having a candlelit supper. Rigsby is peering at the food through the dim light.*

RIGSBY: Miss Jones – I think you've surpassed yourself – this looks exquisite.

RUTH: Do you like Indian food, Mr Rigsby?

RIGSBY: Oh yes. I particularly like the subtle blending of the oriental herbs and spices. (*Looks around*) You haven't got any tomato sauce, have you, Miss Jones?

RUTH: Try it without, Mr Rigsby – I'm sure you'll like it.

RIGSBY: Of course. I must say I do enjoy a good curry – you can tell it's doing you good the way the sweat breaks out on your back. It's the only thing that keeps those poor devils going in Calcutta. (*Modestly*) Actually, I'm a bit of an authority on Indian food. Love a good Tandoori chicken or Bombay duck. (*Begins to fork the food onto his plate*) Ah. What's this little delicacy, Miss Jones?

RUTH: Er … that's a hot flannel, Mr Rigsby. Are you sure you wouldn't like a little more light?

RIGSBY: (*hastily*) No, if you don't mind – I prefer the soft lights. You look very beguiling by candelight, Miss Jones.

RUTH: Are you sure you can see me? When I came back with the curry I found you talking to the chair.

RIGSBY: That was because I was rehearsing a little speech. (*Clears throat*) There was something I wanted to say to you.

RUTH: Oh really – what was it?

Rigsby take the first mouthful of curry and almost chokes. Drinks from fingerbowl.

RUTH: Is it too hot, Mr Rigsby?

RIGSBY: No, very nice. You can understand why those Indians get so excited – it's all that curry powder. I was about to say that I received my decree absolute today. (*Sighs*) A very sad moment, Miss Jones.

RUTH: Sad moment? You didn't look very sad. You were dancing with the postman.

RIGSBY: Ah, that was my first reaction but now I'm in a more sombre mood. I'm a disappointed man, Miss Jones.

RUTH: Yes, I suppose the sea of matrimony can look placid and inviting but there are storms and dangerous currents.

RIGSBY: Precisely. They kept saying 'Come on in the water's lovely'. I didn't know I'd have to swim the Channel.

RUTH: I'm sorry, Mr Rigsby. I know it must be a painful subject for you, but you must look to the future.

RIGSBY: I was coming to that, Miss Jones. That's why I wanted the lights dimmed. It gives me the courage to— (*Pause. Takes out the ring*) I think this will say it more eloquently than I can.

He places the ring on Ruth's plate. Ruth, who is busy loading her plate, fails to see it. Rigsby loses sight of the ring and peers desperately amongst the food.

RUTH: You were saying, Mr Rigsby?

RIGSBY: Man does not live by bread alone, Miss Jones. He's not meant to be a solitary person. He needs warmth and companionship. (*He forks desperately through the food*) He needs a mate – someone to share the long winter evenings and the blazing hearth.

RUTH: (*still concentrating on food*) Oh dear, I've forgotten the poppadoms. I'll get them. Please go on, Mr Rigsby.

Ruth crosses to the sideboard. Rigsby finds the ring among the food. He follows Ruth and goes down on his knees.

RIGSBY: Miss Jones – please take this and wear it as a token of my esteem. Will you do me the honour of – (*Ruth turns from the table and falls over Rigsby. Rigsby bends over her*) Are you all right, Miss Jones?

RUTH: Mr Rigsby! What on earth are you doing down there? Is it your idea of a joke?

RIGSBY: No, this is deadly serious.

RUTH: It's not the curry?

RIGSBY: No, I want you to take this.

He holds out the ring.

RUTH: What?

She turns and knocks the ring from Rigsby's hand.

RIGSBY: Hell!

RUTH: Mr Rigsby! (*Rigsby scrambles for the ring*) What are you doing now? Why do you keep bobbing up and down like that? What are you looking for?

RIGSBY: For this, Miss Jones. (*Brandishes the ring impatiently*) I came here tonight with the ridiculous idea of asking you to marry me. I know you weren't expecting it – I know it's preposterous but that's what I came to say. Will you marry me? What's your answer to that?

RUTH: Yes.

RIGSBY: That's what I thought you'd say. I knew I was wasting my time. I suppose I'm not good enough. All right – forget it. What do I care? I don't want to see this ring again. (*Hurls ring into fireplace*) I knew you wouldn't accept me.

RUTH: But I am accepting you.

RIGSBY: Don't try and make me feel better – don't soften the blow. I knew you'd laugh in my face. I only hope that one day— (*Stops*) Would you mind saying that again, Miss Jones?

RUTH: I said I will marry you.

RIGSBY: Miss Jones!

RUTH: Mr Rigsby.

They embrace. They stare happily at each other, then their expressions change to concern and they dive at the fireplace scrabbling for the ring.

* * *

SCENE 3: *Int. Rigsby's room. Days later.*
Rigsby is trying on morning coat. His manner is nervous and he is irritated with the buttons.
Philip enters. Stops in surprise.

PHILIP: Good Heavens! It's the Aga Khan.

RIGSBY: (*angrily*) If you're going to be funny.

PHILIP: What's the matter? You look nervous.

RIGSBY: I am nervous – we've got her mother coming.

PHILIP: Have you met her before?

RIGSBY: No, she's given me a photograph.

Rigsby hands Philip a snapshot.

PHILIP: She looks a bit severe.

RIGSBY: Well, life's not been easy for her. She was raised in India – and you never get that out of your system. (*Peers at picture*) I wouldn't be surprised if she hasn't got a touch of the Bombay crut.

PHILIP: What's that?

RIGSBY: Well, it's similar to Delhi belly or the Rangoon runs – only worse. It would explain her expression of discomfort.

PHILIP: She looks rather superior to me.

RIGSBY: Of course she does. She was a colonel's daughter. She'd have had a host of servants. A servant for opening the door – a servant for fanning her – a servant for scratching her back. She must have found it difficult coming back to England – learning to dress herself and master the complexities of the twin-tub.

PHILIP: I wonder what she'll think of you?

RIGSBY: That's what worries me. You know what a mother's like – no one's good enough for her daughter. I suppose I'll get a few searching glances. (*Pause*) You don't think I look too old for her, do you?

PHILIP: No, as a matter of fact you seem to look younger.

RIGSBY: I should do – I've darkened my hair. Touched it up with a spot of boot polish. Should be all right – as long as I don't start sweating.

PHILIP: Rigsby, you've been sweating ever since she said yes.

Are you really going to go through with it?

RIGSBY: (*irritably*) I wish you'd stop saying that. Of course I'm going through with it. I can be nervous, can't I? Perfectly normal. Bridegrooms are prone to it. That's why you get them rolling up to church suffering from amnesia.

PHILIP: I didn't know that.

RIGSBY: Oh yes, it happens. They get a distant look in their eyes, turn to the best man and say 'Is this the right bus for Blackpool?' It can be very unnerving.

Rigsby tries on his topper, which sinks gently over his eyes.

PHILIP: (*laughs*) I thought you said it was going to be a quiet wedding?

RIGSBY: It is.

PHILIP: Not if you wear that hat it isn't.

RIGSBY: It only needs packing. I wish you'd shut up. What did you come down for anyway?

PHILIP: There's a man hanging about outside – looks a bit shifty. I thought you ought to know.

They look out of the window.

RIGSBY: Oh yes. I see what you mean. You've only got to look at his features – very furtive – definitely your criminal type.

PHILIP: Any idea who he is?

RIGSBY: Yes – he's my brother.

PHILIP: Your brother! What are you going to do?

RIGSBY: Nothing. Ignore him. He might go away. Now if you'll excuse me I'd like to try my pin-stripes on.

Philip exits bewildered.
Rigsby returns to the mirror. Tries the hat on again. This time it sits on his head. He taps it confidently, it sinks down over his ears.
Ron Rigsby appears around the door. Stares at Rigsby.

RON: Hello, Rupert.

RIGSBY: What do you want?

RON: Now that's no way to greet your brother – not after all this time. (*Rigsby searches for some more packing for hat*) What are you looking for – your rabbit?

RIGSBY: (*sighs. Shuts eyes*) Perhaps it's a bad dream. Perhaps if I shut my eyes and keep calm he'll go away. Look, I don't want you around here – I'm getting married.

RON: I know – that's why I'm here. You don't think I'd desert my brother at a time like this? (*Pause*) You're going through with it then?

RIGSBY: Of course I'm going through with it. (*Frowns*) What made you say that?

RON: Nothing. (*Picks up photograph*) This her? Well, at least you've found someone near your own age. I can't see her making too many physical demands on you – unless you include pushing her wheelchair.

RIGSBY: That's her mother. (*Hands second snap to Ron*) This is her. (*Uneasily*) It's not a very good picture.

Ron examines the picture, turning it this way and that.

RON: Has she got money?

RIGSBY: (*angrily*) No, she hasn't. She's what you'd call a distressed gentlewoman.

RON: (*drily*) She's going to be distressed all right.

RIGSBY: What do you mean by that?

RON: Well, she's hardly your type, is she? You've always liked them with big knockers and come-to-bed eyes. She looks too refined for you.

RIGSBY: Listen, I can be refined. As a matter of fact we've got a lot in common. We share the same intellectual pursuits.

RON: You've never had any intellectual pursuits. You were reading *The Beano* until you were sixteen – and you couldn't do that without moving your lips.

RIGSBY: Well, I didn't have your education, did I? I had to get out to work. I was on the coal cart when I was fourteen. I had to make sacrifices – I'm still picking anthracite out of my pores. (*Hastily*) Not that I've told her that – I've come a long way since then.

RON: I still wonder if you're doing the right thing – looking at these pictures. If you want to know what a woman's going to be like in twenty years time – look at her mother.

Rigsby stares at the pictures then snatches them back hurriedly.

RIGSBY: I've told you, it's a bad picture. She happens to be a warm vibrant woman.

RON: Oh. (*Knowingly*) So that's it.

RIGSBY: What do you mean – 'That's it'?

RON: I wondered what the attraction was. You should keep away from warm, vibrant women at your age.

RIGSBY: There's nothing wrong with me.

RON: But these are your dangerous years. And if she's warm and vibrant she's going to expect a full married life.

RIGSBY: So what?

RON: Well, let's face it, you weren't that successful before – and you were younger then. You could go out like a light. Still, I suppose she'll be provided for – she'll get the insurance.

RIGSBY: There isn't any insurance.

RON: There will be.

RIGSBY: Isn't it amazing? And they say, all the world loves a lover – not around here they don't. Ever since I said I was getting married they've been putting the mockers on it. Well, if that's all you've come for—

RON: Not exactly. I've come for that diamond ring.

RIGSBY: (*shocked*) You can't do that. You gave it to me.

RON: No, I just asked you to keep it for me, that's all. That was my nest egg.

RIGSBY: Ah, well, I don't know where I've put it.

RON: I do – it's on her finger, isn't it?

RIGSBY: Yes, well, you didn't say you wanted it back. You couldn't wait to get rid of it. How do I know it's yours? Where did it come from?

RON: I found it.

RIGSBY: Yes, you've been finding things since you were ten. Why is it you that always find things?

RON: I've got a metal detector.

RIGSBY: You've always got an excuse, haven't you? Like the time they found you at the back

of the Midland Bank at two in the morning – and you said you were looking for a chiropodist.

RON: I was – my feet were killing me.

RIGSBY: They couldn't have been that bad – you were half-way up a ladder. Well, you're not having it back – it's too late.

RON: All right. (*Generously*) You can have it – it'll be my wedding present – on one condition.

RIGSBY: What?

RON: That you let me be best man.

RIGSBY: Oh no. I know why you want to be best man – you want to keep your eye on that ring.

RON: No, I don't. Mind you, if anything goes wrong I shall expect it back.

RIGSBY: Look, things are bound to go wrong if they see you.

RON: (*sharply*) Wait a minute – are you ashamed of me?

RIGSBY: Yes.

RON: (*hurt*) I thought I'd paid my debt to society. I never expected this from my own brother. I only suggested myself for best man because I know mother would have liked it.

RIGSBY: (*uneasily*) I know, Ron, but they're very respectable – they wouldn't understand.

RON: How would they know?

RIGSBY: They'd know. I can just see you in church – standing out in the gloom with your prison pallor – gently shaking the offertory box and talking out of the corner of your mouth.

RON: That's where you're wrong. It's clothes that maketh the man. (*Puts on top hat and tails*) See, now I'm a gentleman.

RIGSBY: No, you wouldn't get away with it. They'd see through you.

Ruth and mother enter. Mother is a majestic memsahib type.

RUTH: Rupert – I've brought mother to meet you.

Mother's eyes alight on Ron and she brightens visibly.

MOTHER: Ah, I must say it's a relief to meet you. When Ruth said an older man I thought she might have meant someone dreadfully decrepit. At least you look as if you have some life left in you. And you wear those clothes beautifully.

RUTH: Er … no, this is Rupert, mother.

MOTHER: (*clearly disappointed*) Oh, yes – I see. He is older, isn't he?

RIGSBY: This is my brother Ron … er … he's the best man.

MOTHER: Yes, so I see.

RON: Delighted to meet you.

(*Looks admiringly at the ring*) What a beautiful ring. But it does look rather loose. I could get it fixed for you. I have friends in the trade.

RUTH: No, I don't want to take it off – it might be unlucky.

RIGSBY: It certain would.

MOTHER: Well, Rupert, you may kiss me. (*Rigsby kisses her clumsily on the cheek. The boot polish leaves a faint smear*) Welcome to the family.

RIGSBY: Charmed. I'd just like to say I'll do my best to make your daughter blissfully happy. (*Sees smear, looks alarmed*)

MOTHER: I'm sure you will. You remind me of someone I knew in India. He was very dependable.

RIGSBY: (*pleased*) Ah, was he a military man?

MOTHER: No, he was a punka wallah – loyal little chap – died of cholera in '46. Do you enjoy good health, Rupert?

RIGSBY: Oh, yes. Never had a day's illness in my life.

MOTHER: Well, that's something. Health's so important in the case of an older man (*Laughs*) We don't want you popping off before we've cut the cake, do we? Are you insured Rupert?

RIGSBY: Er … no.

MOTHER: Never mind, we can

soon put that right. And the house is freehold? Splendid. (*Rigsby and Ron exchange glances*) I'll just have a look round. (*She sees herself in mirror. Stares at the smear. Turns and stares at Rigsby*)

END OF PART ONE.

PART TWO

SCENE 4: *Int. Ruth's room. Wedding morning.*
    Ruth enters from bedroom in wedding dress.

RUTH: Well, how do I look? (*Mother looks at her and sobs*) I didn't think I looked that bad.

MOTHER: (*hugs her*) My poor lamb.

RUTH: Now, don't start crying again, mother.

MOTHER: You're going through with it then?

RUTH: (*tartly*) Well, you don't think I'm off to play badminton. Of course I'm going through with it.

MOTHER: I'm sorry, dear. I shouldn't give way but I wanted it to be so different.

RUTH: But it's what you've always wanted. A white wedding – a beautiful church – the architecture's perpendicular.

MOTHER: That's more than he'll be. I heard the clink of glasses very early this morning.

RUTH: Well, he's bound to be nervous – after the last time.

MOTHER: That's what worries me – the last time. He's already had one failure.

RUTH: That wasn't his fault. He was the innocent party – she left him. That's why the vicar's allowing us to marry in church – he felt he owed him one. It's not normal.

MOTHER: Neither is he.

RUTH: Oh, don't go on, mother. Look, it's a beautiful day. I'm wearing your wedding dress – we're even having your hymn – 'Nearer thy God to thee' – won't that be nice?

MOTHER: I think 'Fight the good fight' would be more appropriate.

RUTH: But what have you go against him?

MOTHER: It's not so much him. Although he's older than you – he never changes that cardigan – his cat's got fleas and he puts boot polish on his hair. (*Sadly*) It's just that I wanted you to marry someone else – someone we're both very fond of. Ever since you were quite small I've had this dream – you know that.

RUTH: (*gently*) I know, mother, and I'm sorry, but there's not much chance of me meeting the Prince of Wales now. I've got to make

526

the best of things. I know he's … I know he's—

MOTHER: I think common's the word you're looking for.

RUTH: I know he's not handsome and dashing, but he's like me – he's lonely – and he's kind – and he must be very fond of me. Look at this beautiful ring – it much have cost the earth.

MOTHER: I know, dear, but you mustn't get carried away with all the glitter and the ceremony – it all has to be paid for. I'm not one to frighten my daughter on her wedding day but men can be beasts. Remember cousin Agnes? Left the church wreathed in smiles and after the wedding night they found her completely gaga.

RUTH: Mother, I don't want to hear anymore. Now go and get ready – it won't be long now.

Mother exits leaving Ruth looking a little thoughtful. She looks at the ring and is reassured. Ron slips round the door.

RON: You look a picture.

RUTH: Thank you.

MOTHER: You're going through with it then?

RUTH: What?

RON: (*confidentially*) It's not too late for you to change your mind. We'd all understand. All you've got to do is return the ring—

RUTH: Why is everyone trying to talk me out of it? I wish you'd all stop it. Even my freesias are wilting.

RON: That's because you're nervous. It's making your hands clammy – second thoughts – doubts are beginning to emerge. Does that ring hurt you?

RUTH: No.

RON: I can understand it – you're wondering what went wrong the first time. It wasn't just because he ate biscuits in bed – we all have our little foibles. No, it goes deeper than that. Rupert was never easy with the opposite sex. If we had a girl to tea he always sat behind the aspidistra. Very shy.

RUTH: Please, Ron – I don't want to hear anymore. I mean, this should be the happiest day of my life. And if I have any doubts about his feelings I only have to look at this ring.

RON: Yes, it's a beautiful ring – perfect setting. I should know – I gave it to him.

RUTH: What?

RON: Oh! I didn't mean to say that. A chapter of my life which is forever closed. I was young and in love. Beautiful girl – tall and graceful – like you. But it wasn't to be – died of consumption.

RUTH: Oh dear, I'm sorry.

RON: I didn't want to see that ring

again. I begged Rupert to take it – the memory was too painful. But now I'm happy to see it on a slim elegant hand once more. (*Great emotion*) Bringing happiness that can never be mine. But for old time's sake – for the memory of a lost love – could I hold it just one more time?

RUTH: I'm afraid it's too tight – my finger's swollen.

RON: What! (*He tugs at the ring. Undignified scramble*) You're right – it won't budge. (*Pause. Sighs*) You know – if only we'd met earlier – you could have helped me to forget.

RUTH: (*pulls away*) Please, Ron. Really!

RON: I'm sorry. I was carried away. I'll withdraw.

Exit Ron. Mother enters from bedroom dressed for the wedding.

MOTHER: Well, how do I look? (*Ruth looks at her and bursts into tears*) Perhaps I should have worn the blue.

* * *

SCENE 5: *Int. attic room.*
Philip is getting ready for church.
Rigsby enters in top hat and tails.

RIGSBY: (*anxiously*) Well, how do I look?

PHILIP: You look marvellous – perhaps a little pale.

RIGSBY: I know. I think I've got flu.

PHILIP: (*smiles*) I thought you might be nervous.

RIGSBY: No, not me. I'm just not well. My voice keeps going – the muscles are contracting in my throat – must be a virus. (*Panicking*) What am I going to do? They won't be able to hear me. She'll be expecting a firm response – a voice resonant with love and sincerity. Not 'Would you say that again, Mr Rigsby?'

PHILIP: I don't think it's important how you say it – as long as you say it.

RIGSBY: Of course it matters. It's got to hit the rafters. 'I do.'

PHILIP: It's 'I will'.

RIGSBY: (*alarmed*) What?

PHILIP: It's not 'I do' it's 'I will'.

RIGSBY: Oh my God! And I've been rehearsing 'I do'! (*He plunges nervously into the prayer book, gabbling at a furious pace and taking all the parts himself*) 'I take thee, Ruth, to be my wedded wife – to have and to hold from this day forward for better for worse, for richer for poorer, in sickness and in health, to love and to cherish, until death us do part.' My voice is going again!

PHILIP: It's only because you're nervous.

RIGSBY: I keep telling you, I am not nervous. (*Wipes his forehead with hanky*) 'With this body I thee ring

– with this worship I thee wed. With my worldly goods ...' What do I do with my worldly goods?

PHILIP: 'With my worldly goods I thee endow.'

RIGSBY: Yes, well, I'll skate over that. 'And now I pledge thee my troth' – put the ring on her finger. Which finger? I've forgotten which finger!

PHILIP: It's the fourth. Now don't panic.

RIGSBY: I'm not panicking. Don't worry about me – just remember your part. Once you've given her away, stand well back. We don't want her marrying the wrong bloke.

PHILIP: That's true. After all, you look more like her father than I do.

RIGSBY: (*angrily*) Now wait a minute. What do you mean by that?

Ron enters carrying a bottle of scotch.

RON: How's he feeling?

PHILIP: He's a bit nervous.

RIGSBY: I am not nervous! Have you got the wedding ring? (*Ron pats his pocket, looks alarmed*) Oh my God! He's lost the ring – he's lost the ring. (*Ron grins and produces the ring*) Did you have to do that?

RON: What you need is a drink – it'll relax you.

RIGSBY: (*hesitates*) No, better not. Might affect the solemnity of the occasion. I don't want the vicar to get a blast of Highland magic each time I respond – he might question my sincerity.

RON: That'll be all right – you can suck a peppermint.

RIGSBY: Yes. No – wait a minute. Peppermint's a dead give away. He'll know I'm sucking the peppermint to hide the whisky.

RON: Right – then have some onions – he'll think you're sucking the peppermint to hide the onions.

RIGSBY: (brightens) Yes. (*Hesitates*) No, he might think I've had the onions to hide the peppermints to hide the whisky.

RON: Please yourself.

He removes bottle. Rigsby snatches it back.

RIGSBY: Well, just one – to ease my throat. (*Takes large draught*)

PHILIP: Do you think he should?

RON: He'll be all right. You'd better keep Ruth happy, Philip – cheer her up a bit.

RIGSBY: (*alarmed*) Why – what's the matter with her?

RON: (*reassuringly*) Nothing. I keep telling you, there's nothing to worry about – she's having a good weep that's all.

RIGSBY: What! I'd better go and see her.

RON: No, you can't do that – not before the wedding – it's unlucky.

PHILIP: I'd better get down to her. (*Philip exits*)

RIGSBY: I bet it's her mother – I can't stand that woman.

RON: You'd better get used to her – she'll be living with you.

RIGSBY: What!

RON: You can say goodbye to that chair by the fire. She'll expect to be waited on hand and foot. You'll be getting the coal in during the winter and fanning her through the summer. It comes from living in India.

RIGSBY: Yes, well, I wish she'd followed the other Indian custom – the one where the widow jumps on the bonfire with her husband.

RON: Well, it's not too late to change your mind.

RIGSBY: Oh no. You're not talking me out of it. This is my day – no one's taking it away from me. After a delightful ceremony the happy couple will depart to explore the south coast – and I'll tell you this, that won't be the exploring I'll be doing. (*Snatches bottle*) No more for you – you're driving. And remember, no confetti in the churchyard – or the verger'll punch your ears. And if the vicar starts rabbitting on

about the state of the spire – ignore him. Oh, and when they take the photographs – tilt your hat down over your eyes. We might make the *Tatler* and I don't want anyone recognising you. And one more thing – keep your hands off the candlesticks. You know, I don't know why you drink this stuff. It's a crutch. I prefer to go to church pure and unsullied. (*Hesitates. Takes long swallow from bottle. Exits*)

* * *

SCENE 6: *Int. Rigsby's room. Three hours later.*
Rigsby enters looking dishevelled. He is followed by Ron in a similar state and sporting a black eye. Rigsby slumps wearily into a chair.

RIGSBY: The happiest day of my life! It was a disaster.

RON: Well, it wasn't my fault.

RIGSBY: Of course it was your fault. I said St Luke's – early perpendicular with Saxon traces and a rood screen. Not St Mark's – late gothic with a vicar to match!

RON: Well, you should have told me we were in the wrong church. Why didn't you say something?

RIGSBY: I wasn't in a condition to say anything. I didn't know what that stuff was like. (*Rubs forehead*) Only drink I've had where you get the hangover first.

RON: We should have known

something was wrong the way the vicar kept frowning at us.

RIGSBY: Oh, that was him, was it? I thought it was a gargoyle. I've never felt so ridiculous in my life. Mind you, I did think the guests looked a bit miserable, but until they wheeled that coffin down the aisle I had no idea it was a funeral. It's a wonder we didn't get lynched.

RON: I still think we should have tried to pass the whole thing off.

RIGSBY: Oh yes? What did you want me to do – spend my honeymoon with the deceased? It was all your fault. If you'd shown some interest in what was going on ... All you could do was look at the roof and say, 'How much lead do you think there is?'

RON: I think I did my duty as best man. I stood up for you when they wanted to bury you instead of the deceased.

RIGSBY: That may be so but it's not the duty of the best man to belt the vicar. I wouldn't mind but you only did it because you thought he was a man of peace – I could have told you he was a boxing blue.

RON: Well, I got you to the right church in the end – I don't know why they couldn't have waited.

RIGSBY: I'll tell you why, because we were three hours late. All we found was a few wilted freesias. How can I explain to that woman? What am I going to say

to her? Left waiting at the church – an object of scorn and ridicule.

RON: I think I'll put something on this eye.

RIGSBY: You'll find plenty of ham at the church Hall – miles of it (*Ron exits. Rigsby stares moodily at Vienna, who comes up wearing a bow tie*) I don't know what you're looking so pleased about. You were supposed to bring us luck. Have you thought about her? Probably sitting there alone staring at the wedding cake – like Miss Haversham. The cobwebs are probably already beginning to form—

Ruth enters. She is still wearing her wedding dress – looks strained.

RIGSBY: Miss Jones. (*Forced cheerfulness*) I must say white really suits you. (*Ruth gives a little sob*) What can I say? Sorry seems hardly adequate under the circumstances. I mean, to have put you through this ordeal—

RUTH: No, Mr Rigsby – I'm the one who should apologise. You poor man. I just couldn't go through with it.

RIGSBY: What!

RUTH: When I think of you standing at that church – and no bride – I feel so ashamed.

RIGSBY: You didn't come?

RUTH: When it came down to it I found my doubts were too strong. Can you forgive me?

RIGSBY: (*magnanimously*) That's all right, Miss Jones, I understand.

RUTH: You're so brave – I must have hurt you dreadfully.

RIGSBY: (*bravely*) That's true. But they do say there's no such thing as a broken heart, and who knows? Perhaps I'll learn to smile again. (*Sighs*) It's just that when I think that by now I could have been exploring the delights of the south coast— (*Ruth hugs him despairingly*)

RUTH: Oh, Mr Rigsby. How can I make it up to you?

RIGSBY: (*a crafty lear crosses Rigsby's face*) Well, there is a way. I mean, we've still got the hotel reservations. The bridal suite's booked to the end of the week.

RUTH: Mr Rigsby, you're not suggesting—?

RIGSBY: Why not, Miss Jones? We could always sprinkle ourselves with confetti – who'd know the difference?

RUTH: Oh, Mr Rigsby.

Ruth falls into his arms. Ron enters.

RON: Now don't get upset, Ruth. I can explain. We went to the wrong church – a perfectly innocent mistake – the amount we'd had.

RUTH: You mean you didn't even arrive?

RON: Yes, we arrived – around tea time.

RUTH: You mean I stood you up and you weren't even standing there?

RIGSBY: Ah, if you'd just listen to me, Miss Jones.

RUTH: No, I've listened to you enough. Mother was right. You're a monster. Here, take the ring back you didn't even bother to buy. I never want to see it again.

Ruth snatches off the ring and hurls it across the room. Exits. Ron and Rigsby stare at each other in silence.

RON: Er … sorry about that.

RIGSBY: Is that all you can say? My whole life's in ruins. I've got nothing left to live for.

RON: Ah, well, you won't be needing the ring then, will you?

They stare at each other for a moment and then dive for the ring as one – fighting and struggling to get under the settee.

THE END

APPENDIX

CAST LISTS

Pilot

The New Tenant (also known as *Rooksby*)
Rehearsals: St. Paul's Church Hall, Sussex Place, Hammersmith, London W6
Recorded: 7/7/74
Original transmission: 2/9/74

Cast:
Rigsby . . . . Leonard Rossiter
Alan . . . . Richard Beckinsale
Ruth . . . . Frances de la Tour
Philip . . . . Don Warrington

Series One

1. *Black Magic*
Rehearsals: St. Paul's Church Hall, Sussex Place, Hammersmith, London W6
Recorded: 3/11/74
Original transmission: 13/12/74

Cast:
Rigsby . . . . Leonard Rossiter
Alan . . . . Richard Beckinsale
Ruth . . . . Frances de la Tour
Philip . . . . Don Warrington

2. *A Night Out*
Rehearsals: St. Paul's Church Hall, Sussex Place, Hammersmith, London W6
Recorded: 17/11/74
Original transmission: 20/12/74

Cast:

Rigsby .... Leonard Rossiter
Alan .... Richard Beckinsale
Ruth .... Frances de la Tour
Philip .... Don Warrington
Spooner .... Derek Newark
Manager .... Frank Gatliff

Extras: Tom Growlin, Penelope Carlisle, Sylvia Stoker, Patrick Lynas, Douglas Quarterman, Norah Blackman, Mark Freeman, Yvonne Sommerling, Stuart Teal, Tom Harrison, Martin le Roy. **Walk-ons**: Peter Newton, Mike Thorley, Alan Frith, Fenella Stone, Conrad Vince, Carl Rae, Angela Elliott, Winifred Williams, Lisa Anning, Joanne Aspey.

3. *Charisma*
Rehearsals: St. Paul's Church Hall, Sussex Place, Hammersmith, London W6
Recorded: 10/11/74
Original transmission: 27/12/74

Cast:

Rigsby .... Leonard Rossiter
Alan .... Richard Beckinsale
Ruth .... Frances de la Tour
Philip .... Don Warrington
Maureen .... Liz Edmiston

4. *All Our Yesterdays*
Rehearsals: St. Paul's Church Hall, Sussex Place, Hammersmith, London W6
Recorded: 24/11/74
Original transmission: 3/1/75
Cast:
Rigsby .... Leonard Rossiter

Alan . . . . Richard Beckinsale
Ruth . . . . Frances de la Tour
Philip . . . . Don Warrington
Spooner . . . . Derek Newark

5. *The Prowler*
Rehearsals: St. Paul's Church Hall, Sussex Place, Hammersmith, London W6
Recorded: 1/11/74
Original transmission: 10/1/75

Cast:
Rigsby . . . . Leonard Rossiter
Alan . . . . Richard Beckinsale
Ruth . . . . Frances de la Tour
Philip . . . . Don Warrington
Baker . . . . George Sewell
Policeman . . . . Michael Stainton

Extra: Non-speaking policeman: Kelwyn Harrison

6. *Stand Up and Be Counted*
Rehearsals: St. Paul's Church Hall, Sussex Place, Hammersmith, London W6
Recorded: 8/12/74
Original transmission: 17/1/75

Cast:
Rigsby . . . . Leonard Rossiter
Alan . . . . Richard Beckinsale
Ruth . . . . Frances de la Tour
Philip . . . . Don Warrington
Labour Candidate . . . . . Michael Ward
Platt . . . . Ian Lavender
De Vere-Brown . . . . Anthony Sharp

Series Two

1. *Permissive Society*
Rehearsals: The Sulgrave Boys' Club, 287 Goldhawk Road, London W12
Recorded: 25/7/75
Original transmission: 7/11/75

Cast:
Rigsby . . . . Leonard Rossiter
Alan . . . . Richard Beckinsale
Ruth . . . . Frances de la Tour
Philip . . . . Don Warrington
Cooper . . . . George A. Cooper

2. *Food Glorious Food*
Rehearsals: The Sulgrave Boys' Club, 287 Goldhawk Road, London W12
Recorded: 18/7/75
Original transmission: 14/11/75

Cast:
Rigsby . . . . Leonard Rossiter
Alan . . . . Richard Beckinsale
Ruth . . . . Frances de la Tour
Philip . . . . Don Warrington

3. *A Body Like Mine*
Rehearsals: The Sulgrave Boys' Club, 287 Goldhawk Road, London W12
Recorded: 1/8/75
Original transmission: 21/11/75

Cast:
Rigsby . . . . Leonard Rossiter
Alan . . . . Richard Beckinsale
Ruth . . . . Frances de la Tour
Philip . . . . Don Warrington

4. *Moonlight and Roses*
Rehearsals: The Sulgrave Boys' Club, 287 Goldhawk Road, London W12
Recorded: 19/9/75
Original transmission: 28/11/75

Cast:

Rigsby	Leonard Rossiter
Alan	Richard Beckinsale
Ruth	Frances de la Tour
Philip	Don Warrington
Desmond	Robin Parkinson
Brenda	Gay Rose

5. *A Perfect Gentleman*
Rehearsals: The Sulgrave Boys' Club, 287 Goldhawk Road, London W12
Recorded: 10/10/75
Original transmission: 5/12/75

Cast:

Rigsby	Leonard Rossiter
Alan	Richard Beckinsale
Philip	Don Warrington
Seymour	Henry McGee

6. *The Last of the Big Spenders*
Rehearsals: The Sulgrave Boys' Club, 287 Goldhawk Road, London W12
Recorded: 17/10/75
Original transmission: 12/12/75

Cast:

Rigsby	Leonard Rossiter
Alan	Richard Beckinsale
Philip	Don Warrington
Brenda	Gay Rose
Flint	Campbell Singer
Gas man	Robert Gillespie
Charlie	Ronnie Brody

7. *Things That Go Bump in the Night*
Rehearsals: The Sulgrave Boys' Club, 287 Goldhawk Road, London W12
Recorded: 24/10/75
Original transmission: 19/12/75

Cast:

Rigsby	Leonard Rossiter
Alan	Richard Beckinsale
Philip	Don Warrington
Brenda	Gay Rose
Vicar	Norman Bird
Curate	David Rowlands

Christmas Special
For the Man Who Has Everything
Rehearsals: The Sulgrave Boys' Club, 287 Goldhawk Road, London W12
Recorded: 19/12/75
Original transmission: 26/12/75

Cast:

Rigsby	Leonard Rossiter
Alan	Richard Beckinsale
Philip	Don Warrington
Brenda	Gay Rose
Fred	Larry Martyn
Lucy	Elizabeth Adare
Gwen	Helen Fraser

Series Three
1. *That's My Boy*
Rehearsals: The Sulgrave Boys' Club, 287 Goldhawk Road, London W12
Recorded: 25/3/77
Original transmission: 12/4/77

Cast:

Rigsby	Leonard Rossiter
Alan	Richard Beckinsale
Ruth	Frances de la Tour

Philip . . . . Don Warrington
Mrs Brent . . . . Ann Beach
Mr Brent . . . . David Daker
Announcer (Radio) . . . . Daphne Oxenford

2. *Stage Struck*
Rehearsals: The Sulgrave Boys' Club, 287 Goldhawk Road, London W12
Recorded: 1/4/77
Original transmission: 19/4/77

Cast:
Rigsby . . . . Leonard Rossiter
Alan . . . . Richard Beckinsale
Ruth . . . . Frances de la Tour
Philip . . . . Don Warrington
Hilary . . . . Peter Bowles

3. *Clunk Click*
Rehearsals: The Sulgrave Boys' Club, 287 Goldhawk Road, London W12
Recorded: 15/4/77
Original transmission: 26/4/77

Cast:
Rigsby . . . . Leonard Rossiter
Alan . . . . Richard Beckinsale
Ruth . . . . Frances de la Tour
Philip . . . . Don Warrington
Mr French . . . . Derek Francis
Peppery Man . . . . James Bree
Caroline . . . . Judy Buxton

4. *The Good Samaritans*
Rehearsals: The Sulgrave Boys' Club, 287 Goldhawk Road, London W12
Recorded: 15/4/77
Original transmission: 3/5/77

Cast:
Rigsby . . . . Leonard Rossiter
Alan . . . . Richard Beckinsale

Ruth .... Frances de la Tour
Philip .... Don Warrington
Mr Gray .... David Swift
Samaritan .... John Clive

Extras: Stretcher-bearers: Buddy Prince & Derek Suthern

5. *Fawcett's Python*
Rehearsals: The Sulgrave Boys' Club, 287 Goldhawk Road, London W12
Recorded: 29/4/77
Original transmission: 10/5/77

Cast:
Rigsby .... Leonard Rossiter
Alan .... Richard Beckinsale
Ruth .... Frances de la Tour
Philip .... Don Warrington
Marilyn .... Andonia Katsaros
Douglas .... Jonathan Elsom

6. *The Cocktail Hour*
Rehearsals: The Sulgrave Boys' Club, 287 Goldhawk Road, London W12
Recorded: 6/5/77
Original transmission: 17/5/77

Cast:
Rigsby .... Leonard Rossiter
Alan .... Richard Beckinsale
Ruth .... Frances de la Tour
Philip .... Don Warrington
Caroline .... Judy Buxton
Mrs Armitage .... Diana King

7. *Suddenly at Home*
Rehearsals: The Sulgrave Boys' Club, 287 Goldhawk Road, London W12
Recorded: 13/5/77
Original transmission: 24/5/77

Cast:
Rigsby .... Leonard Rossiter

Alan . . . . Richard Beckinsale
Ruth . . . . Frances de la Tour
Philip . . . . Don Warrington
Osborne . . . . Roger Brierley

Series Four

1. *Hello Young Lovers*
Rehearsals: The Sulgrave Boys' Club, 287 Goldhawk Road, London W12
Recorded: 17/3/78
Original transmission: 4/4/78

Cast:
Rigsby . . . . Leonard Rossiter
Ruth . . . . Frances de la Tour
Philip . . . . Don Warrington
Robin . . . . Alun Lewis
Father . . . . Robert Dorning

2. *Fire and Brimstone*
Rehearsals: The Sulgrave Boys' Club, 287 Goldhawk Road, London W12
Recorded: 10/3/78
Original transmission: 11/4/78

Cast:
Rigsby . . . . Leonard Rossiter
Ruth . . . . Frances de la Tour
Philip . . . . Don Warrington
Gwyn . . . . John Clive

3. *Great Expectations*
Rehearsals: The Sulgrave Boys' Club, 287 Goldhawk Road, London W12
Recorded: 31/3/78
Original transmission: 18/4/78

Cast:
Rigsby . . . . Leonard Rossiter
Ruth . . . . Frances de la Tour

Philip . . . . Don Warrington
Veronica . . . . Avis Bunnage
Mr Snell . . . . Andrew Sachs
Aunt Maud . . . . Gretchen Franklin

4. *Pink Carnations*
Rehearsals: The Sulgrave Boys' Club, 287 Goldhawk Road, London W12
Recorded: 7/4/78
Original transmission: 25/4/78

Cast:
Rigsby . . . . Leonard Rossiter
Ruth . . . . Frances de la Tour
Philip . . . . Don Warrington
Bride . . . . Helen Fraser
Groom . . . . John Quayle
Mother . . . . Joan Sanderson
Barman . . . . Roy Barraclough

Extras: Colin, Martin & Harry Butterworth, Bob Hargreaves, Audrey
  Worth

Walk-ons: Christine Bell, Patrick Lynas, Caroline Tyson, Honey
  Wheeler, Joy Ash, Chris Driver

5. *Under the Influence*
Rehearsals: The Sulgrave Boys' Club, 287 Goldhawk Road, London W12
Recorded: 14/4/78
Original transmission: 2/5/78
Cast:
Rigsby . . . . Leonard Rossiter
Ruth . . . . Frances de la Tour
Philip . . . . Don Warrington
Ambrose . . . . Peter Jeffrey

6. *Come On In, the Water's Lovely*
Rehearsals: The Sulgrave Boys' Club, 287 Goldhawk Road, London W12
Recorded: 21/4/78
Original transmission: 9/5/78

Cast:
Rigsby . . . . Leonard Rossiter
Ruth . . . . Frances de la Tour
Philip . . . . Don Warrington
Ron . . . . Brian Peck
Mother . . . . Fanny Rowe